プレア・ヴィヘア

アンコール広域拠点遺跡群の建築学的研究 2

付：コンポンスヴァイのプレア・カーン寺院の調査報告

PREAH VIHEAR

———————————

ARCHITECTURAL STUDY ON THE PROVINCIAL SITES
OF
THE KHMER EMPIRE 2

Appendix : Survey Report on Preah Khan Temple of Kompong Svay

Collaborative Project between National Authority for Preah Vihear and Meijo University and Waseda University

2018

監修

中川　武

溝口明則

Editorial Supervisor:

NAKAGAWA Takeshi, MIZOGUCHI Akinori ／中川 武, 溝口 明則

Editorial Assistance:

ISHIZUKA Mitsumasa, KUROIWA Chihiro ／石塚 充雅, 黒岩 千尋

DTP Operator:

ONOE Chihiro, KANEKO Tatsuya, TAKAHASHI Izumi, NARUI Itaru, ISHII Yuka, MIYAZAKI Tamaki, DAMBARA Ko ／
尾上 千尋, 金子 達哉, 高橋 泉美, 成井 至, 石井 由佳, 宮﨑 瑶希, 檀原 江

Translation from Japanese to English, English to Japanese:

Robert McCARTHY, ISHIZUKA Mitsumasa, KOGA Yukako, KUROIWA Chihiro, UCHIDA Etsuo, SUGIYAMA Hiroshi, KUBO
Sumiko, OISHI Takeshi, GLOBAL WORKS ／
ロバート・マッカーシー, 石塚 充雅, 古賀 友佳子, 黒岩 千尋, 内田 悦生, 杉山 洋, 久保 純子, 大石 岳史, グローバル・ワークス

Photographs & Drawings:

© Meijo University and Waseda University

PREAH VIHEAR
ARCHITECTURAL STUDY ON THE PROVINCIAL SITES OF THE KHMER EMPIRE 2
Appendix : Survey Report on Preah Khan Temple of Kompong Svay

2018

Edited by : Collaborative Project Team between National Authority for Preah Vihear and Meijo University and Waseda University

Supervisor : NAKAGAWA Takeshi, MIZOGUCHI Akinori ／中川 武, 溝口 明則

© Collaborative Project Team between National Authority for Preah Vihear, Meijo University and Waseda University,
October 2018

〔本書は独立行政法人日本学術振興会平成 30 年度科学研究費補助金（研究成果公開促進費）の交付を受けた出版である〕
[This publication is supported by Grant-in-Aid for Publication of Scientific Research Results.]

Foreword

Preah Vihear Temple, which was registered as a UNESCO World Heritage Site in 2008, is a special sacred place in the Kingdom of the Khmer dating back to the end of the 9th century and is a very important temple monument for the present Kingdom of Cambodia. It is one of the important representative cultural property monuments in Southeast Asia, and also one of the important monuments in the world.

The temple monument that had been devastated over a long period of time was investigated by EFEO in the 1930s when the first academic survey was conducted. The result was very important, and valuable academic basic data was accumulated. However, this monument did not have the opportunity to go to the next stage of academic investigation until recently.

In 2011, NAPV(National Authority for Preah Vihear) and a joint team of Meijo and Waseda Universities of Japan had signed an MOU to conduct this survey under the research grant from the Ministry of Education, Culture, Sports, Science and Technology of Japan with technical support from JASA (Japan-APSARA Safeguarding Angkor). We had studied this important site for four years from 2012.

This survey report was composed by the results of the survey during 4 years. The results of analysis and research based on these survey materials are included together with the basic academic data. These results will greatly contribute to the future restoration provision for Preah Vihear Temple and also future academic research, conservation and restoration for Khmer temples in various areas of the Kingdom of Cambodia.

NAPV is very pleased to pay a sincere tribute to the co-directors of this project, Prof. Akinori MIZOGUCHI and Prof. Takeshi NAKAGAWA as well as all researchers who joined this survey from each field and all the team members whose efforts made the publication of this report possible.

KIM Sedera

President
National Authority for Preah Vihear

Preface

From 2007 a study team of the ancient Khmer urban plan and monuments centered on the researchers of Meijo and Waseda Universities have implemented to survey of important provincial Khmer monuments of Cambodia. After we had conducted surveys at mainly the Koh Ker Monuments and Beng Mealea Temple from FY2007 to FY2010, we had implemented "Scientific Research on the Spacial Structure of the Khmer Empire and Ancient Khmer Provincial Principal Momuments [Principal Investigator: Akinori MIZOGUCHI, Former Professor of Meijo University]" funded by a Grants-in-Aid for Scientific Research of Ministry of Education, Culture, Sports, Science and Technology of Japan (MEXT) during 4 years from FY2012 to FY2015, and had implemented surveys at Preah Vihear Temple and Preah Khan Temple of Kompong Svay. These surveys were implemented by the excellent cooperation of Ministry of Culture and Fine Arts, the National Authority for Preah Vihear (NAPV), and JASA.

Purpose of our survey from FY2007 is to collect basic academic data of important provincial monuments in the Khmer Empire, and to study and analyze based on these results. In this study, we tried to keep a consistent vision and method for study and collect coessential basic data as much as possible. Only the important monuments in Angkor are not enough to understand the entire aspect of the Khmer Empire at that time. In addition, deterioration of important provincial monuments is definitely proceeding. Therefore, we believe that understanding of present condition of these important monuments and collection of basic data are urgent tasks.

In the original survey plan during 4 years from FY2012, we planned to implement surveys almost equally at Preah Vihear Temple and Preah Khan Temple of Kompong Svay initially, but we changed plan to spend much more time to survey of Preah Vihear Temple because this rare temple monument had showed us multiple fascinating aspects as the survey proceeded. We thought this monument should not be studied summarily in a limited time frame.

We have studied much information from Preah Vihear Temple during this 4 years. The purpose of the publication of this book is to open the results of this survey as much as possible.

We were able to obtain a vast amount of results about Preah Vihear Temple from this study of architecture, petrology, archeology, geography, and highly accurate 3D measurement. We hope the results of these basic academic studies will contribute to the future multiple studies such as study of Khmer and architecture history of Southeast Asia and the future activity and planning of restoration work.

We highly appreciate the excellent cooperation for the study of Preah Vihear Temple by the following people: Mr. President and Chairman of the Boards of NAPV H.E. Mr. Kim Sedara and the Previous President of NAPV H.E. Mr. CHUCH Phoeum, Previous Director General and Present Vice President of NAPV H.E. Mr. UK Top Botra, Present Director General of NAPV HE Mr. Kong Puthikar, Director of Department of Urbanization and Demographic Development Mr. HEM Sinath, Director of Archeology Mr. PHENG Sam Oeurn and the staff of NAPV worked together with the great help at the site from Mr. PIN Sopha, Mr. IN Pheakdey, Mr. NHEM Sonthoun, and Mr. MOUNG Chansey. In addition, we also highly appreciate the excellent cooperation for the study of Preah Khan Temple of Kompong Svay by the Minister of Culture and Fine Arts H.E. PHOEURNG Sackona and staff of the Ministry of Culture and Fine Arts work together at the site Mr. CHEA Vanna, and coordinator of this project Prof. SO Sokuntheary.

February, 2017
MIZOGICHI Akinori

はじめに

　私たち名城大学，早稲田大学を中心としたクメール都市および寺院遺構の調査チームは，2007年よりアンコールから離れたカンボジア各地の重要遺跡の調査を続けてきた。2007年度から2010年度にかけて，コー・ケー都市遺跡とベン・メアレア寺院を対象に現地調査を実施したが，2012年度より2015年度の4年間，独立行政法人日本学術振興会の科学研究費助成金による調査研究「クメール帝国の空間構造と地方拠点都市遺跡に関する研究［研究代表者：溝口明則（名城大学教授，当時）］」を実施し，プレア・ヴィヘア寺院とコンポン・スヴァイのプレア・カーン寺院の調査を進めることになった。これらの調査は，文化芸術省およびプレア・ヴィヘア機構，JASAとともに共同で現地調査を進めたものである。

　2007年以来，私たちが進めてきた調査の目的は，クメール帝国の各地に点在する重要遺跡の学術的な基礎資料を得るとともに，これらの成果に基づいた分析研究を進めることにあった。そこでは，可能な限り一貫した研究視点と調査方法を保ち，同質の基礎資料を網羅的に収集することをめざした。往時の帝国の様相を確かに理解しようとすれば，アンコール地域の重要遺跡だけでは読み解くことが難しい。さらに，地方の重要遺跡の劣化は確実に進行しつつある。このため，各重要遺跡の現況の把握と基礎資料の収集が急務だと考えられたためである。

　2012年から4年間にわたる調査計画では，当初，プレア・ヴィヘア寺院とコンポン・スヴァイのプレア・カーン寺院の現地調査を，およそ均等に実施する予定であった。しかし，調査途上から予定を変更し，プレア・ヴィヘア寺院の学術調査に大きな時間を割くことになった。この稀有な寺院遺構は，調査を進めるに従いさまざまな相貌をみせるようになり，時間を限定して粗略に扱うべき対象ではないと考えられたためである。

　私たちは，この4年間で，プレア・ヴィヘア寺院から多くのことを学んだ。この内容を可能な限り公開することが本書刊行の目的である。

　本調査は，建築学，岩石学，地理学，考古学，そして高精度の三次元測量の分野で実施し，一定の成果を得ることになった。いずれも学術的な基礎調査であり，今後の東南アジア建築史学やクメール学などさまざまな学術的進展の基礎資料として，また今後の遺跡保存活動や修復活動の方針策定などの手がかりとして，少しでも資することを望んでいる。

　末尾に，プレア・ヴィヘア寺院において共同で調査を進めたプレア・ヴィヘア機構現議長キム・セデラー氏，前議長チッ・プン氏，前総裁・現副議長トップ・ボットラー氏，現総裁コン・プティカー氏，都市・人口開発局長ヘン・シナ氏，考古局長ペン・サムウーン氏，そして日々現地でともに調査活動を進めたピン・ソパー氏，イン・ペカダイ氏，ニェン・ソントン氏およびモウン・チャンセイ氏，そしてコンポンスヴァイのプレア・カーン寺院において協力をしていただいた文化芸術省大臣プルン・サッコナ氏，ならびに調査のアレンジの協力をしていただいた文化芸術省スタッフチア・ヴァナ氏およびコーディネーターのソ・ソクンテリー氏に感謝の意を表します。

2017年2月

溝口　明則

Contents

Foreword	1
Preface	2

Chapter 1   Project Overview — 7

1.1 Objective of Study — 9
1.2 Research Organization — 10
1.3 Mission Schedules and Members — 12

Chapter 2   History of Previous Studies of Preah Vihear Temple and Historical Significance of Survey — 15

2.1 Outline of Character and History of Previous Studies of Preah Vihear Temple — 17
2.2 Historical Significance of "Vertically-Oriented Layout Temple" and Subject on Conservation in Preah Vihear Temple — 30

Chapter 3   Study Reports on Preah Vihear Temple — 39

3.1 Geographical Investigations around the Preah Vihear Temple Site (2012 - 2015) — 41
3.2 Determining the Construction Sequence of the Preah Vihear Temple Monument in Cambodia from its Sandstone Block Characteristics — 52
3.3 Archaeological Survey — 65
3.4 Planning of Complex — 75
3.5 Survey of Wood Structure of the Ancient Khmer Ruins and a Chronicle of the Buildings in Preah Vihear Temple — 101
3.6 Construction Order of the Complex I — 121
3.7 Restoration of the Roof of Gopura III — 127
3.8 Reconstructive Study on "田-shape" "口-shape" styles as "Annex Building" — 145
3.9 Planning Method of "Library" in Angkor Period — 159
3.10 Significant Features of the Decorations of the Pediments — 174

Conclusion and Foresight — 185

Biography of Authors — 188

Research achievement from 2012 to 2017 (Preah Vihear) — 194

Final Notes — 196

Appendix I   Monument Inventory — 1

I.1 Singha and Naga Statues in Preah Vihear Temple — 3
I.2 Pediments in Preah Vihear Temple — 29
I.3 Wooden Traces in Preah Vihear Temple — 46
I.4 Pediments in the Other Temples — 61
I.5 Wooden Traces in the Other Temples — 84

Appendix II   Measuring and Drawing Policies and Methods — 97

II.1 Outline of Measuring Work — 99
II.2 Process of the Measuring by Total Station and GPS — 100
II.3 Report on Three-dimensional Measurement — 105
II.4 Process of Making the Drawing — 111

Appendix III   Survey Report on Preah Khan Temple of Kompong Svay — 113

III.1 Survey Report on Preah Khan Temple of Kompong Svay — 115

目次

序文	1
はじめに	2
第1章　調査概要	**7**
1.1 調査目的	9
1.2 調査体制	10
1.3 調査日程・メンバー	12
第2章　プレア・ヴィヘア寺院の研究史と調査の意義	**15**
2.1 プレア・ヴィヘア寺院の概要と研究史	17
2.2 プレア・ヴィヘア寺院における「縦深型寺院」としての歴史的意義と保存修復をめぐる今日的課題	30
第3章　調査および分析	**39**
3.1 プレア・ヴィヘア寺院遺跡とその周辺における地理学的調査（2012-2015年）	41
3.2 石材の特徴に基づくプレア・ヴィヘア寺院遺跡の建造順序の推定	52
3.3 考古学調査	65
3.4 伽藍の計画法	75
3.5 木造屋根の技法とプレアヴィヘア寺院遺構の編年	101
3.6 第1伽藍の造営手順	121
3.7 第3ゴープラの屋根復原	127
3.8「付属建物」としての「田の字」型・「口の字」型建築形式の復原的研究	145
3.9 アンコール期における「経蔵」の設計方法	159
3.10 ペディメントの装飾的特質	174
まとめと展望	185
執筆者略歴	188
業績一覧（2012-2017）（プレア・ヴィヘア）	194
あとがき	196
付章I　インベントリー	**1**
I.1 プレア・ヴィヘア寺院のシンハ・ナーガ像	3
I.2 プレア・ヴィヘア寺院のペディメント	29
I.3 プレア・ヴィヘア寺院の木造痕跡	46
I.4 その他の寺院のペディメント	61
I.5 その他の寺院の木造痕跡	84
付章II　プレア・ヴィヘア寺院における実測・作図の方針と方法	**97**
II.1 測量と図面作成の方針と方法	99
II.2 TPS及びGPSによる実測調査方法	100
II.3 3次元実測調査解説	105
II.4 各種図面の作成方針	111
付章III　コンポンスヴァイのプレア・カーン寺院の調査報告	**113**
III.1 コンポンスヴァイのプレア・カーン寺院の調査概要	115

Plates

1   Drawing Based on Actual Measurement in Preah Vihear Temple

Plate.1   Plan and Section, Preah Vihear Temple
Plate.2   Plan, False Gopura - Gopura II
Plate.3   Plan, Gopura III and Annex Building H, I, H', I'
Plate.4   Plan, Gopura IV
Plate.5   Plan, Gopura V

2   Drawing of the Present Condition of the Each Building in Preah Vihear Temple

■False Gopura

Plate.6   North Elevation, False Gopura
Plate.7   South Elevation, False Gopura
Plate.8   South-North Section, East View, False Gopura
Plate.9   South-North Section, West View, False Gopura
Plate.10 East-West Section, North View, False Gopura
Plate.11 East-West Section, South View, False Gopura

■Central Sanctuary

Plate.12 East Elevation, Central Sanctuary
Plate.13 West Elevation, Central Sanctuary
Plate.14 North Elevation, Central Sanctuary
Plate.15 South Elevation, Central Sanctuary
Plate.16 South-North Section, East View, Central Sanctuary
Plate.17 East-West Section, South View, Central Sanctuary

■Goupra I - Hall N

Plate.18 Plan, Gopura I - Hall N
Plate.19 East Elevation, Gopura I - Hall N
Plate.20 West Elevation, Gopura I - Hall N
Plate.21 North Elevation, Gopura I - Hall N
Plate.22 South Elevation, Gopura I
Plate.23 South-North Section, East View, Gopura I - Hall N
Plate.24 East-West Section, North View, Gopura I - Hall N
Plate.25 East-West Section, South View, Hall N

■Goupra V

Plate.26 Plan, Gopura V
Plate.27 East Elevation, Gopura V
Plate.28 West Elevation, Gopura V
Plate.29 North Elevation, Gopura V
Plate.30 South Elevation, Gopura V
Plate.31 South-North Section, East View, Gopura V
Plate.32 South-North Section, West View, Gopura V
Plate.33 East-West Section, North View, Gopura V
Plate.34 East-West Section, South View, Gopura V

3   Drawing for Restoring the Conjectured Original Design
in Preah Khan Temple of Kompong Svay

Plate.35   Plan, Preah Khan Temple of Kompong Svay

Chapter 1
第 1 章

Project Overview
調査概要

王の名前 King's Name	治世期 Reign
ジャヤヴァルマンII Jayavarman II	802-834
ヤショヴァルマンI Yasovarman I	889-910
ジャヤヴァルマンIV Jayavarman IV	921-941
ハルシャヴァルマンII Harshavarman II	941-944
ラージェンドラヴァルマンII Rajendravarman II	944-968
ジャヤヴァルマンV Jayavarman V	968-1000
スールヤヴァルマンI Suryavarman I	1002-1050
ウダヤディティヤヴァルマンII Udayadityavarman II	1050-1066
スールヤヴァルマンII Suryavarman II	1113-1150
ジャヤヴァルマンVII Jayavarman VII	1181-1218

凡例

本書では、左に示す王の治世期を
基準とする。

Legend

In this publication, we use the King's Reigns as
a table on the left.

1. 調査概要
Project Overview

石塚　充雅
ISHIZUKA Mitsumasa

1.1 調査目的

　名城大学と早稲田大学の共同チームは2007年より
カンボジア地方遺構の調査を行っている。調査の主旨
は，アンコール地域を中心とした調査研究や修復事業
が進展しつつある現在，クメール王国を広域として理
解することが，クメール学の発展にとってきわめて重
要な問題であるという認識と，荒廃が進む地方寺院の
基礎資料を確保することが急務であるという認識に基
づいている。

　私たちは，2007年から2011年にわたる4年間，
コー・ケー遺跡群およびベン・メアレア遺跡群を中心
に現地調査を行った。これは，名城大学及び早稲田大
学の合同チームが日本の独立行政法人日本学術振興会
の科学研究費助成金を得て，JSA，アプサラ機構との共
同プロジェクトとして実施したものである。限られた
時間で実施できた調査は，上記の2つの地方拠点，お
よびチャウ・スレイ・ビボール寺院の伽藍実測，ま
たアンコールとコンポン・スヴァイのプレア・カーン
寺院を繋ぐ街道沿いに分布する宿駅寺院の実測調査で
あった。

　我々はこれまでの経験を生かし，科学研究補助金に
よる「クメール帝国の空間構造と地方拠点都市遺跡に
関する研究」の調査の一環として，2012年よりプレ
ア・ヴィヘア機構協力のもと，プレア・ヴィヘア寺院
において調査を開始した。本調査では，まず学術資料
として各種分析に耐えうる十分な基礎資料（図面，各
種インベントリー）を作成した。それらの基礎資料を
基に，プレア・ヴィヘア寺院において建築的そして都
市計画的な側面を中心とした多角的な分析を行った。

　本調査により作成された基礎資料および研究成果は
将来的な修復事業においても非常に有用なものになり
うると考えられる。

1.1 Objective of Study

　A joint team of Meijo and Waseda Universities in Japan have
implemented a survey of provincial temples in Cambodia from
2007. This survey is based on the realization as follows:
— understanding the expansion of the Khmer empire is a very
important matter for the growth of Khmer study considering that
Khmer study and restoration work are progressing mainly in the
Angkor area.
— there is an urgent need to collect basic data from provincial
temples that are advancing to ruin.

　We had conducted surveys at mainly the Koh Ker Monuments
and Beng Mealea Temple monuments from 2007 to 2011 by
Grant-in-Aid for Scientific Research (KAKENHI) in JAPAN in
cooperation with APSARA National Authority, and JSA. In this
project, we have implemented surveys of two provincial temple
groups as mentioned above and surveys of Chau Srei Vibol
Temple and "Temple d'étape" along the royal road from Angkor
to Preah Khan Temple of Kompong Svay.

　A joint team of Meijo and Waseda Universities implemented a
multidisciplinary survey of Preah Vihear Temple in cooperation
with the National Authority for Preah Vihear as a part of survey
of the grants-in-aid program for the "Scientific Technical
Research on the Spacial Structure of the Khmer Empire and
Ancient Khmer Provincial Principal Monuments". The objective
and outcome of this project is mainly two fold. First, we have
developed basic data such as the detailed drawing made from the
data measured by Total Station, GPS, 3D measurement, and the
inventory of elements. Second, we have done a comprehensive
analysis with a central focus on architecture and planning of each
remains using the basic data made in these surveys.

　The basic data and results of the surveys are very helpful for
planning and implementing restoration work in the future.

Chapter 1 : Project Overview

1.2 調査体制

調査は以下のような体制で行った。なお、括弧内の肩書はいずれも調査当時のものである。

[研究代表者]
・溝口　明則（名城大学理工学部教授, 建築学）

[研究分担者]
・中川　武（早稲田大学理工学術院教授；JSA団長；JASA共同代表, 建築学）
・内田　悦生（早稲田大学理工学術院教授, 岩石学）
・久保　純子（早稲田大学教育・総合科学学術院教授, 自然地理学）
・杉山　洋（独立行政法人国立文化財機構奈良文化財研究所企画調整部長, 考古学）
・池内　克史（東京大学大学院情報学環教授, デジタル3Dデータベース）
・大石　岳史（東京大学大学院情報学環准教授, デジタル3Dデータベース）
・下田　一太（筑波大学人間総合科学研究科助教, 建築学）

[連携研究者]
・小川　英文（東京外国語大学国際社会学部教授, 考古学）
・小野　邦彦（サイバー大学副学長, 建築学）
・佐藤　桂（独立行政法人国立文化財機構東京文化財研究所特別研究員, 建築学）
・南雲　直子（独立行政法人土木研究所 水災害・リスクマネジメント国際センター（ICHARM）水災害研究グループ専門研究員, 自然地理学）
・肥田　路美（早稲田大学文学学術院教授, 美術史）

[調査員]
・内田　賢二（早稲田大学理工研嘱託）
・影沢　政隆（東京大学生産技術研究所助教）
・清水　創大（東京大学大学院情報学環特任准教授）
・鄭　波（東京大学生産技術研究所特任助教）
・佐藤　由似（奈良文化財研究所国際調整室研究補佐員）
・ソ・ケオ・ソバナラ（奈良文化財研究所スタッフ）
・チャン・ヴィタロン（カ国文化省考古部遺物管理局技官）
・猪瀬　健二（東京大学学際情報学府博士課程）
・石塚　充雅（JASAスタッフ）
・下田　麻里子（JASAスタッフ）

1.2 Research Organization

Research organization of this study is as follows. Each status written in parentheses are the one at that time of this study conducted.

[Principal Investigator]
・MIZOGUCHI Akinori (Professor of Faculty of Science and Technology, Meijo University, Architecture)

[Co-Investigator (kenkyu-buntansha)]
・NAKAGAWA Takeshi (Professor of Faculty of Science and Engineering, Waseda University; Director General of JSA; Co-director of JASA, Architecture)
・UCHIDA Etsuo (Professor of Faculty of Science and Engineering, Waseda University, Petrology)
・KUBO Sumiko (Professor of School of Education, Waseda University, Physical Geography)
・SUGIYAMA Hiroshi (Director of Department of Planning and Coordination, Nara National Institute for Cultural Properties, Archaeology)
・IKEUCHI Katsushi (Professor of I.I.S., The University of Tokyo, Digital Three-Dimensional Database)
・OISHI Takeshi (Associate Professor of I.I.S., The University of Tokyo, Digital Three-Dimensional Database)
・SHIMODA Ichita (Assistant Professor of Graduate School of Comprehensive Human Sciences,Tsukuba University, Architecture)

[Co-Investigator (renkei-kenkyusya)]
・OGAWA Hidefumi (Professor of School of International and Area Studies, Tokyo University of Foreign Studies, Archaeology)
・ONO Kunihiko(Vice-president, Cyber University, Architecture)
・SATO Katsura (Research Fellow of Independent Administrative Institution National Institute for Cultural Heritage, Tokyo National Research Institute for Cultural Properties, Architecture)
・NAGUMO Naoko (Researcher of ICHARM, Public Works Research Institute, Physical Geography)
・HIDA Romi (Professor of Faculty of Letters, Arts and Sciences, Waseda University, Art History)

[Research Member]
・UCHIDA Kenji (Research Assistant of Waseda University)
・KAGESAWA Masataka (Research Associate of I.I.S., The University of Tokyo)

Project Overview

・蜂須賀　瞬（早大大学院創造理工学研究科修士課程）
・田淵　奈央（早大大学院創造理工学研究科修士課程）
・出雲　蓮人（早大大学院創造理工学研究科修士課程）
・荻原　周（早大大学院創造理工学研究科修士課程）
・上條　理紗（早大大学院創造理工学研究科修士課程）
・古賀　友佳子（早大大学院創造理工学研究科修士課程）
・中村　みふみ（早大大学院創造理工学研究科修士課程）
・北井　絵里沙（早大大学院創造理工学研究科修士課程）
・黒岩　千尋（早大大学院創造理工学研究科修士課程）
・貞富　陽介（早大大学院創造理工学研究科修士課程）
・松本　奈穂（早大大学院創造理工学研究科修士課程）
・佐藤　広野（早大大学院創造理工学研究科修士課程）
・渡辺　亮太（早大大学院創造理工学研究科修士課程）
・ディン・ミンキアン（早大大学院創造理工学研究科
　修士課程）
・蘆　雨蘇（早大大学院創造理工学研究科修士課程）
・髙橋　泉美（早稲田大学創造理工学部）
・金子　達哉（早稲田大学創造理工学部）
・成井　至（早稲田大学創造理工学部）
・中村　嘉代子（名城大学理工学部）
・水谷　惇志（名城大学理工学部）
・大澤　里美（早稲田大学創造理工学部）
・櫻井　雄一朗（早稲田大学創造理工学部）
・池内　尚史（慶応大学理工学部）
・ピン・ソパー（プレア・ヴィヘア機構）
・イン・ペカダイ（プレア・ヴィヘア機構）
・ニェン・ソントン（プレア・ヴィヘア機構）
・モウン・チャンセイ（プレア・ヴィヘア機構）

1.3 調査日程・メンバー
■2012年度
［第1次ミッション］
調査期間：2012年8月5日〜8月25日
メンバー：溝口明則, 中川武, 池内克史, 久保純子,
大石岳史, 下田一太, 佐藤桂, 南雲直子, 内田賢二,
影沢政隆, チャン・ヴィタロン, 石塚充雅, 下田麻里子,
蜂須賀瞬, 田淵奈央, 出雲蓮人, 荻原周, 古賀友佳子,
中村みふみ, ピン・ソパー, イン・ペカダイ
調査内容：GPS/TPSによる基準点作成, TPS/手ばかり
による図面作成, 3D測量による現状記録, 建築学調査,
地形学調査, 周辺遺構踏査

［第2次ミッション］
調査期間：2012年12月23日〜12月29日
メンバー：溝口明則, 中川武, 池内克史, 大石岳史,
下田一太, 清水創大, チャン・ヴィタロン, 石塚充雅,

・SHIMIZU Sota (Project Research Associate of I.I.S., The University of Tokyo)
・ZENG Bo (Project Research Associate of I.I.S., The University of Tokyo)
・SATO Yuni (Assistant Researcher of International coordination section of Nara National Research Institute for Cultural Properties)
・SOK Keo Sovannara (staff of Nara National Research Institute for Cultural Properties)
・CHAN Vitharong (Staff of Ministry of Culture and Fine Arts)
・INOSE Kenji (Ph.D. Student of Graduate School of I.I.S., University of Tokyo)
・ISHIZUKA Mitsumasa (Technical Staff of JASA)
・SHIMODA Mariko (Technical Staff of JASA)
・HACHISUKA Shun (Master's Course Student of Graduate School, Waseda University)
・TABUCHI Nao (Master's Course Student of Graduate School, Waseda University)
・IZUMO Rento (Master's Course Student of Graduate School, Waseda University)
・OGIHARA Shu (Master's Course Student of Graduate School, Waseda University)
・KAMIJO Risa (Master's Course Student of Graduate School, Waseda University)
・KOGA Yukako (Master's Course Student of Graduate School, Waseda University)
・NAKAMURA Mifumi (Master's Course Student of Graduate School, Waseda University)
・KITAI Erisa (Master's Course Student of Graduate School, Waseda University)
・KUROIWA Chihiro (Master's Course Student of Graduate School, Waseda University)
・SADATOMI Yosuke (Master's Course Student of Graduate School, Waseda University)
・MATSUMOTO Naho (Master's Course Student of Graduate School, Waseda University)
・SATO Hiroya (Master's Course Student of Graduate School, Waseda University)
・WATANABE Ryota (Master's Course Student of Graduate School, Waseda University)
・DING Ming Qian (Master's Course Student of Graduate School, Waseda University)
・LU Yusu (Master's Course Student of Graduate School, Waseda University)
・TAKAHASHI Izumi (Undergarduate Student of Waseda University)

Chapter 1 : Project Overview

荻原周，ピン・ソパー，イン・ペカダイ
調査内容：3D測量による現状記録，建築学調査

■2013年度
［第3次ミッション］
調査期間：2013年3月1日～3月29日
メンバー：中川武，池内克史，下田一太，杉山洋，影沢政隆，鄭波，佐藤由似，石塚充雅，出雲蓮人，荻原周，上條理紗，黒岩千尋，池内尚史，ピン・ソパー，イン・ペカダイ
調査内容：TPS/手ばかりによる図面作成，3D測量による現状記録，建築学調査，考古予備調査

［第4次ミッション］
調査期間：2013年8月2日～9月10日
メンバー：溝口明則，中川武，内田悦生，池内克史，久保純子，下田一太，大石岳史，南雲直子，影沢政隆，鄭波，猪瀬健二，石塚充雅，田淵奈央，出雲蓮人，荻原周，古賀友佳子，中村みふみ，北井絵里沙，貞富陽介，松本奈穂，佐藤広野，大澤里美，ピン・ソパー，ニェン・ソントン
調査内容：TPS/手ばかりによる図面作成，3D測量による現状記録，建築学調査，地形学調査，岩石学調査

［第5次ミッション］
調査期間：2013年12月22日～12月29日
メンバー：内田悦生，池内克史，大石岳史，下田一太，影沢政隆，石塚充雅，佐藤広野，渡辺亮太，モウン・チャンセイ
調査内容：3D測量による現状記録，岩石学調査

■2014年度
［第6次ミッション］
調査期間：2014年2月15日～2月27日
メンバー：溝口明則，中川武，内田悦生，下田一太，杉山洋，佐藤由似，ソク・ケオ・ソバナラ，石塚充雅，渡辺亮太，ディン・ミンキアン，中村みふみ，北井絵里沙，貞富陽介，松本奈穂，ピン・ソパー，ニェン・ソントン
調査内容：建築学調査，岩石学調査，考古学調査

［第7次ミッション］
調査期間：2014年8月21日～8月29日
メンバー：溝口明則，久保純子，南雲直子，杉山洋，佐藤由似，ソク・ケオ・ソバナラ，出雲蓮人，荻原周，古賀友佳子，北井絵里沙，黒岩千尋，貞富陽介，松本

- KANEKO Tatsuya (Undergarduate Student of Waseda University)
- NARUI Itaru (Undergarduate Student of Waseda University)
- NAKAMURA Kayoko (Undergarduate Student of Meijo University)
- MIZUTANI Atsushi (Undergarduate Student of Meijo University)
- OSAWA Satomi (Undergarduate Student of Waseda University)
- SAKURAI Yuichiro (Undergarduate Student of Waseda University)
- IKEUCHI Takashi (Undergarduate Student of Keio University)
- PIN Sopha (Staff of National Authority for Preah Vihear)
- IN Pheakdey (Staff of National Authority for Preah Vihear)
- NHEM Sonthoun (Staff of National Authority for Preah Vihear)
- MOUNG Chansey (Staff of National Authority for Preah Vihear)

1.3 Mission Schedules and Members

■2012

[First mission]

Schedule: 5th August-25th August 2012

Members: MIZOGUCHI Akinori, NAKAGAWA Takeshi, IKEUCHI Katsushi, KUBO Sumiko, OISHI Takeshi, SHIMODA Ichita, SATO Katsura, NAGUMO Naoko, UCHIDA Kenji, KAGESAWA Masataka, CHAN Vitharong, ISHIZUKA Mitsumasa, SHIMODA Mariko, HACHISUKA Shun, TABUCHI Nao, IZUMO Rento, OGIHARA Shu, KOGA Yukako, NAKAMURA Mihumi, PIN Sopha, IN Pheakdey

Mission: Establishing the base point by GPS / TPS, Drawing using by TPS/hand, Recording by 3D measurement, Architectural survey, Geomorphological survey, Field Survey Around the Sites.

[Second mission]

Schedule: 23rd December- 29th December 2012

Members: MIZOGUCHI Akinori, NAKAGAWA Takeshi, IKEUCHI Katsushi, OISHI Takeshi, SHIMODA Ichita, SHIMIZU Sota, CHAN Vitharong, ISHIZUKA Mitsumasa, OGIHARA Shu, PIN Sopha, IN Pheakdey

Mission: Recording by 3D measurement, Architectural survey

■2013

[Third mission]

Schedule: 1st March-29th March 2013

Members: NAKAGAWA Takeshi, IKEUCHI Katsushi, SHIMODA Ichita, SUGIYAMA Hiroshi, KAGESAWA Masataka, ZENG Bo, SATO Yuni, ISHIZUKA Mitsumasa,

奈穂，中村嘉代子，ピン・ソパー，ニェン・ソントン
調査内容：建築学調査，岩石学調査，考古学調査

■2015年度
［第8次ミッション］
調査期間：2015年8月12日〜8月25日
メンバー：溝口明則，内田悦生，久保純子，大石岳史，
南雲直子，石塚充雅，蘆雨蘇，櫻井雄一朗，黒岩千尋，
金子達哉，髙橋泉美，成井至，水谷惇志
調査内容：建築学調査，地形学調査，考古学調査，3D
測量による現状記録

なお、コンポンスヴァイのプレア・カーン寺院の9次にわ
たる調査概要は付章Ⅲに記す。

IZUMO Rento, OGIHARA Shu, KAMIJO Risa, KUROIWA Chihiro, IKEUCHI Takeshi, PIN Sopha, IN Pheakdey
Mission: Drawing using by TPS/hand, Recording by 3D measurement, Architectural survey, Archaeological preliminary survey

[Forth mission]
Schedule: 2nd August-10th September 2013
Members: MIZOGUCHI Akinori, NAKAGAWA Takeshi, UCHIDA Etsuo, IKIEUCHI Katsushi, KUBO Sumiko, SHIMODA Ichita, OISHI Takeshi, NAGUMO Naoko, KAGESAWA Masataka, ZENG Bo, INOSE Kenji, ISHIZUKA Mitsumasa, TABUCHI Nao, IZUMO Rento, OGIHARA Shu, KOGA Yukako, NAKAMURA Mihumi, KITAI Erisa, SADATOMI Yosuke, MATSUMOTO Naho, SATO Hiroya, OSAWA Satomi, PIN Sopha, NHEM Sonthoun
Mission: Drawing using by TPS/hand, Recording by 3D measurement, Architectural survey, Geomorphological survey, Petrology survey

[Fifth mission]
Schedule: 22nd December-29th December 2013
Members: UCHIDA Etsuo, IKEUCHI Katsushi, OISHI Takeshi, SHIMODA Ichita, KAGESAWA Masataka, ISHIZUKA Mitsumasa, SATO Hiroya, WATANABE Ryota, MOUNG Chansey
Mission: Recording by 3D measurement, Petrology survey

■2014
[Sixth mission]
Schedule: 15th February-27th February 2014

Members: MIZOGUCHI Akinori, NAKAGAWA Takeshi, UCHIDA Etsuo, SHIMODA Ichita, SUGIYAMA Hiroshi, SATO Yuni, SOK Keo Sovannara, ISHIZUKA Mitsumasa, WATANABE Ryota, DING Ming Qian, NAKAMURA Mifumi, KITAI Erisa, SADATOMI Yosuke, MATSUMOTO Naho, PIN Sopha, NHEM Sonthoun
Mission: Architectural survey, Petrology survey, Archaeological survey

[Seventh mission]
Schedule: 21th August-29th August 2014
Members: MIZOGUCHI Akinori, KUBO Sumiko, NAGUMO Naoko, SUGIYAMA Hiroshi, SATO Yuni, SOK Keo Sovannara, IZUMO Rento, OGIHARA Shu, KOGA Yukako, KITAI Erisa, KUROIWA Chihiro, SADATOMI Yosuke, MATSUMOTO Naho, NAKAMURA Kayoko, PIN Sopha, NHEM Sonthoun
Mission: Architectural survey, Geomorphological survey, Archaeological survey

■2015
[Eighth mission]
Schedule: 12th August-25th August 2015
Members: MIZOGUCHI Akinori, UCHIDA Etsuo, KUBO Sumiko, OISHI Takeshi, NAGUMO Naoko, ISHIZUKA Mitsumasa, LU Yusu, SAKURAI Yuichiro, KUROIWA Chihiro, KANEKO Tatsuya, TAKAHASHI Izumi, NARUI Itaru, MIZUTANI Atsushi
Mission: Architectural survey, Geomorphological survey, Petrology survey, Recording by 3D measurement

The survey overview of nine missions at Preah Khan Temple of Kompong Svay is mentioned in Appendix III.

Chapter 2
第 2 章

**History of Previous Studies of Preah Vihear Temple and
Historical Significance of Survey**
プレア・ヴィヘア寺院の研究史と調査の意義

Chapter 2 : History of Previous Studies of Preah Vihear Temple and Historical Significance of Survey

凡例
本報告書では，右図に示す建物名を基準とする。建物名に付されたアルファベットは，H. パルマンティエ氏に従う。

Legend
In this report, we use building names as the right drawing. Alphabets of buildings follow the writing of H.Parmentier.

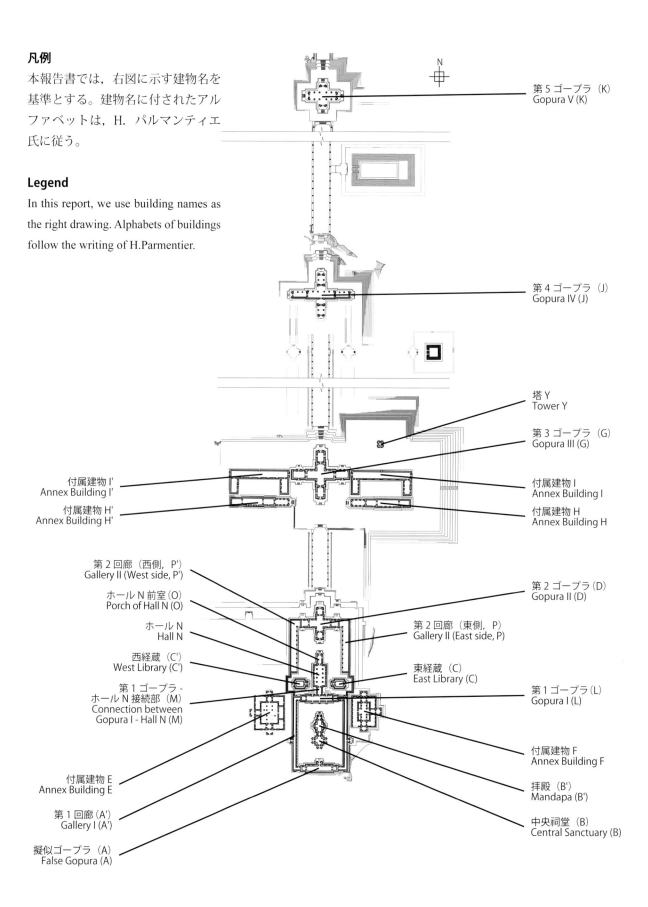

- 第5ゴープラ（K） / Gopura V (K)
- 第4ゴープラ（J） / Gopura IV (J)
- 塔Y / Tower Y
- 第3ゴープラ（G） / Gopura III (G)
- 付属建物 I' / Annex Building I'
- 付属建物 I / Annex Building I
- 付属建物 H' / Annex Building H'
- 付属建物 H / Annex Building H
- 第2回廊（西側，P'） / Gallery II (West side, P')
- 第2ゴープラ（D） / Gopura II (D)
- ホールN前室（O） / Porch of Hall N (O)
- 第2回廊（東側，P） / Gallery II (East side, P)
- ホールN / Hall N
- 西経蔵（C'） / West Library (C')
- 東経蔵（C） / East Library (C)
- 第1ゴープラ-ホールN接続部（M） / Connection between Gopura I - Hall N (M)
- 第1ゴープラ（L） / Gopura I (L)
- 付属建物 F / Annex Building F
- 付属建物 E / Annex Building E
- 拝殿（B'） / Mandapa (B')
- 第1回廊（A'） / Gallery I (A')
- 中央祠堂（B） / Central Sanctuary (B)
- 擬似ゴープラ（A） / False Gopura (A)

2.1 プレア・ヴィヘア寺院の概要と研究史
Outline of Character and History of Previous Studies of Preah Vihear Temple

石塚　充雅　　佐藤　桂　　荻原　周
ISHIZUKA Mitsumasa　　SATO Katsura　　OGIHARA Shu

2.1.1 はじめに

　プレア・ヴィヘア寺院はカンボジアとタイの国境をまたぐダンレック山脈上に位置している。寺院全体の配置は山脈の傾斜を利用し，寺院の最深部を山脈の頂に配置している。本寺院の名称はクメール語の「Preah」＝「神聖な」，「Vihear」＝「仏教僧院」[1]という語を重ねたものである。また，他方タイ側ではカオ・プラ・ヴィハンの名で親しまれている。

　建造時期については，建築史，美術史及び碑文研究の成果から300年間の間に何度も増改築が行われていたと言われており，一般におそらくヤショヴァルマンⅠの統治下で建造が始まり，スールヤヴァルマンⅡの時代で終わったと考えられている。

Photo 2.1-1　Preah Vihear Temple on the cliff of Dangrek Mountains

2.1.2 寺院の概要

　この伽藍は標高約600mの崖の上に位置しており，全長約350m，高低差約100mの中，疑似ゴープラを含む6つのゴープラを結ぶ南北の直線を軸として縦深的に展開している。南から北へと下る地形の傾斜に合わせるように，最深部を頂部である南端の山頂に配置し，そこから北へと降りながら各ゴープラ及び付属施設を配している。本寺院に関しては度重なる増改築

2.1.1 Preface

　Preah Vihear Temple is located on the Dangrek Mountains on the border between Cambodia and Thailand. This temple is arranged by using the slope of the mountain, and the deepest part of this temple is located at the top of the mountain. The name of "Preah Vihear" came from the Khmer words meaning "Preah" meaning "Sacred" and "Vihear" meaning "Buddhist Monastery"[1]. In Thailand, this temple is called "Khao Phra Vihan".

　By the result of study of architecture history, art history and inscriptions, it is generally thought that Preah Vihear Temple has repeated continuous extension and/or alteration construction during the 300 years starting from the period of Yasovarman I and until the period of Suryavarman II.

2.1.2 Outline of Temple

　Preah Vihear Temple is situated on the criff of mountain around 600 m elevation and arranged by centering straight line connecting 6 kinds of Gopura including False Gopura vertically in north – south direction throughout the length of around 700 m and the height of around 100 m. To adjust the slope of terrain declining from south to north, the central part is situated at the south and each Gopura and attached building is arranged to the north. Regarding this temple, it has been pointed out there is possible to have been repeated continuous extension and/or alteration construction. There is a wide space in the west side of the central part at the top so it was possible to take a concentric temple composition which is common in Angkor when monument was extended. Although it seems that it dared to select a vertically-oriented layout. On the other hand, since there are traces of artificial alteration of terrain, it can be thought that monument had been extended by the way that natural shape of terrain had been not used as it was but intentionally modified

17

Chapter 2 : History of Previous Studies of Preah Vihear Temple and Historical Significance of Survey

が行われた可能性が指摘されている一方，頂部に目を向けると中心部西側には広いスペースがあるため，アンコールでは一般的である同心型の寺院構成を取ることも可能ではあったが，あえて縦深的な配置を選択し，拡張していったと思われる。他方，人工的に地形を改変している痕跡も見受けられるため，自然の地形をそのまま利用したわけではなく，当時の計画者の理念に従い，地形を意図的に改変しながら，寺院を拡張していった意図が読み取れる。

　北からの参道以外にも第5ゴープラ東西には古い参道が残っている。特に東側の石造の参道は一部崩壊した状況にあるが，近年整備が進み，参道に沿って木造の階段が整備されており，この参道に沿って麓まで降ることができる。この参道の東端北側の岩盤上にはリンガ・ヨニの彫刻がみられ，さらに参道の先には人工の貯水池，そして古代の集落があったことが確認されている。そのため，この東側の参道が北側の参道同様，あるいは北側の参道の先には麓に通じる道が現在確認されていないため，古代よりプレア・ヴィヘア寺院に通じる参道として重要な役割を果たしていたことが想起される。

　加えて，各ゴープラ間の空間構成が同一ではなく，意図的に変化させていることが本寺院の大きな特徴の一つである。地形，参道，そして参道に付随する階段，石灯籠やナーガ高欄，石敷のペイヴメント，参道両脇の土塁，さらには建物周辺に配される基壇のレイアウトなどを少しずつ変化させることにより，各ゴープラ間の空間演出の差異を生み出している。第5ゴープラ正面の急な階段を上ると，その先の第5ゴープラから第4ゴープラに向かう参道は開かれた形式を取る。他方で，第4ゴープラから第3ゴープラに向う参道の両脇には土塁が配され，閉鎖的な空間に一変する。さらにこの空間より参道の石畳の石一つ一つのサイズがほぼ同一の形式を取ることから，それ以前の空間とは異なる空間であることを明示しているかのようである。その先の第3ゴープラから第2ゴープラまでの空間は一瞬開かれた空間構成となる一方，第2ゴープラから中央祠堂，さらにその背面に配される疑似ゴープラまでは回廊で囲まれ，再び閉鎖的な空間を取るようになるが，その背面は断崖となって，また開かれた空間となる。このようなシークエンスの演出が本寺院の空間構成上大きな特徴であると言えよう。

2.1.3 研究史

　本遺構に関してはアンコール地域から遠く離れた立地条件にあることから，20世紀に調査が十分に実施さ

according to the philosophy of the planner at the time.

　Besides the approach from the north, Gopura V has ancient approaches at east and west side. Particularly the east stone paved approach has collapsed partially, we can go down to the foot along this approach path by wooden staircases set after maintenance has progressed. Sculptures of linga and yoni were seen on the bedrock on the north side of the eastern end of this approach, and it was confirmed that there was an artificial pond and ancient village beyond the approach. As approach to the foot of mountain is not seen at north side of north approach until now, the east approach seems to have played an important role as an approach to Preah Vihear Temple since ancient times as much as or greater than the north approach.

　In addition, it is one of the major features of this monument that spaces between each Gopura are not same and changed intentionally. By gradually changing the layout of terrain, causeway and attached element of the causeway such as step, stone lantern, naga balustrade, stone pavement, earthwork and platform around each building, differences in spatial characteristics between each Gopura were created. When you climb the steep stairs in the front of Gopura V, the approaching path from Gopura V to Gopura IV shows a relatively open space. On the other hand, since the earthwork is arranged around the approaching path from Gopura IV to the Gopura III, it transforms the space into a closed space. Furthermore, since each size of tile stone of stone pavement from this space take almost the same form, it was intended to be a space different from the previous space. Although the space from Gopura III to Gopura II is opened for a moment, the space from Gopura II to the False Gopura set behind Central Shrine is closed by Gallery. The space on the backside of False Gopura has a cliff and become opened again. Such a changing of space is a main feature of this temple. This interpretation of sequence is spatial big feature of this temple.

Photo 2.1-2　Sculptures of linga and yoni

2.1.3 History of Previous Study

Until the 1920's, study for this monument was not implemented enough because of the distance from the Angkor area. A.Bergaigne and A.Barth implemented the study of stele (K382) in Preah Vihear Temple (A.Barth 1885; A.Bergaigne and A.Barth 1893). In the result, they believed this stele was produced in the period of Yasovarman I. After, E.Aymonier tried to review the stele (K382) and he estimates the entire stele (K382), including both its Sanskrit text and its final Khmer text, as composed in 1047 A.D. (E.Aymonier 1897). In "Le Cambodge" devoted to the Siamese provinces of the Angkor Empire, Aymonier offered a summary description of the temple, analysis of the inscriptions in Khmer and Sanskrit, and sketches of Preah Vihear Temple. In this book, he also expressed his idea of the construction date of the entire Preah Vihear Temple as in the period of Suryavarman I. However, this book had some mistakes such as regarding lantern stone as pillar, the characteristic of sandstone, and the recording of the plan of Annex Building E and F in his drawing.

In 1907, E.Lajonquière attempted an architectural description of the monument, visiting from the Thai side (IK, no. 398). In this book, recording of each building was implemented relatively correct, and his drawing from the top of the cliff also was shown.

G.Groslier published his art historical observation by the result of his visit of Preah Vihear Temple in 1913 (G.Groslier 1921-1923).

In 1939, H.Parmentier presented the result of research, cleaning, and study of Preah Vihear Temple monuments in May 1924, March 1929, and February 1930 in "L'Art Khmer Classique. Monuments du Quadrant Nord-Est" (EFEO: Paris). In this book, he showed the detail architectural recording of each building and studied the construction process of each building.

In 1946, after collating the parallel inscription of Preah Vihear Temple (K383) and Phnom Sandak Temple (K194),

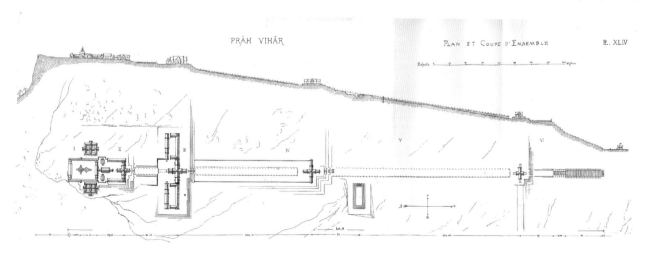

Figure 2.1-1 Plan and section of Preah Vihear Temple (H.Parmentier, 1939)

院（K383）及びプノム・サンダック寺院（K194）の碑文を比較した上で，スールヤヴァルマンⅡの治世期である12世紀の重要な情報が記載されている内容をほぼ完全な形で提示した。また1954年に出版された『Inscriptions du Cambodge』の第6巻において，碑文K380及びK381を解読した。

　1924，1959年，そして1970年代のそれぞれの時代で，Shikhareshvara（シカレシュヴァラ）[2]に言及した碑文（K583）の破片がバプーオン寺院から発見された。L. フィノ，G. セデスそしてC. ジャックは発見された断片を再構成する試みを続けた。

　2008年にはプレア・ヴィヘア寺院が世界遺産に認定された。このとき，10名の国際的なエキスパートが，様々な観点から，遺構の現状，今後のマネージメント及び調査研究に関する問題点に関するレポートを提出している。

　世界遺産に登録された後，しばらくの間，カンボジア－タイ間でプレア・ヴィヘア寺院をめぐる紛争があったため調査が困難な状況が続いたが，近年では沈静化し，再び遺跡まで歩を進める人々が増え始めている。

　最近ではS. サハイが，これまでの研究成果を検証し，プレア・ヴィヘア寺院の建造過程や役割について再検討した。また，B. ブルギエの『Guide archeologique du Cambodge Tome V』においてもコンポン・スヴァイのプレア・カーン寺院，コー・ケー遺跡群と共にプレア・ヴィヘア寺院の報告がなされている。

　上記のような既往研究の中で，プレア・ヴィヘア寺院の建造年代及び過程に関して多くの言及がなされてきた。A. バース，A. バーゲイン，G. セデス，そしてH. パルマンティエは，プレア・ヴィヘア寺院が最初に造営されたのは9世紀，ヤショヴァルマン治世下と考えていた。これは同寺院から発見された石碑に記された碑文（K382）の年代解釈に基づいていたが，E. エイモニエは，この碑文がヤショヴァルマン時代のものではないとして，プレア・ヴィヘア寺院の全体をスールヤヴァルマンⅠによる建立と見なしていた。G. グロリエは，美術史的観点より，プレア・ヴィヘア寺院をコー・ケー遺跡群とワット・プー寺院との間に位置付けていた（G. Groslier 1924-1926）。B. Ph. グロリエは，プレア・ヴィヘア寺院の最初の造営を10世紀，ラージェンドラヴァルマンⅡ治世下と考えていた（B. Ph. Groslier 1961）。C. ジャックによれば，バプーオン寺院の碑文は，プレア・ヴィヘア寺院のシカレシュヴァラ信仰と祠堂の始まりをジャヤヴァルマンⅡの時代であると示している。

G.Cœdès published a nearly complete text giving important information about the site in the 12th century during the reign of Suryavarman II (BEFEO 43), and in Vol. 6 of Inscriptions du Cambodge published in 1954, he deciphered K380 and K381.

The stele of Baphuon Temple (K583), which refers to Shikhareshvara[2], was discovered in pieces from the site on three different occasions in 1924, 1959, and the 1970s. L.Finot, G.Cœdès, and C.Jacques have tried to reconstitute the text following the discovery of various pieces of inscribed slab.

In 2008, Preah Vihear Temple was registered as a World Heritage site. In this time, ten distinguished international experts presented the report on various aspects of the current state of preservation of the monument, and various problems related to the management and recommended further study of the site.

After registered as a World Heritage site, survey and study at site have been difficult to implement because of the conflict between Cambodia and Thailand for Preah Vihear Temple ownership. The situation has corrected itself with possession and responsibility to the Kingdom of Cambodia.

Recently, S.Sahai reviewed the result of study for Preah Vihear Temple until now and reconsiderd the construction process and the role of Preah Vihear Temple. In this book, he referred to the construction process of Preah Vihear Temple. B.Bruguier also reported about Preah Vihear Temple with Preah Khan Temple of Kompong Svay and Koh Ker Monuments in "Guide Archeologique du Cambodge Tome V".

In the previous study above, the date and process of construction of Preah Vihear Temple is an important and interesting theme for every surveyor. A.Barth, A.Bergaigne, G.Cœdès, H.Parmentier believe that the first constructions were made at the site of Preah Vihear Temple in the 9th century, in the period of Yasovarman I. This opinion came from the stele (K382) found from Preah Vihear Temple, but E.Aymonier regarded this stele not as in the period of Yasovarman I but as in A.D 1047 and assigned the constructions at Preah Vihear Temple to the reigns of Suryavarman I and Suryavarman II. From the art-historical point of view, G.Groslier places the constructions at Preah Vihear Temple between Koh Ker Monuments and Vat Phu Temple. According to B.Ph.Groslier (1961, 108), the first construction at the site date back to the reign of Rajendravarman II in the 10th century. To C.Jacques, the inscription of the Baphuon Temple appears to fix without ambiguity the beginning of the existence of a sanctuary consecrated to Shikhareshvara at this place in the epoch of Jayavarman II.

H.Parmentier, who estimated the construction process of Preah Vihear Temple in most particular in the history of study in Preah

同寺院の建造過程について最も詳細に考察を示しているH. パルマンティエは遺跡の観察から，次のような増改築の関係性を指摘した。

1. 第2回廊は第1回廊よりも後に建造された。
2. 第1回廊内では屋根の改築がなされた。
3. 中央祠堂（B）は拝殿（B'）より後に建造された。
4. 第3ゴープラは付属建物H，H'，I，I'（「宮殿」）より後に建造された。
5. 第4ゴープラ正面の穴列群は前身の配置であり，後の時代に放棄された。
6. 第3ゴープラ及び第2ゴープラ前方階段及び斜路の未完成の状態より，当初は各ゴープラに続く単純な斜路であった。
7. 第1回廊西側に開口部があり，後年閉じられた。
8. 付属建物 E，F は中央祠堂及び第1回廊の後に建造された。

さらに碑文の年代解釈を考慮した上で，H. パルマンティエは最終的に次のような7段階の造営過程を推察していた。だが彼自身，これが解決困難な幾つもの問題点を最も都合良く解釈しただけの，あくまでも仮説に過ぎないことを明記しており，この点には注意を要する（H. Parmentier 1939, p. 339）。H. パルマンティエはG. グロリエの説にならい，最初に寺域全体が木造で建造された後，徐々に石造に置き換えられていったものと推察した。彼の説を整理すると，次のようになる。

1. ヤショヴァルマン I
・現在の敷地全体を覆う寺院を建設;
中央祠堂，回廊，5つのゴープラ（木造），ナーガ欄干，北及び東方向から頂部に続く参道，灯篭石（石造）

2. ヤショヴァルマン I の後継者
・第1ゴープラ（L）[3]，ホールN，第2ゴープラ（D），第2伽藍内翼廊（P）（石造・木造瓦葺き屋根）

3. ラージェンドラヴァルマンII，またはジャヤヴァルマンV
・第1回廊（A'）および疑似ゴープラ（A）（石造）
・拝殿（B'）（石造）
・経蔵（C）（石造・レンガ屋根）
・付属建物E，F（石造・木造瓦葺き屋根）

Vihear Temple, proposed for the relationship of the extension or reconstruction from the result of observation as follow;

1. Gallery II was constructed after Gallery I.
2. Reconstruction of the roof was implemented in Gallery I.
3. Mandapa (B') was constructed after Central Sanctuary (B).
4. Gopura III was constructed after Annex Building H, H', I, I' "Palaces".
5. Rows of halls in front of Gopura IV were trace of the earlier arrangement and abandoned in favor of a new arrangement in later period.
6. From the unfinished state of the steps and gradients in front of Gopura III and Gopura II, in a first phase, the rock formations were simply shaped into a steep path leading to the various terraces.
7. In West Gallery I (A') there was a big opening which was later sealed.
8. The two structures, known as Annex Building E and F, were built after the main sanctuary and its enclosure were completed.

H.Parmentier finally estimated the seven step of construction process as below in accordance with result of the previous studies of the period of the stele. However, we need to take care that he also wrote clearly that this idea was only a tentative theory raised from the most convenient aspect to solve a lot of intractable points. He followed the idea of G.Groslier that at first entire building of Preah Vihear Temple was implemented by using wood and reconstruction was implemented by sandstone in later periods. His idea is arranged as follows;

1. Yasovarman I
・ Arrangement of the entire Complex;
Central Sanctuary, the Galleries, the Gopuras I-V (built by wood), the naga decoration, the northern and eastern approaches to sanctuary, the boundary posts (built by sandstone)

2. One of the successors of Yasovarman I
・Gopura I (L)[3], Hall N, Gopura II (D), Gallery of Complex II (P) (built by sandstone with tiled wooden roof)

3. Rajendravarman II or Jayavarman V
・ Gallery I (A) and False Gopura (A') (built by sandstone)
・ Mandapa (B') (built by sandstone)
・ Library (C) (built by sandstone with brick roof)
・ Annex Building E, F (built by sandstone with roof tile)

Chapter 2 : History of Previous Studies of Preah Vihear Temple and Historical Significance of Survey

4．スールヤヴァルマン I
・付属建物H，I，H'，I'（石造・木造瓦葺き屋根）
・第2回廊付属周壁（石造）
・第4ゴープラ（J）及び第5ゴープラ（K）（石造・木造瓦葺き屋根）
・塔Y（石造）
・第3ゴープラ（G）（スールヤヴァルマン I 治世の時点では未完成）

5．ウダヤディティヤヴァルマン II
・中央祠堂（B）（建造中に崩壊，崩壊した瓦礫の除去）（同時に第3ゴープラ（G）の崩落した屋根レンガの除去）

6．スールヤヴァルマン II
・第2回廊内の建物ホールN，第2ゴープラ（D）におけるポーチの改造
・新しい通路の付加

　上記の説を受け，S. サハイは中央祠堂の崩壊した時期，全体計画の時期等に言及するとともに各年代の建造に関して以下のような言及を行っている（S. Sahai 2008）。

○10世紀以前
・ジャヤヴァルマン II の統治期にはすでに有名な Shavite の場所であった
・全体計画がヤショヴァルマン I の時代にできていたかは不明
・自然の高台上に小屋型のアーシュラマの設置
・4つのテラスの整備
・第5ゴープラ（腐りやすい素材）の設置
・中央祠堂～第5ゴープラの建物（mahat dvara）の設置
・ヤショヴァルマン I の時代に北側階段の整備

○10世紀
・中庭 I（第1伽藍）の整備

○11世紀前半
・東の階段の整備
・第1ゴープラの身廊の増築
・第3ゴープラの両脇に Viraçrama もしくは「宮殿」と呼ばれる建物の増築の実施
・第2ゴープラ，経蔵，柱のあるベランダを含む第2回廊（第2伽藍）の整備

4. Suryavarman I
• Annex Building H,I,H',I' (built by sandstone with roof tile)
• Attached Wall of Gallery II (built by stone)
• Gopura IV (J), Gopura V (K) (built by sandstone with roof tile)
• Tower Y (built by sandstone)
• Gopura III (G) (unfinished in the period of Suryavarman I)

5. Udayadityavarman II
• Central Sanctuary (B) (crumbling during construction, cleaning of ruined material)
(at that time cleaning of ruined roof brick of Gopura III (G))

6. Suryavarman II
• Modification of Porch of Hall N, Gopura II (D)
• Add new paths

S.Sahai proposed the process of construction in each period of Preah Vihear Temple as below with some comments such as the date of crumbling of Central Sanctuary and the date of entire planning proposal by H.Parmentier (S.Sahai, 2008);

○ Before 10th century
• Preah Vihear Temple was already famous place as famous Shavite in the period of Jayavarman II
• It is difficult to ascertain entire layout of the site in the time of King Yasovarman I
• On one natural terrace, the first hut-shaped ashrama was built.
• The four terraces were arranged
• The four-faced pavilion (Gopura V) was definitely set up in the time of Yasovarman I by perishable material
• One larger pavilion (mahat dvara) was established between Gopura V and the site of the Central Sanctuary
• The northern stairway was built in the time of Yasovarman I

○ The 10th century
• Court I (Complex I) was built

○ The first half of the 11th century
• The eastern stairway was built
• The narve in front of Gopura I was added
• Additions on either side of Gopura Ill, in the shape of the Viraçrama or the so-called "palaces" was made
• Gallery II with Gopura II, the two Libraries, the pillared verandahs (Complex II) were constructed

○ 11世紀後半
・中央祠堂（石造）の改築

○ 12世紀
・2つの付属建物E，Fの設置
・第4ゴープラ前に傘を設置するための穴の設置
・12世紀終わりに中央祠堂（石造）の崩壊

　ただし、S. サハイの説にしても第3〜5ゴープラへの言及が不十分であったり、建築及び美術的な観点からの言及が部分的にされるのみである。上記のような状況からプレア・ヴィヘア寺院の建造の変遷に関してはいまだ包括的に理解できていないのが現状である。

2.1.4 建築的特徴
　各建物の名称については、前述した先行研究において各研究者によって様々な呼び方がされてきたが、ここではH. パルマンティエによって記され、その後一般的に使用されている名称及び記号を採用して説明を行う。

2.1.4.1 各建物の特徴
○第5ゴープラ（K）
　第5ゴープラ（K）はプレア・ヴィヘア寺院の中で最初の入口として設置された四方に入口を有する十字型平面の建物である。比較的小さな建物ではあるが、壁体はなく柱と梁のみを用いる構成はカンボジアではあまり見られない。このため、プレア・ヴィヘア寺院を象徴する建物となっている。

○第4ゴープラ（J）
　第5ゴープラ（K）と同様の十字型の平面の建物である。ただし、大きさは第5ゴープラ（K）よりも一回り大きく、構成も第5ゴープラ（K）とは異なり南面は窓

○ The second half of the 11th century
・Central Sanctuary made by sandstone was reconstructed

○ The 12th century
・Two impluvium (Annex Building E, F) were added
・The holes for setting large umbrellas in front of Gopura IV were set
・The Sanctuary was collapsed at the close of the 12th century

In the proposal by S.Sahai, suggestion to Gopura III-V was unclear and the comments from a points of architectural and art were partial. As the present situation above, the process of construction of Preah Vihear Temple is not comprehensively understood.

2.1.4 Architectural Features
Regarding the name of each building, various designations have been made by each researcher in the preceding research mentioned above. We explain here by names and sign commonly used by E.Lunet de Lajonquière and H.Parmentier.

2.1.4.1 Features of Each Building
○ Gopura V (K)
Gopura V (K) is a cross-shaped building with entrances on all sides set up as the first entrance in Preah Vihear Temple. Although it is a relatively small building in Preah Vihear Temple, it is a building that symbolizes Preah Vihear Temple because the structure made of only pillars and beams without wall is not seen in Cambodia.

○ Gopura IV (J)
Gopura IV (J) is also cross-shaped building same as Gopura V (K). However, the size is one size larger than Gopura V (K) and the composition is also a little different from Gopura V (K) that

Photo 2.1-3　Gopura V (K)

Photo 2.1-4　Gopura IV (J)

Chapter 2 : History of Previous Studies of Preah Vihear Temple and Historical Significance of Survey

のない壁体を有しており，第5ゴープラ（K）と比べやや閉鎖的な空間となっている。

　往時の木製扉の痕跡に着目すると，通常この種のゴープラに付随する扉は中心部に向って扉が開かれるが，本遺構の南入口には，さらに外方に向うような形で扉が配されている痕跡が残されている。この痕跡や本ゴープラの南側への閉鎖性，さらにはその先に広がる回廊の閉鎖的な空間（第3ゴープラ側）から，このゴープラを境に，異なる意味合いを持つ空間に変化する構成となっている。

　また第4ゴープラ（J）の手前には列状の穴の痕跡がある。こちらについてはS．サハイが装飾的な要素のための穴であり，高僧が各段に旗や傘を配していたと指摘している。ただしこれらの穴が列状に並んでいるため，現在の構造物上に木造の構造物が配されていた可能性も考えられる。

it is a somewhat closed space compared to Gopura V (K) because the south side has a wall without a window.

Focusing on the trace of a wooden door, usually the doors accompanying such gopura are arranged as doors that opened towards the center, but trace of wooden door to open outward remained at the south entrance of Gopura IV (J). This trace and the closing property of this Gopura to the south side and the closed space of causeway from Gopura IV (J) to III (G) by earthwork set at both side of the causeway indicate that the character of space changes from here to space having a slightly different meaning.

There is a traces of row of holes in front of Gopura IV (J). S.Sahai mentioned that these holes were for decorative elements used for arrangement of flags and umbrellas at each stage by high priests. On the other hand, as these holes are arranged in a row, there is a possibility that wooden structures were arranged on the current structure.

○ Gopura III (G) and Annex Building H, I, H', I' ("palaces")

Gopura III (G) is the biggest Gopura in the Preah Vihear Temple. In addition to central entrances, this Gopura has entrances on both sides. On both sides of this Gopura is arranged a building called "palaces" (Annex Building H, I, H', I') to be in contact with the Gopura. The unknown building called "palace" is generally composed of an I-shaped building (H, H') and a U-shaped building (I, I'), has many openings on the south side, and a pair of buildings are arranged so as to sandwich the central axis. Similar types of "palaces" in Preah Vihear Temple were seen at large or middle sized vertically-oriented layout Khmer temples. From gopura or other kinds of building are not arranged between the "palaces" in the other temples had "palaces", plan of Preah Vihear Temple seems unique in the plan of Khmer Temple (for details please see Chapter 3.8 in this document). In these "palaces", collapse of I-shaped building of west "palace" (Annex

Photo 2.1-5 Row of holes

Photo 2.1-6 I-shaped building of west "palace" (H')

Photo 2.1-7 Gopura II

○第3ゴープラ（G）及び付属建物H, I, H', I'（「宮殿」）

　第3ゴープラ（G）はプレア・ヴィヘア寺院の中でもっとも大きなゴープラである。中央の入口のほかに両側面に入口を有している。このゴープラの両脇には「宮殿」（H-I, H'-I'）と呼ばれる付属建物が接するように配置されている。用途不明の「宮殿」と呼ばれる建物は一般的にはIの字型の建物（H, H'）とU字型の建物（I, I'）によって構成され，南側に多くの開口部を有し，一対の建物が中心軸を挟むように配される。類似した形式の建物は，他の縦深型で中規模以上のクメール寺院にも見ることができる。ただし，「宮殿」を有するその他の寺院では，「宮殿」の間にゴープラないし建物が配置されていないため，プレア・ヴィヘア寺院の計画がクメール寺院では特異なものであることが伺われる（詳細はpp. 147〜160参照）。「宮殿」のうち，西側「宮殿」I字型建物（H'）は崩壊が進んでいる。東「宮殿」の北側には東西に開かれた小さな塔Yが独立して配置されている。

○第2 ゴープラ（D）〜疑似ゴープラ（A）及び付属建物 E, F

　プレア・ヴィヘア寺院の最上層には第1回廊（A'）と第2回廊（P, P'）で区画された空間がある。ピミアナカスの迫り出し屋根の構造に似た屋根を有する第1回廊（A'）は第1ゴープラ（L）及び疑似ゴープラ（A）と接続しているが，これらのゴープラと接してはいるものの，直接行き来できる構成にはなっていない。第1回廊（A'）北に位置する第1ゴープラ（L）はホール状の空間（N）を有しており，全体的にT字型のような平面構成をしている。ホールNの柱は頂部に突出部を持つため，当時の屋根構造が二層であった可能性が伺われる。他方，第1回廊（A'）南に位置する疑似ゴープラは南側に開口部を持たない特異なゴープラである。アンコールからコンポンスヴァイのプレア・カーン寺院

Building H') is processing. There is small independent Tower Y opend to east and west at the north side of east "palace".

○ Gopura II (D) - False Gopura (A) and Annex Building E, F

Space circulated in the Gallery I (A') and II is arranged in the uppermost layer of Preah Vihear Temple. Although Gallery I (A'), which has a similar cobel roof structure of Pimianakas, was attached with Gopura I (L) and False Gopura (A). It is not configured to be able to come and go directly between Gallery and Gopuras. Gopura I (L), located on the north side of Gallery I (A'), has a T-shaped plan with Hall N. From pillars of Hall N have protruding parts at top, there is a possibility that the roof structure at the time had a double-layered roof structure. On the other hand, the False Gopura (A), located on the south side of Gallery I (A'), has a unique structure with no opening on the south side. In temples identified of "Temple d'étape" situated along the royal road from Angkor to Preah Khan Temple of Kompong Svay, buildings with a closed south can be seen as well. In the center of the Gallery I (A') there is Central Sanctuary (B) with Mandapa (B'). Although the upper structure of the Central Sanctuary (B) is currently collapsing, by the shape of stones scattered around Central Sanctuary (B), Central Sanctuary (B) seems to have a turret-shaped roof structure. On both sides of the Gallery I (A') there are attached buildings with 田 - shaped Annex Building E, F (please see Chapter 3.8 in this report).

On the north side of Gallery I (A'), there is a U-shaped Gallery II (P, P') with Gopura II (D) on the north. Although the outside of the Gallery is composed of walls the inside is not composed by wall but a column pillar. This Gallery and the Gopura II (D) also have a composition that we can not come and go directly between them like Gallery I (A'). There are Libraries (C, C') in this space surrounded by these Galleries and also enclosure walls along the form of Libraries connected between the Gallery I (A') and II (P, P') (for Libraries, please see Chapter 3.9 in this report).

Photo 2.1-8 Inside Gallery II

Photo 2.1-9 From the top of Central Sanctuary

Chapter 2 : History of Previous Studies of Preah Vihear Temple and Historical Significance of Survey

までの王道沿いに設置された宿駅の寺院においても同様に南側を閉じた構成のゴープラが見られる。第1回廊（A'）の中心には拝殿（B'）を接続させた中央祠堂（B）がある。中央祠堂（B）の上部構造は現在崩壊しているが，周囲に散乱している石材の形状を見ると，往時には砲塔状の屋根形式であったようである。第1回廊（A'）の両脇には田の字型平面をした付属建物（E, F）が位置している。

第1回廊（A'）北側には北面に第2ゴープラ（D）を挟んでU字型の平面をとる特異な形式の第2回廊（P, P'）がある。外側は壁面で構成されているが，内側は列柱で構成されている。この回廊と第2ゴープラも第1回廊（A'）同様，行き来できない構成になっている。またこれらの回廊に囲まれた空間内には経蔵（C, C'）が配され，第1回廊（A'）と第2回廊（P, P'）間には，この経蔵に沿うような形で周壁が配され，2つの回廊を連結している。

2.1.4.2 構造的特徴
○屋根

プレア・ヴィヘア寺院で重要な痕跡の一つは失われた屋根の痕跡である。現在，プレア・ヴィヘア寺院の中で屋根の形状が確認できるのは第1回廊（A'）と中央祠堂（B）の拝殿（B'）のみであるが，当初は木造部材やレンガを使用して屋根を架けていた痕跡が伺える。これまでの研究によると，砂岩造の屋根のほかにレンガ造の屋根（疑似ゴープラ（A），経蔵（C, C'）），木造小屋組・レンガ葺屋根（第3ゴープラ（G）），木造小屋組・瓦葺屋根（第1ゴープラ（L）及びホールN，第2ゴープラ（D），第2回廊（P, P'），第4ゴープラ（J），第5ゴープラ（K），付属建物 H-I, H'-I'，付属建物（E, F））という4種類の屋根構造が混在していたとされている。ただし，プレア・ヴィヘア寺院周辺では岩盤が露出し

2.1.4.2 Structural Features
○ Roof

One of the important traces in Preah Vihear Temple is the trace of the lost roof. Currently, at only Gallery I (A') and Mandapa (B') of Central Sanctuary (B), we can check the shape of the roof in Preah Vihear Temple, but you can see also the traces of roof using brick or wood at that time. According to previous studies, there were 4 kinds of roof structure at least; brick roof structure (False Gopura (A), Libraries (C, C')); wooden roof truss with brick roof (Gopura III (G)), and wooden roof truss with roof tile (Gopura I (L) and Hall N, Gopura II (D), Gallery II (P, P'), Gopura IV (J), Gopura V (K), Annex Building H, I, H', I' and Annex Building E, F in addition to the sandstone roof. From bedrock exposed around Preah Vihear Temple and traces of stone quarries which seemed to have cut out stones at that time were also seen. It seems there was no difficulty to get stones. Under such circumstances, the reasons why other materials were underdeveloped of stone flame and used were thought that there was intention to reduce the load by using wood or brick which is a relatively wood compared to the stone, or that there was also a wooden structure at that time, or that usage of brick was a transitional characteristic replacing wooden structure to sandstone structure (for roof structure, refer to Chapter 3.5, 3.7 and 3.10 in this report).

○ Foundation and upper structure

From the many sandstone quarries around Preah Vihear Temple, it seems that they cut stones from these quarries and used them for construction of the temple. Some lower parts of building composed by cutting directly from natural bedrock are seen at Gallery I (A'), the west side Annex Building E and I - shaped building of Annex Building H'. Focusing on the platform of each building, it is usual to arrange a laterite back-filling structure

Photo 2.1-8 Trace of wooden roof structure

Photo 2.1-9 Trace of brick roof structure

ており，当時石材ブロックを切り出していたと思われる石切場の痕跡も見られるため，石材に困るような状況ではなかったと思われる。このような状況下で，あえて他の部材を使用した理由としては，石造架構が未発達で，石材に比べ比較的軽い素材である木やレンガを使用することにより，荷重を軽減する意図があったことや当初は木造の建造物が建てられていたこと，さらにレンガに関しては木造から砂岩造に置き換えられる際の過渡期的性質であること等の理由が考えられる（屋根形式に関してはpp. 103～122，129～146参照）。

〇基礎構造及び上部構造

　伽藍の周辺を見渡すと，多くの砂岩の石切場が存在していることから，往時はこれらの石切場から砂岩材を切り出し，寺院の建造に使用していたと思われる。また第1回廊（A'）や付属建物E，付属建物I字部H'では建物の下部が岩盤から切り出されている箇所がある。各建造物の基壇部に着目すると，アンコールにおいては砂岩造の建造物の基壇部に関しては砂岩の外装壁と内部の版築基礎の間をラテライトの裏込め構造とするのが常であるが，プレア・ヴィヘア寺院においてはラテライトの裏込め構造が存在しないことが最近のプレア・ヴィヘア機構による第5ゴープラの考古調査の成果から分かった。おそらく周囲から容易に砂岩が採取されることが主な要因であると考えられるが，アンコール地域の寺院との大きな差異の一つかと思われるので，今後の研究と，将来的な修復方針を検討していく際に，着目する必要がある。加えて，先述したように建物下部を岩盤から切り出し，その上に壁を立ち上げる構法は珍しい構法でもある。上部構造に関しては，上記した屋根構造以外には基本的には砂岩ブロックが使用されている。

　砂岩の特徴に着目すると，中央祠堂（B），疑似ゴープラ（A），東側付属建物F，第4ゴープラ（J），第1回廊（A'）の一部および西側付属建物Eの一部では比較的大きな石材が使用される一方，付属建物H，I，H'，I'の一部では寺院内で最も小さな石材が用いられている。使用されている石材の特徴を整理することは建物の建造過程を検討していく上で，重要な要素の一つとなっている（詳細はpp. 54～66参照）。

2.1.4.3 他の寺院のとの比較

　本寺院はシヴァ神（シカレシュヴァラ）に奉祀されたと考えられているが，ダンレック山脈にはその他にも西はタ・ムエン・トム寺院に，東はニャック・ブオス寺院の範囲でシヴァ系の寺院が配置されている。S.

between the sandstone exterior material wall and the interior compaction soil structure on a platform of sandstone buildings in Angkor area. However, it was found that there is no laterite backfill structure inside the platform in Preah Vihear Temple from the result of recent archaeological survey at the Gopura V by National Authority for Preah Vihear. This is probably a result from the situation that sandstone is easily collected from the surroundings. This characteristic is one of the big differences from monuments in the Angkor area, so there is a need to focus the future research and the future restoration policy for this characteristic. In addition, as mentioned above, the construction method that arrangement of the wall on the lower part composed by cutting directly from natural bedrock is rare. Sandstone brock is also used basically for upper structures other than the roof structure mentioned above.

Focusing on the features of sandstone, relatively large stone is used in Central Sanctuary (B), False Gopura (A), east side Annex Building F, Gopura IV (J), part of the Gallery I (A') and part of the west side Annex Building E, while the smallest stone in the temple is used in the part of Annex Building H, I, H', I'. Arrangement of characteristics of sandstone used in Preah Vihear Temple is one of the important factors in considering the construction process of the monument (for details, see Chapter 3.2 in this report).

2.1.4.3 Comparison with Other Temples

This temple is thought to be a fellowship to Shiva (Shikaresvara). In the Dangrek Mountains, other Shiva temples are also arranged in the range from Ta Muen Tom Temple in the west until Neak Buos Temple in the east. From these arrangements and myths remaining around this area, S.Sahai noted that in the Southeast Asia Dangrek Mountains plays the same role of the Himalayas in India.

As similar type of temple which takes the form of vertically-

Photo 2.1-10 Trace of stone quarry site

Chapter 2 : History of Previous Studies of Preah Vihear Temple and Historical Significance of Survey

サハイはこれらの配置と現地に残る神話から，東南アジアにおいてダンレック山脈がインドにおけるヒマラヤの役割を担わされていたと指摘している。

プレア・ヴィヘア寺院と同様に縦深型の形式をとる寺院としては，カンボジア側ではバンテアイ・スレイ寺院，コー・ケー遺跡群のプラサート・トム寺院，ニャック・ブオス寺院やトラペアン・スヴァイ寺院等，タイ側ではプノム・ルン寺院等がある。またその他にもラオスにワット・プー寺院等が存在している。この中で，プラサート・トム寺院やプノム・ルン寺院，ワット・プー寺院にはプレア・ヴィヘア寺院に見られる「宮殿」と呼ばれる形式の建物と同形式の建物がみられ，その共通性が指摘できる。

また，プレア・ヴィヘア寺院のように回廊や周壁が日の字の形になるように配されている遺構はコー・ケー遺跡群のプラサート・トム寺院，セック・タ・ツイ寺院，トラペアン・クニャン寺院，プラタル・チョー寺院等プレア・ヴィヘア州に位置している寺院に類似した形式のものが見られる。

他方，装飾的類似性があることが，カンボジアではバプーオン寺院，バンテアイ・スレイ寺院等，その他の国の遺跡ではムアン・タム寺院，ワット・プー寺院等において指摘される。

以上のように，プレア・ヴィヘア寺院と他の寺院を比較検討した場合，日の字型平面計画のような現在のプレア・ヴィヘア州周辺における独自の縦深型の配置を呈する建築計画の発展過程，そして，配置計画や装飾の特徴等から，クメール帝国の中心であったアン

oriented layout as well as Preah Vihear Temple, there are temples in Cambodia that are similar in deity worship such as Banteay Srei Temple, Prasat Thom Temple in Koh Ker Monuments, Neak Buos Temple and Trapeang Svay Temple and temples in Thailand such as Phnom Rung Temple. There are also temples in Laos such as Vat Phu Temple and others. Among them , Prasat Tom Temple, Phnom Rung Temple, Vat Phu Temple have same type of buildings which are called "palaces" as well as Preah Vihear Temple. So their commonality is considered.

Similar 日 - shaped monuments by Gallery or Enclosure wall such as Preah Vihear Temple, are arranged in Prasat Thom Temple in Koh Ker Monuments, Sek Ta Tuy Temple, Trapean Khyang Temple, Pratal Cho Temple etc. located in Preah Vihear province.

On the other hand, decorative similarity are pointed out in Cambodia such as Baphuon Temple, Banteay Srei Temple and in other countries such as Muang Tham Temple, Vat Phu Temple and others.

As mentioned above, when comparing and examining Preah Vihear Temple and other temples, from the development process of unique vertically-oriented layout plan around area called as Preah Vihear province in present like 日 - shaped plan and the features such as arrangement planning and decoration, the importance of Preah Vihear Temple as node between the ruins of the Angkor area which was the center of the Khmer Empire and the Khmer provincial ruins situated northern from Angkor area.

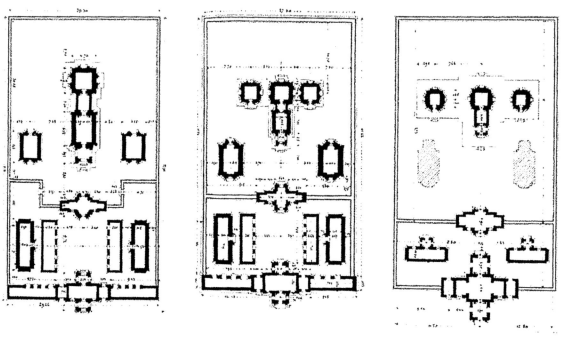

Figure 2.1-2,3,4 Plan of Sek Ta Tuy Temple (left), Trapeang Khyang Temple (center), Pratal Cho Temple (right)(H.Parmentier, 1939)

コール地域の遺跡とアンコール以北に位置するクメール地方遺跡の結節点としてのプレア・ヴィヘア寺院の重要性が窺える。

注

1) "Vihear" は、サンスクリット語とパーリ語の "Vihara" を語源とした語である。

2) "Shikhareshvara" は頂上の支配者としてのシヴァを示す。この用語は碑文ではプレア・ヴィヘアを指し示す際にも使用されている。

3) アルファベット記号はH. パルマンティエによる記載に従ったものである。

Notes

1) "Vihear" originates from "Vihara" meaning "Buddhist Monastery" in Sanskrit and Pali.

2) In the Sanskrit expression, "Shikhareshvara" designates Shiva as the Lord (Ishvara) of the Pinnacle (Shikhara). And this words also denotes the site of Preah Vihear.

3) Alphabets follow the writing of H.Parmentier.

References for Preah Vihear Temple are mainly as fellows;

I) Barth,A., 1885, Inscriptions Sansctrites du Cambodge, Paris.

II) Bergaigne,A., Barth,A., 1893, Inscriptions Sanscrites du Campa et du Cambodge, Paris.

III) Aymonier,E., 1897, Le Cambodge et ses momuments/ Koh Ker, Phnom Sandak, Phnom Preah Vihear,Annales du Musee Guimet, 36, Paris.

IV) Aymonier,E., 1901, Le Cambodge, II: Les Provinces Siamoises, E. Leroux, Paris.

V) Lunet de Lajonquière,E., 1907, Inventaire desctiptif des monuments du Cambodge, II, E. Leroux, Paris.

VI) Groslier,G., 1921, Le Temple de Preah Vihear, AAK, I(3).

VII) Parmentier,H., 1939, L'art Khmer Classique, Monuments du Quadrant Nord-Est 2vols, Paris, EFEO.

VIII) Coedès,G., Dupont,P., 1943-46, La stèle de Sdok Kak Thom, Phnom Sandak et Preah Vihear, BEFEO, 43.

IX) Jaques,C., Freeman,M., 1999, Angkor: Cities and Temples, Riverbook, Bangkok, 1997; Ditto, Ancient Angkor, Riverbook, Bangkok.

X) Roveda,V., 2000, Preah Vihear, Riverbook, Bangkok.

XI) Sahai,S., 2009, Preah Vihear An Introduction to the World Heritage Monument, Phnom Penh, Buddhist Institute Printing House.

2.2 プレア・ヴィヘア寺院における「縦深型寺院」としての歴史的意義と保存修復をめぐる今日的課題

Historical Significance of "Vertically-Oriented Layout Temple" and Subject on Conservation in Preah Vihear Temple

中川　武

NAKAGAWA Takeshi

2.2.1 はじめに

　緑のアンコール平原を見渡すことのできる眺望と共に，大規模且つ典型的な「段台テラス縦深型寺院」の最古の遺構としてプレア・ヴィヘア寺院は重要である。一方で，寺院はカンボジアで2番目の世界遺産として2008年に登録され，現在，保存をめぐる山積みの課題が生じている。

2.2.2 クメールにおけるプレア・ヴィヘア寺院の特質
2.2.2.1 クメール寺院伽藍における「縦深性」について

　クメール寺院はプレ・アンコール期（6世紀）において，インドからの波に洗われるように，カンボジアの南部シャム湾沿いの洞窟内祠堂（プノム・クニャン，プノム・チュゴック）や山上または山腹に単独で建つ祠堂（アシュラム・マハ・ロセイ，プノム・バヤン）をもたらした。これらは神像を安置するためのものであるが，同時にそれ自体礼拝の対象であった。最初期の寺院伽藍の典型は，サンボー・プレイ・クック遺跡群（7～9世紀）で，アプローチのための長い参道と2～3重の周壁，そして中心に向かって少しずつ高めていく段台テラス上に複数の副祠堂と簡易な門を配置し，中心祠堂のシンボル性と正面性を高めるように伽藍が構成されている。しかし，サンボー・プレイ・クック遺跡群の中で最も古いサンボー寺院の中央祠堂（7世紀）が伽藍の東寄りに偏心して配置されているように，中心性の意識もそれほど明快なものではない。

　一方，ワット・プー寺院やプレア・ヴィヘア寺院のように，山岳の麓から中腹や山上へというふうに自然地形を活用して，参道や楼門等の施設を設営するためのテラスを段台状に造築し，それらを最奥の中央伽藍へ向けて繰り返し，中央祠堂とそこに安置されている主尊へ近づくに従ってそのシンボル性を徐々に高めていく空間操作手法が見られる。このような手法は自然

2.2.1 Introduction

　Preah Vihear Temple with the scenery allowing a view of the green Angkor plains, it is important as the oldest remains of large scale and typical "vertically-oriented layout temple on terraced slope". On the other hand, as the 2nd World Heritage Site in Cambodia since 2008, Preah Vihear Temple has stacks of tasks over the conservation.

2.2.2 The Features of Preah Vihear Temple in Khmer
2.2.2.1 "Vertically-Oriented" in Khmer Temple Layout

　In the Pre-Angkor period (6c), as repercussions of India, Khmer temple brought to cave temple along gulf of southern Siam in Cambodia (Phnom Khyang, Phnom Chhugok) and single sanctuary at the top of mountain or mountainside (Asram Moha Russei, Phnom Bayang). These are not only the place for god statues but also the place of worship themselves. The typical temple layout in the earliest period is Sambor Prei Kuk Monuments (7-9c), which complex has composed by long approach, 2 or 3 enclosure and several extra sanctuary and simple gates on terraced slope to symbolize the main sanctuary. In this situation, long approach and temple layout that raises terraces slightly emphasize the main sanctuary and the frontality of temple complex. However, as the oldest sanctuary of Sambor Temple (7c) in Sambor Prei Kuk Monuments has been placed eccentricity by east of complex, the concept of centricity is not so much perspicuous.

　On the other hand, like Vat Phu Temple and Preah Vihear Temple layout, there is a method of space handling by constructing approach and the other facilities on terraced slope that uses topographical environments from the foot to the middle and top of the mountain to make the deepest sanctuary or the main god there symbolically. This method is sometimes seen in temple on a flat plain. For example, Prasat Thom Temple in Koh

の山岳寺院だけでなく，平地伽藍にも見られる。例えば，コー・ケー遺跡群のプラサート・トム寺院やバンテアイ・スレイ寺院が代表的なものである。両者とも中央伽藍の外縁を環濠と最外周壁が囲むが，そのゴープラの外の参道中心軸に対して対称的に副祠堂や直交型長手建物を配置したり，参道に沿って継起的に柱廊を配列して進行方向にリズムを刻んでいる。これらは，施設群の使用目的に沿った機能的な配置であるに留まらず，伽藍中心部の聖性を高めるための空間的効果を発揮している。故に，これもまた縦深型寺院といえるのである。

　そもそも寺院建築は，神座または神像を祀るものであるから，神威の高揚のために建築の内部空間に様々な装置や装飾が発生したり，内部空間の構成に序列性が加わったりする傾向がある。例えば，キリスト教会堂におけるローマ的な有心空間から初期キリスト教会堂→ロマネスク→ゴシックへと変化発展する有軸空間の形成が理解しやすいが，クメール寺院の内部空間は，基本的には特定の儀式以外は一般的な礼拝に供されるものではない。あくまでも，祠堂の周囲あるいは回廊や周壁の外を右回りに回遊しながら礼拝するか，または特定の場合に限られるが，礼拝堂から礼拝する。この場合，四方からほぼ同じ比重の礼拝の場合と正面が明らかに重視されているものがあり，中でもバンテアイ・スレイ寺院の東西方向に延びた拝殿や，正面に拝殿として塔を3基附置したバイヨン寺院の例は，明らかに聖性を高めていることが認められるため，縦深型寺院と呼べなくはない。しかしこれらの例は，あくまでも通常の建築形式の特異な強調的使用例に留まっていて，施設群配置による明快な序列的空間構成の工夫によって神性を高めているものではない。従ってこれらの例は考察対象から除外する。

2.2.2.2 「参道段台テラス縦深型寺院」の形成過程

　この寺院形式で重要なものは，ワット・プー寺院とプレア・ヴィヘア寺院である。ワット・プー寺院の中央祠堂の内陣部は7世紀初め，全体の寺院規模は7世中頃から8世紀初めに計画されたという説がある。また，南北「宮殿」（付属建物）とナンディン堂は当初木造であったと考えられているが年代は不明で，スールヤヴァルマン I の時，石造に造替，その後参道脇の柱廊が作られたらしいことが判っているが，はっきりとした年代は不明である。プレア・ヴィヘア寺院についても事情はあまり変わらない。当初の参道の整備等全体の造成や木造中央祠堂は，ヤショヴァルマン I の時という説があるが根拠は不明である。現遺構の拝殿 I

Ker Monuments and Banteay Srei Temple are representative. Both main sanctuaries are surrounded by the outermost enclosure and a circular moat, however in outside of the outermost Gopura, Extra Sanctuaries and vertical rectangular buildings are symmetrically arranged to the central axis of the approach, the successive colonnades are set along the approach, producing a rhythm in the direction. They are not limited to plot specific functions, in addition, to enhance the sacredness on the center of temple as a spatial effect. Hence it can also be called as the "vertically-oriented layout temple".

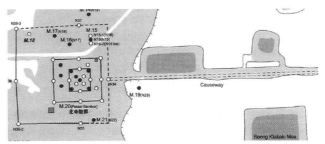

Figure 2.2-1 Sambor Prei Kuk

To begin with temple architecture, for deification the sacred symbol or god statues, it has a tendency to bring about various devices and decorations inside and to add the hierarchy of spatial composition for uplift the god majesty. For instance, it is easy to understand that Roman centripetal space change to an early Christian Church – Romanesque – Gothic into axial space, but in terms of Khmer temple interior is basically not offered except specific religious ceremony. That is clearly just the worship of rotating around the sanctuary or out of the enclosure to the right, or praying from worship hall in particular. There are 2 types of worship, one has equal weight in every direction and another has emphasis upon the front. Above all, Mandapa that extended to the east-west direction of Banteay Srei Temple, 3 religious towers attached to the front of Bayon Temple, clearly acknowledged that emphasize the holiness, so that can be called as "vertically-oriented" in a sense, but these are merely conspicuous usage examples of ordinary styles of architecture, not an example of elaborated spatial composition. Therefore, exclude these examples from the consideration.

2.2.2.2 Formation of "Vertically-Oriented on Terraced Slope"

As "vertically-oriented layout temple", Vat Phu Temple and Preah Vihear Temple are 2 important representatives. The Central Sanctuary of Vat Phu Temple constructed in the early 7th century, and the entire temple complex was carried out in mid-7th to early 8th century. North and south "palace" (Annex Building) and a Nandin hall thought to be made by wood at first, but the date

Chapter 2 : History of Previous Studies of Preah Vihear Temple and Historical Significance of Survey

ンテルの細部様式がバンテアイ・スレイ寺院に近いこと，東西経蔵のレンガヴォールト屋根の技法と西側「口の字」型付属建物H'-I'の主室が石材の帯磁率調査により，プレア・ヴィヘア寺院では最古の部類に属し，ラージェンドラヴァルマンⅡ以降と考えられること以外では，ほぼ全ての施設が スールヤヴァルマンⅠからスールヤヴァルマンⅡまでの時代であると考えられる。これまでの現状遺構調査によれば，プレア・ヴィヘア寺院丘陵の北端の麓より大階段が始まり，参道，第5ゴープラ，参道，第4ゴープラ，参道，第3ゴープラ，参道，第2ゴープラ，第2伽藍（山頂伽藍北半分），第1ゴープラ，第1伽藍（山頂伽藍南半分）へと続く。第5ゴープラ外側基準線より最奥の背面基準線までの水平距離は693,228mmで，造設された各段台テラス上のこれらの施設群は明確な全体計画のもとに配置されている。第5ゴープラの中心と，中央祠堂の中心を結ぶ線は，中間の各ゴープラの中心をも高い精度で直線的に連結していることが確かめられている。しかも，山頂伽藍を構成する第1および第2伽藍は，一体のものとして計画されていながら，第2伽藍の中軸線は，全体の中心線と一致するものではあるが，第1伽藍の中軸線は，東側にズレているのである。クメール寺院伽藍に共通する中央祠堂の中軸線と伽藍の中心線のズレという性格が，この驚異的に長い中心線を持つプレア・ヴィヘア寺院においても貫徹しているのである。

また，断面計画においても，上部へ，深奥へ行くに従って階段の高低差を逓減させる一方で，参道の傾斜角は極力同一に保ち，階段部台座のモールディングのデザインの構成を粗から密へと暫進的に変化させていく技法が報告されている。プレア・ヴィヘア寺院は，全体として極めて意識的計画的に縦深性を強めた有軸空間であって，その完成は，確実なところ11世紀の中頃であったといえよう。同様に検証していくと，ワット・プー寺院の石造伽藍の全体像の完成は11世紀の中頃から12世紀初めにかけてである。

of construction is unknown, under the reign of Suryavarman I these buildings are rebuilt by stone, and the colonnades beside the approach have constructed later. Preah Vihear Temple also has same circumstances. Initially the causeway, wooden main sanctuary and whole temple layout planning are supposed to be established by Yashovarman I, but it is a hypothesis. The ornamental detail on the lintel of present Mandapa is similar to Banteay Srei Temple. Also judging from the technique of vault roof by bricks of east and west libraries and the magnetic susceptibility of the main room in west "口-shaped" Annex Building H'-I', these buildings may belong to the oldest group in Preah Vihear after the reign of Rajendravarman II. Most of other buildings would be under the reign of Suryavarman I to Suryavarman II. From the survey results so far, temple starts from the northernmost foot of the mountain with grand staircase, continue to causeway, Gopura V, causeway, Gopura IV, causeway, Gopura III, causeway, Gopura II, Complex II (a northern half of mountain peak complex), Gopura I and Complex I (a southern half of mountain peak complex). From the outside baseline of Gopura V to the deepest back line, the horizontal distance is 693,228mm and all facilities are under the particular overall planning on terraced slope. A line connecting the center of Gopura V to the center of the Central Sanctuary is recognized linking other Gopuras linearly in a high accuracy. Moreover, even through Complex I and II have planned as a whole, the central line of Complex II fits to the whole central line, but the central line of Complex I is off to the eastside. The common characteristics on a gap of the central lines between the central sanctuary and temple complex go through the Preah Vihear

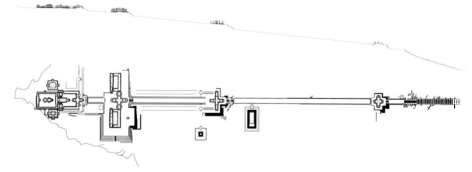

Figure 2.2-2 Plan and Section of Preah Vihear Temple

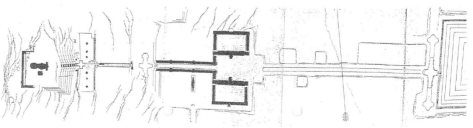

Figure 2.2-3 Vat Phu (H.Parmentier, 1929)

2.2.2.3 「水平縦深型寺院」の形成過程

　後期のアンコール時代になると多数の複合型大型寺院が多かれ少なかれ，水平縦深型の特徴を持つが，先に大まかに述べたように，コー・ケー遺跡群のプラサート・トム寺院とバンテアイ・スレイ寺院が注目される。そして，両寺とも伽藍内のほぼ全ての建物の創建年代が特定される。プラサート・トム寺院は，ジャヤヴァルマン IV が，ほぼその在位中に遷都し，廃都したため，その13年間の前後に建設年代が限られる。また，バンテアイ・スレイ寺院もジャヤヴァルマン V の王師（グル）ヤジャヴァラハによる建立と考えられているため，これも年代が限られるのであり，しかもいずれも，プレア・ヴィヘア寺院や ワット・プー寺院のような参道段台テラス縦深型寺院（山岳式）の全体像の完成よりも，かなり早い時期に水平縦深型形式（水平式）が完成していたことになる。ここからだけ考えると，水平式が山岳式に影響したことになろう。もしそうだとしたら，水平式の縦深性は，どこからやってきたのか，という疑問が残る。また，山岳式の木造前身伽藍が果たして本当にあったのか，あったとしたら，いつ，どの程度の全体像だったのか，等の疑問も解決がつきそうにないのである。

Figure 2.2-4 Pr.Thom Temple

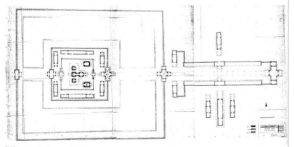

Figure 2.2-5 Banteay Srei Temple (EFEO)

2.2.2.4 クメール寺院における聖山の意味

　クメールの古代都市においては，プレ・アンコール期より，都城と聖山は不即不離の一対の関係とされてきたことが『隋書』や多くの碑文史料から知られている。例えば，メコン川西岸，ワット・プー寺院東側都城址のシュレシュタプラとワット・プー寺院の中央祠堂への参道軸線の北西方向に聳えるカオ山の関係であ

Temple that has a remarkable long central line.

　Also, on the sectional plan, according to go through upward and deeper, the techniques have been reported that one is diminishing the difference in height of stairs, the other is keeping an angle of inclination of approaches, and composing the design of pedestal moldings from rough to minute. On the whole, Preah Vihear Temple has been strengthened as the "vertically-oriented" axial space extremely intentionally, which had completed in the mid-11th century. Similarly, by verifying the Vat Phu Temple, the whole temple had completed in mid-11th to early 12th century.

2.2.2.3 Formation of "Vertically-Oriented on the Plains"

　In the late Angkor period, many complex temples have the character of "vertically-oriented on plains", as to be discussed previously that Prasat Thom Temple of Koh Ker Monuments and Bantey Srei Temple are remarkable. The date of their founding is inferred that Prasat Thom Temple is restricted within 13 years because Jayavarman IV transferred and abolished the capital in Koh Ker Monuments almost under his reign. Also, Banteay Srei Temple has constructed by the King's mentor (guru) of Jayavarman V, Yajnavaraha. From this chronology, the time of completion for "vertically-oriented on the plains" style looks very earlier than for "vertically-oriented on terraced slope" style that is represented by Preah Vihear Temple and Vat Phu Temple. On this point of view, "plains style" infected "terraced slope style". If this hypothesis is correct, there are still doubts that how "vertically-oriented on plains" came from, whether the previous wooden temple complex really existed, and when the previous wooden style completed. As things are, these problems cannot clarify.

2.2.2.4 Significance of Sacred Mountain in Khmer Temple

　In Khmer ancient city, a capital and a sacred mountain are known as one pair from lots of inscriptions and "zuisho" (one of the Chinese historical book) since Pre-Angkor period. For instance, the relationship among the west riverside of the Mekong River, the capital city Shrestapura on the east side of Vat Phu Temple, the sacred mountain Phu Kao rises in northwest direction to the axis of Vat Phu Temple. The connection between a capital and a sacred mountain is widely regarded as an incarnation of belief for ancestors and animism peculiar around Himalayan Mountain Range and the rice-growing monsoons area in Asia. When the time-honored belief faded, foreign new religion intoxicated and compensated it again, also prepared the city and spatial structure for expressing visually to connect its capital and the mountain strongly. Champasak, a cradle of Khmer

る。この都城と聖山の関係は，広くアジアのヒマラヤ山系の周辺やモンスーン稲作地帯に特有な祖先やアニミズム信仰の顕現かもしれない。古来からの土着信仰が薄れゆく時，外来の新宗教がそれを再び覚醒させ，補強させるように，聖山と都城を強く結節するための視覚と空間装置を用意したのではなかったか。山岳式こそが起源であって，そこから水平式へ縦深的有軸空間は広がったのである。カオ山とワット・プー寺院と都城址とメコン川の関係図（Figure 2.2-6）を見る度に，そのことを想う。クメール寺院の全体像を考える上で，プレア・ヴィヘア寺院やワット・プー寺院等，縦深型山岳寺院の占める位置は重要である。

Figure 2.2-6 Bird's-eye view of Vat Phu Temple
©Pierre Pichard (EFEO, 2012)

2.2.3 プレア・ヴィヘア寺院の修復における課題
2.2.3.1 プレア・ヴィヘア寺院における近年の諸介入

プレア・ヴィヘア寺院では1980年代にベトナム軍に占領された際に，多数の塹壕が掘り込まれた他，地雷が埋設された。また，第1回廊・中央祠堂拝殿の迫り出し屋根の目地開きへの遮水対策としてモルタル充填をしたのもこの時のことであるが，遺構の保存を目的としたものではなく，あくまでも野営地としてこの遺跡を使用するための対策であった。1989年から1998年まで，当地はクメール・ルージュに占領され，さらに地雷が追加されたといわれる。ようやく1998年に解放され，2000年から2002年にかけてカンボジア政府によって寺院内の多少の整備が行われた。1998年に解放されて以降はタイ国境側からの入場者がほとんどであり，道路が整備されていなかったカンボジア側の観光客は少数であった。その後，2008年

people, has brought the original form as a relation of sacred mountain-capital city- the Mekong River, and in Preah Vihear Temple, this form developed obviously and surely influenced "plains style". The axial space as "vertically-oriented" has spread out from "terraced slope style" to "plains style". Every time I look at the bird's-eye view drawing of Phu Kao, Vat Phu Temple, capital city and the Mekong River, I remember that thing (Figure 2.2-6). Preah Vihear Temple and Vat Phu Temple as "vertically-oriented layout temple" are important to consider about the whole picture of Khmer temple.

2.2.3 Subjects on Conservation in Preah Vihear Temple
2.2.3.1 Recently Interventions in Preah Vihear Temple

When the Vietnam trops occupied Preah Vihear Temple in 1980s, they dug many trenches and laid mines. At the same time, they filled up the corbel roof of Gallery I and Mandapa with mortar as the water barrier for the purpose that utilizes the ruins for camping. During 1989-1998, this temple was occupied by Khmer Rouge, and added mines more. Finally, temple was released in 1998, maintained by the Cambodian Government till 2000-2002. Since the withdrawal in 1998, most people had visited from Thailand side, only a few visitors from Cambodia because of undeveloped road. In 2008, Preah Vihear Temple was registered as one of the World Heritage. The preceding year, 2007, the removal of landmines has been completed, and in the first half of 2008, timbering and wooden steps for dangerous parts were built. In addition to the record of for the World Heritage, National Authority for Preah Vihear Temple was established. Organized by 6 departments, Dept. of Tourism development, Dept. of Monument and Archaeology, Dept. of Human settlement, Dept. of Environment, Forest and Water, Dept. of Order and Cooperation, and Dept. of Administration, in 2013, about 100 experts, 40 workers, 30 guards were there.

As above, border dispute ballooned into military confrontation with Thailand over the ownership rights after registration, and visitors were forbidden to come in temple again. New trenches were dug in many parts of temple as a military position. The cluster bombs had thrown from Thailand side that temple were damaged in some parts. While the confliction, the road from Cambodian side to climb up the scarp of Dangrek Mountains was developed by compellation of Bayon TV (civil news bureau) for raising money and Chinese Government with a loan agreement. The last steepest slope leads to the Preah Vihear Temple complex was included in the area where Thailand insists the territorial rights so that it is undeveloped. Remaining as the narrow steep road, it will prevent the transportation of machines and materials

にカンボジア第2のユネスコ世界遺産として登録される。その前年，2007年には地雷撤去が完了し，登録直前の2008年前半には倒壊危険箇所への支保工や，一部には木造の階段が設置された。世界遺産登録とあわせてプレア・ヴィヘア国立機構（National Authority for Preah Vihear）が設立される。Dept. of Tourism development, Dept. of Monument and Archaeology, Dept. of Human settlement, Dept. of Environment, Forest and Water, Dept. of Order and Cooperation, Dept. of Administration の6局より構成され，2013年時点では約100名の専門家スタッフの他，約40名の清掃等の作業員，約30名の警備員を擁している。

　世界遺産登録後は，タイとの国境問題が生じ，この遺跡の帰属をめぐり軍事衝突に至り，再び訪問者の入場が閉鎖された。寺院内の各所には新たに塹壕が掘られ，軍事拠点とされた。タイ側から投入されたクラスター爆弾により，寺院内の数ヵ所に被害が報告されている。この軍事衝突の間にカンボジア側からダンレック山脈の上に立つこの寺院へ至る急坂を登坂するための道路が，バイヨンテレビ（民報）による呼びかけによる民間義援金と中国政府の借款事業により整備されるが，寺院群に至る最後の最も急な斜面は，タイ側が国境線を強く主張している地区に含まれるために，道路整備が行われず，いぜんかつての細く急な道路のままであり，将来的な修復工事等に必要となる資機材や重機の昇降を阻んでいる状況にある。こうした事態の中，プレア・ヴィヘア国立機構は十分に機能しない状況が続いていたが，寺院整備作業が進められてきた。

1. チケットセンターやプレア・ヴィヘア機構の事務所の設置
2. 山脈の麓に散在する貯水池での考古学的発掘調査
3. 約1600mにおよぶダンレック山脈の麓から第5ゴープラの東側に至る直線に延びる古代の石造の階段上への木造階段の設置
4. 寺院境内の散乱石材の一部整理
5. 定期的な草刈等のメンテナンス
6. 博物館の設置

2011年末より平静を取り戻し，両軍は一応の武装解除に至った。観光客が徐々に増えつつある中，プレア・ヴィヘア機構も少しずつ活動が活発になり，2013年の前半には寺院への入り口となる最も低い階段の北側5ヵ所で考古学的発掘調査を実施し，博物館の展示等，訪問客の受け入れ態勢を整えつつある。この博物館にはプノンペン国立博物館とアンコール保存事務所に所蔵しているプレア・ヴィヘア寺院関連の遺物の他，プレア・ヴィヘア州内から石彫遺物が移動，展示される

for conservation in future. National Authority for Preah Vihear, under difficult conditions, had been carrying out the temple maintenance projects including:

1. Establishment of ticket center and office
2. Archaeological excavation and survey on basins scattered near foot of the mountain
3. Installing wooden steps along the ancient stone stairs about 1600m in length from foot of the Dangrek Mountains to east side of the Gopura V
4. Sorting of collapsed stone in temple precincts
5. Regular maintenance of weeds
6. Establishment of museum

　Since the end of 2011, both armies unarmed and recovered previous tranquility. The numbers of sightseeing visitors has been increasing recently that activities of National Authority for Preah Vihear are also becoming brisk by degrees. They excavated and researched at 5 points in north side of the lowest altitude stairs in early 2013, and have been preparing for exhibition at museum to welcome the visitors. In this museum, relics related to Preah Vihear Temple from Phnom Penh National Museum and Angkor Conservation Office, and also stone statues and sculptures from Preah Vihear province will be exhibited.

　In 2012, Meijo University and Waseda University made a four-year contract for research program, and started the study on architecture and archaeology in Preah Vihear Temple. The international contract agreement was implemented for the first time after record to the World Heritage, so it is expected to be an opportunity to begin the full-scale activities. This program includes not only academic research by accurate measuring and analysis on dimensional planning but also preliminary survey for conservation in future.

2.2.3.2 Making Risk Map

　With recently periodic maintenance by National Authority for Preah Vihear, the circumstance of temple preservation improved sharply. However, there are some areas not possible to correspond by maintenance, where required serious efforts. The number of the dangerous spots shown in Figure 2.2-7 is as large as 31 in total. The following is a list of main dangerous points.

I. Removal of Trenches and Other Institutions

　This temple is important as the geographical position so that applied for the military base and repeated installation of trenches and mines at several area of temple. Removal these facilities in the right way is demanded.

予定である。
　2012年に名城大学と早稲田大学はプレア・ヴィヘア国立機構と4年間の研究事業契約を締結し、寺院の建築学・考古学調査を開始した。こうした国際的な事業契約の取り決めは、世界遺産登録後には初めてのものとなり、より本格的な諸活動の開始の門戸を開く契機となることが期待されている。本事業は、遺構の正確な実測、寸法計画の分析等の学術調査に加えて、将来的な保存修復工事に必要となる事前調査も含んでおり、本稿ではこれまでの調査の経過を報告するものである。

2.2.3.2 リスクマップの作成
　プレア・ヴィヘア機構による近年の定期的なメンテナンスにより寺院群内の保存状況は大きく改善されつつある。しかしながら、寺院内にはメンテナンスだけでは対応しきれないより本格的な対策が求められる箇所も少なくない。それらの危険箇所のリストはFigure 2.2-7に示される計31ヵ所におよぶ。以下に、そうした危険箇所をその主要な要因毎に分類して列挙する。

I. 塹壕等の施設の撤去
　当寺院は地勢上の重要拠点として、前述のとおり近年に様々な軍事拠点として利用され、そのたびに寺院内各所には塹壕や地雷の設置が繰り返された。こうした軍事施設の適切な形での撤去が求められる。

II. 斜面における排水処置
　寺院全体は南から北側への傾斜地に立地するが、特に北端の石積み階段は急勾配であり、降雨時には石積み下の土砂の流出、それに伴う石積みのスベリ破壊が危惧されている。階段両脇にはオリジナルの排水溝が刻まれており、こうした当初の機能を復元活用する検討も求められよう。

III. 石積み遺構の構造的安定化
　当寺院は岩盤の直上に建てられているために、構造的には比較的安定している。ただし、南から北に下る勾配に加えて、西から東に向かって緩い勾配のある敷地である中、遺構はほぼ左右対称に構築され、東側の遺構は基礎を嵩上げして基壇の高さを揃えているため、嵩上げ部の不同沈下による石積みの変位が生じやすい傾向にある。前述のとおり、寺院群内の各所危険箇所の中でも特に緊急性の高い箇所においては、カンボジア政府により木材やワイヤーを利用した支保工が設置された。ただし、アンコール遺跡群でも木材による支保工は耐用年数が限定されるため、中長期的に維持さ

II. Drainage System on an Incline
Location of the whole temple is on the slope from south to north, specially the northernmost stone stair is steep that worried about sediment outflow and stone crumble in rainy season. There is a drainage gutter on either side of the stair that need to consider the restoration and utilization the original function.

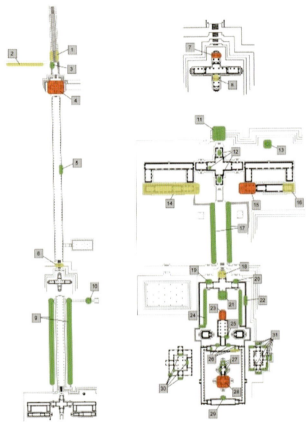

Figure 2.2-7 Risk Map of Preah Vihear Temple

III. Structural Stabilization of Stone Masonry
This temple was built on rock so it is stable structurally. There is a problem, however, the displacement of stone masonry caused by unequal settlement because of gentle slopes from west to east additionally from south to north. The eastern buildings have been constructed symmetrically to west that their platform is raised to make uniform the height, which causes unequal settlement. As mentioned above, the Cambodian government equipped timbering to prop up the risky points. Timbering doesn't last much longer as be seen at Angkor site so that development of long-term materials and construction method are required. There still remains multiple sites needed to rapid structural reinforcement. The west Annex Building of Gopura III called "palace" and Gopura I have risks to collapse by stone displacement for example.

れる支保工の材料・工法の開発が求められる。こうした支保工が既に設置されている箇所の他にも複数個所において早急な構造補強が求められる地点は少なくない。例えば，第3ゴープラの西側に位置する「宮殿」と一般的に呼ばれる付属建物や，第1ゴープラの一部等は，石積みの変形が大きく，更なる崩落が懸念されるものの，現状では未対策のまま取り残されている。

IV. 建築・美術史上重要な彫刻部材の記録・原位置同定・保管

崩落し散乱した石材の中にはリンテルやペディメントといった重要な建築部位，あるいは丸彫りの石彫が含まれている。既にプレア・ヴィヘア国立機構により整備が行われ，崩落個所からは移動されたものも少なくないが，大きく位置を移動されたものはない。これらの石材の原位置の特定と記録が早急に求められる。

V. 今後の保存対策への展望

仮設的な対策を充実させていくことに加えて，今後は緊急な必要性に応じて，より本格的な解体を伴う修復工事を実施するための段階に入ることが予想されよう。中でも寺院の象徴的な存在である「第5ゴープラの復原工事」や「中央祠堂主室の再構築」がその対象となるものと考えられる。今後は修復工事のための学術的事前調査に加えて、プレア・ヴィヘア国立機構の修復保存・建築等の専門家を育成していくことが求められよう。

2.2.4 結論

クメール寺院伽藍におけるプレア・ヴィヘア寺院の特異な意義を考えるために，今後，建築学的特徴の分析のための更なる学術的調査，修復への指標，包括的な人材育成が必要である。

IV. Recording, Identification and Storing of Important Architectural / Art Historical Ornaments

Lintels, pediments and sculptures are important as building components, but they collapsed and scattered in Preah Vihear Temple. National Authority for Preah Vihear moved some of them orderly. Prompt action for position identification and recording is needed.

V. Prospects for the Future Preservation

For the future, it will enter upon a new phase of conducting the restoration work including disassemble in addition to enrich the provision. Even among those "restoration of Gopura V" and "restructuring of the Central Sanctuary" might be significance. To continue the intermittent academic survey for conservation and to develop human resources as expert of architectural conservation in National Authority for Preah Vihear is important.

2.2.4 Conclusions

Considering the singularity significance of Preah Vihear Temple in Khmer temple complex, it is needed to academic survey, measures for the conservation and comprehensive development of human resources for analysis of the architectural features.

References

I) Nakagawa,T. and Mizoguchi,A. and Shimoda,I. (2013) Deterioration condition and conservation plan of the Preah Vihear Temple. Annual Convention of Architectural institute of Japan, 571-572.

II) Tabuchi,N. (2014) Study on the layout planning of Khmer temple complex –Development of vertically-oriented layout temple on terraced slope-Master's thesis of Waseda university.

III) Mizoguchi,A. (2014) On the dimentional planning at Preah Vihear Temple complex. Kinki convention of Architectural Institute of Japan.

IV) Mizoguchi,A. (2014) On the dimentional planning at Preah Vihear Temple complex on the crest: Study on the dimensional plan and the planning method of Khmer architecture (No. 7). Transactions of the Architectural Institute of Japan.

V) Matsumoto,N. (2013) Preah Vihear Temple, a study on configuration planning of stepped-terrace. Graduation thesis of Waseda university.

Chapter 3
第3章

Study Reports on Preah Vihear Temple
調査および分析

3.1 プレア・ヴィヘア寺院遺跡とその周辺における地理学的調査（2012-2015 年）
Geographical Investigations around the Preah Vihear Temple Site (2012-2015)

久保　純子　　南雲　直子
KUBO Sumiko　　NAGUMO Naoko

3.1.1 はじめに

プレア・ヴィヘア寺院遺跡およびその周辺を対象として，地理学・地形学の立場より遺跡の立地環境を明らかにすることを目的として2012年から2015年にわたって調査を実施した。

2012年度はカンボジアとタイで地形図・空中写真等の資料収集を行うとともに遺跡の現地調査を行った。2013～2015年度は遺跡における地形断面測量および基盤岩の走向・傾斜等の測定を実施した。このほか，周辺の遺跡・遺構の踏査を行った。現地調査は2012年8月14・15日，2013年9月5～8日，2014年8月22日，2015年8月21～23日にそれぞれ実施した。

これらにもとづき，地形地質条件と遺跡の立地環境について考察を行った。

3.1.1.1 資料収集

地理学調査に関する資料として，2012年度に地形図ならびに空中写真の収集を行った。プレア・ヴィヘア寺院遺跡はカンボジアとタイの国境付近に位置するため，カンボジアのほか，タイ側でも資料の収集を行った。

カンボジアではプノンペンの関係機関等にて地形図ならびに空中写真を入手した。

カンボジア国1：50,000地形図は1960～1970年代作成のものがプノンペン市中で入手できる。また，カンボジア国1：100,000地形図は日本の国際協力機構（JICA）とカンボジア公共事業運輸省（MPWT）・国土管理都市計画建設省（MLMUPC）により2000年代に発行されたものが入手可能である。

空中写真は縮尺約1：40,000（JICA撮影）をプノンペンのカンボジア国内メコン委員会（CNMC）にて入手した。

タイ国側は，バンコクのタイ王立測量局（Royal Thai Survey Department）にて資料の所在調査を行っ

3.1.1 Introduction

To identify the geographical and geomorphological features of the Preah Vihear Temple site we conducted the following study from 2012 to 2015.

In August 2012, we obtained topographic maps and aerial photographs from agencies in Cambodia and Thailand, along with the field survey. Field investigations during 2012 to 2015 were performed by measuring the dip-strike of base rock as well as longitudinal and cross-sectional surveys. We also performed field reconnaissance on archaeological sites located around the Preah Vihear Temple. Field investigations include those on 14th and 15th August 2012, 5th-8th September 2013, 22nd August 2014, and 21st-23rd August 2015.

We examined the geomorphological condition and environments of the Preah Vihear archaeological site based on these surveys.

3.1.1.1 Obtaining the Study Material

Since the site is located near the border, we obtained topographic maps and aerial photos from agencies in Cambodia and Thailand in 2012.

In Cambodia, we obtained topographic maps and aerial photos in Phnom Penh.

Topographic maps of a scale 1:50,000 published in the 1960s and 1970s are available in the city market. Topographic maps of a scale 1:100,000 prepared by Japan International Cooperation Agency (JICA) and Ministry of Public Works and Transport (MPWT) with Ministry of Land Management Urban Planning and Construction (MLMUPC) for the years after 2000 are also available.

We obtained aerial photos of a scale of approximately 1:40,000 taken by JICA from the Cambodia National Mekong Committee (CNMC) in Phnom Penh.

In Thailand, we visited the Royal Thai Survey Department in

Chapter 3 : Study Reports on Preah Vihear Temple

た。その結果，タイ国1：250,000地形図は入手可能であったが，タイ国1：50,000地形図ならびに空中写真は，国境地帯のために入手できなかった。

3.1.1.2 遺跡現地調査内容

プレア・ヴィヘア寺院遺跡における現地調査としては，プレア・ヴィヘア寺院域の地形・地質踏査および断面測量と，周辺遺跡の踏査を行った。

寺院域の地形・地質については露岩部の地形断面と観察を中心に行った。地形断面測量はレーザーテクノロジー社製TruPulse 360レーザー距離計と反射板のついたポールを用いて2012年，2013年，2015年に行った。

2012年には南北方向で2断面（Line 1,2），2013年には露岩部分で3断面（Line 3-5），2015年には露岩部分2ヵ所および参道と直交方向に4ヵ所の計6断面（Line 6-12），全部で12断面の測量を行った。

また，寺院一帯はおもに砂岩よりなる基盤岩の露岩地域であり，全体として北へ傾斜するケスタ地形を呈している。寺院はこのケスタの背面（バックスロープ，緩斜面）上に展開することから，露岩部において基盤岩の走向と傾斜を測定した。測定はクリノメーターを使用し，層理のなかのこまかなラミナ（葉理）面ではなく層理面の走向・傾斜を測るようにした。

このほか，周辺の遺跡（山麓部）の踏査と周辺の地形観察を行った。

3.1.2 調査結果

プレア・ヴィヘア寺院遺跡はカンボジア・タイ国境地帯をなすダンレック山脈山頂部に位置する（Figure 3.1-1）。ダンレック山脈はチョアン・クサン付近（プレア・ヴィヘア寺院遺跡の約30km東方）の766m（カンボジア1：100,000地形図）をはじめ，プレア・ヴィヘア寺院遺跡周辺では標高600m〜700mに達する。南側（カンボジア側）は比高500mに達する急崖をなし，それに対し北側（タイ側）は緩勾配でコラート高原に続き，明瞭な非対称山稜をなす。カンボジア側の急崖ではやや北へ傾斜する地層の層理が認められ，全体としてケスタ地形をなす。非対称斜面の南側が階崖，北側が背面（バックスロープ）である。

本地域の地質は，既存のカンボジア地質図（1972年，縮尺1：200,000 Tbeng Meanchey）によれば，中部ジュラ系〜下部白亜系砂岩で，シェムリアップ州のクレン山と同じグループに分類されている。ただし，クレン山が水平に近い層理のテーブル状を呈するのに対し，プレア・ヴィヘア寺院周辺のダンレック山脈主稜

Bangkok to obtain maps and aerial photos. A topographic map of a scale 1:250,000 for the Preah Vihear Temple site was available; however, topographic maps of a scale 1:50,000 and aerial photos are restricted because of the presence of international border areas.

3.1.1.2 Field Surveys

We performed the field investigation for geomorphological and geological surveys, longitudinal and cross-sectional surveys, and reconnaissance survey of the surrounding archaeological sites.

The geomorphological and geological surveys focused on the rock exposures in the temple area. Twelve sections were produced in 2012, 2013 and 2015 by using a laser range finder TruPulse 360 (Laser Technology), and a pole with a reflection plate.

Two longitudinal (N-S) sections (Line 1 and 2) were made in 2012, three sections (Line 3 -5) at exposed rock areas were made in 2013, and six sections (Line 6 -12) including two at exposed rock areas and four rectangular sections with the causeway were made in 2015.

The Preah Vihear Temple complex is located on the exposed rocks of a cuesta whose back slope tilts to the north. We measured the strike and dip of the basement rocks with clinometers. We ensured to measure the strike and dip of strata, rather than those of laminations.

In addition, we inspected other archaeological sites and features around the Preah Vihear Temple site.

3.1.2 Results

The temple is located on a hilltop of the Dangrek Mountains (Figure 3.1-1). The mountains rise to 766 m a.s.l. (shown in the 1:100,000 topographic map of Cambodia) near Choam Ksant, some 30 km east of Preah Vihear Temple site, and to 600–700 m a.s.l. near the site. The southern side (Cambodian side) has an abrupt cliff with a relative height of about 500 m. On the contrary, the northern side (Thailand side) has a gentle slope that continues into the Khorat Plateau. This results in a distinct asymmetric slope. The north-tilting strata, in the form of a cuesta, can be observed on the steep slope on the Cambodian side. The southern side (steep) is composed of an escarpment, and the northern side (gentle) consists of the cuesta back slope.

The geological features of this area have been depicted in a 1:200,000 scale geological map (Tbeng Meanchey) published in 1972. According to the map, this area consists of Middle Jurassic to Lower Cretaceous sandstone, similar to Phnom Kulen in Siem Reap province.However,

線部は北方への傾斜が明瞭となる。

　プレア・ヴィヘア寺院は標高655m（高度計による）の山頂から北方へ，次第に高度を下げながら続くケスタのバックスロープ（緩斜面）に位置する。周辺は砂岩の露岩地が広がり，岩盤上に直接，あるいは岩盤を削って構造物が建設されている。このため，自然地形のオリジナルな地表面と砂岩層の傾斜と建築物の立地に注目して調査を行った。

3.1.2.1 断面測量

　2012年・2013年・2015年の断面測量実施位置をFigure 3.1-2に，各断面図をFigure 3.1-3に示す。各断面は南からはじまる。

　Line 1は第1・第2ゴープラの西側の露岩部を南北方向にとったもので，延長は約100 mである。起点から60 m付近まではほぼ平坦で，70 m付近の低くなっているところは第2ゴープラの西側の「池の跡」とさ

while Mt. Kulen shows a table-like form with horizontal strata, the main ridge of the Dangrek Mountains near Preah Vihear Temple shows clear inclination to the north.

The Preah Vihear Temple complex is located on the gently dipping cuesta back slope that begins from the hilltop (655 m a.s.l., by altimeter) spreading to the north. Sandstone strata outcrops can be seen around the site. The building complex was constructed on the sandstone strata. In some places, the rocks have been cut artificially. Therefore, we paid attention to the sandstone strata, ground surface slope, and building locations.

3.1.2.1 Cross-Sectional Surveys

We performed cross-sectional surveys of the original land surface in 2012, 2013 and 2015. Figure 3.1-2 and 3 show the location and sections. Each section starts from the south.

Line 1 stretches from south to north in the rocky field in the western part of Gopura I and II. The length is approximately 100 m. From the starting point to around 60 m, the ground surface is almost level. The lower portion, near 70 m, is believed to have been a water tank.

Line 2 runs parallel to the axis of the buildings and causeways and is located about 50 m west of them. The length is approximately 770 m. We compared this section with that of the axis of the buildings and causeways.

Line 3 is located on the southern tip of the hilltop. The area has an artificial surface caused by a stone quarry. The length is about 65 m. Rough surfaces, where the rock has been quarried, are seen at around 7 m and 30–40 m from the starting point.

Line 4 extends into the rocky field west of Gopura III and IV. The line was set at a

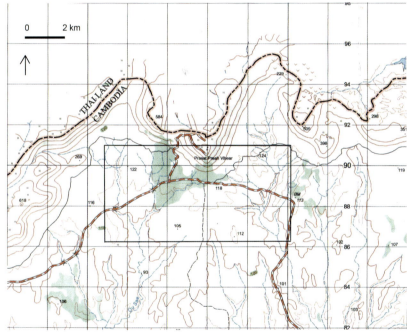

Figure 3.1-1 Location of the Preah Vihear Temple Site (1:100,000 Topographic map "Preah Vihear") The square shows the area of Figure 3.1-6.

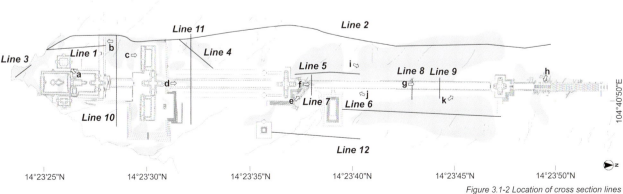

Figure 3.1-2 Location of cross section lines Grey areas present exposed rocks

Chapter 3：Study Reports on Preah Vihear Temple

れる部分である。

　Line 2 は，寺院・参道の中心線の約 50 m 西側を，参道に並行するように測量した。延長は約 770 m である。この自然斜面に沿う断面と建物中軸の断面を別途比較する。

　Line 3 は山頂最南端部で，人工的に露岩部が切られた採石跡の部分である。延長は約 65 m である。起点から 7 m 付近や 30 ～ 40 m 付近は石が切られているため凹凸がある。

　Line 4 は第 3 ゴープラと第 4 ゴープラの間の西側露岩部で，小崖に直交する方向にとった。延長は約 70 m である。起点から 20 ～ 50 m 付近の小崖は，それぞれ人工的な採石の跡である。

　Line 5 は第 4 ゴープラ直下の参道西側露岩部で，参道と並行する方向にとった。延長は約 110 m である。第 4 ゴープラとその下の参道の間は急な階段となっているが，西側の Line 5 はほぼ一様な勾配となっている。

　Line 6 は第 4 ゴープラの北東に位置する長方形のバライ（池）から，参道の東側を参道と平行に第 5 ゴープラの東までの断面である。延長は約 240 m である。全体には北へ向けて下がるものの，途中に明瞭な凹凸があり，参道の縦断面と比べると露岩地の縦断面は起伏に富むことがわかる。

　Line 7 は第 4 ゴープラ階段直下の参道露岩部を，参道と直交方向に断面をとったものである。延長は約 50 m である。ここでは西側に露岩を削り取った垂直な崖（比高約 3 m）があり，この付近では露岩部を削って参道が作られたことがわかる。この崖は北西ー南東方向に参道と斜交して第 4 ゴープラの南東へ連続する。なおこの測線のすぐ脇の階段直下の露岩部分には，直径数十 cm の円形の穴が 6 ヵ所，一列に並んで掘り込まれている。

　Line 8 は第 4 ゴープラと第 5 ゴープラの間の参道に直交する断面である。延長は約 50 m である。西側が露岩部で高く東側が低いため，参道の西半分は露岩だが東側は石積みとなっていることがわかる。

　Line 9 は Line 8 の約 50 m 北に位置し，Line 8 と同じく参道と直交する断面である。Line 8 と同様に西側が高く露岩が見られるが，参道部分は Line 8 と異なり露岩は見られず，比高 1 m 以上の石積みで構築されている。参道東側は再び露岩部となるが，西側の露岩との間には 1 m 以上の落差が見られる。

　Line 10 は第 2 ゴープラと第 3 ゴープラの間の参道と直交する東西方向の断面である。延長は約 160 m である。西側に露岩部があり，参道付近は平坦地となっている。第 2 ゴープラの北側延長部までこの平坦部がテ

right angle to the rock scarps. The length is about 70 m. The rock scarps between 20 and 50 m from the starting point were artificially produced.

Line 5 stretches into the western rocky field parallel to Gopura IV and the causeway. The length is about 110 m. Steep stone steps are located between Gopura IV and the causeway. However, Line 5 shows a smooth section.

Line 6 starts at the northern side of the baray (square water tank) that located in the northwest of Gopura IV, and runs parallel to the causeway to the eastern side of Gopura V. The length is about 240 m. The section shows unevenness while the overall section dips to the north. The longitudinal section of rocky area is uneven in contrast of the smooth section of the causeway.

Line 7 is set at a right angle to the causeway. It crosses the exposed rock portion at the foot of the stairs to Gopura IV. The length is about 50 m. There is a vertical rock scarp (3 m high), showing that the causeway was cut into base rock. This rock scarp extends to the southeast of Gopura IV with a NW-SE orientation that is diagonal to the causeway. Near this section at the foot of stairs to the Gopura, there is a row of six round-shaped rock holes with diameters less than 1 m.

Line 8 is at a right angle to the causeway between Gopura IV and V. The length is about 50 m. The western side with exposed rock is higher than the eastern side. Therefore, the western side of causeway was cut into base rocks while the eastern side was made with stone masonry.

Line 9 is located about 50 m north of Line 8. This also is at a right angle to the causeway. The western part of the line is of exposed rock the same as Line 8. However, the causeway is made of stone masonry. In the eastern side, base rock exposes with the relative height from western side rock a little more than 1 m.

Line 10 is an E-W cross section of the causeway between Gopura II and III at a right angle. The length is about 160 m. Base rock is exposed on the western side. The ground surface is flat along the causeway. This flat surface extends to the north of Gopura II like a terrace. The eastern side of the causeway consists of stone masonry and then the ground surface drops with a steep slope.

Line 11 is another E-W cross section of the causeway in the north of Gopura III. The length is about 120 m. The ground level in the western side is higher than the eastern side and drops with a steep slope as Line 10. Here causeway was cut into the base rock. The southern side of this section's western rim is the basement of stone terraces of Gopura III. Stone stairs are located in front of Gopura III from the causeway the same as Gopura IV.

Geographical Investigations around the Preah Vihear Temple Site (2012-2015)

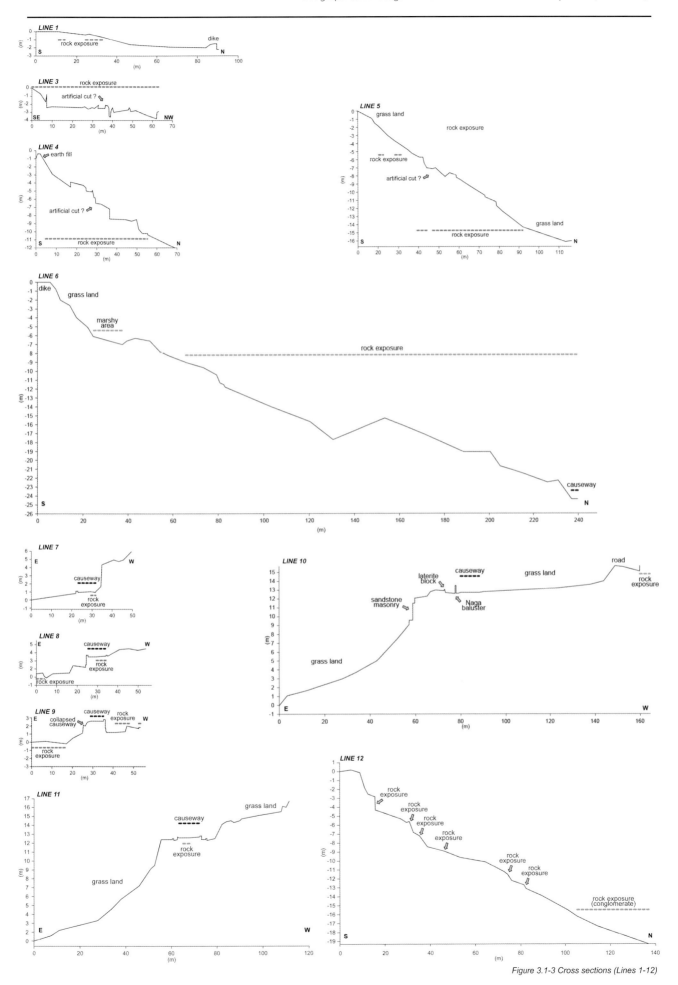

Figure 3.1-3 Cross sections (Lines 1-12)

ラス状に続き，東側の側面は石積みとなり，斜面は急勾配で低下する。

　Line 11 は第3ゴープラの北側の，参道と直交する東西方向の断面である。延長は約120mである。Line 10 と同様に西側が高く，参道の東側では急勾配に低下する。ここでは露岩部を削って参道が作られている。西端部の南側は第3ゴープラの石積みの基部である。第3ゴープラは第4ゴープラと同様に，参道から登る階段が作られている。

　Line 12 は第4ゴープラの南東にある正方形の池の北東隅から，第4ゴープラ北東の長方形のバライの東側までの南北方向の断面である。延長は約140mである。全体に南から北へ急勾配で低下するが，途中に比高約1 m前後の露岩の崖が数箇所に見られる。バライの東方では礫岩の露岩地となり凹凸は見られなくなる。

3.1.2.2 地形断面と建造物断面の比較

　寺院および参道の中軸線と，その西側に並行するほぼ自然状態の斜面であるLine 2との比較，ならびにゴープラ周辺や参道を横断する断面等の検討により，プレア・ヴィヘア寺院の造営にあたり，どのような地形改変が行われたかを推定する。寺院および参道中軸線の断面は建築班の測量結果によるものである。

　Figure 3.1-4 では地形断面との比較のため，断面図の垂直方向を2倍に強調している。

　山頂部（南端）の露岩地には採石跡があり，垂直方向に2m程度の切り取りが行われており（Line 3），地形がかなり改変されている。

　中央祠堂の回廊外西側に位置する付属建物Eは，東側外壁は基盤岩よりなり（Photo a），高さ1.5m程度まで基盤岩を削った状態である。

　第1ゴープラと第2ゴープラの間の西側に「ため池」

　Line 12 is a S-N section that stretches from the northeastern corner of a square pond located in the southeast of Gopura IV to the eastern side of a baray (square water tank). The length is about 140 m. The overall section dips to the north with a steep slope with several base rock scarps that are about 1 m high. To the east of the baray, conglomerate rocks are exposed, and the surface is less rough.

3.1.2.2 Comparison of Ground Surface and Building Structure in Cross Sections

We estimated the artificial transformation of the ground as a result of the construction of the temple complex by comparing the cross section of the central axis of the buildings and causeways with that of Line 2, which runs parallel to the axis. The Architecture Survey Group provided the cross section of the building complex.

The vertical scale of the cross section (Figure 3.1-4) is extended by two times for comparison.

Stone quarries are seen in the rocky field in the southernmost tip. The depth of the rock cut is about 2 m (Line 3), showing the considerable artificial change.

The eastern side of the Annex Building E attached to the outside of the western Gallery of the Central Sanctuary consists of basement rock (Photo a). The height of the basement rock reaches 1.5 m.

A trace of water tank is located in the western side between Gopura I and II. The ground surface is relatively flat (Line 1).

There is a stone bank of the water tank to the west of Gopura II. Basement rocks are exposed at its northern side (Photo b). The terrace and steps attached to Gopura II cut into the basement rock.

The causeway between Gopura II and III shows relatively flat,

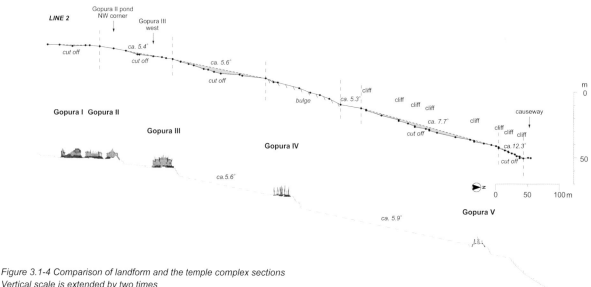

Figure 3.1-4 Comparison of landform and the temple complex sections
Vertical scale is extended by two times

とされる部分があり，ここまでは地表勾配もゆるい（Line 1）。

第2ゴープラの西側にため池の土手のような石積みがあり，その下部（北側）は露岩となっている（Photo b）。第2ゴープラの前のテラス〜石段は基盤岩を削って建設されている。

第2ゴープラと第3ゴープラの間の参道は比較的平坦であり，西側が露岩で，東側は急斜面の上に石積みがされている（Line 10）。

第3ゴープラの西側付属建物H', I'の南側下部は基盤岩を削りだした部分があり，その東側の石積みは不等沈下をおこしている（Photo c）。

第3・第4・第5ゴープラは地形の傾斜変換点にあることがわかる。

第3ゴープラ直下（北側）の参道は基盤岩を削って建設している（Line 11）（Photo d）。また，参道西側の露岩地帯も，採石により階段状を呈する部分がある（Line 4）。これに対し第3ゴープラの東側付属建物H, Iは石積みの高いテラスとなっており，もとの地形の西側が高く東側が低かったため，西側では露岩部を削っている。

第3ゴープラと第4ゴープラの間の参道の平均勾配は5.6°であるが，西側の露岩部では南半分で8°，北半分で7°とより急勾配である。参道の両側には土手がある。

第4ゴープラは地形のバルジ（凸部）に建設されており，直下の（北側）参道にかかる箇所は基盤岩を削って比高約3mの急崖となっている（Line 5，Line 7，Line 12）（Photo e, f）。

第4ゴープラと第5ゴープラの間の参道は平均勾配5.9°で，西側の斜面勾配は上部（南側）が5.3°，下部（北側）が7.7°である。参道上部100mは基盤岩を削り込み（Photo g），下部150mは地形の凹部で参道に石積みが見られる（Line 8，Line 9）（Photo i, j, k）。

第5ゴープラ付近から北側には細礫混じりの砂岩がところどころにあらわれ，ラミナ（葉理）が発達する。第5ゴープラの参道はナーガの石像の下からライオンの石像までは急な石段となり，基盤岩を削りだして階段としている（Photo h）。参道（階段）の両側に基盤岩の崖が階段状に続く。

3.1.2.3 基盤岩の走向・傾斜の測定

寺院周辺の露岩部において基盤岩の走向と傾斜を測定した結果をFigure 3.1-5に示す。南端部（山頂）から北端部まで，おおむねN50°〜N70°Eと一様の傾向を示し，全体として単斜する。ただし，南北方向の地

while rock exposed in the western side and stones are piled over the steep slope in the eastern side (Line 10).

Basement rock was used at the southern side in the western Annex Building H', I' of Gopura III. Because of this, there is subsidence of the neighboring part that is made of stone piles (Photo c).

As seen in the figure, Gopura III, IV, and V are located at the nick points in the cross section.

The causeway connected to Gopura III (northern side) cuts into the basement rock (Line 11; Photo d). The rock field in the west of the causeway also shows step-like features caused by quarrying. On the contrary, the eastern Annex Building H, I of Gopura III is located on a high stone terrace. This is because the original landform is uneven; the higher western area was flattened, and the lower eastern area was elevated with stone blocks.

The average slope of the causeway between Gopura III and IV is 5.6 degrees. However, the original ground surface is steeper, about 8 degrees in the southern part, and 7 degrees in the northern part. There are embankments along both sides of the causeway.

Gopura IV was constructed on the bulge of the slope, and there is a steep rocky cliff below before the causeway (Lines 5, 7 and 12; Photos e and f).

The average slope of the causeway between Gopura IV and V is 5.9 degrees. The original ground surface is about 5.3 degrees in the southern part and 7.7 degrees in the northern part. The uppermost 100 m of the causeway cuts into the basement rock (Photo g), and the lower 150 m is composed of stone blocks as the original section was depressed (Lines 8 and 9; Photos i, j and k).

Sandstones with pebbles partially occur in the area from Gopura V to the north, and laminae are well developed. The causeway of Gopura V consists of steep steps between the naga and lion statues. Stone steps were created by cutting into the basement rock (Photo h).

3.1.2.3 Measurement of the Strike and Dip of Basement rock

Figure 3.1-5 shows the strike and dip of rock around the temple. The entire stretch from the hilltop (southern tip) to the northern part can be characterized by a uniform strike and dip of N50-N70 E and a monoclinal structure. The dip of the strata is about 10 degrees, although the ground surface slope (of the cuesta backslope) is about 7 degrees. This implies that the upper layer is exposed at the downslope toward the north, and that the

Chapter 3 : Study Reports on Preah Vihear Temple

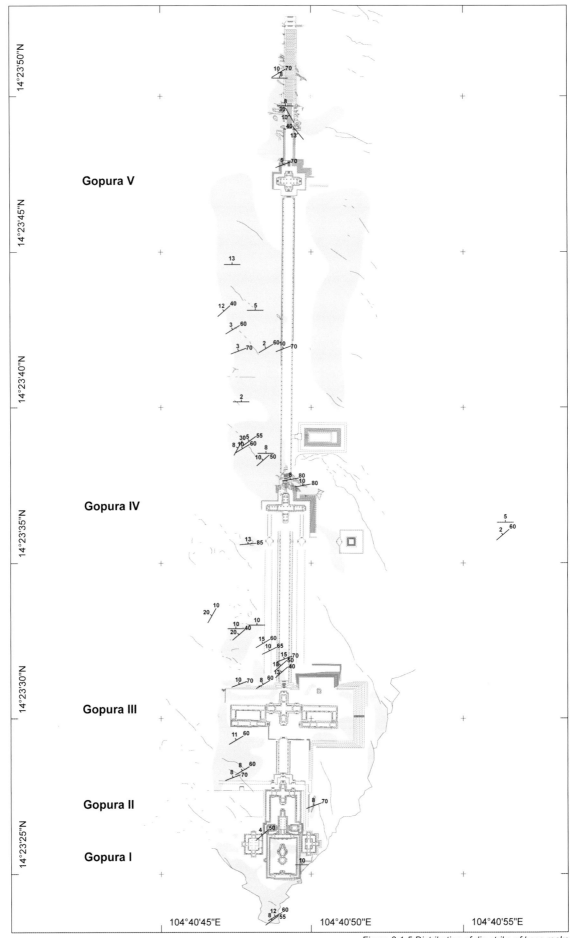

Figure 3.1-5 Distribution of dip-strike of base rocks

表面平均勾配（ケスタのバックスロープ）は約7°であり，地層の傾斜は10°前後である。このため，地表面には南から北へむかってより上位の地層が露出し，岩層の侵食に対する抵抗性の差により表面に起伏が形成されている。

3.1.2.4 山麓部の遺跡踏査

プレア・ヴィヘア機構（NAPV）および佐藤桂博士の情報により，NAPVのソパー氏とともにダンレック山脈山麓部の遺跡分布確認を行った（Figure 3.1-6,7）。各遺跡ではGPSにより位置情報を取得した（2012年）。

プレア・ヴィヘア寺院の南西麓にはヤショタターカとよばれる方形池（バライ）が，南東麓にスールヤターカとよばれる方形池があり，空中写真でも認めることができる。

ヤショタターカの南側にはプラサート・トゥーイ寺院とその東側の方形池がある。プラサート・トゥーイ寺院はラテライトと砂岩からなる。

2012年8月にはヤショタターカは湛水していなかったが，2013年以降は湛水するようになった。

ヤショタターカから約3km西方には，オウアンクロンとよばれる遺物散布地があり，黒陶，中国白磁，青磁などの散布が見られた。途中の道路沿いに小さなバライがあり（14°22' 17.0" N, 104°38' 53" E），内側は水田になっている。

スールヤターカの西側には砂岩とレンガからなる小祠堂がある。またその北西方には，山上の第5ゴープラへ続く石段参道がある。

スールヤターカの南東約3.5 kmの道路沿いには別のバライがあり（14°21' 49.8" N, 104°43' 7.2" E），内側は湿地になっている。西側には「ネアックターの森」がある。

difference in resistance to the erosion of rocks formed the ground surface relief.

3.1.2.4 Distribution of Other Archaeological Features

On the basis of information provided by the National Authority for Preah Vihear (NAPV) and a sketch map made by Dr. Katsura Sato, we visited archaeological sites around the Preah Vihear Temple with Mr. Sopha of the NAPV. We visited and observed the following sites (Figure 3.1-6 and Figure 3.1-7), and obtained their coordinates using a portable GPS instrument in 2012.

In the southwestern side of the mountain slope there is a baray (reservoir) called Yasotataka. Another baray called Suryatataka is located on the southeastern side of the mountain. They can be recognized in aerial photos.

Prasat Touch Temple and its baray are located south of Yasotataka. The Prasat Touch Temple was built using sandstone and laterite blocks.

Although no water was stored in Yasotataka in August 2012, it has been stored there since 2013.

The Ou Ang Krong site is located about 3 km west of Yasotataka, and contains scattered black-grazed pottery and Chinese blue-and-white porcelains sherds. On the way to the site is a small baray (14°22' 17.0" N, 104°38' 53" E) whose interior is now a paddy field.

A small temple built with sandstone and laterite exists west of Suryatataka. The step causeway to the Gopura V of the summit is located northwest of it.

There is another baray along the road, approximately 3.5 km southeast of Suryatataka (14°21' 49.8" N, 104°43' 7.2" E). The interior is swampy and the "Forest of Neak Ta" is located on the western side.

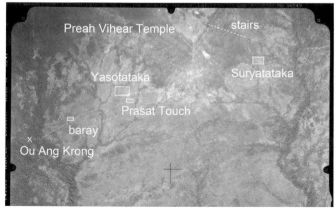

Figure 3.1-6 Distribution of archaeological sites in the environs (modified on the aerial photo taken by JICA) The width of pictured area is about 9 km

Figure 3.1-7 Distribution of archaeological sites in the environs (Google Earth image with our GPS tracks)

Chapter 3 : Study Reports on Preah Vihear Temple

3.1.3 まとめ

2012 ～ 2015年におけるプレア・ヴィヘア寺院と周辺の地形調査により，以下の点が明らかになった。

3.1.3.1 自然地形と建造物の位置

地形断面測量を12ヵ所(南北方向5本，東西方向5本，その他2本)で行い，建造物の立地を考察した。

南北方向のLine 2では，全体として地形は5°～7°の傾斜を示すが，基盤岩の凹凸がところどころに見られ，おおむね基盤岩の突出部にゴープラが位置している。とくに第3・第4・第5ゴープラの位置は基盤地形の傾斜の急変部に対応する。第5ゴープラから下は勾配が急になり，ケスタ地形は不明瞭となる。

東西方向の断面であるLine 10・11は第3ゴープラ周辺のもので，いずれも西側が東側に比べて高く，比高は10m以上となる。ゴープラや参道は標高の高い西側につくられ，基盤岩の突出部では基盤岩を削って参道やゴープラが作られている。第4ゴープラと第5ゴープラの間のLine 7, 8, 9でも西側が高く東側が低い傾向にあり，その間には基盤岩の小崖が分布する。第4ゴープラの東側は基盤岩の凹部であり石積みのテラスが作られ，参道部分もLine 7では基盤岩を削っているが，Line 8・9では基盤岩の凹部を石積みによって高さを補い，参道全体として一定の縦断勾配（平均勾配5.9度）を保っている。この部分の参道は，西側側面は突出部以外は平坦部がある程度連続するため石積みはなく，東側は石積みがみられる部分が長い。

第5ゴープラより北側は基盤岩の急斜面となり（平均勾配12.3度），基盤岩をけずり込んで階段が作られている。

3.1.3.2 ケスタ地形との関係

プレア・ヴィヘア寺院遺跡はダンレック山脈主稜線から北方へ傾斜する中部ジュラ系～下部白亜系砂岩の露岩地に位置し，地層の走向はおおむねN50°～N70°Eと一様の傾向を示し，傾斜は10°前後で全体として北へ単斜する。これに対し，南北方向の地表面平均勾配（ケスタのバックスロープ）は約7°であり，このため，地表面には南から北へむかってより上位の地層が露出し，岩層のうち侵食に対する抵抗性の大きいところでは，やや比高の大きな崖（北西－南東方向）が形成されている。

3.1.3.3 周辺の遺跡立地

プレア・ヴィヘア寺院の東側には，第5ゴープラから東の山麓まで続く石段参道がある。また，山麓には

3.1.3 Concluding Remarks

We clarified the following features as a result of the geomorphological survey around Preah Vihear Temple complex and its vicinity:

3.1.3.1 Landforms and the Locations of Buildings

We measured twelve landform sections (each of five S-N and E-W sections and another two sections) around the temple complex to examine the location of buildings.

The longitudinal S-N direction, Line 2 shows an uneven form with basement rock, and overall inclination about 5-7 degrees. In general, Gopuras are located at these rock bulges. Above all, locations of Gopura III, IV and V correspond to the knickpoints of the longitudinal profile of the basement form. To the downward side from Gopura V, landform slope increases and questa features become unclear.

The E-W cross sections of Lines 10 and 11 are located around Gopura III. They show higher elevations in the western part with relative height of more than 10 m. In this area, the gopura and causeway are constructed in the higher western part. In the bulged area of base rock, these structures are made by cutting into base rock. Lines 7, 8 and 9 between Gopura IV and V also show the higher western part and lower eastern part. Small scarps of base rocks are seen in between. The base rock in the eastern side of Gopura IV is relatively low requiring that piled stone masonry terrace be made. The Line 7 also shows that the causeway below Gopura IV was cut into base rock bulge. On the other hand, Lines 8 and 9 show the pile of stones sustain the uniform slope (average 5.9 degrees). The causeway in this part has no stone masonry on the western side as the ground surface is rather flat and higher, while the eastern side has stone masonry.

To the downward from Gopura V, the ground surface changed steeper (average 12.3 degrees) with exposed rocks, predicating the causeway to be composed of steep stairs.

3.1.3.2 Relationship between Cuesta Landform

The Preah Vihear Temple complex is located on the main divide of the Dangrek Mountains where the Middle Jurassic to Lower Cretaceous sandstone exposes and tilts to the north. The strike of rock shows N50 to N70 E, with the dip being monoclonal as 10 degrees to the north. The landform surface slopes from south to the north (backslope of cuesta landform) about 7 degrees. Therefore the younger (upper) strata is exposed to the north, making small scarps (running NW-SE) of more resistant to erosion

南西側にヤショタターカ，南東側にスールヤタターカと呼ばれるバライがあり，ヤショタターカは湛水させてバライとしての景観が復原された。このほか，バライ周辺に付随するような寺院やマウンド等もいくつか分布するが，詳細な調査は行われていない。

謝辞
現地調査の期間（2012年〜2015年）にはCNMCのブンタン氏，NAPVのソパー氏をはじめとする各位に大変お世話になりました。心よりお礼申しあげます。

3.1.3.3 Archaeological Sites in Surrounding Areas

There is a causeway of long stairs to climb up the Preah Vihear Temple (Gopura V) from the eastern foot of the mountain. There are barays named Yasotataka (in southwest) and Suryatataka (in southeast) respectively at the foot of the mountain. Yasotataka currently stores water and the original landscape was restored. There are several temples and mounds accompanying these barays, but detailed surveys have not been performed.

Acknowledgement

We are grateful to Mr. Bunthan of CNMC, Mr. Sopha and other members of the NAPV, for their support during our surveys (2012 to 2015).

Photos a-k (see manuscript)

51

3.2 石材の特徴に基づくプレア・ヴィヘア寺院遺跡の建造順序の推定
Determining the Construction Sequence of the Preah Vihear Temple Monument in Cambodia from its Sandstone Block Characteristics

内田 悦生　溝口 明則　佐藤 広野　下田 一太　渡辺 亮太
UCHIDA Etsuo　MIZOGUCHI Akinori　SATO Hiroya　SHIMODA Ichita　WATANABE Ryota

3.2.1 まえがき

　プレア・ヴィヘア寺院遺跡は，E. エイモニエ (1897)，E. ラジョンキエール (1907)，G. グロリエ (1921)，H. パルマンティエ (1939)，S. サハイ (2009) により研究が行なわれている。これらの研究は，建築学的な視点，あるいは碑文に基づくものである。それに対し，本研究では，建築学，図像学および碑文学的な観点を考慮に入れながら，遺跡に使用されている石材の特徴に基づき，その建造順序の推定を行なった。

　プレア・ヴィヘア寺院は砂岩材から造られた石造建造物群からなる。古い石切場が周辺に点在しており，これらは遺跡に使用された石材の供給源であると思われる。プレア・ヴィヘア寺院遺跡に使用されている砂岩は，石英質砂岩（石英質アレナイト）であり，アンコール遺跡で使用されている灰色～黄褐色砂岩（長石質アレナイト）とは明らかに異なる (Uchida et al., 1998)。石英質砂岩は，コラート高原やクレン山地域に見られ，白亜紀のものである (Meesok et al., 2011) (Figure 3.2-1)。このような石英質砂岩は，タイのコラート高原上に分布するクメール遺跡の多くに使用されている (Uchida et al., 2010)。カンボジアでも，バッタンバンやプノンペン周辺にある遺跡では石英質砂岩が使用されており，これらの砂岩はカンボジア南西部に位置するカルダモン山脈から供給されたと推測される。アンコール遺跡では，バンテアイ・スレイ寺院においてのみ赤色の石英質砂岩が使われている。アンコール遺跡の他の寺院では，Red Terrain層から供給された灰色～黄褐色砂岩が使用されている。Red Terrain層は石英質砂岩から成るUpper Sandstone層により整合を成して覆われている (Meesok et al., 2011)。灰色～黄褐色砂岩はコラート高原やクレン山の裾野に露出しており，コラート高原上のクメール遺

3.2.1 Introduction

　The Preah Vihear Temple monument was previously studied by E.Aymonier (1897), E.Lajonquiere (1907), G.Groslier (1921), H.Parmentier (1939), and S.Sahai (2009). These studies were conducted from an architectural viewpoint or based on inscriptions. In contrast, this study infers the construction sequence of the monument based on its building stone characteristics, taking into account architectural, iconographic and epigraphic evidence.

　The Preah Vihear Temple consists of masonry buildings constructed from sandstone blocks. Ancient sandstone quarries are located in the area around the monument and are likely the source of its building material. The sandstone used in the Preah Vihear Temple is siliceous sandstone (quartz arenite) and clearly different from the gray to yellowish-brown sandstone (feldspathic arenite) used in the Khmer monuments (Uchida et al., 1998). This siliceous sandstone is found within the Khorat Plateau and Phnom Kulen regions, and dates from the Cretaceous (Figure 3.2-1) (Meesook et al., 2011). Sandstone blocks of this type were also used in many monuments located on the Khorat Plateau (Uchida et al., 2010). Although siliceous sandstone blocks were used in monuments around Battambang and Phnom Penh in Cambodia, these blocks were likely supplied from the Cardamom Mountains in southwestern Cambodia. In the Angkor Monuments, red siliceous sandstone blocks were uniquely used for Banteay Srei Temple. For most of the rest of the Angkor Monuments, the Red Terrain Formation supplied the gray to yellowish-brown sandstone. The Red Terrain Formation is conformably overlaid by the Upper Sandstone Formation, which consists of siliceous sandstone (Meesok et al., 2011). The gray to yellowish-brown sandstone outcrops are found at the foot of the Khorat Plateau and Phnom Kulen, but were not used in the monuments on the Khorat Plateau. In Thailand, the Upper

跡には使われていない。Upper Sandstone層は，タイでは3つの地層に分けられており，下から上に向かってPreah Vihear（Phra Wihan）層，Sao Khua層，Phu Phan層と呼ばれている。各層は必ずしも均質ではなく，色においてバリエーションが見られる。Preah Vihear層は黄褐色を示すことが多く，構成粒子は細粒～粗粒で，0.068×10^{-3} SI unit以下（平均0.020×10^{-3} SI unit）の帯磁率を示す。Sao Khua層は赤色を呈することが多く，細粒～中粒で，$0.016\sim0.086\times10^{-3}$ SI unit（平均0.040×10^{-3} SI unit）の帯磁率を示す。Phu Phan層は白色で，中粒～粗粒であり，0.030×10^{-3} SI unit以下（平均0.008×10^{-3} SI unit）の帯磁率を示す。

平均帯磁率は，Sao Khua層で最も高く，Phu Phan層で最も低くなっており，Preah Vihear層はその中間の値を示している（Uchida et al., 2010）。プレア・ヴィヘア寺院の砂岩は見た目に黄褐色を呈するものが多く（Figure 3.2-2（a）—（d）），中粒～粗粒である。これらの特徴に加え，構成鉱物，化学組成から判断して，内田他の論考（2010）は，プレア・ヴィヘア寺院の砂岩材は，Preah Vihear層に由来すると結論づけている。後で述べる詳細な化学組成や帯磁率測定結果からもこの結論が裏づけされる。

Sandstone Formation is subdivided into three units, from bottom to top, these are the Preah Vihear (Phra Wihan), Sao Khua, and Phu Phan Formations. These formations are not homogeneous and vary in color. The Preah Vihear Formation is mainly yellowish-brown, with fine to coarse grain size, and magnetic susceptibilities of less than 0.068×10^{-3} SI units (0.020×10^{-3} SI units on average) (Uchida et al., 2010). The Sao Khua Formation is primarily red, with fine to medium grain size, and magnetic susceptibilities of $0.016–0.086\times10^{-3}$ SI units (0.040×10^{-3} SI units on average). The Phu Phan Formation is white, with medium to coarse grain size, and magnetic susceptibilities of less than 0.030×10^{-3} SI units (0.008×10^{-3} SI units on average).

Magnetic susceptibilities are highest for the Sao Khua Formation and lowest for the Phu Phan Formation, with the Preah Vihear Formation magnetic susceptibilities falling in the middle (Uchida et al., 2010). The sandstone used at the Preah Vihear Temple is mainly yellowish-brown (Figure 3.2-2 (a) - (d)), and is medium to coarse grained. Based on these characteristics, as well as its constituent minerals and chemical composition, Uchida et al. (2010) concluded that the sandstone blocks used in the Preah Vihear Temple were supplied from the Preah Vihear Formation. Detailed chemical composition and magnetic susceptibility measurements for the sandstone blocks described here support this conclusion.

Figure 3.2-1 Location of the representative Khmer monuments, including the Preah Vihear Temple monument (Uchida et al., 2010) The provenance of sandstones used for constructing the Khmer monuments is also shown in this figure (Geological Survey of Vietnam, 1991; Department of Mineral Resources of Thailand, 1999). The colored asterisks for each monument are correlated with the various sandstone formations used to construct them.

Chapter 3 : Study Reports on Preah Vihear Temple

3.2.2 プレア・ヴィヘア寺院の建造物

プレア・ヴィヘア寺院は，北向きの寺院であり，北側入口（標高約550m）から南端に向かって標高が高くなった斜面上に位置しており，南端部（標高630m）はカンボジア側の平原に対し比高500m程の崖を形成している。北側入口から南端までの全長はおよそ800mである。

寺院は主として4つの建造物群から構成される（Figure 3.2-3）。本研究で使用する建物の記号はH. パルマンティエ（1939）に基づくものである。最も南側の建造物群は規模が最も大きく，疑似ゴープラ（A），中央祠堂（B），拝殿（B'），第1回廊（A'），西側付属建物E，東側付属建物F，第1ゴープラ（L），経蔵（C, C'），ホールN，第2回廊（P, P'），第2ゴープラ（D）からなる。疑似ゴープラ（A），中央祠堂（B），東側付属建物F，第1回廊（A'）の一部および西側付属建物Eの一部では大きな石材が使用されている。また，第1回廊（A'）や西側付属建物Eの一部では岩盤が利用されている。

南側から2番目の建造物群は2番目に規模が大きく，付属建物H, I, H', I'と第3ゴープラ（G）から構成さ

3.2.2 Buildings in the Preah Vihear Temple

Preah Vihear Temple faces north and is located on a slope that increases in altitude from the north entrance (550 m above sea level) to the southernmost end (630 m above sea level), with a relative height of 500 m above the plain of Cambodia. The distance between the north entrance and the south end is approximately 800 m.

The buildings of the Preah Vihear Temple are arranged in four groupings (Figure 3.2-3). The symbols used to identify its constituent buildings are from H.Parmentier (1939). The southernmost group is the largest, and consists of the False Gopura (A), Central Sanctuary (B), Mandapa (B'), Gallery I (A'), Western Annex Building E, Eastern Annex Building F, Gopura I (L), Libraries (C and C'), Hall N, Galleries II (P and P'), and Gopura II (D). Relatively large sandstone blocks were used in the False Gopura (A), Central Sanctuary (B), Eastern Annex Building F, part of the Gallery I (A'), and part of the Western Annex Building E. In addition, bedrock was used for part of the Gallery I (A') and Western Annex Building E.

The second group from the south is the second largest, and

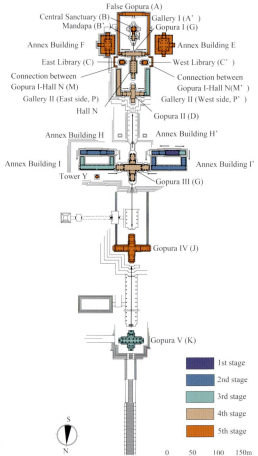

Figure 3.2-2 Photographs of (a) Library (C), (b) Gallery I (A'), (c) Gopura III (G), and (d) Gopura IV (J), (e) and (f) ancient sandstone quaries around the Preah Vihear Temple. Sandstone blocks used for these building have a yellowish-brown color.

Figure 3.2-3 Plan view of the Preah Vihear Temple (Roveda, 2000), showing the name and symbol of each building. The five construction stages established in this study based on sandstone characteristics and pediment style are shown as different colors, grading from blue to red, corresponding to oldest to newest edifices. Arrows indicate the construction sequence with respect to adjacent buildings.

れている。付属建物H'の基壇では一部に岩盤が利用されている。付属建物Iのすぐ北側には小さな塔Yが存在する。3番目の建物は第4ゴープラ（J）のみから，4番目の建物は第5ゴープラ（K）のみからなる。第5ゴープラ（K）の上部構造は崩壊が進んでいる。

3.2.3 調査方法

砂岩材の帯磁率は5cm×5cmの測定面を持つ携帯型帯磁計SM30（ZH instruments，チェコ）を用いて測定を行なった。測定は各建物の各場所において50ヵ所の平らな面に対して行い，その平均値を求めた。表面が藻類や地衣類によって覆われている石材を避けて測定を行なった（Uchida et al., 2003, 2007）。

砂岩材の化学組成分析は，Innov-X Systems社（Waltham, MA, USA）の携帯型蛍光X線分析装置Delta Premiumを用い，「Soilモード」にて測定を行った。日本岩石標準試料（火成岩10試料：JA-1，JA-2，JB-1b，JB-2，JB-3，JG-1a，JG-2，JGb-1，JR-1，JR-2）を用いて分析装置の補正を行った（Imai et al., 1995）。測定時間は1分とした。測定は各建物において藻類や地衣類によって覆われていない5個の砂岩材の平らな面において実施し，その平均値を求めた。

石材の大きさの測定は壁面表面にて行い，幅と厚さの測定を行なった。各建物の各場所において25〜50個の石材に対して測定を行い，その平均値を求めた。これらの測定に加え，砂岩材の層理面方向の調査を行うとともに，破風の形状の調査も実施した。

3.2.4 調査結果

帯磁率の測定結果および携帯型蛍光X線分析装置による化学組成分析結果を，石材の大きさおよび破風の形状とともにTable 3.2-1に示す。遺跡内における上記各項目における違いを以下に示す。Table 3.2-1に示した建造順序は後で詳細に述べるように石材の化学組成，帯磁率，大きさ，破風の形状および隣り合った建物のティンパヌムにおけるレリーフの有無に基づいて推測されたものである。

3.2.4.1 帯磁率

石英質であるプレア・ヴィヘア寺院の砂岩の帯磁率は低く，各建物の平均帯磁率は0.011〜0.068×10⁻³SI unitの範囲にある。それに対し，クレン山の南東裾野から供給されたアンコール遺跡の長石質アレナイトに分類される灰色〜黄褐色砂岩は，0.7〜9.1×10⁻³SI unitの高い平均帯磁率を示している（Uchida et al., 1998, 2003, 2007, 2013）。

consists of the Annex Buildings H, I, H' and I' and Gopura III (G). Here, bedrock were used for part of the platform of the Annex Building H'. A small Tower Y is located north of the Annex Building I. The third group consists only of the Gopura IV (J), and the fourth group only of the Gopura V (K). The upper structure of the Gopura V (K) has almost collapsed.

3.2.3 Methods

Magnetic susceptibility of the sandstone blocks was measured using a portable magnetic susceptibility meter (ZH instruments SM30, Brno, Czech Republic), with a reading surface of 5 cm × 5 cm. Measurements were made on 50 flat surfaces in each section of each building of the monument, and used to calculate average values. Care was taken to avoid blocks covered with algae or lichen (Uchida et al., 2003, 2007).

Chemical analyses of the sandstone blocks were carried out using a portable X-ray fluorescence analyzer (pXRF; Innov-X Systems Delta Premium, Waltham, MA, USA), measuring in soil mode. The instrument was calibrated using 10 reference rocks from the Geological Survey of Japan (JA-1, JA-2, JB-1b, JB-2, JB-3, JG-1a, JG-2, JGb-1, JR-1, and JR-2) (Imai et al., 1995). Measurement time was 1 min. Measurements for 5 sandstone blocks in each building were obtained from flat surfaces, not covered by algae or lichen. These values were averaged.

The size of the sandstone blocks was determined along wall surfaces, showing width and thickness. Dimensions were measured for 25–50 sandstone blocks in each section of each building of the monument, and averaged. In addition to these measurements, bedding plane orientations in the sandstone blocks were recorded, and the style of pediments was described in detail.

3.2.4 Results

The results of magnetic susceptibility and pXRF measurements are summarized in Table 3.2-1, along with information on block size is pediment style. Variation in these parameters within the monument is discussed below. The construction sequence listed in Table 3.2-1, but described in more detail later, is inferred from the chemical composition, magnetic susceptibility, sandstone block size, pediment style, and the presence or absence of relief work on the tympanum of the adjacent buildings.

3.2.4.1 Magnetic Susceptibility

The siliceous sandstone blocks used in the Preah Vihear Temple have low magnetic susceptibilities, with average values in the range of 0.011-0.068×10⁻³ SI units. In contrast, the gray to

Chapter 3 : Study Reports on Preah Vihear Temple

Table 3.2-1 Construction sequence for buildings of the Preah Vihear Temple based on their sandstone block and pediment characteristics.

Stage	Building	MS* (1σ)	K** (1σ)	Ca** (1σ)	Ti** (1σ)	Cr** (1σ)	Mn** (1σ)	Fe** (1σ)	Cu** (1σ)	Zn** (1σ)	Rb** (1σ)	Sr** (1σ)	Y** (1σ)	Zr** (1σ)	Pb** (1σ)	Block size***	Style of pediment ends
1st (Bakheng style period)	Annex Building H' central, upper structure	0.011 (0.009)	2690 (1980)	6300 (200)	1100 (80)	33.6 (38.3)	205 (18)	11800 (880)	10.4 (2.5)	12.8 (4.4)	24 (6.8)	14 (2.9)	12.2 (2.8)	71.8 (11.9)	4.2 (1.8)	Small	
	Annex Building H' central, platform	0.015 (0.007)	2470 (1720)	6800 (450)	1050 (249)	13.4 (6.3)	287 (156)	9580 (2220)	13.8 (6.0)	13.5 (8.3)	20 (5.9)	14 (2.0)	10.2 (1.7)	75.0 (19.1)	5.1 (0.8)	Small	
	Annex Building H' east, lower platform	0.018 (0.010)	4260 (2450)	6760 (410)	1060 (205)	19.8 (2.6)	381 (128)	9500 (1570)	25.8 (27.2)	28.9 (3.3)	30 (11.5)	16 (3.3)	13.2 (2.3)	83.1 (22.7)	5.8 (1.9)	Small	
	Annex Building H' west, platform	0.014 (0.013)	3170 (2450)	6990 (410)	1070 (166)	19.8 (2.6)	196 (128)	11800 (2650)	11.0 (27.2)	22.2 (3.3)	20 (2.6)	14 (1.8)	12.0 (2.3)	75.4 (22.7)	4.9 (1.9)	Small	
2nd (Middle Khleang style period)	Annex Building H' east, upper structure	0.042 (0.019)	5510 (1560)	6210 (120)	1240 (107)	35.4 (16.3)	180 (14)	11500 (1340)	13.2 (1.0)	34.2 (10.6)	44 (4.4)	19 (1.0)	15.3 (3.0)	101.2 (31.9)	5.4 (2.4)	Small	scroll, one block
	Annex Building H' east, upper platform	0.042 (0.019)	7530 (1000)	8330 (2640)	1360 (191)	31.6 (9.8)	184 (19)	11600 (1530)	19.4 (18.9)	27.3 (3.5)	41 (11.2)	19 (3.0)	15.7 (2.1)	116.7 (14.3)	5.2 (1.8)	Small	scroll, one block
	Annex Building H'	0.047 (0.021)	5990 (1750)	6660 (330)	1510 (322)	23.2 (5.2)	205 (40)	10600 (640)	29.2 (22.3)	30.1 (10.6)	33 (7.0)	20 (3.5)	17.0 (2.0)	107.5 (40.3)	3.9 (0.6)	Medium	scroll, one block
	Annex Building I'	0.043 (0.017)	6640 (570)	6270 (250)	1430 (222)	23.0 (3.5)	256 (94)	11400 (670)	15.0 (10.4)	32.2 (5.1)	42 (2.9)	19 (1.6)	18.5 (3.4)	156.0 (68.0)	4.3 (1.9)	Medium	scroll, one block
	Gallery II (West side, P') platform	0.041 (0.025)	6060 (3250)	6300 (220)	1260 (405)	21.4 (10.0)	244 (67)	12400 (2680)	21.6 (10.3)	36.2 (17.0)	36 (14.4)	21 (7.4)	14.3 (3.7)	119.8 (56.2)	11 (6.3)	Medium	
3rd (Late Khleang style period)	Annex Building H' west, upper structure	0.045 (0.018)	2860 (2440)	6170 (220)	1000 (189)	29.4 (16.5)	161 (24)	8300 (2660)	11.4 (2.9)	19.0 (4.6)	24 (14.1)	14 (3.4)	11.8 (6.8)	80.4 (25.5)	3.7 (1.9)	Mediem	scroll, one block
	Annex Building I	0.030 (0.016)	4880 (2380)	6350 (150)	970 (104)	23.6 (13.0)	231 (150)	8600 (1080)	19.2 (8.6)	21.0 (7.5)	27 (7.2)	25 (12.6)	16.7 (5.9)	72.2 (13.2)	7.1 (3.2)	Medium	scroll, one block
	Gopura V (K)	0.023 (0.017)	5530 (5280)	6250 (140)	800 (135)	11.8 (2.3)	142 (12)	8200 (1050)	14.0 (3.0)	12.1 (3.9)	25 (15.2)	15 (4.4)	10.0 (2.8)	66.9 (23.2)	4.9 (0.4)	Large	scroll, one block
	Gallery II (West side, P') upper structure	0.025 (0.013)	2130 (990)	6190 (48)	870 (133)	15.2 (8.2)	159 (20)	8900 (1280)	15.0 (5.5)	25.1 (2.7)	22 (6.8)	19 (5.5)	11.9 (1.3)	70.2 (11.3)	6.0 (1.6)	Medium	scroll, two blocks
4th (End of the Khleang to Baphuon style periods)	Gopura III (G)	0.055 (0.017)	8080 (1710)	6420 (310)	1360 (146)	39.0 (18.3)	217 (70)	15800 (2660)	50.2 (35.6)	38.3 (12.9)	42 (4.6)	23 (5.4)	17.5 (6.1)	133.2 (77.7)	12.8 (8.6)	Large	scroll, one block
	Gopura II (D)	0.057 (0.017)	6460 (1440)	6090 (87)	1370 (179)	32.2 (15.2)	179 (20)	11800 (600)	27.4 (15.1)	35.8 (8.3)	40 (6.8)	19 (2.4)	16.2 (3.0)	92.2 (13.3)	6.9 (0.9)	Medium	scroll, two blocks
	Gallery II (East side, P)	0.051 (0.012)	6580 (1460)	6220 (120)	1420 (91)	19.0 (5.0)	182 (27)	12400 (1410)	17.4 (5.6)	29.9 (10.7)	43 (6.0)	20 (2.6)	17.1 (5.8)	141.4 (26.7)	4.7 (1.7)	Medium	scroll, two blocks
	Hall N	0.067 (0.016)	7400 (1420)	6350 (260)	1460 (261)	28.6 (4.2)	204 (31)	12500 (880)	72.6 (46.6)	64.6 (41.5)	40 (6.7)	27 (7.2)	13.2 (3.1)	130.0 (28.7)	16.0 (14.2)	Medium	scroll, two blocks
	Gopura I (L)	0.049 (0.013)	6090 (2590)	6260 (58)	1480 (238)	29.2 (7.0)	201 (14)	11000 (1640)	32 (9.1)	47.5 (14.3)	37 (11.2)	24 (5.2)	19.5 (6.5)	133.6 (47.9)	34.3 (50.4)	Medium	scroll, two blocks
	Mandapa (B')	0.068 (0.012)	6540 (1640)	7860 (2180)	1330 (126)	142.8 (239.6)	456 (159)	11100 (810)	21.6 (8.8)	51.0 (26.1)	42 (4.9)	21 (2.4)	52.3 (70.1)	108.0 (19.6)	80.2 (59.6)	Medium	five-headed naga
5th (Baphuon to Angkor Vat style periods)	Annex Building E	0.036 (0.007)	2940 (1030)	6240 (210)	1100 (212)	16.6 (4.5)	159 (16)	8900 (1400)	10.6 (6.2)	21.5 (10.8)	25 (7.3)	16 (2.5)	12.5 (2.4)	76.5 (7.1)	5.1 (1.3)	Medium+Large	scroll, two blocks
	Annex Building F	0.042 (0.016)	3950 (3020)	6320 (200)	1140 (340)	21.0 (11.7)	169 (19)	9200 (2060)	10.6 (1.6)	22.5 (10.3)	27 (7.4)	18 (7.0)	11.8 (2.2)	89.1 (32.1)	4.3 (2.3)	Large	scroll, two blocks
	Gopura IV (J)	0.032 (0.019)	4230 (2550)	6160 (96)	1060 (273)	24.8 (10.5)	210 (51)	10500 (2030)	11.2 (3.7)	22.5 (9.6)	29 (13.0)	15 (4.3)	12.2 (3.5)	80.1 (27.8)	10.2 (8.4)	Large	five-headed naga
	Library (C)	0.020 (0.012)	5820 (2930)	6380 (160)	1270 (395)	26.2 (7.5)	175 (21)	9200 (2590)	19.2 (9.9)	37.8 (16.8)	32 (13.5)	58 (32.8)	15.3 (2.1)	114.1 (67.1)	4.7 (2.0)	Large	five-headed naga
	Library (C')	0.019 (0.011)	7430 (1480)	6250 (170)	1135 (243)	34.2 (15.9)	176 (22)	8400 (1610)	80.6 (110.4)	47.7 (15.6)	24 (4.9)	56 (23.4)	14.7 (5.5)	66.0 (10.2)	9.1 (4.1)	Large	five-headed naga
	False Gopura (A)	0.022 (0.011)	3750 (4940)	6200 (140)	1140 (164)	26.6 (11.0)	190 (52)	7600 (690)	78.4 (115.5)	37.5 (39.3)	18 (4.1)	28 (13.7)	18.3 (10.3)	68.5 (10.2)	7.4 (2.7)	Large	five-headed naga
	Central Sanctuary (B)	0.034 (0.018)	4520 (2390)	7280 (940)	1230 (217)	22.2 (7.7)	322 (122)	9300 (720)	26.8 (13.4)	41.2 (33.7)	27 (7.7)	17 (1.8)	12.7 (2.7)	83.6 (24.5)	84.0 (142.7)	Large	
	Gallery I (A') east	0.033 (0.016)	12840 (4540)	7050 (460)	1360 (199)	32.8 (4.3)	244 (69)	11100 (1560)	22.4 (12.2)	82.1 (76.2)	33 (6.8)	30 (12.5)	12.6 (3.6)	93.9 (33.3)	17.2 (19.4)	Medium+Large	five-headed naga
	Gallery I (A') west	0.027 (0.017)	2800 (2280)	6460 (260)	1000 (101)	37.8 (23.7)	336 (251)	8300 (900)	30.6 (27.5)	66.0 (27.1)	20 (5.2)	28 (15.8)	30.0 (22.6)	63.9 (12.4)	12.9 (4.8)	Large	five-headed naga
	Connection between Gopura I-Hall N (M)	0.037 (0.015)	4570 (930)	6240 (360)	1180 (211)	27.2 (12.7)	215 (50)	11600 (1000)	11.4 (3.7)	32.6 (11.3)	33 (1.6)	17 (0.9)	19.4 (3.2)	140.7 (84.1)	6.6 (1.8)	Large	
	Connetion between Gopura I-Hall N (M')	0.024 (0.013)	5040 (4790)	6110 (75)	1040 (300)	20.8 (15.2)	153 (16)	7049 (840)	12.8 (3.9)	21.4 (8.0)	28 (9.4)	15 (4.4)	12.5 (3.6)	123.8 (75.5)	5.7 (1.1)	Large	
	Tower Y	0.036 (0.018)	6690 (1730)	9000 (4380)	1310 (91)	34.0 (7.6)	210 (33)	11300 (1820)	55.6 (39.2)	34.4 (10.3)	32 (7.3)	22 (7.1)	19.0 (4.4)	86.5 (16.5)	4.2 (1.3)	Large	

* MS: Magnetic susceptibility, 10^{-3} SI unit, ** ppm, *** Small: <50 cm in thickness and <50 cm in width, Medium: <50 cm in thickness and 50-100 cm in width, and Large: >50 cm thickness or >100 cm width (on average).

付属建物H'の中央部（第1期）の石材は，プレア・ヴィヘア寺院の中では最も低い帯磁率（0.011×10^{-3} SI unit）を示している。第2期の建物の砂岩材の平均帯磁率は高く，$0.041 \sim 0.047 \times 10^{3}$ SI unitの値を示し，第3期では平均帯磁率が低く，$0.023 \sim 0.045 \times 10^{-3}$ SI unitの値を示している。第4期の拝殿（B'），第1ゴープラ（L），ホールN，拝殿（B'），第2ゴープラ（D）および第3ゴープラ（G）は最も高い帯磁率（$0.049 \sim 0.068 \times 10^{-3}$ SI unit）を示している。第5期の建物では，帯磁率が低く，その平均帯磁率は$0.019 \sim 0.042 \times 10^{-3}$ SI unitの値を示している。

内田他の論考（2010）によれば，Preah Vihear層の砂岩の帯磁率は0.068×10^{-3} SI unit以下であるので，帯磁率のデータは，プレア・ヴィヘア寺院の砂岩材がPreah Vihear層起源であることと整合的である。このことは，砂岩の石切場が，プレア・ヴィヘア寺院の周辺，特に，第4ゴープラ（J）と第5ゴープラ（K）の間の参道の東側および西側に多く見られることと調和的である（Figure 3.2-2（e）および（f））。

3.2.4.2 化学組成

携帯型蛍光X線分析装置によって次の元素が定量的に測定された：K, Ca, Ti, Cr, Mn, Fe, Cu, Zn, Rb, Sr, Y, Zr, Pb。砂岩材から検出されたこれらの元素の内，K, Ti, Fe, Zn, Rb, Zrに関しては系統的な違いが認められた。砂岩材におけるこれらの元素は，第1期および第3期において低く，第2期と第4期において高くなっている。第5期ではこれらの中間的な値を示している。

特に，RbおよびTiは，著しい変化を示している。第1期と第3期の建物ではそれぞれ$20 \sim 30$ ppmおよび$1050 \sim 1100$ ppm，$22 \sim 28$ ppmおよび$800 \sim 1000$ ppmの値を示している。これらの値は，第2期（$33 \sim 45$ ppmおよび$1240 \sim 1510$ ppm）と第4期（$37 \sim 44$ ppmおよび$1330 \sim 1480$ ppm）の建物で高くなっている。第5期の建物では低い値から中間の値（$18 \sim 34$ ppmおよび$1000 \sim 1360$ ppm）を示している。

Srに関しては$14 \sim 58$ppmの範囲の値を示している。経蔵（C, C'）は他の箇所と比べて特徴的に高い含有量（58, 56ppm）を示しており，他の箇所は30ppm以下である。内田他の論考（2010）によれば，Preah Vihear層の砂岩のSr含有量はおよそ40ppm以下である。このことは，プレア・ヴィヘア寺院の砂岩材が，Preah Vihear層由来であることを支持するものである。

yellowish-brown sandstones used in the Angkor monuments, which are feldspathic arenites supplied from the southeastern foot of Phnom Kulen, have higher average magnetic susceptibilities, with values in the range of 0.7-9.1×10^{-3} SI units (Uchida et al., 1998, 2003, 2007, 2013).

The sandstone blocks of the central part of the Annex Building H' (the first stage) have the lowest magnetic susceptibility in the Preah Vihear Temple, averaging 0.011×10^{-3} SI units. The magnetic susceptibility of the sandstone blocks of buildings in the second stage is high, averaging between 0.041-0.047×10^{-3} SI units. It is low in the third stage, with averages in the range of 0.023-0.045×10^{-3} SI units. The Mandapa (B'), Gopura I (L), Hall N, Gopura II (D), and Gopura III (G) edifices belonging to the fourth stage have the highest values, with averages in the range of 0.049-0.068×10^{-3} SI units. The fifth stage buildings have low magnetic susceptibilities, with averages in the range of 0.019-0.042×10^{-3} SI units.

According to Uchida et al. (2010), sandstone of the Preah Vihear Formation has a magnetic susceptibility of less than 0.068×10^{-3} SI units. Hence, all the sandstone blocks of the Preah Vihear Temple have magnetic susceptibility consistent with their supply from the Preah Vihear Formation. This accounts for the abundant ancient sandstone quarries widely distributed around the Preah Vihear Temple, especially in the eastern and western areas, along the causeway between the Gopura IV (J) and Gopura V (K) (Figure 3.2-2 (e) and (f)).

3.2.4.2 Chemical composition

The following elements were quantitatively measured using the pXRF: K, Ca, Ti, Cr, Mn, Fe, Cu, Zn, Rb, Sr, Y, Zr, and Pb. Among these elements, K, Ti, Fe, Zn, Rb, and Zr show systematic changes in content in the sandstone blocks used during construction. The contents of K, Ti, Fe, Zn, Rb, and Zr in the sandstone blocks are relatively low in the first and third stages, but high in the second and fourth stages. They have intermediate values in the fifth stage.

In particular, the contents of Rb and Ti changed markedly. In the first and third stage edifices, their contents had ranges of 20-30 ppm and 1050-1100 ppm, and 22-28 ppm and 800-1000 ppm, respectively. Their contents were higher in the second stage (33-45 ppm and 1240-1510 ppm) and the fourth stage (37-44 ppm and 1330-1480 ppm). The fifth stage had the low to intermediate contents (18-34 ppm and 1000–1360 ppm).

In contrast, the Sr content had a range of 14-58 ppm on average. The Libraries (C, C') had higher Sr contents of 58 and 56 ppm, respectively. The Sr contents in sandstone blocks from the other

3.2.4.3 石材の大きさ

Table 3.2-1では，石材の大きさを次のように分けている：Small；厚さ50cm以下，幅50cm以下，Medium；厚さ50cm以下，幅50〜100cm，Large；厚さ50cm以上あるいは幅100cm以上。Table 3.2-1は，建造時期とともに石材が大きくなっていることを示している。

付属建物H'の中央部には他の箇所や他の建物と異なり，プレア・ヴィヘア寺院の中で最も小さな石材が使用されており，35×43cmの大きさ（厚さと幅）を示している。また，付属建物H'の基壇では砂岩材は薄くなり，23×44cmの大きさとなっている。それに対し，中央祠堂（B），疑似ゴープラ（A），東側付属建物F，第4ゴープラ（J），第1回廊（A'）の一部および西側付属建物Eの一部では60〜80cm×130〜160cmの大きな石材が使用されている。それ以外の場所の建物では，これらの中間の大きさの石材が使用されている。

3.2.4.4 層理面方向

付属建物H'の中央部の上部構造においては，層理面が縦になっている石材の割合が高く，54％に達している。また，付属建物H，I，I'の基壇には正方形の断面を示す石材が多く見られ，このような石材では，およそ半数のものが縦層理を示している。また，第5ゴープラ（K）および第4ゴープラ（J）の基壇にも正方形に近い砂岩材が使用されており，このような石材では縦層理を示すものが半数近くに達している。これに対し，中央祠堂（B），疑似ゴープラ（A），第1回廊（A'）および東側付属建物Fの大きな砂岩材では，水平層理が一般的である。また，疑似ゴープラ（A）および第1回廊（A'）では，層理面が壁面に平行になっている（face bedding）石材も見られる。これらの建物以外では，大きな幅：厚さ比を持ち，水平層理を持つ横長の石材が使用されている。

3.2.4.5 破風の形状

プレア・ヴィヘア寺院に見られる破風は，その先端部の形状に基づき大きく2つに分類される（Figure 3.2-4）。一つは，先端が渦巻状を呈するものである。このような破風は，アンコール時代の初期であるプレア・コー寺院，コー・ケー遺跡群やバンテアイ・スレイ寺院において認められる。もうひとつは，破風の先端に多頭ナーガを有するものである（Figure 3.2-4（f））。このような破風は，広い時代に渡って見られ，アンコール時代の中期から後期であるバンテアイ・スレイ期〜バイヨン期にかけて見られる。さらに，渦巻状の破風は，

buildings were less than 30 ppm. According to Uchida et al. (2010), the Sr content of the Preah Vihear Formation sandstone is typically less than 40 ppm. This also supports the premise that the sandstone blocks used in the Preah Vihear Temple were quarried from the Preah Vihear Formation.

3.2.4.3 Block Size

In Table 3.2-1, block size is listed as "Small", <50 cm in thickness and <50 cm in width; "Medium", <50 cm in thickness and 50-100 cm in width, and "Large", >50 cm in thickness or >100 cm in width. Table 3.2-1 shows that block size became larger over the construction time.

The central part of the Annex Building H', in contrast to other parts or other buildings, was constructed with the smallest sandstone blocks in the Preah Vihear Temple, having an average thickness and width of 35 × 43 cm. Likewise, the sandstone blocks used in the platform of the Annex Building H' are distinctly thin, having a thickness and width of 23 × 44 cm on average. In contrast, large sandstone blocks with dimensions of 60-80 cm × 130-160 cm or larger were used in the Central Sanctuary (B), False Gopura (A), Eastern Annex Building F, Gopura IV (J), part of the Gallery I (A'), and part of the Western Annex Building E. Medium-sized sandstone blocks were used in all other buildings.

3.2.4.4 Bedding Plane Orientations

In the upper structure of the central part of the Annex Building H', 54% of sandstone blocks have vertical bedding planes. Many sandstone blocks with square ends also are observed in the platforms of the Annex Buildings H, I, and I', and almost half of them have vertical bedding planes. Similarly, sandstone blocks with square ends are frequently observed in the Gopura V (K) and Gopura IV (J), and almost half of them have vertical bedding planes. In contrast, the large sandstone blocks used in the Central Sanctuary (B), False Gopura (A), Gallery I (A'), and Eastern Building F have mainly horizontal bedding planes. Sandstone blocks with face bedding are also observed in the False Gopura (A) and Gallery I (A'). In the remaining buildings, horizontally elongated sandstone blocks, with high width/thickness ratios and primarily horizontal bedding planes, were used.

3.2.4.5 Pediment Styles

Preah Vihear Temple building pediments have two styles, based on their terminations (Figure 3.2-4 (F)). One style of a pediment ends in scrolls. Such pediments also are observed in the Preah Ko Temple, Koh Ker Monuments, and Banteay Srei

その先端が一材（Figure 3.2-4 (a)）からなるものと二材（Figure 3.2-4 (b)，(c) および (e)）からなるものとに分けられ，最終的に3つの破風に分けられる。二材渦巻状破風は，石材の調達の容易さから一材渦巻状破風よりも後の様式であると思われる。付属建物H，H'，I，I'，第3ゴープラ（G），第5ゴープラ（K）は，一材渦巻状破風を持ち，第2ゴープラ（D），第1ゴープラ（L），ホールN，第2回廊（P，P'），西側付属建物E，東側付属建物Fは，二材渦巻状破風を持っている。疑似ゴープラ（A），拝殿（B'），第1回廊（A'），経蔵（C，C'），第4ゴープラ（J）は5頭ナーガの破風を持っている。

3.2.5 建造順序・時期に関する考察

前章で述べた結果に基づき，次に述べるようにプレア・ヴィヘア寺院に対し5つの建造時期が推定された（Table 3.2-1，Figure 3.2-2）。特に，砂岩材のTi含有量と帯磁率，破風の形状，および隣接した建物のティンパヌムにおけるレリーフの有無は，これらの建造時期を分けるにあたり重要な要素である（Figure 3.2-5）。

付属建物H'の中央部はプレア・ヴィヘア寺院におい

Temple of the early Angkor period. The other style ends in a five-headed naga at each lower termination point (Figure 3.2-4(f)). These pediments are observed in a wide range of periods, from the Banteay Srei style period to the Bayon style period in the middle to late Angkor period. The scroll-style pediments can be subdivided into pediments that end in scrolls made from one block (Figure 3.2-4(a)) and those that end in scrolls made from two blocks (Figure 3.2-4(b), (c), and (e)), yielding three distinct pediment styles. Pediments in the Preah Ko Temple, Koh Ker Monument and Banteay Srei Temple end in scrolls made from one block. The pediments ending in scrolls made from two blocks are likely to be of a later style, dependent upon more ready procurement of stone. The Annex Building H, I, H' and I', Gopura III (G), and Gopura V (K) have pediments that end in scrolls made from one block; while the Gopura II (D), Gopura I (L), Hall N, Galleries II (P and P'), Western Annex Building E, and Eastern Annex Building F have pediments that end in scrolls made from two blocks. The False Gopura (A), Mandapa (B'), Gallery I (A'), Libraries (C and C'), and Gopura IV (J) have pediments that end in a five-headed naga at each lower termination point.

3.2.5 Construction Sequence and Period

Using results described above, we delineated five construction stages for the Preah Vihear Temple, as described below (Table 3.2-1 and Figure 3.2-2). In particular, the Ti content and magnetic susceptibility of the sandstone blocks, pediment style, as well as the presence or absence of relief work on the tympanum of the adjacent buildings were important factors for determining these stage divisions (Figure 3.2-5).

We believe that the central part of the Annex Building H' was constructed first (Figure 3.2-6). The sandstone blocks in the upper structure of the central part of the Annex Building H' are markedly smaller than those in the eastern and western parts of this Annex Building H', as well as all other buildings in the monument. Their size is similar to sandstone blocks used in the sanctuaries of Phnom Krom and Phnom Bok of the Angkor area, constructed in the Bakheng style period (from the end of the 9th century AD to the beginning of the 10th century AD). The sandstone blocks used in the platforms of Phnom Krom and Phnom Bok also are thin (20-25×35-45 cm) compared with those used in their sanctuaries (Uchida et al., 2001). This block style also

Figure 3.2-4 Images showing pediment styles at the Preah Vihear Temple. (a) A pediment ending in scrolls made from one block (Gopura III (G)), (b) a pediment ending in scrolls made from two blocks (Gopura II (D)), (c) a pediment ending in scrolls made from two blocks (Gallery II (P')), (d) a mortise of a pediment ending in scrolls made from two blocks (Gallery II (P')), (e) a stone block with a tenon that fell from a pediment ending in scrolls made from two blocks (Gallery II (P')), and (f) a pediment ending in a five-headed naga (Gallery I (A')).

Chapter 3 : Study Reports on Preah Vihear Temple

て最初に建造されたと考えられる（Figure 3.2-6）。付属建物H'の中央部の石材は，付属建物H'の東西部分および他の建物と比べて小さくなっている。その大きさは，バケン期（9世紀末〜10世紀初頭）に建造されたアンコール地域のプノム・クロムおよびプノム・ボックの祠堂群に使用されている石材と類似している。また，プノム・クロムおよびプノム・ボックの基壇の砂岩材は祠堂より薄く，20〜25×35〜45cmとなっている（Uchida and Ando, 2001）。このような形状の石材は付属建物H'の基壇にも見られる。また，付属建物H'の中央部の砂岩材の帯磁率は，プレア・ヴィヘア寺院の中で最も低い値を示している。これに加え，付属建物H'中央部の上部構造の石材の54％が縦層理を示している。このような石使いは，付属建物H'の中央部がバプーオン期あるいはそれ以前の建造であることを示している（Uchida et al., 2005）。このように，付属建物H'の中央部の石材とその使い方は，付属建物H'の他の場所や他の建物とは著しく異なっており，その特徴からバケン期の建造であると推測される。なお，付属建物H'の中央および西部基壇と東部の下部基壇も中央部上部構造と同じ時期に建造されたと考えられ（Figure 3.2-6），その砂岩材は低い帯磁率を示している。

第2期として，付属建物H，I'および付属建物H'の東

occurs in the platform of the Annex Building H'. In addition, the magnetic susceptibilities of the sandstone blocks in the upper structure of the central part of the Annex Building H' are the lowest of any of the Preah Vihear Temple. Furthermore, an average of approximately 54% of the sandstone blocks of the upper structure of the central part of the Annex Building H' have vertical bedding planes. This arrangement of blocks suggests that the central part of the Annex Building H' was constructed in or before the Baphuon style period (Uchida et al., 2005). Thus, the sandstone blocks and their arrangement in the upper structure of the central part of the Annex Building H' are markedly different from those of the other parts of the Annex Building H' and the other buildings. Their characteristics suggest that the upper structure of the central part of the Annex Building H' was constructed in the Bakheng style period. The platform of the central and western parts and the lower platform of the eastern part of the Annex Building H' were likely constructed during the same period (Figure 3.2-6), given that their sandstone blocks have similarly low magnetic susceptibilities.

The Annex Buildings H and I' and the eastern part (the upper structure and the upper platform) of the Annex Building H' were constructed during a second stage. Pediments that end in scrolls made from one block are found in all these buildings. The sandstone blocks used in these buildings are relatively rich in K, Ti, Fe, Zn, Rb, and Zr. Although the Annex Building I has pediments that end in scrolls made from one block, its sandstone blocks have different chemical compositions and magnetic susceptibilities from those of the Annex Buildings H and I' and the eastern part of the Annex Building H'. Therefore, the Annex Buildings I likely belongs to a third stage of construction. Given that the tympana of the Annex Buildings I and I' adjacent to the Annex Buildings H and H'. are undecorated, but the other tympanum are decorated, we concluded that the

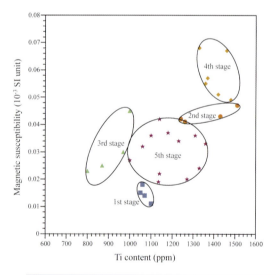

Figure 3.2-5 Plot showing the average Ti contents vs average magnetic susceptibilities for sandstone blocks used in construction of the Preah Vihear Temple. Data given in Table 3.2-1. Values are clearly characteristic of different stages of construction.

Figure 3.2-6 Photograph of the southern face of Annex Building H' showing sections constructed during various stages. The central part (the platform and upper structure), the lower platform of the eastern part, and the platform of the western part were constructed first (first stage); the upper structure and upper platform of the eastern part followed (second stage), and finally, the upper structure of the western part was constructed (third stage).

部（上部構造物および上部基壇）が挙げられる。これらの建物では一材渦巻型の破風が見られる。また、これらの建物の砂岩材は相対的にK，Ti，Fe，Zn，Rb，Zrに富んでいる。付属建物Iは一材渦巻型の破風を持つが、化学組成および帯磁率において付属建物H，I'および付属建物H'の東部とは異なっており、付属建物Iは第3期の建造と考えられる。付属建物H，H'と隣接する付属建物I，I'の破風のティンパヌムにはレリーフが施されていないが、他のものには施されていることから、付属建物I，I'が付属建物H，H'よりも後に建造されたことが推測される。付属建物H'の東部の石材は、付属建物H，I'の石材と同様な化学組成を示しており、このことは、付属建物H'の東部の上部構造が、付属建物H，I'の建造が行なわれているときに増築されたことを示している。付属建物H'西部の上部構造の石材は、付属建物Iの石材と同様な化学組成および帯磁率を示しており、付属建物H'西部の上部構造の増築は、東部の増築（第2期）より明らかに遅く、第3期であると考えられる。

アンコール地域にあるクレアンと付属建物Hとにおける様式の類似性から、第2期はクレアン期のものであると思われる。付属建物Hには碑文（K381）が残されており、この碑文には、1026年の出来事が記されている（Sahai, 2009）。このことから、付属建物H，I'は1026年頃に完成したことが窺われる。

第5ゴープラ（K）は一材渦巻型破風をもつとともに、帯磁率および化学組成において付属建物Iと類似していることから、第3期に建物されたと考えられる。また、第2回廊（P'）の上部構造の砂岩材は、帯磁率および化学組成において付属建物Iと類似しており、第3期に建造されたと推定される。しかしながら、第2回廊（P'）は付属建物Iとは異なり、二材渦巻型の破風をもっている。第2回廊（P'）の基壇に関してはその化学組成や帯磁率から第2期の建造物と同じ砂岩材が使用されていると推測される。このことは、第3期の石材が第2期の石材と比べて低いK，Ti，Fe，Zn，Rb，Zr含有量を示すとともに、低い帯磁率を示していることからも支持される。

砂岩材の高いK，Ti，Fe，Zn，Rb，Zr含有量および高い帯磁率から、第3ゴープラ（G），第2ゴープラ（D），ホールN，第1ゴープラ（L），拝殿（B'）および第2回廊（P）は第4期の建造と考えられる。第3ゴープラ（G）を除いて、中程度の大きさの石材が使用されている。第3ゴープラ（G）は一材渦巻型破風を持つのに対し、拝殿（B'）は多頭ナーガの破風をもっている。他の建物は二材渦巻型破風をもっている。

Annex Buildings I and I' were constructed later than the Annex Buildings H and H'. The sandstone blocks in the upper structure of the eastern part of the Annex Building H' have similar chemical compositions to those in the Annex Buildings H and I'. This suggests that the upper structure of the eastern part of the Annex Building H' was extended while construction of the Annex Buildings H and I' was undertaken. The sandstone blocks in the upper structure of the western part of the Annex Building H' have similar chemical compositions and magnetic susceptibilities to those of the Annex Building I. This suggests that the upper structure of the western part of the Annex Building H' was extended during the third stage, clearly later than the eastern part (second stage).

Given the similarity in style of the Annex Building H to the Khleang in the Angkor area, we believe that the second construction stage corresponds to the Khleang style. The Annex Building H has an inscription (K381), which describes an event that took place in 1026 AD (Sahai, 2009). This suggests that the Annex Buildings H and I' were completed around 1026 AD.

The Gopura V (K) was also likely constructed during the third stage, because it has pediments that end in scrolls made from one block, and its sandstone blocks have similar chemical compositions and magnetic susceptibilities to those of the Annex Building I. The sandstone blocks used in the upper structure of the Gallery II (P') are also similar in chemical compositions and magnetic susceptibilities to those of the Annex Building I, suggesting that the upper structure of the Gallery II (P') was constructed in this third stage. However, the Gallery II (P') has pediments that end in scrolls made from two blocks, which are different from those in the Annex Building I. Given the chemical compositions and magnetic susceptibilities of its constituent blocks, we consider the possibility that the platform of the Gallery II (P') was constructed using the same sandstone blocks as those used in second-stage buildings. This is supported by the fact that the sandstone blocks of the third stage have distinctly lower K, Ti, Fe, Zn, Rb, and Zr contents and magnetic susceptibilities than those of the second stage.

The Gopura III (G), Gopura II (D), Hall N, Gopura I (L), Mandapa (B'), and Gallery II (P) were clearly constructed in a fourth stage, characterized by sandstone blocks with relatively high K, Ti, Fe, Zn, Rb, and Zr contents and magnetic susceptibilities. Medium-sized sandstone blocks were used in all of these buildings, except for the Gopura III (G). The Gopura III (G) has pediments that end in scrolls made from one block, while the Mandapa (B') has pediments that end in a five-headed naga at each lower termination point. The other buildings have

Chapter 3 : Study Reports on Preah Vihear Temple

第3ゴープラ（G）は隣接した付属建物I, I'より後に建造されたと考えられる。なぜならば，付属建物I, I'の破風のティンパヌムにはレリーフが施されているが，隣接する第3ゴープラ（G）の破風のティンパヌムにはレリーフが施されていないからである。破風の様式から判断して，第3ゴープラ（G）に引き続き，第2ゴープラ（D）＋ホールN＋第1ゴープラ（L）＋第2回廊（P），そして，拝殿（B'）の順に建造されたことが推定される。

第2ゴープラ（D）の砂岩材は，帯磁率や化学組成において第2回廊（P）の砂岩材と似ているのに対し，第2回廊（P'）の砂岩材とは異なっている。このことは第2回廊（P）は第2回廊（P'）（第2期〜第3期）とは異なった時期に建造されたことを示している。破風の形式からは，第2回廊（P'）は，第3ゴープラ（G）より後に建造されたことが考えられる。しかしながら，破風の形状から推定される建造順序は，石材の化学組成や帯磁率から推定される建造順序とは矛盾が生じている。

第2ゴープラ（D）の扉の枠材には碑文（K380）が残されており，そこには1018年，1037年，1038年および1049年の出来事が記されている（Sahai, 2009）。このことは，第2ゴープラ（D）が1049年ごろ（クレアン期末期）に建造されたことを示している。このことから，第4期の建物は，クレアン期末期〜バプーオン期の建造であることが推定される。

上記以外の建物は第5期に属すると考えられる。第5期の建物では，第2期および第4期の建物と比べて帯磁率が小さく，また、K, Ti, Fe, Zn, Rb, Zr含有量は，第2期および第4期の建物と第3期の建物の間の値を示している（Figure 3.2-5）。

西側付属建物Eおよび東側付属建物Fは，二材渦巻型破風を持っている。それに対し，5頭ナーガの破風をもつ中央祠堂（B），第1回廊（A'），疑似ゴープラ（A），第4ゴープラ（J）および経蔵（C, C'）は，西側付属建物Eおよび東側付属建物Fより若干後の時期に建造されたと思われる。第4ゴープラ（J）は，その基壇の石材に正方形に近い形をしているものが多く，また、縦層理のものも多いことから，これらの建物の中では最初の建造であると推定される。

他の建物とは異なり，2つの経蔵（C, C'）は，高いSr含有量を示し，また、帯磁率も互いに似ていることから同時期の建造であると思われる。建物の配置から経蔵（C, C'）は，第1ゴープラ（L），ホールN，第2ゴープラ（D）および第2回廊（P, P'）より後に建造されたことが推定される。このことは，経蔵の破風の先端が5頭ナーガとなっているのに対し，経蔵周辺の建物の破風が二材渦巻型になっていることからも裏付けされ

pediments that end in scrolls made from two blocks.

We infer that the Gopura III (G) was constructed after the Annex Buildings I and I' because reliefs were carved on the tympanum of the Annex Buildings I and I', but were left unfinished on those of the Gopura II (D) adjacent to the Annex Buildings I and I'. Judging from the pediment style, construction of the Gopura II (D), Hall N, Gopura I (L), and Gallery II (P), and then Mandapa (B') may have followed the construction of the Gopura III (G).

The sandstone blocks of the Gopura II (D) are similar in chemical compositions and magnetic susceptibilities to those of the Gallery II (P), but differ from those of the Gallery II (P'). This suggests that the Gallery II (P) was constructed at a different time to the Gallery II (P') (during the second to third stages). The style of the pediments suggests that the Gallery II (P') was constructed after the Gopura III (G). However, the construction sequence inferred from the style of the pediments contradicts that derived from the chemical compositions and magnetic susceptibilities of their sandstone blocks.

The inscription (K380) on the door frame of the Gopura II (D) describes events that took place in 1018 AD, 1037 AD, 1038 AD, and 1049 AD (Sahai, 2009). This suggests that the Gopura II (D) was constructed around 1049 AD (the end of the Khleang style period). Therefore, the buildings in the fourth stage are estimated to have been constructed from the end of the Khleang style to the Baphuon style periods.

The remaining buildings at the site belong to a fifth stage. The sandstone blocks of these buildings have lower magnetic susceptibilities than those belonging to the second and fourth stages, and their chemical contents of K, Ti, Fe, Zn, Rb, and Zr fall between those of the second and fourth stages, and those of the third stage (Figure 3.2-5).

The Western and Eastern Annex Buildings E, F have pediments that end in scrolls made from two blocks; thus, we infer their construction slightly before the Central Sanctuary (B), Gallery I (A'), False Gopura (A), Gopura IV (J), and Libraries (C and C'), which all have pediments that end in a five-headed naga at each lower termination point. We believe that the Gopura IV (J) was constructed first among these buildings, because its sandstone blocks have square ends and almost of half of thera vertical bedding planes, which are frequently seen in the platform.

In contrast to the other buildings, the sandstone blocks of the Libraries(C and C') are uniformly high in Sr and have similar magnetic susceptibilities to each other. This suggests that the Libraries (C and C') were constructed at the same time. Given the site layout, we infer that the Libraries (C and C') were constructed after the Gopura I (L), Hall N, Gopura II (D),

る。経蔵（C, C'）は，拝殿（B'）およびホールNと同様に，同時期の他の建物と比べて装飾の完成度が高くなっている。

疑似ゴープラ（A），中央祠堂（B），第1回廊（A'），塔（Y）に使用されている大型の砂岩材は，類似した化学組成および帯磁率を示している。さらに，塔Yを除いてこれらの建物は多頭ナーガの破風をもっており，ほぼ同時期の建造であると推定される。塔Yには装飾が施されておらず，また，積んだだけの未完成の状態にあることから，プレア・ヴィヘア寺院の中でも最末期の建物であると思われる。疑似ゴープラ（A），中央祠堂（B），第1回廊（A'）には大きな石材が使用されており，かつ，層理面方向が基本的に水平であることからアンコール・ワット期の建造であることが推測される。それに対し，東側付属建物F，西側付属建物E，第4ゴープラ（J）および経蔵（C, C'）は，石材の特徴からバプーオン期の建造であり，疑似ゴープラ（A），中央祠堂（B），第1回廊（A'）より前の時期に建造されたと推定される。

プレア・ヴィヘア寺院の建造順序に関しては，Table 3.2-2に示されているようにH. パルマンティエ（1939）およびS. サハイ（2009）によって推定が行われている。H. パルマンティエ（1939）は建築学的な見地から建造順序の推定を行い，S. サハイ（2009）は碑文に基づき建造順序の推定を行っている。本研究における建造順序の推定結果とH. パルマンティエ（1939）およびS. サハイ（2009）による結果とはかなり異なるものである。砂岩材の特徴に基づき，付属建物H'はプレア・ヴィヘア寺院において最も古い建造物であると結論される。このことは，H. パルマンティエ（1939）およびS. サハイ（2009）による建築順序とは一致しない。しかしながら，本研究結果は，付属建物H, I, I'はクレアン期後期の建造であるとの彼らの推定を支持するものである。H. パルマンティエ

and Galleries (P and P'). This is supported by the fact that the Libraries (C and C') have pediments that end in a five-headed naga at each lower termination point, whereas the buildings surrounding the Libraries (C and C') have pediments that end in scrolls made from two blocks. Decoration also is more elaborate on the Libraries (C and C'), as well as on the Mandapa (B') and Hall N, compared with other buildings in this stage.

The large sandstone blocks of the False Gopura (A), Central Sanctuary (B), Gallery I (A'), and Tower Y have similar chemical compositions and magnetic susceptibilities. In addition, these buildings, except for the Tower Y have pediments that end in a five-headed naga at each lower termination point. Given these facts, we infer that these buildings were constructed at nearly the same time. Because the Tower Y has no decoration and is unfinished, it may have been the last construction undertaken at the Preah Vihear Temple. Because large sandstone blocks were used, with bedding planes that are mainly horizontal, the False Gopura (A), Central Sanctuary (B), and Gallery I (A') are consistent with the Angkor Vat style period. In contrast, the Eastern Annex Building F, Western Annex Building E, Gopura IV (J), and Libraries (C and C') belong to the Baphuon style period, and were constructed before the False Gopura (A), Central Sanctuary (B), and Gallery I (A'), based on their sandstone characteristics.

For comparison, the construction sequences for the Preah Vihear Temple previously inferred by H.Parmentier (1939) and S.Sahai (2009) are outlined in Table 2. H.Parmentier (1939) used an architectural viewpoint, while S.Sahai (2009) used inscriptions to establish a sequence. The sequence obtained in this study differs considerably from those obtained by both H.Parmentier (1939) and S.Sahai (2009). Based on its sandstone block characteristics, we concluded that the Annex Building H' is the oldest edifice in the Preah Vihear Temple. This is not consistent with the construction sequences proposed by H.Parmentier (1939) or

Table 3.2-2 Comparison of the constructions sequences for the Preah Vihear Temple proposed by H. Parmentier (1939), S. Sahai (2009) and this study.

Period	King	Parmentier (1939)	Sahai (2009)	This study
Bakheng style (899-910)	Yasovarman I		Gopura IV (J), Gopura V (K)	Central part of Annex Building (H')
Bakheng style (910-923)	Harshavarman I	Gopura I (L), Hall N, Gopura II (D), Galleries II (P, P')	Gallery I (A'), False Gopura (A), Mandapa (B'), Gopura I (L)	
Pre Rup style (944-968) Early Khleang style (968-1001)	Rajendravarman Jayavarman V	Gallery I (A'), False Gopura (A), Mandapa (B'), Libraries (C, C'), Annex Buildings (E,F)		
Late Khleang style (1002-1049)	Suryavarman I	Annex Buildings (H, I, H', I'), Gopura IV (J), Gopura V (K), Connection between Gopura I-Hall N (M, M'), Tower Y, Gopura III (G)	Galleries II (P, P'), Gopura II (D),Hall N, Annex Buildings (H, I, H', I'), Gopura III (G), Connection beween Gopura I-Hall N (M, M'), Libraries (C, C')	Eastern part of Annex Building (H'), Annex Building(H, I')
				Annex Building I, Gallery II (P'), Gopura V (K), Western part of Annex Building (H')
				Gopura III (G), Gallery II (P), Gopura II (D), Hall N, Gopura I (L), Mandapa (B')
Baphuon style (1050-1080)	Udayadityavarman II	Central Sanctuary (B)	Central Sanctuary (B)	
Angkor Vat style (1080-1177)	Suryavarman II		Annex Buildings (E,F)	Annex Buildings (E, F), Gopura IV (J), Libraries (C, C'), False Gopura (A), Central Sanctuary (B), Gallery I (A'), Connection beween Gopura I-Hall N (M, M'), Tower Y

Chapter 3 : Study Reports on Preah Vihear Temple

（1939）およびS．サハイ（2009）は，付属建物H，H'，I，I'よりも拝殿（B'），第1ゴープラ（L），ホールNおよび第2ゴープラ（D）の方が古いと推定している。これに加え，疑似ゴープラ（A）および第1回廊（A'）も付属建物H，H'，I，I'より古いと推定している。本研究を含め，いずれの研究においても第3ゴープラ（G）は，付属建物H，H'，I，I'より後の時期に建造されたと推定している。本研究では，第3ゴープラ（G）と拝殿（B'），第1ゴープラ（L），ホールNおよび第2ゴープラ（D）は，砂岩材の帯磁率，化学組成の類似から同じ頃の時期（後期クレアン期〜バプーオン期）に建造されたと推定している。

中央祠堂（B）が最後に近い時期に建造されたことは3つの研究において一致している。しかしながら，H．パルマンティエ（1939）およびS．サハイ（2009）の研究では，中央祠堂（B）を取り囲む疑似ゴープラ（A）および第1回廊（A'）は，拝殿（B'）と同じ時期に建造されたと推定している。しかしながら，本研究では，それらの砂岩材の特徴はかなり異なっていることを明らかにした。拝殿（B'）とは異なり，疑似ゴープラ（A）および第1回廊（A'）の一部では，中央祠堂（B）と同様に大きな石材が使用されている。これに加え，疑似ゴープラ（A）および第1回廊（A'）の石材は拝殿（B'）の石材とは化学組成および帯磁率において明らかに異なるが，中央祠堂（B）とは類似している。これらのことから，H．パルマンティエ（1939）およびS．サハイ（2009）の建造順序は受け入れ難いものである。

S.Sahai (2009). However, we support their inference that the Annex Buildings H, H', I and I' were constructed in the late Khleang style. Both authors considered that the Mandapa (B'), Gopura I (L), Hall N, and Gopura II (D) were constructed before the Annex Buildings H, H', I and I'. The False Gopura (A) and Gallery I (A') also were inferred to be older than the Annex Buildings H, H', I and I' in their studies. Meanwhile, all studies support that the Gopura III (G) was constructed later than the Annex Buildings H, H', I and I'. We concluded that the Gopura III (G), Gopura II (D), Hall N, Gopura I (L), and Mandapa (B') were constructed during the same period (in late Khleang style to the Baphuon style) based on their similar sandstone block chemical compositions and magnetic susceptibilities.

All three studies agree that the Central Sanctuary (B) was constructed in the final stage. However, H.Parmentier (1939) and S.Sahai (2009) considered the False Gopura (A) and Gallery I (A') surrounding the Central Sanctuary (B) to have been constructed during the same period as the Mandapa (B'). However, we found their sandstone block characteristics to be distinctly different. Large sandstone blocks were used in the False Gopura (A) and part of the Gallery I (A') as well as in the Central Sanctuary (B), in contrast to the Mandapa (B'). In addition, the sandstone blocks of the False Gopura (A) and Gallery I (A') are different in chemical compositions and magnetic susceptibilities from those of the Mandapa (B'), but similar to those of the Central Sanctuary (B). Given these facts, it is difficult to accept the construction sequences for these buildings proposed by either H.Parmentier (1939) or S.Sahai (2009).

References

I) Aymonier,E. 1897. Le Cambodge et ses monuments. Koh Ker, Phnom Sandak, Prah Vihear. In Annales du Musée Guimet. Paris: Ernest Leroux. Revue d'Histoire des Religions 36: 20-54. / II) Department of Mineral Resources of Thailand 1999, Geological map of Thailand (at 1:1,000,000 scale). Geological Survey of Vietnam 1991. /III) Geological map of Cambodia, Laos, and Vietnam (at 1:1,000,000 scale), 2nd eds. Hanoi. / IV) Groslier,G. 1921. Le temple de Preah Vihear, Art et Archéologies Khmères, I, Societé d'Éditions Géographiques, Maritimes et Colonials, Paris 274-294. / V) Imai,N. and Terashima,S. Itoh,S. Ando,A. 1995. 1994 compilation values for GSJ reference samples, "Igneous rock series". Geochem. J. 29: 91-95. / VI) Lunet de Lajonquiere E. 1907. Inventaire descritif des monuments du Cambodge, Paris : Ernest Leroux, vol.II. Publication de l'EFEO 8./ VII) Meesook,A. 2011. Cretaceous. In Ridd, M.F., Barber, A.J. and Crow, M.J. (Eds) The Geology of Thailand, The Geological Society, Lonclon : 169-184. / VIII) Parmentier,H. 1939. L'art khmer classique. Monuments du quadrant Nord-Est. Paris : PEFEO 2: 29. / IX) Roveda,V. 2000. Preah Vihear. Bangkok: River Books. / X) Sahai,S. 2009. Preah Vihear. An introduction to the World Heritage Monument. Phnom Penh: Cambodian National Commission for UNESCO. / XI) Uchida,E, Ando,D. 2001. Petrological Survey 2000. In Annual report on the Technical Survey of Angkor Monument 2001, Japanese Government Team for Safeguarding Angkor 225-247. / XII) Uchida,E. and Cunin,O. Shimoda,I. Suda,C. Nakagawa,T. 2003. The construction process of the Angkor monuments elucidated by the magnetic susceptibility of sandstone. Archaeometry 45: 221-232. / XIII) Uchida,E. Cunin,O. Suda,C. Ueno,A. Nakagawa,T. 2007. Consideration on the construction process and the sandstone quarries during Angkor period based on the magnetic susceptibility. J. Archaeol. Sci. 34: 924-935. / XIV) Uchida,E. Ito,K. Shimizu,N. 2010. Provenance of the sandstone used in the construction of the Khmer monuments in Thailand. Archaeometry 52:550-574. / XV) Uchida,E. Ogawa,Y. Nakagawa,T. 1998. The stone materials of the Angkor monuments, Cambodia – The magnetic susceptibility and the orientation of the bedding plane of the sandstone. J. Petrol. Mineral. Econ. Geol. 93: 411-426. / XVI) Uchida,E. Shimoda,I. 2013. Quarries and transportation routes of Angkor monument sandstone blocks. J. Archaeol. Sci. 40: 1158-1164. / XVII) Uchida,E. Suda,C. Ueno,A. Shimoda,I. Nakagawa,T. 2005. Estimation of the construction period of Prasat Suor Prat in the Angkor monuments, Cambodia, based on the characteristics of its stone materials and the radioactive carbon age of charcoal fragments. J. Archaeol. Sci. 32: 1339-1345.

3.3　考古学調査
Archaeological Survey

杉山　洋　　佐藤　由似
SUGIYAMA Hiroshi　　SATO Yuni

3.3.1.1 第1次調査概要
期間　2014年2月24日から2月27日
調査参加者
　杉山　洋：奈良文化財研究所企画調整部
　佐藤由似：奈良文化財研究所企画調整部
　ソク・ケオ・ソバナラ：奈良文化財研究所
　　　　　　　　　　　カンボジアプロジェクト調査員

3.3.1.2 第1次調査結果
　24日にシェムレアップから現地へ出発し，午後現地で調査の挨拶と調査地点の打ち合わせを行った。翌25日の朝から2ヵ所のトレンチを同時に開け調査を行った。第2トレンチは小規模であるとともに，岩盤を削りだした下部基壇がすぐに検出され，当日中で図面等を含む調査を終了した。第1トレンチは当初2m×3mで設定したが，南側の軍の塹壕とおぼしき遺構が深くその掘削に時間を取られたことから，結局2m×2mの範囲を調査した。午後には第4ゴープラ基壇裾部に断割を入れ，下部基壇の様子を明らかにした。第1トレンチも26日中に調査を終了し，埋め戻しまで完了した。

3.3.1.3 第1トレンチ
　2m×3mのトレンチを設定したが，調査期間の関係から長さ2m分のみを発掘した。トレンチは第4ゴープラの基壇南東部に接するように設定した。
　調査の結果，基壇砂岩石材より北へ60cm内外の所に最近の溝が掘削されており，古代の遺構は検出できなかった。この溝からはビニール袋やアルミの蓋，薬莢などが出土している。この位置からはタイ国境は視認できず，タイとの国境紛争時の掘削ではなく，それより前のベトナム軍駐留時の遺構ではないかとの指摘があった。
　この溝の基壇側の3ヵ所には，成形された砂岩がほ

3.3.1.1 Outline of 1st survey
Period:　February 24th-27th, 2014
Members:
　SUGIYAMA Hiroshi, Planning and Coordination Dept., Nara National Research Institute for Cultural Properties
　SATO Yuni, Planning and Coordination Dept., Nara National Research Institute for Cultural Properties
　SOK Keo Sovannara, Cambodian Project Researcher, Nara National Research Institute for Cultural Properties

3.3.1.2 Result of 1st Survey
　On February 24th, the survey team departed from Siem Reap for Preah Vihear Temple, and in the afternoon, made courtesy calls with regard to the survey and held an onsite meeting about survey spots. On February 25th, two trenches were simultaneously opened and surveyed from the morning. Trench No. 2 was small, and the lower platform that was made by carving the bedrock was immediately found, so the survey, including the drawing of diagrams, was completed in one day. Trench No. 1 was initially planned to be 2m × 3m, but because the structure on the south side that appeared to be a military entrenchment was deep and took time to dig, a 2m × 2m area was surveyed in the end. In the afternoon, A cross section was cut in the base of the platform of Gopura IV, to reveal the condition of the lower platform. Trench No. 1 was completed being surveyed and backfilled on February 26th.

3.3.1.3 Trench No. 1
　A trench 2m × 3m was opened, but only 2m was excavated, due to reasons related to the survey period. It was opened so that it adjoins the southeast portion of the platform of Gopura IV.
　As a result of the survey, a recent ditch was found in a location around 60cm to the north of the platform sandstone element, but

Chapter 3 : Study Reports on Preah Vihear Temple

ぼ等間隔に置かれており，周辺の砂岩石材を利用した足場のような用途が推定される。

今回の調査で第4ゴープラの南側にもモールディングを施した下部基壇があることがわかった。上部基壇のモールディングと同じく，細かく凹凸を作る。今回の調査区東側ではモールディングが未完成な部分がある。この部分の基壇外側の土層は，他の部分とくらべ比較的きれいな粘土が使用されている。部分的な調査であるため断定はできないがこの部分に版築による築地塀が取り付いていた可能性を考えている。次回の調査では，本次調査の南側に調査区を設定する予定であり，築地想定延長部の精査を目指している。

no ancient structure was found. From this ditch, plastic bags, aluminum can tops and empty cartridges were unearthed. The Thailand border was not visible from this location, so it was noted that the ditch was not dug during the border conflict with Thailand, but that it is possibly a structure made before that, during the occupation of the Vietnam army.

In three locations on the platform side of this ditch, shaped sandstone blocks were found placed at roughly even intervals, suggestive of having been used as a foothold, along with the surrounding sandstone elements.

The survey also discovered the existence of a lower platform that was decorated with moldings, on the south side of Gopura IV. The moldings displayed detailed engravings in the same manner as the upper platform. However, a part of the moldings on the east side of the survey area was unfinished. The soil layer on the outside of the platform on this part was made of clay that was relatively cleaner than the rest of the parts. It is possible that a compacted roofed mud wall had been attached to this part, although it is difficult to say with certainty based on only a partial survey. In the next survey, a survey area is planned to be set to the south of this recent survey, with the aim of examining in detail the conjectured extension of the mud wall.

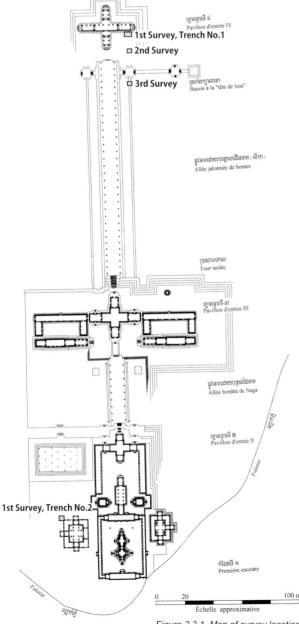

Figure 3.3-1 Map of survey locations

Archaeological Survey

Photo 3.3-1 Trench No. 1: Discovery of stone elements (view from the southeast)

Photo 3.3-2 Trench No. 1: Full view (view from the south)

Photo 3.3-3 Gopura IV: Lower platform

Photo 3.3-4 Gopura IV: Lower platform in detail

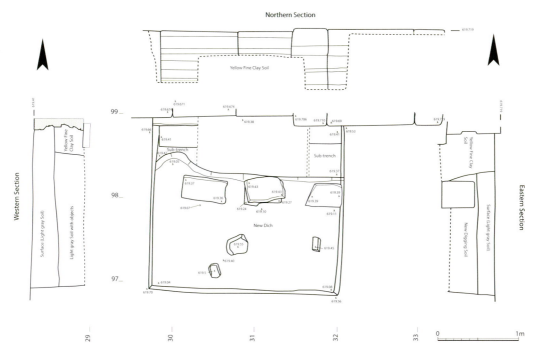

Figure 3.3-2 Trench No. 1: Plan view

3.3.1.4 第 2 トレンチ

第2トレンチは付属建物Eの基壇西北隅に設定した。予想通り岩盤を成形した下部基壇が1段分検出された。

3.3.1.5 遺物

今回は調査期間が短く，かつ調査面積が狭かったため顕著な遺物は出土していない。ただ瓦の破片は比較的多く発見された。いずれも土師質の丸平瓦で，比較的厚い作りのものである。何点か出土している。少数の出土量からの判断は誤解を生む可能性もあるが，これらの瓦を見る限り，付属建物Eからは施釉瓦が数点出土している。第4ゴープラからは土師質の瓦が出土している。

3.3.1.6 まとめ

今回の調査は小面積とはいえプレア・ヴィヘア寺院での発掘として，いくつかの成果をあげる事ができた。まず付属建物E周辺は予想通り岩盤を成形した下部基壇上に，砂岩で組み立てた祠堂が載っていることがはっきりした。第4ゴープラでは地形の影響で南側基壇の下部基壇が埋もれていることがはっきりするとともに，築地の取り付け痕跡を確認した。この築地痕跡については，当該部分から南に延びる堤防状の高まりとの関係が推し量られる。今後はこの堤防状の高まり周辺での調査を予定し，築地遺構の確認に臨みたい。

3.3.1.4 Trench No. 2

Trench No. 2 was opened in the northwest corner of the platform of Annex Building E. As expected, a tier of a lower platform composed of rocks was found.

3.3.1.5 Artifacts

No noteworthy artifacts were unearthed in this survey, as it ran for only a short period, and the survey area was limited. Nevertheless, a relatively large number of roofing tile fragments were found. They were fragments from round tile and flat tile that were plain and unglazed, and were relatively thickly made. Several pieces were unearthed. Any judgment based on a small number of artifacts harbors the risk of misunderstanding, but as far as could be seen by these roof tiles, several glazed roof tiles were found from Annex Building E, while plain, unglazed roof tiles were found from Gopura IV.

3.3.1.6 Summary

The recent survey may have been limited in area, but it made a number of achievements as an archaeological survey at Preah Vihear. It clarified the existence of a sandstone sanctuary on top of a lower platform made of rocks in Annex Building E, as expected. At Gopura IV, it clarified that the lower platform on the south side lies buried in the ground, affected by the landform, and verified traces where a mud wall had been attached. These traces suggest some type of relationship with the levee-like rise extending southward from the said area. In the future, a survey of the area around this levee-like rise is desired, to verify the existence of the mud wall structure.

Photo 3.3-5 Full view of Trench No. 2 (view from the north)

Archaeological Survey

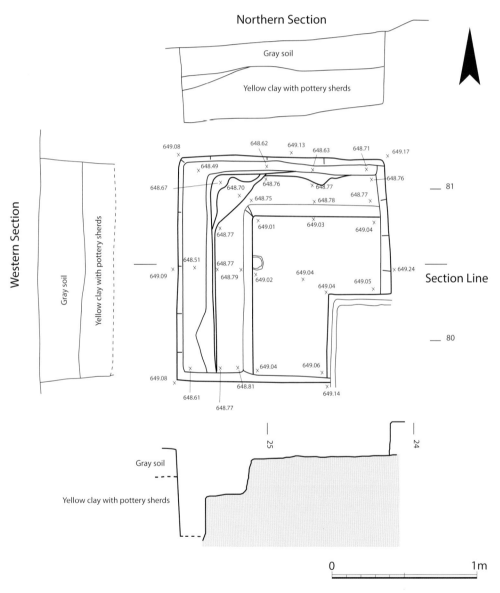

Figure 3.3-3 Plan view of Trench No. 2

69

Chapter 3 : Study Reports on Preah Vihear Temple

Photo 3.3-6 Attachment part of mount, Gopura IV

Photo 3.3-7 Row of stone (from south)

Photo 3.3-8 Entire aspect of trench (from north)

Photo 3.3-9 Ruin on causeway

3.3.2.1 Outline of 2nd Survey

Period:　August 26th-28th, 2014
Members:

　　SUGIYAMA Hiroshi, Planning and Coordination Dept., Nara National Research Institute for Cultural Properties

　　SATO Yuni, Planning and Coordination Dept., Nara National Research Institute for Cultural Properties

　　SOK Keo Sovannara, Cambodian Project Researcher, Nara National Research Institute for Cultural Properties

On August 26th, the survey team departed from Siem Reap for Preah Vihear Temple, and in the afternoon, held an onsite meeting about survey spots. The next morning, a trench was opened on the east side of the row of stones in north-south orientation and surveyed. The soil layer inside the trench was found to be composed of relatively clean, yellow clay, but no remains of a compacted structure were found in particular. Thereafter, the trench was expanded to the west side of the row of stones. In the afternoon of the 27th, records of actual measurements were taken, while opening another trench for verification. In the morning of the 28th, actual measurements were taken of the platform structure and the stone row in the vicinity, before bringing the survey to a close.

3.3.2.2 Survey of the Stone Row

A row of stones in north-south orientation was found from an area 23m south of the southeast wall of Gopura IV and extending 9.5m southward. On the south side of the stone row, there was a platform structure with a staircase oriented in the east-west direction, so it was believed that a roofed mud wall stretching in the north-south direction had existed on top of the stone row as its foundation.

3.3.2.3 Platform Structure

The platform measured approximately 9m east to west and 7m north to south. The outside was made of sandstone, and had a staircase with more than 10 stairs on the east side and another staircase with 5 stairs on the west. On the north side of the platform was an expanse of elaborate, yellow clay, which is thought to be the remains of a mud wall that had been attached to this part of the platform.

3.3.2.4 Summary

The recent survey shed light on the possibility that a roofed mud wall and a shielded facility made of had existed on both sides of the causeway from Gopura IV to Gopura III. It was also assumed that the platform served as a gate for the shielded facility.

The approach, and a structure thought to be a passageway connecting the east and west gate-like platform structures transected the causeway (Figure 3.3-4).

3.3.2.1 第2次調査概要
期間　2014年8月26日から8月28日
調査参加者
　　杉山　洋：奈良文化財研究所企画調整部
　　佐藤由似：奈良文化財研究所企画調整部
　　ソク・ケオ・ソバナラ：奈良文化財研究所
　　　　　　　　　　カンボジアプロジェクト調査員

　26日にシェムレアップから現地へ出発し，午後現地で調査地点の打ち合わせを行った。翌27日の朝から南北に延びる石列の東側にトレンチを開けて調査を開始した。トレンチ内の土層は比較的きれいな黄色粘土層が検出されたが，特に版築などの構造物に相当する遺構は検出されなかった。その後石列の西側にもトレンチを拡張した。27日午後から一部に確認のトレンチを入れながら，実測等の記録を行った。28日午前には基壇遺構や周辺の石列等の実測を行い，調査を終了した。

3.3.2.2 石列の調査
　第4ゴープラの南東壁面から南へ12mほどの所から南へ9.5mにわたって南北石列が観察される。石列の南側には東西に通じる階段を持つ基壇遺構が存在し，石列を基礎の石材とする南北方向の築地塀が存在したと推定した。

3.3.2.3 基壇遺構
　東西約9m，南北約7mの規模で，基壇周りを砂岩で構築し，東には10段以上の階段が取り付き，西には5段の階段が取り付く。基壇北側には築地本体の残りと考えられる，緻密な黄色粘土の広がりが認められ，この部分に築地塀が取り付いていたものと推定される。

3.3.2.4 まとめ
　今回の調査で第4ゴープラから第3ゴープラへの参道両脇に築地塀と土塁の遮蔽施設が存在した可能性が考えられようになった。また基壇遺構は遮蔽施設に開く門としての機能が推定される。同じ構造は参道の西側にも認められ，東西の門状基壇遺構をつなぐ通路と見られる遺構が参道を横断している（Figure 3.3-4）。

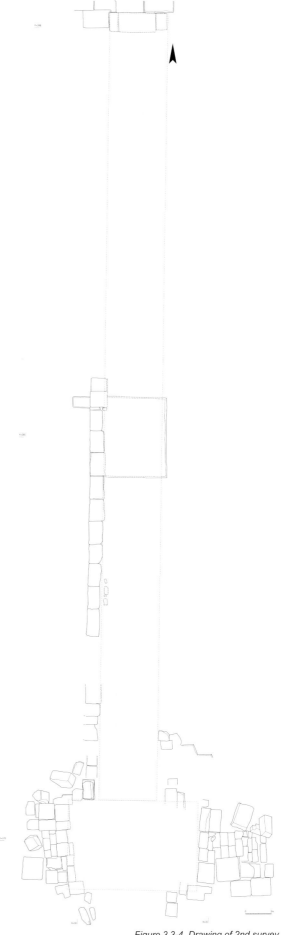

Figure 3.3-4 Drawing of 2nd survey

Chapter 3 : Study Reports on Preah Vihear Temple

3.3.3.1 第 3 次調査概要

期間　2016年1月16日から1月17日

調査参加者

　　杉山　洋：奈良文化財研究所企画調整部

　　佐藤由似：奈良文化財研究所企画調整部

　　今回の調査は第4ゴープラから第3ゴープラへ続く土塁の築成状況を明らかにするために，門状の基壇の南に1m×1mのトレンチを開け，築成状況を見ることとした。

3.3.3.2 築成状況

　　Figure 3.3-5のようにこの土塁は版築ではなく，厚さ20〜30cmほどの土層を交互に積み上げて形成される。各層は砂質土を基本とし，これに黄褐色粘土や砂岩チップを混ぜる。地表から80cmほど下がった所に，砂岩チップが多く混じる厚さ5cmほどの灰褐色土があり，この層を境に築成が2工程に分かれているようである。

4. まとめ

　　今回の3次にわたる調査では，いずれも短期間の調査であったため，大きな成果を上げたとは言い難いが，いくつかの注目すべき点を指摘することができた。なかでも第3ゴープラから第4ゴープラに至る参道部が，ある程度閉塞された空間であった時期のあることが明らかになった点は特筆することができるだろう。

　　第1次調査による第4ゴープラ側面の築地取り付き痕跡の確認，第2次調査による築地積み土の確認，第3次調査による土塁の確認など，これまでの建築学的な調査の追認に終始したとはいえ，この部分に確実に人工的な積み土による塀状の閉塞施設が存在したことを確認できた意義は小さくないであろう。

　　今回の調査で明らかになった閉塞施設は，まず第4ゴープラの取り付き部から，基壇部と呼ぶ門状の遺構までの約26mほどを，黄色いきれいな粘質土によって，おそらくは版築構造の築地状の施設が存在したと推定できる。この築地状施設は第4ゴープラへの取り付き部の痕跡から判断すると，基底部幅約1.6m前後，高さ2.6m前後，で参道に面する西側を砂岩の列石で化粧した遺構と推定できる。

　　当該遺構は門状の基壇部に取り付き，以南の南側は高さ約2mほどの土塁が第3ゴープラ直下まで続く。西側にも今回確認したような施設の痕跡が見て取れ，この部分はある時期参道両側を築地と土塁で閉塞し，1ヵ所に参道を横断できる施設を持った，細長く閉塞され

3.3.3.1 Outline of 3rd Survey

Period:　January 16th-17th, 2016

Members:

SUGIYAMA Hiroshi, Planning and Coordination Dept., Nara National Research Institute for Cultural Properties

SATO Yuni, Planning and Coordination Dept., Nara National Research Institute for Cultural Properties

In this survey, a trench 1m × 1m was opened on the south side of the gate-like platform to examine the construction of the embankment that extends from Gopura IV to Gopura III.

3.3.3.2 Aspect of Construction Condition

As shown in Figure 3.3-5, the embankment is not made of compacted dirt, but of alternating layers of soil each 20 to 30cm deep. Each layer is basically composed of sandy soil, and contains yellow-brown clay and sandstone chips. At a depth of around 80cm from the ground surface, there was a layer of gray-brown soil around 5cm thick containing many sandstone chips. It appears that the construction process was divided in two from this layer.

4. Summary

The three surveys that were recently carried out were all short surveys, so it cannot be said that a large achievement was made, but a number of noteworthy findings has been made, nevertheless. The fact that the survey revealed that there was a period in time when the causeway from Gopura III to Gopura IV had been closed, is particularly worthy of mention.

The 1st survey verified traces of the attachment of a mud wall on the side of Gopura IV, the 2nd survey verified the soil piled mud wall, and the 3rd survey verified the embankment. Thus, it could be said that the surveys mainly focused on verifying the results of previous architectural surveys, but there was more than small significance in having verified for certain the existence of a closed facility surrounded by artificially piled soil.

The closed facility is thought to have been a facility with mud walls made by compacting clean, yellow clayey soil, and occupied a space of roughly 26m between the connection with Gopura IV and the gate-like structure referred to as the platform. Judging from the traces on the connection with Gopura IV, it is believed the facility had a base width of approximately 1.6m and a height of around 2.6m, and was surface-covered with rows of sandstone on the west side that faced the approach.

The structure was connected to the gate-like platform, and an embankment approximately 2m high extended from the south

た施設として存在したことが推定されるに至った。従来，単なる石敷きの参道とのみ考えられていたこの部分が，閉塞された施設と推定されるに至ったことによって，その機能など新たな課題が生じることなったと言える。

side to immediately below Gopura III. Traces of a similar facility were also observed on the west side, leading to the prediction that this part on both sides of the Causeway was at one time closed by dirt walls and a mound, and that a narrow, closed facility existed that transected the Causeway in one place. The new possibility that what was previously thought to simply be a stone-paved causeway was likely a closed facility, has led to the rise of new issues, such as regarding its function.

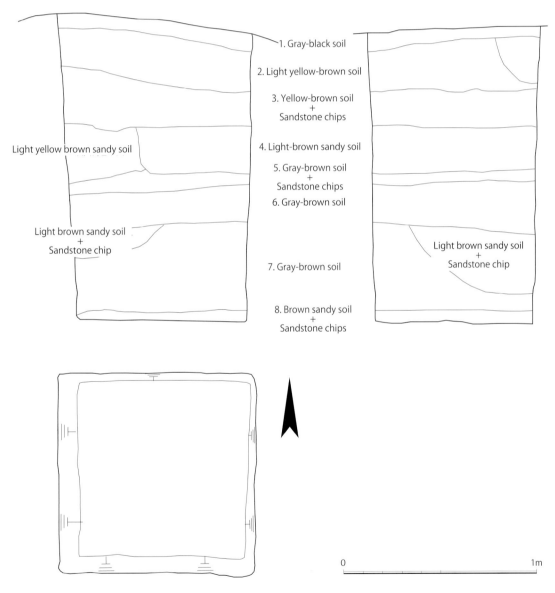

Figure 3.3-5 Trench of 3rd survey

Photo 3.3-10 Dirt mount (view from the north)

Photo 3.3-11 Full view of survey area (view from the north)

Photo 3.3-12 View of the opened trench

Photo 3.3-13 Soil layers

3.4 伽藍の計画法
Planning of Complex

溝口　明則

MIZOGUCHI Akinori

3.4.1 はじめに

　2007年から2010年にかけて，私たちはクメール王国を広域として理解することを目指し，有力な地方拠点であったコー・ケー（Koh Ker）都市遺跡に分布する寺院遺跡群，ベン・メアレア（Beng Mealea）寺院とその周辺遺跡，チャウ・スレイ・ビボール（Chau Srei Vibol）寺院などを対象に，建築学を中心とした現地調査を試みた。これらの地方拠点に残る寺院遺跡は，アンコール地域の寺院遺跡を以て，クメール建築の代表と見なしてしまうことをためらわせる，それぞれ個性ある独特の雰囲気を持っている。これらの経験は，クメール世界をよりよく理解するためには各地の有力な地方拠点に十分な注意を払うべきだという認識を，ますます確かなものにすることとなった[1]。そして2012年夏より，新たな科学研究費助成を得て始まった調査では，プレア・ヴィヘア寺院を対象に，プレア・ヴィヘア機構，JASAとの協同体制で現地調査を進めてきた。

　本節は，クメール建築の設計技術を解明する研究の一環として，長い参道によって構成された伽藍の計画がどのように制御されたのか，また，とりわけ複雑な様相をもつ最奥に造営された山頂伽藍（Complex I，II）を対象に，伽藍の規模計画，寸法計画の手順などを復原的に考察し，計画内容の解明を目指すことを目的とする。

3.4.2 現状と先行研究

　プレア・ヴィヘア寺院は，精確な南北軸に添って直線上に配置された，長大な寺院遺跡である。北端の参道入口を山麓のタイ国境に接し[2]，南端の山頂へ達する距離は南北900mにも及ぶ。検討の対象として，まず，南端の山頂伽藍から始めよう。

　山頂には，北面する前後2つの小規模な伽藍で構成された山頂の伽藍（以下，北半を第2伽藍Complex

3.4.1 Introduction

　Between 2007 and 2010, we conducted on-site surveys at the temple compounds in Koh Ker Monuments, a once flourishing local base, Beng Mealea Temple and surrounding monuments, and Chau Srei Vibol Temple from an architectural point of view with the aiming of gaining a broader perspective of Khmer Empire temple compound layout. The unique and distinctive layouts of these local temple compounds and surrounding monuments have caused us to reconsider the status of Angkor Monuments compound layouts as representative and recognize the need to pay greater attention to local bases in understanding Khmer temple compound layout[1]. Since the summer of 2012, we have surveyed Preah Vihear Temple in concert with National Authority for Preah Vihear and Japan/APSARA Safeguarding Angkor (JASA) with funding from a Grant in Aid for Scientific Research.

　In this section, we examine the extremely complex size and scale relationships of Mountaintop Complex (Complex I, II) built in the innermost section of the compound with the goal of clarifying the overall layout, with a particular focus on the significance of the position of the Complex and the long causeway as a part of research on techniques applied to Khmer temple compound design.

3.4.2 Current Status and Previous Studies

　The Preah Vihear Temple is long and expansive. It is situated along a straight line on the north-south axis. The entrance to the causeway on the north end crosses the Thai-Cambodia border[2], and the distance to the highest point on the mountain on the south end is 900 meters in the north-south direction. Here we describe the layout starting from the Complexes on the south end of the highest point on the mountain.

　At the highest point on the mountain there are two small complexes to the front and back facing to the north. In this

75

Chapter 3 : Study Reports on Preah Vihear Temple

II，南半を第1伽藍Complex Iと呼ぶ）があり，ここより北に向かってゴープラを中心とした3つの施設が直線上に点在する。まとまった先行研究はH. パルマンティエによる1939年の研究が代表的なもので[3]，近年S. サハイによる再検討も発表された[4]。両者は碑文と建築の形式および様式を手がかりに，造営の過程を復原的に捉え，明らかにすることを目指している。その造営過程は，曖昧な点もあるが逐次的に整備されていく過程として捉えているようにもみえる。

study, the one in the north is designated "Complex II" and the one in the south is designated "Complex I". Three buildings are also arranged on a straight line centering on gopuras toward the north. H.Parmentier's 1939 study[3] of these buildings is representative, and a recent reexamination by S.Sahai has also been published[4]. Both studies focused on clarifying the order of construction through restoration with reference to inscriptions as well as architectural structure and style. Although there is some ambiguity, H.Parmentier argues that the buildings were constructed in sequential order.

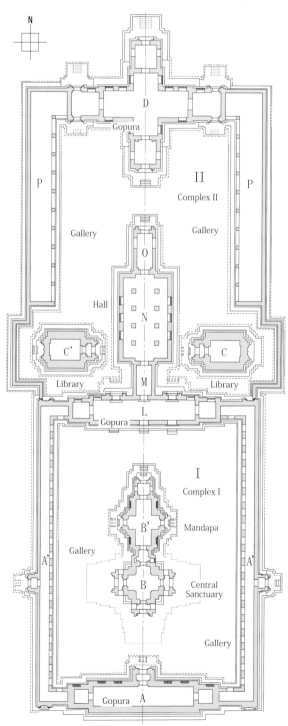

※ Roman numbers and Alphabets follow the writing of H.Parmentier.
Figure 3.4-1 Complexes at the Highest Point on the Mountaintop of Preah Vihear Temple

3.4.2.1 造営の編年

　H. パルマンティエは，伽藍全域の造営の編年をまとめているが，碑文を手がかりに，現在の石造伽藍が造営される以前に木造ないし「軽量」の前身伽藍が存在したと考えている[5]。そのうち山頂伽藍の石造化の順序は，ヤショヴァルマンIの後継者（特定せず。ハルシャヴァルマンIからハルシャヴァルマンIIの時代）によって，まず第2伽藍の第2ゴープラ（D）（以下H. パルマンティエの符号を踏襲する。Figure 3.4-1参照），左右に延びるL字平面の第2回廊（P），中央建物N-O-Mと，これに接続する第1伽藍の第1ゴープラ（L）の4つの建物が造営されたと考えている。その後，ラージェンドラヴァルマンIIまたはジャヤヴァルマンVによって第1伽藍の回廊（A'），拝殿（B'），背面ゴープラ（A）が建立され，ウダヤディティヤヴァルマンIIの時代に中央祠堂（B）が建立されたとするが[6]，倒壊したままの中央祠堂は，完成直前に崩壊したと考えている。第1伽藍では，第1回廊（A'）が完成してから中央祠堂（B）を構築したという手順を想定しており，回廊西辺のポーチに近い転用材で補修された窓間壁を以て，中央祠堂（B）の造営のために開いた回廊の痕跡と捉えている。また，H. パルマンティエが指摘する第2伽藍の2つの経蔵（C, C'）の背後の周壁は，痕跡に明らかなように第2回廊（P）の南端と第1回廊（A'）の北端に突きつけてつくられている。

　一方，S. サハイは，10世紀のうち（したがってジャヤヴァルマンVの時代まで）に第1伽藍が整備された（現状そのままではなく，前身建物を含んだ判断のようである）が，まだ第2伽藍に建物はなく，11世紀前半になって建物N-O-Mが第1ゴープラ（L）に付け加えられ，第2ゴープラ（D），経蔵（C, C'）L字平面の第2回廊（P）も造営され，1037年頃に経蔵（C, C'）の背後の壁が付け加えられたと判断している。また，中央祠堂（B）の建立時期については，H. パルマンティエが指摘した11世紀後半頃の建立という判断を認めながらも，完成直前の崩壊という想定に，明確な根拠がないことを指摘する。

　これら造営の順序に関する編年の試みは，いずれも重要な指摘を含んでいるが，限られた碑文の内容と不明瞭な上に限定された痕跡を辿る困難な作業であるため，再検討すべき余地が残されている。

　第1伽藍の形成について，S. サハイの指摘は曖昧な点も残るが，両者ともに第1回廊（A'）が閉じられた後に中央祠堂が造営されたと捉えている点は無理のある議論といえよう。とくにH. パルマンティエは，第1回廊（A'）西面の補修された窓間壁を以て，中央祠

3.4.2.1 Construction Chronology

　H.Parmentier created a chronology of construction for entire Complex, and noted that there were old structures made with wood or some other light material before the stone structures that we can see at present[5]. The shift from wood or other light material to stone used for the construction of Complexes on the highest point on the mountain began with four buildings, Gopura II (D) in Complex II (named by H.Parmentier; see Figure 3.4.1-1), flat and L-shaped Gallery II (P) extending sideways, Building N-O-M, and Gopura I (L) in Complex I connected to N-O-M, which were built by the successor to Yasovarman I in the rein of Harshavarman I and II, followed by Gallery I (A'), Mandapa (B') and False Gopura (A), built by Rajendravarman II or Jayavarman V, and Mandapa (B'), built in the era of Udayadityvarman II[6]; however, the Central Sanctuary is reported to have collapsed immediately before construction was completed. Central Sanctuary (B) is thought to have been built after Gallery I (A') in Complex I. The piers repaired with secondhand material and located close to the porch on the west side of the Gallery are considered evidence that the Gallery was built for the construction of Central Sanctuary (B). The peripheral wall at the back of Libraries (C and C') in Complex II that were pointed out by H.Parmentier was built to connect to the south end of Gallery II (P) and the north end of the Gallery I (A'), as clearly shown by the traces.

　Meanwhile, S.Sahai argued that Complex I was completed in the 10th century (in Jayavarman V's reign), based not only on the current conditions, but also traces of previously built buildings, and that there was no construction in Complex II until the Building N-O-M was built as additional builng of Gopura I (L) in the first half of the 11th century, followed by Gopura II (D), Libraries (C and C'), and the flat L-Shaped Gallary II (P); and the rear walls of Libraries (C and C') were added around 1037. Although S.Sahai agreed with H.Parmentier that Central Sanctuary (B) was built in the last half of the 11th century, he pointed out that there is no evidence that the Central Sanctuary (B) had collapsed immediately before completion.

　These considerations on the chronological order of construction provide important clues; however, it is very difficult to trace unclear and limited evidence from inscriptions. Therefore, there is a need to reexamine the evidence.

　S.Sahai's suggestion regarding Complex I is also ambiguous. However, it is difficult to think that the Central Sanctuary was built after the closing of Gallery I (A') although both H.Parmentier and S.Sahai considered this to be the case. H.Parmentier considered the repaired piers on the west side of Gallery I (A')

Chapter 3 : Study Reports on Preah Vihear Temple

堂造営のために回廊を開いた痕跡とみるが，あり合わせの材料で補修されている点からみて，窓間壁の損傷に対する後世の補修である可能性が高く，また，中央祠堂の部材を搬入する入口として小さすぎる。さらに，周囲に解体を示す確かな痕跡が見当たらないことにも留意する必要がある。内部の造営を承知して回廊を先に完成させ閉じてしまうことは通例考えがたいから，第1回廊（A'）が早くに造営を始めていたとしても，完成は伽藍造営の最終段階であったと考えるべきである[7]。

　一方，S. サハイの指摘では，第1ゴープラ（L）が10世紀のうちに造立され，11世紀に入って第2伽藍内の建物N-O-Mが接続されたとするが，後に付け加えられたとみなせる明確な痕跡は見出すことができない。第1ゴープラ（L）と同時に造営されたと捉える方が無理のない判断である。

　以上のように，よく知られた寺院遺跡であり，先行研究が興味深い議論を発表しているにもかかわらず，明確な反論が少なく，未だに研究史の成果は多くない。両者の研究についても，多くの未解決の問題を残しているが，造営の編年を整理する作業は，山頂伽藍全体が逐次的に現在の姿にたどり着いたものであったような印象を与えている。編年と同時に考慮すべき問題は，伽藍計画が整合性のある単一の計画に従ったものか，逐次的な計画に従って次第に現在の姿に辿りついたものかを見極めることであろう。

3.4.2.2 伽藍構成の特徴

　プレア・ヴィヘア寺院の山頂伽藍は，他に例のない特殊な構成を持っている[8]。まず，奥行きのある矩形を前後に2分したように見える構成をみせている点であり，また通例は，太い十字形の平面を持つゴープラが第2伽藍のゴープラ（D）にしか見られず，第1伽藍のゴープラ（L）が東西に長い矩形という例外的な平面形状をとっていることである[9]。このゴープラは，第1伽藍の内側に面した壁面に3つの開口を並列させるに留まり，よくみられるゴープラのように回廊の内へ伸びる部位を持たない。さらに経蔵が第1伽藍の回廊の外にあり，ホールNを挟んで向かい合う配置をとっていることも注目すべきであろう。第1伽藍の回廊が簡素であること，第2伽藍の第2回廊（P）は経蔵（C，C'）の手前で終わっており，もともと第2伽藍が閉じていなかったことも注目される。他の遺構では見ることのないこのような構成がなぜ現れたのか，寸法値の分析を始める前に検討を加えておく必要がある。

　バンテアイ・サムレ寺院（12世紀後半）は，内回

to be evidence that Gallery I (A') was built to construct the Central Sanctuary. Since they were, however, repaired with used materials, it is quite possible that the repair was made for damage that took place later. The piers are too small to be used as entrances to carry in materials used for the building of the Central Sanctuary. Furthermore, it is necessary to understand that there is no evidence of dismantlement around the piers. Because it is generally difficult to argue that the Gallery was built first and closed after completion of the inner construction, we should assume that completion of the Gallery was the final stage[7].

　According to S.Sahai, Gopura I (L) was built in the 10th century, followed by Building N-O-M in Complex II in the 11th century; however, this has not been proven by evidence. It is more natural to conclude that Gopura I (L) and Building N-O-M were built at the same time.

　Although, as stated above, Preah Vihear Temple is well known and previous studies have contributed a great deal to our understanding, few studies have examined these issues, leaving researchers with little meaningful information. H.Parmentier and S.Sahai both leave many questions unresolved; however, their chronological studies give the impression that the Complexes on the highest point on the mountain took their current forms in a sequential manner. We believe that it is necessary to consider chronological studies to examine whether planning of the Complexes was based on a consistent and unified plan, or whether the current condition was the result of sequential planning.

3.4.2.2 Character of Complex Composition

　H.Parmentier created a chronology of construction for Complex on the highest point on the mountain at Preah Vihear Temple are unique[8]. They appear as a rectangle divided lengthwise into two parts, front and back, and only Gopura II (D) in Complex II has a bold, cruciform shape. Gopura I (L) in Complex I is rectangular in the east-west direction, which is exceptional[9]. Gopura I (L) has three openings in the wall faced the inner area of Complex I, but it does not have a part, which is often seen, that reaches inside the Gallery. Furthermore, it is also notable that Libraries are placed outside the Gallery in Complex I to face each other across Hall N. It is further notable that the Galleries in Complex I are simple, Gallery II (P) end before Libraries (C, C') in Complex II, and Complex II was not closed. Before looking at size, it is important to consider why these elements, which are not observed in other temple compounds, are present at Preah Vihear Temple.

　Banteay Samre Temple (late 12th century) has two Libraries

廊の中に2つの経蔵を構えるとともに，内回廊の内側に沿って，ゴープラと回廊の基壇上面を拡幅してテラスとして増築した結果，きわめて狭く密度の濃い伽藍に変化している。2つの経蔵の基座南北（短辺）幅は17ハスタ程（後述するように1ハスタを412mmとして換算）で，プレア・ヴィヘア寺院の経蔵よりわずかに小さいが，回廊で囲まれた敷地の南北内法幅は28,720mm程，70ハスタと換算される。2棟の経蔵は，この中にかろうじて配置されている[10]。

　ベン・メアレア寺院群の南に位置するプラサート・チュレイ寺院（12世紀前半か）も，やはり狭小な伽藍に2棟の経蔵を構えている。ただ，この伽藍は回廊を持たず周壁を巡らすため，周壁で囲まれた敷地の南北（短辺）内法幅は意外に大きく29,710mm程で，換算すれば72ハスタ程である。プレア・ヴィヘア寺院第1伽藍の東西（短辺）内法幅は25,735mmであり，2つの伽藍に比べて3mから4m程も狭い。およそ62ハスタにすぎないから，10ハスタ前後の寸法差があることがわかる。つまり第1伽藍の回廊内の敷地は，2棟の経蔵を対称的に配置するには，狭すぎることがあきらかである[11]。

　H．パルマンティエが編年の手がかりとした各建物の様式の特徴は，明瞭といい難い面もあるが前身伽藍をもとに，逐次石造の施設に置き換えていったとする指摘は間違いないと思われる。したがってすでに存在していた，おそらく木造やレンガを主体とした前身伽藍が形成していた南北800mに及ぶ直線の伽藍中心線は，石造化の過程でもそのまま踏襲された可能性が高い。本尊であるシヴァ・リンガ「シカレシュヴァラ」も，この中心線上に配置され続けたと考えられる。伽藍中心線が踏襲されれば，現在の第1伽藍の南東隅が断崖から踏み出しかけている様相から見て，石造化の過程で第1伽藍の東西幅を拡幅できた可能性は考えがたい。つまり，前身建物の伽藍規模を踏襲して第1回廊（A'）を巡らせば，回廊のなかに一対の経蔵を構えることは困難である。このため経蔵（C，C'）は回廊の外に配置されることになったと思われる。経蔵が向かい合って配置された理由は，通例のように，伽藍内の参拝の動線（右回り）に入口を向けたためで，回廊外の動線から見て自然な計画である。

　一般に対になる経蔵の場合，向かって左側のもの（東面する伽藍で南のもの）が実機能をもった施設であると推察される（上部の通気口の存在などから）。ワット・アトビア寺院など寺院が西面しても経蔵は西に開口するが，プレア・ヴィヘア寺院の場合，北面する伽藍において向かって左にある経蔵はやはり西面してい

in the inner Gallery, and the gopura and upper surface of the platform in the Gallery were extended for use as a terrace, which made the Complex extremely narrow and dense. The south-north width of the base of the two Libraries (the shorter side) is about 17 hasta (= 412 mm), slightly shorter than at Preah Vihear Temple, and the internal measurement of the south-north width of the area surrounded by the Galleries (shorter side) was about 28,720 mm (70 hasta). Two Libraries are arranged within[10].

　Prasat Chrei Temple (early 12th century?) located in the southern part of Beng Mealea Temple Monuments also has two Libraries in a narrow Complex. However, this Complex has a peripheral wall without a Gallery. Therefore, the internal measurement of the south-north width of the area surrounded by the peripheral wall (the shorter side) is relatively large at 29,710 mm, or 72 hasta. The internal measurement of the east-west width of Complex I at Preah Vihear Temple (the shorter side) is 25,735 mm, which is 3 m to 4 m narrower than the two Complexes. It is only 62 hasta, an approximate difference of 10 hasta. In other words, the area inside the Gallery in Complex I is too small for the symmetric placement of two Libraries[11].

　The characteristics of the building structures that H.Parmentier employed in his chronological study are less than clear; however, it seems that buildings were replaced with stone material based on the previous Complex in a sequential manner. Therefore, it is highly likely that the straight central line of the previous Complex (800 m long in the north-south direction), which may have been made with wood and bricks, was used during the shift to stone material. It is also thought that the Shikhareshvara, the principal image of Buddha (Shiva linga) was placed on this central line. If the central line of the Complex was followed, it is difficult to imagine that the east-west width of Complex I could be extended during the shift to stone because the south-east corner of Complex I is at the edge of a cliff. It is difficult to place a pair of Libraries in the Gallery if Gallery I (A') was placed based on the size of the previous complex. Because of this, it is probable that Libraries (C, C') were placed outside the Gallery. The two Libraries face each other to allow people to enter in the direction of worship (clockwise) inside the Complex, which is a very natural plan in light of the motion of worshipers outside the Gallery.

　For the pair of Libraries, the one on the left as the observer faces it (situated at southern part of the Complex facing on east) is considered to be the function facility due to the existence of a vent in the upper area. As seen at Vat Athvear Temple, the temple is oriented toward the west, and the Library opens toward the west. However, at Preah Vihear Temple, it is possible to conclude

Chapter 3 : Study Reports on Preah Vihear Temple

るとみることもできる。

経蔵の配置を外に移したことに呼応して，第1伽藍の回廊は最低限の奥行きを持って閉じることとなり，この結果，よく見られる太い十字型の平面を持つゴープラ，つまり回廊の中に突出するポーチなどの部位を持つゴープラを採用することが難しくなり，ゴープラの平面に大きな変形を要することになったであろう。現在，第2伽藍の中央に位置する，形式として拝殿とも見える建物N-O-Mは第1ゴープラ（L）と一体の施設と見なすべきで，いわば，T字型の平面に変形した特殊なゴープラを形成している，と見ることが可能である。南北軸が深くなりすぎているようにも思われ不明な点もあるが，おそらく，通例のゴープラ内部で行われた儀礼のための空間として，ホールNが機能したのではないかと推察される12)。

山頂伽藍は，第2回廊（P）が回廊のようにも見えるため，伽藍全体に回廊を巡らせ，これを前後に区画した伽藍であるかのような印象を与えるが，第2伽藍は，本来，第3ゴープラ以北の他のゴープラと同様に第1伽藍へ至るアプローチ上の施設にすぎない。回廊とも見える第2回廊（P）の構成は，一対の経蔵が回廊の外に配置されたことと関わるであろう。第2回廊（P）は，第1伽藍とのとり合わせと地形の制約から内法幅の確保に限界があるが，区画された聖域内にあるべき経蔵をできる限りとり囲むことを意図して構成されたように思われる13)。経蔵の背後（東西面）を区画する周壁は，後世に付け加えられたことがあきらかだが，経蔵を区画された聖域内に布置しようとする点で，当初の計画の不足を補うものであったと考えられる。

南北800mを超える長大な伽藍は，北から第5ゴープラ，第4ゴープラ，第3ゴープラと東西の付属建物，第2伽藍，第1伽藍の順に，一直線上に配置されている。実測調査の結果，各建物は高い精度で直線上に配置されていることが確かめられた。このうち第2伽藍は，この伽藍中心線上に第2ゴープラ（D）の真を合致させ，東西の翼廊Pは対称性を保っている。一方，第1伽藍は，第1ゴープラ（L）および擬似ゴープラ（A），中央祠堂（B），拝殿（B'）の各建物の中心を貫く中軸線に対し，回廊が東にやや広い構成をとるため，第1伽藍の中心線（回廊の東西全幅を等分する軸線）と第5ゴープラ～第2伽藍の伽藍中心線は合致せず，この伽藍中心線の延長上に，第1伽藍の中軸線（ゴープラ真―拝殿真―中央祠堂真を貫く軸線）を合致させている。

第1伽藍と第2伽藍の中心線同士が食い違う（第2伽藍中心線と第1伽藍中軸線とが合致する）という現象は，逐次的な計画を連想させるもののようだが，伽

that the Library on the left as the observer faces the Complex, which is oriented toward the north, faces toward the west.

In line with the placement of the Libraries, the Gallery in Complex I was closed and had a shallow depth. As a result, it would have been difficult to build a Gopura with a bold, cruciform shape, such as is often seen, or a Gopura stretching out to a Gallery, which would have required a significant change in the surface of the Gopura. Building N-O-M, whose structure in the middle of Complex II is cathedral-like, should be considered a part of Gopura I (L), with its unique structure standing in a T-shaped area. Its south-north axis seems to be too deep, and some points are unclear. However, it is estimated that Hall N functioned as a space for ceremonies that were usually performed at a Gopura[12].

Gallery II (P) in Complex II and Gallery I (A') in Complex I on the highest point on the mountain appear analogous, seemingly functioning to provide front and rear Complexes. However, Complex II is simply a facility on the approach that connects to Complex I, as seen in other Gopuras north of Gopura III. The gallery-like structure of Gallery II (P) is closely associated with the placement of the pair of Libraries outside the Galleries. Gallery II (P) may have been built to surround the Libraries inside the sectioned sanctuary in spite of the limitations imposed by the need to ensure internal width due to the association with Complex I and geographical considerations[13]. The peripheral walls behind the Libraries (east-west side) were obviously added later, probably due to the need to included them inside the sectioned sanctuary to adjust for the original plan.

Gopura V, Gopura IV, Gopura III, auxiliary facilities on the east and west, Complex II, and Complex I are located in order along a straight line in a long and expansive site measuring greater than 800 m in the south-north direction. Actual measurements show that the arrangement of each building on the straight line was highly accurate. The central line of Complex II matches the middle of Gopura II (D), and Gallery II (P) on the east and west sides are symmetrical. Meanwhile, in Complex I, Galleries are slightly wider on the east side against the central axis running through the middle of Gopura I (L) and False Gopura (A), Central Sanctuary (B), and Mandapa (B'), which causes a misalignment between the central axis of Complex I (the axis that equally separates the east and west side of the Gallery) and the central axis running through Gopura V to Complex II. However, the central axis of Complex I (running through the middle of the Gopura, Mandapa, and Central Sanctuary) was aligned with the extension of the central line of Complex II.

The misalignment between the central lines of Complex I and

藍の一方をやや広くとることで伽藍の中軸線を偏向させるという構成は，ほとんど例外なくクメール寺院に認められる特徴である[14]。第１，第２伽藍の中心線同士が食い違うという構成は，結果的に，第２伽藍が第３ゴープラ以北の各ゴープラと同様の施設として位置づけられていたことを示しており，第１伽藍だけが中軸線の偏向を実現する対象と考えられていたことを意味している。したがってこの現象は，第１伽藍と第２伽藍が，それぞれ個別に計画されたということを意味するものではない[15]。

　山頂伽藍の構成は，逐次的に個々の建物の配置が決定されていったとは考え難く，あらかじめ全体として構成された計画が存在していた可能性が予想される。この計画は個々の建物の造営年代とは直接関わらない。造営の年代は，計画の実現過程を示しているにすぎないからである。伽藍構成に関する，以上の予備的考察———第１，第２伽藍を一体として捉えた確かな計画が先行し，これに従って造営された可能性があること———を念頭に置いて分析へ進みたい。

3.4.3 山頂伽藍の分析

　対象遺構の実測調査はGPSおよび光波測定器を用いて行い，CAD図面上に測点をプロットすることで精度の高い実測図面を作成した（Figure 3.4-1, Figure 3.4-3）。この実測資料に基づいて伽藍の規模計画，各部の寸法計画の方法に関する分析を行う。現在までに行ったバンテアイ・サムレ寺院，トマノン寺院，プラサート・スープラＮ１塔，プラサート・トム寺院，プラサート・プラム寺院，ベン・メアレア寺院などの各寺院の実測調査と伽藍寸法分析の結果から，当時の造営尺度（ハスタ，ハッタ，ハト）１単位の実長を412±1mmとみることができる[16]。プレア・ヴィヘア寺院の分析においても，同様の造営尺度を想定する。山頂伽藍は部分的に岩盤上に建てられているため基座が明確ではなく，省略された箇所もある。従来重ねて来た伽藍の分析結果から，寸法計画の基準となる位置は基座外端と考えられるが[17]，基座が省略された位置および未発掘のため基座が確認できない位置（掲載図では破線で示す）では，同一建物のうち，いずれかの位置で確認された基座の寸法を手がかりに，計画上基座が存在したことを想定して分析を行う。

3.4.3.1 伽藍全体の規模計画

　第１伽藍と第２伽藍全体の南北の長さ（回廊（A'）の南面基座外端から第２伽藍の第２回廊（P）北端の基座外端）は，状態のよい西面で87,301mm（211.9

II (alignment of the central line of Complex II and central axis of Complex I) suggested the possibility of sequential planning. However, a slightly wider area on one side of an Complex than the other and deflection of the central axis of the Complex are distinctive characteristics seen at almost all Khmer temples[14]. Misalignment between the central lines of Complex I and II indicate that Complex II had the same function as other Gopuras located north of Gopura III, and only Complex I was thought to produce deflection. Therefore, this does not mean that Complex I and II were planned separately[15].

It is difficult to think that the individual buildings in the Complexes on the highest point on the mountain were sequentially planned and built. It is possible that they were designed as part of a complete plan. This plan is not directly associated with the time that each building was constructed. The time of construction simply shows the progression of the original plan. Based on these preliminary considerations, which suggest the possibility that each building was constructed in accordance with an overall plan for the entire site, including Complex I and II, we will move to the analysis on the structure of the Complexes.

3.4.3 Analysis of Complexes on the Highest Point on the Mountain

We created highly accurate measurement diagrams for the target temple compounds (Figure 3.4-1, Figure 3.4-3) by plotting the measurement points on CAD drawings utilizing GPS and Total Station. We conducted an analysis of the planning for scale and size of the complexes based on the measurement data. According to previous measurements for each temples of Banteay Samure Temple, Tommanon Temple, Prasat Suour Prat Tower N1, Prasat Thom Temple, Prasat Pram Temple, Beng Mealea Temple, etc. and analyses of the sizes of Complexes, the unit of measurement used for construction at that time was calculated as 412±1 mm (hasta, hatta, hato)[16]. We use the same construction scale for the analysis of Preah Vihear Temple. The base of the Complexes at the highest point on the mountain is not clear due to the fact that they are built on rock and there are also some areas that do not have a base. According to the past analysis of the Complexes, the standard point of reference for the dimentional plan is the outer end of the base[17]. For areas with no base or areas that have not yet been excavated (shown with a broken line in the figures), our analysis assumes that there was a planned base utilizing base measurements found in other locations.

Chapter 3 : Study Reports on Preah Vihear Temple

ハスタ）である[18]。また，第2伽藍北端の東西幅（翼
廊（P）の基座外端間）は36,174mm（87.8ハスタ），
第1伽藍南端の東西幅（回廊（A'）の基座外端間。以
下，特記ないかぎり基座外端を基準とする寸法を示
す）は33,752mm（81.9ハスタ）である。したがっ
て南北全長212.0ハスタ，第2伽藍東西全幅88.0ハス
タ，第1伽藍東西全幅82.0ハスタと判断できる。い
ずれも不明瞭な数値だが，南北全長と第2伽藍東西全
幅の合計値が300.0ハスタとなることが注目される[19]。
これは，プラサート・トム寺院の伽藍分析の際に検討
したように，平易な完数による伽藍の規模計画を下敷
きに，そのプロポーションを調整する際に，面積では
なく長短辺の合計値を保持することで，近似的に面積
（規模）を保つ技法であると考えられた[20]。面積を忠
実に保つのではなく外周長の合計値を保つ理由は，長
短辺いずれも完数値が保たれる利便性に由来すると考
えられる。したがって規模計画の考え方は，第1，第
2伽藍を合わせて長辺200.0ハスタ，短辺100.0ハス
タとする基本計画から開始されたと予想することがで
きる。派生して212.0ハスタと88.0ハスタになった原
因は，210.0ハスタと90.0ハスタのプロポーションに
最も近いヴィャマ（ハスタの4倍の長さの度制単位）
で割り切れる値をとったためだと考えられる。これに
対し第1伽藍の東西全幅は，中央祠堂の真から西側が
16,417mm（39.85ハスタ），東側が17,335mm（42.075
ハスタ）であるから，80.0ハスタの幅を基本として
中軸線をずらすため東側に2ハスタを加えた可能性
が予想される。一方，第1回廊（A'）西辺の南北長は
43,922mm（106.6ハスタ）である。山頂伽藍の南北
全長212.0ハスタを2等分した可能性が高いが，後に
検証する。

3.4.3.2 第1伽藍建物の相対位置

　中央祠堂（B）と拝殿（B'）の中心間の距離は
8,315mm（20.2ハスタ），拝殿真から拝殿北端の基座
外端までは8,163mm（19.82ハスタ），いずれも20.0
ハスタを目指した計画と考えられる。中央祠堂の基壇
は崩壊した石材に覆われており輪郭を確認できない
が，平面規模からみてバンテアイ・サムレ寺院やトマ
ノン寺院の中央祠堂に近似する規模を持っている。こ
こから推定される基壇の大きさは,最大でも全幅40.0
ハスタ程と予想されるから[21]，この推定に従えば，中
央祠堂の真から基壇の南端まで20.0ハスタである。し
たがって中央祠堂（B）と拝殿（B'）の南北全長は60.0
ハスタと推定されるが，回廊内の相対的な位置がやや
不明瞭である。その原因は，第1回廊（A'）の南端の

3.4.3.1 Scale Planning for entire Complex

The north-south length of the entire Complex, includin both I and II (from the outer end of the south side of the Gallery I (A') base to the outer end of the north end base of Gallery II (P) in Complex II), is 87,301 mm on the west side and remains in good condition (211.9 hasta)[18]. In addition, the east-west distance of the north end of Complex II (outer end of the base of Gallery II (P)) is 36,174 mm (87.8 hasta), the east-west distance of the south end of Complex I (Outer end of the base of Gallery I (A'): only the sizes are shown hereafter if not otherwise specified) is 33,752 mm (81.9 hasta). Therefore, the total north-south distance is 212.0 hasta, the total east-west distance of Complex II is 88.0 hasta, and the total east-west distance of Complex I is 82.0 hasta. None of these figures show any correlation; however, the total north-south and east-west distances of Complex II are 300.0 hasta, which may be of significance[19]. As we examined the data obtained from the complexes at Prasat Thom Temple, it seems that maintaining the total figure of all sides, that is, not the areas when adjusting the proportion in accordance with the scale of complexes utilizing simple multiples of the measurement unit (MMU), makes it possible to maintain the areas (scale)[20]. The reason for maintaining the total length of outer circumference rather than the areas may have been the convenience of maintaining MMU for both the longer and shorter sides. Therefore, scale planning may have been based on setting the total length of the longer sides in Complex I and II at 200.0 hasta, and the total length of the shorter sides in Complex I and II at 100.0 hasta. The reason for the 212.0 and 88.0 hasta figures for the actual total of the longer and shorter sides may be because these figures were close to 210.0 and 90.0 hasta, which are easily divided by vyama (a unit of length which is four times the hasta). Meanwhile, the total east-west distance of Complex I is 16,417 mm (39.85 hasta) on the west side from the middle of the Central Sanctuary, and 17,335 mm (42.075 hasta) on the east from the middle of the Central Sanctuary. Therefore, it is estimated that 2 hasta was added to the east side to shift the central axis to the east based on 80.0 hasta as the total width. The total north-south distance of the west side of Gallery I (A') is 43,922 mm (106.6 hasta). It is possible that this figure was calculated by dividing the total north-south distance of the Complexes (212.0 hasta) on the mountaintop by two. We will examine this in a later section.

3.4.3.2 Relative Position of the Buildings in Complex I

The distance between the middle of Central Sanctuary (B) and Mandapa (B') is 8,315 mm (20.2 hasta), and the distance between the middle of the Mandapa and outer end of the base

うち，南西隅がやや南に位置し（あるいは南東隅がや
や北に位置する），中央祠堂真から第１回廊（A'）の南
端まで，西面では17,969mm（43.6ハスタ），東面で
は17,761mm（43.1ハスタ）という値をとっているた
めである。このままでは，中央祠堂真から敷地南端ま
での計画が43.0ハスタなのか44.0ハスタなのか判断
が難しい。これはまた，第１回廊の南北幅が，山頂伽
藍全体の南北幅を２等分する位置に合致しているかど
うかの判断に関わる問題である。

まず，第１回廊（A'）を検討しよう。回廊の長辺の
内壁は，等間隔に窓が並ぶが，回廊外の東西に設けら
れたポーチと窓の真とが合致しているように見えるこ
とが注目される。また東西回廊のポーチは，中央祠堂
の真と合致させようとしている。回廊の内壁に，たん
に等間隔に窓を並べても回廊の入口や中央祠堂の真と

at the north end of the Mandapa is 8,163 mm (19.82 hasta). It is possible that both were planned to measure 20.0 hasta. The platform at the Central Sanctuary is covered with collapsed stones and it is hard to see the outlines. According to the planer scale, it seems to be similar to the Central Sanctuary at Banteay Samre Temple and Tommanon Temple. The estimated maximum width of the platform is 40.0 hasta[21], which would make the estimated distance from the middle of the Central Sanctuary to the south end of the platform 20.0 hasta. Accordingly, the total north-south distance between Central Sanctuary (B) and Mandapa (B') is estimated to be 60.0 hasta although the relative positions inside the Gallery are uncertain. The reason for this is because the south-west corner of Gallery I (A') is located slightly more south (or, the south-east corner is located slightly more north), which resulted in the distance between the middle

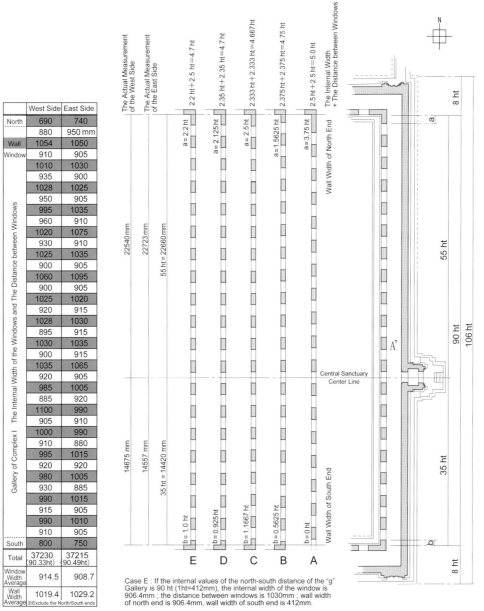

Figure 3.4-2 The Architectural Studies of window Layout in the Gallery

Chapter 3 : Study Reports on Preah Vihear Temple

合致するとはかぎらない。等間隔に配置すれば，かえっ
て真に合致させることが難しいとも予想される。どの
ような計画がなされたのか考えてみよう。

3.4.3.3 回廊の窓割

　回廊の断面幅は，場所によって相違があるが，
4,020mm（9.76ハスタ）から4,124mm（10.01ハスタ）
程の値をとっている。したがって10.0ハスタとする計
画であったと考えられる。このうち内の基座外端から
壁面外面までを820mm（1.99ハスタ）前後としてい
るから，内の壁面から外の基座外端まで8.0ハスタと
いう寸法計画が予想される。第1回廊（A'）の南北全
幅が山頂伽藍全体の南北全幅の半分であったとすれば，
この長さは106.0ハスタのはずで，したがって回廊の
内側の壁面の長さは，106.0ハスタから8.0ハスタの
2倍をさし引いた90.0ハスタのはずである。実測値は，
西面で37,230mm（90.49ハスタ），東面で37,215mm
（90.33ハスタ）である。

　窓の内法幅と窓間壁の幅は，Figure 3.4-2に掲載し
た表のように東西で差があるが，各平均値は909mm
と915mm程，窓間壁の幅は1,019mmと1,030mm程
である。窓内法幅と窓間壁幅の寸法差は，クメール建
築の施工過程を考慮すれば施工誤差の範囲ともみなさ
れる相違だが，両者を同一寸法と見なせるかどうかは
慎重に検討する必要がある。当面，窓内法寸法と南北
端を除く窓間壁の合計の平均値（回廊西1,934mm，同
東1,938mm）を手がかりに検討する。この値は4.7
ハスタ程となってハスタの単位の完数をとらないが，
Figure 3.4-2では窓内法幅と窓間壁の合計値が5.0ハ
スタの場合（A），4と3/4ハスタの場合（B），4と
2/3ハスタの場合（C），4.70ハスタの場合に分け，ま
た4.70ハスタのとき，窓内法幅と窓間壁幅を等分した
2.35ハスタの場合（D）と，それぞれ2.2ハスタと2.5
ハスタとする場合（E），以上5通りの可能性を検討した。

　窓内法幅と窓間影幅の合計が5.0ハスタの場合（A），
窓の中心線と中央祠堂の真（回廊側面入口の真）とを
合致させれば，南端で壁面がとれなくなるから，この
値では窓割が成立しない。また，この値が4.0ハスタ
や4.5ハスタであれば遺構のような窓割は成り立たな
いから，窓内法幅と窓間壁幅の合計寸法にハスタの完
数をとることが困難であったことが明らかである。窓
内法幅と窓間壁幅の合計が4と3/4ハスタの場合（B），
南北両端の壁幅の合計が3ハスタを超える実測値に比
べ，1ハスタ以上も短いため成立しない。同様に窓と
窓間壁の合計値が4と2/3ハスタの場合（C），北端
と南端の壁長さがそれぞれ2.5ハスタと1と2/3ハス

of the Central Sanctuary and the south end of the Gallery I (A')
being 17,969 mm (43.6 hasta) on the west side, and 17,761 mm
(43.1 hasta) on the east side. It is hard to determine whether the
original plan from the middle of the Central Sanctuary to the
south end of the area was 43.0 hasta or 44.0 hasta. This problem
is also associated with the determination of whether the north-
south width of Gallery I is aligned to the point that divides the
north-south width of both Complexes on the mountaintop.

　Let's take a look at Gallery I (A'). Windows were arranged at
equal intervals on the inner wall of the longer side of the Gallery,
and the center of the windows opposite the porches seem to
match the windows in the porches on the east and west sides of
the outside of the Gallery. The porches on the east and west sides
of the Gallery match the middle of the Central Sanctuary. It is
not always true that windows at equal intervals on the inner walls
of the Gallery match the entrance of the Gallery and the middle
of the Central Sanctuary. Arranging windows at equal intervals
may make it more difficult to match the middle of the Central
Sanctuary. Let's think about the original plan.

3.4.3.3 Window Layout in the Gallery

　Cross section widths of the Galleries differ according to location
within the range of 4,020 mm (9.76 hasta) and 4,124 mm (10.01
hasta). This indicates that 10.0 hasta might have been the original
plan. The distance between the outer end of the base and outer
surface of the wall is about 820 mm (1.99 hasta), which allows
for an estimated distance between the inner wall to outer end
of the outside base of perhaps 8.0 hasta. If the total north-south
distance of Gallery I (A') were half the total north-south distance
of both Complexes on the mountaintop, this distance should
be 106.0 hasta, and the length of the inner wall in the Galleries
should be 90.0 hasta when calculated by subtracting the 8.0 hasta
(x2) from 106.0 hasta. The actual measurement of the west side
is 37,230 mm (90.49 hasta), and the east side is 37,215 mm (90.33
hasta).

　The internal width of the windows and the distance between
windows differ between the east and west sides, as shown in
Figure 3.4-2, with the average value of the internal width being
between 909 and 915 mm, and wall distance being between
1,019 and 1,030 mm. Considering Khmer architecture, the
difference in sizes of internal width of windows and distance
between windows is within the range of normal error; however,
it is necessary to carefully examine whether both originally had
the same measurements. We continue examining the planned
measurements utilizing the average of the total values of distance
between windows excluding the internal size of the window and
north-south end (west side of the Gallery: 1,934 mm, east side

タとなって合計4ハスタを超えるが，実測値の合計は，やや伸びがある回廊南北内法寸法の下であってもこの値に届かないから，やはり成立しない。

実測値に近い値が実現する場合は，窓内法幅と窓間壁幅の合計値が4.7ハスタの場合（D，E）である。窓内法幅の平均値は，回廊西で914.5mm（2.22ハスタ），同じく東で908.7mm（2.21ハスタ），一方，南北両端を除く窓間壁の平均値は，回廊西1,019.4mm（2.47ハスタ），同じく東1,029.2mm（2.49ハスタ）であるから，100mm以上の明らかな寸法差がある。したがって窓内法幅を2.2ハスタ，窓間壁幅を2.5ハスタとする寸法計画であった可能性が高いと判断される。

回廊内側の壁面の長さを90.0ハスタと見なせば，中央祠堂の中心まで回廊の北側55.0ハスタ，南側35.0ハスタと算出されるから，窓割計画の技法は，まず，窓内法寸法と窓間壁幅の合計を，一旦5.0ハスタと想定し，この単位をそれぞれ北側に11（55.0ハスタを5.0ハスタで分割）と南側に7（35.0ハスタを5.0ハスタで分割）の合計18とする計画を出発点としたことが予想される。しかしこのままでは，中央祠堂の真が窓と窓間壁との境界に合致してしまう。窓の間隔を調整するため窓を1つ加えて19に等分（4.737ハスタ）することを手がかりとし，その近似値4.7ハスタを以て窓内法幅と窓間壁幅の合計寸法とした上で，窓の真に中央祠堂の真が合致するよう全体の配置を調整したものであろう。回廊南北全幅の内法寸法を90.0ハスタ，窓幅内法寸法は906.4mm（2.2ハスタ），窓間壁幅は1,030.0mm（2.5ハスタ），北端の壁幅は窓内法と同じ2.2ハスタとなり，南端の壁幅は1.0ハスタとなる計画であったと判断することができる。窓間壁の幅2.5ハスタの値は，合計を5ハスタと推定した窓内法幅と窓間壁幅の基本計画で，これを等分するものであったことを示しているのかも知れない。Figure 3.4-2の表に掲載したように，北端の壁幅は小さめで南端の壁幅はかなり大きい。しかし，中央祠堂の中心線と相対する窓の等分線の位置はよく合致しており，その寸法差は回廊東で63mm，西で120mmと算出される。おそらく中央祠堂に相対する窓の位置を先行して決定し，それぞれ南北に向かって窓間壁を施設した結果，個々の施工誤差の集積とともに回廊南北全幅の施工誤差が加わって，南端と北端の壁幅に反映したことが予想される。

以上のように，実測値に従って分析を行った結果，窓内法幅と窓間壁幅の合計計画寸法は4.7ハスタであったと判断された。また，窓幅と窓間壁幅は，それぞれ2.2ハスタと2.5ハスタに割り振ったとみなされた。

of the Gallery: 1,938 mm). This is about 4.7 hasta, which is not an MMU of hasta; however, in Figure 3.4.1-2, the following five cases were examined: (A) Total value of internal width of windows and distance between windows is 5.0 hasta; (B) 4 and 3/4 hasta; (C) 4 and 2/3 hasta; (D) 2.35 hasta calculated by equally dividing the total value of internal width of windows and distance between windows; and (E) 2.2 and 2.5 hasta, respectively.

When total value of internal width of windows and distance between windows is 5.0 hasta (A), matching the central line of the window and central line of the Central Sanctuary (middle of the entrance on the side of the Gallery) makes it impossible to have walls on the south end. Therefore, this value is unrealistic for the placement of windows. If the total were 4.0 or 4.5 hasta, the actual window arrangement at the site would be impossible. Therefore, it is obviously difficult to use MMU of hasta for the total value of internal width of windows and distance between windows. When the total is 4 and 3/4 hasta (B), it is shorter than the actual total (3 hasta) by more than one hasta, and that would be impossible. When the total is 4 and 2/3 hasta (C), the total of the lengths of north and south end walls is 2.5 and 1, and 2/3 hasta, which exceeds 4 hasta; however, the total of the actual measurement values does not reach this even with the internal values of the north-south distance of the Gallery, which makes it impossible.

The total value of internal width of windows and distance between windows of 4.7 hasta (D, E) would be close to the actual measurement value. The average internal width of windows is 914.5 mm (2.22 hasta) on the west side of the Gallery and 908.7 mm (2.21 hasta) on the east. Meanwhile, the average distance between windows is 1,019.4 mm (2.47 hasta) on the west side of the Gallery and 1,029.2 mm (2.49 hasta) on the east. Because there is more than 100 mm difference between them, it is quite possible that the internal width of windows may have been set at 2.2 hasta, and distance between windows may have been set 2.5 hasta.

If we assume the length of the internal wall of the Gallery to be 90.0 hasta, the distance to the middle of the Central Sanctuary would be 55.0 hasta on the north side and 35.0 hasta on the south side. It is estimated that window arrangement was based on a total internal width of windows and distance between windows of 5.0 hasta, allowing 11 units on the north side (dividing 55.0 hasta by 5.0 hasta) and 7 units on the south side (dividing 35.0 hasta by 5.0 hasta), for a total of 18 units. However, this would match the middle of the Central Sanctuary with the border of the windows and walls between windows. One window must have

Chapter 3 : Study Reports on Preah Vihear Temple

南北90.0ハスタの全幅を窓数を1つ加えて19等分すれば端数が現れることは必然だが，4.7ハスタを用いたために切り捨てられた端数分の長さは合計290mm程になる。この値は，南北両端の壁幅の中に吸収されている。この調整の過程で現れた4.7ハスタという値は，ハスタの下位の度制単位が，南アジアのように24（アンギュラ）に区分されたものではなく，数の進法に合わせて10分割した値を用いていたことを暗示しているようである。

以上の検討は，回廊南北全幅（基座外法寸法）が106ハスタか107ハスタかを明確にするための検討であった。検討の結果，回廊（A'）の窓割計画の前提が，回廊南北全幅の内法寸法を，91.0ハスタではなく90.0ハスタとする計画であったことが確かめられたと考えられる。したがって回廊南北全長（基座外端の外法寸法）は106.0ハスタ，つまり第1伽藍の回廊南北長が山頂伽藍全体の南北全長212.0ハスタの半分をとっていることも明確になったと考えられる。また，回廊の幅は10.0ハスタ，回廊北端から拝殿北端まで23.0ハスタ，拝殿真から中央祠堂真まで20.0ハスタ，中央祠堂の基壇が想定通りであれば，中央祠堂真から基壇南端まで20.0ハスタ，基壇南端から回廊南端まで23.0ハスタであったことになる。拝殿真から回廊北端までと中央祠堂真から回廊南端まではいずれも43.0ハスタであるから，回廊内の施設の相対位置は，回廊の南北中央に配置されたことも明らかになった。

3.4.3.4 第1伽藍の規模計画

Figure 3.4-3は，山頂伽藍の各部寸法をハスタに換算し整理したものである。山頂伽藍全体の規模計画および第1伽藍の南北全長の寸法計画は明らかになったが，第2伽藍の東西幅が88.0ハスタであることに対し，第1伽藍の東西幅が82.0ハスタであること，第1伽藍と第2伽藍の中軸線が食い違うなどの問題が残っている。第1伽藍の東西幅の計画，ひいては規模計画について，どのような計画技法が考えられるだろうか。

第1伽藍の南端から建物N-O-Mの北端（ポーチ（O）の北端の基座外端）までの実測値は69,009mmである。この値は167.5ハスタに相当する。わずかに短いが168.0ハスタであれば第1伽藍の東西幅82.0ハスタとの合計が250.0ハスタ丁度の値になることが注目される。この値の輪郭を平面図に重ねたものがFigure 3.4-4である。

南北168.0ハスタ，東西82.0ハスタの矩形の輪郭は，この中に建物N-O-Mばかりでなく2つの経蔵（C，C'）も含んでいる。この矩形の輪郭に対し，東の経蔵（C）

been added to adjust the interval between windows and to ensure that the distance could be equally divided into 19 (4.737 hasta for each). Utilizing 4.7 hasta, which approximates 4.737, for the total internal width of windows and distance between windows, the entire layout must have been adjusted to match the middle of the window and the middle of the Central Sanctuary. As a result, it is estimated that the internal measurement of the north-south width of the Gallery was 90.0 hasta, the internal width of windows was 906.4 mm (2.2 hasta), the distance between windows was 1,030.0 mm (2.5 hasta), the width of the wall on the north end was 2.2 hasta, which was the same as the internal width of windows, and the width of the wall on the south end was 1.0. The distance between windows (2.5 hasta) may indicate that the basic plan set the total value of the internal width of windows and the distance between windows as 5.0 hasta, and the distance between windows (2.5 hasta) was the equally divided value. As shown in Figure 3.4-2, the width of the wall on the north end is relatively small, but that on the south end is quite large. However, the central line of the Central Sanctuary and the bisector of the opposing window match well. The dimentional difference is 63 mm on the east of the Gallery, and 120 mm on the west of the Gallery. It is possible that the location of the window opposing the Central Sanctuary was set first, and then wall between the windows was extended north and south. Accumulated errors in individual construction as well as the errors in the north-south width of the Gallery must have been reflected in the width of the wall on the south and north ends.

As is mentioned above, analysis based on the actual measurements revealed that the total of the internal width of windows and the distance between windows was 4.7 hasta in the original plan. Window width and distance between windows were deemed to be 2.2 hasta and 2.5 hasta, respectively. Dividing the north-south length (90.0 hasta) by 19 (18 windows+1) produces a fraction, which would be approximately 290 mm with 4.7 hasta as the divisor. The 290 mm fraction was included in the width of the wall on the north and south ends. The 4.7 hasta value also seems to imply that the lower unit of hasta was not a unit that was divided by 24 (angular), which was used in South Asia, but a unit divided by 10 according to each number system.

The above-mentioned examinations were undertaken to clarify whether the north-south width of the Gallery (outer dimension of the base) measured 106 hasta or 107 hasta. Results showed that window layout plan for Gallery I (A') was based on an internal north-south width of 90.0 hasta, not 91.0 hasta. Therefore, the total north-south length of the Gallery (outer measurement of the outer end of the base) was 106.0 hasta, which, in other words,

Planning of Complex

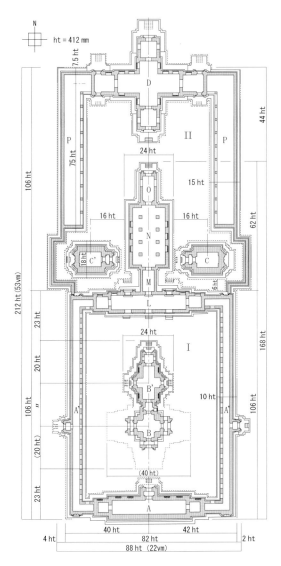

Figure 3.4-3 The Measurements (hasta) of Complex I,II

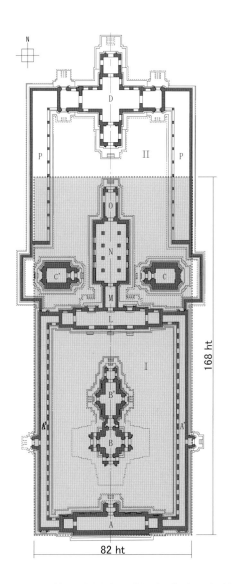

Figure 3.4-4 Scale Planning for Complex I,II

の背面基座は250mm程西にあり，西の経蔵（C'）の背面基座も230mm程西へ踏み出している[22]。したがって2棟の経蔵は，全体として半ハスタ程西へ移動した状態である。建物N-O-Mの北端とともに，いずれもわずかな寸法差があるが，第1伽藍の最大輪郭は，長短辺の合計を300.0ハスタとする山頂伽藍全体の規模計画に対し，その3/4に相当することが判る。しかし，現在まで分析を進めてきた各伽藍では，規模の最大輪郭を体現するものは，回廊や周壁の基座外端であることが通例であり，ここから突出するゴープラのポーチなどを含むものではなかった。したがって，想定された第1伽藍の規模計画が妥当性を持つとすれば，例外的な規模計画と捉えなければならない。理由を検討してみよう。

第1伽藍の構成は，冒頭で述べたように2つの経蔵

means that the north-south length of the Gallery in Complex I is half of the north-south length of the entire Complex at the highest point on the mountain (212.0 hasta). In addition, if the width of the Gallery is 10.0 hasta, the distance from the north end of the Gallery to the north end of the Mandapa would be 23.0 hasta, the distance from the middle of the Mandapa to the middle of the Central Sanctuary would be 20.0 hasta; and if we assume the same for the platform of the Central Sanctuary, the distance from the middle of the Central Sanctuary to the south end of the platform would be 20.0 hasta, and the distance from the south end of the platform to the south end of the Gallery would be 23.0 hasta. The distance from the middle of the Mandapa to the north end of the Gallery, and the distance from the middle of the Central Sanctuary to the south end of the Gallery are 43.0 hasta, which indicates that the position at which the buildings were

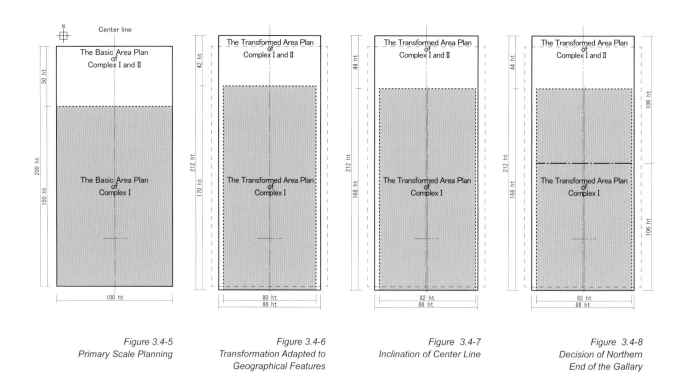

Figure 3.4-5
Primary Scale Planning

Figure 3.4-6
Transformation Adapted to
Geographical Features

Figure 3.4-7
Inclination of Center Line

Figure 3.4-8
Decision of Northern
End of the Gallary

を回廊内に施設する幅を持たないため，第1回廊（A'）はほぼ最低限の規模を持って閉じ，2棟の経蔵を回廊外に配置することになった。この調整に対応して，ゴープラは通例の平面形状から変化し，東西に長い矩形の外方（北方）に拝殿とも見える施設を接続することで，ゴープラの機能を維持しようと試みたように思われる。このため，第1伽藍は，通例の構成に比べて回廊の奥行きが極度に短く，ゴープラの機能を持つ建物N-O-Mが大きく突出することになった。回廊の外に配置された経蔵と大きく突出したゴープラは，回廊を以て伽藍の規模とする通例の計画では，その規模を計画的に把握することが難しいであろう。このように例外的な構成に起因して，伽藍の規模計画が通例と異なる様相を見せたのだと考えられる。

第1伽藍の規模計画は，一応の輪郭を想定できるが，これだけでは回廊の奥行き，南北の長さが決定できない。回廊の奥行きは，山頂伽藍全体の南北長さを等分する位置にあるから，全体の規模計画に依存していることが分かる。つまり，第1伽藍の規模計画は単一の規模計画として成立するものではなく，山頂伽藍全体の規模計画と第1伽藍の規模計画とを，南端を一致させて重ね合わせることで初めて成立する技法であると考えられる。この様相を，Figure 3.4-5 ～ Figure 3.4-8 に示す。

Figure 3.4-5は，基本となる規模を決定する段階で，山頂伽藍の規模を長短辺の合計300.0ハスタ，第1伽

placed symmetrically inside the Gallery was set at the middle of the north-south length of the Gallery.

3.4.3.4 Scale Planning for Complex I

Figure 3.4-3 shows the conversion of each measurement of the Complexes at the highest point on the mountain into hasta. Although the scale plan for the Complex at the highest point on the mountain and the size plan for the north-south length of Complex I have been clarified, some problems remain; namely, the east-west width of Complex I is 82.0 hasta while the east-west width of Complex II is 88.0 hasta, and central axes in Complex I and II differ. Therefore, we examined the plan for the east-west width of Complex I, including its scale plan.

The actual measurement from the south end of Complex I to the north end of Building N-O-M (to the outer end of the base on the north end of the porch O) is 69,009 mm, which is 167.5 hasta. If it is 168.0 hasta, the total of this and the east-west width of Complex I (82.0 hasta) would 250.0 hasta, which merits our attention. The shaded area in Figure 3.4-4 shows the outline of the area obtained from these values.

The outline of the rectangle measuring 168.0 hasta in the north-south direction and 82.0 hasta in the east-west direction includes not only Building N-O-M, but also Libraries (C and C'). Against this rectangular outline, the rear base of Library (C) is 250 mm toward the west, and the rear base of Library (C') is 230 mm toward the west[22]. Therefore, these two Libraries are

藍の規模をその3/4である250.0ハスタとした段階である。Figure 3.4-6は，おそらく地形などが原因となって，やや奥行きのあるプロポーションに変形した段階。南北の長さ210.0ハスタ，東西幅90.0ハスタが目指されたようだが，ヴィャマの単位を優先して212.0ハスタ（53.0ヴィャマ）と88.0ハスタ（22.0ヴィャマ）としたようである。また，第1伽藍の規模を東西幅80.0ハスタ（20.0ヴィャマ）とし，結果的に南北の長さが170.0ハスタに変化した状態である。Figure 3.4-7は第1伽藍の中軸線の偏向を生むために東西幅の東側に2ハスタを加えた段階である。伽藍中心線が先行しているため，敷地輪郭を一方に拡幅し，結果的に伽藍中心線を偏向させるという技法である。この調整に呼応して，南北の長さは168.0ハスタに変化する。Figure 3.4-8は第1伽藍の回廊北端を決定する操作で，山頂伽藍の南北全長を2等分した位置を以て回廊の北端としている。

3.4.3.5 建物配置計画の概要

Figure 3.4-9 ～ Figure 3.4-10のうち Figure 3.4-9は，Figure 3.4-5 ～ Figure 3.4-8の手順で決定した伽藍全体と第1伽藍の輪郭，Figure 3.4-10は，この中に各建物の基座の最大輪郭とヴィャマの単位のグリッドを重ねたものである。各建物に記入した数値は，基座の位置で長短辺の最大幅をハスタの単位で整理したものである。伽藍全体の輪郭はヴィャマの単位のグリッドに合致しているが，先に述べたように，東西幅，南北幅をそれぞれヴィャマの単位を以て整合させた結果である。第1伽藍の規模の輪郭は南北を168.0ハスタとするが，これもヴィャマの倍数である。建物N-O-Mの規模は東西幅24.0ハスタ（8.0ヴィャマ），南北幅60.0ハスタ（15.0ヴィャマ）と判断したが，いずれもヴィャマの倍数の値をとるばかりか，その配置はヴィャマの単位のグリッドに合致する。経蔵の南北幅はいずれも18.0ハスタ（4.5ヴィャマ），東西幅は経蔵によって1ハスタ程の相違があるが，28.0ハスタ（7.0ヴィャマ）を基準としたものであろう。いずれも南端がグリッドに合致し，北端はグリッドの半分に位置している。回廊（A'）の外に配置されたこれらの建物は，いずれもヴィャマの単位のグリッドによく合致するから，これら建物の配置は伽藍全体を覆うヴィャマを単位寸法とする配置計画が潜在したことを示している。

第1伽藍の各ゴープラの規模計画においても，少なくとも1/2ヴィャマの単位の寸法値が認められる。同様に，第1伽藍の拝殿と中央祠堂についても，ヴィャマの単位の寸法計画を窺うことができる。しかし，第

located one-half hasta toward the west. Although there are some small gaps, including the north end of the Building N-O-M, the maximum outline of Complex I is equivalent to 3/4 of the scale of the entire Complex at the highest point on the mountaintop, which sets the total of the longer and shorter sides as 300.0 hasta. According to previous analyses on each Complex, the maximum outline of the scale usually matches the outer end of the base of a Gallery or peripheral wall, not including a porch stretching out of a Gopura. Therefore, the estimated scale plan for Complex I is adequate, and it should be considered exceptional as well.

As was mentioned at the beginning, Complex I does not have sufficient width to accommodate two Libraries inside the Gallery. Therefore, Gallery I (A') only had minimum space and was closed, and the two Libraries were placed outside the Gallery. In line with this adjustment, the shape of one Gopura was also changed from a regular plane to a rectangle stretching out in the east-west direction and was equipped with a facility that appears to be a Mandapa on the north side, which was probably to maintain its function as a Gopura. Therefore, Complex I has an extremely narrow Gallery and Building N-O-M, which functions as a Gopura, extends significantly. The Libraries placed outside the Gallery and the Gopura that is extends significantly must have been difficult to include in a regular plan, whose Gallery defines the scale because it surrounds all the buildings in the Complex. These unusual structural characteristics show that the scale plan for this Complex is different from the standard.

The originally planned outline of Complex I can be estimated; however, this is not enough to determine the depth and north-south length of the Gallery. The Gallery in Complex I stops at a point that equally divides the north-south length of the entire Complex at the highest point on the mountain top, which, therefore, depends on the overall scale plan. In other words, the scale plan for Complex I could not be created as a single scale plan, but needed to be associated with the entire Complex at the highest point on the mountain top by matching the south end. This is shown in Figure 3.4-5 - Figure 3.4-8.

Figure 3.4-5 shows the basic scale of the plan. Here the total of both Complexes at the highest point on the mountain was determined to be 300.0 hasta, that is, the total of longer and shorter sides, and 250.0 hasta, which is 3/4 of 300.0 hasta, as the scale of Complex I. Figure 3.4-6 shows an adjustment with a relatively longer Gallery due to geographical reasons. The north-south length was set as 210.0 hasta while the east-west width was set as 90.0 hasta, and then both were adjusted to 212.0 hasta (53.0 vyama) and 88.0 hasta (22.0 vyama). In addition, for Complex I, the east-west width was set as 80.0 hasta (20.0

Chapter 3 : Study Reports on Preah Vihear Temple

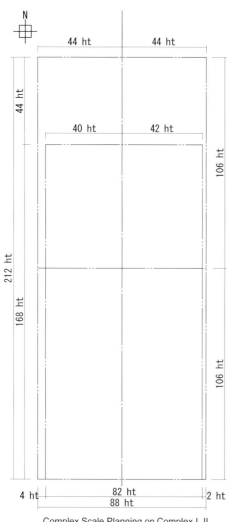

Figure 3.4-9 Scale Planning for Complex I, II

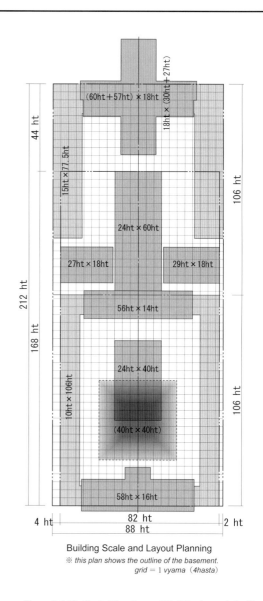

Figure 3.4-10 Scale Planning and Building Layout for Complex I, II

　1伽藍の回廊北端を，伽藍全体の南北の長さを等分する位置に当てたため，回廊の内部ではグリッドの歩みに1/2ヴィャマのずれが起こり，中央に配置した拝殿と中央祠堂の位置は，ヴィャマを単位寸法とする配置計画から1/4ヴィャマ，つまり1ハスタだけ外れることになった。ただこれは，全幅を106.0ハスタとし，その中央に配置する限り必然的なことと考えられる。

　第2伽藍のゴープラ（D）と第2回廊（P）は，ヴィャマの単位からみると，やや曖昧な値をとっているようにみえる。第2ゴープラ（D）は伽藍の外と内で高低差があるため，外側の基座が内側よりも大きく踏み出しており，一見してヴィャマの単位が明確ではないが，基本計画は60.0ハスタ（15.0ヴィャマ）の長さと18.0ハスタ（4.5ヴィャマ）の幅の建物を十字平面に組み合わせた計画とみられる[23]。

　一方，第2回廊（P）は，第1伽藍の回廊（A'）の幅

vyama). Accordingly the north-south length became 170.0 hasta. Figure 3.4-7 shows an adjustment made by adding 2 hasta to the east side of the east-west distance to produce deflection on the central axis of Complex I. The central line of the entire Complex was already determined so that the outline of the area was shifted to one side to produce deflection from the central line. In line with this adjustment, the north-south distance changed to 168.0 hasta. Figure 3.4-8 shows the determination of the north end of the Gallery of Complex I. The north end was placed at the point which divides the north-south length of both Complexes at the highest point on the mountaintop.

3.4.3.5 Building Layout Overview

　Figure 3.4-9 shows the outlines of both Complexes and Complex I determined by the procedures shown in Figure 3.4-5- Figure 3.4-8. Figure 3.4-10 adds the maximum outline of the

10.0ハスタに対し，4.0ヴィヤマ（16.0ハスタ）ではなく15.0ハスタをとっている。長さは，北端で屈曲する第2回廊（P）の真から南端まで75.0ハスタ，南北幅全体で77.5ハスタとなる。これはヴィヤマの単位から大きく離れた値である。しかしこの原因は，経蔵（C，C'）の配置と第2ゴープラ（D）の規模計画を優先した結果ともみえるから，第2回廊（P）の計画と他の建物の計画との間に時代差があることを示すことにはならない。

Figure 3.4-9が示すように，伽藍全体の計画がヴィヤマの単位を以て整った値をとり，各建物の規模計画と配置計画においても同様の単位がよく機能しているように思われる。ヴィヤマを単位とするグリッドは，建物の規模と相対的な位置を明確にするため分析上想定したものにすぎず，グリッドを用いた計画が存在したと主張するものではない。しかしなお，総じて，ヴィヤマを単位とする整合ある単一の全体計画が存在したことを裏付ける結果とみることができる。

ただ，極度に奥行きの小さなポーチを持つ中央祠堂は，拝殿との無理のあるとり付きから推定されるように，当初の計画と異なる可能性が高い。おそらく，ポーチを持たない前身祠堂（レンガ造か）をそのまま残す予定であったものが，拝殿の建立以後，計画途上で変更されたと考えられる。しかし，それでも前身祠堂の位置（本尊の位置）を踏襲した結果，ポーチは，奥行きを縮小せざるを得なくなったのであろう[24]。

中央祠堂の規模に計画変更も予想されるが，伽藍の規模計画と各建物の配置計画は，全体の統一的な計画を予想させるものである。

3.4.4 伽藍全域の特徴

山頂伽藍の基本計画と計画手順について検討してきたが，その結果をもとに，伽藍全域の寸法計画と主要建物の配置計画について検討を行う。一般に伽藍全長は800m程と紹介されるが，北端の階段を入れると850mを超える長大な伽藍である。各建物の配置計画は，配置上の規準点が建物のどの位置に当たるかを特定しない限り判明しない。最も予想される建物真々間の距離は計画的に明確な数値が現れず，試行錯誤を経て，Figure 3.4-11に示した位置を配置の規準点と判断した。

3.4.4.1 第5ゴープラから第4ゴープラ

第5ゴープラ（K）と第4ゴープラ（J）の距離は，第5ゴープラの東西に延びる翼部の北側基座の外端から第4ゴープラの東西翼部南側の基壇外端ま

base of each building and grid by vyama. The values shown at each building are the hasta conversion of the maximum width of the longer and shorter sides at the base position. Both Complexes match the grid by vyama through adjustment for the east-west width and north-south width by vyama. The outline of Complex I shows 168.0 hasta in north-south direction, which is also a multiple of vyama. Building N-O-M was determined to have 24.0 hasta (8.0 vyama) of the east-west width and 60.0 hasta (15.0 vyama) of the north-south width, all of which are multiples of vyama, and whose layout also matches the grid by vyama. The north-south width of the Libraries is the same at 18.0 hasta (4.5 vyama) and the east-west width shows a 1 hasta difference in the two Libraries; however, it can be estimated that they used 28.0 hasta (7.0 vyama) as the standard. The south end of each building matches the grid by vyama, and the north end is at the middle of the areas indicated by the grid. The Libraries placed outside Gallery I (A') match the grid by vyama, which shows that there was a layout plan for both Complexes using vyama as a unit.

The scale plan for each Gopura in Complex I also shows figures utilizing 0.5 vyama. Similarly, the Mandapa and Central Sanctuary in Complex I also show a size plan utilizing vyama as a unit. However, adjusting the north end of the Gallery in Complex I to the point that equally divides the north-south length of both Complexes, which produced a 0.5- vyama gap in the grid inside the Gallery, caused a misalignment in the location of the Mandapa and Central Sanctuary measuring approximately 0.25 vyama (1 hasta) compared with the plan using vyama. This was inevitable because the entire width was determined to be 106.0 hasta and it was necessary to place these buildings in the middle.

Gopura II (D) and Gallery II (P) in Complex II seem to have ambiguous values in terms of vyama. Gopura II (D) has a difference in height between the outside and inside of the Complex so that the base of the outer part stretches out compared with the inside. This makes it difficult to determine the measurements; however, the plan was probably to place two buildings, each of which being 60.0 hasta (15.0 vyama) in length and 18.0 hasta (4.5 vyama) in width, in a cross shape[23].

Meanwhile, Gallery II (P) in Complex II are 15.0 hasta in width, not 16.0 hasta (4.0 vyama) toward the 10.0 hasta width of the Gallery I (A') in Complex I. The length from the middle of the Gallery II (P) that bends from the north end to the south end is 75.0 hasta, and the entire north-south width is 77.5 hasta. These figures are, however, unassociated with vyama, possibly because a priority may have been placed on the layout of Library (C and C') as well as the scale plan for Gopura II (D). If so, it would not indicate any chronological difference between the

Chapter 3 : Study Reports on Preah Vihear Temple

で329,880mmである[25]。繰り返し述べたようにクメール遺構の当時の造営尺度であるハスタの実長は、412mm前後と判断された[26]。この値で上記の実測値を換算すると800.68ハスタとなり、この値から、両

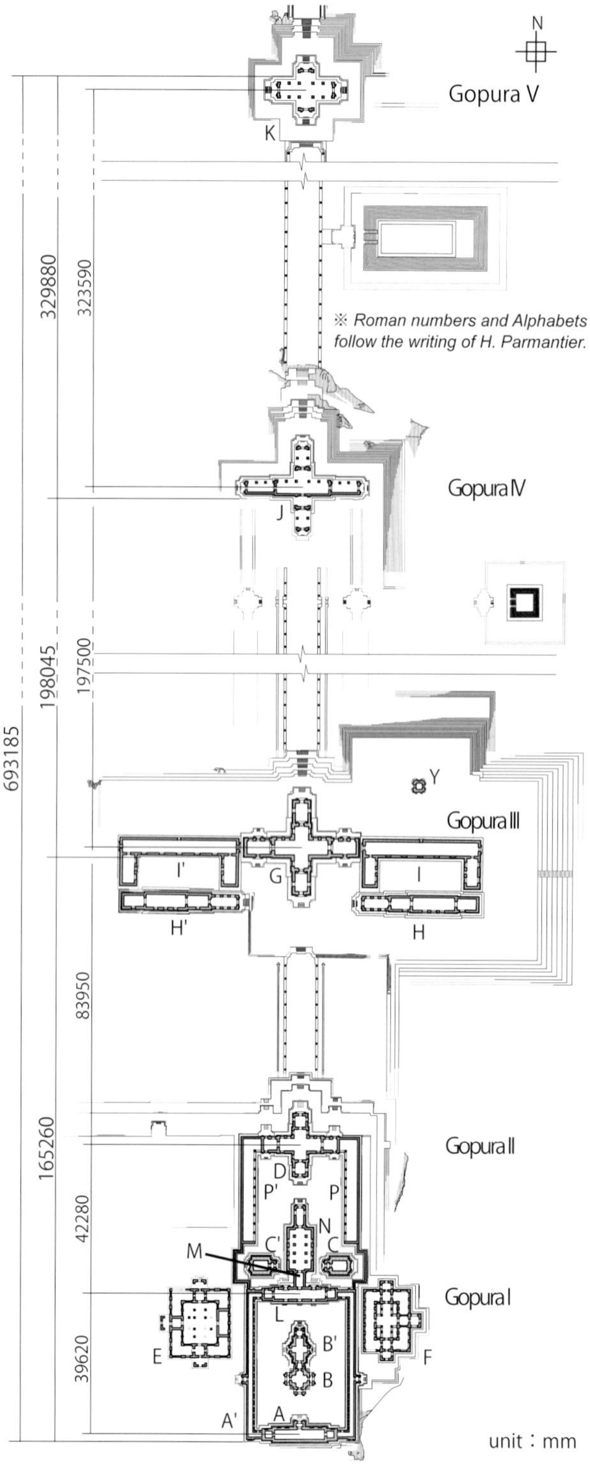

※ Roman numbers and Alphabets follow the writing of H. Parmantier.

unit : mm

Figure 3.4-11 Measurement Map of Each Building of Preah Vihear Temple

plans for Gallery II (P) or other buildings.

As Figure 3.4-9 shows, both Complexes were planned to be adjusted to vyama. The vyama also functions well in the scale and layout plans for each building. The vyama grid was only an assumption for analysis to clarify the scale and symmetrical position of each building, not to argue that there was a plan that utilized vyama for the grid. However, these results suggest the possibly of a plan consistent with the vyama unit.

As is estimated from the gap with the Mandapa and the existence of extremely narrow porches, it is quite possible that the Central Sanctuary differed from the original plan. It is possible that a previous Sanctuary (probably made of brick) without porches had been planned. However, after the Mandapa was built, the plan may have changed. We assume that the building of the Central Sanctuary at the location of the previous (original) Sanctuary (location of the principal image of Buddha) made the porches narrower than the plan had called for[24].

The scale of the Central Sanctuary may have been changed from the original; however, the scale of both Complexes and the layout of each building may have followed a unified plan.

3.4.4 Characteristics of the Entire Complex

We have examined the basic plan and building chronology of Complexes at the highest point on the mountaintop. Based on the results, we examined the planned size for the entire Complex and layout for each building. The total length of entire Complex is 800 m, which is long and expansive, and exceeds 850 m, including the stairs at the north end. The layout for each building cannot be clarified before clarifying the location of the base point of each building. The most accessible measurement is the distance between buildings. Unfortunately, however, no figures were found that could be used to determine the base point. For this reason, we employed a process of trial and error to determine the points shown in Figure 3.4.1-11 as base points for the layout.

3.4.4.1 From Gopura V to Gopura IV

The distance between Gopura V (K) and Gopura IV (J) is 329,880 mm, measured from the outer end of the north side base on the transept running in the east-west direction at Gopura V to the outer end of the platform on the south side of the east-west transept at Gopura IV[25]. As was have repeatedly mentioned, the actual measurement of a hasta, a measurement scale for construction used in the Khmer Empire, was determined to be approximately 412 mm[26]. The above measurement can be converted to 800.68 hasta, which allowed us to estimate the planned distance as 800 hasta (200 vyama). However, the

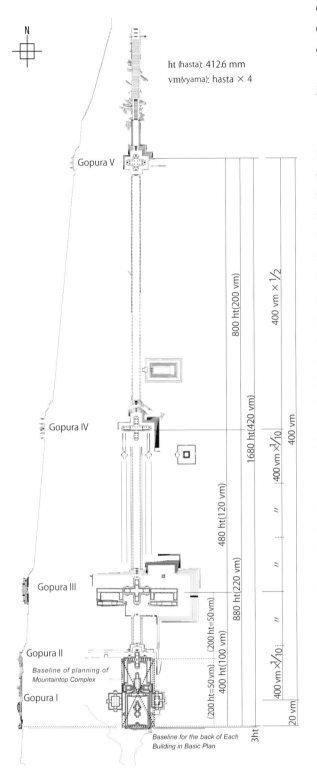

Figure 3.4-12 Building Layout of Preah Vihear Temple

者の距離を800ハスタ（200ヴィャマ）とする計画であったと予想される。これに対し，建物真々寸法325,390mm（789.78ハスタ）では，計画意図が明快とはいい難い値が現れている。

distance between the middle of buildings was 325,390 mm (789.78 hasta), which does not indicate an association with the original plan.

3.4.4.2 From Gopura V to the Back of Both Complexes at the Highest Point on the Mountaintop

Considering the above-mentioned plan, it is possible that the north end of the base of the east-west side room at Gopura V is one of the base points associated with the basic plan for entire Complex. We focus on the entire length of the building layout in the entire Complex from this point to the base of the back of both Complexes at the highest point on the mountaintop. The length is 693,228 mm, or 1,682.59 hasta. It is slightly longer than 1680 hasta, which is 420 vyama. The layout plan for both Complexes at the highest point on the mountaintop suggested in a previously published survey expands 9 hasta to the north and 3 hasta to the south in the north-south direction from the basic rectangle with a north-south length of 200 hasta and an east-west length of 100 hasta.[27] We now consider the possibility that the total length of entire Complex was 1,680+3 hasta.

3.4.4.3 From Gopura IV to III & Back of Both Complexes at the Highest Point on the Mountaintop

It was very difficult to clarify the meaning of the distance from Gopura IV (J) to Gopura III (G), and this difficulty opened a wide range of possibilities. We decided to use the distance from the above-mentioned point at Gopura IV to the outer end of the base on the south side of Annex Building I and I' among the structures around Gopura III, which is 198,045 mm[28]. This is converted to 480.69 hasta, or 480 hasta (120 vyama). The distance from the same point at Gopura III to the back of both Complexes at the highest point on the mountaintop (outer end of the base on the south side of Gallery I (A')) is 165,260 mm, or 401.12 hasta. It is appropriate to consider the distance to be 403 hasta based on the total length of entire Complex and the measurement of each part although there is a small gap between 401.12 and 403 hasta[29]. The basic plan set the length of entire Complex as 1,680 hasta. However, according to the basic plan, which divides the distance from Gopura III to the back of both complexes (100 hasta) into two equal parts, and uses one-half (50 hasta) as the depth of the Complexes, Complex I extended 3 hasta to the south, and Complex II extended 9 hasta to the north. This resulted in a change of the total length of entire Complex to 1,683 hasta.

3.4.4.2 第5ゴープラから山頂伽藍背面

　上記の計画を予想すると，第5ゴープラ東西翼部の基座北端が全体伽藍の基本計画に関わる規準点の一つと考えられる。ここから山頂伽藍背面の基座まで，つまり伽藍内建物配置の全長に注目する。この値693,228mmは1,682.59ハスタに換算される。1,680ハスタ（420ヴィャマ）と見るにはやや長い値である。別稿で指摘した山頂伽藍の配置計画では，基本となる南北200ハスタ，東西100ハスタの規準矩形から，南北方向では北へ9ハスタ，南へ3ハスタ拡大していると考えられた[27]。伽藍全長が1,680＋3ハスタであった可能性を念頭において検討を進めよう。

3.4.4.3 第4ゴープラ〜第3および山頂伽藍背面

　第4ゴープラ（J）から第3ゴープラ（G）の距離は難解で，さまざまな可能性が考えられた。第4ゴープラの上記の位置から，第3ゴープラ周辺の建物のうち付属建物（I，I'）の南側基座外端まで198,045mmという値をとる[28]。換算値は480.69ハスタ，つまり480ハスタ（120ヴィャマ）の計画寸法が予想される。また第3ゴープラの同様の位置から山頂伽藍背面（第1回廊（A'）の南面基座外端）までの距離165,260mmは401.12ハスタに換算される。伽藍全長と各部の値に基づき，やや誤差を含むが403ハスタと捉えることが妥当であろう[29]。したがって基本計画では伽藍全長を1,680ハスタとしたが，山頂伽藍の奥行きを，第3ゴープラから背面までの100ハスタを等分して後半50ハスタに当てるという基本計画に基づき，二次的に南へ3ハスタ，北へ9ハスタ踏み出した。このため，伽藍全長は1,683ハスタに変化したと考えられる。

3.4.4.4 伽藍全体の計画法

　第5ゴープラ東西翼の東基座外端から，山頂伽藍の基本となった東西100ハスタ，南北200ハスタの計画規準線の南端（背面）まで，計画寸法を1,680ハスタ（420ヴィャマ）とし，第5ゴープラの同位置から第4ゴープラの東西翼南面基座（ないし基壇）外端までを800ハスタ（200ヴィャマ）とする。さらに，第4ゴープラの同様の位置から第3ゴープラの東西翼南面基座（ないし基壇）外端までを480ハスタ（120ヴィャマ）とし，第3ゴープラの同位置から基本計画の伽藍背面までを400ハスタ（100ヴィャマ）とする。このうち後半200ハスタを山頂伽藍の基本計画の奥行きとする計画であったと考えられる（Figure 3.4-12）。規準位置に対し，各建物は，基座外端を内法ないし外法に当てて位置決定を進めたと思われる[30]。

3.4.4.4 Planning for Both Complexes

　The distance from the outer end of the east base of the east-west side room at Gopura V to the south end (back) of the planned baseline, which is 100 hasta in the east-west direction and 200 hasta in the north-south direction, was determined to be 1,680 hasta (420 vyama). The distance from the same point at Gopura V to the outer end of the base or platform on the south side of the east-west side room at Gopura IV was determined to be 800 hasta (200 vyama). The distance from the same point at Gopura IV to the outer end of the base or platform on the south side of the east-west side room at Gopura III was determined to be 480 hasta (120 vyama). The distance from the same point at Gopura III to the back of the Complex was determined to 400 hasta (100 vyama). Half of 400 hasta was planned as the depth of both Complexes at the highest point on the mountaintop (Figure 3.4-12). The placement of each building was probably based on the adjustment of the outer end of the base to inner or outer measurements[30].

3.4.5 Conclusion

　Both Complex I and II at the highest point on the mountaintop at Preah Vihear Temple looked as if there were a special layout divided into front and rear sections. However, the Gopura in Complex II and Gallery II (P, P') simply surround the front part of Complex I. The reason for employing such a structure is that the basic scale plan utilizing 100 hasta in the east-west direction and 200 hasta in the north-south direction was insufficient for the placement of two Libraries inside the Galleries, a reality that resulted in their placement outside the Galleries. In response to this, the north-south depth of the Galleries was minimized, which made it difficult to accommodate porches inside the Galleries stretching out from the Gopura built in front of Complex I. Therefore, a building that looks like a Mandapa with depth was attached to the Gopura toward the outside of the Galleries at Complex I to maintain the function of the Gopura. The deformed T-shaped Gopura and the symmetrical layout of the entrance of Libraries may have been a result of the difficulty of retaining sufficient east-west width after these buildings were built based on the central axis of the previous Complexes, which themselves faced geographical limitations. The scale plan for both Complex I and II at the highest point on the mountaintop was a unique combination of the plan for both Complex I and II (100 hasta of the east-west length, 200 hasta of the north-south length) and the plan for Complex I (100 hasta of the east-west length, 150 hasta of the north-south length). The unique structure of Complexes possibly reflected these procedures.

3.4.5 むすび

　プレア・ヴィヘア寺院の山頂伽藍は，一見して前後２つの領域に区分される特殊な配置形態をとっているように見えるが，この配置は第１伽藍の前面を，第２伽藍のゴープラとその第２回廊（P，P'）がとり囲んだものである。このような構成をとった原因は，東西100ハスタ，南北200ハスタを基本とする規模計画では，２つの経蔵を回廊内に収めることができず，回廊外前面に配置したためだと考えられた。呼応して，回廊はほぼ限界まで南北の奥行きを縮小した結果，第１伽藍入口のゴープラは回廊内に突出するポーチを持つことが困難になった。このため第１伽藍の回廊の外へ向けて，拝殿とも見える奥行きのある建物を付属させることでゴープラの機能を維持しようと考えたようである。T字型の平面となったゴープラの変形，入口を向かい合わせた経蔵の配置は，いずれも，地形の制約の下で前身伽藍の中心軸を踏襲したことで，東西幅を十分にとることが困難であったことに起因すると考えられる。伽藍の規模計画は，山頂伽藍全体（東西100ハスタ，南北200ハスタ），と第１伽藍の規模計画（東西100ハスタ，南北150ハスタ）それぞれを重ね合わせた独特の手順が認められた。この技法も，特徴ある伽藍構成が反映したものと判断される。

　結果として，山頂伽藍は，第１伽藍の東西幅を82ハスタ（伽藍中軸線を中心から外すため，東側に２ハスタ大きくとる），第２伽藍の東西幅を88ハスタとし，南北の長さを212ハスタとしてこれを前後に等分するという状態に到達した。このとき，伽藍南端の背面規準線の位置（第１伽藍南回廊基座外端）は，基本計画の位置から３ハスタ南に踏み出したと考えられた。この計画技法の特徴は，逐次的に造営されたようにもみえる伽藍の形成過程の背後に，統一ある規模計画と配置計画が潜在していたことを示している。

　一方，プレア・ヴィヘア寺院全体の伽藍計画は，第５ゴープラの東西翼の北面基座外端から山頂伽藍の基本計画時の背面基準位置まで，1,680ハスタ（420ヴィャマ）と考えられた。また，第５ゴープラの同様の位置から，第４ゴープラの東西翼南面基壇外端（基座外面を目指したか？）まで800ハスタ（200ヴィャマ），第４ゴープラの同様の位置から，第３ゴープラの東西翼南面基壇幅の中央あたり（基座外面か？）まで480ハスタ（120ヴィャマ），第３ゴープラの同様の位置から伽藍背面規準線まで400ハスタ（100ヴィャマ），その後半200ハスタ（50ヴィャマ）を山頂伽藍奥行きの基本計画に当てる，という計画が基本であったと考えられる。現状では山頂伽藍が南端を３ハスタ南へ移

As a result, the total of Complex I and II was equally divided twice of the entire north-south distance (212 hasta) consisting of the east-west distance (82 hasta) of Complex I (shifting 2 hasta toward the east side to keep the central axis of the Complexes away from the center) and the east-west distance (88 hasta) of Complex II. The baseline at the south end of the entire Complex (outer end of the base of the south Gallery in Complex I) extended 3 hasta to the south from the basic plan. This shows that there was a unified scale and layout plan behind the development of the site rather than a simple sequential construction of buildings.

Meanwhile, it was thought that the plan for the entire Preah Vihear Temple site set the total length of the entire Complex, which is from the outer end of the base on the north side of the east-west transepts at Gopura V to the base point at the back of Complex I and II at the highest point on the mountaintop, at 1,680 hasta (420 vyama). The distance from the same point at Gopura V to the outer end of the platform on the south side of east-west transepts at Gopura IV (possibly planned to be the outer surface of the base?) was set at 800 hasta (200 vyama), the distance from the same position at Gopura IV to the middle of the platform width on the south side of the east-west side room at Gopura III (outer surface of the base?) was set at 480 hasta (120 vyama), and the distance from the same point at Gopura III to the baseline at the back of the entire complex was set at 400 hasta (100 vyama), half of which (200 hasta, 50 vyama) was used in the basic plan as the depth of the total of Complex I and II at the highest point on the mountaintop. The current south end of the total of Complex I and II had been shifted to 3 hasta south so that the total distance from the same point at Gopura V to the south end of the entire Complex would measure 1,683 hasta (actual measurement: 1,682.6 hasta).

The plan of Complex exceeds 800 m. However, the center of each building was placed on a straight line without any gaps. Only the center of Gopura V is slightly shifted to the east (80cm). The measurements and the layout on a straight line show the construction was surprisingly accurate.

This analysis was conducted to clarify the size plan of the entire site using CAD drawings based on precise measurement of horizontal distance not taking into account the slope of 5.5 to 6 degrees. The actual measurements taking slope into consideration revealed a difference of more than 4 m over the entire site, in proportion to the length of horizontal projection; and analysis based on these figures revealed gaps. The results of the analysis also show that the site plan did not include adjustment for the slope, but was based on horizontal projection. It will be necessary

動させているため，第5ゴープラの同様の位置から伽藍の南端まで，1,683ハスタ（実測値1,682.6ハスタ）という値である。

800mを超える伽藍計画だが，各建物の中心は，ほとんど誤差なく直線上に載り，僅かに第5ゴープラの中心が80cm程東に寄っている。実測値と直線上の配置は，驚くほどの施工精度を実現している。

伽藍全体の寸法計画の復原を試みた分析は，精密実測調査によって得られたCAD図面上の数値，つまり水平距離に拠ったものであり，5.5°～6°の斜面に沿った値ではない。斜面に沿った実長は，水平投影の長さに比して伽藍全体で4mを超える相違を持っており，この値に従った分析では有意な値を見いだすことが困難であった。分析結果の様相は，当時の伽藍計画においても斜面に沿った計画ではなく，水平投影上で計画されたことを物語っている。この計画を現実の斜面に実現する具体的な方法については，今後の検討課題である。

また，山頂伽藍の基本計画では，本尊の位置から背面まで40ハスタ（10ヴィヤマ）であった。このことに注目しつつ伽藍全体の計画寸法から推定される配置の考え方は，本尊を中心に南北それぞれ40ハスタ，したがって80ハスタ（20ヴィヤマ）四方とする至聖所を計画し，この北面に1,600ハスタ（400ヴィヤマ）のアプローチを接続させた計画が背後に存在した，と考えることも可能である。これはまた，前身伽藍の様相を推定するための手がかりとも考えられるが，あらためて慎重に検討することとしたい。

注

1） 2007年から12年にかけて行った現地調査は，日本学術振興会科学研究費助成事業によって実施された。またその調査，研究成果は，日本学術振興会科学研究費成果公開費により以下の書籍として公開した。中川武，溝口明則共同監修：コー・ケーとベン・メアレア　アンコール広域拠点遺跡群の建築学的研究，中央公論美術出版，2014.3.

2） 北端の施設である第5ゴープラはカンボジア領内だが，参道はタイ国領内にも続いている。

3） Parmentier,H.:L'art Khmer Classique, Monuments du Quadrant Nord-Est 2vols, Paris, EFEO, 1939.

4） Sahai,S.:Preah Vihear An Introduction to the World Heritage Monument, Phnom Penh, Buddhist Institute Printing House, 2009.

5） 碑文に基づいて，ヤショヴァルマンⅠの時代，893年頃に伽藍北端と東からの参道に石造のナーガの高欄がつくられたと判断されることから，この時点で，山頂までの前身伽藍が存在したと判断している。前身伽藍に石造の建造物はなく，すべて「軽量」の材料（レンガと木材を指すのであろう）でつくられていた，と推測している。

to examine specific methods of applying this plan to the actual slope.

In addition, the basic plan for Complex I and II at the highest point on the mountaintop set the distance from the principal image of Buddha to the back at 40 hasta. (10 vyama). It is also possible that the original layout of the entire site was based on a sacred area of 80 hasta (20 vyama) square (40 hasta to the south and north centering on the principal image of Buddha) to the north side connected to an approach measuring 1600 hasta (400 vyama).This would be the key to clarifying the previous Complex; however, it requires additional consideration.

Notes

1) The on-site surveys conducted between 2007 and 2012 were funded by a Grand-in-Aid for Scientific Research by MEXT. The surveys and results were published as a book funded by a Grand-in-Aid for the Publication of Research Results by MEXT as shown below: Jointly compiled under the supervision of Takeshi Nakagawa and Akinori Mizoguchi: Koh Ker and Beng Mealea – Architectural Study on theProvincial Sites of the Khmer Empire, Chuo Koron Bijutsu Shuppan, 2014.3.

2) Gopura V located in the north end of the site is in Cambodia; however, the approach continues to the area in Thailand.

3) Parmentier,H.:L'art Khmer Classique, Monuments du Quadrant Nord-Est 2vols, Paris, EFEO, 1939.

4) Sahai,S.:Preah Vihear An Introduction to the World Heritage Monument, Phnom Penh, Buddhist Institute Printing House, 2009.

5) According to the inscription, it is thought that stone naga motif bridge railing was installed along the approach between the north end to the east in the site around 893, during the era of Yasovarman I ; therefore, the previous site up to the mountaintop had already existed at that time. The previous site did not seem to have stone buildings. They seemed to have been made by light materials, probably brick and wood.

6) The Central Sanctuary had to protrude to the south side of the Mandapa to be connected. This indicates that the Central Sanctuary was built after the Mandapa.

7) The stone outer wall of the Gallery has five layers while the south half of the west side and southeast corner of the east side have three layers of large stones. This may indicate that construction of the Gallery was in several stages. The opening connected to False Gopura (A) is different from other openings, and shows traces of layered stone blocks without longitudinal members for walls between windows or reinforcement by wood joists on the top of the exterior at the openings. Stone size and technique varied, which suggested that there were times that Gallery construction stopped. Parmentier argued that the Gallery was built in the era of Rajendravarman II (944-968) or Jayavarman V (968-1001). It isalso pointed out that the Galleries at this site are similar to those in Phimeanakas. Considering that all galleries are thought to have been built between the rule of Suryavarman I and Udayadityavarman II, it is natural to think they are similar.

H.Parmentier argued that wood roofing was installed on Gallery I (A')

6）中央祠堂は，拝殿の南面に強引に突きつけて接続している
　　から，拝殿より後の造営であることが明らかである。

7）回廊の外壁を構成する石材は5段の石材ブロックを重ねて
　　いるが，西面の南半と東面の南東隅では大材を用いて3段
　　に積載している。これは回廊の造営が複数の段階に分けて
　　行われたこと示している可能性が高い。また，擬似ゴープ
　　ラ（A）に接する開口部の構成は他の開口部と異なり，窓間
　　壁に縦材を用いず石材ブロックを積載し，開口の屋内上部
　　に木造梁を挿入して補強した痕跡を残している。石材の大
　　きさと技法が混在することから，回廊の工事が中断した時
　　期のあったことが予想される。パルマンティエは回廊の建
　　立をラージェンドラヴァルマンⅡないしジャヤヴァルマンⅤ
　　の時代と考えているようである。ピミアナカスの回廊との
　　類似も指摘されているが，いずれもスールヤヴァルマンⅠか
　　らウダヤディティヤヴァルマンⅡの時代の建立と考えれば，
　　様式の類似からみても無理がないであろう。

　　なお，パルマンティエは第1ゴープラ（L）側壁に残る木造
　　梁の仕口痕跡から，一旦，第1回廊（A'）に木造屋根が架け
　　られたと推定するが，仕口痕跡を辿っても十分な小屋組を
　　想定することが難しい。また擬似ゴープラ（A）には同様の
　　痕跡が見いだせない。実際に木造屋根がかかった可能性は
　　考え難く，工事の途上で，早い時期に石造屋根へ変更する
　　ことになったと考えられる。

8）注3）文献の中で，パルマエンティエは，たとえばセック・
　　タ・ツイ寺院，トラペアン・クニャン寺院など，周壁で囲
　　まれた伽藍の内部が前後に2分される平面を持つ寺院遺跡
　　について触れているが，本文にて後述するように，プレア・
　　ヴィヘア寺院の山頂伽藍は，これらの平面形式と同様のも
　　のと考えることができるかどうか，明確ではない。

9）回廊内側に向けてつくられた3つの開口の下部に設けられ
　　た小さな階段は，基壇を構成する石材から作り出されてお
　　り，建立当初のものと見られる。また擬似ゴープラ（A）も，
　　回廊の内部に突出した短いポーチを持つが，背面を閉ざし
　　ている。必ずしも一般的な構成ではないが，通り抜けるこ
　　とのできないゴープラは，各地に類例が認められる。

10）バンテアイ・サムレ寺院は2重の回廊を巡らせるが，4棟
　　の内ゴープラの側壁に残る痕跡から，ゴープラの間に周壁
　　を巡らした時代があり，早い時期に回廊に改修されたこと
　　がわかる。改修された回廊には連子窓以外に開口がなく，
　　回廊屋内には入れない。このためであろうか回廊の内側に
　　沿って，ゴープラを含む基壇上面を拡幅してテラスを巡ら
　　し，ナーガの高欄を設けている。2棟の経蔵の側面基座は，
　　拡幅されたテラスの基座と接している。狭小な印象を与え
　　る回廊内側の敷地は以上の過程を経て実現した。参考文献I）
　　参照。

11）前身伽藍では，周壁が使われていた可能性も残る。そのと
　　き伽藍東西幅が現在と同等であれば，一対の経蔵を配置す
　　るに十分な内法寸法が確保された可能性が高い。

12）第1ゴープラ（L）は，小さな突出部（ポーチ）であれば，
　　拝殿B'の前面に施設することも可能であったかもしれない。
　　しかし伽藍の中央へ向いた2つの経蔵の配置が，第1ゴー
　　プラⅠ（L）の左右に配置された2つの出入口を，通例よりも

due to traces of the joints on the wood joist remaining on the sidewalls at Gopura I (L) However, it is difficult to imagine a roof truss based on traces of the joints. In addition, there were no similar traces at False Gopura (A). Therefore, it is hard to conclude that there was a wooden roof. It is natural to think that the plan was changed to stone at an early stage of the construction.

8) Pr. Sek Ta Tuy and Pr. Trapeang Khyang Temples are described in the literature in Note 3) above. They are separated in the front and back parts and surrounded by peripheral walls. As is described later in this study, it is not yet clear that these layout plans and the one for the Complexes on the highest point on the mountain at Preah Vihear Temple are similar.

9) Small stairs installed in the three openings facing the inside of the Gallery are stone and include a platform. They are thought to have been made at the initial construction. False Gopura (A) in the back has a narrow porch stretching out inside the Gallery, but is closed in the back. It is not a common structure; however, such Gopura structures can also be observed in different regions.

10) Banteay Samre Temple has double-layered galleries. The traces on the sidewalls of the Gopuras inside four buildings show that there was a time at which peripheral walls were built between Gopuras, which were remodeled into Galleries at an early stage. Remodeled Galleries did not have openings other than lattice windows, which made it impossible to enter the Galleries. This is may explain why the upper surface of the platform, including Gopuras along with the interior wall of the Galleries, was expanded and terraces and naga bridge railings were installed. The bases on the side of the two Libraries were contiguous to the base of the expanded terrace. The area inside the Galleries that give the impression of being narrow were constructed through the above-mentioned processes (See the Reference I).

11) The previous site may have peripheral walls too. If the east-west distance of the site is the same as the current site, it is highly possible that internal size was sufficient for a pair of Libraries.

12) It would have been possible to build Gopura I (L) in front of the Mandapa (B') if it had a small porch. However, the layout of the two Libraries facing toward the center of the site seemed to force the installation of two doorways placed on both sides of Gopura I (L) more toward the interior than usual. This caused the arrangement of three doorways at short intervals, which also caused difficulty in installing a porch at the central doorway.

13) There are many cases of layouts with libraries away from the center of the site. It is common to install Libraries in the area surrounded by Galleries or peripheral walls. For example, the Libraries at Ta Kev Temple are installed in the middle of the Galleries. Two Libraries at Beng Mealea Temple and three Libraries at Angkor Vat Temple are similarly installed inside Galleries or peripheral walls.

14) For convenience, we call the axis that equally divides the site looking from the front the "central line", and the axis running through the middle of buildings standing in a line, such as Gopura, Mandapa, and Central Sanctuary, the "central axis". At Hindi temples built in the Khmer Empire, the central lines and central axes do not usually match, but are slightly deflected. Since 1993, we have conducted measurement surveys

Chapter 3 : Study Reports on Preah Vihear Temple

内側に寄せて設けることを強いたようにみえる。このため３つの入口が短い間隔で並ぶことになり，このことも中央の入口にポーチを施設することを難しくしたようである。

13) 経蔵が伽藍の中心から離れて配置された例は多いが，回廊ないし周壁で囲まれた敷地内に配置されることが常法のようである。例えばタ・ケオの経蔵は，中段に位置するが回廊の中に配置される。ベン・メアレア寺院の二対の経蔵もアンコール・ワット寺院の三対の経蔵も，それぞれ回廊ないし周壁の中に配置される点は同様である。

14) 便宜的に，正面から見て伽藍を左右に等分する軸線を「中心線」，ゴープラ―拝殿―中央祠堂など１列に連なる建築群の中心を貫く軸線を「中軸線」と呼称する。クメールのヒンドゥー寺院では，中軸線は中心線に合致せず，僅かに偏向することが通例である。

1993年以後，実測調査の対象としたクメール伽藍は80件を超えるが，例外なく中軸線の偏向が認められる。左右非対称の構成を実現するために，回廊の窓幅あるいは窓間壁の寸法を以て調整する遺構も多く，一見して非対称が判る遺構も多い。なお，中軸線を偏向させる技法は，時代により一定しない。それぞれの技法の特徴については，参考文献VI) にて詳述している。

15) パルマンティエは，第１伽藍と第２伽藍の基壇が一体であることを指摘している。前掲注３）参照。

16) 個々の遺構の分析結果については参考文献I) 〜 IX) を参照。尺度の諸問題については参考文献X) を参照。専制国家の造営事業は単一の長さを持つ公定尺を造営尺度として用いたと考えることが自然である。しかし理念として固定した長さであっても，実際の造営の場面では，遺構ごとにわずかな相違が現れることが通例である。この相違の範囲を含んでハスタの実長を412±1mmと判断している。個々の建築遺構を対象に分析を行なうと，施工誤差が大きく造営尺度の想定に大きな幅が現れるが，伽藍計画の分析を通じて比較的精度の高い造営尺度の実長を抽出することが可能である。

17) 建立当時，寸法基準を体現した位置は，さまざまな可能性が考えられるが，各所で基準位置を仮定し，逐一検討した結果，寸法計画の基準となった位置は，基座の外端位置と判断することになった。参考文献I) では，ジャヤヴァルマンVII時代の宿駅と考えられる東タイに点在する小規模伽藍19件の分析を行っている。この分析で周壁外の基座外端の位置が伽藍規模を体現していることを論じた。また，各伽藍の個々の分析は，参考文献II), IV), VII) にて詳述している。基座の外端の位置は，遺構の最大の輪郭を形成しており，伽藍内の配置計画の際に規模計画としても機能する位置である。

18) 東側の北端（翼廊Pの北面）は基座が省略されており，第１回廊（A'）の南端は断崖に踏み出すためやや変形している。このため南西角の位置の寸法資料を用いる。この値から算出した造営尺度は411.8mm程になるが，実測地点それぞれで値が乱れるため，分析では412mmを用いる。

19) 山頂伽藍の長短辺の合計値が300.0ハスタ丁度になるという指摘は，以下の論考で発表された。

---

at 80 sites in the Khmer Empire. Deflected central axis was observed in all cases. In order to realize an asymmetric structure, many layouts were adjusted based on the window width or distance between windows in Galleries, and clearly show an asymmetric structure. Methods of deflecting the central axis are not consistent. Characteristics of each method are described in reference VI.

15) Parmentier pointed out that the platform of Complex I and II is unified. See Note 3).

16) See Reference I-IX for the results of analysis for the individual sites. See Reference X for issues of scale. It is natural to assume that a dictatorship would often use the official scale unit that had a fixed length. Although the official scale unit had fixed length, it is often the case that small gaps may appear at each site. Including the range of such gaps, we assumed the measurement of hasta was 412±1 mm. Analysis of individual sites reveals significant gaps in construction, which lead to significant gaps in the assumption of construction scale. However, it is possible to obtain the actual length of the construction scale that is relatively accurate through an analysis of the site plan.

17) There are many possibilities for the standard point of reference for the dimentional plan when it was built. However, according to the past analysis conducted by temporarily placing standard points in various sections, we determined it as the outer end of the base. Reference I analyzed 19 small sites, which are considered to be post towns in the eraof Jayavarman VII, scattered around the eastern side of Thailand. In thestudy, we examined whether the location of the outer end of the base determined the size of the complex. In addition, analyses of the individual site are described in References II), IV), and VII). The outer end of the base forms the maximum outline of the site, which also functions as a standard for scale planning when establishing the interior site layout plan.

18) The north end of the east side (north side of Gallery II (P)) does not have a base, and the south end of Gallery I (A') is deformed, perhaps because it was extended to the cliff. Therefore, we used the size at the southwest corner as reference. Construction scale calculated by these figures was 411.8 mm. However, figures varied depending on the measurement points. Therefore, we applied 412 mm for the analysis.

19) The following study pointed out that the total north-south and east-west distance of the Complexes at the highest point of the mountain is 300.0 hasta.

Shu Ogihara: Layout Planning at the Preah Vihear Temple, Waseda University Collection of Theses, 2012. 11

20) Scale planning of the front part of Prasat Thom Temple is based on 400 hasta in east-west direction and 360 hasta in north-south direction centering on the small previous site, adding 1 vyama (4 hasta) to the south and shortening 1 vyama in the east-west direction to 396 hasta. In order to misalign the central axis with the central line that equally separates the site into two we speculated that the proportion of the rectangle was changed without changing the total figure of the outer circumference. See Reference 6.

21) See Reference II for the scale of central sanctuary at Banteay Samure Temple and Thommanon Temple. It stated that the scale was 40 hasta. There is a possibility that the Central Sanctuary at Preah Vihear Temple

荻原周：プレア・ヴィヘアの伽藍配置計画，早稲田大学卒業論文，2012.11

20）プラサート・トム寺院前半部の伽藍規模計画は，小規模な前身伽藍を中央に据えて東西400ハスタ，南北360ハスタとする規模計画をもとに，南に1ヴィヤマ（4ハスタ）の帯を加え，東西を1ヴィヤマ縮小して396ハスタとする。伽藍を2等分する中心線から中軸線を外すため，外周の合計値を変えずに矩形のプロポーションを変更したものと判断した。参考文献Ⅵ）を参照。

21）バンテアイ・サムレ寺院，トマノン寺院の中央祠堂の規模については，参考文献Ⅱ）を参照。同論考にて40ハスタの規模であったことを述べている。プレア・ヴィヘア寺院の中央祠堂は，これより小さく36ハスタ程の規模であった可能性も残るが，回廊内で無理の生じない最大の値を想定した。

22）2棟の経蔵の背面の基座は埋没しており，全体を確認できない。一部地表に露出している基座の長さを参考に推定している。

23）第2ゴープラ（D）の実測値は乱れがあるが，東西翼では北半の東西幅を60ハスタ，南半を57ハスタ，南北翼の北半の長さを真から30ハスタ，南半を27ハスタと判断した。

24）碑文記録から1036年頃の建立が想定されたワット・エク寺院（バッタンバン）の中央祠堂は，プレア・ヴィヘア寺院の中央祠堂とよくにた規模を持つ。プレア・ヴィヘア寺院の中央祠堂のポーチの奥行きは，この遺構の2/3程にすぎず，規模に比べて異例の構成と考えられる。

25）第4ゴープラは斜面に建っており，地表面が低い北面は基座を2段重ね，南面は基壇高さ中程まで埋没している。現状では南面基座が不明なため，一旦基壇外側を手がかりとした。わずかな相違も予想されるが発掘調査を待って再検討したい。

26）参考文献Ⅳ）等

27）溝口明則，中川武，下田一太，佐藤桂，石塚充雅：プレア・ヴィヘア寺院山頂伽藍の寸法計画，クメール建築の造営尺度と設計技術に関する研究（7），日本建築学会計画系論文集697号，pp.817-825，2014.3

28）第3ゴープラの付属建物も基座が埋没しており，推定位置を手がかりとしている。今後，発掘調査によっては，わずかな相違が現れる可能性が残る。

29）実測値では第5〜第4ゴープラ，第4〜第3ゴープラのいずれの距離にも伸びが認められるため，第3ゴープラ以南の値がやや圧迫されたと考えられる。

30）基座外端を規準位置とする考え方は，私たちの感覚からすると違和感がないわけではないが，建物の寸法計画に連動する方法的一貫性に注目すべきであろう。

was 36 hasta, slightly smaller than 40 hasta; however, we assumed the maximum width that would be appropriate for the relative positions inside the gallery.

22) The base in the back of the two Libraries is buried, making it impossible to see the overall structure. This was estimated in reference to the length of the base whose part appears above the ground.

23) Actual Gopura II (D) measurements varied; however, we assumed the east-west distance in the north half to be 60 hasta, east-west distance in the south half to be 57 hasta, the length of north half of the north-south transept to be 30 hasta, and the length of the south half of the north-south side room to be 27 hasta.

24) The structure of central sanctuary at Vat Ek Phnom Temple (Battambang), which was thought to be built around 1036 according to the inscriptions, is similar to the Central Sanctuary at Preah Vihear Temple. The depth of the porch at the Central Sanctuary at Preah Vihear Temple is only 2/3 of this complex, which is unusual compared with the overall scale.

25) Gopura IV is built on a slope. The north side, which stands on lower land, has a double-layered base; and the south side, which stands on higher land, is buried up to the middle of the platform. Current conditions do not allow clarification of the base of the south side; therefore, we used the outside of the platform for estimation. Although there may be some differences from the actual conditions, we would like to reconsider after the excavation survey.

26) Reference IV) etc

27) Akinori Mizoguchi, Takeshi Nakagawa, Ichita Shimoda, Katsura Sato, Mitsumasa Ishizuka: On the Dimensional Planning at Preah Vihear Temple Complex on the Crest: Study on the dimensional plan and the planning method of Khmer architecture No.7, Architectural Institute of Japan Collection of Theses on Architectural Planning, No. 697, pp.817-825, 2014.3

28) The base of the Annex Building of Gopura III is also buried. Therefore, an estimated location was used. There is a possibility that there will be a slight gap from future excavation surveys.

29) The actual distance between Gopura V and IV and Gopura IV and III were longer than the estimates, which shows that the figures in the south from Gopura III were slightly reduced.

30) Although we cannot completely agree with setting the baseline at the outer end of the base, the consistency of building size planning is worth noting.

Chapter 3 : Study Reports on Preah Vihear Temple

References

I) Compiled under the Supervision of Takeshi Nakagawa: Research Reports of the Field Investigation of Asia's Historic Architecture, Waseda University Asian Architecture Study Team, 1999.

II) Akinori Mizoguchi, Takeshi Nakagawa, Takashi Asano, Naoya Saito: On the Dimensional Plan of the Complex in Thommanon and Banteay Samre: Study on the dimensional plan and the planning method of Khmer architecture No. 1, Architectural Institute of Japan Collection of Theses on Architectural Planning, No. 612, pp.131-138, 2007.2.

III) Akinori Mizoguchi, Yasushi Akazawa, Takeshi Nakagawa, Yoshihiko Chubachi: On the Dimensional Plan in Prasat Suor Prat Tower N1: Study on the dimensional plan and the planning method of Khmer architecture No.2, Architectural Institute of Japan Collection of Theses on Architectural Planning, No. 616, pp.175-181, 2007.6.

IV) Akinori Mizoguchi, Takeshi Nakagawa, Katsura Sato, Ichita Shimoda, Daisuke Furukawa: The ancient Khmer's construction measure at the Prang in Koh Ker: Study on the dimensional plan and the planning method of Khmer architecture No.3, Architectural Institute of Japan Collection of Theses on Architectural Planning, No. 640, pp.1449-1455, 2009.6.

V) Akinori Mizoguchi, Takeshi Nakagawa, Katsura Sato, Ichita Shimoda: On the Dimensional Plan in Prasat Pram: Study on the dimensional plan and the planning method of Khmer architecture No.4, Architectural Institute of Japan Collection of Theses on Architectural Planning, No. 651, pp.1273-1278, 2010.5.

VI) Akinori Mizoguchi, Takeshi Nakagawa, Katsura Sato, Ichita Shimoda: On the Dimensional Plan of the Complex in Prasat Pram: Study on the dimensional plan and the planning method of Khmer architecture No. 5, Architectural Institute of Japan Collection of Theses on Architectural Planning, No. 653, pp.1751-1759, 2010.7.

VII) Akinori Mizoguchi, Takeshi Nakagawa, Katusra Sato, Ichita Shimoda, Junya Momose: A Proposed Rational Behind the Ancient Khmer's Dimensional Planning at the Beng Mealea: Study on the dimensional plan and the planning method of Khmer architecture (No.6), Architectural Institute of Japan Collection of Theses on Architectural Planning, No. 671, pp.157-164, 2012.1.

VIII) Compiled under the Supervision of Takeshi Nakagawa: The Master Plan for the Conservation & Restoration of the Bayon Complex, Japanese Government Team for Safeguarding Angkor, 2005.

IX) Compiled under the Supervision of Takeshi Nakagawa: Report on Construction for Restoration of Prasat Suor Prat Tower, Japanese Government Team for Safeguarding Angkor, 2005.

X) Akinori Mizoguchi: Numbers and Architecture – Numbers that Supported Ancient Architectural Techniques, Kashima Shuppankai, 2007.

3.5　木造屋根の技法とプレア・ヴィヘア寺院遺構の編年
Survey of Wood Structure of the Ancient Khmer Ruins and a Chronicle of the Buildings in Preah Vihear Temple

溝口　明則

MIZOGUCHI Akinori

3.5.1 はじめに

　クメールの寺院は，早くからレンガ造であった中央祠堂を除き，伽藍内の多くの施設が木造であったこと，およびこれらの施設が次第に石造に置き換わっていったことは周知の事実である。その途上で，石造の壁体とペディメントを設け，木造の小屋組と瓦葺屋根を載せた木造と石造の混構造の時代が存在したこともよく知られている。プレア・ヴィヘア寺院は，クメール建築が全面的な石造化へ至る過渡期の時代に現れた木造の屋根と木造小屋組の痕跡を残す石造施設が多く残っており，この寺院の特徴のひとつになっている。これらの木造架構については，20世紀の前半のうちにH．パルマンティエによる復原案が示されたが[1]，以後，積極的な議論が少ない。

　木造から石造へ至る途上の段階では，木造架構と石材とを接続するという技術的に特別な状況が現れる。具体的な場面は，石造の壁体上面で起こる，石材と木造梁や垂木を接続するという状況である。この方法は，その上面に残る痕跡から，きわめて多様な技法が存在し，年代によって変化が認められる。建築全体からみて局所的な現象であるが，編年を考えるための手がかりのひとつとして取り扱うべき重要な研究対象である。

　本節では，石造の壁体上面に残る痕跡に注目し，コー・ケー遺跡群の事例やプレア・ヴィヘア寺院を含む同時代の遺構を比較し，技法の発達過程について素描する。またこれらの検討を通じて，プレア・ヴィヘア寺院の施設それぞれの建立年代について，できる限り明らかにすることを目標とする。

　プレア・ヴィヘア寺院は，掲載Figure 3.5-1のように5つの施設から成り立っている。これらは，北から順に第5ゴープラ（K），第4ゴープラ（J），第3ゴープラ（G）とその東西の付属建物H，I，H'，I'，第2伽藍（D，C，C'，P，P'，M，N，O）と第1伽藍（A，A'，B，B'，L）およびその東西の付属建物E，Fである。こ

3.5.1 Introduction

　It is a well-known fact that many facilities within Khmer temple complexes were made of wood, excluding the Central Sanctuary, which was built with bricks from an early period, and that these facilities were gradually replaced by stone facilities. It is also well known that within this process was a period in which wood and stone were used simultaneously. There were facilities with stone walls and pediments and a wooden roof frame on which was placed a tiled roof. Many stone facilities remain at Preah Vihear Temple. They display evidence of wooden roofs and roof frames that appeared when Khmer architecture went through a period of full-scale transition to stone facilities, and have become salient characteristics of the temple. A restoration drawing for these wooden structures was presented by H.Parmentier during the first half of the 20th century[1], but hardly any active discussion has evolved since then.

　During the period of transition from wood to stone, a technically unique circumstance occurred in which wooden structures and stone elements were joined together. This specifically refers to the situation at the top of stone walls, where stone elements were connected to wooden tie beams and rafters. Judging by traces remaining on the top surface, extremely diverse techniques for this method seem to have existed and changed according to era. The method is a local phenomenon when considering architecture as a whole, but it is an important subject for research that should be considered a hint for elucidating temple chronology. This paper compares the ruins of temples from the same time period, including examples at Koh Ker Monuments and Preah Vihear Temple, with a focus on traces remaining on top of the stone walls, and outlines the development process of structural techniques. Additionally, through this examination, an effort will be made to define the dates of construction of the facilities of Preah Vihear Temple as much as possible.

　Preah Vihear Temple is composed of five facilities, as shown

のうち第2伽藍と第1伽藍は接続しており，全体で山頂伽藍を形成している（建物に付した記号はパルマンティエに倣う）。これらの施設のうち，疑似ゴープラ（A）は迫り出し構造のレンガ造屋根を載せた痕跡を残し，中央祠堂（B），拝殿（B'），第2伽藍の2つの経蔵（C，C'），第1伽藍を区画する第1回廊（A'）は石造屋根を載せている。その他の施設は，いずれも木造小屋組の痕跡を残している。

3.5.2 現状と先行研究

　木造小屋組に関する先行研究は限られるが，J. デュマルセによるまとまった提案[2]やこの提案について批判的な検討を加えた澤田知香，上野邦一両氏の提案などがある[3]。J. デュマルセの木造架構の提案は，パルマンティエの復原案などに批判的な検討を加えつつ提案されており，瓦の分析からレリーフに描かれた屋根形式の検討，周辺地域に残る木造架構の類例に至るまで，木造架構のさまざまな手がかりを網羅し検討を尽くそうとしている。とくにカンボジア周辺地域の木造架構の検討を通じ，クメールの木造小屋組が二重の梁と束によって構成されていたとする解釈は，他の可能性を完全に排除しきれてはいないが，強い説得力を持っている。ただ，個々の遺構の木造屋根の復原案については検討の余地が残されたようである。例えばバンテアイ・スレイ寺院付属建物，タ・プロム寺院付属建物の復原案については，澤田知香，上野邦一両氏による再検討が行われ，適切な修正案が示された。

　しかし先行研究は，いずれも木造小屋組全体をとり上げて検討している。寺院建築の石造化の過程で，技術的に大きな問題になったであろう石材と木造屋根部材の接続法については，積極的な検討が進められてきたわけではない。石材と木材の接続法について技術的解決を模索していった過程の検討は，プレア・ヴィヘア寺院の木造小屋組を復原するためにも必須の作業であるとともに，それぞれの施設の編年にとっても重要な手がかりである。

　プレア・ヴィヘア寺院各建物の建立年代を検討するための指標として，パルマンティエが試みた編年のうち木造屋根を持つ遺構に限定して以下に整理する。ただ，パルマンティエは，この編年を仮説に過ぎないとしている点に留意したい。
1）「ヤショヴァルマンの後継者」の時代。
・第1ゴープラ（L），ホールN，第2ゴープラ（D），第2伽藍翼廊（P）。
2）ラージェンドラヴァルマンⅡまたはジャヤヴァルマンⅤの時代。
・付属建物E，F。

in Figure 3.5-1. From the north, they are Gopura V (K); Gopura IV (J); Gopura III (G) and Annex Buildings on its east and west sides (H, I, H', I'); Complex II (D, C, C', P, P', M, N, O); and Complex I (A, A', B, B', L) and Annex Buildings I, I', H, H', E and F on its east and west sides. Complexes I and II are connected, and the facilities as a whole form a Mountaintop complex. (The alphabets given to each building are by Parmentier.) Among these facilities, False Gopura (A) shows traces of a projecting brick roof. Central Sanctuary (B), Mandapa (B'), the two Libraries (C and C') of Complex II, and Gallery I (A') that defines the boundary of Complex I, have a stone roof. The other facilities all show traces of a wooden roof frame.

3.5.2 Present State and Prior Studies

Although prior studies on wooden roof frames are limited, there is the theory compiled by J.Dumarçay[2] and a theory presented by C.Sawada and K.Ueno[3], which incorporates a critical examination of Dumarçay's theory. Dumarçay's theory is based on a critical examination of Parmentier's restoration drawing, and is an attempt to comprehensively study diverse clues regarding wooden structures, ranging from an analysis of roofing tiles to a study of roof styles that display reliefs and comparisons with similar wooden structure remains in the surrounding area. In particular, Dumarçay's interpretation that Khmer wooden roof frames were composed of double tie beams and vertical posts, based on an examination of wooden structures in surrounding areas in Cambodia, is strongly persuasive, even though it does not completely eliminate other possibilities. Even so, there is still room for further examination concerning the restoration drawings for the wooden roof of each ruins. For example, C.Sawada and K.Ueno have reexamined the restoration drawings for the Annex Buildings at Banteay Srei Temple and Ta Prohm Temple and have presented a proper revised drawing.

These prior studies deal with wooden roof frames as a whole, however. Active studies have not necessarily focused on the method of connecting stone elements and wooden roof elements, which probably posed a large technical issue in the process of the transition of temple architecture to stone. Conducting a study of the process through which technical solutions had been sought for connecting stone and wooden elements is necessary for restoring the wooden roof frames of Preah Vihear Temple, and an important clue to assessing the chronology of the facilities.

As an index for assessing the date of construction of each buildings of Preah Vihear Temple, the chronology attempted by Parmentier is organized as shown below with regard to ruins with a wooden roof. It should be noted, however, that Parmentier developed this chronology as no more than a theory.

3）スールヤヴァルマンIの時代
- 第3ゴープラ付属建物H，IおよびH'，I'，第4ゴープラ（J），第5ゴープラ（K），第3ゴープラ（G）（未完）。

4）ウダヤディティヤヴァルマンの時代
- 第3ゴープラ（G）（崩落した屋根レンガ材の除去と瓦屋根の造営）。

5）スールヤヴァルマンIIの時代
- ホールNのポーチ，第2ゴープラ（D）のポーチの改造。

一方，S. サハイの編年の整理では，第3ゴープラ東西の付属建物を11世紀後半とするほかは，木造屋根の痕跡を持つ建物については積極的な言及が少ない[4]。

1) The era of Yasovarman I's successor
 ・Gopura I (L) and Hall N, Gopura II (D) and Gallery II (P) of Complex II
2) The era of Rajendravarman II or Jayavarman V
 ・Annex Buildings E and F
3) The era of Suryavarman I
 ・Annex Buildings H, I, H', and I' of Gopura III, Gopura IV (J), Gopura V (K), Gopura III (G) (unfinished)
4) The era of Udayadityavarman
 ・Gopura III (G) (removal of collapsed brick elements of the roof)
5) The era of Suryavarman II
 ・Renovation of the porch of Hall N and the porch of Gopura II (D)

Note that in S.Sahai's chronological organization, the Annex Buildings on the east and west sides of Gopura III are dated to the latter half of the 11th century, but there is little mention of buildings with a wooden roof trace[4].

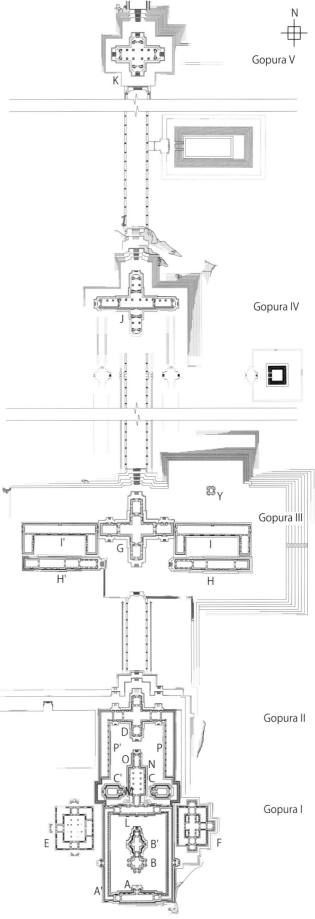

Figure 3.5-1 Each Structure Plan of Preah Vihear Temple

3.5.3 木造小屋組と壁体上部の収まり

石造壁体上部と木造小屋組の接合法について、私たちが知ることのできる最初の事例はコー・ケーが首都であった時代の遺跡群である。年代的にみて、この時代以前の建物はおそらくまだ、石造構造体と木造架構が混在する構造はほとんど存在しなかった。したがってこの時代を嚆矢として混構造が発生したと捉えてよいであろう。以下時代に沿ってそれぞれの様相を見ていこう。

3.5.3.1 コー・ケー遺跡群

コー・ケー遺跡群のプラサート・トム寺院の付属建物やプラサート・クラチャップ寺院のゴープラ付属翼廊では、木造梁を用いるが木造軒桁を持たず、いずれもラテライトの壁体最上部に載せられた砂岩材に、直接仕口を刻んで梁を接合している。壁体はいずれもラテライト造だが、仕口はかなり複雑なものであるから、仕口の加工のために最上部材に限って砂岩材を採用したのだと考えられる。垂木はこの石材の上面に下端を引っかけ固定するための浅い溝を掘り、ここに直接当てている[5]。Figure 3.5-2はその様相を図示したもので、左図は複雑な形状だが「相欠」に類する接合法を持つ。同様の形式は、プラサート・トム寺院の付属建物の複数の建物においても認められる[6]。右図は「あり落とし」（ダブ・テイル）の形状を持つ仕口で、局所に限定して使われている[7]。これらの例は、いずれもコー・ケー遺跡群が首都であった時代、10世紀前半に遡ると考えられる。

3.5.3 The Assembly of Wooden Roof Frames and Upper Walls

The first known example of the method of joining the top of the stone walls and a wooden roof frame is that which is seen in ruins dating from a period when the capital was located in Koh Ker Monuments. In terms of chronology, buildings made of both stone and wood structures scarcely existed before then. Therefore, stone-wood mixed structures can be said to have appeared for the first time during this period. Below is a description of the appearance of each method of assembly, in chronological order.

3.5.3.1 Koh Ker Monuments

At Koh Ker Monuments, the Annex Buildings at Prasat Thom Temple and the Gallery besides Gopura at Prasat Krachap Temple had wooden tie beams but no wooden eave girders. In both cases, joints were made directly in sandstone elements placed on the laterite walls, and the tie beams were attached to these joints. The walls were all made of laterite, but because the joints were complex, sandstone elements were used as the topmost elements of the walls to process the joints in addition to creating moldings. To hook and secure the bottom of the rafters on the stone elements, a shallow groove was made in the top surface of the stone elements, and the bottom of the rafters was placed directly in contact with the groove[5]. This is shown in Figure 3.5-2. The drawing on the left in Figure 3.5-2 appears complex, but shows a joining method that uses a type of cross lap joint. A similar method is also seen in multiple buildings composing the Annex Buildings of Prasat Thom Temple[6]. The drawing on the right in Figure 3.5-2 is a dovetailed tenon, found in restricted locations[7]. It is thought that these examples date back to the first half of the 10th century, during the era when the capital was located in Koh Ker Monuments.

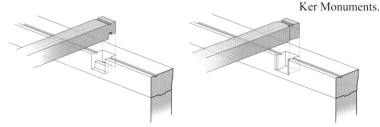

Figure 3.5-2 Gallery besides Gopura at Prasat Krachap Temple

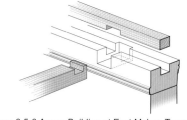

Figure 3.5-3 Annex Building at East Mebon Temple

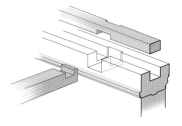

Figure 3.5-4 Annex building at Pre Rup Temple

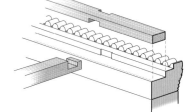

Figure 3.5-5 Central part of an Annex Building at Ta Kev Temple

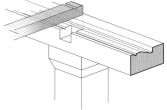

Figure 3.5-6 Porch of an Annex Building at Ta Kev Temple

3.5.3.2 東メボン寺院，プレ・ルプ寺院

　東メボン寺院の付属建物に見られる木造軒桁は，壁体上面に沿って石材の中央に埋め込まれる（Figure 3.5-3）。この収まりは，プロポーションにやや相違を持つものの，プレ・ルプ寺院の付属建物も同様である（Figure 3.5-4）。壁体頂部の石材は，軒桁の断面に合わせて深く彫り込まれて凹型の断面を持つ。軒桁の上面は壁体上面に合致し，垂木を受けるために露出していたと思われる。壁体上面に高さを合わせた木造梁は，コー・ケーの時代と同様の位置を維持するが，石材の中で，埋め込まれた軒桁と仕口によって接合される。この接合部は，おそらく簡単な「相欠」に類する仕口であった。埋め込まれた軒桁は，梁を固定し垂木を受けるための部材と考えられるが，一方，木造梁は構造材である。このため梁は軒桁よりも一段と太い[8]。したがって軒桁よりも低い敷面を取るから，両者が接合する位置の石材は，やや複雑な形状に加工されている。

3.5.3.3 タ・ケオ寺院

　一方，タ・ケオ寺院の付属建物では，壁体の上面に軒桁を載せ，軒先瓦を並べた形状を持つ石材が，軒桁外側の面に接するように置かれる。軒桁の敷面と梁の敷面を同一面とするため，仕口の様相はさまざまに考えられるが，軒桁の「成」に比して構造材である梁の成はおそらく一段と高かった可能性が大きい。明確な痕跡が認められないが，梁を下方，軒桁を上方とする「相欠」様の仕口であったと考えられる。とすれば，Figure 3.5-5に描画したような収まりが予想される。

　ところがポーチでは，Figure 3.5-6に示したように，石梁上面に，垂木を架ける浅い溝と瓦を収めるやや深く広い溝が直接施設され，石材に，梁の端を落とし込む簡単な仕口が施されている。木造の軒桁を用いず石材に直接梁と垂木を架ける点はコー・ケー遺跡群の技法と同様だが，梁を受ける石材に複雑な仕口を設けることはない。

3.5.3.4 バンテアイ・スレイ寺院

　バンテアイ・スレイ寺院の伽藍中心部四周に配置された付属建物の木造小屋組については，先に述べたように澤田，上野両氏によって再検討された。この議論はJ. デュマルセの復原案に批判的検討を加え，改造が行われたとする的確な復原案が提出されているが[9]，この復原案に補足的な検討を加えたい。

　改造痕跡は壁体の嵩上げを伴うもので，現在のペディメントよりも少し背の低いペディメントが存在していた時代が予想されている。当初の軒桁は，凹型断

3.5.3.2 East Mebon Temple, Pre Rup Temple

Wooden eave girders seen in the Annex Buildings at East Mebon Temple were embedded directly in the center of the stone elements in line with the top surface of the wall (Figure 3.5-3). This type of assembly is also found in the Annex Buildings of Pre Rup Temple, although they differ slightly in terms of proportion (Figure 3.5-4). The stone elements on the walls have a deep U-shaped cross section to match the cross section of the eave girders. The top surface of the eave girders matches the top surface of the walls and was probably exposed to receive the rafters. The wooden tie beams that were made to match the height of the top surface of the walls remain in the same position as during the Koh Ker period, but were joined by an eave girder and joint embedded in the stone element. This was probably a type of cross lap joint, judging by the relative height of its bench, the shape of its cross section and traces left by the end of a tie beam. While the embedded eave girders probably served to fix the tie beams in place and receive the rafters, the wooden tie beams were structural components. For this reason, the tie beams were thicker than the eave girders[8]. Because the tie beams had a lower bench than the eave girders, the part of the stone elements where the two were joined had a rather complex appearance.

3.5.3.3 Ta Kev Temple

In the Annex Buildings at Ta Kev Temple, eave girders were placed on the walls, and stone elements that appear to be decorated with eave tiles were placed so that they connect to the outer face of the eave girders. As the benches of the eave girders and tie beams were the same, various joints could be imagined, but it is likely that the tie beams, as a structural component, were slightly higher in height than the eave girders. Although no clear traces were found, the tie beams and eave girders probably formed a type of cross lap joint, with the tie beam on the bottom and eave girder on top. If so, the assembly as shown in Figure 3.5-5 could be assumed.

In the porch, however, stone beams had a shallow groove for receiving the rafters and a rather deeper and wider groove for fitting the tiles carved directly in their top surface, as shown in Figure 3.5-6, and a simple joint for installing the ends of the tie beams was made in the stone elements. The method of directly placing tie beams and rafters on the stone elements without using wooden eave girders is the same as at Koh Ker Monuments, but the stone elements that receive the tie beams did not have a complex joint.

3.5.3.4 Banteay Srei Temple

The wooden roof frames of the Annex Buildings positioned

面の最上部材（ラテライト）に埋め込まれていた痕跡を残しており，東メボン寺院，プレ・ルプ寺院と同様の収まりであった。しかし後の改造時に，軒桁を取り去ってラテライト材の外半を極小の庇屋根の形状に整形し，軒桁が収まっていた空隙をレンガで埋めた痕跡が確認される[10]。そしてこの上に，背の低い腰壁と軒の形をつくりだした砂岩のブロックを重ね，ごく小さな形状だが，経蔵などにみられる庇屋根を持つ姿に改造している。この砂岩ブロックは，削り直された小さな庇屋根の形状を確保しようとして不安定な位置に置かれている。このためブロックどうしを上面の「契り」で繋ぐ処理が施されている。改造時に積載したこの石材は，上部室内側に軒桁を載せる整形が施されており，全体として太いL字型の断面を持っている。タ・ケオ寺院の付属建物では別材を用いるが，外側を立ち上げた石材の上面に軒桁を据える点で同様の技法であり，改造前に見られた軒桁を石材に埋め込む技法とは異なっている。

改造後の梁の痕跡は，残存状態が悪く確認できないが，改造過程で当初の軒桁を取り去っているから，軒桁と接合する仕口を持った梁だけがそのまま残ることは考え難い。したがって改造前と同位置の直上に，あらたに架け直されたと考えられる（Figure 3.5-7）。改造後の梁の相対位置は，タ・ケオ寺院の事例などから，新しい軒桁と上面どうしを合わせた位置であったと考

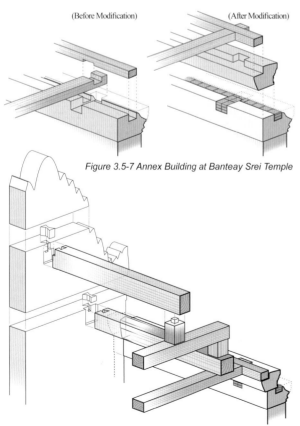

Figure 3.5-7 Annex Building at Banteay Srei Temple

Figure 3.5-8 Annex Building at Banteay Srei Temple: restoration of the roof frame after modification

on the four sides of the central area of Complex of Banteay Srei Temple have been reexamined by Sawada and Ueno, as mentioned earlier. They added a critical examination of J.Dumarçay's restoration drawing and submitted a proper restoration drawing of modifications that were assumed to be made[9]. Below is a supplementary observation to this restoration drawing.

There were traces of modification indicating that the walls were raised, and suggest that a pediment slightly lower than the present pediment had existed at one time. There are traces showing that original eave girders were embedded in the topmost elements (laterite) that displayed a U-shaped cross section, as at East Mebon Temple and Pre Rup Temple. However, there were traces showing that the eave girders were removed in later modifications, and that the outer half of the laterite elements was shaped into a small eaves roof and the spaces where the eave girders were mounted were filled with bricks[10]. A low spandrel wall and sandstone blocks shaped like eaves were stacked on top of these bricks to create the appearance of an eaves roof, which although small, was often seen in library buildings. The sandstone blocks were placed in an unstable position, unnaturally lowered toward the chamber side, to retain the shape of the re-carved small eaves roof. For this reason, the top surfaces of the blocks were connected by butterfly joints. These stone elements that were installed at the time of modification were shaped to receive the eave girders on their upper chamber side, and display a thick L-shaped cross section as a whole. The Annex Buildings at Ta Kev Temple use a different type of material, but display the same technique of mounting the eave girders on top of stone elements that have a higher outer side, and differ from the technique of embedding the eave girders in the stone elements as seen before the modification.

Traces made by tie beams after modification are in poor condition and cannot be confirmed, but since the original eave girders had been removed in the modification process, it is not reasonable to think that only the tie beams that were joined with the eave girders were left as they are. Thus, it is thought that new tie beams were installed in the same positions as before the modification (Figure 3.5-7). Since the height of the top surface of the eave girders correspond to traces of the lower edge of purlin dado joints that remain on the pediment, the top surface of the tie beams that were installed between the dado joints probably matched the top surface of the eave girders. This is the same type of assembly as the case examples at Ta Kev Temple. This also means that the roof frame directly supported the purlins without using vertical posts on the tie beams (Figure 3.5-8).

The laterite elements at the top of the walls in the corners of

えられる。桁と梁の上面の高さは，ペディメントに残る母屋桁の大入れ痕跡の下端に当たる。したがって梁上に束を用いず，母屋桁を直接載せた小屋組であったと考えられる（Figure 3.5-8）。

建物隅に位置する壁体上部のラテライト材も，当初材の軒桁を受けていた痕跡を残している。改造後に屋根型に削られ変形しているが，それでも当初の軒桁が妻側に突き抜け，木口を見せていた痕跡が認められる。これは東メボン寺院やプレ・ルプ寺院の妻側に見られる痕跡と同様で，軒桁の端と木造の破風板が接合していたことを予想させる。Figure 3.5-10はプレ・ルプ寺院の付属建物に見られる痕跡から，破風板との収まりを推定した図である。Figure 3.5-9は東メボン寺院の壁体上部の砂岩材にある妻側の痕跡である。主室上部のいずれの砂岩材も，軒桁が突き抜けていた痕跡とともに，その下部に破風板の下端を載せた突出部がみてとれる。木造破風板の形状については不明だが，この突出部の形状から，石造に置き換えられた姿と極端に異なることはなかったと予想される[11]。破風板が木造であり，壁体上面に木造の桁が埋め込まれた痕跡を残すから，妻壁もまた木造であったであろう[12]。したがって，バンテアイ・スレイ寺院付属建物の当初のペディメントも木造であった。

現在の妻壁には母屋桁の浅い大入れ跡が残り，大入れ痕跡の中に「契り」を用いた痕跡を残している[13]。この痕跡はすべて，ペディメントを構成する石材上面の水平目地に合わせて施設されるから，母屋桁の高さに合わせて石材ブロックの高さを調整し，妻壁の石材と母屋桁とを交互に組むという作業過程が予想される。これらの特徴は，妻壁が薄いことに起因する工夫であったことが指摘されているが，当初，木造妻壁に合わせて下部の壁体を比較的薄い扱いとしたことに，本来の原因があったと考えられる。したがって一連の改造は，主に木造ペディメントを石造化しようとするものであった。その過程で軒桁の収まりの技法に変化が

the building have also left traces that show that they received the original eave girder elements. After modification, they became shaved down and deformed by the roofing, but the traces still indicate that the original eave girders had extended outside the gable side so that butt ends of the girders were visible. The same traces were also found on the gable side at East Mebon Temple and Pre Rup Temple, and suggest that the ends of the eave girders were joined to a wooden gable board. Figure 3.5-10 shows a drawing of the assembly of the eave girder with the wooden gable board, estimated from traces found in the annex building at Pre Rup Temple. Figure 3.5-9 shows traces that were found on the sandstone elements on top of the wall on the gable side at East Mebon Temple. All sandstone elements at the top of the main room clearly show traces that indicate that the eave girders extended beyond the gable side, and a projection at the bottom where the bottom edge of the gable board had been mounted. The shape of the wooden gable board is unknown, but judging by the shape of the projection, it probably did not differ much from its stone replacement[11]. The gable walls were also probably made of wood, since the gable boards were wood and remaining traces show that wooden girders were fitted onto the walls[12]. Thus, it is thought that the original pediments of the Annex Buildings at Banteay Srei Temple were also made of wood.

The present gable walls have shallow dado joints that received purlins, with some of them showing traces of having used butterfly joints[13]. Since these traces match the horizontal joints of the top surface of the stone elements that compose the pediment, it is thought that the height of the stone blocks were adjusted to match the height of the purlins, and the stone elements of the gable walls and purlins were assembled alternatingly. It is said that these features were applied as a measure to compensate for the gable walls that were thin, but the real reason was probably because the lower walls were originally made relatively thin to match the wooden gable walls. This is why the series of modifications mainly attempted to replace the wooden pediment

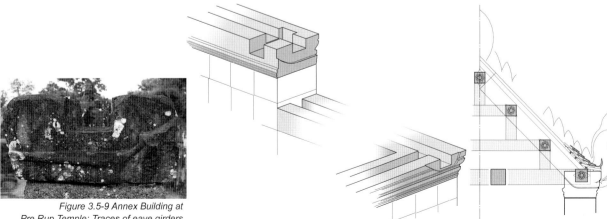

Figure 3.5-9 Annex Building at Pre Rup Temple: Traces of eave girders and estimation of a wooden gable wall

Figure 3.5-10 Annex Building at East Mebon Temple: Traces of eave girders and wooden gable

現れている。技法の特徴から見て，この改造は，タ・ケオ寺院付属建物の時代とそれほど離れない時代に行われたと考えられる。

3.5.4 プレア・ヴィヘア寺院の木造屋根に見られる軒桁と梁の様相
3.5.4.1 第1，2ゴープラ，付属建物H，ホールN

タ・ケオ寺院付属建物の主室（Figure 3.5-5）によく似た収まりは，プレア・ヴィヘア寺院の第1，第2ゴープラにも見られる。これらの建物のうち，第1，第2ゴープラでは，軒先の石材は立ち上がりが低く軒先瓦の形状も持たず，上面は外に向かって緩やかに下る勾配をとっている（Figure 3.5-11, 12）。勾配を持つ外半の上面は仕上げが粗く，別の石材を載せた形跡がないから，おそらく石材上面に，漆喰等で固定した軒先瓦を載せたと思われる。いずれも軒桁と梁の敷面を同一高さとするが，よく観察すると木造梁の輪郭に合わせて敷面をわずかに沈めている個所があることから，梁を下にして軒桁を被せた「相欠」様の接合であったとみられる。

第2伽藍のホールNの壁体上面の収まりも，第1，第2ゴープラなどと同様で，軒桁を内面に合わせて配置するよう削りとられた砂岩材を最上部に載せている。梁の端を収めた痕跡は第2ゴープラに比べて大きく，敷桁と梁が簡単な「相欠」様の仕口で接合されていたことを予想させる。敷面は，ポーチで梁の敷面をやや沈めた痕跡があり，第1，第2ゴープラと同様に，梁を下に敷き軒桁を被せた「相欠」様の接合法が予想される（Figure 3.5-13）。

3.5.4 Eave Girders and Tie Beams of Wooden Roofs at Preah Vihear Temple
3.5.4.1 Gopuras I & II, Annex Building H, Hall N

The assembly similar to that seen in the main room of the Annex Buildings at Ta Kev Temple (Figure 3.5-5) is also found in Gopuras I and II at Preah Vihear Temple. Of these buildings, the stone eave elements in Gopuras I and II are low, do not display shapes of eaves tiles, and have a top surface that gradually slopes down toward the outside (Figure 3.5-11, 12). The outside half of the sloping top surface has a rough finish, and there are no traces of having placed a different stone element, so it is thought that eaves tiles were placed on the stone elements and secured with stucco or other such material. The benches of the eave girders and tie beams are the same height, but close examination reveals that they are slightly lowered in some places to match the shape of the wooden tie beams. Thus it is thought that the joints were a type of cross lap joint, with the tie beam on the bottom covered by an eave girder from above.

The assembly at the top of the walls of Hall N in Complex II is similar to that in Gopuras I and II, with sandstone elements carved to match the inside surface of the eave girders placed at the top. The traces where the ends of the tie beams had been inserted are larger than those in Gopura II, and suggest that the eave girders and tie beams were simply joined by a type of cross lap joint. Traces show that the benches of the tie beams in the porch were slightly lowered, and like Gopuras I and II, it is thought that the joints were a type of cross lap joint, with the tie beam on the bottom covered by an eave girder from above (Figure 3.5-13).

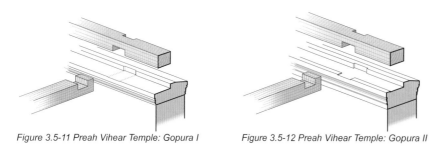

Figure 3.5-11 Preah Vihear Temple: Gopura I　　*Figure 3.5-12 Preah Vihear Temple: Gopura II*

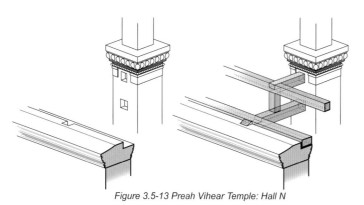

Figure 3.5-13 Preah Vihear Temple: Hall N

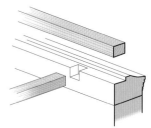

Figure 3.5-14 Preah Vihear Temple: Annex Building E

3.5.4.2 付属建物 E

付属建物Eでは，軒桁を壁体上面に載せ，梁は壁体上面に梁上端が位置するよう石材に直接架ける。したがって梁の位置は，軒桁に対し梁成ひとつ分下に位置する。石材はコー・ケー遺跡群のような仕口を持たず，タ・ケオ寺院付属建物のポーチの梁の収まりと同様である。軒桁は，梁の端を上から抑えるように積載される（Figure 3.5-14）。したがって軒桁と梁は上下に重なり接することになるが，直接的な接合がなかったか，ダボなどを用いて接合した可能性が高い。

3.5.4.3 第3ゴープラ付属建物 H, I, H', I'

第3ゴープラ付属建物H, I, H', I'は，一見して東西いずれも「口の字」平面の建物にみえるが，南辺に位置する「一の字」平面の建物と他の三方の辺を構成する「コの字」平面の建物とで構成されており，2つの建物の基壇は突きつけて接合しているから同時に計画されたものではない。構成は，まず「一の字」平面の建物が建ち，中庭を囲むように「コの字」平面の建物が後から接続されたと考えられる。この施設は第3ゴープラを挟み，対称性を以て東西に配置される。

2つの付属建物は一見してよく似ているが細部がかなり異なっている。とくに西建物のうち「一の字」平面建物H'は，東端ポーチを後から増築したことが明らかで，また同様の改造が西端でも見てとれる。西端は，連子窓を含んでこの位置から端まで改造が加えられたが未完成のままである。

西「一の字」平面建物H'の前身は建物中央部に残っており，確認できる範囲が限られるが，壁体最上部の砂岩材の仕口跡から，軒桁から1段下げて梁を架けて

3.5.4.2 Annex Building E

In Annex Building E, eave girders were placed on the walls, and tie beams were placed directly on the stone elements so that the top of the beams matched the top surface of the walls. The position of the tie beams, therefore, was one tie-beam height lower than the eave girders. The stone elements had the same assembly as the tie beams in the porches of the annex buildings at Ta Kev Temple, rather than that seen at Koh Ker Monuments. The eave girders were placed as though to hold down the ends of the tie beams from above (Figure 3.5-14). This means that the eave girders and tie beams were arranged on top of each other, but it is highly possible that they were not directly joined together, or were joined using doweled joints.

3.5.4.3 Annex Buildings H, I, H', I' of Gopura III

The Annex Buildings H, I, H', I' on the east and west sides of Gopura III appear to have a square ground plan, but they actually consist of a building with a linear ground plan forming the south side and a building with an U-shaped ground plan forming the other three sides. Moreover, the platforms of the two buildings are simply abutted against each other, meaning that they were not planned at the same time. It is thought that the linear buildings were built first, and the U-shaped buildings built later as through to enclose a courtyard. These facilities flank Gopura III, and are symmetrically arranged on the east and west.

The two Annex Buildings are similar at a glance, but significantly differ in their details. Of the buildings on the west, linear Annex Building H', in particular, clearly has a porch that was later added onto the east end, and a similar modification can also be seen on the west end. This portion of the west end,

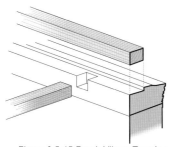

Figure 3.5-15 Preah Vihear Temple : Annex Building H' on west side of Gopura III

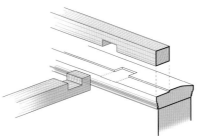

Figure 3.5-16 Preah Vihear Temple: Annex Building I' on west side of Gopura III

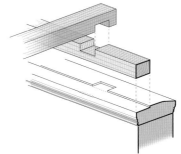

Figure 3.5-17 Preah Vihear Temple: Annex Building I on east side of Gopura III

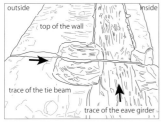
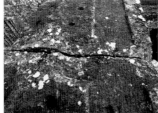

Figure 3.5-18 Preah Vihear Temple: Annex Building I on east side of Gopura III

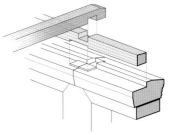

Figure 3.5-19 Preah Vihear Temple: traces at the top of the wall in porch of Annex Building H on the east side of Gopura III

いたことが判る（Figure 3.5-15）。この技法は付属建物Eと同様である。しかし西「コの字」平面の建物I'では、軒桁と梁が同一の敷面上で接続する。ただ、砂岩材の敷面を観察すると、梁が載った位置で、梁の輪郭に合わせて軒桁の敷面よりもわずかに沈めた形跡があるため、梁が下に、軒桁が上に位置する「相欠」様の接合であったことが判る（Figure 3.5-16）。

東側の付属建物のうち、「一の字」平面の建物Hの壁体上面の軒桁の敷面でも、同様に梁位置を軒桁敷面よりもわずかに沈めており、梁が下に軒桁が上に位置した接合であった。しかしポーチについては様相が異なる。ポーチ上部では、2つの砂岩材に跨ってつくり出された奇妙な仕口（背の低い矩形が敷面から作り出される）が認められる。これは窓間小壁の上で、石梁どうしを、軒桁を用いて繋ごうとした簡単な仕口の形状だと考えられる。したがって軒桁は、敷面およびつくりだした仕口に直接載ることになるから、木造梁は軒桁に対し上から接合したと考えるほかはない。東「一の字」平面建物Hのポーチでは、例外的に軒桁が下、梁が上という関係をとる（Figure 3.5-19）。

一方、東「コの字」平面の建物Iの敷面の状態は、反対に、梁と軒桁が交差する位置の敷面で、梁端が載る敷面がわずかに沈み、両者が交差する位置では軒桁の高さが維持される例がみられる（Figure 3.5-18）[14]。したがって、梁が上に軒桁が下に位置する接合であった（Figure 3.5-17）。

3.5.4.4 付属建物F

付属建物Fの外壁上部では、軒桁と梁が敷面を同じくして接合されたと見られるが、一部で梁の輪郭に合わせて軒桁敷面よりわずかに沈めた痕跡が残っている。したがって、梁が下、軒桁が上に位置する「相欠」様の接合が予想される。中庭に建つ石柱の上に木造桁の上面に梁を載せた痕跡が残り、木造桁は石梁下部の内側に施設される。一方、外壁上部では、石材が軒桁の上面を覆った形跡は認められない。これをFigure 3.5-20に示す。この図では、外壁上面の様相とともに、中庭の隅柱上の軒桁と梁の様子を復原している。

from the lattice window to the end, had been modified but left unfinished.

The predecessor of linear Annex Building H' on the west remains in the central part of the building. Although only limited scope can be confirmed, traces of the joints of the sandstone elements on top of the walls indicate that tie beams were installed in a position slightly below the eave girders (Figure 3.5-15). This technique is the same as that seen in Annex Building E. However, in U-shaped Annex Building I' on the west, the eave girders and tie beams were connected on the same bench. Nevertheless, a close observation of the benches on the sandstone elements reveal that at the positions of the tie beams, the benches were made slightly lower than the eave girders to match the shape of the tie beams. This means that the joints were a type of cross lap joint, with the tie beam on the bottom and eave girder on top (Figure 3.5-16).

Of the Annex Buildings on the east side, the benches of the eave girders at the top of the walls in linear Annex Building H were also made slightly lower than the benches of the eave girders at the positions of the tie beams, and indicated joints where the tie beam was positioned on the bottom and the eave girder on top. However, the situation differed in the porch. At the top of the porch, peculiar joints that saddled two sandstone elements were found (a low rectangular shape was formed by the benches). This is thought to be a simple joint adopted to connect two stone beams together using eave girders above the walls between windows. Since this means that the eave girders were placed directly on the bench and the joint that was created, the wooden tie beams had to have been joined from above the eave girders. Thus, in the porch of linear Annex Building H on the east, eave girders were positioned on the bottom and the tie beams on top, as an exception (Figure 3.5-19).

On the other hand, in U-shaped Annex Building I on the east, there were contrary examples in which the bench at positions where the tie beam and eave girder crossed each other was made slightly lower than the bench on which tie beam ends were placed, and where the two crossed each other, the height of the benches of the eave girders were retained (Figure 3.5-18) [14]. This indicated joints in which the tie beam was positioned on top and the eave girder on the bottom, as shown in Figure 3.5-17.

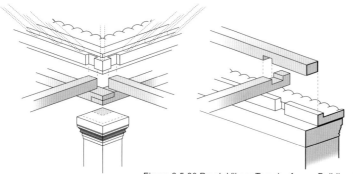

Figure 3.5-20 Preah Vihear Temple: Annex Building F

中庭の独立柱上に載る，一見して軒桁ともみえる部材は，梁よりも1段下という異例の位置に置かれるが，この位置では低すぎて垂木尻を収めることが難しい。したがって，独立柱上に載る木造桁は，軒桁ではなく石梁を支持し補強するための桁と考えなければならない。垂木は，石梁の形状から見て石梁上部の内角につくり出した隅に直接掛けていたと考えられる[15]。

3.5.4.5 第3，第4，第5ゴープラ

プレア・ヴィヘア寺院第3，第4，第5ゴープラでは，軒先瓦の形状を刻んだ石材は，軒桁側面ばかりでなく上面を，垂木の下端も含めて高い位置で覆うように加工される（Figure 3.5-21, 22, 23）。この収まりは，現存する石材の積載の様相からみて，壁体上面を加工して軒桁を設置し，さらに垂木を固定した後，軒瓦型を持つ石材を被せるように施設するという手順が予想される（Figure 3.5-21）。第1，第2ゴープラ，付属建物Eなどの考え方とは大きく異なっている。また，いずれのゴープラも太い十字形平面を持つため，軒桁の中間は，平面中央の交差部で中空に架かるから，この位置で梁に変化することになる。このため軒桁と梁は同一の部材となり同一の高さに架かる。軒桁と梁は，もともと性格の異なる部材だが，部材としての相違が消失すると考えてよい（Figure 3.5-22, 23）。敷面はよく整形され痕跡が明確ではないが，軒桁に架かる梁は，おそらく「相欠」様の仕口が開かないように軒桁を下に置き上から被せたとみられる[16]。この判断は，先に述べた第3ゴープラ東付属建物Hの出現によって，技法が推移したことが理解できるためである。

3.5.4.6 技法の整理

プレア・ヴィヘア寺院の木造屋根の遺構を検討するため，少ないながらも他の事例を集めて軒桁と梁の様相を整理した。壁体上部に施設された木造梁と軒桁を巡る様相は，以上のように多様な変化が見られる。

壁体上部の石材に直接仕口を施し，木造梁を架けようとしたコー・ケー遺跡群の事例を嚆矢として，東メボン寺院，プレ・ルプ寺院，バンテアイ・スレイ寺院改造前の各事例では，木造の軒桁が出現する。これは上面を見せて石材に完全に埋め込む収まりであった。木造梁は構造材であるため軒桁よりも一回り大きな断面を持つが，軒桁と上面を揃えて施設された。石材の痕跡は，梁が下から軒桁と噛み合う「相欠」様の仕口が存在したことを物語っている。しかしこの後，タ・ケオ寺院，プレア・ヴィヘア寺院の第1，第2ゴープラ，ホールN，第3ゴープラ付属建物H'，I，付属建物Eなどでは，軒桁は壁体上部に据えられ，外側面に石材

3.5.4.4 Annex Building F

At the top of the external wall of Annex Building F, eave girders and tie beams seem to have been joined on the same bench, but in some parts, there are traces that show that the benches of the tie beams were made slightly lower than the benches of the eave girders to match the shape of the tie beams. This suggests a type of cross lap joint in which the tie beam was positioned on the bottom and the eave girder on top. On top of a stone post that stands in the courtyard, there are traces showing that a beam was placed on a wooden girder. The wooden girder had been installed on the inside below the stone beam. At the top of the external wall, however, no traces have been found that show that a stone element covered the top surface of the eave girders. Figure 3.5-20 shows the appearance of the top surface of the external wall and a restoration drawing of an eave girder and tie beam on top of a corner post in the courtyard.

The element placed on the independent post in the courtyard, which appears to be an eave girder at a glance, is unusually positioned slightly below the tie beam, but this position is too low to fit the rafter end. Thus, the wooden girder that was placed on the independent post was not an eave girder, but was probably a girder to support and reinforce the stone beam. It is also thought that the rafters were placed directly on the corner of the upper stone beam whose inside corner had been carved[15].

3.5.4.5 Gopuras III, IV and V

In Gopuras III, IV and V in Preah Vihear Temple, the stone elements carved with the shapes of eaves tiles were assembled so that not only the side faces of the eave girders but also their top surface were covered at a high position, including the bottom edge of the rafters (Figure 3.5-21, 22, 23). From the stacking of the existing stone elements, it is estimated that this assembly was made by processing the top surface of the walls, installing the eave girders, and after securing the rafters, installing the stone elements carved with eaves tiles as though to cover the eave girders (Figure 3.5-21). This technique largely differs from the standard technique seen in Gopuras I and II and Annex Building E. Additionally, since all Gopuras have a wide cruciform ground plan, the center of the eave girders cross the central intersection of the ground plan in midair, and change into beams at this position. For this reason, the eave girders and tie beams are same elements installed at the same height. They differ in character in the first place, but it can be said that their differences as elements disappeared (Figure 3.5-22,23). None of the three Gopuras provide clear evidence of the benches of the stone elements that receive the eave girders and tie beams. However, from the faint traces that remain, it appears that the tie beams that spanned

が置かれる（あるいは石材に段差が設けられて外側を高くとる）という収まりに変化する。つまり，木造軒桁は上面と室内側を露出させる収まりである。付属建物Ｅでは，軒桁は壁体上面に載るが，梁は壁体最上部材の大入れの仕口に上端を揃えて挿入される。両者は梁成分の段差を持ち，梁が下方に位置する。この収まりは第3ゴープラに付属する西の「一の字」建物Ｈ'の前身部分にも認められた。他の例はいずれも軒桁と梁の敷面の高さを同一とするが，一部で梁の敷面をかすかに沈めようとした痕跡が認められたことから，上方の軒桁に下方から梁が接続する「相欠」様の仕口が予想された。部材の上下関係を示唆する痕跡がみいだせないタ・ケオ寺院付属建物や痕跡を消失している改造後のバンテアイ・スレイ寺院も，おそらく同様の収まりであったと考えられる。

しかし，第3ゴープラ東付属建物の「コの字」建物Ｉ，プレア・ヴィヘア寺院の第3，第4，第5ゴープラで，軒桁と梁の敷面高さを同一としながら，かすかに残る痕跡から，軒桁を下方に梁を上方にする仕口が存在したことが判る。また，軒桁上に梁を積載する付属建物Ｆの中庭独立柱上では，軒桁の上に，単に木造梁を載せた事例も認められた。また，プレア・ヴィヘア寺院の第3，第4，第5ゴープラおよび付属建物Ｆ（中

the eave girders were joined by placing the eave girders below them and covering them so that the type of cross lap joint that was used does not open[16]. As mentioned earlier, a reversal of the order of the eave girders and tie beams occurred after Annex Building H on the east side of Gopura III was constructed.

3.5.4.6 Summary of Techniques

In order to study the wooden roofed ruins of Preah Vihear Temple, an attempt was made to collect other case examples, although limited in number, to study the assembly of their eave girders and tie beams. As described above, diverse changes could be seen in the assembly of wooden tie beams and wooden eave girders at the top of the walls according to era.

Beginning with the examples at Koh Ker Monuments, in which joints were made directly in the stone elements at the top of the walls to install wooden tie beams, the examples of Annex Buildings at East Mebon Temple, Pre Rup Temple and Banteay Srei Temple prior to its modification indicate the emergence of wooden eave girders. As a creative measure to firmly fix rafter ends in place, it is thought that they were completely embedded in the stone elements face up. Wooden tie beams had a slightly larger cross section than eave girders, as structural components, but they were installed with their top surfaces matching the top surfaces of the eave girders. Traces on the stone elements indicate that a type of cross lap joint existed in which the tie beams interlocked with eave girders from the bottom. However, this changed thereafter, such that eave girders were installed on top of the walls and stone elements placed on the outer side (or a level difference was made in the stone elements to make the outer side higher) at Ta Kev Temple and at Gopuras I and II, Hall N, Annex Buildings H' and I of Gopura III and Annex Building E at Preah Vihear Temple. In other words, the top surface and chamber side of the wooden eave girders were left exposed. In Annex Building E, eave girders were placed on top of the walls, but tie beams were inserted in dado joints in the topmost part of the walls with their top edges aligned. Both had a level difference equal to the height of the tie beams, with the tie beams positioned below them. This assembly was also found in the predecessor part of linear Annex Building H' attached to the west side as an Annex Building of Gopura III. In all other examples, the benches of the eave girders and tie beams were the same height, but because there was evidence that the bench was slightly lowered in some of the tie beams, a type of cross lap joint could be envisioned, with the tie beams having connected to the eave girders from the bottom. Similar assemblies were probably employed in the annexed buildings at Ta Kev Temple and Banteay Srei Temple that has lost its relevant traces after

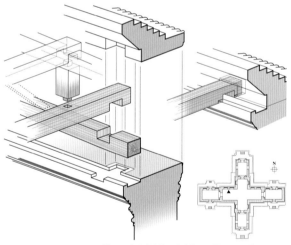

Figure 3.5-21 Preah Vihear Temple: Gopura III

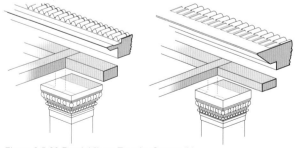

Figure 3.5-22 Preah Vihear Temple: Gopura IV
Figure 3.5-23 Preah Vihear Temple: Gopura V

庭）では，壁体上面に軒桁を施設して外側面に石材を置くばかりでなく，軒桁に固定される垂木の下端を含め，軒桁上方を石材で覆うようになる。

3.5.5 壁体上部の収まりの変遷過程と技法の編年

石造の壁体と木造梁，木造軒桁のさまざまな収まりについて，可能な限りそれぞれの時代の特定を行いたい。

木造の軒桁を持たないコー・ケー遺跡群内プラサート・トム寺院付属建物，プラサート・クラチャップ寺院のゴープラ翼廊の事例は，コー・ケー首都時代，ジャヤヴァルマンⅣとハルシャヴァルマンⅡの時代と判断される。この技法は石造と木造の接合法として，木造梁に対しては石材に精緻な仕口を刻むが，簡単な溝を掘る垂木との接合法が粗略である（Figure 3.5-2）。クメールの垂木は扠首に近いため，石材上面に確実に接合できず外れることがあれば，おそらく大量の瓦が落下し事実上屋根の崩落という結果になったであろう。

垂木の接合を確実にするためには，壁体上面に木造部材が必要になるとともに，その木造材が壁上で確実に固定されることが必要になる。このための工夫は，木造軒桁を壁体上面に埋め込む東メボン寺院，プレ・ルプ寺院，バンテアイ・スレイ寺院付属建物（改造前）に見られる技法である（Figure 3.5-3，4，7）。この方

Photo 3.5-1 East pediment of the main room of Gopura III (main room side)

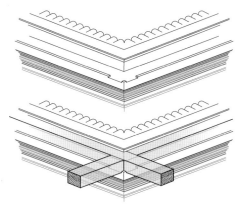

Figure 3.5-24 The assembly of girders that intersect in the corner of the main room of Gopura III

modification, although no evidence could be found that suggests the top-bottom relationship of elements.

However, in the U-shaped Annex Building I on the east side of Gopura III and in Gopuras III, IV and V at Preah Vihear Temple, faintly remaining traces reveal that joints existed in which the eave girders was positioned below the tie beams even though their benches were the same height. Additionally, with regard to the independent post in the courtyard of Annex Building F, on which a tie beam was mounted on top of an eave girder, there were examples in which a wooden tie beam was simply placed on the eave girder. In Gopuras III, IV and V and Annex Building F (courtyard) at Preah Vihear Temple, not only were stone elements placed on the outer side of the eave girders installed on top of the walls, but the top of the eave girders, including the bottom edge of the rafters fixed onto the eave girders, was also covered with a stone element.

3.5.5 Chronology of the Transition of the Assembly and Assembly Techniques at the Top of the Walls

Below, the various assemblies of stone walls, wooden tie beams and wooden eave girders will be dated as much as possible.

The examples seen at the Annex Building of Prasat Thom Temple and the Gallery besides Gopura at Prasat Krachap Temple in Koh Ker Monuments, which do not have wooden eave girders, are dated to the period of reign of Jayavarman IV and Harshavarman II, when the capital was located in Koh Ker Monuments. The technique seen here to join stone and wooden elements involves carving a subtle joint in the stone element for the wooden tie beams, but the technique for joining the rafters to the stone element by carving a simple groove is crude (Figure 3.5-2). In Khmer architecture, the rafters are close to the diagonal braces that are used to form the triangular frame, so if they fail to be firmly joined to the top surface of the stone element and become detached, a large number of tiles would likely fall and cause the roof to collapse.

In order to securely attach the rafters, a wooden element is needed at the top of the walls, and that wooden element needs to be firmly secured to the wall. This was achieved by embedding the wooden eave girders into the top surface of the walls, as seen at East Mebon Temple, Pre Rup Temple and the Annex Buildings of Banteay Srei Temple (before modification) (Figures 3.5-3, 4, 7). In this method, the eave girders were completely embedded in the stone elements on top of the walls, but it is thought that an attempt was made to realize strong connections between such wooden elements as eave girders, tie beams and rafters, while retaining the appearance that was achieved in eras when eave girders were not used. As joints were made between wooden

法は，軒桁を壁体最上部石材に完全に埋め込むが，軒桁を用いなかった前時代の形状を踏襲しつつ，軒桁，梁，垂木など木材どうしの強固な接合を実現することを目指したと考えられる。仕口は木材どうしで刻むから，石材加工に比較的繊細な作業を求めずにすみ，軒桁と梁，軒桁と垂木の接合も容易かつ確実になる。

垂木の下端は確実に固定できるようになったと思われるが，凹型断面の石材に木造の軒桁を埋め込んだため，漏水が溜まるとともに抜けにくく，軒桁の腐朽を促すことになったと思われる。これら3遺構は，いずれもラージェンドラヴァルマンⅡの時代の建築で，最も早い東メボン寺院が952年の建立と考えられているから，木造軒桁を導入し壁体最上部の石材に埋め込むという工夫は，10世紀後半に入って現れたと考えられる。

上記の方法に対し，タ・ケオ寺院，プレア・ヴィヘア寺院第1，第2ゴープラ，第3ゴープラ付属建物西「コの字」平面建物I，東「一の字」平面建物Hなどにみられる方法は，軒桁を埋め込まずに壁体上部に積載し，外面を石材で保護するという方法をとるから，相対的に漏水が留まり難く乾燥しやすい（Figure 3.5-5, 11，12，16，17）。したがっておそらく，先行する東メボンおよびプレ・ルプ寺院の方法の改良版であった。この時代はジャヤヴァルマンⅤの治世に該当する。ただ，壁上に軒桁を載せ，この外面を石材で覆うため，壁体上面を基準とすればコー・ケー時代よりも軒がやや高い位置をとる。タ・ケオ寺院の付属建物では，独立柱上に石梁を架けるポーチに限り木造軒桁を用いず，石材上面に直接垂木と瓦を施設した痕跡を残している（Figure 3.5-6）。壁上では問題にならないが，石梁であるため，上部に厚みが出てしまうことを避けようとしたためであろう。詳細が不明だが，改造後のバンテアイ・スレイ寺院付属建物もおよそこの時代に属すると考えられる。

上記の技法は，いずれも前時代の方法の名残を受け，軒桁と梁を同一敷面上で接合するが，いずれも梁を下方，軒桁を上方とする「相欠」様の仕口である。それでは，プレア・ヴィヘア寺院の建物E（Figure 3.5-14），第3ゴープラに付属する西の「一の字」建物H'の中央部（前身建物）（Figure 3.5-15）に見られた，タ・ケオ寺院のポーチのように梁を架けながらも壁体に軒桁を載せる技法は，どのように考えればいいだろう。

同様の事例は少なく考えにくいが，木造梁は，複雑な仕口を刻むことはないが壁体最上の石材に直接接合している点は，コー・ケー遺跡群や東メボン寺院，プレ・ルプ寺院などに共通する。しかし軒桁を石材に埋め込むのではなく上面に載せる点は，東メボン寺院，

elements, the relatively delicate task of processing stone elements was eliminated, and joints between eave girders and tie beams, and between eave girders and rafters, were able to be made easily and securely.

The bottom edges of the rafters were probably able to be secured, but because wooden eave girders were embedded in the stone elements with a U-shaped cross section, leaked water pooled and remained pooled in the stone elements, thereby causing the eave girders to decay. The above-mentioned three ruins were built during the era of Rajendravarman II, with East Mebon believed to be built earliest among them, in 952. Therefore, it is estimated that the measure of introducing wooden eave girders and embedding them in the stone element on top of the walls emerged during the latter half of the 10th century.

In contrast to the above, the method seen at Ta Kev Temple and at Preah Vihear Temple, in Gopuras I and II, U-shaped Annex Building I' of Gopura III on the west side, and linear Annex Building H of Gopura III on the east side, the eave girders were installed on top of the walls without being embedded, and their outer faces were protected with stone. Leaked water was thus relatively prevented from pooling, but the wooden elements were prone to drying (Figures 3.5-5,11,12,16,17). It was likely an improvement on the preceding method seen at East Mebon Temple and Pre Rup Temple. This era corresponds to the reign of Jayavarman V. However, because the eave girders were placed on the walls and covered on the outside with a stone element, the eaves during this era were slightly higher than the top of the walls, compared to that of the Koh Ker period. At Ta Kev Temple, wooden eave girders were not used in the porch, where stone beams were mounted on independent posts. There, there is evidence indicating that rafters and tiles were installed directly on the stone elements (Figure 3.5-6). Placing stone beams on the walls was not a problem, but this method was probably employed to avoid the thickness that stone beams would have created in the upper part. The details are not known, but it is thought that the annexed buildings of Banteay Srei Temple after modification also belong to this period.

The above techniques conform to the method of their previous period and join eave girders and tie beams on the same bench, and had a type of cross lap joint in which the tie beam was positioned on the bottom and the eave girder on top. If so, how should the technique of mounting tie beams directly on the stone elements but placing the eave girders on the walls be interpreted, as seen in Annex Building E (Figure 3.5-14) and in the center (predecessor building) of linear Annex Building H' that was attached to Gopura III on the west side (Figure 3.5-15), as in the porch at Ta Kev Temple?

プレ・ルプ寺院よりも新しい技法と考えられる。とはいえ，タ・ケオ寺院，プレア・ヴィヘア寺院第１，第２ゴープラなどのように，木造梁が壁体の上で軒桁と同一敷面の位置まで上らず，壁体と上面を揃える位置に留まっている点は古風である。したがって，建物Ｅの時代はジャヤヴァルマンⅤの治世の早い時期と考えられる[17]。この時代の末期，およそ1000年頃に建立されたタ・ケオ寺院のポーチの技法も，軒桁は用いていないが梁の収まりが共通している。

プレア・ヴィヘア寺院第３ゴープラ付属建物（西H'，I'，東H，I）の４つの建物は，梁上面を壁体上面に揃える西「一の字」平面建物（Figure 3.5-15）と軒桁，梁の敷面高さを揃え，梁を下，軒桁を上とする仕口を持つ西「コの字」平面建物（Figure 3.5-16），そして同様だが軒桁と梁の上下が逆転する東「一の字」平面建物（Figure 3.5-19）および東「コの字」平面建物（Figure 3.5-17）の３種類であった。このうち東「一の字」平面建物は，碑文から1026年頃までに建立されたと考えられている。したがって，スールヤヴァルマンⅠの治世中頃の建築である。おそらく時間を置かずに，対称性を保つため西「一の字」平面建物に改造と増築が施されたと思われる。前身建物は，先に記したように10世紀の第３四半期頃と考えられる。

西「コの字」平面建物と東「一の字」平面建物には木造架構の技法に差が認められないから，西「一の字」平面建物増改築に呼応して，西「コの字」平面建物もほぼ同時に建立されたと考えてよさそうである。しかし東「コの字」平面建物は，1026年頃に建立された東「一の字」平面建物に，後代になって接続しており，木造架構の技法においても少し時代が下ると考えられる。

プレア・ヴィヘア寺院第３，第４，第５ゴープラ（Figure 3.5-21，22，23，24，Photo 3.5-1）に見られる顕著な特徴は３点ある。第１は壁体上面で接合する軒桁と梁の関係が逆転し，梁が上に位置する仕口に変化することである。これは，屋根荷重を受ける梁の変形を考慮すれば，仕口が口を開けないよう梁を上から被せる「相欠」とするのは，梁の垂下を抑え，より構造的に安定する接続法をとろうとしたためである。この工夫は，第３ゴープラ東付属建物Ⅰを除き，プレア・ヴィヘア寺院の他の木造痕跡では見られない。

第２に，軒桁と個々に接続される垂木の下端を含め，上部を石材で覆う工夫が見られる。建物Ｆおよび第４，第５ゴープラをみると，独立柱の間に架け渡された石造梁の底に木造梁が一部入り込んでいる。建物Ｆでは，木造桁は石造梁の補強を意図した部材とみえるが，第４，第５ゴープラでは軒桁の機能をかねている。この２つの建物では，石造梁の自重変形に対処する意図も

Although there are few similar examples and thus difficult to ascertain, this is similar to the annex buildings at Koh Ker Monuments, East Mebon Temple and Pre Rup Temple, in that wooden tie beams were directly connected to the stone elements on top of the walls without creating a complex joint. However, it displays a newer technique than that seen in East Mebon Temple and Pre Rup Temple, in that eave girders were simply placed on the walls and not embedded in the stone elements. At the same time, it is also old-fashioned in that the wooden tie beams fall short of the height of the bench with the eave girders on top of the walls as in the annexed buildings at Ta Kev Temple and in Gopuras I and II at Preah Vihear Temple, but are aligned with the top surface of the walls. Thus, Annex Building E could be dated to the latter half of the reign of Jayavarman V[17]. The technique seen in the porch of the annexed building of Ta Kev Temple, built toward the end of this period, around 1000, does not use eave girders, but display the same assembly of tie beams.

The 4 Annex Buildings of Gopura III at Preah Vihear Temple (west H', west I', east H, and east I) could be classified into three types: linear Annex Building H' on the west in which the top surface of the tie beams matches the top surface of the walls (Figure 3.5-15); U-shaped Annex Building I' on the west (Figure 3.5-16) that have joints with the tie beam on the bottom and eave girder on top; and linear Annex Building H on the east (Figure 3.5-19) and U-shaped Annex Building I on the east (Figure 3.5-17) that is similar but the opposite, with the tie beam on top and the eave girder on the bottom. Among these, the linear building on the east is thought to have been built around 1026, judging by an inscription. If so, it was built around the middle reign of Suryavarman I. It is likely that the linear building on the west was modified and expanded soon thereafter, to retain symmetry. The predecessor building was probably built during the third quarter of the 10th century, as mentioned earlier.

Since there is no difference in wooden frame technique between U-shaped Annex Building I' on the west and linear Annex Building I on the east, it seems reasonable to assume that U-shaped Annex Building I' on the west was also built at around the same time in conjunction with the modification of linear Annex Building H' on the west. However, U-shaped Annex Building I on the east was later attached to linear Annex Building H on the east, which was built around 1026, so the wooden frame technique could also be dated to a later period.

Three salient characteristics could be seen in Gopuras III, IV and V at Preah Vihear Temple (Figure 3.5-21, 22, 23, 24, Photo 3.5-1). The first characteristic is the modification of joints between the eave girders and tie beams on top of the walls so that the tie beams were positioned on top and the eave girders on

含まれるように見えるが，そのような意図だけであれば，壁体だけで構成される第3ゴープラに同様の工夫が現れる理由がない。したがって軒桁上部に石材が被るようになる工夫は，軒桁が壁体上面に載るようになってのち，上部の漏水が軒桁にかからないよう保護する工夫が一段と進んだ結果と考えられる。木造軒桁を使わない時代から軒桁を埋め込む時代を経て，軒桁が壁体上面に載せられるようになった一連の工夫の過程からみて，軒桁の腐朽を促す漏水に対し，一貫して対処しようとしてきた結果と考えられる。

　第3に，これら3つのゴープラはいずれも太い十字平面を持つが，この平面形式では，独立柱や壁体の上部に載った軒桁は，交差部で中空に跨がる位置では梁の役割に変化する。したがって軒桁と梁は同一断面の部材となり，先行する時代のように，軒桁が細く梁が太いという部材の相違が消失する。

　以上の特徴から，付属建物Fは，建物外壁上部の軒桁と梁の収まりをみる限り，軒桁と梁の敷面高さが揃ってはいても，まだ梁を下に軒桁を上にする仕口が認められること，また中庭の独立柱の上で，木造梁が木造桁上面に仕口を持たずに積載されるが，この桁は石梁の補強のために石梁下端に挿入されたもので，垂木は石梁の上部に直接掛けられている。第4，第5ゴープラのように軒桁と梁とが同一の部材として認識される以前の段階であることを示している。

　一方，第3，第4，第5ゴープラは，上記のように建物Fよりもはるかに洗練された木造架構を持っている。とくに石梁を支持する木造梁が軒桁がひとつの材で兼ねるようになり，さらに軒桁と梁の相違が消失し同一の部材を使い分ける。これらの特徴は，これらのゴープラが早くともスールヤヴァルマンI時代の後期以後，おそらく11世紀後半の時代以後に至って造立されたことを物語っている。

　以上の考察を編年としてまとめると以下のようになる[18]。

1）ジャヤヴァルマンIV頃：プラサート・トム付属建物，プラサート・クラチャップゴープラ翼廊
2）ラージェンドラヴァルマンII・10世紀第3四半期：東メボン，プレ・ルプ，バンテアイ・スレイ付属建物（改造前）
3）ジャヤヴァルマンV・10世紀第4四半期？：プレア・ヴィヘア西「一の字」平面建物の前身（H'中央部），付属建物E
4）スールヤヴァルマンI・10世紀末〜11世紀第1四半期：プレア・ヴィヘア第1，第2ゴープラ，第3ゴープラ付属建物西「コの字」平面建物H'，東「一の字」平面建物I，付属建物F，バンテアイ・

the bottom. When considering how the weight of the roof could deform the tie beams that support it, the transition to a type of cross lap joint, in which the tie beams were mounted from above to prevent the joint from opening, was a measure to prevent the tie beams from sagging and ensure structural stability. No wooden assembly traces at Preah Vihear Temple indicate this measure, except for U-shaped Annex Building I on the east side of Gopura III.

The second characteristic is the measure to cover the upper portion, including the bottom of the rafters that are connected to each eave girder, with a stone element. A look at Annex Building F and Gopuras IV and V shows that wooden tie beams partly dug into the bottom of the stone beams that bridge the independent posts. In Annex Building F, the wooden girders appear to be elements that were installed to reinforce the stone beams, but in Gopuras IV and V, they also served as eave girders. In these two buildings, it seems there was also the intention to prevent the self-weight deformation of the stone beams, but if this were the only intention, there is no reason for it to be employed in Gopura III, which was composed of walls only. Thus, the measure to cover the top of the eave girders with a stone element is regarded as a further advancement of the measure to protect the eave girders from water leakage from above, after the eave girders came to be placed on top of the walls. From an era in which no wooden eave girders were used, through to the era in which eave girders were embedded, the development of the series of measures which led to the eave girders being placed on top of the walls imply that consistent efforts were made against the possible decay of the eave girders by water leakage.

The third characteristic is the wide cruciform ground plan of the three Gopuras, in which eave girders placed on the independent posts and the top of the walls took on the role of beams in midair at the intersection of the ground plan. Eave girders and tie beams came to be elements with the same cross section, and the differences that were seen in previous eras between the two elements—i.e., thin eave girders and thick tie-beams—disappeared.

Compared to the above characteristics, the assembly of eave girders and tie beams at the top of the external walls of Annex Building F was such that they were connected by joints in which the tie beam was positioned on the bottom and the eave girder on top, although the height of their benches were the same. Additionally, on top of the independent posts in the courtyard, wooden tie beams were mounted without creating a joint on top of the wooden girders, but these girders were positioned below the stone beams to reinforce the stone beams, and rafters were directly placed on top of the stone beams. In Gopuras IV and V,

スレイ付属建物（改造後）

5）スールヤヴァルマンI・11世紀第2四半期：プレア・ヴィヘア東「コの字」平面建物I

6）スールヤヴァルマンI末期以後・11世紀後半：プレア・ヴィヘア第3，第4，第5ゴープラ

上記に記したように，編年は6期に区分されるが，いずれも現存遺構を手がかりに可能性の上限を想定したものである。技法の変遷は，古い技法と新しい技法が併存する可能性も考慮に入れておく必要がある。また，第4期までに比べ，第5期がどの王の治世に相当するかは明確ではなく，これも上限の時期を想定したものである。このため第6期はさらに時代が不明瞭であり，いずれも大きく時代が下る可能性も考えられる。

3.5.6 むすび

石造の壁体や独立柱の上に木造屋根を載せることは容易ではなく，両者を確実に接続する方法はさまざまに工夫された。その過程は，上記のように，木造梁をどのように接続するかという問題を含みながら，木造軒桁の発生と腐朽を防ぐ工夫と複合して発達したと考えられる。その過程は，およそ1世紀を超えて進展したが，その後は石造屋根に置き換わっていった。

比較的短期間に次々に多様な工夫が現れたが，その様相からプレア・ヴィヘア寺院の各遺構のおよその編年を読みとることができる。この局所的な技法に限定してみる限り，パルマンティエの提案にあった，第1ゴープラ（L），ホールN，第2ゴープラ（D），第2伽藍翼廊（P，P'）の建立年代と推定された「ヤショヴァルマンIの後継者」の時代は，まだ木造の軒桁が生まれていない時代であり，さらに東メボン寺院やプレ・ルプ寺院に見られる技法とも異なっている。この工夫は，早くとも10世紀の第4四半期から1000年頃の技法であり，西「一の字」平面建物の前身や付属建物Eの方が古式であることが判る。また第3ゴープラ付属建物は同時代の建立ではなく，碑文（K381）から東「一の字」平面建物の建立を1026年と見れば，それ以前の西「一の字」平面建物の前身建物，同時代の西「コの字」平面建物，そして時代が下る東「コの字」平面建物に区分される。そして第3，第4，第5ゴープラは，さらに時代が下ると考えられた。これら3つのゴープラが造立された時期の前後については，詳細は不明である。

本節では，局部の技法に限定して注目することで遺構の編年を試みた。したがって，この試みは限定的なものである。遺構の編年については，今後もさまざまな視点から検討を加え，総合的に判断していく必要がある。

which have independent posts, the eave girders that received the rafters also served to reinforce the stone beams, and eave girders and tie beams were treated as the same element. Annex Building F does not display this state of organization.

Gopuras III, IV and V have a far more refined wooden frame than Annex Building F, as described above. These characteristics indicate that they were all built after the later years of the reign of Suryavarman I, at the earliest. When considering the distance in technique with Annex Building F, they were probably built from the latter half of the 11th century to the 12th century.

The above observations could be chronologically summarized as follows [18].

1) Jayavarman VI and thereabouts: Annex Buildings of Prasat Thom Temple, Gallery besides Gopura at Prasat Krachap Temple

2) Rajendravarman II, 3rd quarter of the 10th century: East Mebon Temple, Pre Rup Temple, Annex Buildings at Banteay Srei Temple (before modification)

3) Jayavarman V, 4th quarter of the 10th century?: Predecessor to the West Linear Annex Building (central part of H') , Building E at Preah Vihear Temple

4) Suryavarman I, late 10th century to the 1st quarter of the 11th century: Gopuras I and II, U-shaped Annex Building I' on the west and linear Annex Building H on the east attached to Gopura III, Annex Building F at Preah Vihear Temple, annex buildings at Banteay Srei Temple(after modification)

5) Suryavarman I, 2nd quarter of the 11th century: U-shaped Annex Building I on the east at Preah Vihear Temple

6) After Udayadityavarman II, late 11th century to the 12th century: Gopuras III, IV and V at Preah Vihear Temple

As shown above, the chronology is divided into six stages, based on an estimation of their upper limits. It should be noted that within the transition in technique, there may have been stages when old and new techniques existed simultaneously. Additionally, compared to stages up to the fourth stage, it is not clear under which king's reign stage 5 corresponds, so stage 5 is also an estimation of the upper limit. For this reason, the dates of stage 6 are even more unclear, such that the dates for stages 5 and 6 may largely go forward in time.

3.5.6 Summary

Placing a wooden roof on stone walls or independent posts is not technically easy, and various measures were taken to steadily connect the two components. As discussed above, it is thought that this process involved measures that went through a complex developmental process in which wooden eave girders emerged to receive the rafters and measures were taken to prevent their

注

1）参考文献 I ）

2）参考文献 II ）

3）参考文献 III ）

4）Sahai,S.:Preah Vihear An Introduction to the World Heritage Monument, Phnom Penh, Buddhist Institute Printing House, 2009.

5）垂木を受ける浅い溝の断面はコの字型の輪郭を持つが，垂木の勾配に合わせて室内側に傾斜をつけている。

6）プラサート・トム寺院東ゴープラのすぐ内側に位置する付属建物にて調査を行った。また伽藍東端の「宮殿」においても，同様の仕口とともに垂木を受ける線状の溝の痕跡が認められる。コー・ケー遺跡群においても遺構の残存状態は良好ではなく，木造架構の様相を残す事例は限られる。

7）いわゆる「あり落とし」状の仕口は，妻壁に近接する梁の仕口に限って使用されている。他はいずれも「相欠」様の仕口を持つ。意図的に使い分けられていることは明らかだが，意図に不明な点も残る。

8）実測数値は実測場所によってかなりの相違がみられるが，以下に大略を示す。東メボン寺院付属建物の軒桁と梁の痕跡は，軒桁断面が幅240mm前後，高さは130mm前後である。梁断面を幅と高さいずれも240mm程とする。プレ・ルプ寺院付属建物では軒桁痕跡の幅と高さが200mmと250mm程。梁断面の痕跡は，幅，高さともに280mm程である。軒桁の断面は高さに比して幅が大きい。垂木を受ける材であるから不自然な形状ではない。一方，梁の断面は幅，高さをほぼ同寸とし，軒桁に比べて一回り太いことが明らかである。いずれも，軒桁，梁の上面が石材上面と同一面を保っていたと仮定している。

9）参考文献 III ）

10）限られた位置だがレンガを充当した痕跡がある。当初材の軒桁が埋められていた跡は，改修後に建物の外に露出する位置である。したがってこのまま放置すれば雨水が溜まるなどの不具合が起きる。充当したレンガの痕跡は限定されるが，充填材を用いて埋められたことは確実である。

11）木造時代の棟木，母屋桁，軒桁の木口は，破風板を当て，表から釘で留めたと予想される。破風板は，浸水に弱い妻壁と屋根面の接合部を保護するとともに，同様に弱点である母屋桁や棟木の木口を被覆し保護する部材である。しかしこれを釘留めにすると，木質繊維の断裂した位置から浸水を起こす。このため，釘留めの位置をさらに被覆する部材（日本名：釘隠し）が必要である。石造の破風の頂部と両端のほか，通例，胴部に2つ設ける花紋は，この釘の頭を被覆する部材が形象化されたものとみられる。木造時代にすでにある程度装飾化が進んでいた可能性もあるが，石造化を契機に装飾的な変形が進んだと考えられる。

12）木造の妻壁であった可能性は，詳細な言及はないが参考文献 II ）にて指摘されている。

13）母屋桁の端を加工して「あり落とし」の仕口を設けた可能性も残るが，「あり落とし」部分の高さが小さいため「契り」を用いたと考えたい。

14）第3ゴープラの東付属建物に限られたことではないが，本来，梁と軒桁の敷面は同一面を目指して施工されている。

decay, while at the same considering how to connect wooden tie beams. This process likely took place over a period of more than a century, before all buildings of temple complexes were replaced by stone roofs thereafter.

Diverse measures emerged in succession over a relatively short period of time, and suggest the approximate chronology of the buildings of Preah Vihear Temple. As far as local techniques go, wooden eave girders had not yet emerged during the period of construction of Gopura I (L), Hall N, and Gopura II (D) and Galleries II (P and P') in Complex II as estimated by Parmentier, or in other words the period of Yasovarman I's successor. The technique seen in the following period at East Mebon Temple and in the annex buildings at Pre Rup Temple also differs. The measure of connecting wood and stone thus emerged during the period from the 4th quarter of the 10th century to around 1000 at the earliest, and that seen in the predecessor to linear Annex Building H' on the west and Annex Building E is an old technique. In addition, the Annex Buildings of Gopura III were not all built in the same period. If linear Annex Building H on the east is assumed to have been built in 1026 as indicated in an inscription (K381), the construction could be classified into three periods: that of the predecessor building to west linear Annex Building H' built prior to it; that of west U-shaped Annex Building I' built in the same period; and that of east U-shaped Annex Building I built later. Gopuras III, IV and V were built even later. The date and order of construction of these three Gopuras is unclear, however, as they display no significant differences in technique.

This paper attempted to determine the chronology of buildings by focusing solely on a local technique. Therefore, the attempt itself was limited in scope. Continued efforts need to be made to comprehensively determine the chronology of buildings from various other perspectives as well.

Notes

1) See Reference I).

2) See Reference II).

3) See Reference III).

4) Sahai,S.: Preah Vihear: An Introduction to the World Heritage Monument, Phnom Penh, Buddhist Institute Printing House, 2009.

5) The shallow groove that receives the rafters has a U-shaped cross section, but is sloped toward the chamber side to match the gradient of the rafters.

6) A survey was conducted at the annexed building located immediately inside the east Gopura at Prasat Thom Temple. Also in the "palace" at the east end of the Complex, traces were found of similar joints and traces of a linear groove that had received the rafters. However, the

しかし，実際に軒桁や梁を石材の上面に据える段階で，部材の座りが悪かったり収まりにくかったりすると，おそらくその場で石材の表面を調整したのだと思われる。このため，結果的にかすかな整形の痕跡が残されることになった。ただ，これはどの遺構においても例外的な存在であり，多くの仕口では敷面に明確な調整の跡を持たない。さらに時代が下るほど，この種の痕跡の判別が難しくなる傾向もみられる。

15）石梁上部内角を削りとった加工の状態は，敷面の凹凸が大きく木造桁などを施設できる丁寧な整形ではない。したがって，垂木尻を直接掛けるための加工であったと判断する。

16）第5ゴープラの独立柱上で，かすかだが桁を下に梁を上に設置した痕跡が残る。

17）黒岩千尋，中川武，溝口明則：プレア・ヴィヘア寺院の「口の字」型・「田の字」型建築形式について―「付属建物」に見るクメール建築変遷史の考察，日本建築学学会計画系論文集719号，pp.195-202，2016.1
　上記論文では，プレア・ヴィヘア寺院付属建物EとFの建立年代を，内田悦夫氏（岩石学）の調査結果に従い，ほぼ同時代の建立として扱う。本節では，局部的な部材の扱いに限定して編年を試みるが，そのように見たとき，両建物の建立はもう少し遡るようであり，さらに付属建物Eの建立年代は，付属建物Fより遡るようである。

18）編年の指標として，タ・ケオ寺院付属建物の建立年代を1000年，第3ゴープラ東「一の字」平面建物Iの建立を1026年とする。
　注記：各図版に描いた木造の梁，軒桁は，いずれも収まりの様相を示すためのものである。それぞれの部材の大きさや断面のプロポーション等は，仕口跡から想定された仮定にすぎないことを付記する。

buildings at Koh Ker Monuments remain in poor condition, and cases that show any appearance of wooden frames is limited.

7) The dovetailed tenon is used only in the joints of tie beams near the gable wall. The other joints are all of a type of cross lap joint. The two are clearly used selectively, but unclear points also remain regarding their purpose.

8) Measured values differ considerably depending on the measured location, but can be roughly summarized as follows. The traces left by eave girders and tie beams in the Annex Building at East Mebon Temple show that the cross section of the eave girder was around 240mm wide and 130mm high, and that of the tie beam was 240mm in both width and height. In the Annex Building at Pre Rup Temple, the cross section of the eave girder was 200mm wide and 250mm high, and that of the tie beam was around 280mm in both width and height. The cross section of the eave girder was wider than its height. This is not unnatural as an element that received the rafters. On the other hand, the tie beam had a cross section that was almost the same in width and height, and was clearly thicker than the eave girder. In both cases, it is assumed that the top surfaces of the eave girders and tie beams were aligned with the top surface of the stone elements.

9) See Reference III).

10) There is evidence that bricks were used, although in restricted positions. Traces showing that original eave girders were embedded were found in positions that were exposed outside the building after modification. Therefore, if they had been left as they are, rainwater would have pooled and caused a problem. The brick traces are limited, but it is certain that they were applied using a filling material.

11) In the wood era, it is thought that the butt ends of ridges, purlins and eave girders were pressed against a gable board and secured by nails from the outside. The gable board protected the connections of the gable wall and roof, which were vulnerable to water, as well as covered and protected the butt ends of purlins and the ridge, which were also vulnerable in the same way. However, if nails were used, water immersion would occur from where the wood-fiber is torn by the nails. For this reason, another element to cover the nail heads (called "kugi-kakushi" in Japanese, literally meaning "hiding the nails") was needed. The flower design that appears at the top and both ends of stone gables and commonly in two locations on the body is regarded as a figurative expression of elements that were used to cover the nail heads. Decorative motifs may have already been used to a certain degree in the wood era, but it is thought that elements were decoratively deformed when replacing wood with stone.

12) Although there is no detailed description, Reference II) points to the possibility that it may have been a wooden gable wall.

13) There is the possibility that the ends of the purlins were processed into a dovetailed tenon, but since the height of the traces is small, it seems more like that a butterfly joint was used.

14) Although not limited to the east Annex Buildings of Gopura III, tie beams and eave girders were originally processed so that they shared the same bench joint. However, when actually mounting the eave girder or tie beam on top of the stone element, any instability or poor fit between elements was probably adjusted on the spot by the surface of the stone

Chapter 3 : Study Reports on Preah Vihear Temple

element. For this reason, subtle shaping marks came to be left. However, such shaping was an exception in all buildings, and most joints show no clear traces of adjustment on their bench joint. As the era advanced, this type of mark tends to become more difficult to discern.

15) The state of the upper stone beam whose inside corner had been carved is such that the bench joint is largely uneven and not carefully shaped for the installation of a wooden girder. Thus, it is thought that the beam was processed to directly place the butt end of the rafters on the beam.

16) On an independent post in Gopura V, there are faint traces showing that the girder was positioned on the bottom and the tie beam on top.

17) Kuroiwa Chihiro, Nakagawa Takeshi, Mizoguchi Akinori: "□-shape" "田-shape" Aechitectural Styles in Preah Vihear Temple -Consideration on transition of Khmer architecture through the example of "Annexed Building"-, Transactions of AIJ: Journal of Architecture, Planning and Environmental Engineering vol. 719, pp. 195 – 202, Jan. 2016.

In the above paper, Annex Buildings E and F at Preah Vihear Temple were assumed to have been built during the same period, around the reign of Jayavarman VI (1080 – 1107), conforming to the results of a study by Uchida Etsuo (petrology). However, when the buildings are chronologized solely by the treatment of local elements as attempted in this paper, the dates of construction of both buildings go slightly further back in time, with Annex Building E dating to an earlier time than Annex Building F.

18) As a chronological index, the annex buildings at Ta Kev Temple are dated to 1000, and east linear Annex Building I of Gopura III to 1026.

Remarks: Wooden tie beams and eave girders depicted in each drawing show the appearance of how they were assembled. Note that the size, cross-section dimensions, etc. of each element are simply assumptions based on the traces of joints.

References

I)   Parmentier, H.: L'art Khmer Classique, Monuments du Quadrant Nord-Est 2vols, Paris, EFEO, 1939.

II) Dumarçay, J.: Khmer roofs and tiles, Report of the Joint Study on Cultural Heritage Protection in Angkor, Nara National Research Institute of Cultural Properties, 1997.

III) Sawada, Chika & Ueno, Kunikazu: A reconstruction of wooden roof frames at Banteay Srei and Ta Prohm—Woodworking techniques in Khmer architecture, Transactions of AIJ: Journal of Architecture, Planning and Environmental Engineering vol. 623, pp 221 – 226, Jan. 2008.

3.6 第1伽藍の造営手順
Construction Order of the Complex I

溝口　明則

MIZOGUCHI Akinori

3.6.1 はじめに

　山頂伽藍の形成過程は，複雑であるとともに時代を決定づける手がかりに乏しく難解な問題である。しかしこの問題は，すでにH. パルマンティエによって検討されている。彼の編年案は仮説であることを明言しているが，この提案をさらに再検討したS. サハイの議論も提出されている。これらの先行研究を手がかりとしつつ，今回の調査によって得られた資料をもとに，第1伽藍の形成過程について，あらためて整理したい。

3.6.2 造営過程の検討

　H. パルマンティエは，山頂の第1伽藍と第2伽藍が同一の基礎の上に立っていることを指摘している。「3.4 伽藍の計画法」で検討したように，山頂伽藍全体の寸法計画は，この2つの伽藍がひとつの統合された設計過程に従って構成されたことを示しており，両伽藍の基礎が連続していることの意味が裏付けられたと考えられる。第1伽藍の西の回廊の北半は，岩盤を削りだして床面を形成し，基壇も岩盤上に砂岩ブロックを載せて形成しているが，西面の外の基壇は，通例の上半だけがつくられている。西に露岩があり，北に向かって下がる地形に合わせ，山頂伽藍全体が整地された時代があったと思われる。

　H. パルマンティエは，第1ゴープラ（L）の造営年代を「ヤショヴァルマンIの後継者」の時代，およそ，ハルシャヴァルマンIからIIが王位に就いていた10世紀前半の時代と判断している[1]。第1ゴープラ（L）は，平面形式が簡素で素朴な印象を与え，時代が遡るように見えるが，おそらく第1伽藍の中で最古の建築であっても，「3.5 木造屋根の技法とプレア・ヴィヘア寺院遺構の編年」で指摘したように，壁体上面で工夫が繰り返された木造屋根の積載技法の変遷過程から見ると，10世紀の最後の四半世紀（おそらく1000年に

3.6.1 Introduction

Elucidating the development process of the Mountaintop Complex is a difficult issue, as the process is Complex, and there are few clues to determining its period of construction. However, this issue has been addressed by H.Parmentier. Parmentier notes that the chronology he proposes is a hypothesis, but S.Sahai has also submitted a discussion based on a review of Parmentier's theory. While taking a cue from these previous studies, this paper attempts to define the development process of Complex I also using materials acquired in a recent survey.

3.6.2 Study of the Construction Process

H.Parmentier points out that Complexes I and II on the Mountaintop were built on the same foundation. As discussed in Chapter "3.4 Planning of Complex", the dimentional plan of the Mountaintop Complex as a whole indicates that the two Complexes were built according to a single integrated design, and thus corroborates the meaning that the two have a continued foundation. The northern half of the west Gallery of the first ComplexI was developed by carving the bedrock to create the floor and placing sandstone blocks on the bedrock to create the platform. However, only what corresponds to the upper half of a regular platform has been created outside the west face. As bare rocks are found on the west and the landform slopes downward toward the north, it is thought that the Mountaintop Complex as a whole was developed in conformity to the landform at one point in time.

H.Parmentier judges that Gopura I (L) was built during the period of Yasovarman I's successors, around the first half of the 10th century during the reign of Harshavarman I and II [1]. Gopura I (L) gives the impression of a simple and unsophisticated ground plan and appears to go considerably back in time. Even if were the oldest architecture within Complex I, however, it displays

121

近い時期)から11世紀の最初の四半期までに現れた技法が認められる。この技法は,10世紀の第3四半期にはまだ認められないため,およその建立年代を限定することが可能である。同様の技法が認められるホールN,および両者の接続部(M)と比較すると,ホールNの壁体上部の整形の方がより洗練されているように思われるため,造営の順番は,第1ゴープラ,ホールN,接続部(M)の順である。

中央祠堂は,H. パルマンティエによってバプーオン様式の要素が指摘されており,S. サハイの意見も同様である[2]。ウダヤディティヤヴァルマンII時代頃の建立と考えられているが,この時代が第1伽藍の整備の最終段階にあたるであろうことは,大きく異ならないと考えられる。したがって第1伽藍の形成過程は,早くとも10世紀最後の四半期,おそらく10世紀末から11世紀の中頃までに収まるであろう。

砂岩の迫り出し構造の屋根を持つ拝殿(B)は,スー

a construction technique that appeared sometime between the last quarter of the 10th century (probably around 1000) to the first quarter of the 11th century, in terms of the transition of the technique that was repeatedly modified to mount a wooden roof onto the walls, as described in Chapter "3.5 Survey of Wood Structure of the Ancient Khmer Ruins and a Chronicle of the Buildings in Prear Vihear Temple". As this technique did not yet exist in the third quarter of the 10th century, it provides a hint for identifying the approximate construction date of buildings. When comparing Hall N which also display the same technique and the Connecting Part between Gopura I and Hall N, the top of the walls in Hall N appears to be more refined, so Gopura I was built first, followed by Hall N and Connecting Part (M).

In the Central Sanctuary, H.Parmentier points out elements of the Baphuon-style, and S.Sahai also holds the same view[2]. The building is thought to have been built during the reign of Udayadityavarman II, but there is no large discrepancy in

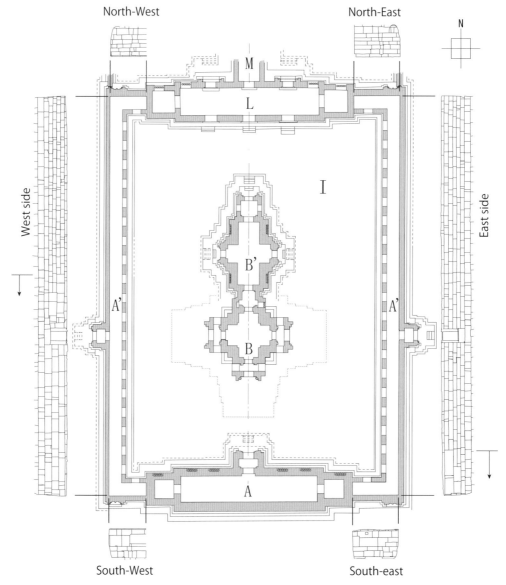

Figure 3.6-1 Stone joints in the outer walls of the Gallery I

ルヤヴァルマンI時代の建立と考えられてきたが，中央祠堂との取り付きで，一旦完成したレリーフを削り取った跡が残っており，また中央祠堂との接続部では，中央祠堂のポーチが拝殿の妻庇に入り込んでいる。これらの様相は，明らかに予定外の調整であったことを示している。この原因は，拝殿の造営の時点では，おそらく中央祠堂の前身建物がまだ存在していたためである。前身建物はレンガ造でポーチを持たない形式の塔であったと考えてよいであろう。拝殿の造営工事が原因であったかどうか明らかではないが，当初の予定と異なり，中央祠堂をつくりなおす必要が生じたため，時代に合わせて四方にポーチ（拝殿側はアンタラーラ：相の間を形成する）を付属させる祠堂の造営を試みたのだと思われる。

1036年頃の建立が想定されているバッタンバンのワット・エク・プノム寺院の中央祠堂は，ポーチを付属させる最初期の遺構のひとつだと思われるが，この遺構と比較したとき，祠堂の規模はほぼ同大で，わずかにプレア・ヴィヘア寺院祠堂の方が大きい[3]。ところが，ポーチの内法長さに注目すると，プレア・ヴィヘア寺院中央祠堂はワット・エク・プノム寺院中央祠堂の60％に届かず，規模に比べて極端に小さなポーチを接続したことが判る。

塔状の中央祠堂のポーチは，構造的に，横力などに対応するバットレスとして機能するから，プレア・ヴィヘア寺院中央祠堂は，当初から構造上やや不安定な形状であった可能性がある。ポーチの長さを極端に小さくした理由は，北側に近接する拝殿が完成していたためで，拝殿との取り合いで可能な大きさのポーチを作ったためである。ヒンドゥー寺院ではよく見られることだが，本尊シカレシュヴァラの位置を動かすことは禁忌に触れる。本尊の位置を変えずに祠堂を建立するためには，ポーチを小さくとること以外に選択肢がなかったのであろう。

中央祠堂の造営は，予定外とはいえ大きな工事である。したがってこのときに回廊が閉じていた可能性は考えられない[4]。Figure 3.6-1は，第1回廊（A'）の壁面にみられる石目地を記録したものである。石目地の様相は，西辺の回廊の南側半分と南東隅の石材だけが他と異なり，大材を使っていることを示している。石材の大きさの全体的な傾向は，床上から迫り出し構造が始まる迫り元までの壁高さを，石材を7段積むことで実現しているが，先の特別な部分では，同じ高さを5段の石材で賄っており，とくに中段の3段の石材に大材を使っている。大材使用箇所の分布が明確に区分されることから，全回廊のうち，先に挙げた2ヵ所

the view that the final stages of development of the Complex I corresponded to this period. The Complex I was therefore developed in the last quarter of the 10th century at the earliest, and probably falls somewhere between the late 10th century and the mid-11th century.

The Mandapa (B) with a sandstone corbel roof has been dated to the era of Suryavarman I. At the end that connects to the Central Sanctuary, there are traces which show that a relief was scraped away after it was completed, and at the connection with the Central Sanctuary, the porch of the Sanctuary digs into the gable eave of the Mandapa. These conditions indicate adjustments that were clearly unplanned, since the predecessor building of the Central Sanctuary probably did not yet exist at the time the Mandapa was built. It can be assumed that the predecessor building was a brick tower that did not have a porch. For reasons that may or may not have been associated with the construction of the Mandapa it became necessary to rebuild the Central Sanctuary, though not originally planned, and a Sanctuary with porches on its four sides came to be built following the trend of the times (the Mandapa side is an antarala (space between two structures)).

The Central Sanctuary of Vat Ek Phnom Temple in Battambang, believed to be built around 1036, is considered one of the buildings of the earliest period to which a porch was attached. Compared with this building, the Central Sanctuary at Preah Vihear Temple is roughly the same size, but just slightly larger[3]. However, when focusing on the inside length of the porch, the Central Sanctuary at Preah Vihear Temple is not even 60% the length of the Central Sanctuary at Vat Ek Phnom Temple. This means that a considerably small porch was attached compared to the size of the Sanctuary.

The porch of tower-shaped central sanctuaries structurally serves as a buttress against lateral force, so the Central Sanctuary at Preah Vihear Temple may have been structurally rather unstable from the beginning. The length of the porch was made extremely small, because the Mandapa was already built adjoining the north side, and the porch had to be a size that fits in the space between the Sanctuary and worship hall. Relocating the main deity Sikharesvara was considered taboo, as was commonly believed in Hindu temples. Therefore, in order to build the Sanctuary without changing the location of the main deity, there was probably no other choice but to make the porch small.

The construction of the Central Sanctuary was a large task, regardless of it being unplanned. The possibility that the Gallery I (A') was closed at this time is therefore inconceivable[4]. Figure 3.6-1 is a record of the stone joints of the walls of the Gallery.

Chapter 3 : Study Reports on Preah Vihear Temple

は，他の箇所と造営時期を異にする可能性が予想される。したがってこれらの箇所は，回廊が最後に閉じられた場所であったと考えられる。回廊の造営が2つの時期に区分できるとすれば，その原因は，予定外の中央祠堂の造営工事に由来するであろう。とすれば，回廊の竣工時期は，中央祠堂の完成の直後と考えることも必然である[5]。

回廊の工事が一部未完成のままであった理由は，拝殿の石材の搬入のためであり，拝殿の造営工事がある程度進んだ段階まで，回廊の工事が始まらなかったと推察される。その後，回廊が閉じる前に，予定外の中央祠堂の造営が始まったと考えられるから，この時期は拝殿の竣工直後である。したがって拝殿は，スールヤヴァルマンI時代の最末期からウダヤディティヤヴァルマンII時代にかかる頃に造営されたと考えてよい。つまり11世紀中頃のことと思われる。

第1ゴープラの側面に，木造屋根を架けたと考えられた母屋桁の大入れ跡の痕跡が残っている。この痕跡は，パルマンティエによって，現在の回廊に一時期木造屋根がかけられた痕跡と考えられた。東の妻壁は大入れの痕跡が不足しており，西の妻壁は，間隔が極度に狭い大入れ跡が並んでいる。さらに回廊内壁の外にはみ出す痕跡もある。したがってこれらの痕跡を辿っても，現在の回廊とうまく接合する木造屋根を想定することは難しい（Figure 3.6-2）。回廊は当初，基壇だけが完成し，比較的長い時間そのままとなっていた可能性が高い。この時期に差し掛けの木造屋根が敷設された可能性があり，現在の回廊とは直接関係のない痕跡であったと考えられる。

拝殿の造営が始まり，おそらく，拝殿の石材の搬入と関わりを持ちにくい回廊東辺の工事がまず開始され，拝殿の石材搬入作業が一段落した後に，回廊西辺の工事が開始されたとすれば，この途上で疑似ゴープラの工事も開始されたと考えてよいであろう。他の遺構でよく見られるように思われる工事の手順は，前後（と

It shows that the stone elements of the southern half of the west side of the Gallery and those in the southeast corner differ from the rest, and utilize large elements. As an overall trend in the sizes of the stone elements, the height of the wall from the floor to the root of the corbel structure is composed of a tier of seven stone elements. However, in the above-mentioned parts, the same height is achieved by stacking five stone elements, with large stone elements used particularly for the middle three elements. As the locations where large elements are used can be clearly distinguished, there is the possibility that the two said locations were constructed at a different time than the rest of the walls. Furthermore, it can be assumed that the two locations were where the Gallery was closed at the very end. If indeed the Gallery was constructed in two different periods, the reason probably lies in the unplanned construction of the Central Sanctuary. If so, the completion of the Gallery should logically be considered to have immediately followed the completion of the Central Sanctuary[5].

The construction of the Gallery was left partly unfinished, presumably to transport in the stone elements for the Mandapa, and the construction probably did not begin until the Mandapa was constructed up to a certain point. Thereafter, since the unplanned construction of the Central Sanctuary probably began prior to closing the Gallery, this must have been immediately after completion of the Mandapa. Thus, the Mandapa could be dated to the period from around the end of the reign of Suryavarman I to the reign of Udayadityavarman II, or in other words, around the mid-11th century.

On the side faces of Gopura I, there are traces of dado joints for purlins on which a wooden roof was installed. Parmentier interpreted these traces as indicating that the present Gallery had a wooden roof at one point. However, the east gable wall displays no traces of dado joints, and the west gable wall shows traces of dado joints placed extremely close together. Furthermore, some of the traces penetrate the inside wall of the Gallery. Even if these traces are traced, it is difficult to imagine a wooden roof that had been properly joined to the present Gallery (Figure 3.6-2). It is likely that only the platform of the Gallery was initially completed, and that the construction was left in this state for a relatively long period of time. A sloping wooden roof may have been installed at this time, but the traces probably have no direct relevance to the present Gallery.

Construction of the east side of the Gallery probably began after the construction of

Figure 3.6-2 Traces of a wooden roof in the gable wall in Gopura I

the Mandapa began, as it was unrelated to the transporting in of stone elements for the Mandapa, and construction of the west side of the Gallery probably began after the stone elements for the Mandapa were finished being transported. If so, it can be assumed that the construction of the False Gopura also began during this process. The construction order that is commonly seen in other ruins is such that the front and False (and left and right) Gopuras were completed before connecting the two with a Gallery. However, in the Complex I of Preah Vihear Temple, it is unclear whether the False Gopura existed from an early stage, as its two ends appear to have been connected to the Gallery at the final construction stage of the Gallery. Be that as it may, although the False Gopura is physically attached to the Gallery, it has side walls that prevent any access to and from the Gallery. These side walls include unshaped stone elements and were closed off (Figure 3.6-3), indicating that the False Gopura stood independently of the Gallery at one time, and the side walls were blocked, intended for a short period of time[6]. Thus, the False Gopura had probably already been completed before completion of the Gallery. However, unless the slight difference in time is considered, no explanation could be found in regard to the brick corbel structure compared to Gopura I, which had a wooden roof.

3.6.3 Summary of the Construction Process

Based on the above estimations, the construction process of the Complex I could be summarized as follows.

1) Completion of Gopura I (late-10th century?), foundation work of the Gallery, False Gopura, etc. (Hall N and Connecting Part M – first quarter of the 11th century).

2) Commencement of construction of the Mandapa (second quarter of the 1000s).

3) Construction mainly of the east side of the Gallery, after a slight delay. The False Gopura is constructed at around the same time.

4) Completion of the Mandapa (mid-1000s). Rebuilding of the Central Sanctuary immediately thereafter. The construction of the Gallery is suspended, leaving the southern portion of the west side and southeast corner unfinished.

5) Completion of the Central Sanctuary (third quarter of the 1000s). The Gallery is closed immediately thereafter.

Gopura II is believed to have been built by the second quarter of the 11th century, as was Gopura I, since it also had a wooden roof made using the same technique as Gopura I. It gives a rather rustic impression, but eave girders serve as tie beams at the central intersection of the ground plan, and appear to exhibit a stage in which the two elements became integrated. It

Figure 3.6-3 Gable wall in the False Gopura

第2ゴープラも，第1ゴープラと同様の技法で木造屋根を載せるため，同様に11世紀の第2四半期までに建立されたと考えられる。やや素朴な印象を与えるが，交差部では軒桁が梁として機能し，両者が統合した段階のように見える。第1ゴープラよりも後の時代と考えられる。L字平面の第2回廊（P，P'）は第2ゴープラとほぼ同じ時代が予想されるが，いずれも11世紀の第1四半期の建立と考えてよさそうである。第2伽藍の構成は，経蔵が最後に建立されたと見られるから，経蔵の建立は，拝殿の完成とほぼ同じ頃だったと予想される。

3.6.4 むすび

プレア・ヴィヘア寺院山頂伽藍の造営過程について編年を整理した。先行研究の指摘のほか，ごく限られた手がかりから推定したものである。具体的な手がかりがきわめて乏しいため，上記の編年はひとつの試みに過ぎない。今後も，さまざまな視点から年代の判定作業を進め，総合的に判断を下していく必要があると思われる。

注

1 ）Parmentier,H.：L'art Khmer Classique, Monuments du Quadrant Nord-Est 2vols, Paris, EFEO, 1939.

2 ）Sahai,S.：Preah Vihear An Introduction to The World Heritage Monument, Cambodian National Commission for UNESCO with the support of UNESCO office in Phnom Penh and National Authority for Preah Vihear, 2009.

3 ）ワット・エク・プノム寺院の中央祠堂の内法最大値（入口枠間の内法寸法）は4,604mm，ポーチの内法1,429mmに対し，プレア・ヴィヘア寺院中央祠堂の内法最大値は4,907mmとやや大きいにも関わらず，ポーチの内法はわずか825mmに過ぎない。

4 ）パルマンティエは，回廊西辺の入口近くの窓間壁が転用材を使って補修されていることに注目し，一旦閉じた回廊の中で中央祠堂の工事を実施し，この窓間壁の位置を資材搬入口と捉えようとしている。崩壊後の祠堂の散乱部材を見れば，この程度の窓間壁を1つ取り去って工事ができるとは，到底考えられない。パルマンティエの意見は，事態を十分に承知した上でのエスプリ，とも取れる。

5 ）中央祠堂が完成するまで回廊が閉じていなかったとすれば，パルマンティエが推論した中央祠堂の崩壊時期，つまり完成直前ないし直後に倒壊したとする判断は保留される。回廊が開いていれば，崩壊した中央祠堂の散乱石材を，現在のように放置したままとする理由が考えがたいためである。一方，サハイは，中央祠堂の崩壊を12世紀末と判断している。

6 ）現在は未整形の石材の間をレンガで塞いでいる。レンガは最近の補修であるが，当初，石材で側壁が完全に塞がれていたかどうか不明である。

was probably built at a later time than Gopura I. The L-shaped Galleries II (P, P') are thought to have been built at around the same time as Gopura II, probably in the first quarter of the 11th century. Within the Complex II, the Libraries appear to have been built last, so they probably date back to the around the same period as the completion of the Mandapa.

3.6.4 Conclusion

Above, the chronology of the process of construction of the Preah Vihear Temple Mountaintop Complex has been estimated based on the findings of previous studies and other limited clues. However, it is no more than a theory, as concrete clues are absolutely lacking. It is necessary hereafter to determine construction dates from various other perspectives to make a comprehensive judgment.

Notes

1) Parmentier,H.: L'art Khmer Classique, Monuments du Quadrant Nord-Est 2vols, Paris, EFEO, 1939.

2) Sahai,S.: Preah Vihear An Introduction to The World Heritage Monument, Cambodian National Commission for UNESCO with the support of UNESCO office in Phnom Penh and National Authority for Preah Vihear, 2009.

3) At Vat Ek Phnom Temple, the maximum inside dimension (inside dimension between the entrance frame) of the Central Sanctuary is 4,604 mm, and the inside dimension of the porch is 1,429 mm. In comparison, the maximum inside dimension of the Central Sanctuary at Preah Vihear Temple is 4,907 mm and slightly larger, but the inside dimension of the porch is a mere 825 mm.

4) Parmentier focused his attention on the fact that the wall between windows near the entrance on the west side of the Gallery had been repaired using diverted elements, and interprets this as meaning that the construction of the Central Sanctuary was performed inside the Gallery that was "temporarily" closed, and that materials were transported in from the area corresponding to the wall between windows. However, a look at the scattered elements of the Sanctuary after its collapse shows that it is hardly possible for construction to have gone on simply by removing a wall of this size. Parmentier's view may be regarded as his "esprit" based on a full understanding of the situation.

5) If the Gallery had not been closed until completion of the Central Sanctuary, Parmentier's estimation that the Central Sanctuary collapsed some time immediately before to immediately after its completion should be put on hold. If the Gallery had been open, there should have been no reason to leave the scattered elements of the collapsed Central Sanctuary abandoned as they are today. Sahai, on the other hand, dates the collapse of the Central Sanctuary to the late-12th century.

6) The spaces between the unshaped stone elements are blocked with bricks, at present. The bricks are from a recent restoration, but it is not clear whether or not the side walls were originally completely blocked with stone elements.

3.7 第3ゴープラの屋根復原
Restoration of the Roof of Gopura III

溝口　明則　　古賀　友佳子
MIZOGUCHI Akinori　　KOGA Yukako

3.7.1 はじめに

　本節では，第3ゴープラの当初の小屋組と屋根の姿がどのようなものであったか，検討を行う。H. パルマンティエは，第3ゴープラの屋根が，当初レンガ葺であったことを指摘し，中央祠堂の建立直後の崩壊に伴い，第3ゴープラのレンガ葺の屋根が崩壊した可能性を挙げた。そして彼は，その後に瓦葺の屋根に変更された姿について復原案を提示している[1]。

　クメールの寺院建築は，早くからレンガ造であった中央祠堂を除き，伽藍を形成するさまざまな建物が木造建築から石造建築へ移行するが，その過程で，石造の壁体上に木造屋根を載せる多数の試みが現れたことは，各地に残る遺構によってよく知られていることである。プレア・ヴィヘア寺院の第3ゴープラもまた，この変遷の過程で現れた希少な試みの1つであったと思われる。当初，厚みのあるレンガ葺屋根を載せていた痕跡が見られる点に大きな特徴があるが，これは，クメール建築が木造の瓦葺屋根から石造の迫り出し屋根へ移行する過渡期に，ごく短期間，木造小屋組とレンガ造などの屋根が併存する時期があった可能性を予想させるものである。

　本節の目的は，第3ゴープラの建立当初の姿を復原し，架構で試みられた内容を理解することを目指す。

3.7.2 先行研究

　木造小屋組とレンガや石材が混在した構造が存在した可能性について言及した先行研究は限られるが，いくつかの試みが見られる。

3.7.2.1 バコン寺院

　バコン寺院のゴープラは，四方それぞれに建つ同形式の小さな建物である。屋根の表面を直線的に葺き下ろしており，後の時代の屋根に見られる曲線的な輪郭

3.7.1 Introduction

　This chapter examines what the roof frame and roof of Gopura III originally looked like. H.Parmentier points out that Gopura III originally had a brick roof, and raises the possibility that it collapsed accompanying the collapse of the Central Sanctuary immediately after its construction. He then presents a restoration drawing showing the appearance of the Gopura after it was modified to a tiled roof [1].

　In Khmer temple architecture, the various buildings that compose a temple Complex underwent a transition from wood to stone, excluding the Central Sanctuary, which was made of brick from early on. In this process, a number of attempts have been made to place a wooden roof on top of stone walls, as has become well known through ruins that remain in various regions. Gopura III of Preah Vihear Temple is also considered one such rare attempt which emerged in this process of transition. A salient characteristic lies in the traces that show the building initially had a solid brick roof. This suggests the possibility that wooden roof frames and brick roofs co-existed at one time for a brief period during the transition from wooden tiled roofs to stone corbel roofs in Khmer architecture.

　The goal of this chapter is to restore the appearance of Gopura III at the time of its construction, and to shed light on the structural attempts that have been made.

3.7.2 Previous Studies

　Previous studies that address the possibility of mixed structures that had a wooden roof frame combined with brick and stone elements are limited, but a few do exist.

3.7.2.1 Bakong Temple

　The Gopuras at Bakong Temple are small, same-style buildings that stand in each of the four directions. The surface of the

が見られない。中央祠堂以外では，おそらく石造屋根のもっとも古い時代に属する遺構と思われる。J. デュマルセは，バコン寺院のゴープラ屋根について，薄い石材ブロックで構成された屋根を木造の母屋桁が支持するともみえる復原案（Figure 3.7-1-01）を提示している[2]。

このゴープラについて注目すべき最大の特徴は，平面全幅の半分程度を占めるに過ぎない狭小な内部空間を持ち，反対に異常に厚い壁体を持っている点である。木造の母屋桁が架かっていた明確な形跡がみられないことも指摘されているが，もし母屋桁が石造屋根を支持するのであれば，特別な厚さを持つ壁体がつくられた意味が不明瞭になる。厚い壁と狭い内部空間は，迫り出し構造で覆う壁体間の距離を縮めるとともに，直線的に葺き下ろす屋根形状の実現を目指した理由として受け止めることができる。上に掲げたこの遺構の顕著な特徴は，石材かラテライト材，あるいはレンガを用いて迫り出し構造の屋根を掛けようとしたことを強く示唆している。

Figure 3.7-1-02は，EFEOの所蔵図面に基づいて加筆したものである。想定した迫り出し構造の上部構造は，垂直2に対し水平1程の勾配を持つから，構造として無理のない範囲に収まることが分かる。したがって，バコン寺院のゴープラに，木造と石造の混構造の屋根が載っていた可能性は暫定的な提案の範囲にあり，確実な復原とはいいきれない。

roof slopes linearly downward, and shows no curves that were commonly seen in roofs built in later periods. Aside from the Central Sanctuary, they probably belong to the oldest group of buildings with a stone roof. J.Dumarçay presents a restoration drawing of the roof of the Gopuras at Bakong Temple (Figure 3.7-1-01), in which wooden purlins appear to support a roof made of thin stone blocks [2].

The largest characteristic of these Gopuras worth noting is that they have a narrow inside space that occupies only around half the entire width of the ground plan, but conversely have exceptionally thick walls. It has also been pointed out that no clear traces have been found that show evidence of wooden purlins, but if purlins had supported a stone roof, it becomes unclear why the walls were made especially thick. The thick walls and narrow inside space could be interpreted as a measure to shorten the distance between the walls that was covered by a corbel structure, and to realize a linearly sloping roof shape. The above-mentioned salient characteristics strongly suggest an effort to install a corbel roof using stone or laterite elements or brick.

Figure 3.7-1-02 shows a drawing with additions made based on a drawing in possession of EFEO. It shows that the upper part of the envisioned corbel structure had a gradient with a vertical to horizontal ratio of 2 to 1, and was thus a reasonably stable structure. Therefore, the possibility that the Gopuras at Bakong Temple had a roof made of a combination of wood and stone is merely a provisional proposal, and cannot be said to be an indisputable restoration.

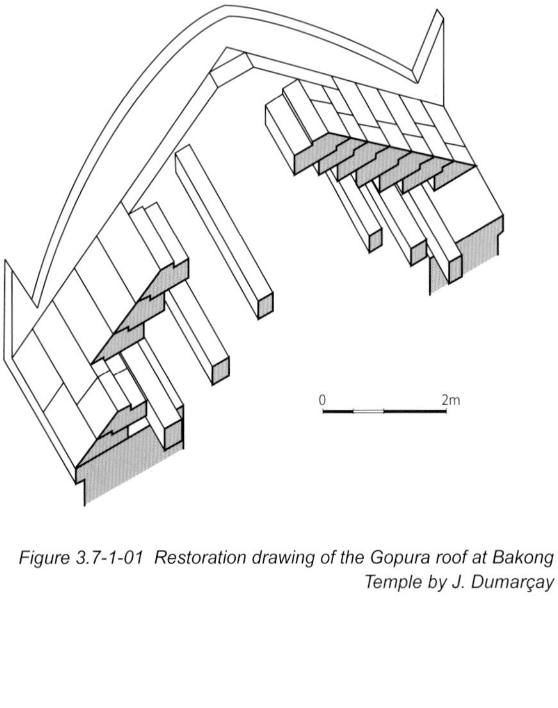

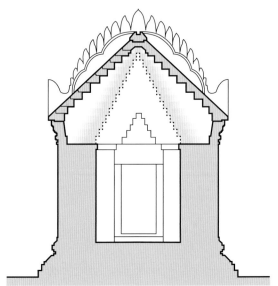

Figure 3.7-1-01 Restoration drawing of the Gopura roof at Bakong Temple by J. Dumarçay

Figure 3.7-1-02 Possibility of a corbel structure for the Gopura at Bakong Temple (additions by the writers to a drawing in possession of EFEO)

3.7.2.2 北クレアン

J. デュマルセによる，よく知られた北クレアンの屋根構造の復原案は[3]，透視図を用いて表現された（Figure 3.7-2-01，02参照）。木造小屋組の架構上に石造のブロックを重ねるという，意欲的な提案である。一見して興味深い提案だが，透視図で示されたアイデアを母屋桁の痕跡の図面に従って断面図として起こしてみると，上部が提案よりもかなり高い位置をとり，棟木の痕跡から推定される屋根高さは，壁面の破風型装飾に接しかねず，棟飾はこの装飾を飛び越えてさらに高い位置を占めている。また，上部の石材ブロックは，母屋桁との取り合いを考慮すると，下方の石材ブロックに比べて背の高い大きなブロックを想定する必要が生ずる（Figure 3.7-2-03）。実際の母屋桁と棟木の痕跡から予想される木造架構の位置と，母屋桁の位置を考慮して置かれた石材ブロックは，取り合いが難しい点を残している。J. デュマルセの復原案が描かれた透視図の石材の形状は，もちろんひとつの可能性を示したものに過ぎないであろうが，それでもこの復原案は，意欲的ではあるが，まだ十分な検討が尽くされていないようである。

母屋桁の配置に支配されながらも，その母屋桁に直接石材を積載し，また背後の面を当てて収めようとするアイデアは，混構造として奇妙なものである。石材ブロックはたんに葺かれているのではなく，迫り出し構造を体現する。そしてこの石材ブロックと木造架構が併存するという提案である。つまり，２つの架構技術が補完的に併存するという提案だが，木造小屋組は，石材を葺くという特殊な状況に合わせて当然考慮されるべき工夫が一切みられず，木造瓦葺屋根の場合とまったく同様の小屋組をそのまま転用していることになる。このような事態が本当に起きえたことなのか，という疑問を覚える提案である。

3.7.2.2 North Khleang

J.Dumarçay's restoration drawing of the well-known roof structure at North Khleang[3] is expressed in perspective view (Figure 3.7-2-01, 02). It is a bold theory that assumes stone blocks were stacked onto a wooden roof frame. It is an interesting theory at a glance, but when the idea presented in the perspective view is translated into a cross section view based on the drawing of purlin traces, the top occupies a considerably higher position than that which is suggested in the theory, the height of the roof that is estimated from the traces of the ridge purlin does not necessarily reach the gable-like decoration on the walls, and the cresting appears in an even higher position beyond the decoration. Furthermore, when considering the connection with the purlins, it becomes necessary to envision upper stone blocks that were higher in height than the lower stone blocks (Figure 3.7-2-03). A difficulty remains in explaining the connection

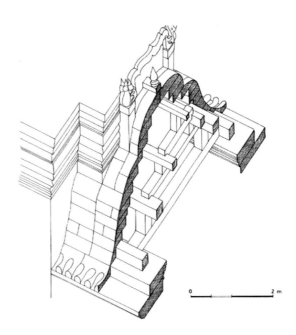

Figure 3.7-2-02 Restoration drawing of a wood-stone mixed structure
Restoration drawing by J. Dumarçay;
c.a. beginning of the 11th century

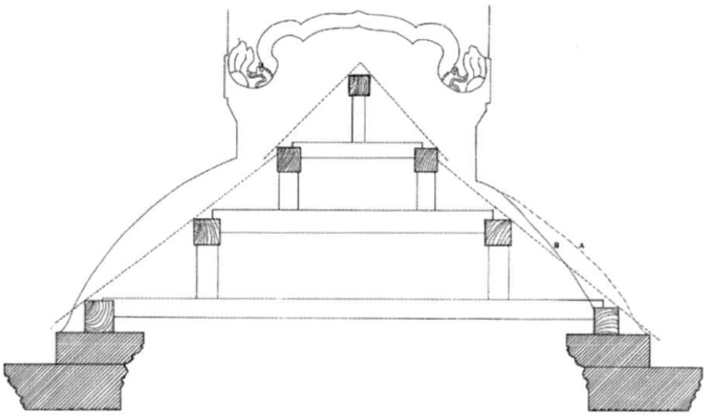

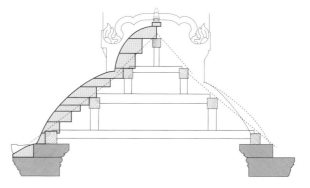

Figure 3.7-2-01 Restoration drawing of a wooden roof frame
13th century wooden roof by J. Dumarçay

Figure 3.7-2-03 Composite drawing of Figures. 2-01 and 2-02
(by the writers)

Chapter 3 : Study Reports on Preah Vihear Temple

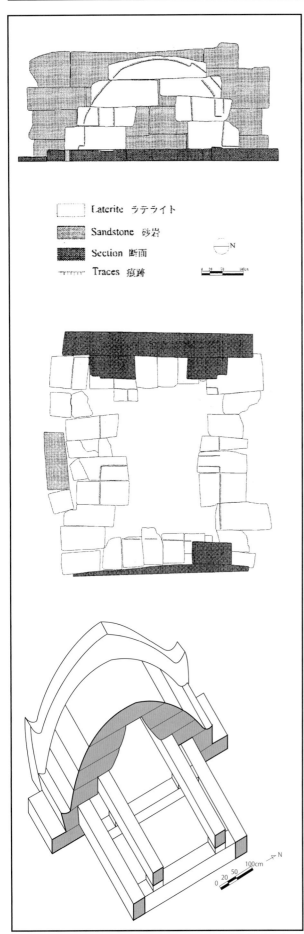

Figure 3.7-3 Traces and restoration drawing of Prasat Suor Prat N6 tower

between the positions of the wooden structure estimated from the actual purlins and traces of the ridge purlin and the stone blocks that were placed in consideration of the positions of the purlins. The perspective view of stone blocks shown in J.Dumarçay's restoration drawing may simply display a possibility, but the drawing leaves much to be examined, although it certainly shows a bold effort.

As a mixed structure, the idea of directly stacking stone elements on the purlins in line with the arrangement of the purlins, and fixing them in place by supporting them from behind seems peculiar. Dumarçay's theory is that the stone blocks were not used to simply tile the roof, but to also realize a corbel structure, and that these stone blocks and wooden structure coexisted. That is, it proposed that two structural techniques coexisted in complement with each other. However, the wooden roof frame displays no marks of any effort whatsoever that would normally need to be made to accommodate the exceptional case of creating a roofing with stone elements, and a roof frame that was completely the same as that of a wooden tiled roof was used as it is. The proposed theory thus invites the question of whether such a situation actually took place.

3.7.2.3 Prasat Suor Prat

H.Hattori and S.Nishimoto produced a restoration drawing of the roof of a Prasat Suor Prat tower using J.Dumarçay's restoration drawing of the Khleang as a hint[4]. As it shows traces of both a laterite corbel structure and wooden structure, it is assumed to be a mixed structure that combines wood and stone. However, it is hard to think that a laterite corbel roof alone was inadequate to cover a span of a mere 1.5m. The drawing appears to be deduced from the large purlin traces that are almost exaggerated compared to the size of the structure, but it seems even more exaggerated if a wooden roof frame was built and a laterite roof that could fully support a corbel structure had been placed on it.

An analysis of traces of a wooden structure that remains on the inner side walls of the pediment and at the top of the walls of each Prasat Suor Prat tower shows that the traces largely differ from each other and no unified style seems to exist. Thus, it is more natural to assume that when the laterite roof was damaged, a wooden roof was built as appropriate to the situation. In other words, it is highly unlikely that this small roof was a combination of wood and stone.

As shown above, it can be said that no sound argument exists at present regarding mixed structures in which a wooden roof frame and a corbel structure made of stone blocks coexisted.

3.7.2.3 プラサート・スープラ

J. デュマルセのクレアン復原案を手がかりとして考察された，服部と西本によるプラサート・スープラ塔の屋根の復原案では[4]，ラテライトの迫り出し構造と木造架構の痕跡のいずれもが観察されるため，木造架構とコーベル・アーチの混構造を想定している。しかし，わずか1.5m程のスパンを覆うために，ラテライト造の迫り出し屋根だけで不都合が生じたとは考え難い。これは，規模に比べて過剰とも思える母屋桁の大きな痕跡に由来する判断のようだが，木造小屋組をつくり，さらにこの上に迫り出し構造で十分に実現できるラテライトブロックの屋根を重ねたとすれば，さらに過剰な構造体である。

プラサート・スープラ各塔のペディメント内側面と壁体上面に残る木造架構の痕跡を辿れば，それぞれに大きな相違があって統一した形式が認めがたい。このことから，ラテライト造の屋根が破損した際に，その都度，状況に合わせて木造屋根を架けていたと受け止める方が自然である。つまり，この小さな屋根に，混構造が存在した可能性はきわめて低いと判断される。

以上に挙げたように，木造の小屋組と石造ブロックの迫り出し構造とが併存する混構造に関する確かな議論は，いまのところ存在しないといってよい。木造屋根から石造屋根へ遷る発達の過程を考慮すれば，いずれの提案もあらためて検討を要する提案である。現在の先行研究の様相から見れば，レンガを葺いた例であるが，プレア・ヴィヘア寺院第3ゴープラは，木造屋根から石造屋根へ推移していくクメール建築の変遷過程を考えるにあたり，きわめて重要な実例であり，貴重な位置を占める存在であることが判る。

3.7.3 第3ゴープラの屋根形式の復原
3.7.3.1 第3ゴープラの木造小屋組の編年からみた特徴

石造の壁体上で起こる木造屋根との接続法については，前節にてその発達の過程について述べた。第3ゴープラは，この発達の過程の最終段階にあたる事例である。ここでは，この時代の特徴として，以下3点を挙げる。

1）軒桁と梁に部材寸法の相違がないこと。

前代では，軒桁と梁は部材として別なものであり，軒桁に比べて梁が一段と太いという相違を持っていた。しかし，第3ゴープラは太い十字形の平面を持つため（Figure 3.7-4），壁体上面に載った軒桁は交差部を通過する際に中空を渡る。つまり軒桁は，交差部では梁として機能する。したがって軒桁と梁は，部材として相違を持つ理由を失い，同一の断面を持つ部材として扱

When considering the process of development from wooden roof to stone roof, all theories require further examination. From the perspective of previous studies, Gopura III of Preah Vihear Temple is an extremely valuable case example, although it is an example of a brick roof, and is clearly a precious existence in elucidating the transition of Khmer architecture from wooden roof to stone roof.

3.7.3 Restoration of the Roof Style of Gopura III
3.7.3.1 Characteristics of the Wooden Roof Frame of Gopura III from a Chronological Perspective

The method of connecting a wooden roof onto the top of a stone wall has been discussed in the previous chapter with regard to its process of development. Gopura III is a case example that represents the final stage of that development process. Below are three characteristics of this period.

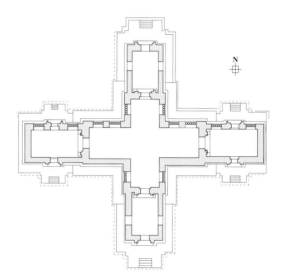

Figure 3.7-4 Ground plan of Gopura III

1) There is no difference in the dimensions of eave girders and tie beams.

In previous eras, eave girders and tie beams were different elements, and tie beams were thicker than eave girders. However, as Gopura III has a wide cruciform ground plan (Figure 3.7-4), eave girders that were placed on the walls crossed the intersection in midair. This means they functioned as tie beams at the intersection. Thus, eave girders and tie beams came to have no meaning in being different elements, and were treated as elements with the same cross section.

2) It is thought that tie beams and eave girders had a type of cross lap joint, and were connected with the eave girder covering the tie beam from the top.

From the first half of the 10th century, when eave girders were not used and tie beams were mounted on the walls by making a joint directly in the stone elements, the tie beams were positioned

われる。

2）梁は軒桁と「相欠」様の仕口を持ち，軒桁に対し
上から被る接続法であったと考えられたこと。

もともと軒桁を持たず，壁体上部の石材に直接仕口
を刻んで梁を架けていた10世紀前半の時代から，梁の
位置は壁体上面に梁上面を合わせる位置にあった。10
世紀後半になって木造の軒桁を用いるようになり，壁
体上面に埋め込む時代になっても，また，この軒桁が
壁体上面に載せられるようになった初期の段階，おそ
らく10世紀第4四半期頃でも梁は同様の位置を守って
いた。梁は常に軒桁よりも下の位置を占めていたから，
軒桁と梁がいずれも壁体上面に載り，接続するように
なった10世紀第1四半期になっても，「相欠」様の仕
口の構成は，梁が下に軒桁が上に位置していた。梁は，
束を経由して屋根荷重を受ける構造材だが，軒桁の発
生の経緯は，垂木を受けて固定するための部材として
の性格が強い。したがって両者は断面のプロポーショ
ンが異なり，梁は一段と太い部材が使われていた。

しかし，一連の発達過程の最終段階に入って，この
位置関係が逆転する。束を通じて屋根荷重を受けて下
方に湾曲する梁の仕口は，軒桁を下から接続している
場合，荷重変形によって仕口の口が開くためである。
荷重による梁の変形を考慮すれば，梁は上から軒桁と
接続されるものである。梁と軒桁の相互関係を含んだ
複雑な発達の経緯によって，この接続法はなかなか現
れなかったが，1000年代の第2四半期の後，おそらく
1000年代中頃に至って実現することになる。

3）壁体上面の外側に置かれた石材は，軒桁の外側面
と軒桁と垂木尻をともに上部から覆うようになる。

この石材の形状は，軒桁を雨水から保護するという
前代から続く工夫の最終段階と考えられる。同様の工
夫は，第4，第5ゴープラにも見ることができるが，
2つのゴープラはいずれも瓦葺であるため，第3ゴー
プラの石材とは断面形状がやや異なっている。第3
ゴープラの石材は，外側に勾配を付けて細かなステッ
プを刻んでおり，ここにレンガが積まれたことが明ら
かで，外面と上面がレンガで覆われていた。

以上3点の特徴は，10世紀前半から続く，軒桁と梁
に関する複雑な発達の経緯の結果として，第3ゴープ
ラの構成に辿り着いている。これらの特徴を十分に考
慮しつつ復原作業を進めよう。

so that the their top surface matched the top surface of the walls. Wooden eave girders came to be used from the latter half of the 10th century, but even when they came to be embedded in the top surface of the walls, tie beams were kept in the same position they were placed during the initial stages when eave girders were placed on top of the walls, around the fourth quarter of the 10th century. Tie beams were generally placed below the eave girders, so even in the first quarter of the 10th century, when both eave girders and tie beams came to be placed on top of the walls and connected, their cross lap joints were made so that the tie beam was positioned on the bottom and the eave girder on top. Tie beams are structural elements that receive the load of the roof via struts, but eave girders emerged primarily as elements that receive rafters and fix them in place. The two elements therefore had cross sections that differed in size, with the tie beams being thicker than eave girders.

However, the relationship of the two elements reversed in the final stage of the development process. This was because as tie beams receive the load of the roof via struts and tend to sag, their joints would open due to deformation under load if they were to be positioned below the eave girders. When considering the deformation of the tie beams caused by an upper load, it is natural to connect them with eave girders from the top. It took some time for this method of connection to emerge, due to a Complex development process that included the mutual relationship between tie beams and eave girders, but it finally emerged after the second quarter of the 1000s, probably around the mid-1000s.

3) Stone elements placed on the outer side of the top surface of the walls came to cover both the outer faces of the eave girders and rafter ends from above.

This stone element shape is thought to be the final stage of measures that have continued from the previous era to protect the eave girders from rain. Similar measures can be seen in Gopuras IV and V, but as these two Gopuras have a tiled roof, their stone elements have a slightly different cross section compared to those in Gopura III. The stone elements in Gopura III have small graded steps on the outside, on which bricks were clearly laid, and their outer and upper faces were covered by bricks.

The above three characteristics culminate in the structure of Gopura III as a result of a Complex development process involving eave girders and tie beams that continued from the first half of the 10th century. Restoration activities shall be pursued in full consideration of these characteristics.

Restoration of the Roof of Gopura III

3.7.3.2 各部の痕跡と復原
3.7.3.2.1 壁体上面の痕跡

　主室の壁体上面は，敷面を少し下げて丁寧に加工されており，軒桁と妻壁上の敷桁を積載していた位置の輪郭が，明瞭につくり出されている。木造軒桁は，妻の壁上面の敷桁も含め，主室を構成する全ての壁上に載る。南ペディメントの西側の足下にて，軒桁と敷桁を接続した痕跡が確認できたが，この様相から「相欠」様の仕口を持っていたことが判る。主室の敷面の加工の様子は，敷桁の敷面がやや低く加工されていることから，敷桁が下に，軒桁が上に位置した接合であったと判断される（Figure 3.7-5）。

3.7.3.2 Traces and Restoration of Each Part
3.7.3.2.1 Traces at the Top of the Walls

The top surface of the walls of the main room was carefully processed with benches slightly lowered, and clearly shows the outlines of eave girders and the positions where eave girders were mounted on the gable wall. Wooden eave girders, including walls plates on the top of the gable side walls, were placed on all walls that compose the main room. Traces showing the connection of eave girders and wall plates that were found at the bottom of the south pediment on the west side indicate that they had a type of cross lap joint. As the bench of the eave girders were made slightly lower than the wall plate in the main room, it is thought that the connections were made so that the wall plate

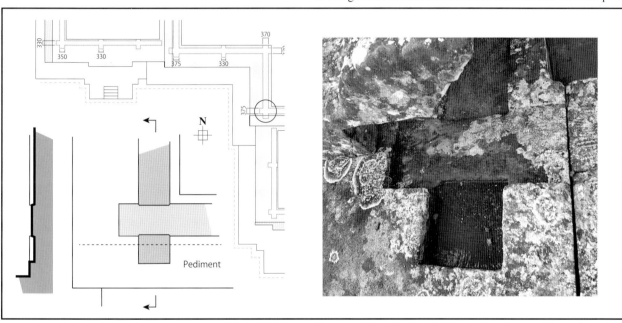

Figure 3.7-5 Traces of an eave girder and wall plate in the southwest corner of the south pediment

　先に述べたように，主室交差部の角の壁上を越えると，軒桁はそのまま中空に架かって梁として機能する。軒桁どうしが交差していた状態を示す痕跡が残るが，敷面にかすかな痕跡があり，南北方向の軒桁を下に敷いた「相欠」様の仕口であったと考えられる。南北方向の敷面に鑿跡の痕跡がよく残り，さらに砂岩材の南端の痛みが激しい（Figure 3.7-6）。これは南北方向にかけた軒桁が下にあるため仕口が開きやすく，東西方向よりも垂下が大きくなって砂岩材の端を痛めたことを物語っている。

　主室平面形状は太い十字形を形成し東西の腕を長くとるが，この2本の腕の中央に梁を架けた痕跡が残る（Figure 3.7-7）。東西の腕に架けられた梁の痕跡は，寸法から見て軒桁と同一部材が使われたとみられる。太い十字形の平面を持つ遺構では，付属建物Eの中庭の構成にみられるように，軒桁と梁を別材とし，高さを変えて架けることで交差部に梁を用いた例がみられる。

was positioned on the bottom and the eave girder on top (Figure 3.7-5).

As discussed earlier, eave girders cross the intersection of the main room in mid-air after extending beyond the walls forming the corners of the intersection, and function as tie beams. There are traces that suggest that eave girders crossed each other. From the faint traces on their benches, it is thought that a type of cross lap joint was used, with the eave girders in the north-south direction positioned on the bottom. The benches of the eave girders in the north-south direction have clear traces of chisel marks, and the south end of the sandstone elements was severely damaged (Figure 3.7-6). This indicates that the joints tended to open because the north-south eave girders were positioned on the bottom and their sagging became larger than the east-west girders, thus damaging the ends of the sandstone elements.

The main room has a wide cruciform ground plan with long east and west arms, and there are traces showing that a tie beam

133

しかし第3ゴープラの時代になると，軒桁と梁を同一部材として扱い，同一の高さに架ける。この結果，軒桁が交差部にかかる範囲で梁の役割を担うことが可能になる。そしてこれは，主室の東西の腕の中央に架かる梁にも当てはめられた。いずれも当初の仕口の状態を示す手がかりに乏しいが，梁の端は軒桁を超えて外側に延び，軒を構成する石材は，梁の端が収まるように加工されている。したがって相欠に類する仕口であったことは確実であり，さらに，梁が上，軒桁が下という接合法であったと考えられる。

was placed across the center of these two arms (Figure 3.7-7). Judging from the dimensions of these traces, it appears that the same element as the eave girders was used. In buildings that have a wide cruciform ground plan, there were examples in which eave girders and tie beams were different elements, and a tie beam was installed over the intersection by changing its height, as seen in the structure of the inner courtyard of Annex Building E. However, in the period of Gopura III, eave girders and tie beams were treated as the same element and installed at the same height. As a result, it became possible for eave girders to take on the role of a tie beam at the intersection of the cruciform ground plan. This was also applied to the tie beam that crossed the center of the east and west arms of the main room. In either case, there is a lack of hints on the state of the original joints, but the ends of tie beams extended outside beyond the eave girders, and stone elements that compose the eave were processed to fit the ends of the tie beams. Therefore, it is certain that the joints were a type of cross lap joint, and it is thought that the elements were connected with the tie beam on top and the eave girder on the bottom.

The eave girder that was installed on the walls on the gable

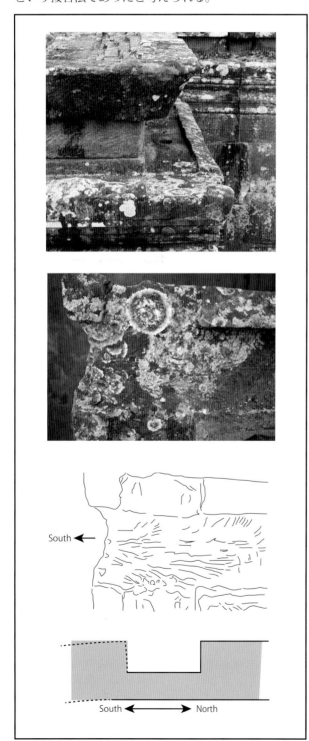

Figure 3.7-6 Traces of an eave girder in the corner of the intersection

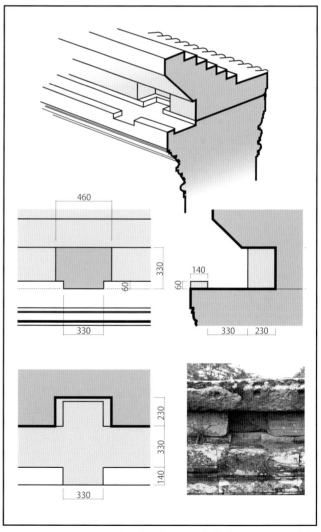

Figure 3.7-7 Traces of a tie beam and eave girder

妻側の壁上に施設された敷桁は，ペディメントの張り出しの下に半ば潜り込む位置にあり，軒桁の外面と上部に被る石材は，先に施設してしまえば木造の軒桁を挿入することが困難である。さらに，梁の端が収まる軒の石材の加工の様子は，梁端の大きさに比べてずいぶん大きくとっており，あらかじめ梁端のおよその位置を予想して加工したもののように見える。いずれの様相も，まず，壁体上面を加工して木造の敷桁と軒桁を施設し，さらに梁を架けた後に，ペディメントの石材と軒を構成する石材を積載するという手順を予想させるものである。とすれば，ペディメントが完成した後，次の段階で母屋桁と棟木が施設されるという手順が想定される（Figure 3.7-8）。

side was positioned so that it half slides in under the projection of the pediment. If the stone element that covers the outer side and top of the eave girder had been installed first, it would have been difficult to insert the wooden eave girder. Furthermore, the stone element of the eave where the end of the tie beam was fitted was processed to a much larger size compared to the size of the tie-beam end, and appears as though it was processed in advance in anticipation of the estimated position of the tie-beam end. The above all point to an estimated procedure in which the top surfaces of the walls were processed first, wooden wall plates and eave girders were installed on them, and after installing the tie beams, stone elements of the pediment and stone elements that compose the eave were loaded. If so, the next step that could

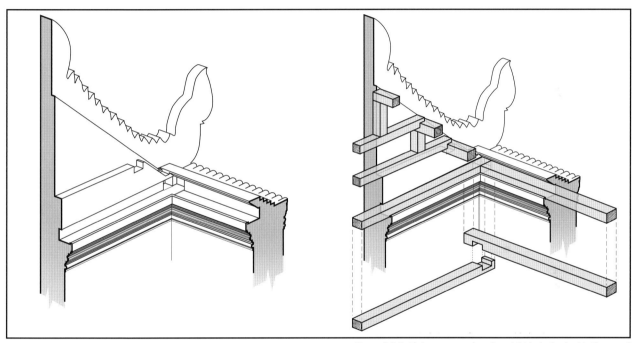

Figure 3.7-8 Main room, east pediment (side facing inside the room)

四方の側室では，主室側のペディメントにレリーフを施し，主室側を除く三方の壁上に軒桁と敷桁を施設して中央に梁を架ける。軒桁と梁の様相は主室とほぼ同様である。つまり，妻の壁上では，敷桁はペディメントの下部に半ば潜り込むように施設される。軒桁どうしは相欠の仕口で接合するが，敷面を観察する限りいずれの軒桁が上に位置したか明瞭ではない。側室の梁は東西側室にそれぞれ2本，南北の側室に1本ずつ施設された痕跡が残っている。軒桁と梁の接合部の痕跡は，主室と同様に梁端が軒桁を超えて跨がるから，相欠によって接合されていたことが理解できる。敷面は同一だがここでも梁が上の位置を占めていたであろう。軒桁の外面と上面に被る石材の様相も主室と同様だが，後述のように，側室外側のペディメントのうち，南側と西側の室内面はやや様相が異なる。

be envisioned after completing the pediment is the installation of the purlins and ridge purlin (Figure 3.7-8).

In the side rooms in the four directions, the pediments on the main room side were decorated with a relief, eave girders and wall plates were installed on the three walls excluding the wall on the main room side, and a tie beam was installed in the center. The eave girders and tie beam were roughly the same as in the main room. That is, on the gable side walls, the eave girders were installed as though to partly slide in under the bottom portion of the pediment. Eave girders were connected together by a type of cross lap joint, but as far as the benches are observed, it is not clear which eave girder was placed on top. There are traces that show that two tie beams each were installed in the east and west side rooms and one each in the north and south side rooms. Traces of the connections between the eave girders and tie beams

3.7.3.2.2 主室ペディメント

ペディメントは室内側で下方を張り出し，下の2本の母屋桁をこの張り出し部の頂部で受けている。そしてペディメントの底部両端（壁体上面に下面が位置する）に軒桁の大入れ痕跡を持っているが，張り出し部より上の面では，頂部の棟木，上方の左右2本の母屋桁ともに痕跡を残していない。また垂木を施設した跡，葺材であるレンガを密着させた痕跡が残っており，ペディメントに接する垂木は足下の石材に載っていた痕跡を残し，上に述べた張り出し部の両端は，垂木の勾配に合わせて整形されている。垂木を密着させた痕跡の内側に沿って，三角形の形状に合わせて厚みを増している（Figure 3.7-9）。

Figure 3.7-9 Main room east pediment (side facing inside the room)

上記の状態は，主室の四方に立つペディメントの主室側全ての面に共通するが，南面だけは，下部の張り出しがほとんどない。南ペディメントは残存状態が悪く上部を失っているが，下部の張り出し位置が残っており（Photo 3.7-1），上面に母屋桁を受けた，奥行きの浅い痕跡が残ることから，張り出しは，後の時代に削り取られたと思われる[5]。

主室の室内側の木造小屋組は，通例の通り棟木，上方2本の母屋桁，下方2本の母屋桁，2本の軒桁で構成されたと思われるが，このうち下方2本の母屋桁は，ペディメント下部の張り出し部上部に直接架け，この上に梁を渡して束を立てて上方の2本の母屋桁を支持

show that the ends of the tie beams straddled the eave girders as in the main room. Thus it can be understood that they were connected by a cross lap joint. The bench faces are the same, but the tie beams are thought to have been on top. The stone elements that covered the outer and top faces of the eave girders were also the same as in the main room, but as will be discussed later, among the pediments on the outer sides of the side rooms, those on the chamber side on the south and west sides appear slightly different from the rest.

3.7.3.2.2 Main Room Pediments

The lower part of the pediments projects outward into the chamber side, such that the top of the projection receives the bottom two purlins. Both bottom ends of the pediment (where the bottom surface connects with the top surface of the wall) have traces of a dado joint of eave girders, but in the area above the projection, neither the top of the ridge purlin nor the two upper purlins on the left and right have left any traces. There are also traces showing that rafters had been installed, traces where roofing bricks were attached, and traces where rafters adjoining the pediment had rested on stone elements below them, and the two ends of the above-mentioned projection were shaped to match the gradient of the rafters. They increase in thickness in conformity with the triangular shape, in line with the inner side of the traces showing where rafters were attached (Figure 3.7-9).

The above condition is common to all faces of the four pediments of the main room that face inside the room, but only that in the south side hardly has any projection at the bottom. The south pediment has remained in poor condition and has lost its upper part, but the bottom projection remains (Photo 3.7-1) and shows shallow traces of having received purlins on top, so the projection is believed to have been carved away in later years[5].

The wooden roof frame on the inner side of the main room is thought to have consisted of a ridge purlin, two upper purlins, two lower purlins and two eave girders, as customary. However, it can be assumed that the structure had two bottom purlins placed directly on the top of the projection at the bottom of the

Photo 3.7-1 Main room south pediment (side facing inside the room)

し，さらに梁を渡して中央に束を立て棟木を支持する架構であった，と考えることができる。

　ペディメント下部の張り出し部は，壁体上面と同位置に桁材を施設するため，壁体上面から敷桁１本分の高さで底部を抉りとっている。この下に施設された桁は，通例，大入れ痕跡を持たないペディメントに接して木造小屋組を組むとき，束を受ける最下部の部材として妻の壁体上面に載る部材である。ところが第３ゴープラでは，上述の張り出しが，下方の母屋桁を受けるため，最下段に束を用いない。したがってこの桁材は，通常の使い方と異なっており，施設された理由が不明瞭である。この部材は，両端をそれぞれ軒桁と接合する。したがって軒桁どうしの間隔を固定するという意味合いを持つかもしれない。また，妻の壁面に施設された開口部の上部に位置するから，ペディメントの荷重を受け，補強する意味合いがあったのかもしれない。

　主室ペディメントの外面は，いずれもレリーフを持ち，やや浅い傾向にあるが棟木，上方２本の母屋桁，下方２本の母屋桁，および２本の軒桁を，いずれも大入れとした痕跡が残っている。これはレリーフのために木造小屋組を施設しない通例の技法だが，南面のペディメントに関しては，外面に屋根勾配に合わせた三角形の張り出しを設けて中央にレリーフを施し，三角形の２辺の輪郭に合わせて棟木，母屋桁を上部から落とし込む仕口としている（Figure 3.7-10）。後述のように，側室のペディメントも同様の仕口がみられる。なぜ南のペディメントだけ仕様が異なるのか，現段階で

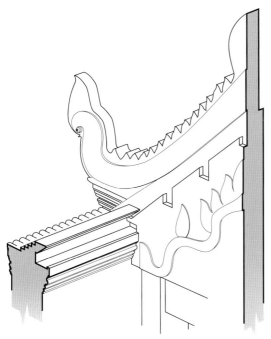

Figure 3.7-10 Main room south pediment (side facing the side room)

Restoration of the Roof of Gopura III

pediment, a tie beam placed on them to support the upper two purlins with struts, and another tie beam to support the ridge purlin with a strut in the center.

The bottom of the projection at the bottom of the pediment was gouged out a certain amount from the top surface of the wall equal to the height of one wall plate, in order to install a girder element at the same position as the top surface of the walls. The girder installed below this was usually placed on the wall of the gable as the bottommost element that receives the struts when assembling a wooden roof frame adjoining a pediment that has no traces of dado joints. In Gopura III, however, the above-mentioned projection received the bottom purlins, so no struts were used in the bottommost tier. This girder element was therefore used differently from usual, and was installed for an unknown reason. The ends of this element connected with an eave girder, so it may have served to fix the interval between eave girders. Also, since it was positioned above the opening in the gable wall, it may have served to receive the load of the pediment as reinforcement.

The outer face of the main room pediments are decorated with a relief, and have traces, although rather shallow, that show that the ridge purlin, two upper purlins, two lower purlins, and two eave girders were connected by dado joints. This was a common technique when not installing a wooden roof frame in order to preserve the relief, but the pediment on the south face has a triangular projection on the outer face matching the gradient of the roof and displaying a relief in the center, and has joints where the ridge purlin and purlins were dropped in from the top to match the shape of the two sides of the triangle (Figure 3.7-10). As will be discussed later, the same type of joints is also seen in the pediments in the side rooms. It is difficult at this stage to determine why only the specification of the south pediment differs.

All four pediments of the main room show clear traces on the outside where brick roofing elements that were attached to the side rooms came in close contact with the main room.

3.7.3.2.3 Side Room Pediments

Of the traces in the four side rooms attached to the main room, the chamber side of the pediments that stand on the outside are the same as those on the inside of the main room, as far as the east and north pediments are observed. However, the west and south pediments have a shallow projection, and traces of purlins that were placed on the projection are also shallow. The south face, in particular, has faint chisel marks that appear to show that struts were erected to support the purlins that were closely

Chapter 3 : Study Reports on Preah Vihear Temple

は判断が困難である。

　主室の四方いずれのペディメントも，その外面に，側室に葺かれていたレンガを密着させた痕跡が明瞭に残っている。

3.7.3.2.3 側室ペディメント

　四方に付属する側室の痕跡の内，外側に立つペディメントの室内側は，東および北のペディメントを見る限り主室の内側と同様である。ところが西および南のペディメントでは，張り出し部の奥行きが少なく，この上に載る母屋桁の痕跡も奥行きが浅い。とくに南面では，奥行きの浅い張り出しに密着させて母屋桁を支持する束を立てていたと思われるかすかな鑿跡があり，上部の面には，棟木と上方2本の母屋桁の痕跡を残している。この痕跡は，ペディメント中央部に作り出された，屋根形状に合わせてつくり出された厚みのある三角形の輪郭に合わせ，上から桁材を落とし込む仕口である（Figure 3.7-11）。西面は上方のペディメント部材が失われており，同様の痕跡が存在したかどうか確認ができない。南，西の2つの面は，いずれも鑿跡の様子から，後の時代になって下部の張り出しを削り，束を立てる架構に修正したと考えられる。南面上方の屋根構造の輪郭に合わせた三角形の張り出しに設けられた，上部から落とし込む仕口の痕跡は，このとき施設されたものとも，オリジナルのものとも考えられ判定が難しい。これは，南の主室ペディメントの仕口に対応しており，両ペディメントに棟木と桁材を上から落とし込むことで構成が可能だからである。

　以上の検討から，オリジナルの形状は，東と北のペディメントに残る形状であり，主室と同様の形式を持っていたことが判る。

3.7.3.2.4 屋根面と葺材の痕跡

　ペディメントの痕跡は，木造小屋組の仕口ばかりでなく，二等辺三角形を形成する垂木の痕跡の外周に，レンガを当てた痕跡が残っている。レンガの痕跡が砂岩の表面に残った理由は，レンガとペディメント面を密着させて漏水を防ごうとしたためであろう。この痕跡をみると，水平方向で320mmから400mmの幅があり，レンガの奥行き2枚分ほどに相当し，葺き厚をかなりとっていることが判る（Figure 3.7-12）。また，壁体上面で採取したレンガ片は，一方に勾配を持っていることから葺材であった可能性が予想された。このレンガ片は，石造の軒構成材に刻まれたステップによく馴染むように見える（Photo 3.7-2）。

　同様のレンガ痕跡を残す遺構は，プノム・チソール

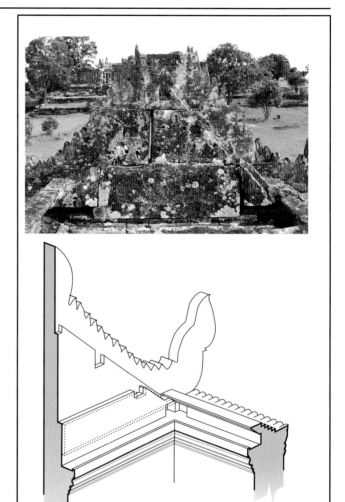

Figure 3.7-11 South side room pediment (side facing inside the room)

installed against the shallow projection, and the top surface has traces of the ridge purlin and two upper purlins. These traces are joints where girder elements were dropped in from the top to match the outline of the thick triangle that was formed in the shape of the roof in the center of the pediment (Figure 3.7-11). On the west face, the top elements of the pediment are missing, so it cannot be confirmed whether similar traces existed or not.

Judging from the chisel marks, it is thought that the lower part of the projection on the south and west faces was carved away in later years and modified to create a structure with struts. The traces of joints that were made in the triangular projection to match the outline of the roof structure at the top of the south face to drop in elements from the top may have been made at this time, or perhaps they were originally made; it is difficult to determine. This is because the joints correspond to the joints in the south pediment of the main room, and it is possible that the structure was made by dropping in the ridge purlin and girder elements into the pediments from the top.

From an examination of the above, it is clear that the east and north pediments display the original appearance, and that they

寺院の第3ゴープラやワット・プー寺院の「口の字」型平面を持つ付属建物にも見いだすことができる。いずれの例も直線的に葺き下ろす点、葺き厚を大きくとっている点は同様だが[6]、壁体上部の収まりの様子は大きく異なり、プレア・ヴィヘア寺院第3ゴープラのように軒桁の上部が砂岩材で覆われ、軒桁とレンガが確実に分離している例は見いだせない。ただ、当然のことだが、いずれも瓦葺屋根と比較すると、このままでは屋根荷重が異常な重量になることが予想される。したがってレンガ葺の遺構では、実際に施工されたかどうかはともかく、瓦形などの形状を削り出し、結果として軽量化することを目指していた可能性が高い。

プレア・ヴィヘア寺院第3、第4、第5ゴープラの石造の軒構成材は、いずれも垂木尻とともに軒桁の上面を覆うような形状を持っているが、その下面は、垂木の勾配に合わせて全面を整形している（Figure 3.7-13-01, 02）。つまり、垂木がどの位置に立とうとも対応が可能な形状である。これはおそらく、垂木の間隔がかなり狭く施設されたことを物語っている[7]。垂木の間隔は明瞭ではなく、時代によって多様であった可能性もあるが、初期の例であるコー・ケー遺跡群の壁体上面に残された痕跡が線状を呈していることから（Photo 3.7-3）かなり狭い間隔をとって並べることが

were made in the same style as the main room pediments.

3.7.3.2.4 Surface of the Roof and Traces of Roofing Elements

The traces on the pediments include not only traces of joints of a wooden roof frame, but also traces made by bricks around the perimeter of the traces of rafters that create an equilateral triangle. The traces of bricks probably remained on the surface of sandstone elements, because the bricks were closely adjoined to the pediment surface in order to prevent water leakage. They were 320mm to 400mm in width in the horizontal direction, equaling a depth of two bricks, and display a considerable roofing thickness (Figure 3.7-12). Additionally, brick fragments collected from the top of the walls had a gradient in one direction, so they were presumed to be roofing elements. These brick fragments appear to fit naturally with the step carved in the stone eave elements (Photo 3.7-2).

Photo. 3.7-2 Brick fragment remaining on the wall and steps carved in the stone eave component

Similar brick traces can also be seen in Gopura III of Phnom Chisor Temple and in the ancillary building with a square ground plan at Vat Phu Temple. Both examples are similar in that they slope straight downward and have a considerable roofing thickness[6], but the assembly at the top of the walls differ significantly. No examples similar to Gopura III at Preah Vihear Temple have been found in which the top of the eave girders was covered by a sandstone element and the eave girders and bricks were definitely separated. However, needless to say, compared to tiled roofs, the load of the roof would become abnormally heavy. Therefore, in brick-roofed buildings, it is likely that the shape of the elements was shaved and made lighter, leaving aside whether or not such a structure was actually built.

The stone eave components in Gopuras III, IV and V at Preah Vihear Temple are such that the top surface of the eave girders were covered along with rafter ends, but their bottom surface

Figure 3.7-12 Main room east pediment (side facing inside the room)

通常の技法であったと思われる。

しかしそれでも，垂木の間隔がレンガの幅より小さいことは考え難いので，垂木の上面に直接レンガを葺くことは困難だったであろう。つまり，垂木の上面には下地板が張られていたと考えなければならない。

was wholly shaped to match the gradient of the rafters (Figure 3.7-13-01, 02). In other words, they were shaped to fit regardless of the position of the rafters. This suggests that the rafters were installed extremely close together[7]. The actual spacing of the rafters is not clear, and may have differed according to era, but

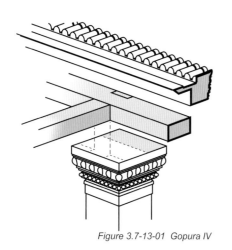

Figure 3.7-13-01 Gopura IV

Photo 3.7-3 Prasat Krachap (Koh Ker Monuments)

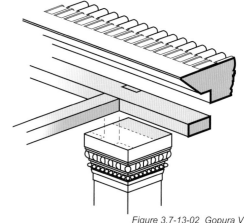

Figure 3.7-13-02 Gopura V

since there are linear traces (Photo 3.7-3) remaining on the top of the walls at Koh Ker Monuments, considered to be an early example, it is thought that installing the rafters rather close together had been a common technique.

Even so, since it is unthinkable that the rafter spacing was smaller than the width of the bricks, it would have been difficult to directly install the bricks on the rafters. In other words, it is natural to think that a base board had been placed on the rafters.

3.7.4 屋根構築の手順

以上の検討を踏まえ，以下にレンガ葺屋根の構築手順を整理する。各部の痕跡を見る限り，側室と主室に手順の差はみとめられず，さらに手順として独立していると考えられるため，主室を中心に整理する。

1. 4 ヵ所の妻壁上の敷桁を施設する。
2. 石造壁体の上面に，南北方向の木造軒桁を施設する（軒桁上面には，あらかじめ垂木を受ける仕口が施されていたか，あるいは手順4までに準備）。
3. 同様に，東西方向の木造軒桁を施設する。
4. 東西1本ずつ梁を施設する。
5. 石造ブロックを重ねて四方のペディメントを構築し壁体上部外側に石造軒構成材を積載する。
6. ペディメント下部の梁出し上に8本，交差部を跨ぐ4本の軒桁上に8本，東西2本の梁上4本，計20本の束を立てる。
7. 東西方向8本，南北方向4本の梁とペディメント下部の張り出しを繋ぐ下方の母屋桁を架ける。
8. 下方母屋桁上に，東西6本，南北4本の中段の梁を架ける。
9. 中段の梁上に東西12本，南北8本の束を立てる。
10. 上方の母屋桁を架ける。
11. 最上段の小梁，東西6本，南北4本を架ける。
12. 小梁の中央に，10本の束を立てる。
13. 交差する2本の棟木を載せる。
14. 垂木を施設する（谷の4本の垂木も含まれる）。
15. 垂木の上面に下地板を張る。
16. レンガを葺く。

3.7.4 Roof Construction Procedure

Based on the above examination, the construction procedure of the brick roof is summarized below. From the traces in each part, there does not seem to be any difference in procedure between the side rooms and main room. Furthermore, since the procedure seems to be independent among the structures, the procedure mainly of the main room will be described.

1. Wall plates were installed in four locations on the gable wall.
2. Wooden eave girders in the north-south direction were installed on the stone walls. (Joints for receiving the rafters were made in the top surface of the eave girders in advance, or until step 4.
3. Wooden eave girders in the east-west direction were installed in a similar manner.
4. Tie beams were installed on the east and west sides.
5. Stone blocks were stacked to create the four pediments, and stone eave components were loaded onto the outer side of the top of the walls.
6. A total of 20 struts were erected: 8 on the projection at the

17. 棟飾りを施設する（詳細不明）。

18.（屋根表面に瓦形を削りだす。）

　以上の手順のうち，木造部材の仕口等の加工は，構築される以前にあらかじめ施されていたであろうが，ある程度は現場で調整を施したことも予想される。また石材の痕跡の様子は，木造の部材を当てた場面で頻繁に現場調整を行っていたことを物語っている。

　以上の手順の整理から，レンガ葺のプレア・ヴィヘア寺院第3ゴープラは，Figure 3.7-14のように復原することができる。ここでは屋根面の瓦形の整形については手がかりがないため省略している。

3.7.5 レンガ葺屋根に予想される問題点

　先に述べたように，垂木の上面は，おそらく下地板が張られていた。下地板の表面にレンガを積載することは容易だが，しかしこれは，レンガを屋根面にどのように固定するかという問題を生むことであったとも考えられる。高さ60mm，長手300mm，短手150mm程のレンガを，おそらく小口を外に向けて内外に2列程度を積載する理由は，1列だけであれば，瓦形に削り出すことで各所に小片が生まれ，下地板のため固定しきれず剥離する恐れが生ずるためであろう。また，過剰とも見える葺き厚の荷重が木造小屋組に与える負担を承知していても，2列程度の厚さを以て葺き，さらに壁体上面で勾配を緩めて十分な厚さをとることで，全体の重量を以てレンガ屋根が安定することも期待されたのではないかと思われる。

　葺材の膨大な荷重は，母屋桁を押し下げ，梁中央部の垂下を招くことになったであろう。しかしペディメントに接する小屋組は，敷桁を壁体上に置くから小屋組の垂下や変形が小さい。プレア・ヴィヘア寺院第3ゴープラでも，下方の母屋桁を石材で受けるが，同様の事態が起こったことが十分に予想される。このためペディメントの位置では屋根の垂下は抑制され，建物の中央ほど垂下が大きくなるという変形が予想される。この結果，棟木が中央で撓み，屋根全体の変形を起こす結果を招き，ペディメントに密着していたレンガ屋根は上部ほど大きく剥離し漏水を招いた可能性が高い。異常な屋根荷重が木造架構に大きな負担を与えるという予想ばかりでなく，ペディメントに接する架構が中央部と異なることで起きる変形と漏水が，木造架構の寿命を一段と短くしてしまう原因になったと思われる。H．パルマンティエが予想した第3ゴープラ屋根の崩壊時期の真偽は不明だが，レンガ葺屋根の竣工後，短期間で深刻な問題を抱えることになり，早い時期に瓦葺に改修せざるを得なくなった可能性が高い。

bottom of the pediments, 8 on the four eave girders that cross the intersection, and 4 on the east and west tie beams.

7. Lower purlins were installed to connect the 8 east-west tie-beam and 4 north-south tie beams with the projection at the bottom of the pediments.

8. 6 middle-level tie beams were installed in the east-west direction and 4 in the north-south direction on the lower purlins.

9. 12 east-west struts and 8 north-south struts were erected on the middle-level tie beams.

10. The upper purlins were installed.

11. 6 small tie beams were installed in the east-west direction and 4 in the north-south direction on the topmost tier.

12. 10 struts were erected in the center of the small tie beams.

13. 2 intersecting ridge purlins were installed.

14. Rafters were installed (including the four valley rafters).

15. A base plate was affixed to the surface of the rafters.

16. Brick tiles were installed.

17. Cresting was applied (details unknown).

18. (The shape of roof tiles was carved on the surface of the roof.)

Within the above procedure, the joints of wooden elements were probably processed in advance before construction of the building, but adjustments may have been made to a certain degree onsite. Traces on stone elements also indicate that onsite adjustments were frequently made when wooden elements were pressed against them.

Following the above procedure, the brick-roofed Gopura III at Preah Vihear Temple could be restored as shown in Figure 3.7-14. It omits the tile shapes carved on the roof surface, as no hints have been found regarding them.

3.7.5 Expected Issues Concerning the Brick Roof

As mentioned earlier, a base plate was probably affixed to the top surface of the rafters. It is easy to load bricks onto the base plate, but this probably posed the issue of how to secure the bricks to the roof. Bricks that were 60mm high, 300mm in the lengthwise direction and 150mm in the widthwise direction were probably laid with their header facing outward and front to back in two rows, because a single row would have created small fragments throughout when carving them into tile shapes, making the bricks difficult to secure on the base plate and ultimately causing them to fall. Even knowing that the load of the apparently excessive tile thickness would weigh heavily on the wooden roof frame, the brick tiles were laid almost two-rows thick, but by reducing the gradient on the top of the walls and

Chapter 3 : Study Reports on Preah Vihear Temple

3.7.6 レンガ葺屋根の歴史的位置と構造的特徴

第3ゴープラの建立時期は明瞭ではないが，前節で述べたように，壁体上部の工夫や梁と軒桁の統合など，発達した技法が見られることから，早くとも11世紀後半より後に建立されたとみられる。したがって小規模な回廊などであれば，すでに迫り出し構造のレンガ造や石造屋根が実現していた時代である。ただ，第3ゴープラのように規模が大きく，交差部を持つような建築に石造屋根を載せることは，いまだに困難な時代であった。このため木造架構であるにも関わらず，レンガ葺の屋根を載せるという工夫が生まれたのだと思われる。つまり，木造瓦葺屋根から石造屋根に至る過渡期に生まれたアイデアの一つに違いないであろうが，おそらく，すでに実現し発達しつつあった石造屋根に触発されて現れた屋根形式であった。

プレア・ヴィヘア寺院第3ゴープラは，上記のように特徴的な，過剰とも見える葺き厚を持ちながらも直線的に葺き下ろすレンガ葺屋根を載せており，レンガ造のコーベル・アーチが持つ構造的性格や技術的特徴は一切みられない。この屋根の構造は，梁と束と母屋桁を組み合わせた純粋な木造架構である。レンガ葺であるプノム・チソール寺院のゴープラやワット・プー寺院の付属建物も，構造上，木造架構の屋根である点はまったく同様である。

これらの遺構が意味するものは，桁，梁，束を組み合わせる木造架構技術とブロックを重ねる迫り出し構造という，相互に独立した二つの技術の系統があり，容易に相互補完的に併存し機能できるものではない，ということであろう。つまり，これらレンガ葺の遺構は，冒頭で取り上げた先行研究の提案，つまり木造と石造の混構造が存在したとする提案に対し，あらためて検討を促す事例だと考えられる。クメール建築が木造屋根から石造屋根へ転換していく過程は，学術的にみてもきわめて興味深い問題である。私たちはこの問題に，慎重な姿勢を以て立ち向かうべきである。

securing an adequate thickness, the entire weight was probably expected to stabilize the brick roof.

The huge load of the tile elements probably pushed down on the purlins and caused the center of the tie beams to sag. However, the roof frame that adjoined the pediment displayed minor sagging and deformation, because wall plates were placed on the walls. Also in Gopura III at Preah Vihear Temple, stone elements received the load of the lower purlins, so the same situation might have occurred. The sagging of the roof was probably controlled at the position of the pediment, so the sagging probably became greater toward the center of the building. As a result, it is likely that the ridge purlins sagged in the center, causing a deformation of the entire roof, and the brick roof that adjoined the pediment largely delaminated toward the top and caused water leakage. It is thought that the abnormally heavy roof not only placed a large burden on the wooden structure, but the difference between the structure joined to the pediment and the central part of the building also caused deformation and water leakage, and in effect shortened the life of the wooden structure. Whether or not H.Parmentier's estimation of when the roof of Gopura III collapsed is true is not known, but it is highly probable that after completion of the brick roof, the building became burdened with a serious problem in a short period of time, and it became necessary to repair the roofing at an early period.

3.7.6 Historical Significance and Structural Features of Brick Roofs

The date of construction of Gopura III is not clear, but as discussed in the previous section, measures at the top of the walls, the integration of tie beams and eave girders, and other such developed techniques suggest that it was built after the latter half of the 11th century at the earliest. This is a period when small galleries already had a brick corbel structure or stone roof. However, it was still difficult at this time to place a stone roof on a large building with an intersection, like Gopura III. It was probably for this reason that measures were derived for placing a brick roof on a wooden structure. In other words, it was undoubtedly an idea that was born during the period of transition from a wooden tiled roof to a stone roof, but it was also a roof style that probably emerged inspired by the stone roof that had already been realized and was gradually developing at the time.

Gopura III at Preah Vihear Temple had a brick roof that sloped linearly downward even while having a characteristic roofing thickness that appeared exaggerated, as mentioned above, and showed no structural properties or technical characteristics of a brick structure with a corbel arch. This roof structure was purely a wooden structure built of a combination of tie beams, struts and purlins. The brick Gopura at Phnom Chisor Temple and Annex Building at Vat Phu Temple are structurally the same in that they have a wooden roof frame.

These buildings signify that there were two systems of techniques that were mutually independent—the wooden structural technique that combined girders, tie beams and struts, and the corbel structure made by stacking blocks. However, they cannot easily coexist and function in complement to each other. In other words, these brick buildings could be regarded as case examples that urge a review of the theory proposed by previous studies mentioned at the beginning of this chapter, that mixed structures made of both wood and stone had existed. The process through which Khmer architecture underwent a change from having a wooden roof to a stone roof is an extremely intriguing issue even from an academic perspective, and needs to be addressed with a careful attitude.

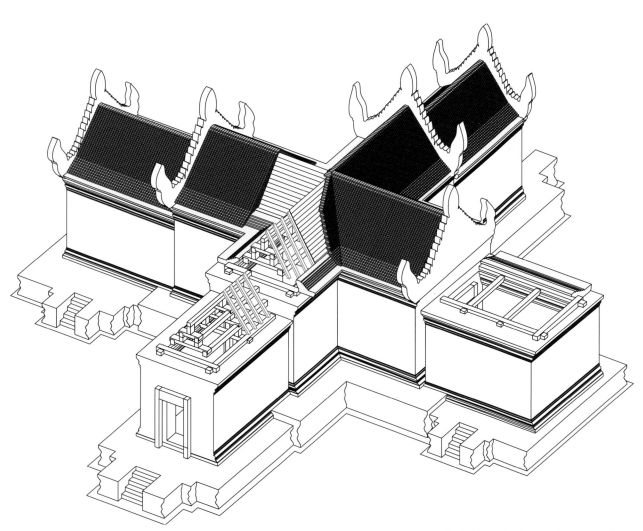

Fig. 3.7-14 Restraotion drawing of the brick roof

注

1）Parmentier,H.：L'art Khmer Classique, Monuments du Quadrant Nord-Est 2vols, Paris, EFEO, 1939.

2）Dumarçay,J.：Charpentes et Tuiles Khmeres，EFEO, 2005.

3）J.デュマルセ：クメールの小屋組と瓦，アンコール文化遺産保護共同研究報告書，奈良国立文化財研究所，1997.

4）服部博紀：プラサート・スープラ塔頂部屋根の痕跡調査と屋根の復原，アンコール遺跡調査報告書，日本国政府アンコール遺跡救済チーム，2003.

5）ペディメント下部の張り出しを削り取った理由は不明だが，敷桁の腐朽によって取り換える必要が生じたのではないかと推察される。その際に，おそらく敷桁の上部に被る張り出しを，ペディメントを解体して外した上で再構築するより，張り出し部分を削りとる作業がより簡便だと判断されたのであろう。敷桁を取り換えた後，この部材上に束を立てることで，問題なく小屋組の再構築が可能である。

6）プノム・チソール寺院の葺き厚は500mmを超え，ワット・プー寺院の葺き厚は300mm前後である。葺き厚の相違が何に由来するのか明瞭ではないが，壁間の距離が大きいと葺き厚が増加する傾向がある。なお，プノム・チソール寺院第3ゴープラの壁体上部は，外側にラテライトの軒構成材（内面にレンガの当たり痕跡が残る）を置き，内側に施設した軒桁との間をレンガで埋めている。梁端は，軒桁を超えて軒構成材に向かって伸びるため，おそらくレンガの中に埋設された。

ワット・プー寺院の「口の字」型平面の付属建物の壁体上部では，外側に軒瓦の形を刻んだ砂岩の軒構成材を配置し，内側に向けてステップが2段下がり，最下段に軒桁を施設していたと見られる。中段はレンガで充当し，最上段の軒構成材の上面の一部にもレンガが置かれたようである。

7）石造加工と木造加工はおそらく分離しており，石造軒構成材の工程の段階では，精確な垂木の位置が把握できずに加工を施していた可能性がある。しかしそれでも，垂木の間隔が十分に大きければ，石造の軒構成材の加工は垂木の当たる位置に合わせたものになったであろう。

Notes

1) Parmentier,H.: L'art Khmer Classique, Monuments du Quadrant Nord-Est 2vols, Paris, EFEO, 1939.

2) Dumarçay,J.: Charpentes et Tuiles Khmeres, EFEO, 2005.

3) Dumarçay,J.: Khmer roof frames and tiles, Report on the joint study for protection of the cultural heritage of Angkor, Nara National Research Institute for Cultural Properties, 1997.

4) Hattori,H.: Survey of roof traces at the top of Prasat Suor Prat and restoration of the roof, Angkor Monument Survey Report, Japanese Government Team for Safeguarding Angkor, 2003.

5) The reason why the projection at the bottom of the pediment was carved away is unknown, but it is thought that the wall plates needed to be replaced due to decay. When doing so, it was probably judged easier to carve away the projection that covered the top of the wall plates than to dismantle rebuild the pediment. After replacing the wall plates, it was possible to rebuild the roof frame without problem, by erecting struts on them.

6) The roofing thickness at Phnom Chisor Temple exceeded 500mm, and that at Vat Phu Temple was around 300mm. It is not clear what the difference in roofing thickness arose from, but roofing thickness tended to increase when the distance between the walls was large. In Gopura III at Phnom Chisor Temple, the top of the walls is such that laterite eave components were placed on the outer side (brick marks were found on the inner side), and the gap with the eave girder installed on the inner side was filled with brick. The ends of tie beams extended past the eave girders and toward the eave components, so they were probably embedded in the bricks.

In the Annex Building with a square ground plan at Vat Phu Temple, it seems that sandstone eave components whose outer side was carved in the shape of brick tiles was placed on top of the walls, and eave girders were placed on the bottom step of two steps going down toward the inside. Bricks were applied to the middle step, as well as to part of the top surface of the topmost eave components.

7) Stone processes and wood processes were probably separate, and at the stage of processing stone eave components, rafters may have been processed without knowing their accurate positions. However, even so, if the rafters were spaced sufficiently apart from each other, stone eave components would nevertheless have probably been processed to match the positions of the rafters.

3.8 「付属建物」としての「田の字」型・「口の字」型建築形式の復原的研究
Reconstructive Study on "田-shape" "口-shape" Styles as "Annex Building"

黒岩　千尋
KUROIWA Chihiro

3.8.1 はじめに

プレア・ヴィヘア寺院の顕著な特徴の一つに「田の字」型,「口の字」型の平面をもつ付属建物が併存することが挙げられる（Figure 3.8-1）。これらは南北に伸びる中軸線に対して,「田の字」型建物が山頂伽藍の東西に,「口の字」型建物が第3ゴープラの東西に, 対となり配置される。「田の字」型,「口の字」型の対の建物が連続的・継起的に見られるのは, プレア・ヴィヘア寺院のみである。しかし, その性質や機能の詳細はわかっていない。「口の字」型, さらに「田の字」型建築形式を詳細に分析する必要がある。

従来より, 寺院に付属する「付属建物」として「宮殿[1]」と称される建物が, クメールの既往文献において度々登場する。平面形式から「口の字」型,「日の字」型,「田の字」型建物とも類別される。しかし, ほとんどの既往研究が概略的な説明に留まり, その性質や機能面に関しては, 深く考えられてこなかった。クメール建築の変遷において, 祠堂・経蔵等の主たる建築形式と機能には大きな変化が見られない。一方で,「田の字」型のような建築形式の劇的な出現と急激な変容は注目に値する。「田の字」型建築形式が段階を経て, 変化を受容したものであるとすれば, 今まで「付属建物」と呼ばれてきた建物が, クメール建築の変遷とその意義を考察する上でふさわしい対象であると考えられる。

プレア・ヴィヘア寺院の詳細な調査と他寺院の「付属建物」の空間的特徴の比較から, その意義に関して推考する。

3.8.1 Introduction

One of the greatest characteristics in Preah Vihear Temple is the coexistence of "田-shape" "口-shape" Annex Buildings (Figure 3.8-1). "田-shape" located on the east and west side of the Complex on the mountain top and "口-shape" located on the east and west side of Gopura III along long south-north axis in temple. There is no temple that has 2 pairs of "田-shape" and "口-shape" except Preah Vihear Temple. However, it's not apparent that functions and features of these "Annex Building". It is necessary to study more on the architectural styles of "田-shape" "口-shape" buildings in consideration of temple Complex enlargement.

The building called "palace[1]" are confirmed as "Annex Building" in Khmer previous study. They are also confirmed as "田-shape" "口-shape" "日-shape" buildings from their plan. Previous studies are almost limited to guideline about them, and they were not deemed about functions and features. Originally, in Khmer temple history, the architectural styles and functions of the main buildings such as temple towers and Libraries are not particularly changed, by contrast, vigorous emergence of "田-shape" architectural style is remarkable. If "田-shape" architectural style has changed gradually, the "annexed" buildings of temples would be a significant subject to consider the transition of Khmer architecture.

Consider about significance of "Annex Building" by survey on these buildings in Preah Vihear Temple and the other temple for comparison on the spatial characteristics.

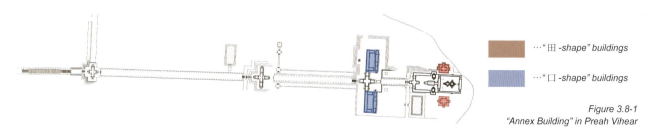

…"田-shape" buildings

…"口-shape" buildings

Figure 3.8-1
"Annex Building" in Preah Vihear

3.8.2 The Architectural Characteristics of "Annex Building" in Preah Vihear Temple

"L'Art Khmer Classique[2]" by H.Parmentier (1939) and "Carte archéologique du Cambodge[3]" by EFEO (2007) have previous drawings of Preah Vihear Temple. These drawings include mistakes and different notes from actual buildings.

Through the several terms of survey in Preaeh Vihear Temple, we measured each building by TPS instrument, 3D measurement, and hand mesurement, precise plans of "Annex Buildings" have drawn (Figure 3.8-2 - 3.8-5).

The roof of these buildings has lost in nature over many years, because it supposed to have wooden structural frames. There are several kinds of traces, which show the original appearance with roof-tiling.

3.8.2.1 Revision from a Plan Drawing of the Past

Figure 3.8-6 - 3.8-9 shows the past drawing of east and west "田-shape" "口-shape" buildings. There are some differences between new plan drawings and the past drawings.

I. West "田-shape" Building (Annex Building E)

· Each dimension	· Pilaster
· Wall of the porch	· Steps
· Number of window lattice	· Connection of wall

In the past plan of east building, 4 ponds is seen in the inner side encircled by pillars, but we couldn't find them because of soil on the ground. At the connection of inner wall and outer wall, a window overlaid with wall, and carved the lattice from vertical wall masonry stone directly (Photo 3.8-1). This part

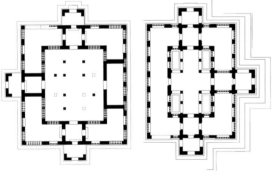

Figure 3.8-2 West "田-shape" building   *Figure 3.8-3 East "田-shape" building*

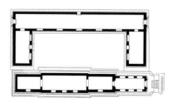   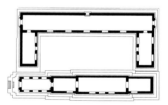

Figure 3.8-4 West "口-shape" building   *Figure 3.8-5 East "口-shape" building*

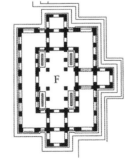

Figure 3.8-6 West "田-shape" building (past)   *Figure 3.8-7 east "田-shape" building (past)*

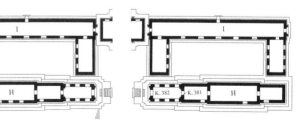

Figure 3.8-8 West "口-shape" building (past)   *Figure 3.8-9 East "口-shape" building (past)*

る壁材から直接窓の連子子が刻まれる（Photo 3.8-1）。これは，壁の取付後に窓の彫刻を施したものであろう。つまりは，この建物が改築された可能性が挙げられる。

II. 東側「田の字」型建物（付属建物 F）

・各部寸法	・付け柱
・建物内部の柱下部の段差	・窓の連子子の数

柱下独立部の段差は，4つの水盤をそれぞれ囲むように存在する。

III. 西側・東側「口の字」型建物（付属建物 H, I, H', I'）

・各部寸法	・ステップ
・窓の数	・窓の連子子の数
・基壇の形状	

西側「口の字」型建物の南辺，「一の字」型部分の窓のみ，連子子が5本で構成され，それ以外は7本である。また，既往図面からは西側建物の「コの字」型部分西壁面に窓が存在するが，実際には見られない。

3.8.2.2 木造痕跡の記録

各「田の字」型，「口の字」型建物から木造架構の痕跡が確認された。木造架構の痕跡図は，付章Ⅰに別途示す。また，木造架構の復原研究は，「3.5 木造屋根の技法とプレア・ヴィヘア寺院遺構の編年」を参照。

I. 西側「田の字」型建物

西側「田の字」型建物の中央部分には，12本の柱が存在したが，そのうち4本は倒壊している。柱天端面には，梁受けの痕跡が見られる。対応して，壁には梁受け大入れ痕が存在する（Photo 3.8-2）。中央とポーチを繋ぐ3つの部屋の上部四方にはペディメントがあり，それぞれのペディメントには5つの桁穴が存在する。ポーチと主室部分を直接繋ぐ壁は無いが，梁受け大入れ痕を確認され（Photo 3.8-3），梁が存在したことが理解される。内側壁面や柱側には，庇の架構痕跡が見られる（Photo 3.8-4）。中央とポーチを繋ぐ部屋の周囲の開口部は，ステップと木造扉の痕跡を有する。

II. 東側「田の字」型建物

東側建物の中央部分にも，8本の柱が存在するが，柱下部に段差を有する。柱天端面には，石材の梁が載る（Photo 3.8-5）。天端面に桁受けの痕跡があるため，柱と石梁の間には桁が通っていたと考えられる。中央部分とポーチをつなぐ部屋の上部四方にはペディメントがあり，5つの桁穴が存在する。建物の四隅にもペディメントを有する。窓枠下部と柱側面には小さなほ

might be curved after vertical wall has stood. It is supposed to be the modification of the west "田-shape" building.

II. East "田-shape" Building (Annex Building F)

・ Each dimension	・ Pilaster
・ Steps of pillar's foot	・ Number of window lattice

There are steps of pillar's foot independence parts as to surroud the 4 ponds.

III. "口-shape" Buildings (Annex Building H, I, H', I')

・ Each dimension	・ Steps
・ Number of window	・ Number of window lattice
・ Shape of Platform	

There are only 5 window lattices at the part of " 一 -shape" in west building, the other windows have 7 lattices. In the past drawing, there are windows at the west wall of "コ-shape" building in west building, actually there is no windows.

3.8.2.2 Survey Records of Wooden Trace

Each "田-shape" "口-shape" buildings have wooden structural traces. Appendix I shows the wooden trace drawings from these records. Also, reconstructive study is mentioned in Chapter 3.5.

I. West "田-shape" Building

In inner side of the west building, there were 12 pillars but 4 pillars already collapsed. There are traces of beam props at upper surface of pillars. Correspondingly, large props on the wall (Photo 3.8-2). Top of the chamber which connect the porch and inner side, 4 pediments in all directions make cross shape roof split into individual chambers which surrounding the inner side and corridor of inner side. Each pediment has 5 beam seats. Also, the porch is independent from the main body so that has large beam prop as connection with the one (Photo 3.8-3). On the wall surface and pillar side surface, traces are seen and were considered to there were the provisional eaves (Photo 3.8-4). Each door has step and wooden door trace.

II. East "田-shape" Building

In inner side of the east building, there are 8 pillars with bumps connecting each 2 pillars. There are stone trusses at upper surface of pillars (Photo 3.8-5) and traces of beam props on the wall enclosed by stone truss. Top of the chamber which connect the porch and inner side, there are 4 pediments to make cross shape roof split into individual chambers which surrounding the inner side and corridor of inner side. Each pediment has 5 beam seats. Also pediments are existence in 4 corners of this building. On

ぞ穴や痕跡が見られ，仮設的な庇が設けられていたことが想定される（Photo 3.8-6 〜 3.8-7）。

III. 西側・東側「口の字」型建物

東西の「口の字」型建物における木造架構痕跡は，細部に差異が確認されるが，痕跡位置や数は同様である。西側「一の字」型建物の上部は崩壊が激しく，痕跡の位置確認が不可能であった。東側建物の主室部分においては，4本分の梁受け痕跡が確認され，主室前方の側室とポーチでは2本ずつの梁受け痕跡が見受けられる。ポーチ部分の痕跡は他箇所と異なり，木材を引っ掛けるような形状をとる（Photo 3.8-8, Figure 3.8-10）。東西の「コの字」型建物の長辺部分の梁受け痕跡は，共に12本分であるが，痕跡間のスパンが異なっている。木造架構ではないが，窓や扉の上部には石材の荷重を軽減するための痕跡が見られ，木材が嵌め込まれていた可能性が考えられる（Photo 3.8-9）。

the lower part of window frame and pillar side surface, smaller traces are seen and were considered to there were the provisional eaves (Photo 3.8-6 - 3.8-7).

III. East and West "口-shape" Building

In west and east building, there are some detailed differences of wooden structure traces, but almostly they have same traces. Upper part of " 一 -shape" in west building have almostly corrapsed that we couldn't find traces. The main room of " 一 -shape" part in east building, there are 4 beams traces on each walls. In side room of the main room and porch space, each has 2 beams traces. At porch, the beam traces are differ from the other traces that for hook a timber (Photo 3.8-8, Figure 3.8-12). The long sides of east and west " コ -shape" part, there are 12 beams traces for each, but it is different in the span of traces. There are load reduction traces on upper part of window frames and door frames, which probably timber is fitted instead (Photo 3.8-9).

Photo 3.8-1 Connection of wall

Photo 3.8-2 Beam prop and Large prop

Photo 3.8-3 Large beam prop of porch

Photo 3.8-4 Eaves traces on the wall

Photo 3.8-5 Stone truss

Photo 3.8-6 Eaves traces on the wall

Photo 3.8-7 Eaves traces on piller side

Photo 3.8-8 Trace of hook timber

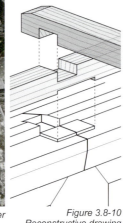
Figure 3.8-10 Reconstructive drawing

Photo 3.8-9 Load reduction

3.8.2.3 Differences in East and West Building

It is considered each "田-shape" and "口-shape" building in Preah Vihear Temple is to be as pairs, but there are some differences in details between east and west building.

I. Differences in "田-shape" Building

· Types of window	· Stone truss
· Plan scale	· Pediment position
· Number of rooms	

There are 3 types of window in the west building. First, type ① is a window with frame formatted by separate stone from wall masonry, which has lattices with molding decoration (Photo 3.8-10), type ② is a window with feigned frame that curved directly from the wall stone that uses 2 types of lattice, one has molding decoration and stands in outer line of window and another has no decoration and stands in inner line of window (Photo 3.8-11), type ③ is a window with no frame and its lattices are curved directly from wall stone with no decoration (Photo 3.8-12).

Compare to west building, east one has same number and same plot of windows, but has only one type of window, which with feigned frame that just curved directly to the stone (Photo 3.8-13). Figure 3.8-14 shows types and its plots of window in west building. Type ① window is regularly plotted 2 windows for each direction on outerwall, type ② is arranged the other

Photo 3.8-10 With stone frame (the west building)

Photo 3.8-11 Feigned curved frame (the west building)

Photo 3.8-12 No frame (the west building)

Photo 3.8-13 Feigned curved frame (the east building)

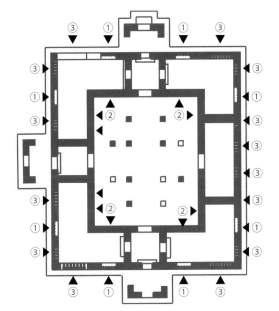

① with frame (*Photo 3.8-10*)
② with feigned curved frame (*Photo 3.8-11*)
③ no frame (*Photo 3.8-12*)

Figure 3.8-11 Window plot

所を占める。③の窓は，内側壁のすべてを占める。②・③の窓が，積んだ石材より直接彫られていることや，Photo 3.8-1で示したように，直行する壁から窓の格子が直接掘られていることから，西側建物の窓は①のタイプが先に計画され，②・③は建造後に増設された可能性が考えられる。また，1種類のみの窓をもつ東側建物は，西側の窓の増設計画を遂げた後に，対の建物として建造されたと見做すことが可能だと思われる。

東西建物において，平面規模・部屋の数・構法（窓枠・石張りの有無・ペディメントの位置）にも，差異が見られる。平面規模について，西側建物の外側壁面における規模は南北20.4m，東西18.7mである[4]。東側建物の規模は南北18.6m，東西15.3mであり，西側建物に比べ南北方向に約1.8m，東西方向に約3.3m縮小される。特に，十字柱列を有する建物内部の縮小率が大きく，一方で外側壁面と内側壁面の間の距離[5]は，東西建物各部で2.7m前後の一定値を保つ。この事実から，同建物では計画の優位性が建物周囲の両壁面に挟まれた空間にあり，この閉鎖的で連続的な回廊のような空間を主空間と見做すことが可能であろう。

構法に関しても，東西建物には差異が見られる。東側建物では，4つの水盤を囲む柱の上部に石材の梁が載り，西側に想定される木造梁に比べ後発的な技術が見られる。この敷桁の構法は，第4・第5ゴープラにも見られる。また，東側建物は西側建物にはない建物四隅のペディメントが確認される。

パルマンティエは，その平面規模の相違から中央祠堂の計画後に東西の「田の字」型建物が増築されたとしている[6]。東側建物は崖際に立地するため，地形の制約により規模を縮小せざるを得なかったことが推測される。このことからも，東側建物は西側建物の計画後に対として増築された可能性が高いが，さらなる検討が必要とされる。

II.「口の字」型建物の差異

・窓の配置	・窓の連子子の数

東側建物の「コの字」型部分において，東面壁体部には窓が存在する（Photo 3.8-14）。東西建物の窓は基本的に壁体下方より正方形に近い窓をもつが（Photo 3.8-15），東面壁体上方のみ横長の矩形の窓である。東西の建物は対称の計画に見えるが，西側建物にこの窓は確認できない。西側建物の「一の字」型部分で，窓の連子子の本数は5本である（Photo 3.8-16）。「コの字」型部分と東側建物では，7本である（Photo 3.8-14 ～ 3.8-15）。さらに西側「一の字」型部分において，主室と前方の側室の窓は窓枠材を有し，連子子のほぞ

---

windows except type ① of outerwall, and type ③ occupies all windows of innerwall. Type ② and ③ are curved directly from stone masonry, also window that curved directly and intersecting wall overlaid as we can see from Photo 3.8-1, it is considered type ① window has planned at first and added type ② and ③ in the west building. Also, the east building, which has 1 type of window, has a possibility that is planned as a pair building after the addition of windows to the west building.

In the east and west building, there are differences in plan scale, the number of rooms, and constructive methods (window, stone truss, pediment position). Focused on dimentions of plan, the west building size on the outer wall[4] is 20.4m from north to south, 18.7m from east to west. The east building size is 18.6m from north to south, 15.3m from east to west, that the east building is 1.8m on north-south direction and 3.3m on the east-west direction smaller than the west building. The inner area of building which have pillars lined in closs-shape is especially reduced its dimention, however the interval distance between the outer and inner wall[5] keeps 2.7m in each part of both buildings. This narrow and gallery-liked space is predominant on planning, and can be considered as the main space in this building.

In the east building there are stone trusses on the pillars surrouding 4 basins, that looks late technique compare to the west building supposed wooden trusses. This method of partition cap is seen at Gopura IV and V. There are 4 pediments to the corners only in the east building.

Parmentier mentioned the both "田-shape" buildings are planned after the construction of main shrine from the dfference of the both buildings scale[6]. The east building stands very limits to the edge of cliff because of topographical restriction. There is a possibility that the west building constructed first and the east building added later in that limitation. It is necessary to further architectural survey and comparative study with other examples.

II. Differences in "口-shape" Building

· Window plot	· Number of lattices of window

In " コ -shape" part of the east building, there are windows on the east wall (Photo 3.8-14). Basically, in the east and west building, windows are composed by nearly square shape from lower part of wall (Photo 3.8-15), only this east wall has windows constituted by wide shape from upper part of wall. The east and west buildings seem to be symmetry, but no windows in the west building. In the west " 一 -shape" part, the number of window lattices is 5 (Photo 3.8-16), and the other parts are 7 (Cf Photo 3.8-14,15). Furthermore, main room and the frontal side room in " 一 -shape" of the west building have stone window

穴は四角である（Photo 3.8-17）。後方の側室は窓枠材を持たず，ほぞ穴は丸である（Photo 3.8-18）。

内田悦生氏の岩石調査は[7)]，パルマンティエとサハイによる既存の諸説に対して新たな編年を提案し，さらに各建物内での増改築を詳述している。西側「一の字」型部分の東西側室は，後の改造の痕跡が認められ，建物の中核部は寺院内の最も初期の石造建築である可能性が指摘されている。その過程は，「コの字」型建物の付加による「一の字」型から「口の字」型への平面形式の改変と捉えることも可能だろう。一方，「付属建物」が何故増改築を経たのか，その経緯は判然としない。

3.8.3 「付属建物」の空間的特徴

「付属建物」を，寺院伽藍内における祠堂や経蔵，ゴープラ，回廊等の主要建物を除く機能・性質が不明なものと捉えると，そのような建物を有する遺構は，現在図面化されている全てのクメール遺跡中，41遺構から174棟がこれに比定される。これら全体を通して傾向を捉えることは難しい。各「付属建物」の伽藍内配置，平面形式，寺院の伽藍形式，他空間との類似性から総合的に分類を行う必要がある。以下の5類型への分類を試みた（Table 3.8-1）。

　①第1周壁/廻廊内に位置する「付属建物」
　②廻廊に類似する「付属建物」
　③「日の字」型寺院内の「付属建物」
　④参道沿いに位置する「付属建物」
　⑤複合型寺院における「付属建物」

frame and square mortises for lattice (Photo 3.8-17). Rear side room has feigned curved frame and round mortise (Photo 3.8-18).

Stone survey results by E.UCHIDA[7)], he proposed new chronicle of building construction in detail. The both ends of the west "一-shape" part have traces of modification, and the central part has a possibility of the most earliest stone building in this temple. That process can be considered as an alteration of building plan from "一-shape" to "口-shape" by addition of "コ-shape" building. However, the reason of the transition of "Annex Building" architectural style is unclear.

3.8.3 Spatial Characteristics of "Annex Building"

"Annex Building" is defined as the buildings that function and characteristics are unclear, and except the main buildings of temple Complex like a Central Sanctuary, Libraries, Gopuras and galleries. There are 174 "Annex Buildings" in 41 temples within the past studies and drawings of Khmer temples. It is difficult to find some tendencies of "Annex Building" totally. Consider about plot on temple complex, type of plan, type of temple layout, similarity of spatiality, comprehensive classification is needed. I classified "Annex Building" into 5 characteristics (Table 3.8-1).

　① plotted inside of Enclosure I/ Gallery I
　② similar to corridor
　③ figured in "日-shape" temple layout
　④ plotted along the temple approach
　⑤ figured in complex layout temple

Photo 3.8-14 Window of the east wall (the east building)

Photo 3.8-15 The other window (the east building)

Photo 3.8-16 5 lattices window (the west building)

Photo 3.8-17 Square mortise (the west building)

Photo 3.8-18 Round mortise (the west building)

Table 3.8-1 Classification of "Annex Building"

① plotted inside of 1st enclosure	② similar to corridor	③ figured in "日-shape" temple layout	④ plotted along the temple approach	⑤ figured in complex layout temple

Chapter 3 : Study Reports on Preah Vihear Temple

このうち，プレア・ヴィヘア寺院と類似性のある④⑤の21遺構58棟を比較対象とする。他類型に関しては「付属建物」の全体像を大まかに把握した上で比較検討を進めるために略筆した。対の建物，窓，材料，構法，寺院伽藍形式等を比較すると，4つの「付属建物」の空間的性質が明らかとなった。

3.8.3.1 対の建物の増改築

プレア・ヴィヘア寺院の調査結果より，西側「田の字」型建物の建設後に東側建物が増築された可能性が指摘される。また，「口の字」型建物においても，はじめに西側の「一の字」型建物が建立され，その後「コの字」型建物と東側建物が増築された可能性が考えられる。

クメール寺院において，「付属建物」が対として増築された例は他にも見られる（Table 3.8-2）。例えば，トラペアン・スヴァイ寺院では，「一の字」型建物と特異な平面をもつ「口の字」型建物が，第2ゴープラ脇に軸線を挟んで対に見られる。「一の字」型建物がまず建立され，その後「口の字」型に改築されたと推測されている（Figure 3.8-12）[8]。これらの事例から，「付属建物」には変遷の過程が存在することが想定される。

3.8.3.2 窓の種類とその配置

クメール建築の連子窓には，大別して以下の2種類が見受けられる。
①壁面低位置から正方形に近い形状の窓
②壁面上方に横長の長方形によって構成される窓
（①Photo 3.8-19，②Photo 3.8-20）
プレア・ヴィヘア寺院において，「田の字」型建物は②の窓を全ての面に有する。一方，「口の字」型建物で

Type ④ and ⑤ have similarities with Preah Vihear Temple, so 58 buildings in 21 temples are selected for comparative study. Other types are omitted to grasp the entire structure of "Annex Building" for comparison.

Comparison of window, material, constructive methods and temple layout, there are 4 common characteristics of "Annex Building".

3.8.3.1 Enlargement as a pair

From survey results as mentioned above, "田-shape" buildings have a possibility that enlarged east building after construction of west building. Also, "口-shape" buildings have a possibility that enlarged west + part and east building after construction of west "一-shape" part (Figure 3.8-16).

In Khmer temple complex, there are some examples to show the fact that "Annex Building" modified as a pair (Table 3.8-2). For example, in Trapeang Svay Temple, there are strange form "Annex Building", which are "一-shape" "口-shape" building oppositely near Gopura II along the temple axis. It is said these building altered from a original pair of "一-shape" in east and west building to altered to "口-shape" in east building later (Figure 3.8-12)[8]. These models suggest that "Annex Building" goes through the transformation process.

3.8.3.2 Window Types and Plots of "Annex Building"

In Khmer temple, there are 2 types of lattice window,
① lower positioning square window (Photo 3.8-19)
② higher positioning wide rectangular window (Photo 3.8-20)
In Preah Vihear, "田-shape" building has only type ② in all directions, and "口-shape" building has almostly type ① in south

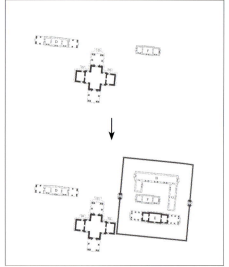

Figure 3.8-12 Modification of "口-shape" building in Trapeang Svay

Photo 3.8-19
① Lower positioning Square window

Photo 3.8-20
② Higher positioning Wide window

Photo 3.8-21 Platform height DIfference in "口-shape"

Table 3.8-2 Spatial Characteristics of "Annex Building"

	Plan	Pair/ Single	Type of Window and Plot	Material (wall part)	Height Defference of Platform	Temple Layout V-O : Vertically-Oriented C-L : Complex Layout
Pr.Thom	"—-shape"	pair	① east	laterite	—	"V-O" plain
//	"□-shape"	pair	① south, east	laterite	—	//
Pr. Banteay Srei	"—-shape"(east)	pair	① east	laterite	—	"V-O" plain
//	"—-shape"(west)	pair	① west	laterite	—	//
Preah Theat Preah Srei	"—-shape"	pair (different plan)	unclear	laterite	—	"V-O" plain
//	"□-shape"		unclear	laterite	—	"V-O" mountain
Pr. Neak Buos	"—-shape"	single	① south	laterite	—	//
//	"—-shape"	pair	① south(east bldg.), ① south&north(west bldg.)	brick	—	"V-O" mountain
//	"□-shape"	single	① south	sand stone ("—-shape"), laterite("□-shape")	—	//
Pr. Trapeang Svay	"—-shape"	single	① south	laterite	—	"V-O" mountain
//	"□-shape"	pair (different plan)	① south, ② east&west ("□-shape" east part)	sand stone ("—-shape"), brick (center"—-shape"), laterite ("□-shape")	○	//
Pr. Khnar	"—-shape"	single	① east	laterite	—	plain
//	"□-shape"	single	① south, east&west ("□-shape" east part), west ("□-shape" west part)	sand stone ("—-shape"), laterite ("□-shape")	○	//
Khleang	"□-shape"	pair[25]	① east&west ("—-shape") ② east (north bldg."□-shape"east part)	sand stone ("—-shape"), laterite ("□-shape")	○	plain
Pr. Dap	"—-shape"	pair	unclear	laterite	—	("V-O" plain)
Phnom Sandak[26]	"□-shape"	single	① south, inner area ("□-shape")	sand stone ("—-shape"), laterite ("□-shape")	○	"V-O" mountain
Pr. Phnom Thom	"□-shape"	single	unclear	laterite	—	"V-O" mountain
Preah Theat Toek Chha[27]	"□-shape"	single	unclear	laterite	○	"V-O" mountain
Pr. Phanom Rung	"□-shape"	single	① south, east (※ "—-shape"part composed by pillars, and opens to south&north)	laterite	○	"V-O" mountain
Vat Phu	"—-shape"	pair[28]	① east	sand stone	—	"V-O" mountain
//	"□-shape"	pair	① east, south, approach("—-shape") ② west	sand stone (south bldg. "—-shape"), brick (south bldg. "□-shape" west part), laterite (other)	○	//
Pr. Preah Vihear	"□-shape"	pair	① south, inner part ("□-shape") ② east (east bldg. "□-shape"east part)	sand stone	○	"V-O" mountain
//	"田-shape"	pair	② all side(outer&inner)	sand stone	—	//
Chau Srei Vibol	"田-shape"	single	① all side(inner) ② all side(outer)	sand stone	—	mountain
Phimai	"日-shape"	single	① south, east	sand stone	—	("C-L" plain)
//	"日-shape"	pair	① all side(inner) (※ no window in outer side)	laterite	—	//
Beng Mealea	"日-shape"	pair (different plan)	① south&north(inner) ② west	sand stone	○	"C-L" plain
//	"田-shape"		① all side(closs-shape) ② all side(outer&inner)	sand stone	—	//
//	"田-shape"	pair	unclear	unclear	—	//
Ta Prohm	"日-shape"	single	② all side(outer) (※ no lattice window in inner side)	laterite	—	"C-L" plain
//	rectangle	single	unclear	laterite	—	//
Preah Khan	"日-shape"	single	② south&north (※ no lattice window in inner side)	laterite	—	"C-L" plain
//	"日-shape"	single	(※ no window in outer side, no lattice window in inner side)	laterite	—	//
//	rectangle	single	② south&north	laterite	—	//
Pr. Banteay Chhmar	"日-shape"	single	unclear	unclear	—	"C-L" plain
//	rectangle	single	unclear	unclear	—	//
Banteay Kdei	"日-shape"	single	(※ no window in outer side, no lattice window in inner side)	laterite	—	"C-L" plain

は南側と「コの字」型の中庭に面する壁に①の窓を持ち、東側建物の東壁面のみに②の窓を持つ。

Table 3.8-2の「Type of Window and Plot」の項目に、各「付属建物」の窓種類と箇所を示した。「一の字」型建物や「口の字」型建物の主室や前室では、ほとんどの建物で南面と東面のみに連子窓を有する。例外的にワット・プー寺院の「口の字」型建物が参道沿いに連子窓を持ち、プノム・サンダック寺院の「口の字」型建物が中庭に面して連子窓を持つが、これらの平面形式の建物では、概して南と東の方位に対して開放優位性を有することが考えられる。これは「一の字」型建物からの性質であり、「口の字」型建物にもその傾向が引き継がれる。

一方、「日の字」型建物や「田の字」型建物では、全方位に窓を有している。とりわけ、外側壁面に②のタイプの窓、内側壁面に①のタイプや連子子を持たない開口部が確認される。外部に閉鎖的であり、且つ、廻廊状の連続空間に対して全方位の開口部から同等に光を取り込もうとする意識を捉えることができる。但し、ピマイ寺院南側参道沿いの「日の字」型建物は前者の性格に類し、特例として挙げられる。

「付属建物」は開口部とその空間性において変容プロセスの存在が認められる。

3.8.3.3 「付属建物」における空間の序列化

「付属建物」の壁体部における材料構成を確認する（Table. 3.8-2「Material」の項）。特に、「口の字」型建物内での、材料の差別化の傾向が窺える。ニャック・ブオス寺院等「口の字」型建物では「一の字」型部分に砂岩材が使用され、「コの字」型部分にラテライトが使用されている。ワット・プー寺院とトラペアン・スヴァイ寺院の「口の字」型建物では、各辺によって3種類の材料がそれぞれ使用され、複雑な構成であるが、いずれも「一の字」型建物には砂岩材が用いられる。材料の差別化により建物内の序列化が意図されている可能性が挙げられる。つまりは「一の字」型部分と「コの字」型部分における材料差がそのまま、空間のヒエラルキー差を表現しているという見方である。

基壇部の高さも「一の字」型と「コの字」型部分とで異なる。プレア・ヴィヘア寺院やパノム・ルン寺院の「口の字」型建物では、「一の字」型部分の基壇が高く、「コの字」型部分は低くなる（Photo 3.8-21）。

「口の字」型建物では、材料と高さの調整が「空間の序列化」を表現する手法として見られることを注意しておきたい。一方で、「田の字」型や「日の字」型建物では、1つの建物内では同一材が用いられ、「空間の

and facing innerside of " コ -shape" part, also only east wall of east building has type ② .

Table 3.8-2 "Type of Window and Plot" shows types of windows and its plots of each "Annex Building". Typical " ― -shape""□-shape" architectural styles have lattice windows on south and east wall. Exceptionally, "□-shape" buildings in Vat Phu Temple have windows along the temple approach and "□ -shape" building in Phnom Sandak Temple has windows towards the inner space of building. The tendency of these buildings shows the characteristics of the predominant openness to south and east. This is a tendency from " ― -shape" building and succeed to "□-shape" building.

On the other hand, "田-shape" and "日-shape" styles have a tendency to make windows in all directions. They have type ② window towards can see at the outer wall of building and type ① and window with no lattice can see at the innerside. They are closed to the outside, and succeed gallery-liked space is lightened by windows of all directions equally. Exceptionally, "日-shape" building on south approach in Phimai Temple belongs to the former tendency. "Annex Building" has a transition process on its window and space.

3.8.3.3 Hyerarchical Factors of "Annex Building"

Consider the material composition of the building wall of "Annex Building" (Table. 3.8-2 "Material"), there is a tendency that "□-shape" building has a differentiation of materials. In "□-shape" building of Neak Buos Temple, " ― -shape" part is composed by sand stone and " コ -shape" part is constructed by laterite. In "□-shape" building of Vat Phu Temple and Trapeang Svay Temple, " ― -shape" part is constructed by sand stone and each side of "コ-shape" part is composed by 3 materials. The differentiation of materials between " ― -shape" and "コ-shape" part shows a hierarchy of space signification.

There is tendency that " ― -shape" parts of "□-shape" buildings are made by sandstone and " コ -shape" parts are made by laterite. Distinction of materials shows the hierarchy of each building.

Also, height of platform is different in " ― -shape" and " コ -shape". In "□-shape" building in Preah Vihear Temple and Phanom Rung Temple, " ― -shape" part platform is higher than "コ-shape" part (Photo 3.8-21).

In "□-shape" building, "spatial hierarchy rises" by distinction of materials and height. On the other hand, "田-shape" and "日 -shape" building use same material into one building, which has no meaning of "spatial hierarchy". In Complex layout temples like Preah Khan Temple, the main shrine and galleries

序列化」の手法は認められない。プレア・カーン寺院等の複合型寺院では，祠堂・回廊に砂岩材が用いられるのに対し「付属建物」は主にラテライトが用いられ，寺院内では顕著にヒエラルキー差を示す。開口部の配置とともに，「付属建物」の各平面形式における空間性の相違を生み出す手法として，石材の種類及び基壇部高さの差に注目する必要がある。

3.8.3.4 「付属建物」を有する寺院の伽藍形式

　プレア・ヴィヘア寺院は，山岳の斜面地を利用する「山岳式縦深型寺院」である。プラサート・トム寺院は縦深性の強い伽藍を有しながら平地に立地する「平地式縦深型寺院」[9]，プレア・カーン寺院は平地に複合的に展開する「平地式複合型寺院」である。G. セデスは東南アジア固有の基層文化として山岳地への信仰による寺院造営を挙げているが[10]，その根拠は述べていない。プレア・ヴィヘア寺院等の「縦深型寺院」では，「口の字」型，「一の字」型建物が多く造営され，寺院参道を挟みもしくは片側に，訪れた者を迎えるかのように立地する。ピマイ寺院等の「複合型寺院」では，「田の字」型，「日の字」型建物が見られ，寺院の周壁外や廻廊外側に位置する。その中で，プレア・ヴィヘア寺院の「田の字」型建物のみが山岳式縦深型寺院に位置することから，寺院が平地式複合型寺院に見られる性格を有していたと推定されるが，考察を必要とする。

3.8.4 「付属建物」の機能

　碑文資料から，ヤショヴァルマンⅠの頃に各地に木造の「アーシュラマ（açrama）」が建てられたことが理解される。「アーシュラマ」については諸説見られるが，「僧房」としての解釈が散見され，プレア・ヴィヘアの東側「口の字」型建物の碑文（K381）より，スールヤヴァルマンⅠが苦行者タパスヴィンドラパンディタに「ヴィラシュラマ」という僧房を寄進した事実が見られる[11]。「アーシュラマ」の語は，「付属建物」を有するその他の寺院碑文からも確認される。また，バンテアイ・クデイ寺院は仏教僧院だが，複数の建物から陶器等の日常生活に供する出土品が発見されている。バンテアイ・スレイ寺院の碑文からはクメール寺院における師（Guru）の存在が窺え，「付属建物」は師と修行僧の学林のための場として用いられていたことが１つの可能性として挙げられる。

3.8.5 「付属建物」の変遷過程に関する現時点での整理

　「付属建物」が如何に変容したのか，既往研究と碑文資料，および増改築の痕跡の比較考察から，「付属建物」

are constructed by sand stone, however "Annex Buildings" are mainly constructed by laterite, which shows hierarchical composition apparently. It is considered the plot of window type, material composition and height of platform are the methods to create the differentiation of spatial hierarchy.

3.8.3.4 Temple Layout of "Annex Building"

Preah Vihear Temple is one of the "vertically-oriented" temples on terraced slope of the mountain. Pr. Thom and Banteay Srei Temple is "vertically-oriented" temple on the plains[9]. Preah Khan Temple is one of the "Complex layout" temples on the plains. G.Coedes mentioned that one of the fundamental cultures in Southeast Asian countries is a construction of temple to the mountains from a belief to the holy mountain[10], however he didn't note the reasons. "Vertical-oriented" temples like Preah Vihear Temple have mainly "口-shape" "一-shape" building, which are located on both or one side of approach. "Complex layout" temples like Phimai Temple have mostly "田-shape" "日-shape" building, which are located on outside of temple enclosure. The architectural style of "Annex Building" seems to depend on the style of temple layout, the only "田-shape" building in Preah Vihear Temple is located on "vertically-oriented" temple in the mountain. It is considered it had a nature of "Complex layout" in the plains. Further consideration is needed.

3.8.4 Functions of "Annex Building"

Supposition from temple's inscription, the monastic building "açrama" have constructed in each area of the empire during the reign of Yasovarman I . There are various opinions on the meaning of "açrama" and many are interpreted as a monastry. The inscription K381 in the east "口-shape" building of Preah Vihear Temple shows Suryavarman I honored the ascetic Tapasvindrapandita with the monastic building "Viraçrama"[11]. Similarly, "açrama" words are found in other temples which have "Annex Buildings". Banteay Kdei Temple are known as Buddhist monasetry, where burial goods like ceramics were found in several buildings. "Annex Building" is considered to be for the ascetic practice of teacher (Guru) and students by the inscription of Banteay Srei Temple, however it is needed furthermore study on this subject.

3.8.5 Transision of "Annex Building"

Many "Annex Buildings" didn't been clarified its transition process. I considered the process from research of the past studies, the inscriptions, and traces of alterations of building,

Chapter 3 : Study Reports on Preah Vihear Temple

の変遷を推定した（Table 3.8-3）。窓の種類，構成材料，
伽藍形式等の空間構成要素の特徴と併せると，以下の
2つの時期に「付属建物」の移行期が確認される。

I. 10 世紀後半〜 11 世紀始め

ワット・プー寺院，パノム・ルン寺院等において，
多くの「口の字」型建物が建立される。「一の字」型
から「口の字」型への移行事例が見られる。特定方位
での連子窓の設置，異材料の使用と基壇部高低差より，
「空間の序列化」を確認した。主に，「平地式」から「山
岳式」の縦深型寺院に「付属建物」が立地する傾向が
ある。

II. 11 世紀後半〜 12 世紀始め

「口の字」型建物は確認されず，「田の字」型「日の字」
型建物へと移行する。それ以前は，正方形の窓が東と
南面に優位に見られたが，この時期より，壁面上方の
横長長方形の窓が全方位に見られ，中庭に向けて大き
な開口部をもつ傾向がある。「空間の序列化」は消失し，
平地の複合伽藍に「付属建物」は建立される。

その中で，プレア・ヴィヘア寺院の「田の字」型建
物のみが「山岳式縦深型寺院」であることが特筆され
るが，この意義は寺院がダンレック山脈に位置し，交
通の結節点の性格を有すること，寺院がアンコール平
原を志向し，クメール王国の中心地アンコールを眺望
することから，王国内で特殊な位置付けを占め，地方
拠点として重要性を帯びたことが，主な理由として考
えられる。寺院は後期に，「平地式複合型寺院」と同様
の役割も担うようになった可能性が挙げられる。

3.8.6 結論

プレア・ヴィヘア寺院の「付属建物」の建築的特徴
を手掛かりに，代表的な寺院との比較考察を行った。
クメールの隆盛期に，山岳地のみならず，平地の縦深
型寺院にも「付属建物」が多く造営されたこと，それ
らの開口部，構成材料，基壇部の段差，廻廊状の連続
空間等における変容プロセスを指摘することができた。
山岳寺院としての性質を示すとともに，12世紀以降，
複合型大寺院が大都市・拠点を担うことに伴って，「付
属建物」は長期的な礼拝・学林のための，複合型寺院
へと収束する。プレア・ヴィヘア寺院は両方の傾向が
クロスする性格を持ったと考えられる。

completed Table 3.8-3 in the following page. Including spatial characteristics of window type, material composition, and temple layout, there are 2 transitional stages of "Annex Building".

I. Late 10th Century-Early 11th Century

Many "□-shape" buildings have constructed which is seen at Vat Phu Temple and Phanom Rung Temple. Some examples show the transformation from " — -shape" to "□-shape". The spatial hierarchy risen by window uses in specific directions, differentiation of materials and platform height. Temple layout has altered from "plains style" to "terraced slope style".

II. Late 11th Century-Early 12th Century

Instead of "□-shape" construction, "田-shape" "日-shape" mostly have configured. The large square window which opens to south and east predominantly, specifically has changed into the higher positioning rectangular window which open to all direction and large window which open to inner side. The spatial hierarchy disappeared and temple layout has transferred into Complex layout temple.

Only "田-shape" building in Preah Vihear Temple located on "vertically-oriented" temple on terraced slope. Preah Vihear Temple is located on Dangrek Mountains that has a nature as a node point of transportation, pointed out and look over the Angkor Plains from top of the mountain. There is a possibility that temple took a role as same as "Complex layout" temple on the plains in the later period of the empire because of its uniqueness as a regional base.

3.8.6 Conclusion

I considered architectural characteristics of "Annex Building" in Preah Vihear Temple through the comparative study. The fact is that "Annex Buildings" are configured on "vertically-oriented" temple on terraced slope and also on the plains in Khmer prosperous time, and there is a transition process considered by windows, materials, height of platform and gallery-liked space. "Annex Building" concluded into Complex layout temple for long-term worship and ascetic practice after 12th century along with the change of large Complex temple to the provincial principal base. It is considered that Preah Vihear Temple has both sides of characteristics.

Reconstructive Study on "田-shape" "口-shape" Styles as "Annex Building"

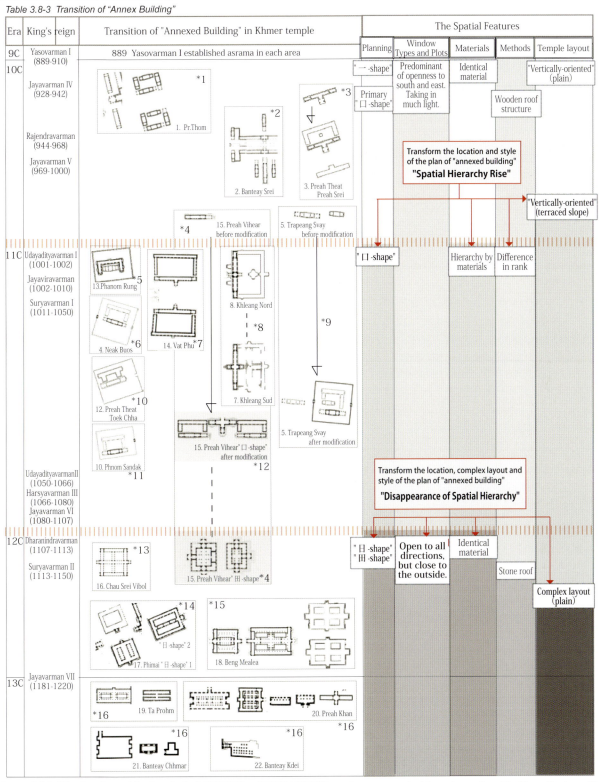

Table 3.8-3 Transition of "Annex Building"

*1 Katsura SATO, "Site Overview and Previous Studies", KOH KER and BENG MEALEA -two large monuments at the eastern portion of the Khmer Empire-, p.29-31, 2011.   *2 Georges Coedès, "Inscription du Cambodge I", p.143-147, "Inscription du Cambodge II" p.62/105/170, 1910-.   *3 Supposition from the following document Georges Coedès, "Inscription du Cambodge V", p.32-34, p.170.   *4 Stone survey results by Etsuo UCHIDA, and Shun HACHISUKA, "Study of Chronology about Preah Vihear by using 3D models", 2010.   *5 Shoji ITO, "Khmer ancient heritage, Phanom Rung Temple", Journal of Asian and African Studies, No.23, 1982.   *6 Supposition from the following document   Georges Coedès, "Inscription du Cambodge VI", p.236.   *7 Kunikazu UENO, "On the roof construction of Palace in Wat Phu, Laos", Annual Convention of Architectural institute of Japan, 1991.   *8 Pascal ROYERE, "Le Khleang Sud'd Angkor Thom : Quelques éléments liés à l'histoire architecturale du monument", BEFEO84,1997.   *9 Bruno BRUGUIER, "Preah Khan, Kor Ker et Preah Vihear Les provinces septentrionales", p.442-449.   *10 Supposition from the following document   Georges Coedès, "Inscription du Cambodge II", p.105, p.170, "Inscription du Cambodge V", p.222.   *11 Supposition from the following document   Georges Coedès, "Inscription du Cambodge VI", p.247.   *12 Shoji ITO, "Khmer ancient heritage, Preah Vihear", Journal of Asia and Africa Studies, No.26, 1983.   *13 Ichita SHIMODA, "Architectural Survey of the Chau Srei Vibol Monument", KOH KER and BENG MEALEA -two large monuments at the eastern portion of the Khmer Empire-, 2011.   *14 UNESCO world heritage centre website "http://whc.unesco.org/en/tentativelists/1919/", 2004.   *15 Akinori MIZOGUCHI, "A Proposed Rational behind the Ancient Khmer's Dimentional Planning at the Beng Mealea", 2012.   *16 Olivier CUNIN, "De Ta Prohm au Bayon", Tome I/II, p.22/41

注

1） J.Moura.: Le Royaume du Cambodge, II, Paris, 1883, p.247. L.Lajonquiere.: Inventaire descriptif des monuments du Cambodge, Paris, 1902/1907/1911.

2） H.Parmentier.: L' art khmer classique, Monuments du quadrand Nord-Est, PEFEO, Paris, 1939, pp.45-73.

3） Carte archéologique du Cambodge Ministère de la culture et des beaux-arts ; École française d'Extrême-Orient, 2007.

4） ポーチ部分は含まない。

5） 壁の外法を基準とする。

6） 注2）に同じ。

7） 「3.2 石材の特徴に基づくプレア・ヴィヘア寺院遺跡の建造順序の推定」（内田悦生）を参照のこと。

8） B.Bruguier.: Preah Khan, Kor Ker, et Preah Vihear Les provinces septentrionals, Guide archeologique du Cambodge Tome V, 2013, pp.447-448.

9） 中川武:クメール寺院伽藍における縦深型祠堂の形成過程カンボジア プレア・ヴィヘア寺院に関する研究（7），日本建築学会大会，2014年，pp.673-674。

10） G.Coedes.: The Indialized states of Southest Asia, The University Press of Hawaii, 1963.

11） 伊東照司:クメール古跡プラ・ウィハーン寺院：タイ国クメール遺跡調査報告（3），アジア・アフリカ言語文化研究，第26号，1983年11月，pp.220-234。

Notes

1) J.Moura.: Le Royaume du Cambodge, II, Paris, 1883, p.247. L.Lajonquiere.: Inventaire descriptif des monuments du Cambodge, Paris, 1902/1907/1911.

2) H.Parmentier.: L' art khmer classique, Monuments du quadrand Nord-Est, PEFEO, Paris, 1939, pp.45-73.

3) Carte archéologique du Cambodge Ministère de la culture et des beaux-arts ; École française d'Extrême-Orient, 2007.

4) Not including porch part.

5) Measured between the wall surface.

6) Refer to 2).

7) Refer to "3.2 Determining the Construction Sequence of the Preah Vihear Temple Monument in Cambodia from its Sandstone Block Characteristics" by E. UCHIDA.

8) B.Bruguier.: Preah Khan, Koh Ker, et Preah Vihear Les provinces septentrionals, Guide archeologique du Cambodge Tome V, 2013, pp.447-448.

9) T.NAKAGAWA.: Formation Process of a Khmer Temple strung out along acclivitous axis - Studies on Preah Vihear Temple, Cambodia (7) -, Architectural Institute of Japan, 2014, pp.673-674.

10) G.Coedes.: The Indialized states of Southest Asia, The University Press of Hawaii, 1963.

11) S.ITO.: On the Khmer Temple, Prasat Phra Viharn in Thailand, Journal of Asian and African studies, 1983, pp.220-234.

3.9　アンコール期における「経蔵」の設計方法
Planning Method of "Library" in Angkor Period

貞富　陽介　　成井　至
SADATOMI Yosuke　　NARUI Itaru

3.9.1 はじめに

　クメール寺院を構成する一要素である「経蔵」と呼ばれる建物は，寺院内において中央祠堂を正面にして左側，あるいは対となって存在する建物を指す。クメール建築では「経蔵」と呼ばれる建物に経典や書典が納められていたという記録は残っていないが，周辺諸国の例としてタイのホ・トライやミャンマーのピダガッ・タイには書庫としての機能が確認されており，配置傾向や構造形式からもクメールと同種であると考えられるものが特に「経蔵」と呼ばれている。G. セデスのクメール碑文研究ではその建物に類する語と関連した記述が複数確認されており，pustakàçramah を宝物庫（プラサート・クナ寺院，プラサート・コック・サック寺院碑文より），dravyâçramah を寺院の財産庫や宝物庫（ワット・プー寺院碑文より），vidyâçramah を神学校（プラサート・コンパス寺院碑文より），krakå glåñ を聖なる倉（ワット・バセット寺院碑文より）と解釈している。結果的にこれらの語が指す意味的範囲の共通項としてフランス語の「Bibliothéque」の訳語として「経蔵」という語を用いている。G. セデス，M. グレイス，J. ボワスリエ，C. ジャック，荒樋久雄各諸氏によってこの建物に関する研究が行われてきた。特に近年のC. ヴィタロン，藤田達哉，原智子各諸氏は自身の研究において，経蔵の建築学的特徴と碑文研究から用途や機能に関する分析を行っている。具体的には左側の経蔵において換気システムが備えられている点，対となる経蔵で遺物が異なることから，儀式の内容が異なっていたであろう点などが指摘されている[1]。

3.9.2 研究目的

　プレア・ヴィヘア寺院の2つの「経蔵」は，第1回廊の外に配置されている点，対になる経蔵の正面が向かい合う点など，一見して他遺構との相違が明白である。だがこの建物の包括的な設計方法は未だ明らかに

3.9.1 Introduction

　The so-called "Library" building is one component that generally configures a Khmer temple complex. It has a tendency to be located on the left side in front of a Central Sanctuary as a single or on the both sides as a pair of buildings. In Khmer history, there are no records that indicate that inscriptions or some other book-like manuscripts were placed in a "Library". However, there are some examples of building in neighboring countries that have similar characteristics of structural style and disposition of arrangement to that of Khmer which are collectively called "Library". For example "Ho-trai" in Thailand and "Pitakat-taik" in Myanmar have been confirmed that they function as the actual library. In the study of Khmer inscriptions by G.Coedes, he mentioned that the words and relative sentences relating to the "Library" building appeared, and can be interpreted as "pustakàçramah" a treasure house (inscription in Prasat Khna Temple and Prasat Kok Sak Temple), "dravyâçramah" as a storehouse or a treasure house of the temple (inscription in Vat Phu Temple), "vidyâçramah" as a theological school (inscription in Prasat Kompas Temple), and "krakå glåñ" (inscription in Vat Basaet Temple) as the sacred warehouse. As a result, the building was designated as a "Bibliothéque" in French as a common denominator of meaning. G.Coedes, M.Glaise, J.Boisselier, C.Jacques, and H.Arahi are major researchers of this building style. More recently researches C.Vitharong, T.Fujita, and T.Hara mentioned the uses and functions of "Library" through their study of architecture features and inscriptions. It has been noted that only the left "Library" had a ventilator system implying different functionality[1].

3.9.2 Purpose of Study

　The two "Libraries" in Preah Vihear Temple have clear differences from other "Libraries" in as much as they are situated outside of the Gallery I, and this pair of Libraries face each other.

Chapter 3: Study Reports on Preah Vihear Temple

されておらず，プレア・ヴィヘア寺院においても「経蔵」の建物単体の基本計画や寸法計画の研究はなされていない。

一方で近年のクメール伽藍寸法研究は一定の成果を見せつつある。造営尺度が1ハスタ＝約412mmとみなせること，基座輪郭が規模決定の際に基準となることなどが寺院伽藍の全体計画を対象とした分析によって指摘されている[II]。しかし伽藍規模での平面計画の研究が進む一方で，建物単体を対象とした研究は少ない。さらにそのほとんどは平面計画を対象とした分析であり，平面と立面の関係性を明らかにする研究は少ない。そこで本研究は対となる経蔵の寸法差，及び平面―立面の関係性を同時代，同形式の遺構との比較を通して経蔵の基本計画とプレア・ヴィヘア寺院の特徴を考察する基礎的研究とする（以下，本研究では経蔵と統一して表記する）。

3.9.3 分析対象遺構の選定

既往研究であるEFEOの図面分析，編年考察，他の経蔵に関する既往研究を踏まえて，以下の点でプレア・ヴィヘア寺院と比較有用な遺構を本研究の分析対象として選定した（Figure 3.9-1）。
①10世紀以降に見られる主室，庇の形式をもつもの。
②前室，疑似扉を有する，10世紀以降に見られる経蔵の一般的な形式である。
③残存状況が良く，平面計画と立面計画において関係性を考察するに適切である。

対象遺構は以下に挙げた，プレア・ヴィヘア寺院を含めた5遺構である。
・プレア・ヴィヘア寺院（10世紀）
・タ・ケオ寺院（10世紀末～11世紀初）
・チャウ・サイ・テヴォダ寺院（12世紀初）
・トマノン寺院（12世紀初）
・バンテアイ・サムレ寺院（12世紀半）

3.9.4 測量方法

本節では現地での実測調査において採取された寸法データを基に，各選定遺構における経蔵の平面図および立面図を作成し，その各部寸法分析から比較考察を行う。

なお，各部寸法の抽出に際して写真測量ソフト「Agisoft PhotoScan Professional 1.1.6」をTPS測量と併用して用いている。当ソフトはデジタル写真測量ソフトの1つであり，市販のカメラによって対象物を複数の角度から撮影した写真を用いた重複箇所と距離から，3D化・モデルを作成するものである。近年の技術

However, the comprehensive study about the planning methods of this particular type of building is not clear, and also in Preah Vihear Temple, the study of a primary planning and a dimentional planning about the "Library" building alone has yet to be completed.

On the other hand, recent studies about dimentional planning of Khmer temple complex achieved certain results. The module of the dimension is considered to be about 1hasta = 412 mm. The outline of a base define the plan scale of the building are mentiond based on analyzing of whole temple planning[II]. However the study about planning method on each building scale is exiguous meanwhile same study on temple scale is progressed further. In addition, most of those studies focused on plan, and a relation between planning and elevation is scanty.

Therefore, the overall objective of this study is to conduct basic studies on differences of dimensions and the relationship between plan and elevation of the pair of Libraries in Preah Vihear Temple through a comparison with other temples of the same time frame, and same style. (Hereinafter, we call "Library" building as the Library uniformly.)

3.9.3 Selection of Temples for Comparative Study

Considered from the results of the previous plan drawings of EFEO, chronology, and previous research about other Libraries, target temples for comparartive study were selected on some points of view (Figure 3.9-1).
1. Library has nave and eave after 10th century
2. Library has a porch and a false door, which is a generic form after 10th century
3. Satisfies 1 and 2, and in a reasonable state of preservation

Therefore 5 temples including Preah Vihear Temple were selected for comparison:
・Preah Vihear Temple (10th century)
・Ta Kev Temple (end of 10th century - beginning of 11th century)
・Chau Say Tevoda Temple (beginning of 12th century)
・Thommanon Temple (beginning of 12th century)
・Banteay Samre Temple (middle of 12th century)

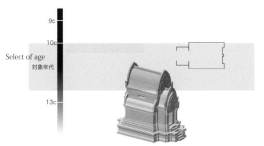

Figure 3.9-1 Selection of Age for Comparison

進歩により，従来の専門性の高い写真測量技術に匹敵するレベルで対象物の 3D 化を行うことができる。本研究では立面方向など，手ばかりが困難な箇所において寸法抽出を行うことができるという点，ある程度手ばかりによって採取したデータよりも客観性がある点で，この方法を採用している。なお，この方法は当時の石材位置を示す痕跡が埋没しているような崩壊の激しい箇所では，モデルの作成が困難であるというデメリットがあるが，本研究で抽出する箇所はこれに該当しない範囲であるため，問題はないと考えられる。

3.9.4.1 平面寸法の抽出方法

以下の手順を用いて調査対象遺構の平面寸法抽出を行った。

1. TPS 測量を用いて各部ポイントを記録，基準線の作成を行う。
2. 細部において現地での手ばかり実測値を採取，TPS 測量における測点と照合する。
3. この際に生じた歪みを各部において分散，平均化する。
4. 崩壊，損傷が激しい箇所に限りクメール建築の対称性に乗っ取り，該当箇所と考えられる寸法を転用する。
5. 写真測量を用いて経蔵の全体規模を把握，TPS 測量および実測数値における結果と照合する。
6. 対象遺構に対して共通した寸法抽出箇所を規定して寸法比較を行う。

なお，経蔵の建物主室の平面寸法抽出箇所において，本研究では選定した遺構の形式的特徴から，主室，側面平庇，前室部分の各箇所において寸法の抽出を行っている。本論文中では，平庇を除いた主室を構成する壁を「主室壁」，平庇を構成する壁を「側面庇壁」，前室部分を構成する壁を「前室壁」と略称する（Figure 3.9-2）。

3.9.4.2 立面寸法の抽出方法

以下の手順を用いて調査対象遺構の立面寸法抽出を行った。

1. 写真測量により東西南北各面において正対させたものを画像化し，CAD に取り込むか，3D 編集ソフト内の測量ツールを用いて，立面形状を把握する。
2. 対象遺構に対して共通した寸法抽出箇所を規定して寸法比較を行う。

3.9.4.3 寸法分析に際した単位長と誤差の扱い

本研究におけるクメール造営尺度の単位長として，

3.9.4 Method of Measurement

Based on measurement survey on-site we conducted the comparative consideration on dimensions of each element from the plan and elevational drawings of Libraries.

We used the photographic measurement software "Agisoft Phtotoscan Professional 1.1.6" with TPS measurement. This software is a type of the digital photographic software that can create a 3D model based on distances and overlap elements of photos taken by a normal camera from several angles. Recent techniques enable the creation of a 3D model of an object in high quality much the same as the past professional photographic measurement technique. In this study, this measurement method is useful to extract the dimensions of some elements like high places that are hard to measure by hand, and also has much more objectivity rather than the data measured by hand. Still it has a difficulty to make the 3D model of elements that collapsed or are seriously damaged to know the original position of stones at the time.

3.9.4.1 Method on Extraction of Dimensions from Plan Drawings

We extracted each dimension of the Library according to the following process:

1. Record several points of each element of building by TPS measurement and draw the criterion lines.
2. Measure the detail demensions by hand on-site and collate with TPS measurement data.
3. Scatter and average the error demensions accrued by process 1 and 2.
4. Apply the dimension to the element that is slightly collapsed or damaged based on symmetrical planning characteristic of Khmer architecture.
5. Collate TPS measurement data and 3D model data by photographic measurement and comprehend the totality of the plan.
6. Establish the common elements, extract the dimensions of each temples and compare each temples and pair of the Libraries.

In this study, we extracted the dimensions of body element, side eaves element and porch element of selected temples by considering architectural style. In our analysis, we call the walls configuring the main "main wall", walls configuring the side eaves "side eave wall", and walls configuring the porch "porch wall" (Figure 3.9-2).

Chapter 3 : Study Reports on Preah Vihear Temple

JSA（日本国政府アンコール遺跡救済チーム）が行ったバイヨン寺院南北経蔵の比較分析で提案された，1ハスタ＝412mm，また1ヴィヤマ＝4ハスタ（＝1648mm）を分析考察において手がかりとする。

また，本研究の分析に関して寸法を抽出する際に以下の理由から誤差が発生する可能性が挙げられる。
1. 調査時の測量誤差
2. 経年変化，経年劣化による誤差
3. 建設当時の施工誤差

1及び2に関しては発生する誤差は数十mm程度である。3に関しては，本研究で対象にする経蔵が石造であること，またクメール建築における施工方法を考慮すると，200mm程度の仕事斑を含む可能性が考えられる。この誤差は一様な方法で処理できるものではない。したがってこの誤差を評価しながら実寸法を計画意図を考慮したうえで適宜換算する必要がある。

3.9.4.2 Method on Extraction of Dimensions from Elevational Drawings

We extract the dimensions of elevational drawings according to following process:

1. Retrieve the elevational forms of each direction by using software for editing 3D data or CAD application to capture, and measure the confronting position photos which are captured by photographic measurement system.
2. Extract and compare dimensions of the common elements in each temple.

3.9.4.3 Transaction of Tolerance and Module on Dimentional Analysis

In this study, we regard "hasta", the module of dimension in Khmer architecture, as 412 mm refered to the research of north and south library in Bayon conducted by JSA (Japanese Government for Safeguarding Angkor). In addition, we used the module "vyama" (1 vyama=4 hasta=1,648 mm) for consideration.

For analysis in this study, there are some possibilities of accruing the tolerance of dimension extracton for the following reasons:

1. Tolerance occurred by measuring survey on site
2. Tolerance along aged deterioration
3. Tolerance occurred during initial construction

In 1 and 2, the tolerance of dimensions are considered to be several tens of mm. In 3, the tolerance of construction works based on construction method in Khmer architecture are considered to be about 200 mm. There are no consistent way to transact the tolerance of dimensions. Therefore, it is necessary to convert actual dimensions considering the intension of the primary planning of each building.

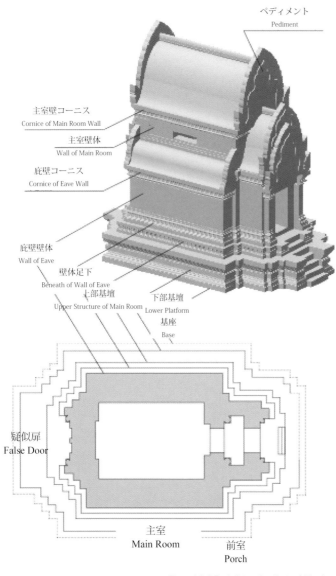

Figure 3.9-2 Each Extraction Parts of Libraly

3.9.5 各遺構寸法抽出
3.9.5.1 各遺構平面寸法抽出

Table 3.9-1 The Parts of Dimensions on Planning

3.9.5 Extraction of Dimensions of Each Temple
3.9.5.1 Extraction of Dimensions from Plan Drawings of Each Temple

Table 3.9-1-01 The Parts of Dimensions on Planning (Preah Vihear Temple, Banteay Samre Temple)

Each Element		Preah Vihear Temple – East Library mm	hasta	Convergence Value	West Library mm	hasta	Convergence Value	Difference of Dimension	Banteay Samre Temple – South Library mm	hasta	Convergence Value	North Library mm	hasta	Convergence Value	Difference of Dimension
Base a	X1	11577.51	28.10	28.00	11152.83	27.07	27.00	424.68	11833.00	28.72	28.50	12213.00	29.64	29.50	-380.00
	X2	10394.77	25.23	25.00	10532.41	25.56	25.50	-137.64	10350.00	25.12	25.00	10289.00	24.97	25.00	61.00
	X3	9818.21	23.83	24.00	9963.18	24.18	24.00	-144.97	9614.00	23.33	23.50	9561.00	23.21	23.00	53.00
	X4	8307.06	20.16	20.00	8295.18	20.13	20.00	11.88	7448.00	18.08	18.00	7449.50	18.08	18.00	-1.50
	X5	7712.63	18.72	18.50	7765.48	18.85	19.00	-52.85	6890.70	16.72	16.50	6829.00	16.58	16.50	61.70
	X6	2145.51	5.21	5.00	2103.34	5.11	5.00	42.17	3226.00	7.83	8.00	3407.83	8.27	8.50	-181.83
	X7	1719.37	4.17	4.00	1284.00	3.12	3.00	435.37	1716.00	4.17	4.00	1976.17	4.80	5.00	260.17
	Y1	7426.76	18.03	18.00	7466.67	18.12	18.00	-39.91	7163.27	17.39	17.50	7084.26	17.19	17.00	79.01
	Y2	5967.15	14.48	14.50	5903.83	14.33	14.50	63.32	5707.87	13.85	14.00	5626.19	13.66	13.50	81.68
Lower Platform b	X1	11057.51	26.84	27.00	10632.83	25.81	26.00	424.68	11589.34	28.13	28.00	11973.00	29.06	29.00	-383.66
	X2	9874.77	23.97	24.00	10012.41	24.30	24.50	-137.64	10090.00	24.49	24.50	10049.00	24.39	24.50	41.00
	X3	9298.21	22.57	22.50	9497.18	23.05	23.00	-198.97	9354.00	22.70	22.50	9321.00	22.62	22.50	33.00
	X4	7787.06	18.90	19.00	7775.15	18.87	19.00	11.91	7188.00	17.45	17.50	7208.66	17.50	17.50	-20.66
	X5	7192.63	17.46	17.50	7245.48	17.59	17.50	-52.85	6631.00	16.09	16.00	6569.50	15.95	16.00	61.50
	Y1	6906.76	16.76	17.00	6946.67	16.86	17.00	-39.91	6904.25	16.76	17.00	6844.26	16.61	16.50	60.00
	Y2	5447.15	13.22	13.00	5383.76	13.07	13.00	63.39	5447.87	13.22	13.00	5386.00	13.07	13.00	61.87
Upper Platform c	X1	9427.98	22.88	23.00	9567.17	23.22	23.00	-139.19	10016.00	24.31	24.50	9998.77	24.27	24.50	17.23
	X2	8978.32	21.79	22.00	8901.89	21.61	21.50	76.43	9248.00	22.45	22.50	9254.00	22.46	22.50	-6.00
	X3	8355.37	20.28	20.50	8305.08	20.14	20.00	50.29	8603.00	20.88	21.00	8558.00	20.77	21.00	45.00
	X4	6805.19	16.52	16.50	6765.12	16.42	16.50	40.07	6326.00	15.35	15.50	6331.00	15.37	15.50	-5.00
	X5	6266.00	15.21	15.00	6275.17	15.23	15.00	-9.17	5754.39	13.97	14.00	5781.14	14.03	14.00	-26.74
	Y1	5994.66	14.55	14.50	5976.36	14.51	14.50	18.31	6049.36	14.68	14.50	6069.90	14.73	14.50	-20.54
	Y2	4490.94	10.90	11.00	4457.04	10.82	11.00	33.90	4638.92	11.26	11.50	4585.00	11.13	11.00	53.92
Under Structure of Main Element d	X1	8538.62	20.72	20.50	8524.62	20.69	20.50	14.01	8769.00	21.28	21.50	8758.68	21.26	21.50	10.32
	X2	7916.49	19.21	19.00	7893.80	19.16	19.00	22.69	8078.00	19.61	19.50	8063.50	19.57	19.50	14.50
	X3	6366.74	15.45	15.50	6354.31	15.42	15.50	12.43	5865.00	14.24	14.00	5846.64	14.19	14.00	18.36
	X4	5827.67	14.14	14.00	5865.17	14.24	14.00	-37.50	5314.00	12.90	13.00	5315.00	12.90	13.00	
	Y1	5564.94	13.51	13.50	5581.97	13.55	13.50	-17.02	5541.63	13.45	13.50	5560.00	13.50	13.50	-18.37
	Y2	4061.23	9.86	10.00	4037.04	9.80	10.00	24.19	4145.50	10.06	10.00	4061.00	9.86	10.00	84.50
Wall of Main Element e	X1	8129.49	19.73	19.50	8111.12	19.69	19.50	18.37	8299.50	20.14	20.00	8289.50	20.12	20.00	10.00
	X2	7505.99	18.22	18.00	7480.30	18.16	18.00	25.69	7612.60	18.48	18.50	7609.55	18.47	18.50	3.05
	X3	5965.77	14.48	14.50	5940.81	14.42	14.50	24.96	5367.00	13.03	13.00	5415.27	13.14	13.00	-48.27
	X4	5417.17	13.15	13.00	5451.67	13.23	13.00	-34.50	4830.00	11.72	11.50	4800.00	11.65	11.50	30.00
	Y1	5154.44	12.51	12.50	5150.78	12.50	12.50	3.67	5063.17	12.29	12.50	5088.24	12.35	12.50	-25.07
	Y2	3644.62	8.85	9.00	3623.54	8.80	9.00	21.08	3621.65	8.79	9.00	3621.00	8.79	9.00	0.65
Chancel of Main Room f	X1	4554.00	11.05	11.00	4643.58	11.27	11.50	-89.58							
	Y1	2927.70	7.11	7.00	2820.00	6.84	7.00	107.70							

Table 3.9-1-02 The Parts of Dimensions on Planning (Chau Say Tevoda Temple, Ta Kev Temple)

Each Element		Chau Say Tevoda Temple – South Library mm	hasta	Convergence Value	North Library mm	hasta	Convergence Value	Difference of Dimension	Ta Kev Temple – North Library mm	hasta	Convergence Value	South Library mm	hasta	Convergence Value	Difference of Dimension
Base a	X1	13811.34	33.52	33.50	14260.12	34.61	34.50	-448.78	12469.30	30.27	30.50	12467.14	30.26	30.50	-2.16
	X2	11876.88	28.83	29.00	11899.72	28.88	29.00	-22.84	10876.63	26.40	26.50	10902.55	26.46	26.50	-25.92
	X3	11265.24	27.34	27.50	11011.27	26.73	26.50	253.97	10394.63	25.23	25.00	10361.91	25.15	25.00	-32.71
	X4	8835.06	21.44	21.50	8722.88	21.17	21.00	112.17	8188.13	19.87	20.00	8149.55	19.78	20.00	-38.57
	X5	8302.11	20.15	20.00	8356.00	20.28	20.50	-53.89	7607.05	18.46	18.50	7542.69	18.31	18.50	-64.36
	X6	3794.23	9.21	9.00	4138.19	10.04	10.00	-343.96	3223.90	7.82	8.00	3292.00	7.99	8.00	68.10
	X7	1717.57	4.17	4.00	1765.93	4.29	4.50	-48.35	1638.35	3.98	4.00	1632.44	3.96	4.00	-5.91
	Y1	7282.00	17.67	17.50	7248.30	17.59	17.50	33.70	6987.82	16.96	17.00	6973.12	16.93	17.00	-14.70
	Y2	5686.76	13.80	14.00	5592.80	13.57	13.50	93.96	5424.86	13.17	13.00	5423.00	13.17	13.00	-61.86
Lower Platform b	X1	13165.23	31.95	32.00	13569.50	32.94	33.00	-404.27	12239.28	29.71	29.50	12147.16	29.48	29.50	-92.12
	X2	11232.20	27.26	27.50	11254.81	27.32	27.50	-22.61	10626.50	25.79	26.00	10600.16	25.73	25.50	-26.34
	X3	10599.16	25.73	25.50	10484.01	25.45	25.50	115.15	10144.50	24.62	24.50	10059.52	24.42	24.50	-84.98
	X4	8222.14	19.96	20.00	8091.60	19.64	19.50	130.54	7913.50	19.21	19.00	7807.64	18.95	19.00	-105.86
	X5	7664.11	18.60	18.50	7638.50	18.54	18.50	25.61	7332.42	17.80	18.00	7264.58	17.63	17.50	-67.84
	Y1	6657.79	16.16	16.00	6555.25	15.91	16.00	102.54	6702.00	16.27	16.50	6612.03	16.05	16.00	-89.97
	Y2	5015.22	12.17	12.00	4927.89	11.96	12.00	87.33	5150.24	12.50	12.50	5060.62	12.28	12.50	-89.62
Upper Platform c	X1	11333.78	27.51	27.50	11476.00	27.85	28.00	-142.22	10518.00	25.53	25.50	10531.87	25.56	25.50	13.87
	X2	10382.19	25.20	25.00	10468.08	25.41	25.50	-85.89	9930.00	24.10	24.00	9975.26	24.21	24.00	45.26
	X3	9711.06	23.57	23.50	9598.26	23.30	23.50	112.80	9414.50	22.85	23.00	9405.66	22.83	23.00	-8.84
	X4	7293.50	17.70	17.50	7166.73	17.39	17.50	126.46	7186.50	17.44	17.50	7126.57	17.30	17.50	-59.93
	X5	6726.62	16.33	16.50	6664.10	16.18	16.00	62.52	6634.00	16.10	16.00	6628.68	16.09	16.00	-5.32
	Y1	5699.15	13.83	14.00	5603.19	13.60	13.50	95.96	6032.00	14.64	14.50	6005.52	14.58	14.50	-26.48
	Y2	4145.05	10.06	10.00	4059.25	9.85	10.00	85.80	4470.02	10.85	11.00	4442.85	10.78	11.00	-27.17
Under Structure of Main Room d	X1	9930.36	24.10	24.00	9843.83	23.89	24.00	86.53	9587.51	23.27	23.50	9546.37	23.17	23.00	-41.14
	X2	9227.76	22.40	22.50	9109.40	22.11	22.00	118.36	8952.75	21.73	21.50	9010.00	21.87	22.00	57.25
	X3	6728.27	16.33	16.50	6690.73	16.24	16.00	37.54	6772.18	16.44	16.50	6735.00	16.35	16.50	-37.18
	X4	6139.52	14.90	15.00	6190.45	15.03	15.00	-50.93	6218.93	15.09	15.00	6231.02	15.12	15.00	12.08
	Y1	5143.21	12.48	12.50	5139.91	12.48	12.50	3.30	5615.30	13.63	13.50	5604.00	13.60	13.50	-11.30
	Y2	3473.72	8.43	8.50	3498.44	8.49	8.50	-24.72	4048.93	9.83	10.00	4029.09	9.78	10.00	-19.84
Wall of Main Room e	X1	9457.21	22.95	23.00	9418.74	22.86	23.00	38.47	9073.04	22.02	22.00	9063.24	22.00	22.00	-9.81
	X2	8754.61	21.25	21.00	8749.55	21.24	21.00	5.06	8457.93	20.53	20.50	8527.76	20.70	20.50	69.83
	X3	6276.60	15.23	15.00	6245.00	15.16	15.00	31.60	6312.96	15.32	15.50	6298.00	15.29	15.50	-14.96
	X4	5685.94	13.80	14.00	5830.60	14.15	14.00	-144.66	5766.48	14.00	14.00	5802.19	14.08	14.00	35.71
	Y1	4666.29	11.33	11.50	4780.05	11.60	11.50	-113.76	5147.95	12.50	12.50	5147.35	12.49	12.50	-0.60
	Y2	3084.00	7.49	7.50	3090.48	7.50	7.50	-6.48	3552.22	8.62	8.50	3578.25	8.69	8.50	26.02
Chancel of Main Room f	X1														
	Y1														

Convergence Value：The Value that is Rounding Criteria based on 0.5 hasta

■ : 300 ~ of diffirence ranges   ■ : 200 ~ 300   □ : 100 ~ 200

Chapter 3 : Study Reports on Preah Vihear Temple

Table 3.9-1-03 The Parts of Dimensions on Planning (Thommanon Temple)

Each Elemant		Thommanon Temple South Library		
		mm	hasta	Convergence Value
Base a	X1	13074.34	31.73	31.50
	X2	11152.5	27.07	27.00
	X3	10468.375	25.41	25.50
	X4	8363.5	20.30	20.50
	X5	7729.12	18.76	19.00
	X6	3216.88	7.81	8.00
	X7	2128.342	5.17	5.00
	Y1	7434.618	18.05	18.00
	Y2	5752.543	13.96	14.00
Lower Platform b	X1	12853.092	31.20	31.00
	X2	10952.5	26.58	26.50
	X3	10268.375	24.92	25.00
	X4	8163.5	19.81	20.00
	X5	7475.944	18.15	18.00
	Y1	7234.618	17.56	17.50
	Y2	5552.543	13.48	13.50
Upper Platform c	X1	10985.723	26.66	26.50
	X2	10124.139	24.57	24.50
	X3	9433.976	22.90	23.00
	X4	7270.5	17.65	17.50
	X5	6487.019	15.75	15.50
	Y1	6245.008	15.16	15.00
	Y2	4714.180	11.44	11.50
Under Structure of Main Room d	X1	9401.663	22.82	23.00
	X2	8680.261	21.07	21.00
	X3	6423.582	15.59	15.50
	X4	5660.941	13.74	13.50
	Y1	5465.450	13.27	13.50
	Y2	不可		
Wall of Main Room e	X1	9003.436	21.85	22.00
	X2	8281.261	20.10	20.00
	X3	6023.582	14.62	14.50
	X4	5323.832	12.92	13.00
	Y1	5065.450	12.29	12.50
	Y2	Unrecordable		
Chancel of Main Room f	X1			
	Y1			

Convergence Value : Tht Value that is Rounding Criteria based on 0.5 hasta
■ : 300～ of diffirence ranges   ▓ : 200～300   ░ : 100～200

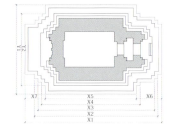

Figure 3.9-3 Extraction Parts of Base "a" on Plannning

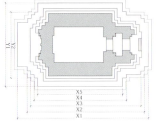

Figure 3.9-4 Extraction Parts of Lower Platform "b" on Plannning

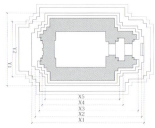

Figure 3.9-5 Extraction Parts of Upper Platform "c" on Plannning

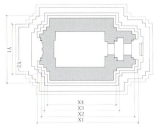

Figure 3.9-6 Extraction Parts of Under Structure Main Room "d" on Plannning

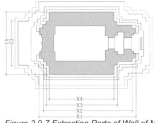

Figure 3.9-7 Extraction Parts of Wall of Main Room "e" on Plannning

3.9.5.2 各遺構平面縮減値抽出 / 3.9.5.2 The Reductional Dimensions of Each Temple

Table 3.9-2 The Reductional Dimensions of Each Element on Planning
Table 3.9-2-01 The Reductional Dimensions of Each Element on Planning (Preah Vihear Temple)

					Preah Vihear Temple										
					East Library						West Library				
				mm	hasta	Degression	Convegence Value	Estimated hasta	Estimated mm	Difference of Dimension	mm	hasta	Degression	Convegence Value	Estimated hasta	Estimated mm	Difference of Dimension
Main Room	Longer Side x	Wall of Main Room e	X3	5965.77	14.48		14.50	14.50	5974.00	8.23	5940.81	14.42		14.50	14.50	5974.00	33.19
		Under Structure of Main Room d	X3	6366.74	15.45	-0.97	15.50	15.50	6386.00	19.26	6354.31	15.42	-1.00	15.50	15.50	6386.00	31.69
		Upper Platform c	X4	6805.19	16.52	-1.06	16.50	16.50	6798.00	-7.19	6765.12	16.42	-1.00	16.50	16.50	6798.00	32.88
		Lower Platform b	X4	7787.06	18.90	-2.38	19.00	19.00	7828.00	40.94	7775.15	18.87	-2.45	19.00	19.00	7828.00	52.85
		Base a	X4	8307.06	20.16	-1.26	20.00	20.00	8240.00	-67.06	8295.18	20.13	-1.26	20.00	20.00	8240.00	-55.18
	Shorter Side y	Main Element e	Y2	3644.62	8.85		9.00	9.00	3708.00	63.38	3623.54	8.80		9.00	9.00	3708.00	84.46
		Under Structure of Main Room d	Y2	4061.23	9.86	-1.01	10.00	10.00	4120.00	58.77	4037.04	9.80	-1.00	10.00	10.00	4120.00	82.96
		Upper Platform c	Y2	4490.94	10.90	-1.04	11.00	11.00	4532.00	41.06	4457.04	10.82	-1.02	11.00	11.00	4532.00	74.96
		Lower Platform b	Y2	5447.15	13.22	-2.32	13.00	13.50	5562.00	114.85	5383.76	13.07	-2.25	13.00	13.50	5562.00	178.24
		Base a	Y2	5967.15	14.48	-1.26	14.50	14.50	5974.00	6.85	5903.83	14.33	-1.26	14.50	14.50	5974.00	70.17
Eave Room	Longer Side x'	Main Room e	X4	5417.17	13.15		13.00	13.50	5562.00	144.83	5451.67	13.23		13.00	13.50	5562.00	110.33
		Under Structure of Main Room d	X4	5827.67	14.14	-1.00	14.00	14.50	5974.00	146.33	5865.17	14.24	-1.00	14.00	14.50	5974.00	108.83
		Upper Platform c	X5	6266.00	15.21	-1.06	15.00	15.50	6386.00	120.00	6275.17	15.21	-1.00	15.00	15.50	6386.00	110.83
		Lower Platform b	X5	7192.63	17.46	-2.25	17.50	18.00	7416.00	223.37	7245.48	17.59	-2.36	17.50	18.00	7416.00	170.52
		Base a	X5	7712.63	18.72	-1.26	18.50	19.00	7828.00	115.37	7765.48	18.85	-1.26	19.00	19.00	7828.00	62.52
	Shorter Side y'	Main Part e	Y1	5154.44	12.51		12.50	12.50	5150.00	-4.44	5150.78	12.50		12.50	12.50	5150.00	-0.78
		Under Structure of Main Room d	Y1	5564.94	13.51	-1.00	13.50	13.50	5562.00	-2.94	5581.97	13.55	-1.05	13.50	13.50	5562.00	-19.97
		Upper Platform c	Y1	5994.66	14.55	-1.04	14.50	14.50	5974.00	-20.66	5976.36	14.51		14.50	14.50	5974.00	-2.36
		Lower Platform b	Y1	6906.76	16.76	-2.21	17.00	17.00	7004.00	97.24	6946.67	16.86	-2.36	17.00	17.00	7004.00	57.33
		Base a	Y1	7426.76	18.03	-1.26	18.00	18.00	7416.00	-10.76	7466.67	18.12	-1.26	18.00	18.00	7416.00	-50.67

Table 3.9-2-02 The Parts of Reductional Dimensions of Each Element on Planning (Banteay Samre Temple)

					Banteay Samre Temple										
					South Library						North Library				
				mm	hasta	Degression	Convegence Value	Estimated hasta	Estimated mm	Difference of Dimension	mm	hasta	Degression	Convegence Value	Estimated hasta	Estimated mm	Difference of Dimension
Main Room	Longer Side x	Wall of Main Room e	X3	5367.00	13.03		13.00	13.00	5356.00	-11.00	5415.27	13.14		13.00	13.00	5356.00	-59.27
		Under Structure of Main Room d	X3	5865.00	14.24	-1.21	14.00	14.25	5871.00	6.00	5846.64	14.19	-1.05	14.00	14.25	5871.00	24.36
		Upper Platform c	X4	6326.00	15.35	-1.12	15.50	15.50	6386.00	60.00	6331.00	15.37	-1.18	15.50	15.50	6386.00	55.00
		Lower Platform b	X4	7188.00	17.45	-2.09	17.50	17.50	7210.00	22.00	7208.66	17.50	-2.13	17.50	17.50	7210.00	1.34
		Base a	X4	7448.00	18.08	-0.63	18.00	18.00	7416.00	-32.00	7449.50	18.08	-0.58	18.00	18.00	7416.00	-33.50
	Shorter Side y	Wall of Main Room e	Y4	3621.65	8.79		9.00	9.00	3708.00	86.35	3621	8.79		9.00	9.00	3708.00	87.00
		Under Structure of Main Room d	Y4	4145.50	10.06	-1.27	10.00	10.25	4223.00	77.50	4061.00	9.86	-1.07	10.00	10.25	4223.00	162.00
		Upper Platform c	Y5	4638.92	11.26	-1.20	11.50	11.50	4738.00	99.08	4585.00	11.13	-1.27	11.00	11.50	4738.00	153.00
		Lower Platform b	Y5	5447.87	13.22	-1.96	13.00	13.50	5562.00	114.13	5386.00	13.07	-1.94	13.00	13.50	5562.00	176.00
		Base a	Y5	5707.87	13.85	-0.63	14.00	14.00	5768.00	60.13	5626.189	13.66	-0.58	13.50	14.00	5768.00	141.81
Eave Room	Longers Side x'	Wall of Main Room e	X4	4830.00	11.72		11.50	11.50	4738.00	-92.00	4800.00	11.65		11.50	11.50	4738.00	-62.00
		Under Structure of Main Room d	X4	5314.00	12.90	-1.17	13.00	12.75	5253.00	-61.00	5315.00	12.90	-1.25	13.00	12.75	5253.00	-62.00
		Upper Platform c	X5	5754.39	13.97	-1.08	14.00	14.00	5768.00	13.61	5781.14	14.03	-1.13	14.00	14.00	5768.00	-13.14
		Lower Platform b	X5	6631.00	16.09	-2.13	16.00	16.00	6592.00	-39.00	6569.50	15.95	-1.91	16.00	16.00	6592.00	22.50
		Base a	X5	6890.70	16.72	-0.63	16.50	16.50	6798.00	-92.70	6829.00	16.58	-0.63	16.50	16.50	6798.00	-31.00
	Shorter Side y'	Wall of Main Room e	Y1	5063.173	12.29		12.50	12.50	5150.00	86.83	5088.24	12.35		12.50	12.50	5150.00	61.76
		Under Structure of Main Room d	Y1	5541.631	13.45	-1.16	13.50	13.75	5665.00	123.37	5560.00	13.50	-1.15	13.50	13.75	5665.00	105.00
		Upper Platform c	Y1	6049.36	14.68	-1.23	14.50	15.00	6180.00	130.64	6069.90	14.73	-1.24	14.50	15.00	6180.00	110.10
		Lower Platform b	Y1	6904.25	16.76	-2.07	17.00	17.00	7004.00	99.75	6844.26	16.61	-1.88	16.50	17.00	7004.00	159.74
		Base a	Y1	7163.27	17.39	-0.63	17.50	17.50	7210.00	46.73	7084.26	17.19	-0.58	17.00	17.50	7210.00	125.74

Planning Method of "Library" in Angkor Period

Table 3.9-2-03 The Reductional Dimensions of Each Element on Planning (Chau Say Tevoda Temple)

				Chau Say Tevoda Temple — South Library						Chau Say Tevoda Temple — North Library					
				mm	hasta	Degression	Convegence Value	Estimated hasta	Estimated mm	Difference of Dimension	mm	hasta	Degression	Convegence Value	Estimated hasta	Estimated mm	Difference of Dimension
Main Room	Longer Side x	Wall of Main Room e	X3	6276.60	15.23		15.00	15.00	6180.00	-96.60	6245.00	15.16		15.00	15.00	6180.00	-65.00
		Under Structure of Main Room d	X3	6728.27	16.33	-1.08	16.50	16.00	6592.00	-136.27	6690.73	16.24	-1.08	16.00	16.00	6592.00	-98.73
		Upper Platform c	X4	7293.19	17.70	-1.37	17.50	17.50	7210.00	-83.19	7166.73	17.39	-1.16	17.50	17.50	7210.00	43.27
		Lower Platform b	X4	8222.14	19.96	-2.25	20.00	19.50	8034.00	-188.14	8091.60	19.64	-2.24	19.50	19.50	8034.00	-57.60
		Base a	X4	8835.06	21.44	-1.49	21.50	21.00	8652.00	-183.06	8722.88	21.17	-1.53	21.00	21.00	8652.00	-70.88
	Shorter Side y	Wall of Main Room e	Y4	3084.00	7.49		7.50	7.50	3090.00	6.00	3090.48	7.50		7.50	7.50	3090.00	-0.48
		Under Structure of Main Room d	Y4	3473.72	8.43	-0.88	8.50	8.50	3502.00	28.28	3498.44	8.49	-0.99	8.50	8.50	3502.00	3.56
		Upper Platform c	Y5	4145.05	10.06	-1.63	10.00	10.00	4120.00	-25.05	4059.25	9.85	-1.36	10.00	10.00	4120.00	60.75
		Lower Platform b	Y5	5015.22	12.17	-2.11	12.00	12.00	4944.00	-71.22	4927.89	11.96	-2.11	12.00	12.00	4944.00	16.11
		Base a	Y5	5686.76	13.80	-1.63	14.00	13.50	5562.00	-124.76	5592.80	13.57	-1.61	13.50	13.50	5562.00	-30.80
Eave Room	Longer Side x'	Wall of Main Room e	X4	5685.94	13.80		14.00	14.00	5768.00	82.06	5830.60	14.15		14.00	14.00	5768.00	-62.60
		Under Structure of Main Room d	X4	6139.52	14.90	-1.10	15.00	15.00	6180.00	40.48	6190.45	15.03	-0.87	15.00	15.00	6180.00	-10.45
		Upper Platform c	X5	6726.62	16.33	-1.43	16.50	16.00	6592.00	-134.62	6664.10	16.18	-1.15	16.00	16.00	6592.00	-72.10
		Lower Platform b	X5	7664.11	18.60	-2.28	18.50	18.50	7622.00	-42.11	7638.50	18.54	-2.37	18.50	18.50	7622.00	-16.50
		Base a	X5	8302.11	20.15	-1.55	20.00	20.00	8240.00	-62.11	8356.00	20.28	-1.74	20.50	20.00	8240.00	-116.00
	Shorter Side y'	Wall of Main Room e	Y1	4666.29	11.33		11.50	11.50	4738.00	71.71	4780.05	11.60		11.50	11.50	4738.00	-42.05
		Under Structure of Main Room d	Y1	5143.21	12.48	-1.16	12.50	12.50	5150.00	6.79	5139.91	12.48	-0.87	12.50	12.50	5150.00	10.09
		Upper Platform c	Y1	5699.15	13.83	-1.35	14.00	13.50	5562.00	-137.15	5603.19	13.60	-1.12	13.50	13.50	5562.00	-41.19
		Lower Platform b	Y1	6657.79	16.16	-2.33	16.00	16.00	6592.00	-65.79	6555.25	15.91	-2.31	16.00	16.00	6592.00	36.75
		Base a	Y1	7282.00	17.67	-1.52	17.50	17.50	7210.00	-72.00	7248.30	17.59	-1.68	17.50	17.50	7210.00	-38.30

Table 3.9-2-04 The Reductional Dimensions of Each Element on Planning (Ta Kev Temple)

				Ta Kev Temple — South Library							Ta Kev Temple — North Library					
				mm	hasta	Degression	Convegence Value	Estimated hasta	Estimated mm	Difference of Dimension	mm	hasta	Degression	Convegence Value	Estimated hasta	Estimated mm	Difference of Dimension
Main Room	Longer Side x	Wall of Main Room e	X3	6298.00	15.29		15.50	15.50	6386.00	88.00	6312.96	15.32		15.50	15.50	6386.00	73.04
		Under Structure of Main Room d	X3	6735.00	16.35	-0.96	16.50	16.50	6798.00	63.00	6772.18	16.44	-1.11	16.50	16.50	6798.00	25.82
		Upper Platform c	X4	7126.57	17.30	-0.95	17.50	17.50	7210.00	83.43	7186.50	17.44	-1.01	17.50	17.50	7210.00	23.50
		Lower Platform b	X4	7807.64	18.95	-1.65	19.00	19.00	7828.00	20.36	7913.50	19.21	-1.76	19.00	19.00	7828.00	-85.50
		Base a	X4	8149.55	19.78	-0.83	20.00	20.00	8240.00	90.45	8188.13	19.87	-0.67	20.00	20.00	8240.00	51.87
	Shorter Side y	Wall of Main Room e	Y2	3578.25	8.69		8.50	8.50	3502.00	-76.25	3552.22	8.62		8.50	8.50	3502.00	-50.22
		Under Structure of Main Room d	Y2	4029.09	9.78	-0.92	10.00	9.50	3914.00	-115.09	4048.93	9.83	-0.90	10.00	9.50	3914.00	-134.93
		Upper Platform c	Y2	4442.85	10.78	-1.00	11.00	10.50	4326.00	-116.85	4470.02	10.85	-1.02	11.00	10.50	4326.00	-144.02
		Lower Platform b	Y2	5060.62	12.28	-1.50	12.50	12.50	5150.00	89.38	5150.24	12.50	-1.65	12.50	12.50	5150.00	-0.24
		Base a	Y2	5363.00	13.02	-0.73	13.00	13.00	5356.00	-7.00	5424.86	13.17	-0.67	13.00	13.00	5356.00	-68.86
Eave Room	Longer Side x'	Wall of Main Room e	X4	5802.19	14.08		14.00	14.00	5768.00	-34.19	5766.48	14.00		14.00	14.00	5768.00	1.52
		Under Structure of Main Room d	X4	6231.02	15.12	-1.04	15.00	15.00	6180.00	-51.02	6218.93	15.09	-1.10	15.00	15.00	6180.00	-38.93
		Upper Platform c	X5	6628.68	16.09	-0.97	16.00	16.00	6592.00	-36.68	6634.00	16.10	-1.01	16.00	16.00	6592.00	-42.00
		Lower Platform b	X5	7264.58	17.63	-1.54	17.50	17.50	7210.00	-54.58	7332.42	17.80	-1.70	18.00	17.50	7210.00	-122.42
		Base a	X5	7542.69	18.31	-0.68	18.50	18.50	7622.00	79.31	7607.05	18.46	-0.67	18.50	18.50	7622.00	14.95
	Shorter Side y'	Wall of Main Room e	Y1	5147.35	12.49		12.50	12.50	5150.00	2.65	5147.95	12.50		12.50	12.50	5150.00	2.05
		Under Structure of Main Room d	Y1	5604.00	13.60	-1.11	13.50	13.50	5562.00	-42.00	5615.30	13.63	-1.13	13.50	13.50	5562.00	-53.30
		Upper Platform c	Y1	6005.52	14.58	-0.97	14.50	14.50	5974.00	-31.52	6032.00	14.64	-1.01	14.50	14.50	5974.00	-58.00
		Lower Platform b	Y1	6612.03	16.05	-1.47	16.50	16.50	6798.00	185.97	6702.00	16.27	-1.63	16.50	16.50	6798.00	96.00
		Base a	Y1	6973.12	16.93	-0.88	17.00	17.00	7004.00	30.88	6987.82	16.96	-0.69	17.00	17.00	7004.00	16.18

Table 3.9-2-05 The Reductional Dimensions of Each Element on Planning (Thommanon Temple)

				Thommanon Temple — South Library						
				mm	hasta	Difference of Dimension	Convegence Value	Estimated hasta	Estimated mm	Difference of Dimension
Main Room	Longer Side x	Wall of Main Room e	X3	6023.58	14.62		14.50	14.50	5974.00	-49.58
		Under Structure of Main Room d	X3	6423.58	15.59	-0.97	15.50	15.50	6386.00	-37.58
		Upper Platform c	X4	7270.50	17.65	-2.06	17.50	17.50	7210.00	-60.50
		Lower Platform b	X4	8163.50	19.81	-2.17	20.00	20.00	8240.00	76.50
		Base a	X4	8363.50	20.30	-0.49	20.50	20.50	8446.00	82.50
	Shorter Side y	Wall of Main Room e	Y2	3343.00	8.11		8.00	8.00	3296.00	-13.49
		Under Structure of Main Room d	Y2	3743.00	9.08	-0.97	9.00	9.00	3708.00	-35.00
		Upper Platform c	Y2	4714.18	11.44	-2.36	11.50	11.50	4738.00	23.82
		Lower Platform b	Y2	5552.54	13.48	-2.03	13.50	13.50	5562.00	9.46
		Base a	Y2	5752.54	13.96	-0.49	14.00	14.00	5768.00	15.46
Eave Room	Longer Side x'	Wall of Main Room e	X4	5323.83	12.92		13.00	13.00	5356.00	32.17
		Under Structure of Main Room d	X4	5660.94	13.74	-0.82	13.50	14.00	5768.00	107.06
		Upper Platform c	X5	6487.02	15.75	-2.01	15.50	16.00	6592.00	104.98
		Lower Platform b	X5	7475.944	18.15	-2.40	18.00	18.50	7622.00	146.06
		Base a	X5	7729.12	18.76	-0.61	19.00	19.00	7828.00	98.88
	Shorter Side y'	Wall of Main Room e	Y1	5065.45	12.29		12.50	12.00	4944.00	-121.45
		Under Structure of Main Room d	Y1	5465.45	13.27	-0.97	13.50	13.00	5356.00	-109.45
		Upper Platform c	Y1	6245.01	15.16	-1.89	15.00	15.00	6180.00	-65.01
		Lower Platform b	Y1	7234.62	17.56	-2.40	17.50	17.50	7210.00	-24.62
		Base a	Y1	7434.62	18.05	-0.49	18.00	18.00	7416.00	-18.62

Convergence Value : Tht Value that is Rounding Criteria based on 0.5 hasta
estimated hasta : Dimensions Estimated based on the Considering
■ : 300 ~ of diffirence ranges   ▨ : 200 ~ 300   □ : 100 ~ 200

Table 3.9-3 Dimensions of Each Parts on Planning based on "Table 3.9.5.2"

	Element	Side	Base a	Lower platform b	Upper platform c	Under structure of main room d	Wall of main room e
Preah Vihear Temple	Eave Wall	Longer Side	19.00	18.00	15.50	14.50	13.50
		Shorter Side	18.00	17.00	14.50	13.50	12.50
	Main Room	Longer Side	20.00	19.00	16.50	15.50	14.50
		Shorter Side	14.50	13.50	11.00	10.00	9.00
Banteay Samre Temple	Eave Wall	Longer Side	16.50	16.00	14.00	12.75	11.50
		Shorter Side	17.50	17.00	15.00	13.75	12.50
	Main Room	Longer Side	18.00	17.50	15.50	14.25	13.00
		Shorter Side	14.00	13.50	11.50	10.25	9.00
Chau Say Tevoda Temple	Eave Wall	Longer Side	20.00	18.50	16.00	15.00	14.00
		Shorter Side	17.50	16.00	13.50	12.50	11.50
	Main Room	Longer Side	21.00	19.50	17.50	16.00	15.00
		Shorter Side	13.50	12.00	10.00	8.50	7.50
Thommanon Temple	Eave Wall	Longer Side	19.00	18.50	16.00	14.00	13.00
		Shorter Side	18.00	17.50	15.00	13.00	12.00
	Main Room	Longer Side	20.50	20.00	17.50	15.50	14.50
		Shorter Side	14.00	13.50	11.50	9.00	8.00
Ta Kev Temple	Eave Wall	longer side	18.50	17.50	16.00	15.00	14.00
		shorter side	17.00	16.50	14.50	13.50	12.50
	Main Room	longer side	20.00	19.00	17.50	16.50	15.50
		shorter side	13.00	12.50	10.50	9.50	8.50

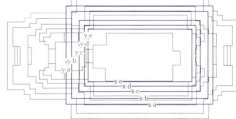

Figure 3.9-8 Main Parts of Reductional Dimensions on Planning

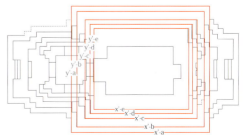

Figure 3.9-9 Eave Parts of Reductional Dimensions on Planning

165

3.9.5.3 各遺構立面寸法抽出

Table 3.9-4 The Parts of Dimensions on Elevational Plannning

Name of Temples	Pair of Library	Lower Platform	Upper Platform	Height of Platform	Eave Part	Main Room	Height of Pediment
Preah Vihear	East Library	2.01ht(830.00mm)	0.75ht(308.19mm)	2.76ht(1138.19mm)	6.51ht(2683.38mm)	6.34ht(2612.96mm)	
	West Library	2.10ht(865.00mm)	0.88ht(364.47mm)	2.98ht(1229.47mm)	6.47ht(2665.54mm)	6.39ht(2632.93mm)	
	Difference of Dimension	35mm	56.28mm	91.28mm	17.84mm	19.97mm	
Banteay Samre	South Library	2.71ht(1116.19mm)	0.85ht(352.00mm)	3.56ht(1468.20mm)	7.26ht(2991.19mm)	6.44ht(2651.58mm)	7.97ht(3285.57mm)
	North Library	2.56ht(1053.52mm)	0.79ht(326.48mm)	3.35ht(1380.00mm)	7.46ht(3073.76mm)	6.35ht(2617.90mm)	8.01ht(3302.15mm)
	Difference of Dimension	62.67mm	25.53mm	88.2mm	82.57mm	33.68mm	16.59mm
Chau Say Tevoda	South Library	2.05ht(845.57mm)	0.80ht(330.72mm)	2.85ht(1176.19mm)	6.48ht(2670.92mm)	6.19ht(2550.27mm)	6.49ht(2672.74mm)
	North Library	2.08ht(858.62mm)	0.86ht(352.76mm)	2.94ht(1211.39mm)	6.55ht(2697.43mm)	6.29ht(2591.92mm)	
	Difference of Dimension	13.15mm	22.04mm	35.2mm	26.51mm	41.65mm	
Thommanon	South Library	2.3ht(949.05mm)	0.82ht(338.91mm)	3.13ht(1287.97mm)	6.88ht(2836.54mm)	6.05ht(2492.01mm)	6.63ht(2731.50mm)
Ta Kev	South Library	1.44ht(591.37mm)	0.87ht(358.58mm)	2.31ht(949.95mm)	7.22ht(2972.85mm)	5.98ht(2464.80mm)	6.88ht(2835.41mm)
	North Library	1.46ht(600.64mm)	0.83ht(343.95mm)	2.29ht(944.58mm)	7.22ht(2974.31mm)	5.92ht(2439.52mm)	6.95ht(2862.19mm)
	Difference of Dimension	9.27mm	14.63mm	5.36mm	1.46mm	25.57mm	26.78mm

3.9.5.3 Extraction of Dimensions from Elevational Plan of Each Temple

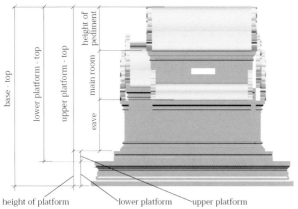

Figure 3.9-10 Extraction Parts on Elevational Plannning

3.9.6 各遺構の比較考察
3.9.6.1 対になる経蔵の基本計画について

前述したように，クメール建築史の中で経蔵は対になって配される場合と，伽藍の中で経蔵を1つしか持たない場合が存在する。また，既往研究の中でも，対の経蔵には，通気口の有無や材料の差，平面寸法の差など，左右に差異を持っていることがわかっている。そこで経蔵には共通の基本計画が存在し，一方はこの計画のままとし，他方はこの計画にわずかな操作を加えて差異を作り出している，と考えることが自然である。したがって，ここではまず対となる経蔵のどちらが基本計画となっていたかを類推する必要性がある。

ここで対の経蔵の各部位（Table 3.9-1を参照）を見てみると，経蔵を1つしか持たないトマノン寺院，寸法差がほとんど認められないタ・ケオ寺院を除いた3遺構に関して，明確な寸法差が表れる箇所，経蔵の長辺方向基座（a-X1），および下部基壇全幅（b-X1）に共通して約1ハスタの寸法差が設けられていることがわかる。いずれの遺構も上部基壇以上の各部寸法値に明確な差異は見られず，左右の経蔵の意図的な平面計画の相違が行われていたとは認められない。

この約1ハスタの寸法差は，疑似扉側出幅（a-X7）あるいは前室側出幅（a-X6）に現れる。プレア・ヴィヘア寺院においては東経蔵疑似扉側出幅（a-X7）が4ハスタ（＝1ヴィヤマ），西経蔵疑似扉側出幅（a-X7）

3.9.6 Comparative Consideration of Each Library
3.9.6.1 Primary Planning on the Pair of Libraries

According to previous section, the disposition of library in Khmer history have 2 patterns; situated as a pair or only one in a temple complex. Previous study reveals that there are some differences between a pair of Libraries, for example, existence of vent hole, materials, and dimensions of plan. It is presumed that there is common planning between a pair of Libraries, and one of them is designed differently in a slight control based on primary planning. Therefore, at first, it is necessary to consider which plan is the primary planning vehicle in a pair of buildings.

Focusing on each element of the Libraries (refer to Table 3.9-1), long side length of base (a-X1), total length of lower platform (b-X1). Some elements which have clear differences in a pair building of three temples have 1 hasta differences between a pair of libraries. Exceptions are Thomanon Temple that has only one library and Ta Kev Temple that the differences of dimensions are not clearly recognized. Differences of dimensions could not be recognized clearly in elements upon the lower platform of each temple. Therefore, it can not be assumed that there was intentional manipulation of plan dimensions.

One hasta differences of dimensions appear in the depth of false door side (a-X7) and depth of porch side (a-X6). In Preah Vihear Temple, the depth of the false door side (a-X7) of east library is 4 hasta (=1 vyama), and that (a-X7) of west is 3 hasta (=4-1 vyama). Therefore, if the planning that regards a module of vyama as a unit, it is considered that 3 hasta in false door depth (a-X7) of west Library is planned, and is a shortening of 1 hasta from 1 vyama of the primary planning. Depth of porch side (a-X6) of each Library has no intentional manipulation of dimensions and they are same 5 hasta number. In Banteay Samre, the false door depth (a-X7) of the south Library is confirmed as 4 hasta (=1 vyama), and that of north false door depth is confirmed as 5 hasta. Both porch depths (a-X6) are the integer number 8 hasta. Therefore, it is inferred that the primary planning in based on 8 hasta=2 vyama.

Planning Method of "Library" in Angkor Period

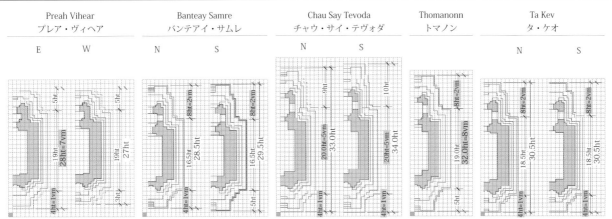

Figure 3.9-11 Dimensions of Longer Side of Libraries on Base Plannning

が３ハスタ（＝４－１ハスタ）であるから，１ヴィヤマをユニットとした計画であった場合，１ヴィヤマの基本計画から１ハスタ縮減して３ハスタが計画された可能性がある。前室側出幅（a-X6）に関しては意図的な寸法操作の傾向は見られず，東西経蔵とも５ハスタで一致する。バンテアイ・サムレ寺院では南経蔵疑似扉側出幅（a-X7）が４ハスタ（１ヴィヤマ）として計画され，北経蔵同一箇所において１ハスタの拡幅がみられた。前室側出幅（a-X6）においては南北経蔵とも８ハスタで一致しており，８ハスタ＝２ヴィヤマの計画が類推される。

チャウ・サイ・テヴォダ寺院においてはこの１ハスタの寸法差が前室側出幅（a-X6）にみられ，北経蔵では前室側出幅（a-X6）において10ハスタ，南経蔵ではこの距離を９ハスタとしている。10ハスタを完数とする計画性を優先したとすれば，９ハスタの出自には，１ハスタの縮減という操作が予想される。また，チャウ・サイ・テヴォダ寺院では疑似扉側出幅（a-X7）に明確な寸法操作は見られないものの，南北経蔵ともに４ハスタ（＝１ヴィヤマ）という値を示すことは，ヴィヤマを単位として設計計画が行われた可能性を強める。プレア・ヴィヘア寺院に関しては，前室側出幅（a-X6）において小さな値をとるが，前室に窓を持たないことを考慮すれば８ハスタ以上もの出幅が必要なかったものと推測できる。さらに狭小な伽藍内で，ホールＮを挟んで正対する配置に起因することも予想される。

このように両経蔵の寸法差が下部基壇以下かつ疑似扉側か前室側長辺方向にあらわれるという点は，いずれも中央祠堂を正面として左側の経蔵を基準として，４ハスタ＝１ヴィヤマをユニットとした基本計画があった可能性を指摘できる。したがって，以降の分析においては，上部基壇以上に関して基本的に同一の設計計画であり，その基本計画を中央祠堂を正面として左側の（東面する伽藍では南側の経蔵。経蔵が一棟の伽藍

In Chau Say Tevoda Temple, this 1 hasta differences are seen at porch depth (a-X6), and that of the north Library is 10 hasta; that of south Library is 9 hasta. If the primary planning that has dimension of the integer number is adopted, it is presumed that 9 hasta of south Library was shortened 1 hasta based on that of north Library. In Chau Say Tevoda Temple, it was not observed that the difference of dimension in false door depth (a-X7), however, it is estimated that the primary planning is based on vyama because of the dimensions are 4 hasta (=1 vyama). In Preah Vihear Temple, porch depth (a-X6) is shorter than that of other temples. However, it is inferred that the dimension does not need to widen beyond 8 hasta, considered that there is no window in the porch element. In addition, another factor is presumed that the Libraries are situated in a limited space of the Complex and faced each other in between the Hall N.

The differences of dimensions are observed in the element lower than lower platform at the longer side of porch element or false door side. On these tendencies, it is presumed the left Library in front of Central Sanctuary has the possibility that its dimensions were used as primary planning based on a unit of 4 hasta=1 vyama. Thus, in the following analysis we consider that a pair of Libraries is designed based on the same ideal plan upon upper platform and the left Library in front of Central Sanctuary (south Library in temples facing east. If there is only one Library, it is situated in the south. Hereinafter referred to as left Library.) is planed as priority.

3.9.6.2 Primary Planning of Dimensions Based on Reduction Numbers in Each Element

In the analyzing the dimensions of Prasat Suor Prat N1 tower by JSA, it was indicated that each element was reduced by the same dimensions [III]. In brief, it is considered that reduction distances are controlled from the outline of a base that is 23 units×27 units (1 unit=412 mm), to the outline of bottom of the wall, whole

167

Chapter 3 : Study Reports on Preah Vihear Temple

構成では南に配置する）経蔵（以下，左経蔵とする）を基調に考察していく。

3.9.6.2 縮減値を基に想定される基本計画寸法

JSA によるプラサート・スープラ N1 塔の寸法分析において，各部位が同一の値で逓減することが指摘されている[III]。すなわち，最下部の基座の四隅を結ぶ矩形 23 × 27u（1unit=412mm とみなす）の輪郭線から初層の四隅を繋ぐ矩形までが，前室部を除いて 4u の間隔を保っており，この間隔の中に，外から順に 1.5u（下部基壇まで），1u（上部基壇まで），0.5u（初層基座まで），1u（初層壁体まで）という間隔を保って各部の寸法を縮減して制御する，と考えられている。

このような見方を対象の各寺院に適応させ，各部の寸法値に関して縮減する値を，同一遺構の長辺方向と短辺方向の対応箇所において統一させて 0.25 〜 0.5 ハスタ程度増減させたものが想定ハスタ，すなわち想定基本寸法である。各部寸法値の分析は収束値ではなく，この想定ハスタ を扱うこととする。

以上の前提を踏まえた上で，各寺院の左経蔵の各部縮減値を，主室壁部と庇壁部で比較考察する。各部の寸法値をまとめると以下のようになる。

「側面庇壁体長辺幅（x-e）に関して」

最大縮減幅は，プレア・ヴィヘア院とバンテアイ・サムレ寺院を除く寺院の値が 13 ハスタもしくは 14 ハスタに近似していることが分かる。

「主室壁体長辺幅（x'-e）に関して」

最大縮減幅は長辺方向の傾向と同様に，バンテアイ・サムレ寺院を除く他のすべての寺院の値が 14.5 〜 15.5 ハスタの範囲で近似している。

「側面庇壁体短辺幅（y-e）に関して」

最大縮減幅は全寺院が完数の 12 ハスタを目指していた可能性が伺える。12 ハスタ＝ 3 ヴィマャであり，4 ハスタのユニットを想定した値とも考えられる。

「主室壁体短辺幅（y'-e）に関して」

最大縮減幅は多少ばらつきが見られる。ただし，チャウ・サイ・テヴォダ寺院，トマノン寺院，タ・ケオ寺院の 3 遺構をみれば 8 ハスタ＝ 2 ヴィマャを目指した可能性が伺える。その視点では，プレア・ヴィヘア寺院，バンテアイ・サムレ寺院は 9 ハスタと大きい値をとる。

reduction dimensions except porch elements keep 4 units, each from the outside is; from a base to lower platform is 1.5 units, from lower platform to upper platform is 1 unit, from upper platform to a base is 0.5 units, from a base to bottom of wall is 1 unit.

We converted the actual measurement value into estimated primary dimensions that control the dimensions about 0.25-0.5 hasta integrated corresponding to the elements of longer side and shorter side based on previous consideration. In the analyzing chapter, we used not the actual dimensions, but the estimated primary dimensions.

Based on the above, the reduction of each element of left Library in each temple is considered in Main Room and side eave. Each dimension is as follows:

「Length of Longer Side of Side Eave Wall (x-e)」

Max dimension of the reduction is estimated as 13 hasta or 14 hasta except Preah Vihear Temple and Banteay Samre Temple.

「Length of Longer Side of Main Room Wall (x'-e)」

Max dimensions of the reduction is estimated as the same as the side eave wall length, that is 14.5-15.5 hasta except Banteay Samre Temple.

「Lengh of Shorter Side of Side Eave Wall (y-e)」

Max dimensions of the reduction is estimated as 12 hasta in all temples, which is an integer number. There is a possibility that was intended to be 12 hasta = 3 vyama based on a unit of 4 hasta.

「Length of Shorter Side of Main Room Wall (y'-e)」

Max dimensions of the reduction looks varied. However in three temples, Chau Say Tevoda Temple, Thomanonn Temple and Ta Kev Temple, the dimensions intended to be 8 hasta=2 vyama. On this view, those of Preah Vihear Temple and Banteay Samre Temple are 9 hasta.

3.9.6.3 Analyzing of the Dimensions in Plan
3.9.6.3.1 Analyzing of the Dimensions of Longer Side

The followings are tendencies on the planning of dimensions of the longer side in each temple.

「Total Lengh of Longer Side of Base (a-X1)」

According to the previous section, total lengh of base (a-X1) and total lengh of lower platform (b-X1) in the longer side of plan are implemented under different control. All of the dimensions are different in each temple. The dimension of the

Planning Method of "Library" in Angkor Period

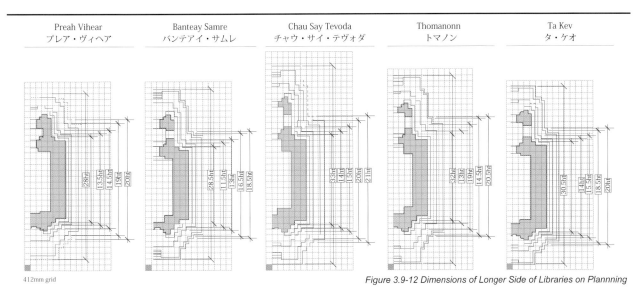

Figure 3.9-12 Dimensions of Longer Side of Libraries on Plannning

3.9.6.3 平面計画の分析
3.9.6.3.1 長辺方向の寸法分析

以下，各遺構の平面長辺方向の計画法について，その傾向を整理する。

「基座長辺方向全幅（a-X1）について」

前述したように，平面長辺方向の基座全幅（a-X1），および下部基壇全幅（b-X1）は各遺構において異なる寸法操作を行っており，トマノン寺院，タ・ケオ寺院を含めても，同一箇所において寸法値が合致することはなかった。プレア・ヴィヘア寺院の該当箇所の寸法値でもっとも近似している遺構はバンテアイ・サムレ寺院の 0.5 ハスタ差であり，その他遺構とは 2 ハスタ以上の寸法差がある。

「側面庇壁基座長辺幅（x'-a）に関して」

想定値を見比べると，バンテアイ・サムレ寺院を除く寺院の値がほぼ 18.5 〜 20 ハスタに近似する。明快な完数としての傾向は見られないがこの類似性は特筆すべきである。

「主室基座長辺幅（x-e）に関して」

バンテアイ・サムレ寺院を除く寺院の値がほぼ 20 〜 21 ハスタに近似することが分かる。庇壁部からの出幅がそれぞれ 1 ハスタないしは 1.5 ハスタで一貫していることから，傾向は変わらず，バンテアイ・サムレ寺院は 18 ハスタと比較的短い。

3.9.6.3.2 短辺方向の寸法分析

以下，各遺構の平面短辺方向の計画法について，その傾向を整理する。

element in Banteay Samre Temple is similar to that of Preah Vihear Temple, that is the difference is 0.5 hasta, and in the other temples it is 2 hasta ormore.

「Lengh of Side Eave Base in Longer Side (x'-a)」

To compare the estimated primary dimensions, it approaches about 18.5-20 hasta except Banteay Samre Temple. It is not confirmed that is a clear integer number, however, it should be mentioned as a similarity.

「Length of Main Base in Longer Side (x-e)」

In all temples except Banteay Samre Temple, the dimensions approach 20-21 hasta. Each of the depths from the side eave elements are consistently 1 hasta or 1.5 hasta, so that the tendency is the same as previous dimensions. Only in Banteay Samre Temple, the dimension is 18 hasta whichh is comparatively shorter than the others.

3.9.6.3.2 Analyzing of the Dimensions of Shorter Side

The followings are tendencies on the planning of dimensions of the shorter side in each temple:

「Lengh of Side Eave Base in Shorter Side (y'-a)」

The actual dimensions on measurement survey in each temple are approaching 17.5-18 hasta except that of Ta Kev Temple. It is inferred that there was the common intention on planning compared to the longer side.

「Length of Main Room Base in Shorter Side (y-a)」

All of the reduced dimensions are 3.5 or 4 hasta from shorter side of side eave base (y'5). The dimensions of the shorter side of the body base (y5) are estimated to be about 14 hasta in 4

169

Chapter 3 : Study Reports on Preah Vihear Temple

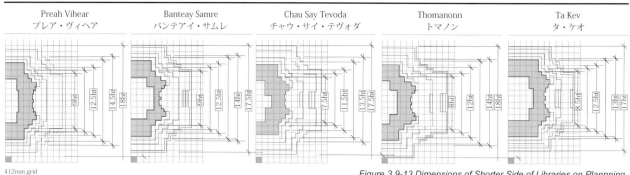

412mm grid

Figure 3.9-13 Dimensions of Shorter Side of Libraries on Plannning

「側面庇壁基座短辺幅（y'-a）に関して」

　各遺構の実測値をみると，タ・ケオ寺院以外の遺構で 17.5 〜 18 ハスタという近似した値を得られ，長辺方向に比べて同一の計画意図があったことが考えられる。

「主室基座短辺幅（y-a）に関して」

　全遺構とも庇壁部基座短辺幅（y'5）からの縮減値が 3.5 ハスタないし 4 ハスタで一貫しており，主室壁部基座短辺幅（y5）は 5 遺構中 4 遺構が 14 ハスタであると推測される。プレア・ヴィヘア寺院の縮減値が 3.5 ハスタと短いが，全遺構の縮減値の傾向から 14 ハスタを目指していた可能性を伺える。

3.9.6.3.3 縮減値と平面計画を含めた考察

　上述の各部の傾向と平面計画から，類似する値を抽出しそれぞれの部位に予想される寸法値を得た。また，長辺方向に比べて，短辺方向の値が良く近似していることを確認した。短辺方向では庇壁部と主室壁部の差を 4 ハスタ＝ 1 ヴィャマとして，基座と壁体の差を 6 ハスタの間隔で制御する基本計画が推測される。つまり，18-14-12-8（ハスタ）という関係を見ることができる。プレア・ヴィヘア寺院及びバンテアイ・サムレ寺院の腰壁部壁体短辺幅は 8 ハスタ以外にも 9 ハスタの完数が予想されている。他 3 遺構に比べて傾向が分散しており，計画意図を読み取りづらい。

3.9.6.4 立面計画の比較考察

　以下，各遺構の立面方向の計画法の傾向を整理する。

「全高（基座上端から最頂部）に関して」

　プレア・ヴィヘア寺院はペディメント欠損のため不明であるが，チャウ・サイ・テヴォダ寺院とトマノン寺院，タ・ケオ寺院が比較的類似した高さで，バンテアイ・サムレ寺院は明らかに高い。各経蔵全高においても明快な完数による制御を見出すことができない。

temples. The reduction in Preah Vihear Temple is 3.5 hasta. It is possible to aim to be 14 hasta of length of the shorter side of the body base by the tendency of all reduced dimensions.

3.9.6.3.3 Consideration Including Planning on Plan and Dimension of Reduction

According to the tendency of each of the elements and planning on plan, the dimensions of each element is estimated. The tendency of the dimensions of the shorter side is constant than those of the longer side. The primary planning of shorter side has inferred that the difference of reduction from side eave wall to main room wall is planned as 4 hasta=1 vyama and the difference of that from base to wall is planned as 6 hasta. There is a relationship of dimensions that is 18-14-12-8 (hasta). Length of spandrel wall in the shorter side is comsidered not only 8 hasta but also 9 hasta as integer number in Preah Vihear Temple and Baneay Samre Temple. Compared to the other 3 temples it is difficult to estimate the primary planning because of a dispersed tendency.

3.9.6.4 Comparative Consideration of Elevational planning

Tendencies of elevational planning are as follows:

「Total Height (From Top of Base to the Top of Building)」

Total height in Preah Vihear Temple can not be measured because of the collapsed pediment, however Chau Say Tevoda Temple, Thomanonn Temple, and Ta Kev Temple have similar dimensions comparatively while Banteay Samre is clearly highest. Integer numbers to control the total height is not be considered in these temples.

「Platform Height」

The total height of base is similar at about 3 hasta, and the height of upper platform is commonly 1 hasta. Therefore, the difference of dimension appeared under the lower platform.

Planning Method of "Library" in Angkor Period

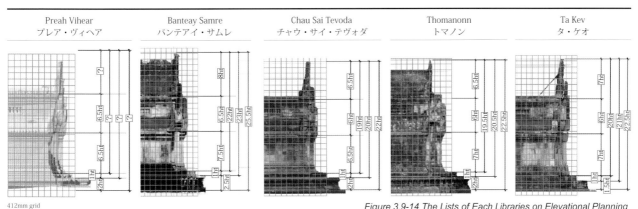

Figure 3.9-14 The Lists of Each Libraries on Elevational Planning

「基壇部に関して」

　基壇全高はいずれも3ハスタ程度と類似した高さを示すが，上部基壇が高さが1ハスタと共通するため，0.5ハスタの寸法差は下部基壇以下にみられる。

「庇壁部（上部基壇上端―庇壁コーニス上端）に関して」

　トマノン寺院とタ・ケオ寺院が7ハスタで類似するが，バンテアイ・サムレ寺院のみ明らかに高い。

「腰壁部（庇壁コーニス上端―腰壁コーニス上端）に関して」

　プレア・ヴィヘア寺院とバンテアイ・サムレ寺院が6.5ハスタで類似し，チャウ・サイ・テヴォダ寺院とトマノン寺院，タ・ケオ寺院が6ハスタで類似することが分かる。ペディメント部（腰壁コーニス上端―最頂部）に関して，プレア・ヴィヘア寺院はペディメントが欠けているため不明，チャウ・サイ・テヴォダ寺院とトマノン寺院が6.5ハスタで類似することが分かる。タ・ケオ寺院はそれより0.5ハスタ高く，バンテアイ・サムレ寺院はさらに1ハスタ高い。

　これら3層を見比べると，1，3層目に近似した値を割り付け，2層目でやや短い値を用いて寸法操作を行う傾向が見て取れる。またバンテアイ・サムレ寺院は1層目，3層目において他遺構より大きな値を示す。上部基壇上端―最頂部の高さをみると，プレア・ヴィヘア寺院は不明，バンテアイ・サムレ寺院は22ハスタ，チャウ・サイ・テヴォダ寺院は19ハスタ，トマノン寺院は19.5ハスタ，タ・ケオ寺院は20ハスタとなり，20ハスタ＝5ヴィヤマとする計画の可能性が窺える。上部基壇高さが全遺構とも1ハスタであることから，上部基壇を含めた場合は全ての遺構で基本計画に1ハスタを足すことになり，チャウ・サイ・テヴォダ寺院のように20ハスタ＝5ヴィヤマの完数を得る可能性も考えられるが，バンテアイ・サムレ寺院は2ハスタほど大きな値をとる。

「Side Eave Wall Height (Top of Side Eave Wall Cornice-Top of Spandrel Wall Cornice)」

　The heights in Preah Vihear Temple and Ta Kev Temple approach 7 hasta. However Banteay Samre Temple is clearly higher than the others.

「Spandrel Wall Height (Top of Side Eave Wall Cornice-Top of Spandal Wall Cornice)」

　The heights in Preah Vihear Temple and Banteay Samre Temple approach 6.5 hasta, and those in Chau Say Tevoda Temple, Thomanonn Temple, and Ta Kev Temple approach 6 hasta.

　Concerning the pediment element (top of spandal wall cornice-top of building), the height in Preah Vihear Temple was not examined because of collapse. In Chau Say Tevoda Temple and Thomanonn Temple, it approachs 6.5 hasta and they are similar. Ta Kev is 0.5 hasta higher than these temples, and Banteay Samre Temple is 1 hasta higher than Ta Kev Temple.

　Comparing these three layers, the tendency is that the first and third layer were designed similarly on their dimensions, and second layer was designed with a shorter dimension. The first layer and third layer in Banteay Samre Temple are higher than the others. Observing the dimensions from the top of upper platform to the top of the building, Preah Vihear Temple cannot be confirmed; Banteay Samre Temple is 22 hasta, Chau Say Tevoda Temple is 19 hasta, Thomanonn Temple is 19.5 hasta, and Ta Kev Temple is 20 hasta. Thus, there is the primary planning that the height is planned as 20 hasta=5 vyama in integer number. Including the upper platform, the dimensions in all of the temples are added 1 hasta to previous dimensions. In this case, Chau Say Tevoda Temple is considered to be 20 hasta=5 vyama as integer number, even Banteay Samre Temple as examined is 2 hasta higher.

171

Chapter 3 : Study Reports on Preah Vihear Temple

3.9.6.5 平面計画と立面計画の関係性の一考察

他遺構と比較してバンテアイ・サムレ寺院では明らかに平面長辺方向と高さ方向の規模変化が見て取れる。本研究では明確な関係性を見て取れることはできなかったが，試論として半周長の保持について各部を検証していく。半周長の保持とは，建物の規模計画を行う際に，極端な規模やプロポーションの変化を抑えるために，伽藍の長短辺を足し合わせた結果が一定となる原則を立てることである。その結果，主室壁部下部基壇長辺幅（x4）と下部基壇上端～最頂部の高さを足し合わせた数値が全遺構とも40ハスタを得るという傾向がみられた。40ハスタという値は10ヴィヤマという非常に明快な完数を示す。この結果から，平面長辺方向×立面方向が20ハスタ×20ハスタの関係をみることができる。寺院ごとによって寸法が微妙に異なる理由は，この基本計画を基にしつつも増減が施された結果であると見ることができそうである。基座の出幅を1ハスタ程度と考え，短辺方向で想定した理論値において基座～壁体への縮減幅が6ハスタであることを踏まえれば，主室壁部基座長辺幅（x5）から内側に向かって21-20-15-14（ハスタ）という関係が成り立つと推察される。

しかしこの法則に関しては，平面長辺方向と立面方向というやや不自然な値の関係性について言及しており，また平面長辺方向の対象箇所が主室壁部長辺方向の寸法値を対象としている面から，推論の域を出ていない。経蔵における平面方向と立面方向の基本計画の類推にはより確かな分析が必要であるため，ここでは可能性の指摘にとどめることとする。

なお，半周長の関係が保持されるとすれば，プレア・ヴィヘア寺院経蔵は，主室壁部基座長辺幅（x5）19ハスタ（東：18.90ハスタ，西：18.87ハスタ）であることから，長辺方向は1ハスタ程度基本計画より小さい値で計画される。プレア・ヴィヘア寺院は最頂部が崩壊しているが，40ハスタの保持により下部基壇上端～最頂部は21ハスタであると推測される。ペディメント高さは7ハスタと予想され，これに呼応して主室壁部壁体短辺幅（y1）が調整されるが，一方でその他の短辺幅は基本計画に近い値を用いる可能性があり，多少の寸法操作を短辺方向にも適用させなければならない。

3.9.7 結論

本研究における形式の経蔵には，共通した計画性とある程度の差を許容する箇所が確認される。特に短辺方向の平面計画においては，多少の寸法差を許容しな

3.9.6.5 One of the Considering Between the Plan and Elevational Plan

On comparing Banteay Samre Temple to other temples, we illustrate the maintaining of the total figure of all sides by the relationship between the transformation plan of the longer side and the elevational plan. In this study, we are not able to reveal the factor of transformation. However, we consider the relationship that they have the law in sum of dimensions of total figure and all sides. The maintaining of the total figure of all sides is an established rule that states that the total length of the circumference of a temple complex is constant to make it possible to maintain the areas and scale in the primary planning. As a result, it is confirmed that the total dimension of the main room of the lower platform height in the longer side (x4), and height from top of the lower platform to top the of building is intended to be 40 hasta in all of the temples. The number 40 hasta is same as 10 vyama that is a clear integer number. From this result, the relation between the longer side of the plan × elevation is regarded to be 20 × 20 hasta. The proposed reason for the diverse dimensions in each temple is that the dimensions are added or reduced based on an ideal plan. As the depth of the base is about 1 hasta, it is inferred that the relationship is 21-20-15-14 (hasta) from the length of the main room base on the longer side (x5) to the inner is determined by the dimension of the primary planning of 6 hasta from the estimated hasta of base to wall on the shorter side.

However, this rule mentions that there is an unnatural relationship between the longer side of the plan and height of elevation, and in the detail of the plan, the length of the main room wall on the longer side is the target in that rule, but it is but tentative theory in this study. In the future, it is necessary to continue verification.

If the maintaining of a total figure of all sides is realized, the whole dimensions of longer side of Library in Preah Vihear Temple is designed shortened about 1 hasta from primary planning based on the analyzing that the main room base length in the longer side (x5) is 19 hasta (east: 18.90 hasta, west: 18.87 hasta). In this view, the height from the top of the lower platform to the top of the building is regarded to be 21 hasta with the collapsed pediment considered to provide a maximum height of 40 hasta. The height of the pediment is estimated at 7 hasta, and the main room wall length on the shorter side (y1) is controlled according to the size of the pediment. However, there is a possibility that the other dimensions in the shorter side are adopted close to the primary planning. In this case, it is necessary to control the dimensions in the shorter side.

がらも一貫した計画性を見て取ることができ，いくつ
かの箇所において4ハスタ＝1ヴィヤマを単位とした
計画性が考えられることを確認できた。しかし，長辺
方向の平面計画及び立面方向の高さは，今回確認した
遺構すべてに明確かつ一貫した計画があったとは言え
ず，特にバンテアイ・サムレ寺院において大きな差異
がみられた。バンテアイ・サムレ寺院を除く各遺構の
寸法の類似性から，ペディメントが一部崩壊している
プレア・ヴィヘア寺院経蔵では，ある程度の高さを予
想することができた。今後の研究によって平面計画長
辺方向の寸法と立面方向の高さ関係が明らかになると，
さらにこの精度が上がる可能性がある。プレア・ヴィ
ヘア寺院とバンテアイ・サムレ寺院における左右の
経蔵の寸法差が1ハスタずつ縮減，拡幅している点や，
主室壁部壁体短辺幅（y1）が9ハスタ（2ヴィヤマ+1
ハスタ）である点など，ヴィヤマを1つの単位系とし
ているだけでなく，さらに意図的に寸法操作が行われ
ている箇所も確認できた。この計画意図をさらに検証
することで，プレア・ヴィヘア寺院だけでなく同時代，
同形式の他遺構においても復原案を類推できる可能性
が考えられる。

また，中央祠堂に向かって左側に1つだけのもの，
対になる経蔵を持つものを含めて，必ず入口が西向き
である建物があること，左右に対になる経蔵を有する
とき，同形式であっても寸法差を設けられる遺構が多
いことを考えると，左右では主機能に差異があり，そ
れによって寸法操作が発生するとも考えられる。本研
究では一貫した経蔵の基本計画を類推し，左経蔵の基
本計画を思索，それを基にさらに右側の経蔵において
寸法操作が行われている可能性を論じた。そこには具
体的な建築的意義までは踏み込めないものの，左右の
経蔵の計画意図の相違や，対の建物における設計手法
の理念の違いがあったとも考えられよう。

3.9.7 Conclusion

Through the Libraries with the same style in this study the common planning is confirmed while some elements show allowing for a discrepancy to the planning. Especially on the plan of the shorter side, the common planning is confirmed based on a unit of 4 hasta=1 vyama, with a few inadequate elements in each temple. However, in the plan of the longer side and elevation, the common tendency is not followed especially in Banteay Samre Temple. From the similarity of each temple, except Banteay Samre Temple, the height of the pediment in Preah Vihear Temple can be estimated. If the relation between the plan of the longer side and elevation is identified in the future study, estimates will be improved. From some facts that differences of dimension between a pair of the libraries is shortened or widened for 1 hasta in Preah Vihear Temple and Banteay Samre Temple, and also main room wall legth of shorter side (y1) is 9 hasta (=2 vyama + 1 hasta), these tendencies suggest the plan is based on vyama as one of the units. Moreover, some of the dimensions are presumed controlled intentionally based on vyama. There is a possibility to speculate the restoration plan not only in Preah Vihear Temple, but other temples of same times and same styles by research about planning intentions.

In addition to those tendencies, the control of the dimension is based on differences of the main functions of the left and right Libraries in front of the Central Sanctuary. Considered must be given to the fact that there is necessarily a building which has a door open to west whether it is situated as a pair or only one in temple, There are many Libraries that have differences of dimensions in a pair in spite of the same style. This study presumed the common primary planning of Libraries and mentioned that there was a possibility to control the dimension in the right Library based on the ideal plan of the left Library. Until the concrete uses of Libraries are determined, , we can only suggest the possibility that there are differences in the planning intention, and principle of design when Libraries are in pairs.

References

I)   Chan Vitharong: Hotrai 'Library' of Ancient Khmer Temples.

II) Akinori Mizoguchi: The Dimensional Plan of the Bayon Temple - A Comparison between the Bayon Northern Library and Southern Library-, The Master Plan for the Conversation &Restoration of the Bayon Complex, JSA, June, 2005.

III) Akinori Mizoguchi, Yasushi Akazawa, Takeshi Nakagawa & Takahiko Nakabachi: On the Dimensional Plan in Prasat Suor Prat Tower N1 - Study on the dimentional plan and the planning methods of Khmer architecture No. 2, J. Archit. Plann., AIJ, No. 616, 175-181, Jun, 2007.

3.10 ペディメントの装飾的特質
Significant Features of the Decorations of the Pediments

金子　達哉　　北井　絵里沙
KANEKO Tatsuya　　KITAI Erisa

3.10.1 はじめに

プレア・ヴィヘア寺院では，建物によって異なる形式のペディメントが見受けられる。クメール寺院のペディメント形式として，直線的な輪郭をもち，両下端に渦巻型をもつ三角形破風形式，および曲線の輪郭をもち，両下端にアクロテリオン形式の多頭ナーガをもつ火炎型破風形式という2通りの破風形式が確認されている。通例はいずれか一方の破風がみられることが多いが，プレア・ヴィヘア寺院においては両方の形式が混在している。屋根を構成する部材の中にレンガを使用したと見られる建物がある点もプレア・ヴィヘア寺院の特徴である。アンコール地域の北東に位置し，このように様々な形式のペディメントが混在するプレア・ヴィヘア寺院は，クメール全体の木造屋根を考察していく上で時代的にも地域的にも非常に重要であると考えられる。本研究は，プレア・ヴィヘア寺院における木造小屋組痕跡が確認されたペディメントに関して，比較考察を行いつつその特徴を明らかにしていくものである。

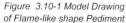

Figure 3.10-1 Model Drawing of Flame-like shape Pediment　　*Figure 3.10-2 Model Drawing of Triangle Pediment*

3.10.2 研究方法

プレア・ヴィヘア寺院のそれぞれの建物におけるペディメント形式及びペディメント上の木造痕跡の特徴を明らかにしていく。方法としてはまず，ペディメント上に確認できる木造部材を支持したであろう痕跡の寸法を，プレア・ヴィヘア寺院のみではなく，他の地域における遺構の痕跡と比較していくことで，クメール寺院建築に共通する傾向と，プレア・ヴィヘア寺院

3.10.1 Introduction

In Preah Vihear Temple, there are different types of pediment in each building. Khmer temples have 2 types of pediments, one is triangle pediment with straight outline which has spiral-shape in both bottom corner of the pediment, and another is flame-like shape pediment with multi-headed nagas as acroteria. There are both types of pediments in Preah Vihear Temple although just one type of pediment for one temple is often seen. Another significant feature of Preah Vihear Temple is a building whose roof was made of a mixture of wood and brick. Thus, Preah Vihear Temple, which stands in the northeast part of Cambodia, is very important temple to consider a chronological transition, and the regional characteristics of Khmer wooden roofs. This study reveals features of wooden roof construction and its pediment by comparing traces of wooden roof structures.

3.10.2 Method of Study

The objective of this study is to clarify the types of pediment as well as the features of wooden traces on pediments in Preah Vihear Temple. In the beginning, the study compares Preah Vihear Temple with other Khmer temples by the dimensions of wooden traces on pediments which appear to have supported a wooden roof structure which reveals a common tendency of Khmer architecture, and the significant tendency of Preah Vihear Temple. The analysis on the disposition of wooden traces on pediment will also take the structural devices of the lost wooden roofs into consideration. In addition, it considers a relation between the disposition of wooden traces on backside of pediment and decorations on the frontside of it for each triangle and flame-like shape type. Through cross-sectional comparison of pediments in each era and region, it will become more evident that the transition of pediment types and decorations, had influences on the regional and chronological characteristics of pediment styles.

における特徴的な傾向を明らかにする。同時に痕跡の
配置から，失われた木造屋根の構造的な工夫を考察
する。また三角形破風と火炎型破風それぞれにおいて，
痕跡位置とペディメント上の装飾との関係性を考察し
ていく。各時代地域のペディメントの特徴も横断的に
比較することで，ペディメント自体の装飾形式の変遷
も明らかにし，最終的にペディメント装飾の変遷を明
らかにした上で，その形式の地域性と時代性による影
響を明らかにしたい。

3.10.3 プレア・ヴィヘア寺院におけるペディメントの概要

プレア・ヴィヘア寺院における屋根構法に関して，
先行研究においては「砂岩造」「木造」「木造（レンガ
造）」の存在が報告されている。屋根架構が「木造」で
あったことを示す木造小屋組痕跡が確認できた箇所は，
第5ゴープラ，第4ゴープラ，第3ゴープラとその東
西の付属建物（H, H', I, I'），第2伽藍，第1伽藍と
その東西の付属建物（E, F）である。そのうち第3ゴー
プラにおいては，合わせてレンガを葺いた痕跡も確認
された。各建物の残存するペディメントは，「付章 I.
2 プレア・ヴィヘア寺院のペディメント」にて立面図
一覧を記載する。

第5ゴープラは崩壊の度合いが激しいため，木造小
屋組の痕跡が見られるペディメントは限られていた。
ペディメントの形状は三角形破風でありペディメント
裏には母屋桁跡とともに垂木もしくは瓦のあたりと思
われる痕跡が存在している。壁体上部の砂岩材は，軒
桁の上に砂岩材が覆い被さるように配されていたと思
われる痕跡が残存しており，その外面には瓦当を模し
た装飾が施されていることから，瓦葺きの屋根であっ
たと想定される。

第4ゴープラにおけるペディメントの形式は火炎型
破風であり，計9つのペディメントが残存する。その
うちの1つは建物の内部空間を仕切るために設けられ
た壁体であり，桁がペディメント上方を貫通して桁の
中央の位置を支えるような収まりになっている。桁は
軒桁を合わせて4段で計7つの桁痕跡が確認された。
壁体上部の砂岩材には，第5ゴープラと同じく瓦当を
模した装飾が施されている。母屋桁跡に関しては，軒
桁，1段目，2段目，棟木と上部の桁になるにつれて
断面の大きさが小さくなっている。

第3ゴープラのペディメントは三角形破風である。
ペディメント内側の面にはレンガを葺いたと見られる
階段状の痕跡が残存しており，壁体上部の砂岩材にも
レンガのあたりとみられる5段ほどの階段状痕跡が確

3.10.3 Overview of Pediment Characteristics in Preah Vihear Temple

Existance of "sandstone structure", "wooden structure", "wooden structure (including brick)" were reported as the construction methods of Preah Vihear Temple. The evidence of wooden frames are confirmed in Gopura V, Gopura IV, Gopura III, and Annex Buildings located on its east and west sides (H, H', I, I'), Complex II, Complex I and Annex Buildings on its east and west sides (E, F). The traces of a roof with bricks are confirmed only at Gopura III. Elevation drawings of all remaining pediments of each building are showed as a list in "Appendix I.2 Pediments in Preah Vihear Temple".

In Gopura V, the existence of a pediment with evidence of the wooden frame is limited because of the severe collapse of the building. From its pediment shape, it is classified as a triangle type. There is evidence of rafters or roof tiles touching on the backside of the pediment. The evidence was confirmed from stones on the top part of wall which is considerd to cover the wooden gave girders. The decorations on the surface of these stones look like the end of roof tiles. Therefore Gopura V seems to be roofed with tiles.

Nine pediments of the flame-like shape type are left in Gopura IV. One of the pediments seems to be built for separating inside space, and the purlins of the roof structure pierced the upper part of the pediment for supporting the center part. The purlins are confirmed as 4 steps including gave girder. Therefore the total number of purlin traces is 7. Sandstone on the top of wall is decorated like roof tiles the same as Gopura V. The size of traces of purlins become gradually smaller by the higher dispositions from gave girder to 1st step, 2nd step and the ridge purlin.

Gopura III has triangle type pediments. The stair-casing traces are left on the inside surface of the pediment and that implies there was brick as a roofing. Five steps of the stair-casing traces of bricks also remain in the sandstone on the top of the wall. The brick trace angles correspond to the rafter position, and it constitutes a straight outlines in both inside and outside.

Triangle type pediments, which are same with Gopura IV, are also confirmed in the Annex Buildings that are locate on both sides of Gopura III (H, H', I, I'). However, none of decorated pediments exist in the Annex Buildings on the east and west sides of Complex I (E, F), nor can be confirmed the type of pediment while the evidences of the wooden frame are left on the pediments of the room borders.

In the Complex II, pediments of a triangle type were used in Gopura II, and the outside wall of the Galleries whose plan is "L" shaped. Most of the pediments in Hall N, standing at the center

認できる。垂木の位置に相当するレンガ部の角度は内外ともに直線的であった。

　付属建物H，H'，I，I'においても，第4ゴープラと同様に三角形破風形式のペディメントが見られるが，付属建物E，Fに関しては，装飾を有するペディメントの痕跡が残存していないため，その形状は把握することができないが，木造屋根の痕跡については，この建物の各室を隔てる仕切壁のペディメントにおいて確認する事が出来る。

　第2伽藍では，第2ゴープラとL字形の平面をもつ回廊の外壁で三角形破風形式のペディメントが用いられた。また，第2伽藍中央のホールN部分におけるペディメントは，全体的に崩壊が激しいが，側廊端にハーフペディメントが残っており，その装飾から，この建物も三角形破風形式であったと判断される。

　第1伽藍内では，背面ゴープラ，中央祠堂および拝殿，経蔵では石材やレンガによるコーベルアーチの迫り出しを用いた屋根形式が採用されており，木造小屋組の跡が確認された遺構は第1ゴープラのみであった。その形式が三角形破風であったことは確認できるが，全体として崩壊が激しく全容は不明である。

　これらをまとめると，プレア・ヴィヘア寺院における木造小屋組跡が確認されたペディメントでは第4ゴープラのみが火炎型破風，それ以外は全て三角形破風となっている。全体の傾向として，三角形破風をもつ遺構は木造屋根，火炎型破風をもつ例はレンガ造ないし石造屋根を載せるが，火炎型破風に木造屋根を組み合わせる例も認められることは，プレア・ヴィヘア寺院の特徴である。

3.10.4 ペディメント上に見られる木造痕跡の比較考察

　前項で述べたように，プレア・ヴィヘア寺院の各建物に残るペディメントに，木造小屋組を有していたと考えられる母屋桁大入れ跡が確認された。木造痕跡を有するペディメントに関して，他遺構と比較考察を行う。対象遺構は，プレア・ヴィヘア寺院と同じく，ペディメントに木造痕跡が確認されたコー・ケー遺跡群のプラサート・トム寺院，プラサート・クラチャップ寺院，アンコール遺跡群のバンテアイ・スレイ寺院，タ・ケオ寺院各遺構の付属建物とする。なお，コー・ケー遺跡群の2つの寺院は，コー・ケーが首都であった928年から944年頃の都市整備に伴う建立と考えられ，バンテアイ・スレイ寺院（碑文では968年建立）の付属建物は，建立後に屋根の高さを増す大きな改造が予想されるため，現存するペディメントは10世紀末～11世紀初頭頃の改造後の様相を示すと考えられる。

of the Complex II are almost collapsed, but the decoration of its half-pediments of both side eave shows the pediments would be triangle type.

In the Complex I, a corbel roof with stones or bricks was used as the roof style for the false gopura, Central Sanctuary, and its Mandapa and Libraries. The evidence of wooden roof frame is left only in Gopura I. That pediment type seems to be a triangle, but the whole shape is still unknown because of the heavy damage to the building.

To summarize, only Gopura IV has flame-like shape type pediments, and the other buildings that have evidences of a wooden frame used triangle type pediments. As a tendency in Khmer temples, usually buildings with triangle type pediments have wooden roof, and with flame-like shaped type pediments have a stone or brick roof, however Preah Vihear Temple has the combination of flame-like shape type pediments and wooden roof in a same building that is a significant architectural feature of this temple.

3.10.4 Comparative Consideration on Wooden Traces on Pediments

As mentioned above, dado traces for purlin as evidence of a wooden frame are confirmed in each existing pediment in Preah Vihear Temple. The following description compares this with other temples having pediments with wooden traces. The temples for comparison are Prasat Thom and Prasat Krachap Temples at Koh Ker Monuments, Banteay Srei and Ta Kev Temples at Angkor Monuments; all of them showing wooden traces on pediments. Two temples at Koh Ker Monuments are considered to be built along with urban development around 930~940 A.D. when Koh Ker was the capital city of the Khmer Empire. Annex Buildings in Banteay Srei Temple (built in 968 A.D.) are estimated to have been improved extensively for increasing building height after foundation. Therefore, the remaining pediments seem to show a style from the end of the 10th century to the beginning of the 11th century. Annex Buildings in Ta Kev Temple are also considered to be built at the beginning of the 11th century.

3.10.4.1 Comparative Consideration on Dimension of Purlin Trace

This section begins with the comparison of the dimension of the dado traces for purlin. In Prasat Thom Temple in Koh Ker Monuments, 3 steps of traces including the ridge purlin are confirmed except the gave girders laid on the wall directly are the same as Preah Vihear Temple. Comparing height, width and

タ・ケオ寺院の付属建物も同様に11世紀初頭頃の建立と考えられる。

3.10.4.1 母屋桁大入れ跡の寸法値に関する比較考察

まず，母屋桁大入れ跡の寸法値について比較を行う。コー・ケー遺跡群のプラサート・トム寺院では，プレア・ヴィヘア寺院と同様に壁上に直接載る軒桁の痕跡と考えられるものを除き，棟木跡を含めて3段の痕跡が確認できる。大入れ痕跡の高さと幅，奥行を比較すると，各寺院の値は均一ではないが，最上段の棟木跡よりも下段の痕跡の方が，寸法値が大きくなる傾向が鮮明である（Figure 3.10-3）。この傾向は，初期の遺構であるプラサート・トムの第2ゴープラ，また，プレア・ヴィヘア寺院においても同様である。同一のペディメント内で対になっている痕跡の寸法は，左右でばらつきが存在することが多い。おそらくこの原因は，ペディメントを建てた後に母屋桁をはめ込むため，石材側の仕口を余裕をもって加工したためだと考えられる。

3.10.4.2 母屋桁大入れ跡の配置に関する比較考察

次に，母屋桁大入れ跡の相対的な位置関係，配置間隔に関して比較考察を行う。まず鉛直方向については，プラサート・トム寺院，プラサート・クラチャップ寺院では，棟木と壁体上部を3等分して大入れを配しているとみられるものと，上部段に上るにつれて痕跡同士の高さの間隔が狭くなるものがみられる。一方でタ・ケオ寺院の付属建物では，ペディメントの壁体上端から大入れ跡最下段までの距離だけが，それより上部の段における痕跡の間隔に比べて広くなる様子が確認される。水平方向の配置については，多くの遺構で室内の短辺内法間を，およそ6等分して配している。プレア・ヴィヘア寺院の第3ゴープラ，バンテアイ・スレイ寺院の第4ゴープラ，タ・ケオ寺院の矩形建物では，1段目から3段目を均等の間隔で配しているものの，

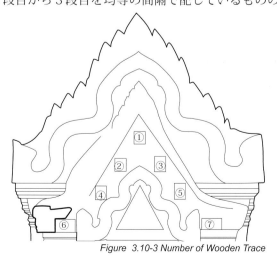

Figure 3.10-3 Number of Wooden Trace

depth of dado traces for purlin in comparison temples, they are not of a uniform dimension, but there is a clear tendency that traces of the lower steps are bigger than the upper ridge purlin trace (Figure 3.10-3). This tendency is the same with Gopura II of Prasat Thom and Preah Vihear Temples. Many pairs of the same step traces in the same pediment have a gap in dimensions between right side and left side of the pediment. The reason for the gap might be joints which are processed with enough size for putting purlins into mortices after the erection of the pediment.

Table 3.10-1 Dimensions of Wooden Trace

Temple	Facility	Position of Pediment	Position of Trace	X mm	X hasta	Y mm	Y hasta
Prasat Thom	East Gopura II	South Side Room (Backside)	①	205	0.50	135	0.33
			②	210	0.51	160	0.39
			③	235	0.57	150	0.36
			④	165	0.40	275	0.67
			⑤	170	0.41	260	0.63
			⑥				
			⑦				
		Main Room	①	195	0.47	215	0.52
			②	215	0.52	215	0.52
			③	215	0.52	215	0.52
			④	260	0.63	240	0.58
			⑤				
			⑥				
			⑦				
	Annex Building in cause way	Main Room (South Frontside)	①	310	0.75	300	0.73
			②	310	0.75	310	0.75
			③	335	0.81	335	0.81
			④	290	0.70	310	0.75
			⑤	345	0.84	360	0.87
			⑥				
			⑦				
		Main Room (South Backside)	①	320	0.78	515	1.25
			②	325	0.79	330	0.80
			③	300	0.73	330	0.80
			④	335	0.81	330	0.80
			⑤	325	0.79	305	0.74
			⑥				
			⑦				
Preah Vihear	Gopura IV	Main Room (West Frontside)	①	170	0.41	170	0.41
			②	200	0.49	210	0.51
			③	205	0.50	225	0.55
			④	240	0.58	320	0.78
			⑤	180	0.44	260	0.63
			⑥	400	0.97	325	0.79
			⑦	235	0.57	235	0.57
	Gopura III	Main Room (East Frontside)	①	265	0.64	395	0.96
			②	290	0.70	485	1.18
			③	275	0.67	490	1.19
			④	305	0.74	525	1.27
			⑤	285	0.69	525	1.27
			⑥	280	0.68	235	0.57
			⑦	235	0.57	270	0.66
		Main Room (West Frontside)	①	220	0.53	240	0.58
			②	280	0.68	150	0.36
			③	280	0.68	270	0.66
			④	285	0.69	320	0.78
			⑤	310	0.75	175	0.42
			⑥				
			⑦	310	0.75	300	0.73
		Main Room (North Frontside)	①	235	0.57		
			②	170	0.41	120	0.29
			③	295	0.72	235	0.57
			④	300	0.73	290	0.70
			⑤	275	0.67	180	0.44
			⑥	415	1.01	260	0.63
			⑦				
		Main Room (South Frontside)	①				
			②	250	0.61	425	1.03
			③	255	0.62	465	1.13
			④	300	0.73	420	1.02
			⑤	270	0.66	535	1.30
			⑥	295	0.72	300	0.73
			⑦	320	0.78	225	0.55

▨ Unrecordable

Chapter 3 : Study Reports on Preah Vihear Temple

Table 3.10-2 Horizontal Placement Dimension of Wooden Trace

Temple	Facility	Position of Pediment	Average of ①-②,①-③ mm	hasta	Average of ②④,③⑤ mm	hasta	Average of ④⑥,⑤⑦ mm	hasta	Bottom-Wall mm	hasta
Preah Vihear	Gopura IV	Main room(E-F)	160	0.39	135	0.33	350	0.85	350	0.85
		Main room(W-F)	195	0.47	190	0.46	355	0.86	375	0.91
		Main room(N-F)	145	0.35	165	0.40	340	0.83	340	0.83
		Main room(S-F)	150	0.36	145	0.35	380	0.92	400	0.97
	Gopura III	Main room(E-F)	310	0.75	280	0.68	570	1.38	550	1.33
		Main room(W-F)	300	0.73	270	0.66	550	1.33	550	1.33
		Main room(N-F)			165	0.40	340	0.83	340	0.83
		Main room(S-F)			340	0.83			495	1.20
		Side room(B)	365	0.89	280	0.68			460	1.12
	Annex Building H',I'	Main room(E-B)	290	0.70	305	0.74			540	1.31
		Side room(W-B)	340	0.83	400	0.97			415	1.01
	Annex Building H,'	Main room(W-B)	390	0.95	390	0.95			615	1.49
		Side room(E-B)	320	0.78	300	0.73			400	0.97
Banteay Srei	Structure C	Main room(S)	425	1.03					220	0.53
		Side room(N)			240	0.58			290	0.70
	Structure D	Main room(N)	380	0.92					557	1.35
	West Gopura II	Side room(E)	445	1.08					405	0.98
	Gopura IV	Main room(E)	365	0.89	355	0.86			655	1.59
	East Gopura II	Main room(E)	340	0.83						
Ta Kev	Structure A	Main room1(F)	110	0.27	270	0.66	315	0.76	315	0.76
		Main room2(B)	220	0.53	230	0.56	430	1.04	430	1.04
		Main room2(F)	160	0.39	360	0.87	340	0.83	340	0.83
	Structure B	Main room1(F)	215	0.52	180	0.44	340	0.83	340	0.83
		Main room1(B)	220	0.53	230	0.56	415	1.01	405	0.98
		Main room2(F)			215	0.52			370	0.90
		Main room2(B)			160	0.39			365	0.89
	Structure D	Main room1(F)	155	0.38	190	0.46			340	0.83
Prasat Thom	East Gopura II	Side room(S-B)	300	0.73	350	0.85			325	0.79
		Main room(B)	330	0.80	340	0.83			305	0.74
	Annex Building in Causeway	Main room(S-F)	390	0.95	310	0.75			365	0.89
		Main room(S-B)	360	0.87	385	0.93			365	0.89
Prasat Krachap	West Gopura II	Side room(S)	250	0.61	250	0.61			210	0.51
		Main room(W-F)	302	0.73	305	0.74			265	0.64
		Main room(B)	295	0.72	262	0.64			265	0.64

▨ Unrecordable

Table 3.10-3 Vertical Dimension of Wooden Trace

Temple	Facility	Position of Pediment	Top-2nd trace mm	hasta	2nd trace-Bottom mm	hasta	Bottom-Wall mm	hasta
Preah Vihear	Gopura IV	Main room(E-F)	220	0.53	245	0.59	620	1.50
		Main room(W-F)	300	0.73	270	0.66	630	1.53
		Main room(N-F)	280	0.68	220	0.53	605	1.47
		Main room(S-F)	280	0.68	190	0.46	610	1.48
	Gopura III	Main room(E-F)	120	0.29	180	0.44	690	1.67
		Main room(W-F)	170	0.41	220	0.53	1355	3.29
		Main room(N-F)			195	0.47	1455	3.53
		Main room(S-F)			75	0.18	1435	3.48
		Side room(B)	165	0.40	440	1.07	750	1.82
	Annex Building H',I'	Main room(E-B)	365	0.89	310	0.75	745	1.81
		Side room(W-B)	330	0.80	470	1.14	730	1.77
	Annex Building H,'	Main room(W-B)	385	0.93	205	0.50	770	1.87
		Side room(E-B)	375	0.91	340	0.83	625	1.52
Banteay Srei	Structure C	Main room(S)	365	0.89			270	0.66
		Side room(N)	300	0.73	130	0.32	95	0.23
	Structure D	Main room(N)	370	0.90			385	0.93
	West Gopura II	Side room(E)	440	1.07			160	0.39
	Gopura IV	Main room(E)	230	0.56	190	0.46	710	1.72
	East Gopura II	Main room(E)	295	0.72			620	1.50
Ta Kev	Structure A	Main room1(F)	165	0.40	245	0.59	290	0.70
		Main room2(B)	180	0.44	230	0.56	510	1.24
		Main room2(F)	180	0.44	220	0.53	490	1.19
	Structure B	Main room1(F)	200	0.49	210	0.51	285	0.69
		Main room1(B)			200	0.49	520	1.26
		Main room2(F)			120	0.29	460	1.12
		Main room2(B)			180	0.44	450	1.09
	Structure D	Main room1(F)	225	0.55	195	0.47	265	0.64
Prasat Thom	East Gopura II	Side room(S-B)	460	1.12	365	0.89		
		Main room(B)	405	0.98	380	0.92	330	0.80
	Annex Building in Causeway	Main room(S-F)	445	1.08	430	1.04	470	1.14
		Main room(S-B)	480	1.17	475	1.15	535	1.30
Prasat Krachap	West Gopura II	Side room(S)	265	0.64	210	0.51	320	0.78
		Main room(W-F)	345	0.84	305	0.74	300	0.73
		Main room(B)	235	0.57	170	0.41	325	0.79

▨ Unrecordable

Figure 3.10-4
Drawing of Gopura III Pediment
(Front:Thin line, Back: Bold line)

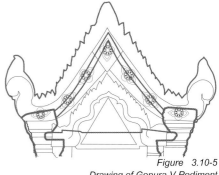

Figure 3.10-5
Drawing of Gopura V Pediment
(Front:Thin line, Back: Bold line)

３段目から壁体端までがやや大きな値をとっていることが確認された。

3.10.5 装飾と痕跡の関連性

前項ではペディメントに見られる母屋桁大入れ跡の寸法値の傾向，後期寺院における建物幅を広げるための構造的な工夫が確認された。一方で，ペディメント表面に施された装飾と裏面の木造痕跡がいかに連関していたのかは不明である。しかしペディメント表面の装飾は，本来，木造の妻壁に使われた形式を踏襲していると考えられるため，石造化以後は単なる装飾であるにも関わらず，背面の木造屋根の形式と計画上一定の関連を持ち続けていたことも予想される。装飾は三角形破風と火炎型破風の２タイプに大きく分類することができるが，両タイプについてそれぞれ木造痕跡との関連性を考察する。

3.10.5.1 三角形破風装飾の痕跡の比較考察

まず木造ペディメントの表れとされる形式を置き換えようとしたであろう石造ペディメントの三角形破風装飾から比較を行う。東メボン寺院やプレ・ルプ寺院の付属建物では，木造の妻壁が建っていたとみられる痕跡が残されているが，残念ながらその全容を理解させる例は残っていない。木造小屋組痕跡が確認された石造ペディメントの中で三角形破風装飾が確認されたのは，プラサート・トム寺院，プラサート・クラチャップ寺院，バンテアイ・スレイ寺院，および第４ゴープラを除くプレア・ヴィヘア寺院の木造屋根遺構である。またプレア・コー寺院においても三角形破風装飾に特有の渦巻装飾の一部が確認された。三角形破風形式は，９世紀後半から10世紀前半頃にかけて各地で使用され，一部の地域で11世紀初頭まで続いた形式のようである。

三角形破風の破風板に当たる装飾の上には，釘隠しとみられる形を表現した菱形の装飾が確認される。これは，木造妻壁の時代に，母屋桁木口に，これを覆う目的で幅の広い破風板を当て，破風板の外から母屋桁に釘止めとした収まりに起因すると考えられる。釘隠しは，破風板表面の釘の腐食と釘周辺の木材の腐朽を防ぐ目的で，破風板表面の釘の頭に被せた部材である。石造化された後の様相から推察される木造時代の釘隠しの大きさは，かなり大きな部材であるので，これは金属製ではなく木製であったと考えられる。しかし，木造時代の破風板は，背後の瓦と垂木の側面，母屋桁の木口などを覆っていたと考えられるため，釘隠しの位置が破風板の幅の中央ではなく，下方に寄っていたと思われる。一方，石造化後の釘隠しは，破風板の幅

3.10.4.2 Comparative Consideration on Arrangement of Purlin Traces

Comparative consideration on the positional relation and the interval arrangement of dado traces for purlin was made. In Prasat Thom Temple and Prasat Krachap Temple, there are 2 types of trace arrangements which are set by dividing into 3 equal spans between the ridge purlin and gave girder, and by a narrowing of the interval gradually on raising every step of the purlin traces. On the other hand, in Annex Building of Ta Kev Temple, only the span between the gave girder and the lowest step of the purlin traces is wider than the other spans. In a horizontal direction, purlin traces are set by dividing the span of the inside measurent of building into 6 equal spans in many temples. But, in Gopura III at Preah Vihear Temple, Gopura IV at Banteay Srei Temple, and rectangle buildings at Ta Kev Temple, a span between the third step of purlins and the gave girder is a little longer, while the other spans from first to third steps of traces are almost equal dimensions.

3.10.5 Relevance of Decoration and Wooden Trace

In the preceding section, it is confirmed that there is a tendency that the dimensions of dado traces for purlin on pediments and the structural device to expand the width of temple buildings in the late period. However, the relevance between decorations on the frontside of pediments and wooden traces on backside of pediments is still unclear. Decorations on the frontside of pediments seem to follow a style of wooden pediment. So it is expected that it has a fixed relation to a style of wooden roof traces on the backside of the pediments even though it has been changed to a kind of decorations with the transfer to masonry buildings. Decorations on pediments are classified into two types and the relevance between wooden traces and decorations would be considered in the following section.

3.10.5.1 Comparative Consideration on Traces of Triangle Type Pediment

Decorations of triangle pediments, which shows a clue of former wooden pediments, are considered in this section. In the Annex Buildings in the East Mebon Temple and Pre Rup Temple, there are traces of wooden pediments, however the complete shape of the pediments is still unknown. Triangle masonry pediments with traces of the wooden frame are confirmed in Prasat Thom Temple, Prasat Krachap Temple, Banteay Srei Temple, and Preah Vihear Temple except Gopura IV. In Preah Ko Temple, there is also a fragment of spiral-shape which is a feature of a triangle type pediment. Thus, triangle pediments

Chapter 3 : Study Reports on Preah Vihear Temple

の中央に位置しており，石造化に伴う装飾的扱いが介在したことが予想される。

釘隠し装飾の位置は，プレア・ヴィヘア寺院の第5ゴープラを除き，最上部の釘隠し装飾と背面の棟木の位置がほぼ一致している。また，プラサート・トム寺院，プラサート・クラチャップ寺院，バンテアイ・スレイ寺院の各寺院では，各母屋桁の位置が表面の釘隠し装飾の位置と概ね一致していることが確認された。プレア・ヴィヘア寺院の第5ゴープラでは，釘隠し装飾と母屋桁は一致しなかったが，垂木の角度に沿うように破風板の装飾が配されていることが確認された。破風板の装飾位置は，概ね垂木位置に対応している傾向がうかがえたが，プレア・ヴィヘア寺院の第5ゴープラのように必ず一致するわけではない。しかし，全体の傾向は，石造三角形破風の裏面の小屋組各部材と表面の装飾の位置関係は，強く意識してつくられた可能性が考えられる。釘隠し装飾や三角型の破風板は，クメール建築が木造であった頃の要素が石造化した際に装飾として形式化して引き継がれ，さらに木造時代の位置関係をよく踏襲しようとしたものであったと考えられる。

3.10.5.2 火炎型破風装飾と痕跡の比較考察

プレア・ヴィヘア寺院の火炎型破風では，三角形破風装飾と異なり釘隠し装飾が施されない。第4ゴープラ以外の遺構はレンガ造ないし石造の屋根を載せるため，もともと母屋桁位置と釘隠し装飾を合わせる計画は存在しようがない。一方，タ・ケオ寺院及びバンテアイ・スレイ寺院の周壁内付属建物にみられる木造屋根と火炎型破風の組み合わせた例でも，釘隠し装飾のない例が確認された。

しかし後代の火炎形破風は，釘隠し装飾をもつことが通例である。したがって初期の火炎型破風の形式は，木造屋根とは無関係に，おそらく当初から石造等の屋根に合わせて成立したもので，これに木造破風の時代の形式が装飾化して合体したものだと思われる。石造火炎型破風に使われるようになった釘隠し装飾は，曲線をもつナーガの胴体の上に施されるが，頂部の装飾から壁体直上の下端の装飾まで，一直線に配置される。したがってこれは，配置を含めて木造破風時代の特徴を残していると考えてよいであろう。

後代の様相は，初期の釘隠し装飾をもたない火炎型破風の時代でも，木造屋根の様相が反映するような技法が潜在していた可能性が高い。木造屋根と火炎型破風を組み合わせた遺構の装飾配置を確認すると，ナーガ・マカラの胴体は曲線を描くが，この曲線の複数の

seem to be used from the latter half of the 9th century to the first half of the 10th century in various regions, and continued to the beginning of the 11th century in specific regions.

The lozenge-shaped decorations expressing nail covers which conceals the head of a nail are confirmed on a gable decorative plate of the triangle pediments. This is considered to be the origin of the structural detail of a wooden gable in that period. Covering the cut end of purlins by a wide gable plate, and nails are inserted from the outside of the gable plate. Nail covering is a method for covering the surface of the nail to prevent corrosion of the nail and wood around a nail stem. Nail covering might be made of wood not metal because its size is large by judging from decorations on pediments of the period after the transition to stone masonry. In the period which wooden pediments were used, gable plates seem to have been covering tiles, side of rafters, and end of purlins behind it, so nail covers seem to be set to a lower than center of a gable plate. In contrast, nail covers are set to a center of gable plate after the transition to stone masonry pediment. This shows that nail covers are stylized as a decoration to stone masonry.

The position of the top of the nail cover is almost corresponding to the ridge purlin except for Gopura V in Preah Vihear Temple. In Prasat Thom Temple, Prasat Krachap Temple and Banteay Srei Temple, each decorative of nail cover is almost corresponding to the purlin position on the backside of the pediment. Only in Gopura V in Preah Vihear Temple does the decoration of a nail cover not correspond to the purlin, but decorations on gable plate have a tendency to be arranged corresponding to angle of the rafter. The decoration position on the gable plate of the other buildings in Preah Vihear Temple seems to generally match to the rafter position, but not the same as Gopura V. As the overall tendency, there is a possibility the parts of wooden frame on the backside and decorations on frontside of stone triangle pediments were set to correspond with each other. Decorations of nail covers and triangle-shaped gable plates with stone masonry are considered as a formality of elements in the former wooden Khmer architecture to decorations in later stone masonry buildings. Furthermore, the relationship of element positioning also remains as well.

3.10.5.2 Comparative Consideration on Decorations and Traces of Flame-like Shaped Type Pediment

In Preah Vihear Temple flame-like shaped type pediments do not have nail covers unlike that of triangle-shaped pediments. Roofs which have flame-like shape pediments, except Gopura IV, are made of brick or stone so it is natural that there is no original

頂点を結ぶ接線が，背面の垂木下面にほぼ接する高さで，垂木勾配に並行する傾向がみられる。

3.10.6 ペディメント装飾の変遷と地域性

前項まで，各装飾形式と木造痕跡の関連に関しての考察を重ねてきたが，装飾形式の選択に関しては未だ不明な点が多い。本項では，三角形破風や火炎型破風といった装飾形式がいかにして選択されてきたのか，時代地域を横断して比較することによりその変遷をみていこう。

3.10.6.1 ペディメント装飾形式の時代の変遷

10世紀前半，初期の木造小屋組を有する石造ペディメントには，コー・ケー遺跡群のプラサート・トム寺院やプラサート・クラチャップ寺院にみられるような三角形破風装飾が施されていた。一般的な三角形破風装飾の端部は渦巻型であるが，プラサート・トム寺院の伽藍東端に位置する「宮殿」と称される建物では渦巻きは通常と反対向きに巻かれていることが確認された。木造屋根が石造ペディメントに組み込まれた最初期の遺構であるプラサート・トム寺院では，伝統的な木造建築部材を模した三角形破風を使用する計画がなされたが，細部の装飾形式は定まっていなかったことが推測される。その後，バンテアイ・スレイ寺院やプレア・ヴィヘア寺院以降，多くの遺構で，火炎型破風に移行していったことが確認できる。

Photo 3.10-1 Pediment (Prasat Thom Temple)

plan to correspond the purlins to nail covers. There are also some examples of flame-like shape pediments without the decoration of nail covers which are seen at Ta Kev Temple and Annex Buildings inside the enclosure in Banteay Srei Temple.

Flame-like shaped type pediments with a wooden roof in the latter period often have nail cover decorations. Therefore, the early style of flame-like shape pediments with a wooden roof would be originally formed as to correspond to stone masonry roofs without any relationship to wooden roofs, and that decorations are added with wooden gable plate style. Nail cover decorations are arranged above the curve-shaped naga on flame-like shaped stone pediments which are set straight from a top decoration to the bottom. Thus, these pediments included the positioning of decorations representing features of wooden pediments.

This aspect of the latter period shows that even the early style of flame-like shape pediments without nail cover decorations would possibly have reflected the style of wooden roofs. The curve line of naga and makara bodies on flame-like shape pediments of wooden roofs have a tendency that the tangential line of linking top points of the curve line is almost parallel to its rafter line degree.

3.10.6 Transition and Regional Tendency of Pediment Decoration

Relevance between each type of pediment decoration and wooden trace is much considered as described above, however the way for initially determining the type of pediment decoration is still unclear. In this section, the process of how they chose pediment types like triangle and flame-like shaped type would be considered through a chronological and regional comparison.

3.10.6.1 Time Transition of Pediment Decoration Type

In the first part of 10th century, triangle type pediment decorations were applied to the early stone pediments with wooden roofs which are found in Prasat Thom Temple and Prasat Krachap Temple in Koh Ker Monuments. The bottom ends of triangle type pediments have generally spiral-shaped decorations, however the spirals are reversed at buildings so-called "palace" at the eastern end of Prasat Thom Temple. This temple is confirmed as the primary temple that used wooden roofs with stone masonry pediments. The traditional triangle type pediments are planned, but details of decoration styles seem not to be decided. After the era of Banteay Srei and Preah Vihear Temples, the main stream of pediment style shifted to flame-like shape pediments.

Chapter 3 : Study Reports on Preah Vihear Temple

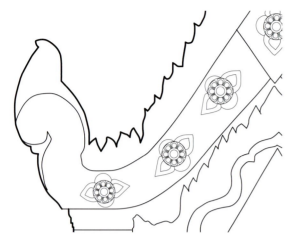

Figure 3.10-6
Pediment (Preah Vihear Gopura V)

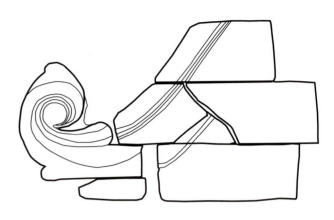

Figure 3.10-7
Pediment (Prasat Thom Temple)

3.10.6.2 ペディメント装飾形式の変遷に見られる地域性

木造屋根に火炎型破風が初めて使用された例は，おそらくバンテアイ・スレイ寺院付属建物の改造時，タ・ケオ寺院付属建物建立の頃，つまり11世紀に入って間もない時期である。アンコール地方で木造屋根が使用された例は東メボン寺院，プレ・ルプ寺院においても確認できるが，この両寺院では，壁体木口に残る破風板を受けた痕跡から，木造のペディメントが存在したことが明らかであり，したがっておそらく，直線の破風と両端の渦巻型が存在したであろう。したがって10世紀中頃は，まだ木造の破風をもつ時代であり，11世紀に入って妻壁が火炎型の石造破風に置き換えられたと考えられる。その後，木造小屋組を有する石造ペディメントとして，プノム・サンダック寺院の付属建物で三角形破風がみられるものの，主流は火炎型破風に移行していく。しかし，時代の推移からみれば，プレア・ヴィヘア寺院の三角形破風は，やや遅い時代の建立と考えられる。また，プレア・ヴィヘア州のトラペアン・スヴァイ・トム寺院は，建立年代は不明なものの中央祠堂のハーフペディメントにおいて，端部が渦巻模様の三角形破風形式がみられる。

さらに，ワット・プー寺院中央祠堂拝殿のハーフペ

3.10.6.2 Regional Tendency through the Transition of Pediment Decoration Type

The first examples of a wooden roof building applied to flame-like shape pediments was around the time that a Annex Building in Banteay Srei Temple was altered and Annex Building in Ta Kev Temple was constructed, which is the beginning of the 11th century. In the Angkor region, evidences of wooden roofs are confirmed in East Mebon Temple and Pre Rup Temple. In addition, it is clear the existence of wooden gable plate by traces on the edge wall that would have received the plate in both temples. Hence, it is considered there was a gable of straight outline and spiral-shape at both ends. Therefore, wooden gables were still used in the middle of the 10th century and transferred gradually to stone gables of flame-like shaped type in the 11th century. Triangle type pediments are still confirmed in Phnom Sandak Temple while the mainstream has changed to flame-like shaped type pediments. Triangle type pediments in Preah Vihear Temple seem to be constructed slightly later than the others. Triangle pediments with spiral-shaped decorations are also confirmed in half pediments of a half vaulted roof of the Central Sanctuary of Trapeang Svay Thom Temple in Preah Vihear Province whose construction age is unknown. Furthermore in

Photo 3.10-2 Pediment in Trapeang Svay Thom Temple

Photo 3.10-3 Half Pediment in Trapeang Svay Thom Temple

ディメントは11世紀以降のものと考えられているが，三角形破風に端部装飾に多頭ナーガを組み合わせたともみえる形式をとり，三角形破風と火炎型破風の両要素が確認される。火炎模様の様式が主流となった11世紀においても，プレア・ヴィヘア州やラオスなど，クメール帝国北部の寺院では伝統的な木造形式の装飾が，断片的ながら継承されていることがわかる。

　ナーガ・マカラの胴体を持ち，その上部に火炎を並べる装飾は，形状は異なるがミャンマーのバガン王朝時代の遺構などにもみられる。したがってこの形式は，広域に広がった形式であった可能性が高い。一方，三角形破風の形式は，渦巻型のナーガなどを含め，クメールに固有の木造建築の形式に由来すると考えられる。これらは2つの形式は，おそらく起源を異にするもので，木造屋根とレンガ造・石造屋根との相違に関わるものであったと考えられる。したがって，この2つの破風の形式が移行する過程は，大局的にみれば木造屋根から石造屋根への移行に並行し付随するものであった。しかし，その変遷の途上で，木造屋根をもちながらも火炎型破風を設ける遺構が，やや例外的に現れたと考えられる。この過渡的な組み合わせは，建築の規模が大きい，あるいは独立柱を多用する比較的脆弱な構造を選択したことなどに起因して，石造屋根を目指しつつも困難な状況で現れた，と考えるべきかも知れない。

3.10.7 結論

　三角形破風や火炎型破風といったペディメントの装飾形式と木造小屋組痕跡に関して，それぞれの関係性と変遷を中心に考察を行った。ペディメント上の木造小屋組痕跡からは，拡大する傾向にある内部空間に対する試行錯誤の様相を垣間みることができた。またとくに三角形破風形式のペディメントにおいては，それらの痕跡と装飾の配置に関連性がみられ，火炎型破風には痕跡位置に関連する装飾が確認できなかったことからも三角形破風形式が石造化の流れの初期のものであり，その後火炎型破風形式に移行していったと考えられる。装飾形式に関して，直線的な三角形破風は木造としてごく自然な形象であり，地域よりも木造から石造へ変化していったペディメントの初期の段階で一時的に現れた時代的なものである可能性が考えられる。プレア・ヴィヘア寺院における三角形破風の使用は，クメール北東部における復古的な風潮を示すという捉え方もあるが，三角形破風装飾が使われた形跡は，プレア・コー寺院を含む多数の地域で確認される。プレア・ヴィヘア寺院における三角形破風（と木造屋根）

Photo 3.10-4 Picture of Half Pediment in Vat Phu Temple

the Mandapa of the Central Sanctuary of Vat Phu Temple, which is considered to be constructed after the 11th century, it can be confirmed that half pediments with multi-headed nagas at the bottom ends show a combination of both elements of flame-like shape and triangle type pediment. As described, even in the 11th century after flame-like shaped type pediments became mainstream, decorations imagining traditional wooden structure are partly inherited in the northeast part of the Khmer empire like Preah Vihear Temple and Vat Phu Temple.

Decorations of flame-like shaped form above naga and makara body are also confirmed at temples of the Bagan dynasty in Myanmar although its form is a little different from that of Khmer. Therefore, this pediment type probably had wide spread acceptance. On the other hand, triangle type including spiral-shape decoration seem to have come from Khmer wooden architecture. Both types have probably different origins which relate to the difference of wooden, brick or stone roofs. Thus the transition process of 2 types of pediment generally corresponds in parallel to the transition of the roof from wooden to stone masonry. In spite of the fact, buildings of a wooden roof with flame-like shape pediments appeared in the middle of the transition. This transient combination might have to be considered as a correspondence to the difficult situations with a scale-up of building or a selection of quite vulnerable structure composed by independent columns, while tried to make a stone masonry roof.

3.10.7 Conclusion

In this study, relationships between decoration types of triangle and flame-like shape pediments and wooden traces are considered. Trial-and-error procedure could be seen along with the expansion of the inside space of building confirmed from traces of the wooden roof structure on pediments. Especially in

の使用は，各ゴープラの建築規模の大きさや独立柱を多用する構造の問題が潜在している。ペディメント発展段階の途上の様相であって，必ずしも地域性を意味するとはいえないであろう。ペディメント形式の選択における地域性と時代性の関係に関しては，今後のさらなる研究が期待される。

triangle type pediment, a relationship between the arrangement of decorations and traces is confirmed while some of the flame-like shape pediments do not have a relationship to wooden traces. It seemed that triangle type pediments were the primary type in the transition to stone masonry building, and flame-like shape type pediments appeared subsequently. Concerning pediment decoration types, the triangle type with straight outline seems to be a natural phenomenon as the primary and temporary period of transition from wooden architecture to stone rather than consider as one of the regional characteristics. There is a hypothesis that triangle pediments in Preah Vihear Temple denotes a stream of revivalism in the northeast part of the Khmer empire, however evidences of use of triangle pediments are confirmed in some areas including Preah Ko Temple. Using triangle pediments (and wooden roofs) in Preah Vihear Temple has a relation to structural problems like a scale of building or independent columns. It shows the middle step of pediment development and does not necessarily mean to reflect a regional tendency. Further research on the relationship between regional tendency and the time transition of pediment type selection is expected.

Table 3.10-4 Chronology of Type of Pediment

Age	Temple	Facility	Type of Pediment
Harshavarman I	Prasat Thom	Gopura II	Triangle
		Gopura IV	Triangle
		Annex Building	Triangle
Ishanavarman II	Prasat Krachap	1st Gopula	Triangle
Jayavarman IV	Prasat Thom	South "Palace"	Triangle
		North "Palace"	Triangle
Jayavarman V	Banteay Srei	Gopura II (front)	Triangle
		Gopura II (Back)	Flame-like
		Gopura IV	Concave
		Annex building	Flame-like
	Ta Kev	Annex building	Flame-like
	North Khleang		Flame-like
Suryavarman I	Phnom Chisor	Gopura II	Flame-like
		Gopura III	Flame-like
	Preah Vihear	Annex building (H,I)	Triangle
		Gopura II	Triangle
		Gopura III	Triangle
		Gopura IV	Flame-like
		Gopura V	Triangle
Dharanindravarman I		Annex Building (E)	Concave
Suryavarman II		Annex Building (F)	Concave

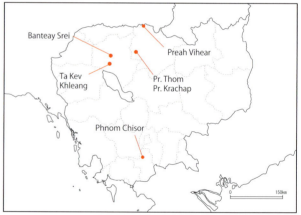

Figure 3.10-8 Plot Map

Conclusion and Foresight

MIZOGUCHI Akinori

Since 2007, our team have been researching of regional significant position as Kor Ker, Beng Mealea and so on, and we have spent much time in researching Preah Vihear Temple. It is because that we have understood the meaning and the worth of Preah Vihear Temple in the evolutional history of Khmer temples and in the reign of land and the vision of the universe in Khmer Empire, as we have made a progress on research.

The fundamental purpose of our research is covering all significant heritages as much as possible while not changing the research method and the research view. In the near future, this research will enable to compare and examine it and it will contribute to finding the aspect of Khmer Empire as fundamental document that is difficult to find only by Angkor ruins. However, Preah Vihear Temple was very suggestive heritage and it should be discussed more. It is one reason that the temple is a precious temple of "vertically-oriented" layout planning.

The "vertically-oriented" temple is planned from the North to the South accurately over 800 meters. The layout planning is drawn by precision survey, and it proved the existence of accurate planning. The approach from Gopura V to Gopura IV is open, but the archeological excavation demonstrated that a side of the approach from Gopura IV to Gopura III is closed probably by rammed earth wall, and by mud wall in the shape of mound at present. This relates that the back wall of Gopura IV is closed. This coordination of the approach from Gopura V to Gopura III is unusual pattern that have not reported many times. It is confirmed that the relative planning method of each Gopura follows the accurate layout planning of temple complex, by superimposing excavation document of buried Gopura foundation by archaeological team based on the precise

まとめと展望

溝口　明則

2007年以来，コー・ケー都市遺跡，ベン・メアレア寺院遺跡など地方の重要拠点の調査を続けてきた私たちのチームは，2012年以後，プレア・ヴィヘア寺院に多くの時間を割くことになった。調査が進展するにつれて，クメール帝国の宇宙観や領土の統治において，またクメール寺院建築の発達史にとって，プレア・ヴィヘア寺院遺構の意味や価値の大きさを少しずつ理解することになったためである。

私たちのクメール寺院遺構の調査の基本的な目的は，各地の重要遺跡を可能なかぎり同一の調査方法と研究視点を維持しながら網羅することにある。それらは近い将来，相互に比較検討を可能にし，アンコール遺跡群だけでは難しいクメール帝国の様相を見いだすための基礎資料として機能することが期待される。

しかしプレア・ヴィヘア寺院は，もう少し踏み込んで検討すべき，多くの示唆に富んだ遺跡であった。それはまず，縦深型の計画をみごとに実現した数少ない貴重な寺院であることにある。

正確に南北を向き，800ｍを大きく越える直線的な配置計画は，精密実測調査によって図面が起こされ，精度の高い配置計画が存在したことが確かめられた。第5ゴープラから第4ゴープラへのアプローチは，開放的な視野の中を登るが，第4ゴープラから第3ゴープラへ至る参道は，考古学班の発掘調査によって参道脇がおそらく版築の壁体と現在はマウンド状の土壁によって閉じられていたことが明らかになった。これは第4ゴープラの背面が壁面で閉じていることとも呼応する。第5ゴープラから第3ゴープラへ至るこのような参道の演出は，いままであまり報告された

survey document. Also it is confirmed by geography team that the location of long linear approach of approximate equivalent slope and dotted Gopuras was executed after large-scaled leveling ground by banking and scraping bedrock. In general, the clue of build era of each attached architecture around Preah Vihear Temple is very little. This is why many research for the forming process of temple complex remains invisible. We tried to research about the build era of each architecture as much as possible because a complicated transition process of Temple complex had assumed and previous research in early 20th century had raised a doubt in Preah Vihear Temple. By this achievement, the chronology from the research of magnetic susceptibility of stone by petrology team and the chronology from the research using traces of wooden roof structure by architecture team is suggested. This suggestion is tries of solving the forming process to current temple complex which have considered previous architecture replaced one by one in the frame of layout planning of temple complex in 9th century.

About the roof of Gopura III, a work making restoration scheme of the repaired tiled roof by collapse is under progress, but the form of an original tiled roof remained unclear. Architecture team tried the restoration of an original form of tiled roof on Gopura III, compare and study the case of Vat Phu Temple that has the same traces of roofing and submitted the restoration scheme. In a short period, the unusual roofing form that roofed bricks on wooden structure is confirmed exactly. Also Architecture team is trying re-study the mutual relation between the layout and dimentional planning of temple complex on the top of the mountain and build era of corridor and central tower. Also the restoration by archaeological team demonstrated that temple complex on the top of the mountain is constructed by a part of the bedrock under foot which is processed and used as some walls in this architecture.

The Preah Vihear Temple has the precious feature in the layout planning and the coordination of the approach and has a significant meaning in the transition process of Khmer temple complex. And also it is the significant features that extinct techniques in the various transition process are confirmed: the leveling ground and layout planning that enable Preah Vihear

ことのない演出手法である。

　精度の高い測量資料に基づいて，各ゴープラの相対的な位置決定の計画法は，考古学班による埋もれたゴープラ基壇の発掘調査資料と重ね合わせることで，明確な伽藍配置計画に従っていることが確認された。また，直線を構成しほぼ均等の勾配を持つ長いアプローチと各所に点在するゴープラの立地は，地理学班よって，土盛や岩盤を削り出す大きな整地を行って実現していることが確かめられた。

　一般に，伽藍中枢部の建築はともかく，周辺に位置する付属建築の建立年代は，手がかりがきわめて少ない。このため，伽藍の成立過程が不明なままの事例が多い。プレア・ヴィヘア寺院では，伽藍の複雑な変遷過程が予想されてきたことと20世紀前半の先行研究に疑義が生じたため，各建物の建立年代についてできる限りの調査を試みた。この成果は，岩石班による帯磁率などを手がかりとした調査からの編年と，建築班による木造屋根架構の痕跡からの編年の提案である。9世紀に遡る伽藍配置を骨格として，前身建物を逐次置き換えて現在の伽藍に至ると考えられてきた成立過程を，少しでも解明しようとしたものである。

　第3ゴープラの屋根については，崩落による改修後の瓦葺屋根の復原案が試みられているが，当初のレンガ葺の屋根の形式は不明な点が残されていた。建築班は，第3ゴープラのレンガを葺いた当初の屋根形式の復原を試み，同様の屋根を載せた痕跡をもつワット・プー寺院の事例等と比較検討し，復原案を提出した。ごく短期間，木造小屋組にレンガを葺いた例外的な屋根形式がたしかに存在したことが認められた。また建築班は，山頂伽藍の配置と寸法計画，回廊と中央塔の建立年代の相互関係の再検討などを試みている。さらに山頂伽藍は，足下の岩盤を加工し，一部を壁体など建物に取り込んで構築しているが，これらも考古学班による発掘を経て確認が進められた。

　プレア・ヴィヘア寺院は配置計画や参道の演出に特徴があり，クメール伽藍の編成過程にとって重要な意味を持つ

Temple to exist, the trace on wooden roof of each Gopura expected that it was roofed in the transition process of wooden roof structure, the form of central tower which is concerned in the earliest era of poach, the form of the bricks roofed on the structure of brick vault and wooden roof, and so on. It seems that any transition processes studied from various research aspect take part of this temple. It is the most significant heritage in the history of Khmer architecture.

At first, Preah Khan Temple of Kompong Svay was the subject of this research. However, there was no choice than to take this research method of making plan as examining restoration in detail over and over again about this broken down temple. In this report, there is just provisional restoration planning because this method could not be finished in a short term. There is remained a big temple complex except for this ruin, and besides the temple ruins of "vertically-oriented" layout planning of temple complex should be considered as the future research object.

Our research is not enough to find entire forms and not enough to research deeply at the sight of each temple ruin. There are many research tasks in Preah Vihear Temple, and I would like to research more if I have an opportunity next time. Thanks for giving us full and especial care from Ministry of Culture and Fine Arts, National Authority for Preah Vihear, JASA, and every research members, this research has been realized. Also the support from a Grants-in-Aid for Scientific Research of Ministry of Education, Culture, Sports, Science and Technology of Japan (Scientific Research (A) Overseas Academic Research：19254005) enabled this research, and Grant-in-Aid for Publication of Scientific Research Results (Scientific Literature：No.18HP5242) to publish the results. Finally I would like to offer my profound appreciation for all.

ている。そしてこれを実現する地形整備と配置計画法，ほぼコー・ケー遺跡群から始まる木造屋根架構の変遷途上に位置づけられる各ゴープラの木造屋根痕跡，ポーチを持つ最初期の時代に該当する中央塔の形式，レンガのヴォールト構造と木造屋根にレンガを葺いた形式等々，変遷の途上で消滅して行ったさまざまな過渡期の技法が認められる点も大きな特徴である。さまざまな研究視点からみた変遷過程は，いずれもこの寺院遺跡で交差するように思われる。クメール建築史上きわめて重要な遺跡である。

今回の調査では，当初，コンポン・スヴァイのプレア・カーン寺院についても調査の対象としていた。しかし崩壊の激しいこの寺院は，細部の復原考察を繰り返しつつ平面図を作成するという研究方法を進めるほかはない。これは短期間で実施できることではないため，本報告書では暫定的な平面図を掲載するに留めた。この遺構以外にも大伽藍は残っており，さらに縦深型伽藍配置を持つ寺院遺構についても，今後の調査対象として考慮しなければならない。

私たちの調査は，まだ全体を網羅するに至らず，さらに個々の寺院遺構としてみれば踏み込みが不十分である。プレア・ヴィヘア寺院もまだ多くの問題を残しており，今後も機会があればぜひ調査を進めたいと考えている。

今回の調査では，カ国文化芸術省，プレア・ヴィヘア機構，JASAの各位から，全面的かつ特別なご配慮を，そして調査メンバー各位の大変なご努力をいただいたことで，はじめて実現することができた。また，日本学術振興会科学研究費助成金（基盤研究（A）海外：19254005）の支援によって調査を実施することができ，さらにその成果を，2018年度の科学研究費助成金・研究成果公開促進費（課題番号：18HP5242）の助成により本書として刊行するに至った。末尾ながら各位に深甚な感謝の意を表します。

Biography of Authors
執筆者略歴

[Principal Investigator / Supervisor / Author 研究代表者／監修者／著者]

MIZOGUCHI Akinori 溝口明則（1951〜）
Former Professor, Meijo University, Faculty of Science and Technology
名城大学理工学部教授（当時）
Currently Visiting Professor, Faculty of Science and Engineering
早稲田大学理工学術院客員教授（現）
Dr. Engineering
工学博士

1. T.Nakagawa, A.Mizoguchi eds, "KOH KER AND BENG MEALEA - ARCHITECTURAL STUDY ON THE PROVINCIAL SITES OF THE KHMER EMPIRE", Chuo Koron Bijutsu Shuppan, 2014.
   中川武,溝口明則監修,『コー・ケーとベン・メアレア─アンコール広域拠点遺跡群の建築学的研究』,中央公論美術出版, 2014.
2. A.Mizoguchi, T.Nakagawa, I.Shimoda, K.Sato, M.Ishizuka, "ON THE DIMENSIONAL PLANNING AT PREAH VIHEAR TEMPLE COMPLEX ON THE CREST: Study on the dimensional plan and the planning method of Khmer architecture No. 7", J. Archit. Plann., AIJ, 79(697), pp.817-825, 2014.
   溝口明則, 中川武, 下田一太, 佐藤桂, 石塚充雅,「プレア・ヴィヘア寺院山頂伽藍の寸法計画:クメール建築の造営尺度と設計技術に関する研究(7)」,日本建築学会計画系論文集,第79巻, 第697号, pp. 817-825, 2014.
3. A.Mizoguchi, T.Nakagawa, K.Sato, I.Shimoda, "THE ANCIENT KHMER'S DIMENSIONAL PLANNING AT THE PRASAT THOM IN KOH KER: Study on the dimensional plan and the planning method of Khmer architecture No.5", J. Archit. Plann., AIJ, 75(653), pp.1751-1759, 2010.
   溝口明則, 中川武, 佐藤桂, 下田一太,「プラサート・トムの伽藍寸法計画:クメール建築の造営尺度と設計技術に関する研究(5)」,日本建築学会計画系論文集,第75巻, 第653号, pp. 1751-1759, 2010.

[Supervisor / Author 監修者／著者]

NAKAGAWA Takeshi 中川武（1944〜）
Professor Emeritus, Waseda University, Faculty of Science and Engineering, Dr. Engineering, Director, The Museum MEIJI-MURA.
早稲田大学理工学術院名誉教授, 博物館明治村館長（現）
Dr. Engineering
工学博士

1. T.Nakagawa, "Research on the Ancient Architectural and City Ruins of Phnom Kulen and Quarries in the Surrounding Area", The 17th Science Council of Asia Board Meeting and International Symposium, Manila, Philippine, 2017.
2. T.Nakagawa, "Bayon Great Buddha Restoration, Reconstruction and Reinstallation Project", The 15th Science Council of Asia Board Meeting and International Symposium, Siem Reap, Cambodia, pp.55-58, 2015.
3. T.Nakagawa, "Significance of "Vertically-Oriented Layout Temple" and Subject on Conservation in Preah Vihear Temple, Cambodia", Proceeding of the 10th International Symposium on Architectural Interchanges in Asia, (II), Hangzhou, China, pp.792-797, 2014.

[Author 著者]

IKEUCHI Katsushi 池内克史（1949〜）
Professor Emeritus, The University of Tokyo
東京大学名誉教授
Dr. Engineering
工学博士

1. K.Ikeuchi and D.Miyazaki, 'Digitally Archiving Cultural Objects', Springer, 2008.
2. A.Banno, T.Masuda, T.Oishi and K.Ikeuchi, "Flying Laser Range Sensor for Large-Scale Site-Modeling and Its Applications in Bayon Digital Archival Project", International Journal of Computer Vision, Vol.78, No.2-3, pp.207-222, 2008.07.
3. K.Ikeuchi, T.Oishi, J.Takamatsu, R.Sagawa, A.Nakazawa, R.Kurazume, K.Nishino, M.Kamakura and Y.Okamoto, "The Great Buddha Project: Digitally Archiving, Restoring, and Analyzing Cultural Heritage Objects", International Journal of Computer Vision, Vol.75, No.1, pp.189-208, 2007.10.

ISHIZUKA Mitsumasa 石塚充雅（1986〜）
Technical Assistant, Japanese Government Team For Safeguarding Angkor
日本国政府アンコール遺跡救済チーム技術補佐
M. Architecture
修士（建築学）

1. M.Ishizuka, T.Nakagawa, A.Mizoguchi, I.Shimoda, K.Sato, "Study on arrangement planning of Chau Sray Vibol", Summ. Tech. Paper of Annual Meeting, F-2, AIJ, pp.423-524, 2011.
   石塚充雅, 中川武, 溝口明則, 下田一太, 佐藤桂,「チャウ・スレイ・ビボールにみる配置計画に関する一考察」,日本建築学会大会学術講演梗

概集, F-2, 日本建築学会, pp. 423-424, 2011.

2. M.Ishizuka, "Principle of the placement plan in the Khmer district large size temple ", Master Thesis, Laboratory of Architectural History, Waseda Univ., 2012.
石塚充雅,「クメール地方大型寺院にみる配置計画の原理」, 早稲田大学建築史研究室修士論文, 2012.

3. M.Ishizuka, T.Nakagawa, A.Mizoguchi, I.Shimoda, K.Sato, "Annexes so Called 'palace' at Beng Mealea(1-1) : Studies on Beng Mealea Monuments, Cambodia(1) ", Summ. Tech. Paper of Annual Meeting, F-2, AIJ, pp.591-592, 2010.
石塚充雅, 中川武, 溝口明則, 下田一太, 佐藤桂,「ベン・メアレア寺院の〈宮殿〉と呼ばれる付属建物に関する考察(1-1): カンボジア ベン・メアレア遺跡群に関する研究(1)」, 日本建築学会大会学術講演梗概集, F-2, 日本建築学会, pp. 591-592, 2010.

KAGESAWA Masataka　影澤政隆（1962〜）

University of Tokyo, Institute of Industrial Science
東京大学生産技術研究所
Dr. Engineering
博士(工学)

1. 小林哲也, 影澤政隆, 大石岳史,「物理モデルベース非剛体位置合わせによる木製文化財の３次元デジタル復原」, 情報処理学会, 第169回コンピュータグラフィックスとビジュアル情報学研究発表会, 2018.

2. T.Morimoto, K.Inose, M.Kagesawa, N.Kuchitsu, K.Ikeuchi, "Investigation on the Colors of Kokadani Tomb Using Micrograph and Multispectral Imageing", Abstracts. Annual Meening of the Japan Society for Scientific Studies on Cultural Property, Vol.31, pp.256-257, 2014.
森本哲郎, 猪瀬健二, 影澤政隆, 朽津信明, 池内克史,「顕微鏡写真解析および分光画像解析による弘化谷古墳の彩色調査」, 日本文化財科学会大会発表要旨集, 31巻, pp.256-257, 2014.

3. Z.Wang, M.Kagesawa, S.Ono, A.Banno, T.Oishi, K.Ikeuchi, "Detection of Emergency Telephone Indicators in a Tunnel Environment", International Journal of Intelligent Transportation Systems Research, 2014.

KANEKO Tatsuya　金子達哉（1993〜）

Former Master Course Student, Waseda University, Graduate School of Creative Science and Engineering
早稲田大学創造理工学研究科修士学生(当時)
M. Architecture
修士(建築学)

1. T.Kaneko, T.Nakagawa, A.Mizoguchi, M.Koiwa, C.Kuroiwa, "Transition of type of Pediments Decorations, Consideration on transition of roof structure of Khmer architecture", Summ. Tech. Paper of Annual Meeting, AIJ, pp.843-844, 2017.
金子達哉, 中川武, 溝口明則, 小岩正樹, 黒岩千尋,「ペディメント装飾形式の時代変遷―クメール建築における屋根発展の考察―」, 日本建築学会大会学術講演梗概集, 日本建築学会, pp. 843-844, 2017.

2. T.Kaneko, "The chronology of wooden roof of Khmer Architectures", Graduated Thesis, Laboratory of Architectural History, Waseda Univ., 2016.
金子達哉,「クメール遺跡における木造架構屋根の編年分析」, 早稲田大学建築史研究室卒業論文, 2016.

KITAI Erisa　北井絵里沙（1992〜）

Former Master Course Student, Waseda University, Graduate School of Creative Science and Engineering
早稲田大学創造理工学研究科修士学生(当時)
M. Architecture
修士(建築学)

1. E.Kitai, "Design Plan of Pediment in Khmer Architecture with a Wooden Roof ", Master Thesis, Laboratory of Architectural History, Waseda Univ., 2016.
北井絵里沙,「木造屋根を有するクメール建築のペディメント設計計画」, 早稲田大学建築史研究室修士論文, 2016.

2. E.Kitai, "Study of Preservation Plan of Preah Vihear Temple", Graduated Thesis, Laboratory of Architectural History, Waseda Univ., 2014.
北井絵里沙,「プレア・ヴィヘア寺院の保存計画に関する考察」, 早稲田大学建築史研究室卒業論文, 2014.

KOGA Yukako　古賀友佳子（1990〜）

Former Master Course Student, Waseda University, Graduate School of Creative Science and Engineering
早稲田大学創造理工学研究科修士学生(当時)
M. Architecture
修士(建築学)

1. Y.Koga, "Preah Vihear Gopura III Reconstruction Study of the Roof Part, A Consideration of the Characteristic and the Transition of the ［Wooden Brick Roof］", Master Thesis, Laboratory of Architectural History, Waseda Univ., 2015.
古賀友佳子,「プレア・ヴィヘア寺院第3ゴープラの屋根部に関する復原研究－［木造レンガ積屋根］の特性と位置付けに対する考察－」, 早稲田大学建築史研究室修士論文, 2015.

2. Y.Koga, T.Nakagawa, A.Mizoguchi, I.Shimoda, M.Ishizuka, M.Shimada, "PreahVihear Temple Restoration Study of Wooden Roof Truss of The Mundapa of GopuraI: Studies on Preah Vihear temple. Combodia(6)", Summ. Tech. Paper of Annual Meeting, AIJ, pp.581-582, 2013.
古賀友佳子, 中川武, 溝口明則, 下田一太, 石塚充雅, 島田麻里子,「プレア・ヴィヘア寺院ゴープラI拝殿の木造小屋組の復原考察: カンボジア プレア・ヴィヘア寺院に関する研究(6)」, 日本建築学会大会学術講演梗概集, 日本建築学会, pp. 581-582, 2013.

3. Y.Koga, "Preah Vihear Reconstruction inquiry of the roof truss at Mandapa of Gopura I", Graduated Thesis, Laboratory of Architectural History, Waseda Univ., 2013.
古賀友佳子,「プレア・ヴィヘア寺院ゴープラI拝殿の木造小屋組の復原考察」, 早稲田大学建築史研究室卒業論文, 2013.

KUBO Sumiko 久保純子 (1959 ～)

Professor, Waseda University, School of Education and Integrated Arts and Sciences
早稲田大学教育・総合科学学術院教授
Dr. Science
博士（理学）

1. S.Kubo, N.Nagumo, M.Chhum, I.Shimoda, "Radiocarbon ages and stratigraphy in the city area of the Sambor Prei Kuk Pre-Angkor archaeological site", Cambodia, Bulletin of the Graduate School of Education, Waseda University, No.26, pp.43-55, 2016.
2. S.Kubo, 'Landforms and Environmental Analysis', "KOH KER AND BENG MEALEA -ARCHITECTURAL STUDY ON THE PROVINCIAL SITES OF THE KHMER EMPIRE (from A. Mizoguchi, T. Nakagawa eds)", Chuo Koron Bijutsu Shuppan, pp.26-32, 2014.
   久保純子,「遺跡群周辺の地形と立地環境」,『コー・ケーとベン・メアレア—アンコール広域拠点遺跡群の建築学的研究（中川武・溝口明則監修）』, 中央公論美術出版, pp. 26-32, 2014.
3. Y.Kojo, S.Kubo, "A preliminary report of the investigations in Sambor Prei Kuk Archaeological site (7th century), central Cambodia -results in 1998 and 1999-", Bulletin of the Graduate School of Education, Waseda University, No.13, pp.15-31, 2003.
   古城泰, 久保純子,「カンボジア中部、ソンボープレイクック遺跡（7世紀）の調査―1998・1999年度調査より―」, 早稲田大学大学院教育学研究科紀要, No.13, pp. 15-31, 2003.

KUROIWA Chihiro 黒岩千尋 (1991～)

Doctor Course Student, Waseda University, Graduate School of Creative Science and Engineering
早稲田大学創造理工学研究科博士課程学生
M. Architecture
修士（建築学）

1. C.Kuroiwa, T.Nakagawa, A.Mizoguchi, "The Significance of "āçrama" system in Khmer Empire", SCA-16 Abstracts and Proceedings, SCA 16 Committee, pp.63-68, 2016.05.
2. C.Kuroiwa, T.Nakagawa, A.Mizoguchi, ""口-SHAPE" "田-SHAPE" ARCHITECTURAL STYLES IN PREAH VIHEAR TEMPLE - Consideration on transition of Khmer architecture through the example of "Annexed Building" - ", J. Archit. Plann., AIJ, 81(719), pp.195-202, 2016.
   黒岩千尋, 中川武, 溝口明則,「プレア・ヴィヘア寺院の『口の字』型・『田の字』型建築形式について―『付属建物』に見るクメール建築変遷史の考察―」, 日本建築学会計画系論文集, 第81巻, 第719号, pp.195-202, 2016.
3. C.Kuroiwa, "Study on Khmer Regional Bases – Analysis of Empire Social Structure on "āçrama" and Architectural Iconographical Changes-", Waseda University Master's Thesis, 2016.
   黒岩千尋,「Khmer地方拠点研究 – āçramaと建築・図像変化における帝国の構造 -」, 早稲田大学修士論文, 2016.

NAGUMO Naoko 南雲直子 (1981～)

Research Specialist, International Centre for Water Hazard and Risk Management (ICHARM), Public Works Research Institute
国立研究開発法人土木研究所水災害・リスクマネジメント国際センター専門研究員
Dr. Environment
博士（環境学）

1. N.Nagumo, T.Sugai, S.Kubo, "Fluvial Geomorphology and Characteristics of Modern Channel Bars in the Lower Stung Sen River, Cambodia", Geographical Review of Japan series B, Vol.87 No.2, pp.115-121, 2015.
2. N.Nagumo, T.Sugai, S.Kubo, "Late Quaternary floodplain development along the Stung Sen River in the Lower Mekong Basin, Cambodia", Geomorphology, 198: pp.84-95, 2013.
3. N.Nagumo, T.Sugai, S.Kubo, "Location of a pre-Angkor capital city in relation to geomorphological features of lower reach of the Stung Sen River, central Cambodia", Geodinamica Acta 23/5-6, pp.255-266, 2010.

NARUI Itaru 成井至 (1994～)

Doctor Course Student, Waseda University, Graduate School of Creative Science and Engineering
早稲田大学創造理工学研究科博士課程学生
M. Architecture
修士（建築学）

1. I.Narui, T.Nakagawa, A.Mizoguchi, M.Koiwa, M.Ishizuka, C.Kuroiwa, "Consideration on the Initial Plan about the Corridor with pillar in Angkor Site; Study on Preah Khan de Kompong Svay, Cambodia part3", Summ. Tech. Paper of Annual Meeting, AIJ, pp.839-840, 2017.
   成井至, 中川武, 溝口明則, 小岩正樹, 石塚充雅, 黒岩千尋,「アンコール期大型寺院における列柱回廊の計画方法の分析　カンボジア コンポン・スヴァイのプレア・カーン寺院に関する研究 (3)」, 日本建築学会大会学術講演梗概集, 日本建築学会, pp. 839-840, 2017.
2. I.Narui, " Analysis on planning of Angkor Thom capital", Graduated Thesis, Laboratory of Architectural History, Waseda Univ., 2016.
   成井至,「アンコール・トム都城における計画意図の分析」, 早稲田大学建築史研究室卒業論文, 2016.

OGIHARA Shu 荻原周 (1990～)

Former Master Course Student, Waseda University, Graduate School of Creative Science and Engineering
早稲田大学創造理工学研究科修士学生（当時）
M. Architecture
修士（建築学）

1. S.Ogihara, "Planning method of "vertically-oriented" layout temple in Khmer Architecture, Comparative Study on Preah Vihear, Phnom Chisor, Baphuon, Banteay Srei", Master Thesis, Laboratory of Architectural History, Waseda Univ., 2015.
荻原周, 「クメール建築における縦深型伽藍の設計方法－プレア・ヴィヘア、プノム・チソール、バプーオン、バンテアイ・スレイの比較を通して－」, 早稲田大学建築史研究室修士論文, 2015.
2. S.Ogihara, "Restoration Study in the peripheral wall of the deployment plan of Preah Vihear", Graduated Thesis, Laboratory of Architectural History, Waseda Univ., 2013.
荻原周, 「プレア・ヴィヘア寺院周壁内計画手順の復原的考察」, 早稲田大学建築史研究室卒業論文, 2013.

OISHI Takeshi 大石岳史（1976～）

Associate Professor, The University of Tokyo, Institute of Industrial Science
東京大学生産技術研究所准教授
Dr. Interdisciplinary Information Studies
博士(学際情報学)

1. K.Ikeuchi, T.Oishi, '3D Digital Archive', University of Tokyo Press, 2010.
池内克史, 大石岳史（編著）, 「3次元デジタルアーカイブ」, 東京大学出版会, 2010.
2. A.Banno, T.Masuda, T.Oishi, K.Ikeuchi, "Flying Laser Range Sensor for Large-Scale Site-Modeling and Its Applications in Bayon Digital Archival Project," International Journal of Computer Vision, Vol.78, No.2-3, pp.207-222, 2008.
3. K.Ikeuchi, T.Oishi, J.Takamatsu, R.Sagawa, A.Nakazawa, R.Kurazume, K.Nishino, M.Kamakura, Y.Okamoto, "The Great Buddha Project: Digitally Archiving, Restoring, and Analyzing Cultural Heritage Objects," International Journal of Computer Vision, Vol.75, No.1, pp.189-208, 2007.

SADATOMI Yosuke 貞富陽介（1992～）

Former Master Course Student, Waseda University, Graduate School of Creative Science and Engineering
早稲田大学創造理工学研究科修士学生（当時）
M. Architecture
修士(建築学)

1. Y.Sadatomi, "Study on dimensional planning of "Library" of temple Preah Vihear", Graduated Thesis, Laboratory of Architectural History, Waseda Univ., 2016.
貞富陽介, 「アンコール期における経蔵と呼ばれる建物の設計方法」, 早稲田大学建築史研究室修士論文, 2016.
2. Y.Sadatomi, "Design Method of "Library" built in Angkor Period", Master Thesis, Laboratory of Architectural History, Waseda Univ., 2014.
貞富陽介, 「プレア・ヴィヘア寺院「経蔵」の寸法計画に関する研究」, 早稲田大学建築史研究室卒業論文, 2014.

SATO Hiroya 佐藤広野（1990～）

Former Master Course Student, Waseda University, Graduate School of Creative Science and Engineering
早稲田大学創造理工学研究科修士学生（当時）
M. Engineering
修士(工学)

1. E.Uchida, A.Mizoguchi, H.Sato, I.Shimoda, R.Watanabe, "Determining the construction sequence of the Preah Vihear monument in Cambodia from its sandstone block characteristics", Heritage Science, 5-42, pp.1-15, 2017.
2. H.Sato, "Clasification of the sandstones used in the Khmer monuments and the estimation of the construction sequence of Preah Vihear", Master Thesis, Laboratory of Geochemistry of Mineral Resources, Waseda Univ., 2013.
3. H.Sato, "Experiments on the simultaneous ion partitioning of rare earth element between xenotime and supercritical hydrothermal solution", Graduated Thesis, Laboratory of Geochemistry of Mineral Resources, Waseda Univ., 2012.
佐藤広野, 「ゼノタイムと超臨界熱水間における希土類元素の分配挙動に関する実験」, 早稲田大学資源地球化学研究室卒業論文, 2012.

SATO Katsura 佐藤桂（1972～）

Former Associate Fellow, National Research Institute for Cultural Properties, Tokyo
東京文化財研究所アソシエイトフェロー（当時）
Currently Project Researcher, Japan Cultural Heritage Consultancy
株式会社文化財保存計画協会特任研究員（現）
Dr. Architecture
博士(建築学)

1. K.Sato, 'Sanctuaries after descended from the mountain. The development of Khmer cities from the 7th to 10th centuries', "Comprehensive Study on the Ancient History of Southeast Asia", Research Report on the Grant-in-Aid for Scientific Research (Basic Research B) 2013/2015, pp.51-56, 2016.
佐藤桂, 「山を降りた聖域　7世紀から10世紀におけるクメール都市の展開」, 『東南アジア古代史の複合的研究』, 2013～2015年度科学研究費補助金(基盤研究B)研究成果報告書, pp. 51-56, 2016.
2. K.Sato, 'Modifications during the construction of Ta Nei temple', "The World Architectural History", Papers commemorating the retirement of Professor Takeshi Nakagawa, Chuokouron Art Publication, pp.147-154, 2015.
佐藤桂, 「タ・ネイ遺跡に見られる建造途中の改変について」, 『世界建築史論集：中川武先生退任記念論文集』, 中央公論美術出版, pp. 147-154, 2015.
3. K.Sato, "Ancient Khmer City "Chok Gargyer" reviewed", Doctoral Dissertation submitted to the Graduate School of Science and Engineering, Waseda University, 2010.

佐藤桂，「クメール古代都市『チョック・ガルギャー』研究序説」，早稲田大学大学院理工学研究科学位請求論文，2010.

SATO Yoshihiro　佐藤啓宏（1976〜）

Institute of Industrial Science, the University of Tokyo
東京大学生産技術研究所
D. Engineering
博士（工学）

1. S.Kudoh, P.Vinayavekhin, Y.Sato, K.Ikeuchi, "Imitation of Human Regrasping Motion with a Robotic Hand Based on Tangle Topology," Journal of The Robotics Society of Japan, Vol.33, No.7, pp.514-523, 2015.
   工藤俊亮, ビナヤウェキンポンタリン, 佐藤啓宏, 池内克史, "タングルトポロジーを用いたロボットハンドによる人間の持ち替え動作の模倣", 日本ロボット学会誌, Vol. 33, No. 7, pp. 514-523, 2015.
2. Y.Sato, T.Oishi, K.Ikeuchi, "Development of the Sound System for the MR-Mobility System," Journal of the Virtual Reality Society of Japan, Vol.19, No.2, pp.247-254, 2014.
   佐藤啓宏, 大石岳史, 池内克史, 「VR/MRガイドツアーシステムの開発と運用」, 日本バーチャルリアリティ学会論文誌, Vol.19, No.2, pp. 247-254, 2014.
3. Y.Sato, Y.Narasaki, T.Oishi, K.Ikeuchi, "Development and Practice for the VR/MR Guided-Tour System", Journal of the Virtual Reality Society of Japan, Vol.19, No.2, pp.185-193, 2014.
   佐藤啓宏, 楢崎雄太, 大石岳史, 池内克史, 「移動型ＭＲにおけるサウンドシステムの開発」, 日本バーチャルリアリティ学会論文誌, Vol.19, No.2, pp. 185-193, 2014.

SATO Yuni　佐藤由似（1981〜）

Expert, International Cooperation Section, Department of Planning and Coordination, Nara National Research Institute for Cultural Properties
奈良文化財研究所国際遺跡研究室専門職
M. Arts
修士（文学）

1. Y.Sato, "Demand and Distribution of Ceramics from the Royal Capital Area in Early Modern Period of Cambodia", Archaeology for the Middle and Early Modern Period Ceramics IV, pp.207-228, 2016.
   佐藤由似, 「中近世カンボジア王都周辺地域における陶磁器の需要と流通」, 佐々木達夫編, 『中近世陶磁器の考古学　第四巻』, pp. 207-228, 2016.
2. Y.Sato, "New Elements of Theravada Buddhism Found at Western Prasat Top", Annual Report on the Research and Restoration Work of the Western Prasat Top Dismantling Process of the Southern Sanctuary, II, pp.56-64, 2015.
3. Y.Sato, "Investigations of Burials and Artefacts Found at the Krang Kor Site, Cambodia", Advancing Southeast Asian Archaeology 2013, Selected Papers from the First SEAMEO SPAFA International Conference on Southeast Asian Archaeology, pp.5-14, 2015.

SHIMODA Ichita　下田一太（1976〜）

Agency for Cultural Affairs
文化庁
Technical Expert, Japanese Government Team For Safeguarding Angkor (~2013), Assistant Professor, Graduate School of Comprehensive Human Sciences, World Heritage Studies, University of Tsukuba (2013~2015)
日本国政府アンコール遺跡救済チーム技術顧問（〜2013），筑波大学大学院人間総合科学研究科世界遺産専攻助教（2013〜2015）
Dr. Architecture
博士（建築学）

1. I.Shimoda, T.Haraguchi, T.Chiba, M.Shimoda, "The Advanced Hydraulic City Structure of the Royal City of Angkor Thom and Vicinity Revealed through a High-resolution Red Relief Image Map", Archaeological Discovery, 4 (1), pp.22-36, 2016.
   下田一太, 原口強, 千葉達朗, 下田麻里子, 「高解像能赤色立体図によって解明された王都アンコールトムとその近傍における高度な水利都市構造」, Archaeological Discovery, 4(1), pp. 22-36, 2016.
2. I.Shimoda, Quarrying Technique of Khmer Monuments Sandstone Blocks, J. Archit. Plann., AIJ, 79 (705), pp.2543-2551, 2014.
   下田一太, 「クメール建築の砂岩採石技法に関する考察」, 日本建築学会計画系論文集, 第79巻, 第705号, pp. 2543-2551, 2014.
3. I.Shimoda, S.Shimamoto, "Spatial and Chronological Sketch of the Ancient City of Sambor Prei Kuk", Aseanie, 29, pp.11-74, 2012.
   下田一太, 嶋本紗枝, 「古代都市サンボー・プレイ・クックの空間的年代的な素描」, Aseanie, 29, pp. 11-74, 2012.

SUGIYAMA Hiroshi　杉山洋（1956〜）

Deputy Director, Nara National Research Institue for Cultural Properties
奈良文化財研究所副所長
M. Archaeology
考古学修士

1. H.Sugiyama, "Annual Report on the Research and Restoration Work of the Western Prasat Top -Dismantling Process of the NorthernSanctuary-", 2016.

杉山洋編著,『西トップ遺跡調査修復報告 北祠堂解体編』, 2016.
2. H.Sugiyama, "Report of the Archaeological Excavation of Veal Svay Kiln No.1", 2016.
　杉山洋編著,『ヴィエルスヴァイ窯跡発掘調査報告書』, 2016.
3. H.Sugiyama, "A study of the Mirror in Cambodia", Journal of Southeast Asian Archaeology, No.35, pp.31-41, 2015.
　杉山洋,「カンボジアの鏡雑感」, 東南アジア考古学, 第35号, 東南アジア考古学会, pp. 31-41, 2015.

TAKAHASHI Izumi　髙橋泉美（1993〜）

Former Master Course Student, Waseda University, Graduate School of Creative Science and Engineering
早稲田大学創造理工学研究科修士学生（当時）
M. Architecture
修士（建築学）

1. I.Takahashi, T.Nakagawa, A.Mizoguchi, M.Koiwa, M.Ishizuka, C.Kuroiwa, "Consideration on the 1st Gallery; Preah Khan of Kompong Svay Study on Preah Khan de Kompong Svay, Cambodia Part 2," Summ. Tech. Paper of Annual Meeting, AIJ, pp.837-838, 2017.
　髙橋泉美, 中川武, 溝口明則, 小岩正樹, 石塚充雅, 黒岩千尋,「コンポン・スヴァイのプレア・カーン寺院第1回廊における形状の復原的考察　カンボジア　コンポン・スヴァイのプレア・カーン寺院に関する研究(2)」, 日本建築学会大会学術講梗概集, 日本建築学会, pp. 837-838, 2017.
2. I.Takahashi, " Spatial theory of "gallery" in Khmer Architecture", Graduated Thesis, Laboratory of Architectural History, Waseda Univ., 2016.
　髙橋泉美「クメール寺院伽藍における回廊空間の構成原理」, 早稲田大学建築史研究室卒業論文, 2016.

UCHIDA Etsuo　内田悦生（1955〜）

Professor, Waseda University, Faculty of Science and Engineering
早稲田大学理工学術院教授
Dr. Science
理学博士

1. E.Uchida, K.Tsuda, I.Shimoda, "Construction sequence of the Koh Ker monuments in Cambodia deduce from the chemical composition and magnetic susceptibility of its laterites", Heritage Science, 2, pp.1-11, 2014.
2. E.Uchida, I.Shimoda, "Quarries and transportation routes of Angkor monument sandstone blocks", Journal of Archaeological Science, 40, pp.1158-1164, 2013.
3. E.Uchida, K.Ito, N.Shimizu,"Provenance of the sandstone used in the construction of the Khmer monuments in Thailand", Archaeometry, 52, pp.550-574, 2010.

WATANABE Ryota　渡辺亮太（1989〜）

Former Master Course Student, Waseda University, Graduate School of Creative Science and Engineering
早稲田大学創造理工学研究科修士学生（当時）
M. Engineering
修士（工学）

1. E.Uchida, A.Mizoguchi, H.Sato, I.Shimoda, R.Watanabe, "Determining the construction sequence of the Preah Vihear monument in Cambodia from its sandstone block characteristics", Heritage Science, 5-42, pp.1-15, 2017.
2. E.Uchida, R.Watanabe, S.Osawa, "Precipitation of manganese oxides on the surface of construction materials in the Khmer temples, Cambodia", Heritage Science, 4-16, pp.1-17, 2016.
3. E.Uchida, D.Niikuma, R.Watanabe, "Regional Differences in the Chemical Composition of Cuneiform Clay Tablets", Archaeological Discovery, 3, pp.179-207, 2015.

ZHENG Bo　鄭波（1977〜）

Institute of Industrial Science, University of Tokyo
東京大学生産技術研究所
Dr. Information Science and Technology
博士（情報理工学）

1. B.Zheng, Y.Zhao, J.Yu, K.Ikeuchi, S.-C.Zhu, "Scene Understanding by Reasoning Stability and Safety", International Journal of Computer Vision (IJCV), 2015.
2. B.Zheng, J.Takamatsu, K.Ikeuchi, "An Adaptive and Stable Method for Fitting Implicit Polynomial Curves and Surfaces", IEEE Trans. on Pattern Analysis, Machine Intelligence (PAMI), vol. 32, no. 3, pp. 561-568, 2011.
3. B.Zheng, R.Ishikawa, J.Takamatsu, T.Oishi, K.Ikeuchi, "A Coarse-to-fine IP-driven Registration for Pose Estimation from Single Ultrasound Image", Computer Vision and Image Understanding (CVIU), Available online 24, 2013.

Research achievement from 2012 to 2017 (Preah Vihear)
業績一覧（2012-2017）（プレア・ヴィヘア）

2012

A.Mizoguchi, "Technique of planning of building in Khmer Temple Monuments", meeting for restoration technique of Angkor monuments and preservation study of palece of Hue in Vietnam (Meeting for Angkor and Hue in Vietnam), Tokyo, 2012.
溝口明則,「クメール寺院遺跡における建築設計技術について」, アンコール遺跡修復技術 ベトナム・フエ王宮復原研究報告会（アンコールとベトナム・フエの会）, 東京, 2012.

T.Nakagawa, "Special Axial Space at Ancient Egypt and Angkor Monuments : Axial Space Connecting Significant Points generate Historical Story", The journal of survey, 62, Japan Association of Surveyors, pp.6-11, 2012.
中川武,「古代エジプトとアンコール遺跡における超有軸空間について：有意な点と点を結ぶ有軸空間が歴史物語を生む」, 測量, 62, 日本測量協会, pp.6-11, 2012.

S.Hachisuka K.Sato, M.Chhum, T.Nakagawa, "Traces of the modifications of Preah Vihear temple", Summ. Tech. Paper of Annual Meeting, F-2, AIJ, pp.481-482, 2012.
蜂須賀瞬, 佐藤桂, チュンメンホン, 中川武,「プレア・ヴィヘア寺院の増改築の痕跡について」, 日本建築学会大会学術講演梗概集, F-2, 日本建築学会, pp.481-482, 2012.

2013

N.Tabuchi, T.Nakagawa, A.Mizoguchi, I.Shimoda, M.Ishizuka, "The Characteristics of Preah Vihear temple complex as a temple strung out along acclivitous axis of the terraced slopes of a hill: Studies on Preah Vihear temple, Cambodia (2)", Summ. Tech. Paper of Annual Meeting, F-2, AIJ, 2013, pp.573-574.
田淵奈央, 中川武, 溝口明則, 下田一太, 石塚充雅,「参道テラス縦深型祠堂としてのプレア・ヴィヘア寺院の特徴：カンボジア プレア・ヴィヘア寺院に関する研究（2）」, 日本建築学会大会学術講演梗概集, F-2, 日本建築学会, pp. 573-574, 2013.

C.Kuroiwa, T.Nakagawa, A.Mizoguchi, I.Shimoda, M.Ishizuka, N.Tabuchi, "A state and features of "Four-chamber" in Preah Vihear temple: Studies on Preah Vihear temple, Cambodia (3)", Summ. Tech. Paper of Annual Meeting, F-2, AIJ, 2013, pp.575-576.
黒岩千尋, 中川武, 溝口明則, 下田一太, 石塚充雅, 田淵奈央,「プレア・ヴィヘア寺院の『田の字型』建物の現状と特徴：カンボジア プレア・ヴィヘア寺院に関する研究（3）」, 日本建築学会大会学術講演梗概集, F-2, 日本建築学会, pp. 575-576, 2013.

A.Mizoguchi, T.Nakagawa, K.Sato, I.Shimoda, M.Ishizuka, "Study on the dimentional planning at the Preah Vihear temple complex on the crest: Studies on Preah Vihear temple, Cambodia (4)", Summ. Tech. Paper of Annual Meeting, F-2, AIJ, 2013, pp.577-578.
溝口明則, 中川武, 佐藤桂, 下田一太, 石塚充雅,「プレア・ヴィヘア寺院の山頂伽藍計画について：カンボジア プレア・ヴィヘア寺院に関する研究（4）」日本建築学会大会学術講演梗概集, F-2, 日本建築学会, pp. 577-578, 2013.

K.Sato, "Reread of "L'Art khmer classique" part 4: Chapter 4 Preah Vihear", Study Report collection of Kanto Branch of AIJ, 83(II), pp.733-736, 2013.
佐藤桂,「『クメール古典美術』の再読：その4『第4章プレア・ヴィヒア』」, 日本建築学会関東支部研究報告集, 83(II), pp. 733-736, 2013.

2014

A.Mizoguchi, T.Nakagawa eds, "KOH KER AND BENG MEALEA -ARCHITECTURAL STUDY ON THE PROVINCIAL SITES OF THE KHMER EMPIRE -", Chuo Koron Bijutsu Shuppan, 2014.
中川武, 溝口明則監修,『コー・ケーとベン・メアレア—アンコール広域拠点遺跡群の建築学的研究』, 中央公論美術出版, 2014.

A.Mizoguchi, T.Nakagawa eds, Preliminary Report on the Ancient Khmer Provincial Principal Monuments -Preah Vihear-, National Authority for Preah Vihear, Meijo University, Waseda University, Siem Reap, Cambodia, 2014.

A.Mizoguchi, T.Nakagawa, I.Shimoda, K.Sato, M.Ishizuka, "ON THE DIMENSIONAL PLANNING AT PREAH VIHEAR TEMPLE COMPLEX ON THE CREST:Study on the dimensional plan and the planning method of Khmer architecture No. 7", J. Archit. Plann. 79(697), AIJ, pp.817-825, 2014.
溝口明則, 中川武, 下田一太, 佐藤桂, 石塚充雅,「プレア・ヴィヘア寺院山頂伽藍の寸法計画：クメール建築の造営尺度と設計技術に関する研究（7）」, 日本建築学会計画系論文集, 第79巻, 第697号, 日本建築学会, pp. 817-825, 2014.

T.Nakagawa, "Significance of "Vertically-Oriented Layout Temple" and Subject on Conservation in Preah Vihear Temple, Cambodia," Proc. of the 10th International Symposiumon Architectural Interchanges in Asia, (II), ISAIA, Hangzhou, China, pp.792-797, 2014.

C.Kuroiwa, "Reconstructive Study on "田-shape" "口-shape" as "annexed building" in the "Vertically-Oriented" layout temple, Preah Vihear Temple, Cambodia", ISAIA2014, Hangzhou, China, Proceeding of the 10th International Symposium on Architectural Interchanges in Asia, (II), pp.798-803, 2014.

T.Nakagawa, A.Mizoguchi, M.Ishizuka, C.Kuroiwa, "Formation Process of a Khmer Temple strung out along acclivitous axis : Studies on Preah Vihear Temple, Cambodia(7)", Summ. Tech. Paper of Annual Meeting, AIJ, pp.673-674, 2014.
中川武, 石塚充雅, 溝口明則, 黒岩千尋,「クメール寺院伽藍における縦深型祠堂の形成過程：カンボジア プレア・ヴィヘア寺院に関する研究（7）」, 日本建築学会大会学術講演梗概集, 日本建築学会, pp. 673-674, 2014.

C.Kuroiwa, T.Nakagawa, A.Mizoguchi, M.Ishizuka, "History of spatial features and functional study on the "attached-building" in Khmer temples : Studies on Preah Vihear temple, Cambodia(8) ", Summ. Tech. Paper of Annual Meeting, AIJ, pp.675-676, 2014.
黒岩千尋, 中川武, 溝口明則, 石塚充雅, 「クメール寺院における「付属建物」の空間的特徴の変遷と機能について : カンボジア プレア・ヴィヘア寺院に関する研究(8)」, 日本建築学会大会学術講演梗概集, 日本建築学会, pp. 675-676, 2014.

A.Mizoguchi, T.Nakagawa, M.Ishizuka, "Study on the dimentional planning at the Preah Vihear temple complex : Studies on Preah Vihear temple, Cambodia(9)", Summ. Tech. Paper of Annual Meeting, AIJ, pp.677-678, 2014.
溝口明則, 中川武, 石塚充雅, 「プレア・ヴィヘア寺院の伽藍全体計画について : カンボジアプレア・ヴィヘア寺院に関する研究(9)」, 日本建築学会大会学術講演梗概集, 日本建築学会, pp. 677-678, 2014.

T.Nakagawa, "Significance of "Vertically-Oriented Layout Temple" and Subject on Conservation in Preah Vihear Temple, Cambodia", JSPS Core-to-Core Program (B.Asia-Africa Science Platform Program) Establishment of the Network for Safeguarding and Development of the Cultural Heritage in the Mekong Basin Countries - Human Resources Development and its Major Issues through Technical Activities of Restoration and Conservation in the World Heritage Site Vat Phou -, Champasak, Laos, 2014.

C.Kuroiwa, "Reconstructive Study on "田-shape" "囗-shape" as "annexed building" in the "Vertically- Oriented" layout temple, Preah Vihear Temple, Cambodia", JSPS Core-to-Core Program (B.Asia-Africa Science Platform Program) Establishment of the Network for Safeguarding and Development of the Cultural Heritage in the Mekong Basin Countries - Human Resources Development and its Major Issues through Technical Activities of Restoration and Conservation in the World Heritage Site Vat Phou -, Champasak, Laos, 2014.

E.Uchida, A.Mizoguchi, H.Sato, I.Shimoda, R.Watanabe, "Construction sequence of the Preah Vihear monument in Cambodia deduced from the characteristics of its sandstone blocks", The Japan Society for Scientific Studies on Cultural Properties, Nara University of Education, 2014.
内田悦生, 溝口明則, 佐藤広野, 下田一太, 渡辺亮太, 「砂岩材の特徴に基づくプレア・ヴィヘア遺跡の建造順序の推定」, 日本文化財科学会, 奈良教育大学, 2014.

2015

A.Mizoguchi, "Asian Characteristic in the Complex Plan", Essays on World Architecture History: Essays in honour of Professer Takeshi Nakagawa, Chuo Koron Bijutsu Shuppan, 2015.
溝口明則, 「伽藍計画のアジア的特質」, 『世界建築史論集：中川武先生退任記念論文集』, 中央公論美術出版, 2015.

T.Nakagawa, "Research in Preah Vihear: Collaborative Project between National Authority for Preah Vihear, Meijo University and Waseda University", International Coordinating Committee for the Safeguarding and Development of the Historic Site of Preah Vihear (ICC-Preah Vihear), Siem Reap (Cambodia), 2015.

C.Kuroiwa, T.Nakagawa, "The Origin of Khmer City Structure by Comparison of Vat Phu and Preah Vihear", The 15th Science Council of Asia Board Meeting and International Symposium, Siem Reap (Cambodia), Presentation, 15th SCA Conference and International Symposium, pp.45-48, 2015.

S.Kubo, N.Nagumo, "Geomorphological and geological investigations around Preah Vihear temple in northern Cambodia", Proceedings of the General Meeting of the Association of Japanese Geographers, 87, p.104, 2015.
久保純子, 南雲直子, 「カンボジア北部プレアヴィヒア寺院周辺の地形地質調査」, 日本地理学会発表要旨集, 87, p. 104, 2015.

B.Zheng, X.Huang, R.Ishikawa, T.Oishi, K.Ikeuchi, "A New Flying Range Sensor: Aerial Scan in Omini-directions," In Proc. International Conference on 3D Vision (3DV), pp.623-631, 2015.

R.Ishikawa, B.Zheng, T.Oishi, K.Ikeuchi, "Rectification of Aerial 3D Laser Scans via Line-based Registration to Ground Model," IPSJ Transactions on Computer Vision and Applications, Vol.7, pp.89-93, 2015.

2016

A.Mizoguchi, "History of Study for scale of Khmer Architecture", Architecture History, 66, pp.53-67, 2016.
溝口明則, 「クメール建築の造営尺をめぐる研究史」, 建築史学, 66, pp. 53-67, 2016.

C.Kuroiwa, T.Nakagawa, A.Mizoguchi, M.Ishizuka, ""囗-SHAPE" "田-SHAPE" ARCHITECTURAL STYLES IN PREAH VIHEAR TEMPLE: Consideration on transition of Khmer architecture through the example of "Annexed Building" ", J. Archit. Plann. 81(719), AIJ, pp.195-202, 2016.
黒岩千尋, 中川武, 溝口明則, 「プレア・ヴィヘア寺院の「口の字」型・「田の字」型建築形式について : ―「付属建物」に見るクメール建築変遷史の考察―」, 日本建築学会計画系論文集, 第81巻, 第719 号, pp. 195-202, 2016.

2017

E.Uchida, A.Mizoguchi, H.Sato, I.Shimoda, R.Watanabe, "Determing the construction sequence of the Preah Vihear monument in Cambodia from its sandstone block characteristics", Heritage Science, 5, pp.1-15, 2017.

A.Mizoguchi, T.Nakagawa, M.Koiwa, M.Ishizuka, C.Kuroiwa,"ON THE TECHNIQUES OF THE WOOD FRAMES ON THE STONE-WALLS IN KHMER ARCHITECTURE" 7", J. Archit. Plann. 82(741), AIJ, pp.2969-2978, 2017.
溝口明則, 中川武, 小岩正樹, 石塚充雅, 黒岩千尋, 「クメール寺院の石造壁と木造架構の接続技法」, 日本建築学会計画系論文集, 第82巻, 第741号, 日本建築学会, pp. 2969-2978, 2017.

Final Notes

On December 2014, at a conference room of APSARA Authority in Siem Reap city, the 1st meeting of ICC Preah Vihear was conducted. It was based on achievements of ICC Angkor for 20 years of history, Government of Cambodia prepared to establish that after a registration of Preah Vihear Temple as one of UNESCO World Heritage Sites in 2008. I should say it was a very difficult start because the situation got worse by a border dispute between Cambodia and Thailand.

I visited Preah Vihear Temple for the first time on August 1993 when there was transient secuare condition. No one can forget the view of beauty, vast and completely green Angkor Plains from the peak of the deepest point of vertically-oriented and axial space. This exceptional and overwhelming hierarchical space unmistakably indicates the direction to holy ground, Angkor. The role of this place was realized beyond as the transportational base on the Dangrek Mountains which connects Angkor and the northeast part of Thailand.

Our studies also took a long time, however I am really delighted that many specialists in several fields especially architecture took part for this significant heritages and we could do the fandamental academic survey. In the future, restoration work will be promoted, I would be pleased if our investigation are applied as a basic information for future survey.

I would like to express my respect and appreciate to all members of Natinal Authority for Preah Vihear, everyne who has a concern in the survey and makes a great effort to publish this report.

February 2017
NAKAGAWA Takeshi

あとがき

2014年12月，シェムリアップ，APSARAの大会議場にて，第1回ICC－プレア・ヴィヘアの会議が行われた。もう既に20年の歴史を持つICCアンコールの成功実績のもとに，カンボジア政府が，2008年のプレア・ヴィヘア寺院遺跡のUNESCO世界遺産リストの登録以降，準備してきたものであるが，カンボジア・タイ国境紛争等に巻き込まれたこともあって，前途多難を思わせる出発であったといえよう。

私がはじめて，プレア・ヴィヘア寺院遺跡を訪れたのは，1993年の8月で，この地が瞬の間の小康状態にあった。崖上に展開する，縦深的な強い有軸空間が行きついた最深部の崖上から見た，一面の緑のアンコール平原の広大さと，美しさが忘れられない。この特異，かつ，圧倒的な序列空間が指し示す方向は，まぎれもなく，聖地アンコールであって，アンコールとタイ東北部を結ぶダンレック山脈上の交通の拠点以上の意味が，実感されたのである。

私たちの調査もまた，長い時間を要したが，この意義深い遺跡について，建築学を中心とした関連分野の専門家に参加いただき，基本的な学術調査ができたことを嬉しく思っている。今後，進められていくであろう，保存修復工事や，さらなる精査のための基本情報として，活用していただければ幸いである。

国立プレア・ヴィヘア機構のみなさまや，調査に参加され，成果の取りまとめと報告書の執筆，報告書の発刊に努力されたみなさまに敬意を表し，御礼申し上げたい。

2017年2月
中川　武

Appendix I
付章 I

Monument Inventory
インベントリー

＊この章は、プレア・ヴィヘア寺院のシンハ・ナーガ像、ペディメント装飾、木造屋根痕跡、および、比較寺院の木造屋根痕跡に関するインベントリーである。各節のはじめに、概要を英語にて示した。

＊ This chapter is the inventory of Singha / Naga statues, pediment decorations, wooden roof traces in Preah Vihear Temple, and wooden roof traces in other Khmer temples. The head of each section has the outline in English.

I.1　プレア・ヴィヘア寺院のシンハ・ナーガ像
Singha and Naga Statues in Preah Vihear Temple

In Preah Vihear Temple, 43 statues of Singha and 4 statues of Naga (Some of them are the pairs of head and tail.) are found. We numbered the statues from the deepest area of temple complex, Singha No.1-43 and Naga No.1-4. Figure I.1-2 is a location map of each statue. The red marks are statues of Singha and the green marks are statues of Naga.

The following pages are the inventory of Singha and Naga statues in Preah Vihear Temple. Each item has a location map and 5 confronting photos of front, back, right, left and over side of statue.

Statues are put to 6 groups in order to the location area in the temple complex, starting from the deepest "Gopura II" to "Great Staircase". The list of groups are as follows;

I.1.1　Gopura II
I.1.2　Gopura III
I.1.3　Gopura IV
I.1.4　Basin
I.1.5　Gopura V
I.1.6　Great Staircase

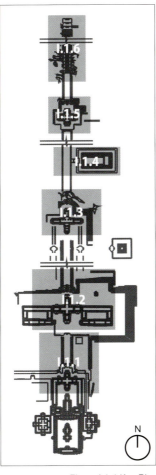

Figure I.1-1 Key Plan

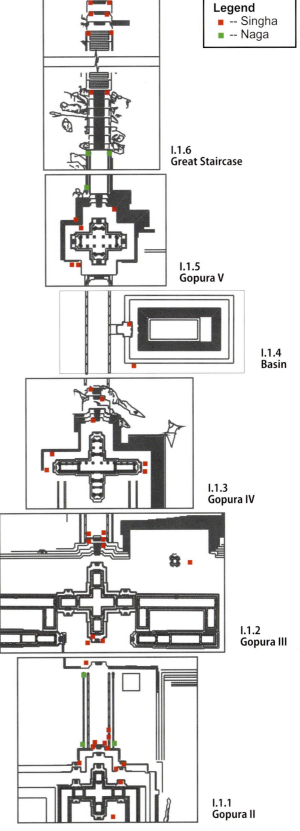

Figure I.1-2 Location of Singha and Naga Statues

Appendix I : Monument Inventory

I.1.1 Gopura II (Singha No.1-12)

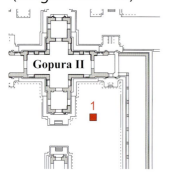

Singha No.1 - Location

*All drawings are north upward.

Singha No.1 - Front Side

Singha No.1 - Back Side

Singha No.1 - Over Look

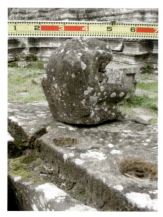

Singha No.1 - Right Side

Singha No.1 - Left Side

Singha No.2 - Location

Singha No.2 - Front Side

Singha No.2 - Back Side

Singha No.2 - Over Look

Singha No.2 - Right Side

Singha No.2 - Left Side

Singha and Naga Statues in Preah Vihear Temple

Singha No.3 - Location

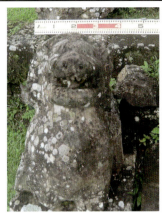
Singha No.3 - Front Side

Singha No.3 - Back Side

Singha No.3 - Over Look

Singha No.3 - Right Side

Singha No.3 - Left Side

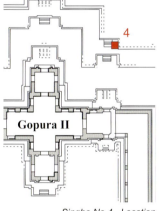
Singha No.4 - Location

Singha No.4 - Front Side

Singha No.4 - Back Side

Singha No.4 - Over Look

Singha No.4 - Right Side

Singha No.4 - Left Side

Appendix I : Monument Inventory

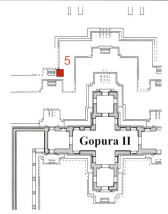
Singha No.5 - Location

Singha No.5 - Front Side

Singha No.5 - Back Side

Singha No.5 - Over Look

Singha No.5 - Right Side

Singha No.5 - Left Side

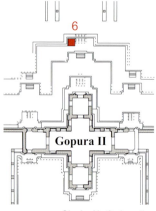
Singha No.6 - Location

Singha No.6 - Front Side

Singha No.6 - Back Side

Singha No.6 - Over Look

Singha No.6 - Right Side

Singha No.6 - Left Side

Singha and Naga Statues in Preah Vihear Temple

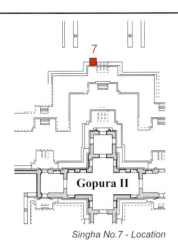
Singha No.7 - Location

Singha No.7 - Front Side

Singha No.7 - Back Side

Singha No.7 - Over Look

Singha No.7 - Right Side

Singha No.7 - Left Side

Singha No.8 - Location

Singha No.8 - Front Side

Singha No.8 - Back Side

Singha No.8 - Over Look

Singha No.8 - Right Side

Singha No.8 - Left Side

Appx. 7

Appendix I : Monument Inventory

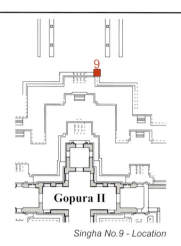
Singha No.9 - Location

Singha No.9 - Front Side

Singha No.9 - Back Side

Singha No.9 - Over Look

Singha No.9 - Right Side

Singha No.9 - Left Side

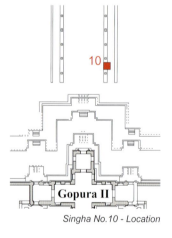
Singha No.10 - Location

Singha No.10 - Front Side

Singha No.10 - Back Side

Singha No.10 - Over Look

Singha No.10 - Right Side

Singha No.10 - Left Side

Singha and Naga Statues in Preah Vihear Temple

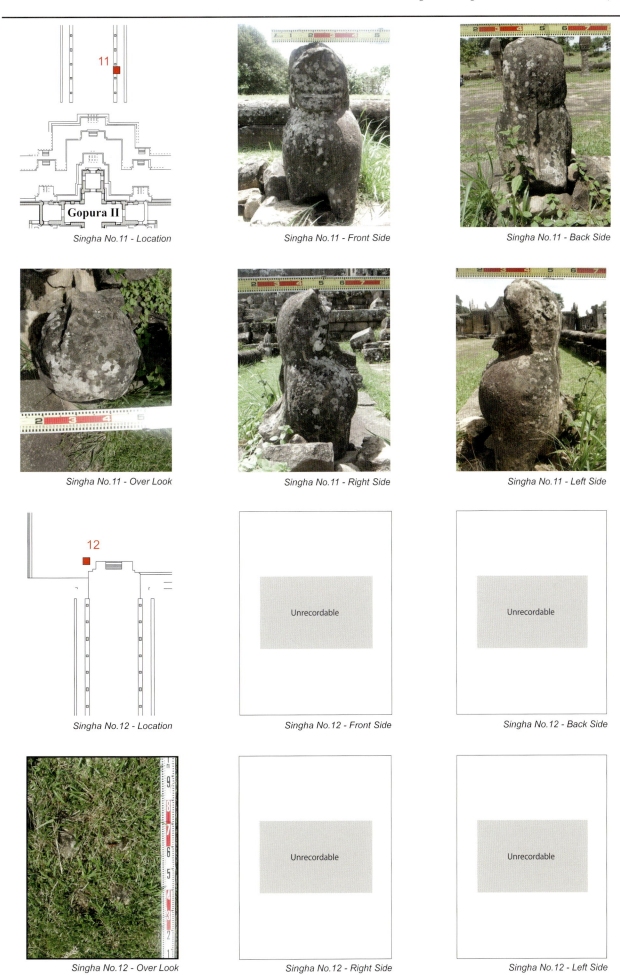

Appx. 9

Appendix I : Monument Inventory

I.1.2 Gopura III
(Singha No. 13-21)

Singha No.13 - Location

Singha No.13 - Front Side

Singha No.13 - Back Side

Singha No.13 - Over Look

Singha No.13 - Right Side

Singha No.13 - Left Side

Singha No.14 - Location

Singha No.14 - Front Side

Singha No.14 - Back Side

Singha No.14 - Over Look

Singha No.14 - Right Side

Singha No.14 - Left Side

Singha and Naga Statues in Preah Vihear Temple

Singha No.15 - Location

Singha No.15 - Front Side

Singha No.15 - Back Side

Singha No.15 - Over Look

Singha No.15 - Right Side

Singha No.15 - Left Side

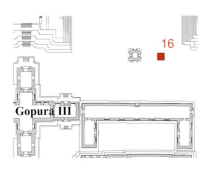
Singha No.16 - Location

Singha No.16 - Front Side

Singha No.16 - Back Side

Singha No.16 - Over Look

Singha No.16 - Right Side

Singha No.16 - Left Side

Appendix I : Monument Inventory

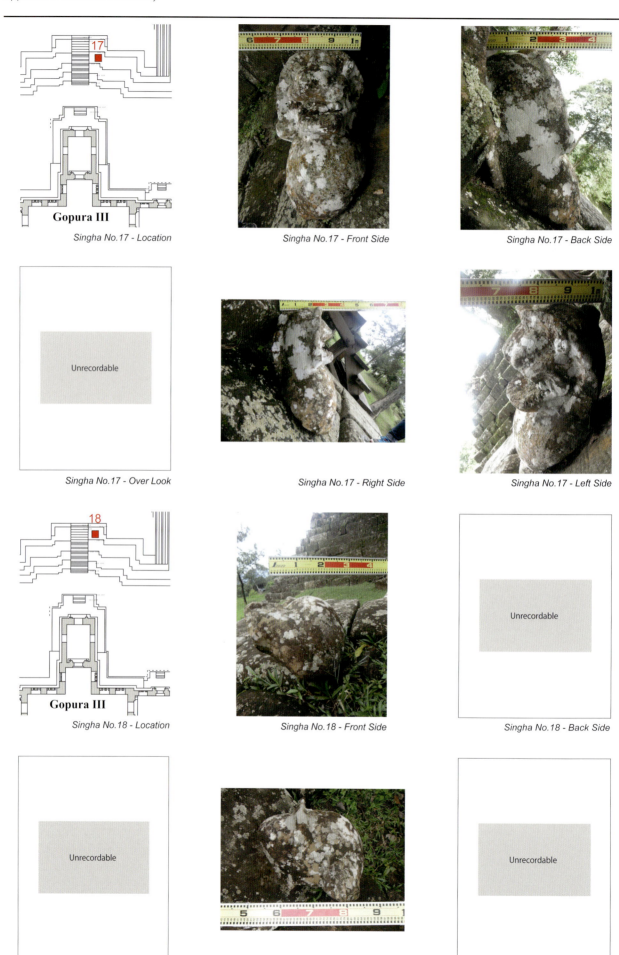

Singha and Naga Statues in Preah Vihear Temple

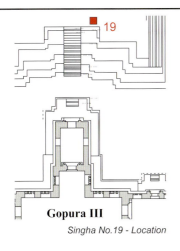
Gopura III
Singha No.19 - Location

Singha No.19 - Front Side

Singha No. 19 - Back Side

Singha No.19 - Over Look

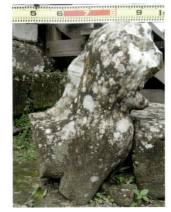
Singha No.19 - Right Side

Singha No.19 - Left Side

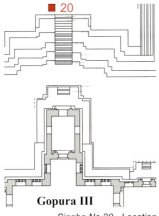
Gopura III
Singha No.20 - Location

Singha No.20 - Front Side

Singha No.20 - Back Side

Singha No.20 - Over Look

Singha No.20 - Right Side

Singha No.20 - Left Side

Appx.
13

Appendix I : Monument Inventory

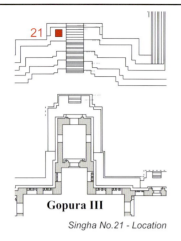
Singha No.21 - Location

Singha No.21 - Front Side

Singha No.21 - Back Side

Singha No.21 - Over Look

Singha No.21 - Right Side

Singha No.21 - Left Side

I.1.3 Gopura IV (Singha No. 22-28)

Singha No.22 - Location

Singha No.22 - Front Side

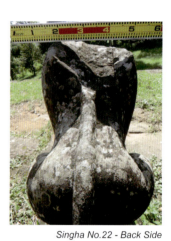
Singha No.22 - Back Side

Singha No.22 - Over Look

Singha No.22 - Right Side

Singha No.22 - Left Side

Singha and Naga Statues in Preah Vihear Temple

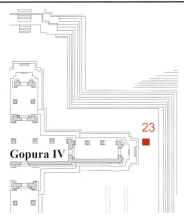
Singha No.23 - Location

Singha No.23 - Front Side

Singha No.23 - Back Side

Singha No.23 - Over Look

Singha No.23 - Right Side

Singha No.23 - Left Side

Singha No.24 - Location

Singha No.24 - Front Side

Singha No.24 - Baack Side

Singha No.24 - Over Look

Singha No.24 - Right Side

Singha No.24 - Left Side

Appx.
15

Appendix I : Monument Inventory

Singha No.25 - Location

Singha No.25 - Front Side

Singha No.25 - Back Side

Singha No.25 - Over Look

Singha No.25 - Right Side

Singha No.25 - Left Side

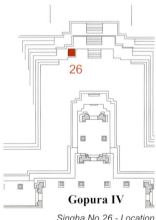
Singha No.26 - Location

Singha No.26 - Front Side

Singha No.26 - Back Side

Singha No.26 - Over Look

Singha No.26 - Right Side

Singha No.26 - Left Side

Singha and Naga Statues in Preah Vihear Temple

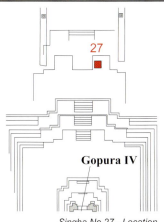
Singha No.27 - Location

Singha No.27 - Front Side

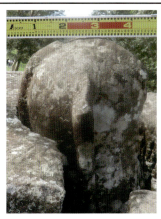
Singha No.27 - Back Side

Singha No.27 - Over Look

Singha No.27 - Right Side

Singha No.27 - Left Side

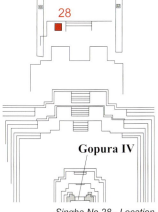
Singha No.28 - Location

Singha No.28 - Front Side

Singha No.28 - Back Side

Singha No.28 - Over Look

Singha No.28 - Right Side

Singha No.28 - Left Side

Appendix I : Monument Inventory

I.1.4 Basin (Singha No. 29-30)

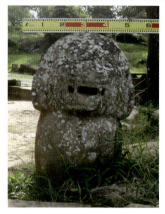

Singha No.29 - Location

Singha No.29 - Front Side

Singha No.29 - Back Side

Singha No.29 - Over Look

Singha No.29 - Right Side

Singha No.29 - Left Side

Singha No.30 - Location

Singha No.30 - Front Side

Singha No.30 - Back Side

Singha No.30 - Over Look

Singha No.30 - Right Side

Singha No.30 - Left Side

Appx.
18

Singha and Naga Statues in Preah Vihear Temple

I.1.5 Gopura V
(Singha No. 31-35)

Singha No.31 - Location

Singha No.31 - Front Side

Singha No.31 - Back Side

Singha No.31 - Over Look

Singha No.31 - Right Side

Singha No.31 - Left Side

Singha No.32 - Location

Singha No.32 - Front Side

Singha No.32 - Back Side

Singha No.32 - Over Look

Singha No.32 - Right Side

Singha No.32 - Left Side

Appendix I : Monument Inventory

Singha No.33 - Location

Singha No.33 - Front Side

Singha No.33 - Back Side

Singha No.33 - Over Look

Singha No.33 - Right Side

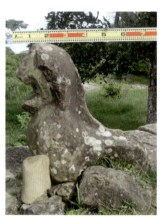
Singha No.33 - Left Side

Singha No.34 - Location

Singha No.34 - Front Side

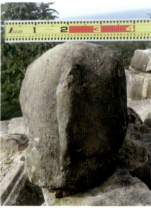
Singha No.34 - Back Side

Singha No.34 - Over Look

Singha No.34 - Right Side

Singha No.34 - Left Side

Singha and Naga Statues in Preah Vihear Temple

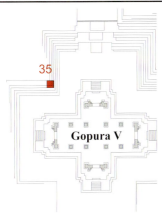
Singha No.35 - Location

Singha No.35 - Front Side

Singha No.35 - Back Side

Singha No.35 - Over Look

Singha No.35 - Right Side

Singha No.35 - Left Side

I.1.6 Great Staircase (Singha No. 36-43)

Singha No.36 - Location

Singha No.36 - Front Side

Singha No.36 - Back Side

Singha No.36 - Over Look

Singha No.36 - Right Side

Singha No.36 - Left Side

Appendix I : Monument Inventory

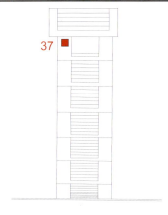
Singha No.37 - Location

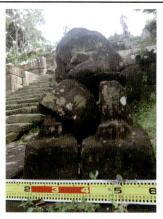
Singha No.37 - Front Side

Singha No.37 - Back Side

Singha No.37 - Over Look

Singha No.37 - Right Side

Singha No.37 - Left Side

Singha No.38 - Location

Singha No.38 - Front Side

Singha No.38 - Back Side

Singha No.38 - Over Look

Singha No.38 - Right Side

Singha No.38 - Left Side

Singha and Naga Statues in Preah Vihear Temple

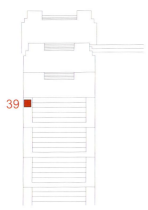
Singha No.39 - Location

Singha No.39 - Front Side

Singha No.39 - Back Side

Singha No.39 - Over Look

Singha No.39 - Right Side

Singha No.39 - Left Side

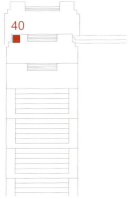
Singha No.40 - Location

Singha No.40 - Front Side

Singha No.40 - Back Side

Singha No.40 - Over Look

Singha No.40 - Right Side

Singha No.40 - Left Side

Appx.

Appendix I : Monument Inventory

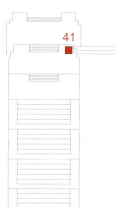
Singha No.41 - Location

Singha No.41 - Front Side

Singha No.41 - Back Side

Singha No.41 - Over Look

Singha No.41 - Right Side

Singha No.41 - Left Side

Singha No.42 - Location

Singha No.42 - Front Side

Singha No.42 - Back Side

Singha No.42 - Over Look

Singha No.42 - Right Side

Singha No.42 - Left Side

Singha and Naga Statues in Preah Vihear Temple

Singha No.43 - Location

Singha No.43 - Front Side

Singha No.43 - Back Side

Singha No.43 - Over Look

Singha No.43 - Right Side

Singha No.43 - Left Side

Appx.
25

Appendix I : Monument Inventory

I.1.1 Gopura II (Naga No. 1-2)

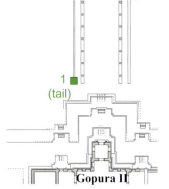
Naga No.1 (tail) - Location

Naga No.1 (tail) - Front Side

Naga No.1 (tail) - Back Side

Naga No.1 (tail) - Over Look

Naga No.1 (tail) - Right Side

Naga No.1 (tail) - Left Side

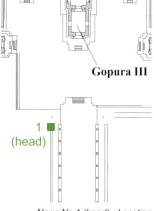
Naga No.1 (head) - Location

Naga No.1 (head) - Front Side

Naga No.1 (head) - Back Side

Naga No.1 (head) - Over Look

Naga No.1 (head) - Right Side

Naga No.1 (head) - Left Side

Singha and Naga Statues in Preah Vihear Temple

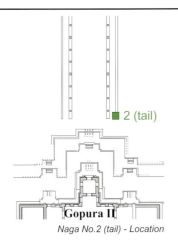
Naga No.2 (tail) - Location

Naga No.2 (tail) - Front Side

Naga No.2 (tail) - Back Side

Naga No.2 (tail) - Over Look

Naga No.2 (tail) - Right Side

Naga No.2 (tail) - Left Side

I.1.5 Gopura V (Naga No. 3)

Naga No.3 - Location

Naga No.3 (tail) - Front Side

Naga No.3 (tail) - Back Side

Naga No.3 (tail) - Over Look

Naga No.3 (tail) - Right Side

Naga No.3 (tail) - Left Side

Appx.
27

Appendix I : Monument Inventory

I.1.6 Great Staircase (Naga No. 3-4)

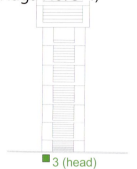
Naga No.3 (head) - Location

Naga No.3 (head) - Front Side

Naga No.3 (head) - Back Side

Naga No.3 (head) - Over Look

Naga No.3 (head) - Right Side

Naga No.3 (head) - Left Side

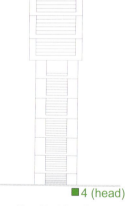
Naga No.4 (head) - Location

Naga No.4 (head) - Front Side

Naga No.4 (head) - Back Side

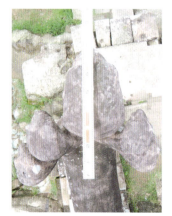
Naga No.4 (head) - Over Look

Naga No.4 (head) - Right Side

Naga No.4 (head) - Left Side

I.2　プレア・ヴィヘア寺院のペディメント
Pediments in Preah Vihear Temple

In Preah Vihear Temple, we confirmed 2 decoration types of pediments. One is triangle pediment with straight outline which has spiral-shaped nagas in both bottom corner of the pediment, and another is flame-like shape pediment has multi-headed nagas as acroteria. For the details about each decoration, see Chapter 3.10 "Significant Features of the Decorations of the Pediments".

Figure I.2-1 is a location map of buildings which have pediments, starting from "Central Sanctuary" to "Gopura V". The following pages show the inventory of pediment drawings of each building.

Each item has a map of pediment number and elevational drawings of pediments. The pediment number is composed by "direction+number from inside". For example, the most inner side pediment of South direction is named as "S1". Exceptionally, "D1" shows the door attached to the wall, and "H1" shows the half-pediment which is seen at Hall N. The elevational drawing is based on the present situation of pediments. It is composed by outline of building shape and decorations.

The list of buildings are as follows;
I.2.1　Central Sanctuary
I.2.2　Gallery I
I.2.3　False Gopura
I.2.4　Gopura I・Hall N
I.2.5　West Library
I.2.6　East Library
I.2.7　Annex Building E
I.2.8　Annex Building F
I.2.9　Gallery II
I.2.10　Gopura II
I.2.11　Gopura III
I.2.12　Annex Building H'-I'
I.2.13　Annex Building H-I
I.2.14　Gopura IV
I.2.15　Gopura V

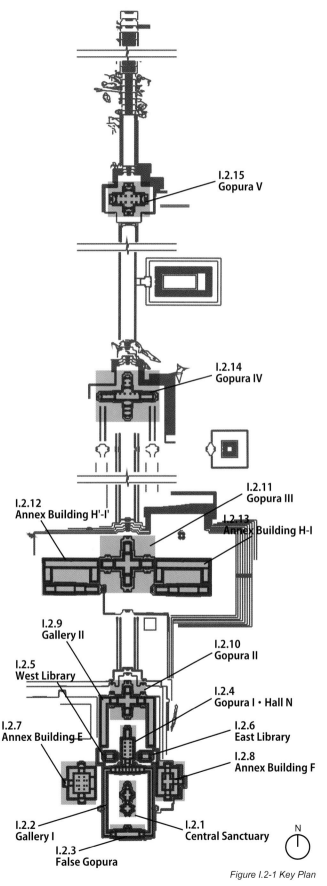

Figure I.2-1 Key Plan

Appendix I : Monument Inventory

I.2.1　Central Sanctuary

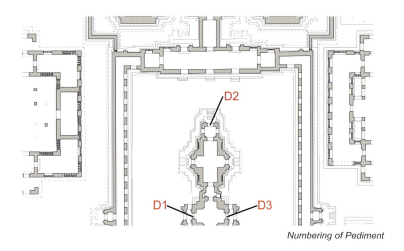

Numbering of Pediment

Legend
X1 -- Remain
X1 -- Collapse

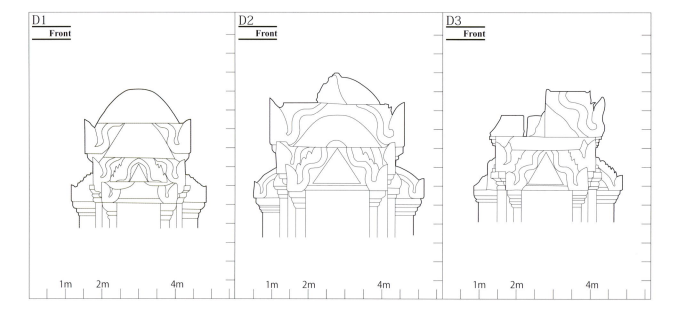

Pediments in Preah Vihear Temple

I.2.2 Gallery I

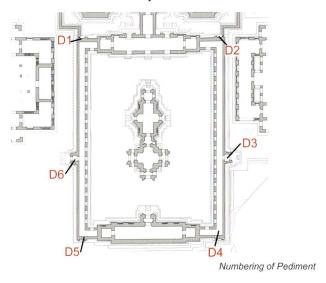

Numbering of Pediment

Legend
X1 -- Remain
X1 -- Collapse

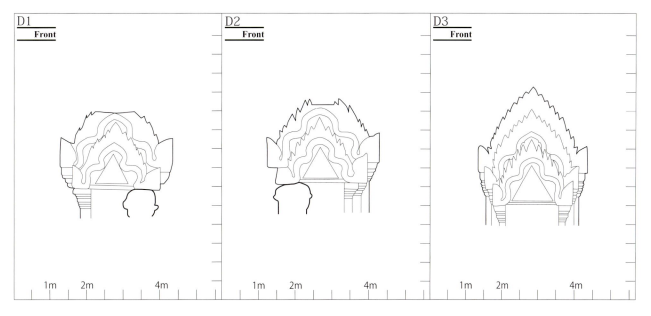

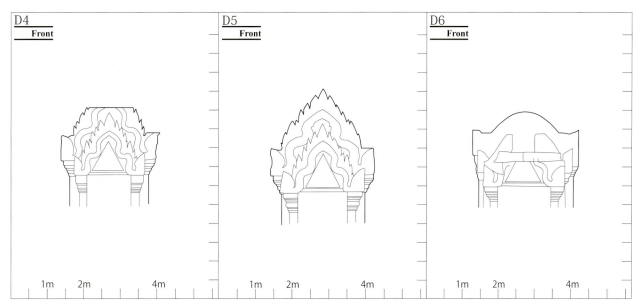

Appx.
31

Appendix I : Monument Inventory

I.2.3　False Gopura

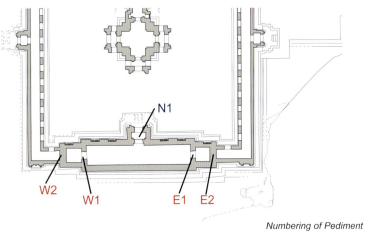

Numbering of Pediment

Legend
X1 -- Remain
X1 -- Collapse

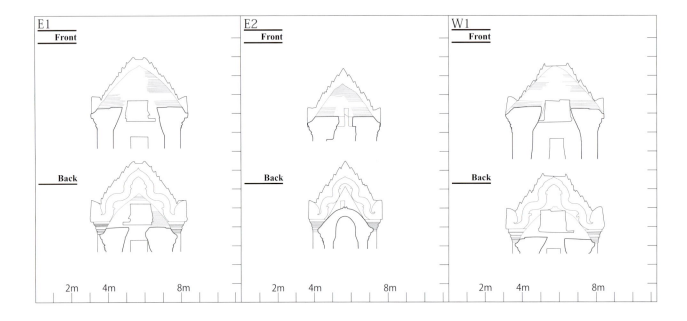

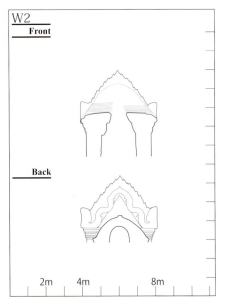

I.2.4 Gopura I · Hall N

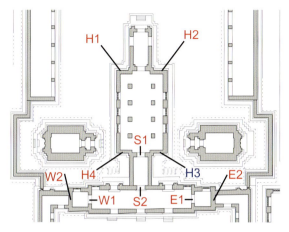

Numbering of Pediment

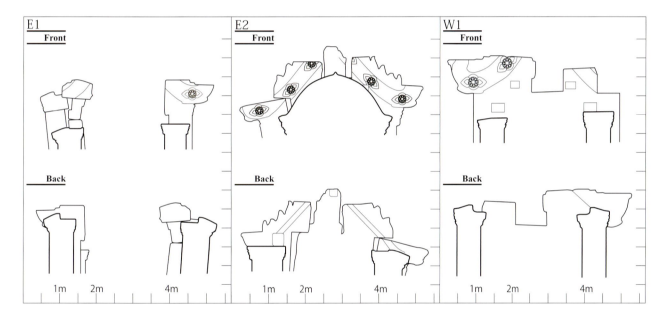

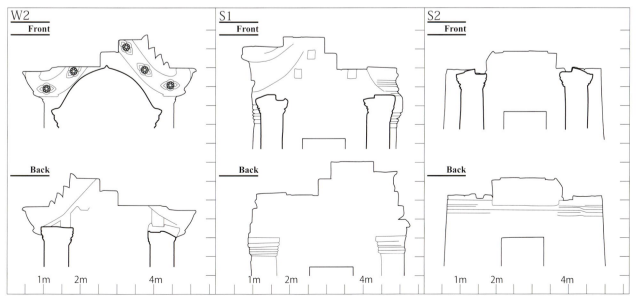

Appendix I : Monument Inventory

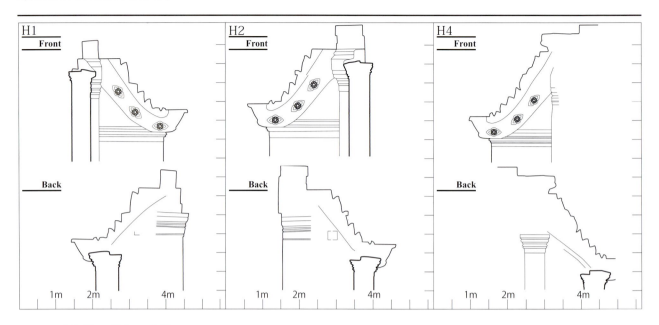

I.2.5 West Library

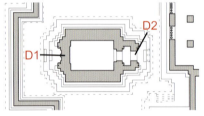

Numbering of Pediment

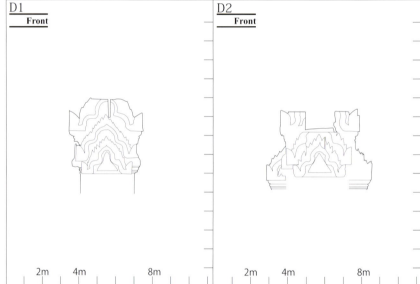

I.2.6 East Library

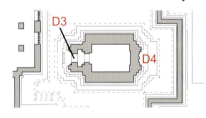

Numbering of Pediment

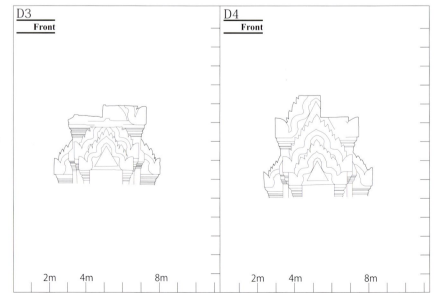

I.2.7 Annex Building E

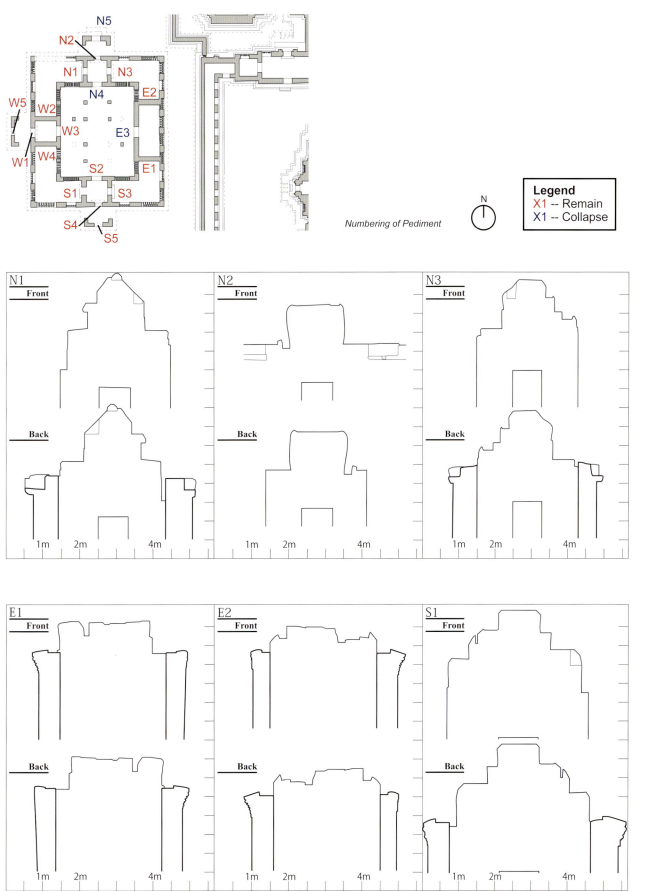

Appendix I : Monument Inventory

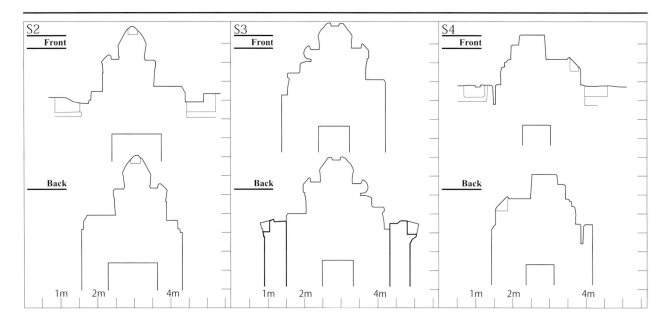
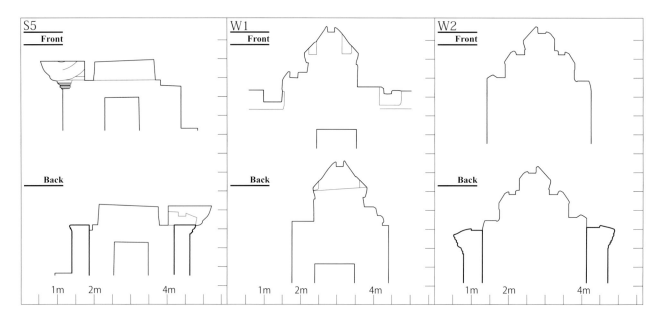
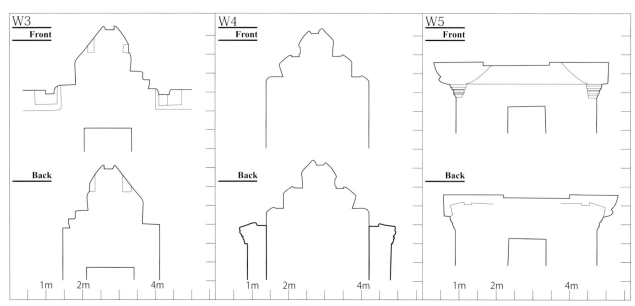

I.2.8 Annex Building F

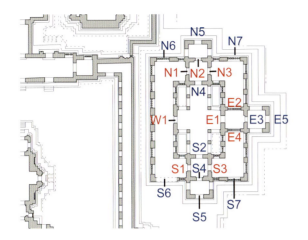

Numbering of Pediment

Legend
X1 -- Remain
X1 -- Collapse

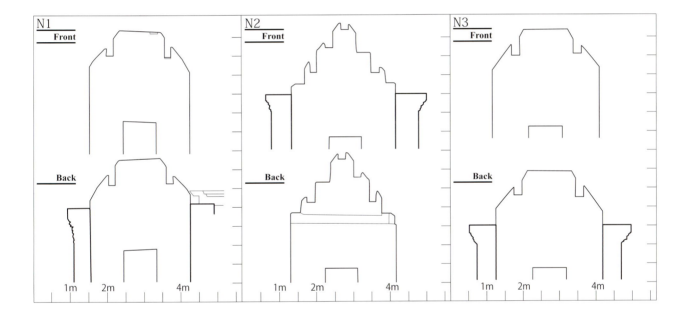

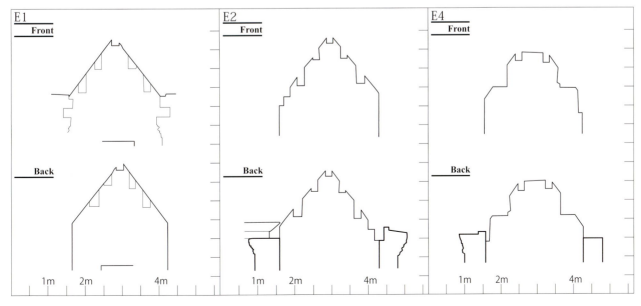

Appendix I : Monument Inventory

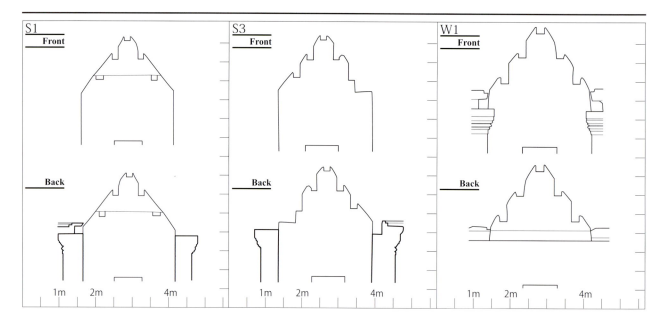

I.2.9 Gallery II

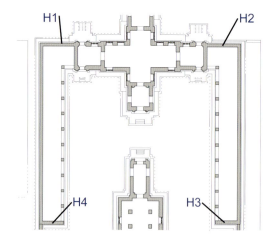

Numbering of Pediment

Legend
X1 -- Remain
X1 -- Collapse

I.2.10 Gopura II

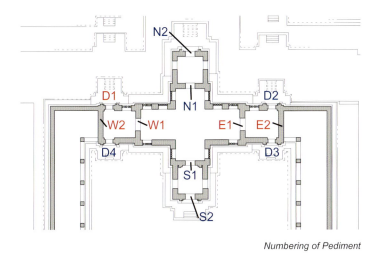

Numbering of Pediment

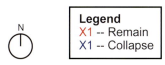

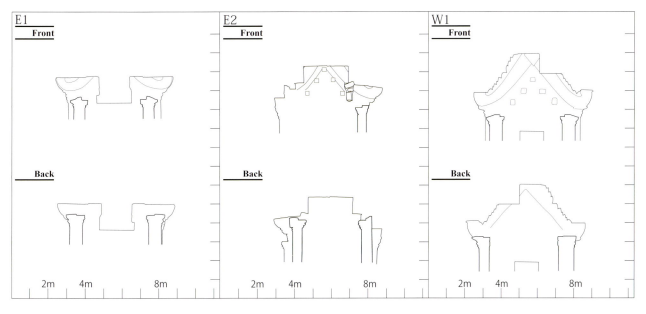

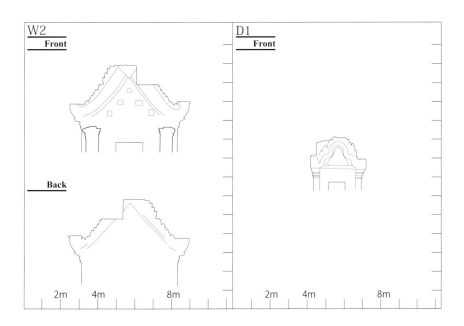

Appendix I: Monument Inventory

I.2.11 Gopura III

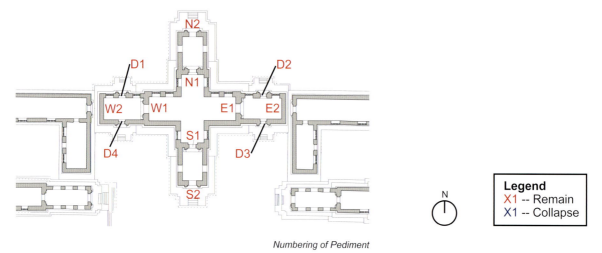

Numbering of Pediment

Legend
X1 -- Remain
X1 -- Collapse

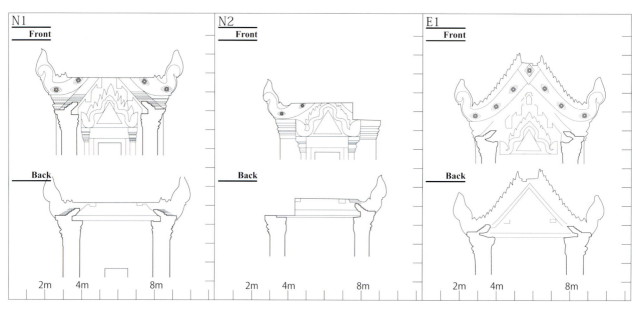

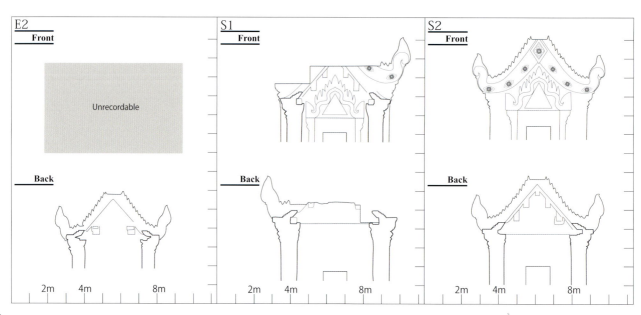

Pediments in Preah Vihear Temple

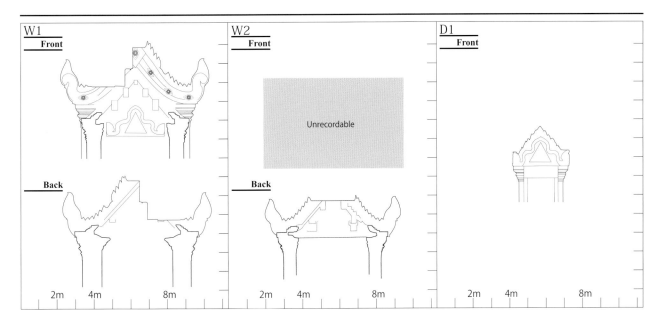
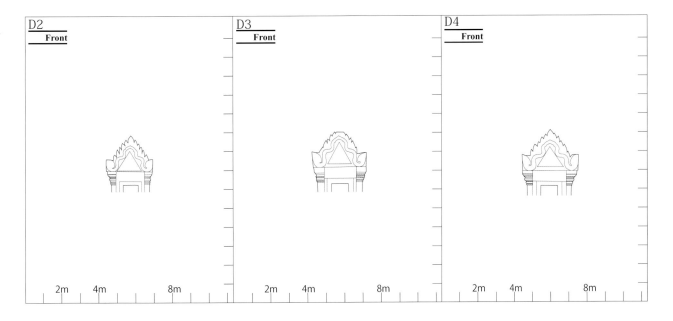

Appx.
41

Appendix I : Monument Inventory

I.2.12 Annex Building H'-I'

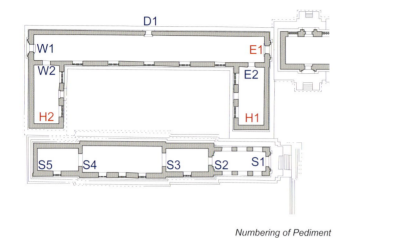

Numbering of Pediment

Legend
X1 -- Remain
X1 -- Collapse

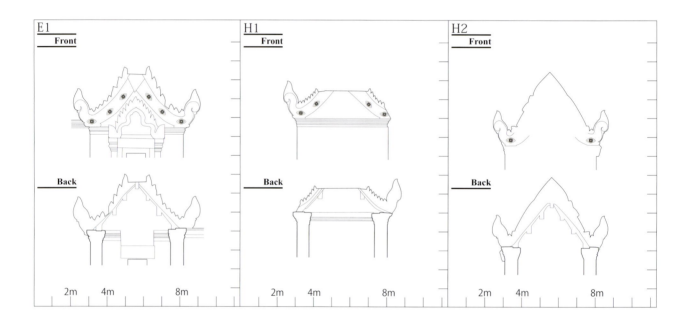

I.2.13 Annex Building H-I

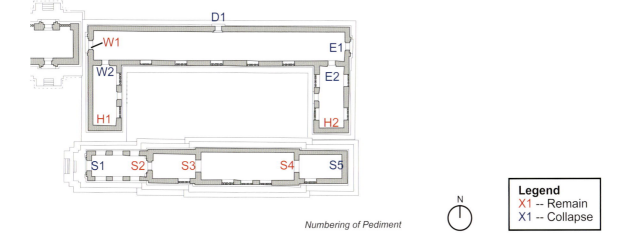

Numbering of Pediment

Legend
X1 -- Remain
X1 -- Collapse

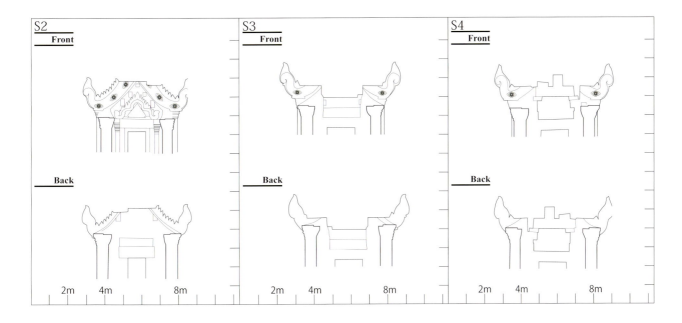

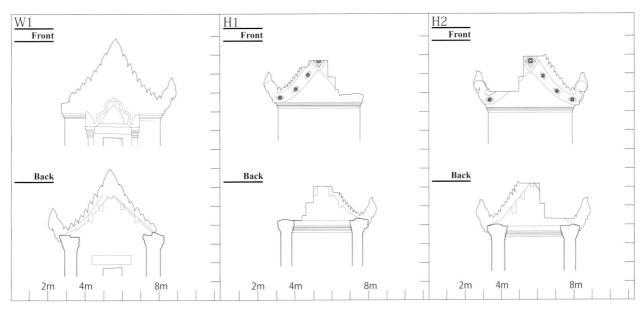

Appx.
43

Appendix I : Monument Inventory

I.2.14 Gopura IV

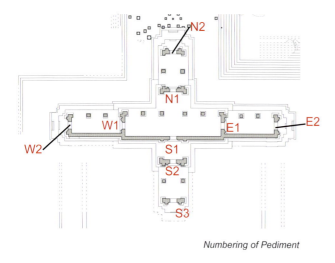

Numbering of Pediment

Legend
X1 -- Remain
X1 -- Collapse

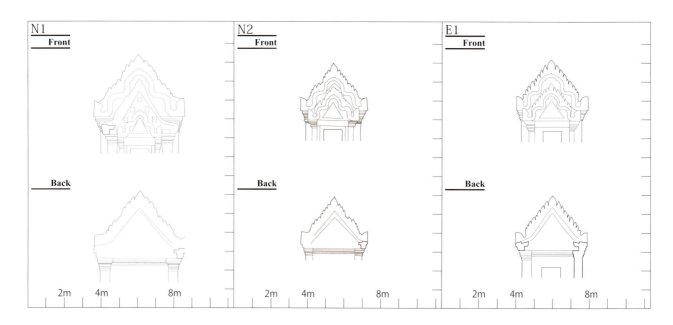

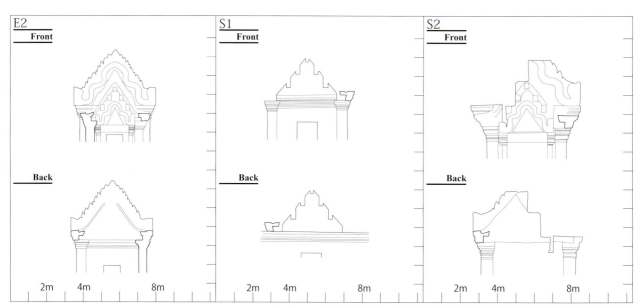

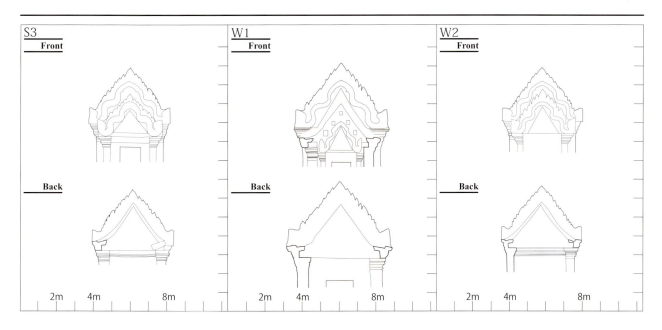

I.2.15 Gopura V

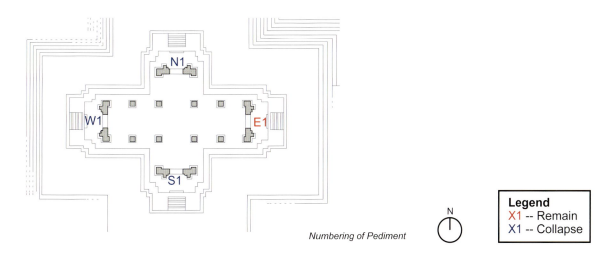

Numbering of Pediment

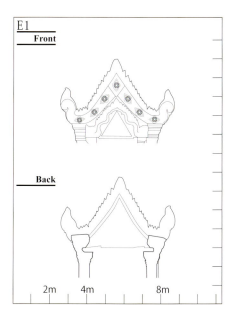

I.3 プレア・ヴィヘア寺院の木造痕跡
Wooden Traces in Preah Vihear Temple

Gopuras and Annex Buildings in Preah Vihear Temple have traces of wooden roof structure. It is considered there were 4 types of roof in this temple, stone masonry roof, wooden roof, a roof of brick work (False Gopura (A)) and a roof of mixture of wooden structure and brick. Also, there are different and unique techniques of joint of wooden structures and stone wall. For the details about wooden roof of Preah Vihear Temple, see Chapter "3.5 Survey of Wood Structure of the Ancient Khmer Ruins and a Chronicle of the Buildings in Preah Vihear Temple" and Chapter "3.7 Restoration of the Roof of Gopura III".

Figure I.3-1 is a key plan of buildings which have traces of wooden structure, starting from "Gopura I" to "Gopura V". The following pages show the inventory of traces of wooden structure in Preah Vihear Temple.

Each item has a drawing of wooden traces, map of trace number and photos of traces. The drawing of wooden trace is baced on the measuring survey of upper wall part of the present building. The dotted line is a supposition by other parts of same building. For some distinguished traces of each temple, we made the reconstructive drawings of wooden structure.

The list of buildings are as follows;

I.3.1 Gopura I
I.3.2 Hall N
I.3.3 Annex Building E
I.3.4 Annex Building F
I.3.5 Gopura II
I.3.6 Gopura III
I.3.7 Annex Building H'-I'
I.3.8 Annex Building H-I
I.3.9 Gopura IV
I.3.10 Gopura V

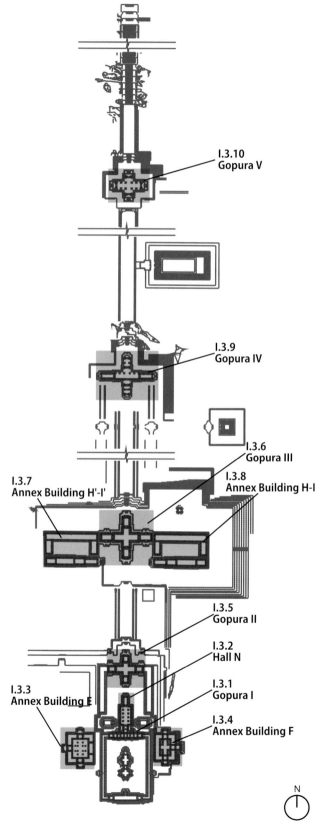

Figure I.3-1 Key Plan

I.3.1 Gopura I

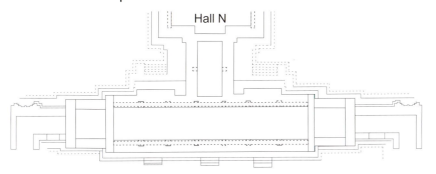

Drawing of Wooden Trace

Legend
— Based on Measurement
···· Supposition

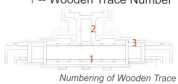

Numbering of Wooden Trace

1   *Overview of wooden traces (from East side)*

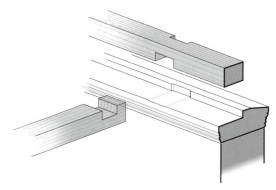

2   *Reconstruction of wooden frames of trace No.1*

3   *Trace No.1 of main room (from East side)*

4   *Trace No.2 of connecting room (from North side)*

5   *Trace No.3 of East side room (from East side)*

Appendix I : Monument Inventory

I.3.2 Hall N

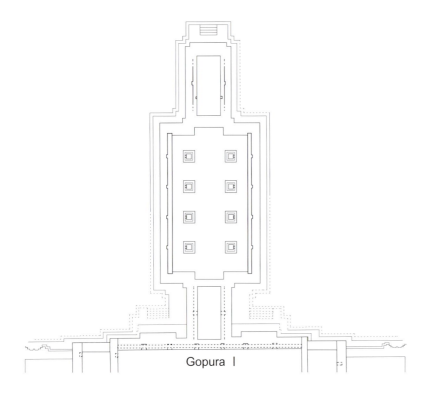
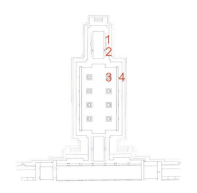

Drawing of Wooden Trace   *Numbering of Wooden Trace*

1   Overview of wooden traces (from Northwest side)   *2   Trace No.1 & No.2 of porch (from South side)*

3   Trace No.1 of porch (from South side)   *4   Trace No.2 of porch (from South side)*

Wooden Traces in Preah Vihear Temple

5   *Trace No.3 on side-face of pillar of main room (from East side)*   6   *Trace No.4 of main room (from North side)*

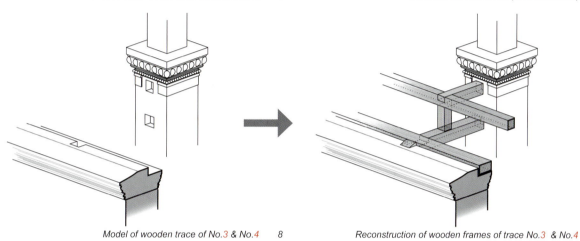

7   *Model of wooden trace of No.3 & No.4*   8   *Reconstruction of wooden frames of trace No.3 & No.4*

I.3.3   Annex Building E

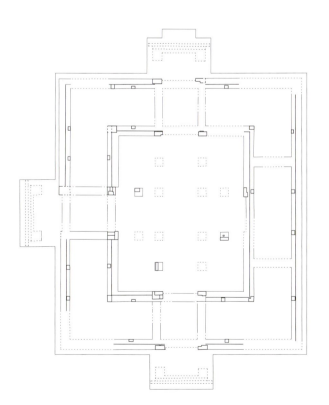
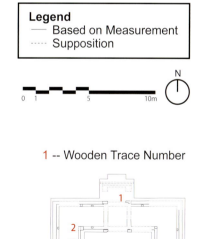

Drawing of Wooden Trace   *Numbering of Wooden Trace*

Appx.
49

Appendix I : Monument Inventory

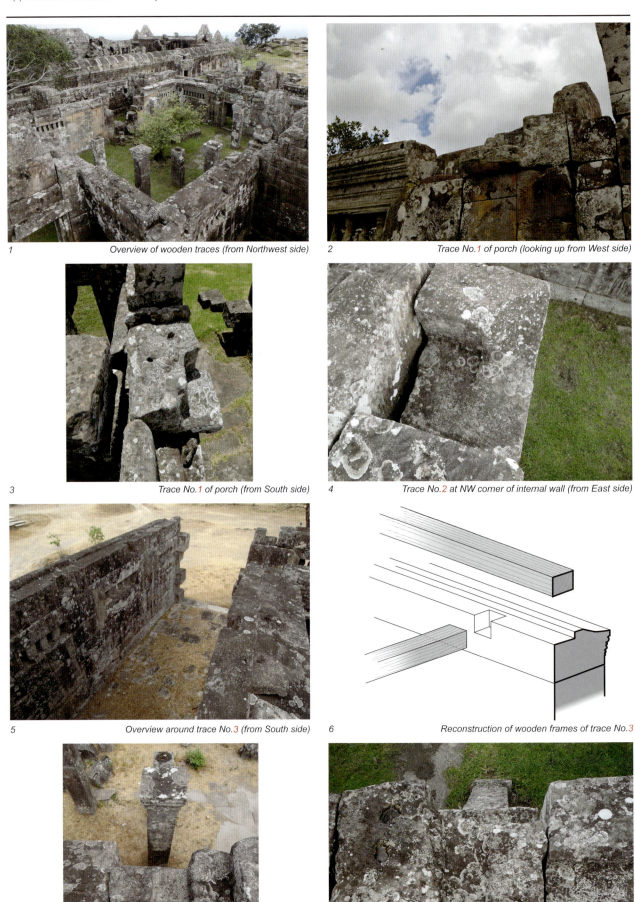

1 Overview of wooden traces (from Northwest side)
2 Trace No.1 of porch (looking up from West side)
3 Trace No.1 of porch (from South side)
4 Trace No.2 at NW corner of internal wall (from East side)
5 Overview around trace No.3 (from South side)
6 Reconstruction of wooden frames of trace No.3
7 Trace No.4 & No.5 in the cross gallery (from West side)
8 Trace No.6 at SW part of the cross gallery (from West side)

Wooden Traces in Preah Vihear Temple

9   Trace No.6 at SW part of cross gallery (from South side)

10   Trace No.7 on the pillar in cross gallery (from South side)

I.3.4   Annex Building F

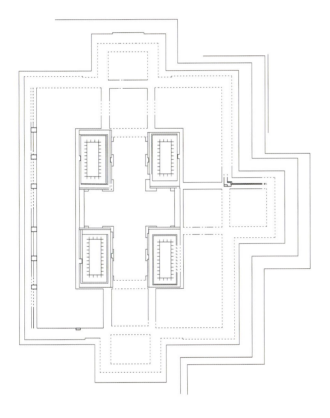

Drawing of Wooden Trace

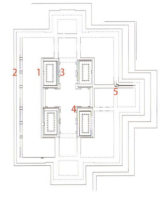

Numbering of Wooden Trace

1   Overview of wooden traces (from Northeast side)

2   Trace No.1 on internal wall (from North side)

Appx.
51

Appendix I : Monument Inventory

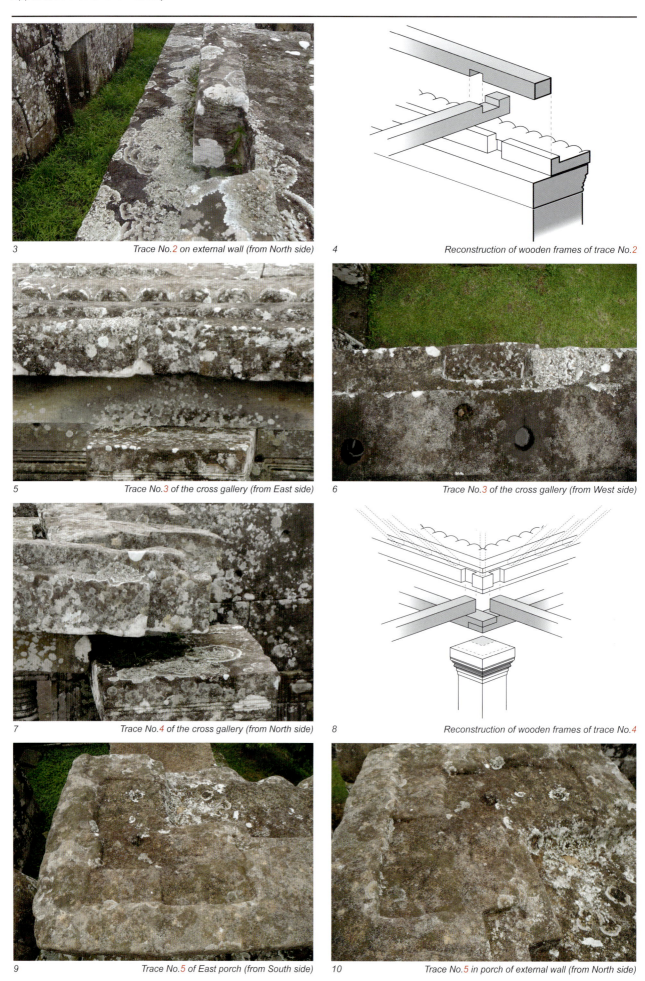

3　　Trace No.2 on external wall (from North side)

4　　Reconstruction of wooden frames of trace No.2

5　　Trace No.3 of the cross gallery (from East side)

6　　Trace No.3 of the cross gallery (from West side)

7　　Trace No.4 of the cross gallery (from North side)

8　　Reconstruction of wooden frames of trace No.4

9　　Trace No.5 of East porch (from South side)

10　　Trace No.5 in porch of external wall (from North side)

Wooden Traces in Preah Vihear Temple

I.3.5 Gopura II

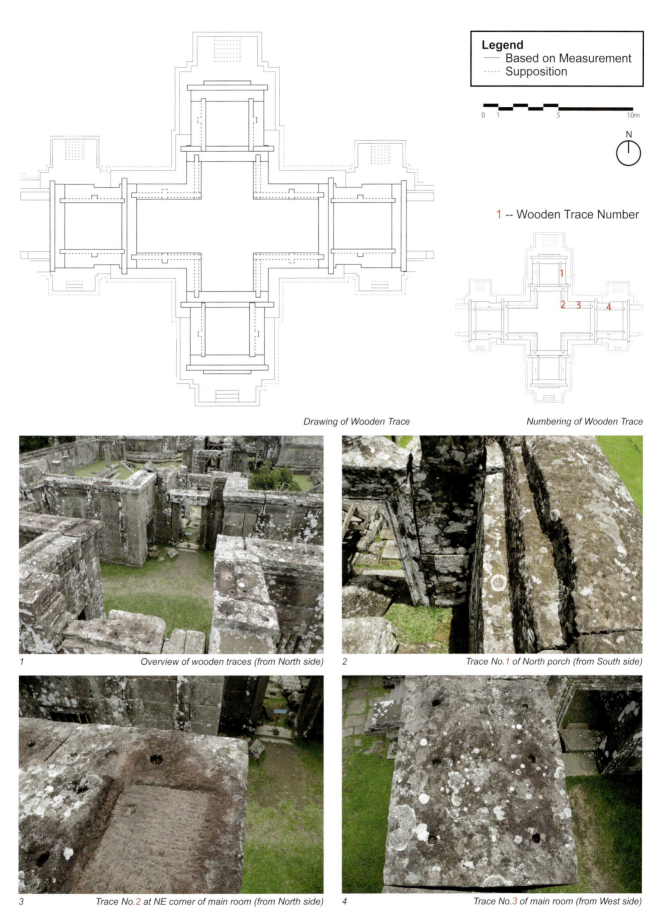

Drawing of Wooden Trace   *Numbering of Wooden Trace*

1   *Overview of wooden traces (from North side)*

2   *Trace No.1 of North porch (from South side)*

3   *Trace No.2 at NE corner of main room (from North side)*

4   *Trace No.3 of main room (from West side)*

Appx.
53

Appendix I : Monument Inventory

5　　　　　　　　　Trace No.4 of East side room (from East side)　　　6　　　　　　Reconstruction of wooden frames of trace No.4

I.3.6　Gopura III

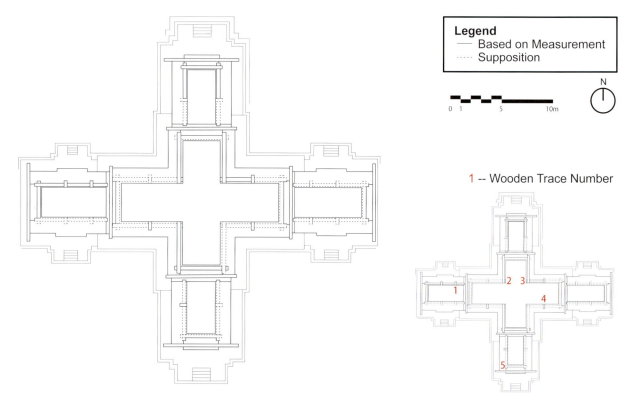

Drawing of Wooden Trace　　　　　　　　　　　Numbering of Wooden Trace

1　　　　　　　　　Overview of wooden traces (from North side)

2　　　　　　　　　Trace No.1 of West side room (from South side)

Wooden Traces in Preah Vihear Temple

3   *Trace No.2 of main room (from West side)*

4   *Trace No.2 of main room (from West side)*

5   *Trace No.3 of main room (from North side)*

6   *Trace No.3 of main room (from West side)*

7   *Trace No.4 of main room (from North side)*

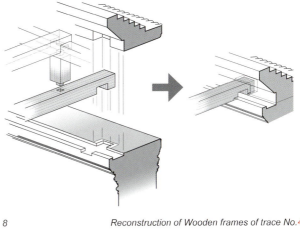
8   *Reconstruction of Wooden frames of trace No.4*

9   *Trace No.5 of South side room (from East side)*

Appx.
55

Appendix I : Monument Inventory

I.3.7   Annex Building H'-I'

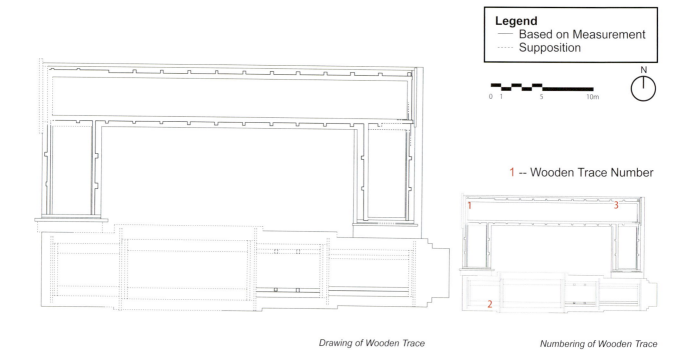

Drawing of Wooden Trace

Numbering of Wooden Trace

1   Overview of wooden traces (from East side)

2   Trace No.1 at NW corner of Northern building (from West side)

3   Trace No.2 of porch of Southern building (from North side)

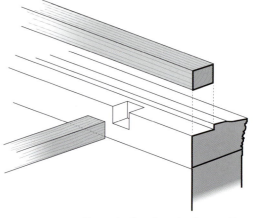

4   Reconstruction of wooden frames of trace No.2

Wooden Traces in Preah Vihear Temple

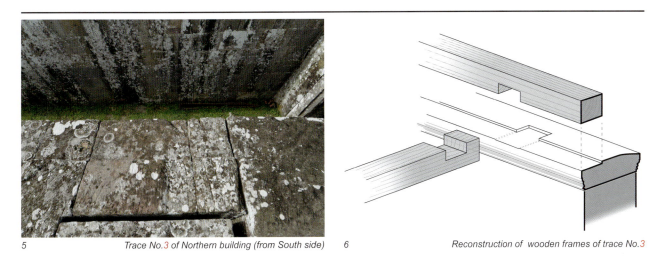

5   *Trace No.3 of Northern building (from South side)*   6   *Reconstruction of wooden frames of trace No.3*

I.3.8   Annex Building H-I

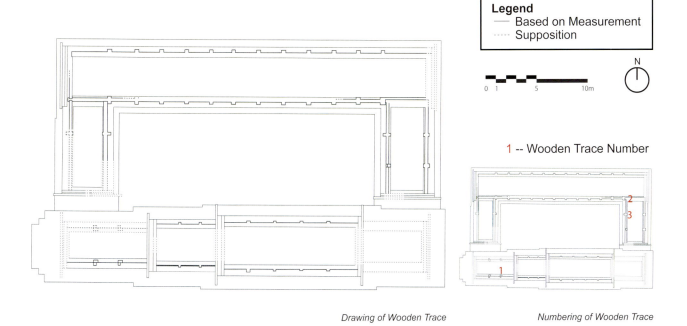

Drawing of Wooden Trace   *Numbering of Wooden Trace*

1   *Overview of wooden traces (from West side)*   2   *Trace No.1 of porch of Southern building (from West side)*

Appx.
57

Appendix I : Monument Inventory

3 *Trace No.1 of porch of Southern building (from West side)*

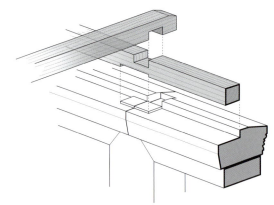

4 *Reconstruction of wooden frames of trace No.1*

5 *Trace No.2 of Northern building (from East side)*

6 *Trace No.3 of East side room of Northern building (from South side)*

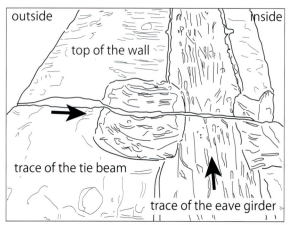

7 *Drawing around trace No.3*

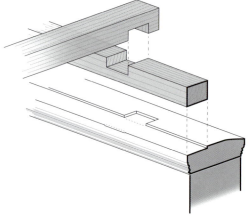

8 *Reconstruction of wooden frames of trace No.3*

Appx.
58

I.3.9 Gopura IV

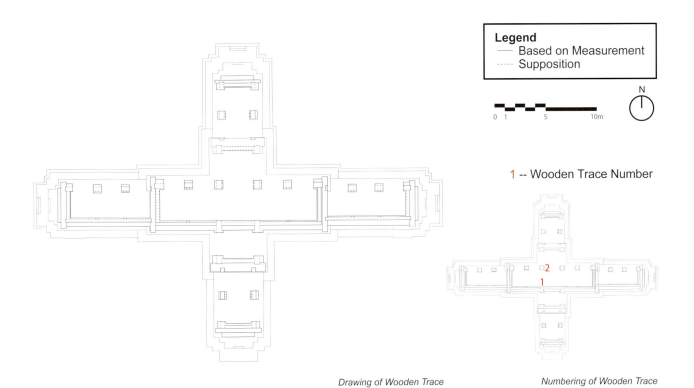

Drawing of Wooden Trace *Numbering of Wooden Trace*

1 Overview of wooden traces (from West side)

2 Trace No.1 of main room (from East side)

3 Trace No.2 on the pillar of main room (from South side)

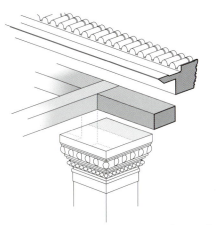

4 Reconstruction of wooden frames of trace No.2

Appendix I : Monument Inventory

I.3.10 Gopura V

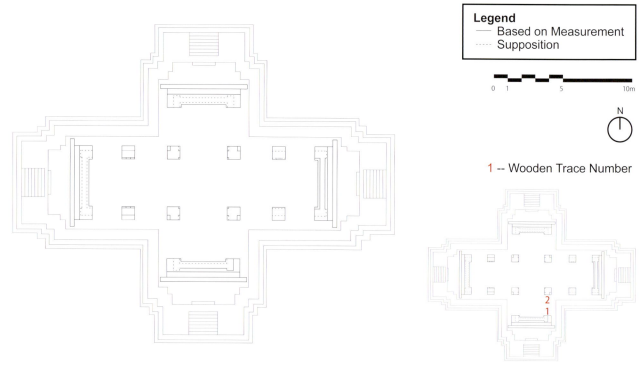

Drawing of Wooden Trace   *Numbering of Wooden Trace*

1   *Overview of wooden traces (from West side)*

2   *Trace No.1 at South end (from North side)*

3   *Trace No.2 on pillar of main room (from Northwest side)*

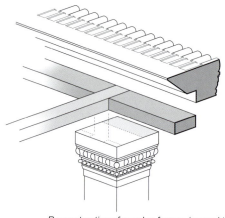

4   *Reconstruction of wooden frames (around trace No.2)*

I.4 その他の寺院のペディメント
Pediments in the Other Temples

In Khmer temples, there are some other examples of pediment which considered to have wooden roof structure. To compare the pediments of Preah Vihear Temple, we investigated pediments of temple buildings that had wooden roofs, especially in Angkor Monuments, Koh Ker Monuments and Phnom Chisor Temple. For the details about Khmer pediments, see Chapter "3.10 Significant Features of the Decorations of the Pediments".

Figure I.4-1 - I.4-6 are the key plan drawings of temples and buildings we investigated. The following pages show the inventory of pediments which had wooden roof structure in Khmer temples.

Each item has a map of temple, pediment number and confronting photos of pediments. For some pediments, we also conducted the measuring survey, which are drawn as elevational drawings. The pediment number is composed by "direction+number from inside". For example, the most inner side pediment of South direction is named as "S1". The elevational drawing is drawn based on the present situation of pediments. It is composed by outline of building shape, wooden traces and decorations.

The list of temples and buildings we surveyed is as follows;
I.4.1 Prasat Thom Temple
: Gopura II, Gopura IV, Rectangle Building, Palace
I.4.2 Prasat Krachap Temple
: Gopura I, Galleries besides Gopura I
I.4.3 Banteay Srei Temple
: Rectangle Buildings in Enclosure I, II
I.4.4 Ta Kev Temple
: Rectangle Buildings in Enclosure I, II
I.4.5 North Khleang
I.4.6 Phnom Chisor Temple : Gopura II, Gopura III

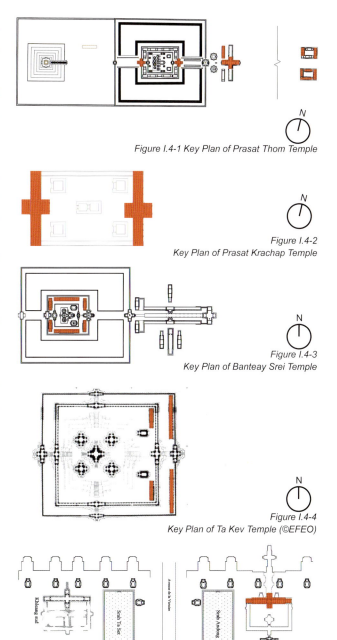

Figure I.4-1 Key Plan of Prasat Thom Temple

Figure I.4-2 Key Plan of Prasat Krachap Temple

Figure I.4-3 Key Plan of Banteay Srei Temple

Figure I.4-4 Key Plan of Ta Kev Temple (©EFEO)

Figure I.4-5 Key Plan of Khleang (©EFEO)

Figure I.4-6 Key Plan of Phnom Chisor Temple (©EFEO)

Appx.
61

Appendix I : Monument Inventory

I.4.1 Prasat Thom Temple : Gopura II

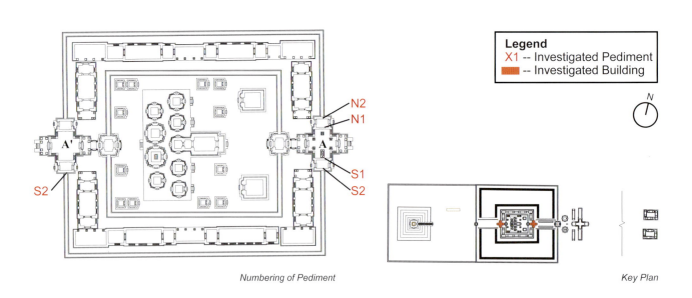

Numbering of Pediment

Key Plan

1	Front view of N1 (Building A)
2	Back view of N1 (Building A)
3	Front view of N2 (Building A)
4	Back view of N2 (Building A)

Pediments in the Other Temples

5   *Front view of S1 (Building A)*   6   *Back view of S1 (Building A)*

7   *Front view of S2 (Building A)*   8   *Back view of S2 (Building A)*

9   *Front view of S2 (Building A')*   10   *Back view of S2 (Building A')*

Appx.

Appendix I : Monument Inventory

Prasat Thom Temple : Gopura IV and Rectangle Building

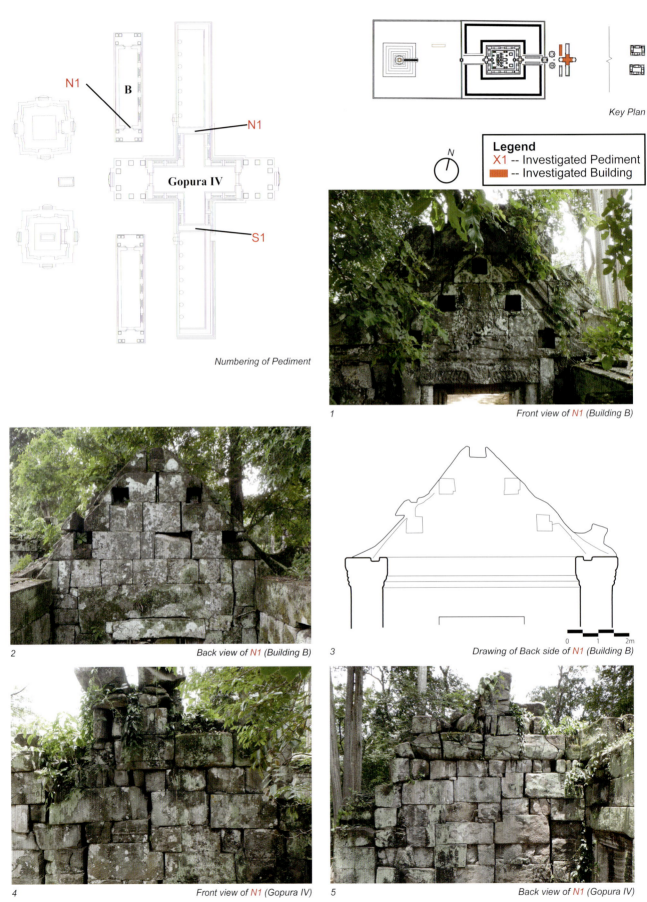

Pediments in the Other Temples

6 *Front view of S1 (Gopura IV)*

7 *Back View of S1 (Gopura IV)*

Prasat Thom Temple : Palace (Annex Building)

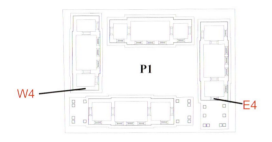

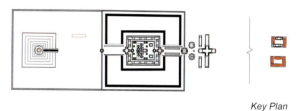
Key Plan

Legend
X1 -- Investigated Pediment
▥ -- Investigated Building

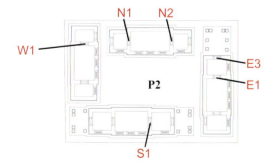
Numbering of Pediment

1 *Front view of W4 (Building P1)*

2 *Back view of W4 (Building P1)*

Appx.
65

Appendix I : Monument Inventory

3　　Front view of E4 (Building P1)　　　4　　Back view of E4 (Building P1)

5　　Front view of W1 (Building P2)　　　6　　Back view of W1 (Building P2)

7　　Front view of N1 (Building P2)　　　8　　Back view of N1 (Building P2)

9　　Front view of N2 (Building P2)　　　10　　Back view of N2 (Building P2)

Pediments in the Other Temples

11   *Front view of E1 (Building P2)*   12   *Back view of E1 (Building P2)*

13   *Front view of E3 (Building P2)*   14   *Back view of E3 (Building P2)*

15   *Front view of S1 (Building P2)*   16   *Back view of S1 (Building P2)*

Appendix I : Monument Inventory

I.4.2 Prasat Krachap Temple : Gopura I, Galleries besides Gopura I

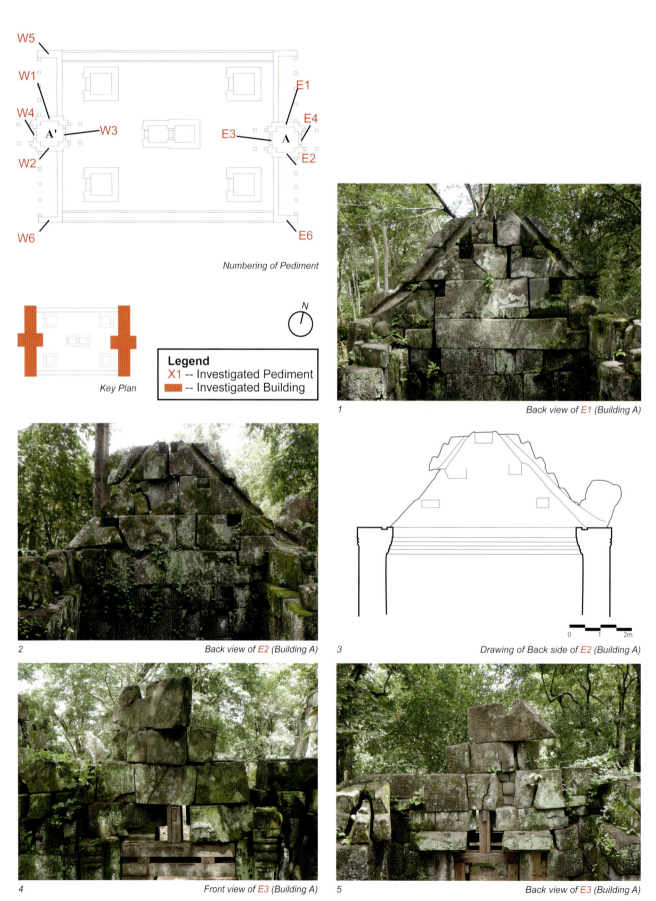

Pediments in the Other Temples

6 Front view of E4 (Building A)

7 Back view of E4 (Building A)

8 Back view of E6 (Building A)

9 Front view of W1 (Building A')

10 Back view of W1 (Building A')

11 Front view of W2 (Building A')

12 Back view of W2 (Building A')

Appx.
69

Appendix I : Monument Inventory

13 Front view of W3 (Building A')
14 Back view of W3 (Building A')
15 Front view of W4 (Building A')
16 Drawing of Front side of W4 (Building A')
17 Back view of W4 (Building A')
18 Drawing of Back side of W4 (Building A')
19 Back view of W5 (Building A')
20 Back view of W6 (Building A')

I.4.3 Banteay Srei Temple : Rectangle Buildings in Enclorsure II

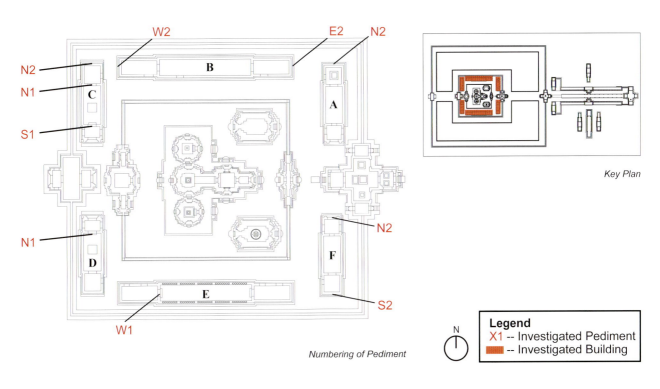

Numbering of Pediment

Key Plan

Legend
X1 -- Investigated Pediment
-- Investigated Building

1   *Front view of N2 (Building A)*   2   *Back view of N2 (Building A)*

3   *Front view of E2 (Building B)*   4   *Back view of E2 (Building B)*

Appendix I : Monument Inventory

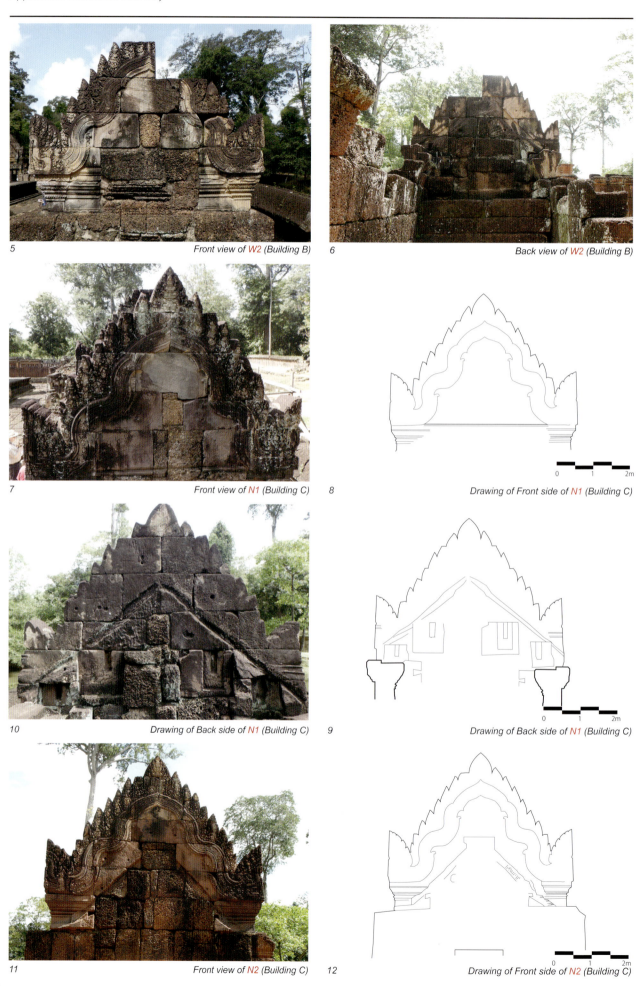

5 Front view of W2 (Building B)
6 Back view of W2 (Building B)
7 Front view of N1 (Building C)
8 Drawing of Front side of N1 (Building C)
10 Drawing of Back side of N1 (Building C)
9 Drawing of Back side of N1 (Building C)
11 Front view of N2 (Building C)
12 Drawing of Front side of N2 (Building C)

Pediments in the Other Temples

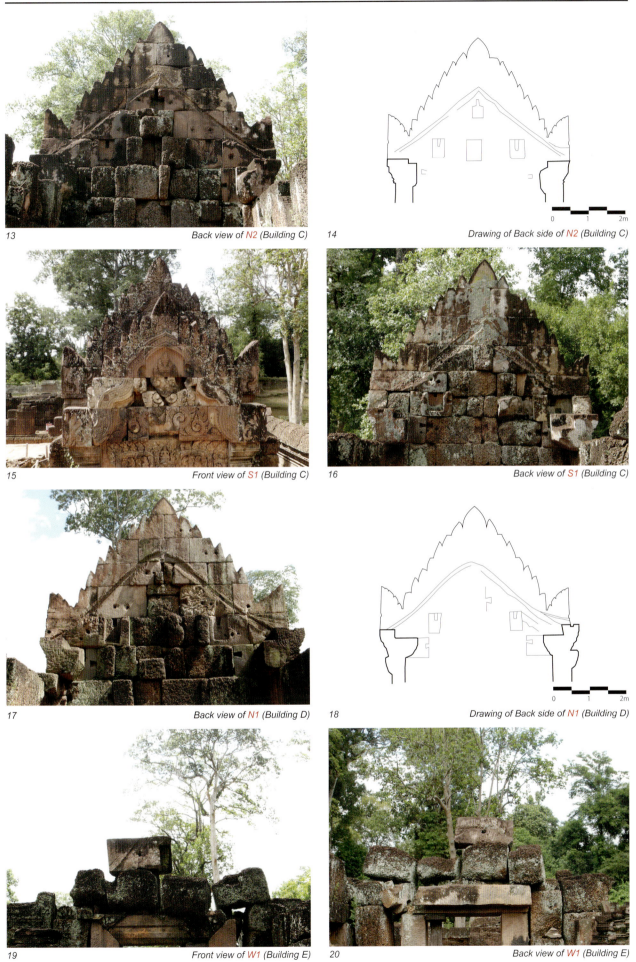

13 Back view of N2 (Building C)
14 Drawing of Back side of N2 (Building C)
15 Front view of S1 (Building C)
16 Back view of S1 (Building C)
17 Back view of N1 (Building D)
18 Drawing of Back side of N1 (Building D)
19 Front view of W1 (Building E)
20 Back view of W1 (Building E)

Appx.
73

Appendix I : Monument Inventory

21 Front view of N2 (Building F)
22 Back view of N2 (Building F)
23 Front view of S2 (Building F)
24 Back view of S2 (Building F)

I.4.4 Ta Kev Temple : Rectangle Buildings in Enclosure I, II

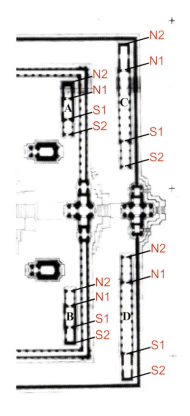

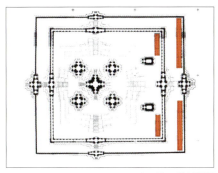

Key Plan (©EFEO)

Numbering of Pediment (©EFEO)

1   *Front view of N1 (Building A)*

2   *Back view of N1 (Building A)*

3   *Front view of N2 (Building A)*

4   *Back view of N2 (Building A)*

Appendix I : Monument Inventory

5   *Front view of S1 (Building A)*   6   *Back view of S1 (Building A)*

7   *Front view of S2 (Building A)*   8   *Back view of S2 (Building A)*

9   *Front view of N1 (Building B)*   10   *Back view of N1 (Building B)*

11   *Front view of N2 (Building B)*   12   *Back view of N2 (Building B)*

Pediments in the Other Temples

13 Front view of S1 (Building B)
14 Back view of S1 (Building B)
15 Front view of S2 (Building B)
16 Back view of S2 (Building B)
17 Front view of N1 (Building C)
18 Back view of N1 (Building C)
19 Front view of N2 (Building C)
20 Back view of N2 (Building C)

Appendix I : Monument Inventory

21 Front view of S1 (Building C)   22 Back view of S1 (Building C)
23 Front view of S2 (Building C)   24 Back view of S2 (Building C)
25 Front view of N1 (Building D)   26 Back view of N1 (Building D)
27 Front view of N2 (Building D)   28 Back view of N2 (Building D)

Pediments in the Other Temples

29 Front view of S1 (Building D)

30 Back view of S1 (Building D)

31 Front view of S2 (Building D)

32 Back view of S2 (Building D)

I.4.5 North Khleang

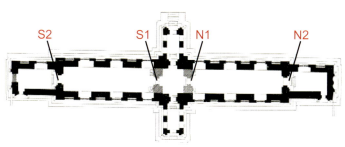
Numbering of Pediment (©EFEO)

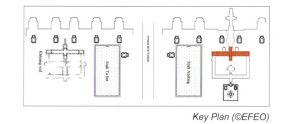
Key Plan (©EFEO)

Legend
X1 -- Investigated Pediment
-- Investigated Building

1 Front view of N1

2 Back view of N2

Appx.
79

Appendix I : Monument Inventory

3　　　　　　　　　　　　　　　　　　Front view of S1

4　　　　　　　　　　　　　　　　　　Back view of S2

I.4.6　Phnom Chisor Temple : Gopura II, Gopura III

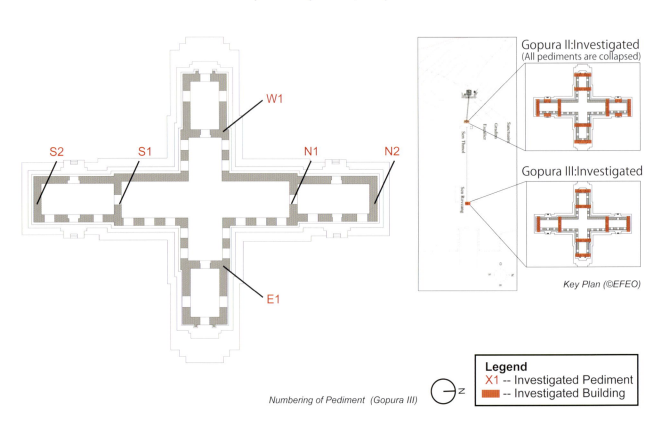

Numbering of Pediment (Gopura III)

Key Plan (©EFEO)

Legend
X1 -- Investigated Pediment
▬ -- Investigated Building

1　　　　　　　　　　　　　　　Front view of N1 (Gopura III)

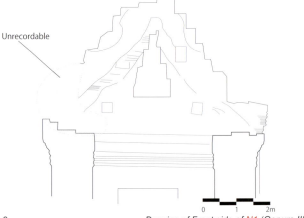
2　　　　　　　　　　　Drawing of Front side of N1 (Gopura III)

Pediments in the Other Temples

3 Back view of N1 (Gopura III)

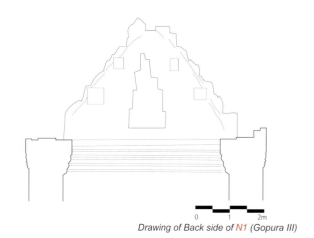
4 Drawing of Back side of N1 (Gopura III)

5 Front view of N2 (Gopura III)

6 Back view of N2 (Gopura III)

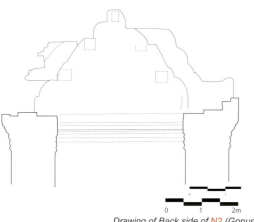
7 Drawing of Back side of N2 (Gopura III)

8 Front view of E1 (Gopura III)

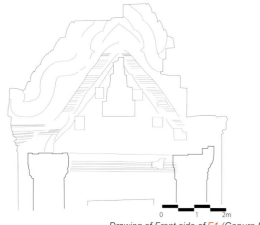
9 Drawing of Front side of E1 (Gopura III)

Appx.
81

Appendix I : Monument Inventory

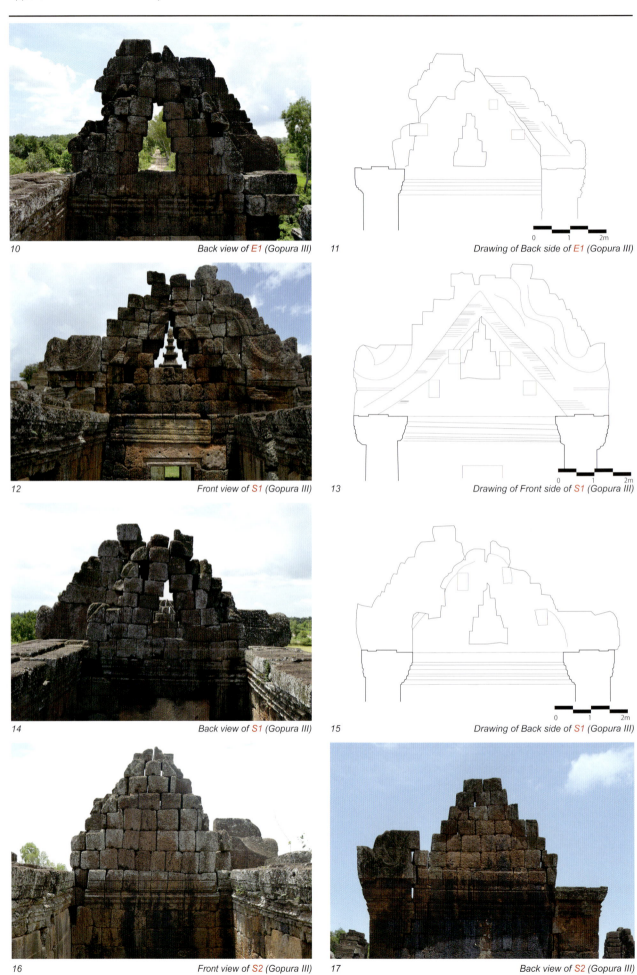

10 Back view of E1 (Gopura III)
11 Drawing of Back side of E1 (Gopura III)
12 Front view of S1 (Gopura III)
13 Drawing of Front side of S1 (Gopura III)
14 Back view of S1 (Gopura III)
15 Drawing of Back side of S1 (Gopura III)
16 Front view of S2 (Gopura III)
17 Back view of S2 (Gopura III)

Pediments in the Other Temples

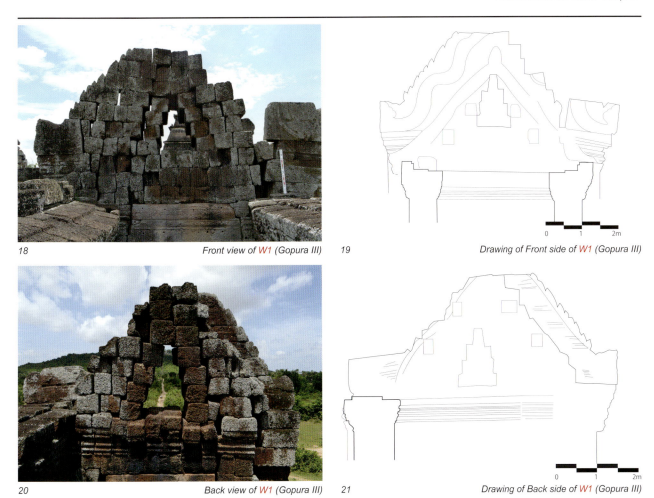

18 Front view of W1 (Gopura III)
19 Drawing of Front side of W1 (Gopura III)
20 Back view of W1 (Gopura III)
21 Drawing of Back side of W1 (Gopura III)

I.5 その他の寺院の木造痕跡
Wooden Traces in the Other Temples

In Khmer temples, there are some other examples of buildings with wooden traces which used to have wooden roof structure. To compare the wooden techniques of Preah Vihear Temple, we investigated the other temple buildings that had wooden roofs, especially in Angkor Monuments, Koh Ker Monuments and Phnom Chisor Temple. For the details about wooden roofs, see Chapter 3.5 "Survey of Wood Structure of the Ancient Khmer Ruins and a Chronicle of the Buildings in Preah Vihear Temple" and Chapter 3.7 "Restoration of the Roof of Gopura III".

Figure I.5-1 - I.5-8 are the key plan drawings of temples and buildings that we investigated. The following pages show the inventory of wooden traces which had wooden roof structure in Khmer temples.

Each item has a drawing of wooden traces, map of trace number and photos of traces. The drawing of wooden traces is baced on the measuring survey of the upper wall part of the present building. The dotted line is a supposition by other parts of same building. For some distinguished traces of each temple, we made the reconstructive drawings of wooden structure.

The list of temples and buildings we surveyed is as follows;
I.5.1 Prasat Thom Temple
 : Rectangle Building
I.5.2 Prasat Krachap Temple : Galleries besides Gopura I
I.5.3 Banteay Srei Temple : Rectangle Buildings
I.5.4 Pre Rup Temple : Rectangle Buildings
I.5.5 East Mebon Temple : Rectangle Buildings
I.5.6 Ta Kev Temple : Rectangle Building
I.5.7 South Khleang
I.5.8 Phnom Chisor Temple : Gopura III

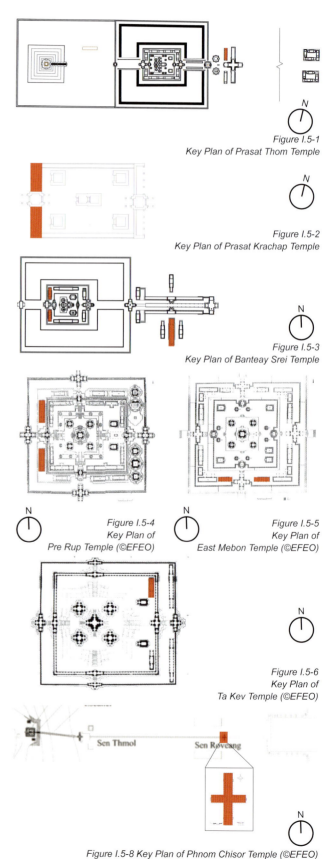

Figure I.5-1 Key Plan of Prasat Thom Temple

Figure I.5-2 Key Plan of Prasat Krachap Temple

Figure I.5-3 Key Plan of Banteay Srei Temple

Figure I.5-4 Key Plan of Pre Rup Temple (©EFEO)

Figure I.5-5 Key Plan of East Mebon Temple (©EFEO)

Figure I.5-6 Key Plan of Ta Kev Temple (©EFEO)

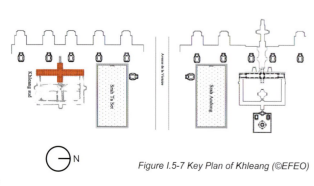

Figure I.5-7 Key Plan of Khleang (©EFEO)

Figure I.5-8 Key Plan of Phnom Chisor Temple (©EFEO)

Appx.
84

Wooden Traces in the Other Temples

I.5.1   Prasat Thom Temple ：Rectangle Building

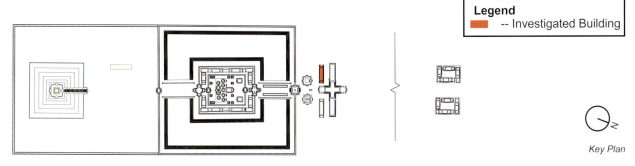

Key Plan

＊ We conducted the measurement survey partly.

1   *Wooden beam trace*　　2   *Wooden beam trace*　　3   *Trace of rafter edge (with roof tiles edge)*

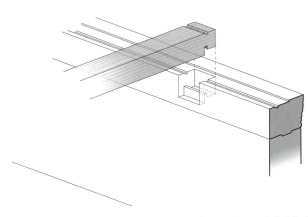

4   *Trace of rafters edge (with roof tiles edge)*　　5   *Recinstruction of wooden frames (Rectangle Building)*

Appx.
85

Appendix I : Monument Inventory

I.5.2 Prasat Krachap Temple : Galleries besides Gopura I

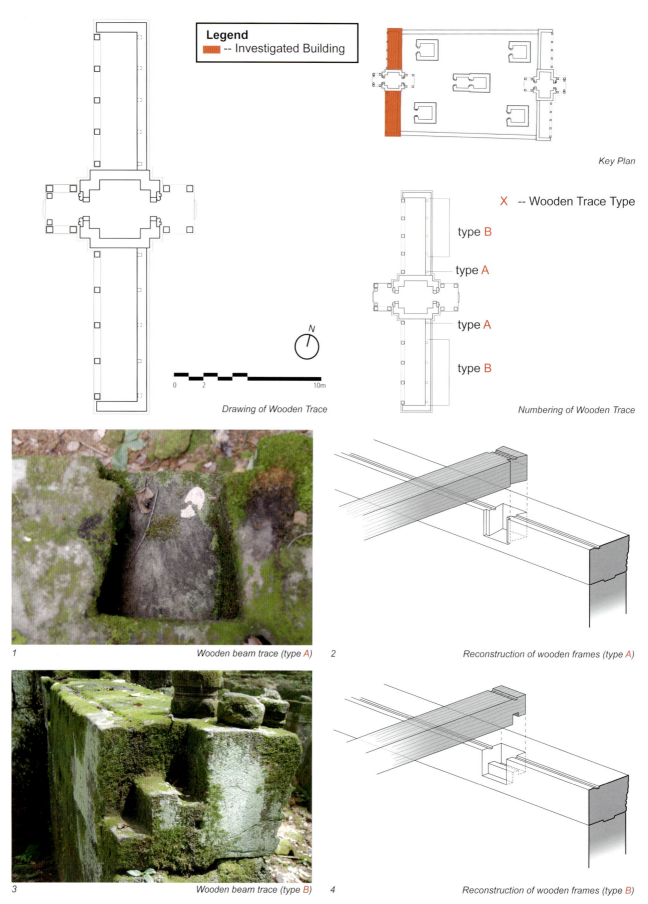

Key Plan

Drawing of Wooden Trace

Numbering of Wooden Trace

1 *Wooden beam trace (type A)*
2 *Reconstruction of wooden frames (type A)*
3 *Wooden beam trace (type B)*
4 *Reconstruction of wooden frames (type B)*

Wooden Traces in the Other Temples

5 *Trace of root tiles edge*

6 *Trace of rafters edge (with roof tiles edge)*

I.5.3 Banteay Srei Temple : Rectangle Buildings

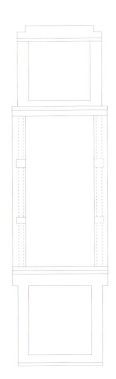

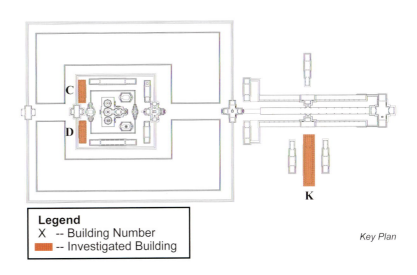
Key Plan

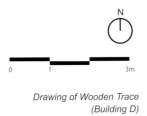
Drawing of Wooden Trace (Building D)

1 *Overview of wooden traces (Building D)*

Appx.
87

Appendix I: Monument Inventory

2 *Wooden beam trace (Building D)*

3 *Wooden trace (Building D)*

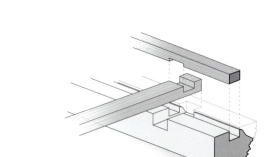

4 *Reconstruction of wooden frames before alteration (Building D)*

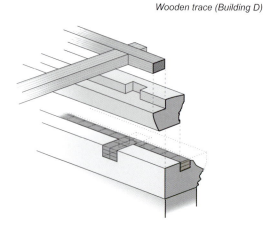

5 *Reconstruction of wooden frames after alteration (Building D)*

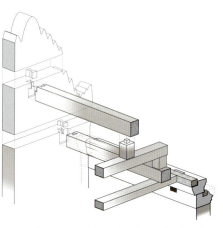

6 *Reconstruction of wooden frames after alteration (Building D)*

7 *Overview of wooden traces (Building C)*

8 *Wooden beam trace (Building K)*

9 *Wooden beam trace (Building K)*

Wooden Traces in the Other Temples

I.5.4 Pre Rup Temple : Rectangle Buildings

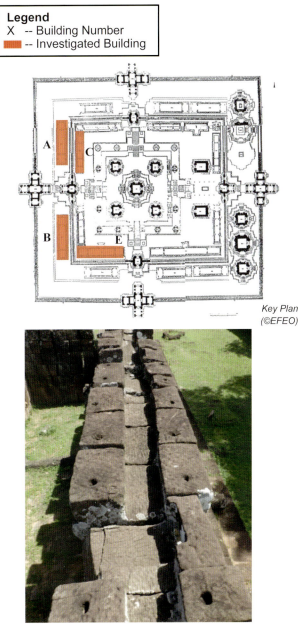

Key Plan
(©EFEO)

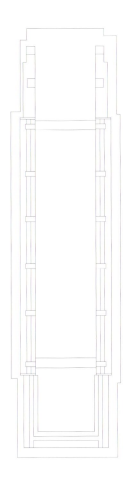

Drawing of Wooden Trace (Building B)

1 *Overview of wooden eave girder traces (Building A)*

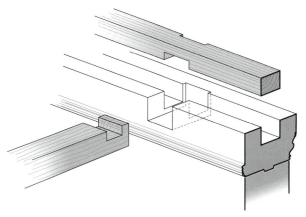

2 *Wooden beam trace (Building A)*   3 *Reconstruction of wooden frames (Building A)*

Appx.
89

Appendix I : Monument Inventory

4   Wooden trace (Building B)

5   Edge of ridge purlin trace (Building B)

6   Edge of ridge purlin trace (Building B)

7   Overview of wooden traces (Building C)

8   Wooden beam and eave girder trace (Building E)

9   Wooden eave girders trace (Building E)

I.5.5 East Mebon Temple : Rectangle Buildings

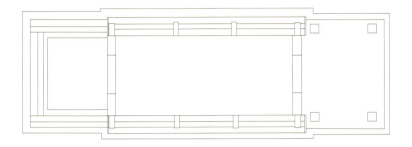

Drawing of Wooden Trace (Building E)

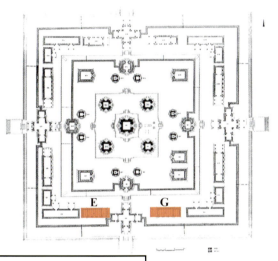

Key Plan (©EFEO)

Legend
X -- Building Number
▬ -- Investigated Building

2 *Wooden beam and eave girder trace (Building E)*

3 *Wooden trace (Building E)*

4 *Wooden trace (Building E)*

1 *Overview of wooden traces (Building E)*

Appx.
91

Appendix I : Monument Inventory

5 *Edge of ridge purlin trace (Building G)*

6 *Edge of ridge purlin trace (Building G)*

7 *Overview of wooden traces (Building G)*

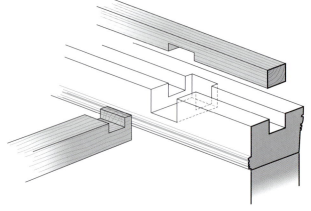

8 *Reconstruction of wooden frames (Building G)*

Appx.
92

I.5.6 Ta Kev Temple : Rectangle Building

Key Plan(©EFEO)

1 — Trace of rafter edge (with roof tiles edge)

2 — Wooden trace in porch

3 — Wooden trace in porch

4 — Wooden trace in main room

5 — Wooden trace in main room

Appendix I : Monument Inventory

I.5.7 South Khleang

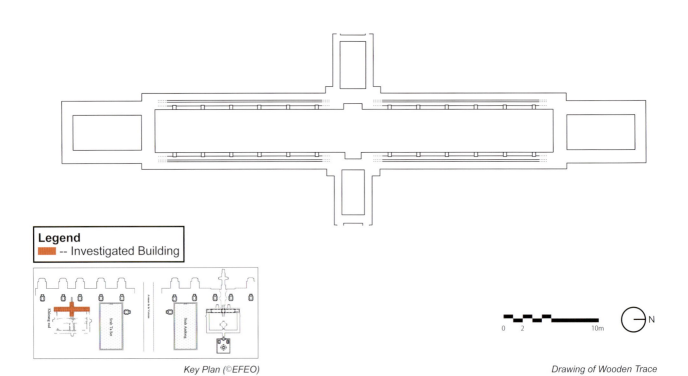

Key Plan (©EFEO)

Drawing of Wooden Trace

1   *Overview of South part in main room (from North side)*

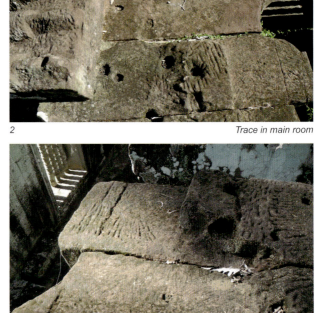

2   *Trace in main room*

4   *Connection of beam-and-girder trace and roofing tiles*

Wooden Traces in the Other Temples

I.5.8 Phnom Chisor Temple : Gopura III

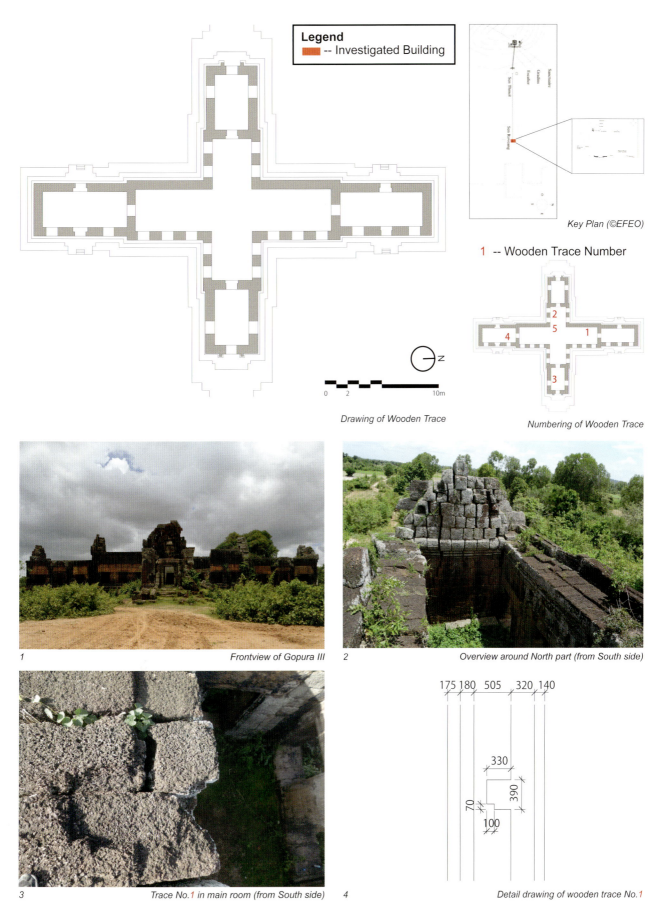

Appx.
95

Appendix I : Monument Inventory

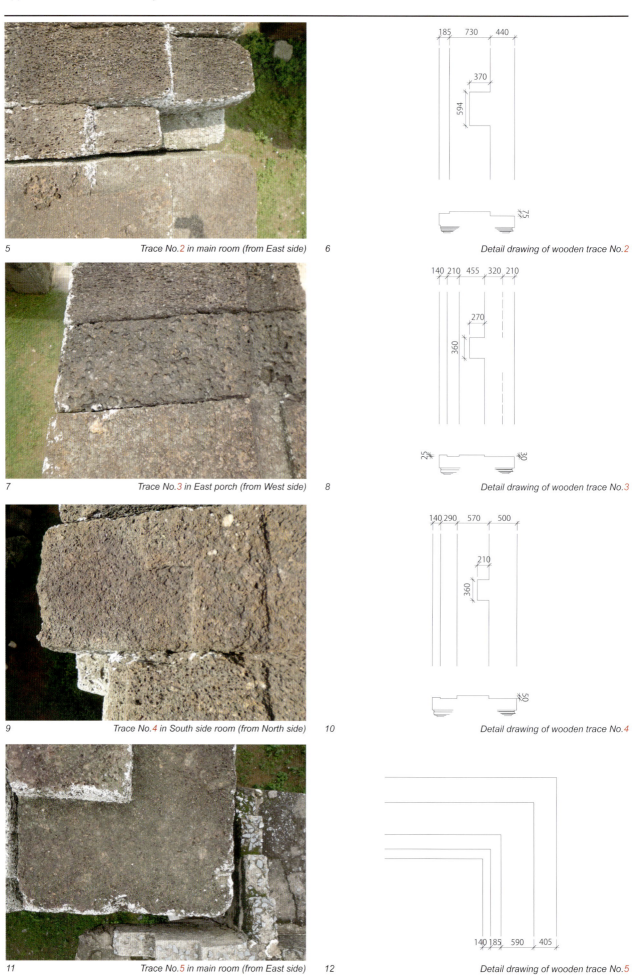

5   *Trace No.2 in main room (from East side)*   6   *Detail drawing of wooden trace No.2*

7   *Trace No.3 in East porch (from West side)*   8   *Detail drawing of wooden trace No.3*

9   *Trace No.4 in South side room (from North side)*   10   *Detail drawing of wooden trace No.4*

11   *Trace No.5 in main room (from East side)*   12   *Detail drawing of wooden trace No.5*

Appendix II
付章 II

Measuring and Drawing Policies and Methods in Preah Vihear Temple
プレア・ヴィヘア寺院における実測・作図の方針と方法

II.1 測量と図面作成の方針と方法
Measuring and Drawing Policies and Methods

石塚　充雅
ISHIZUKA Mitsumasa

II.1.1 実測の概要

2007年から2011年にかけて進められた前回の研究事業に引き続き，今回の研究事業においても遺構の正確な記録を目的とした実測調査及び図面作成を実施している。2012年よりプレア・ヴィヘア寺院にて実施している調査では，前回と同様，建設完成時の姿をできる限り正確に復原するために，GPS及びTPSを利用して測量を行い，そのデータを基に図面を作成した。

加えて，今回の調査では，現状を正確に記録するために，3D測量も同時に実施している。また，そのデータを利用して，崩壊の状況が著しい遺構及び木造屋根構造解明のための木造痕跡の調査対象となっている遺構に対して優先的に現状図面を作成している。

なお，立面図および断面図の作成に関しては，測量データにもとづき，細部装飾を含めてチャン・ヴィタロン氏が描画を担当した。

本稿では，本寺院で実施した測量及び図面の作図方法についての概要を記載する。

II.1.1 Outline of Measuring Work

Following the previous project study implemented from 2007-2011, in this study project we have continued the measuring and drawing for the purpose of the accurate recording of the monuments. In this survey at Preah Vihear Temple from 2012 as is the case in previous study we have implemented the measuring by using GPS and TPS for recapturing the original appearance of the buildings at the time of initial construction as much as possible and the drawing based on the result of measuring data.

In addition, in this study project, we also have implemented 3D measurement for recording the correct present condition. By using this data, we have implemented the drawing of the present condition in priority to the studies of ruins in a collapsed condition, and the ruins for study of wooden trace for clarification of the previous wooden roofing.

Furthermore, the drawings of elevation and section with the ornamental details are implemented by Mr. CHAN Vitharong based on the measuring data.

In this paper we provide an overview of the measuring and drawing methods for this temple.

Appx.

II.2　TPS 及び GPS による実測調査方法
Process of the Measuring by Total Station and GPS

石塚　充雅
ISHIZUKA Mitsumasa

II.2.1　使用した機材
本測量において使用した測量器材を以下に記載する。

・TPS…	TCR1205
	TCR1103

・GPS… 基準局	アンテナ　ATX1230 GG	
	コントローラー　RX1250X	
移動局	アンテナ　AX1202GG	
	コントローラー　RX1210T	

II.2.2　座標系の設定

　座標系に関しては，2通りの座標系を用意した。世界的に一般的に利用されている UTM 座標系そしてプレア・ヴィヘア寺院独自の座標系である。

　このように2通りの座標系を用意した理由は UTM 座標系が全世界を60等分して球面上に位置している全ての位置情報を一律に平面へと変換する図法であるため，距離及び方位に関しての補正が多くかかってしまう図法だからである。距離に関して言えば本図法については中央経線上にて最大99.96%程度の補正がある。また，方位については UTM 座標系の地図に見られる北は「地図上の北」「grid north」と言われており，「真北」「true north」とは異なるものとして扱われている。本調査の目的のうちの一つが建築計画の復原であることから，プレア・ヴィヘア寺院の建築計画を分析する際にはこれらの補正のかかってしまう要素を排除するため独自の座標系を使用する。またその一方で，広域に広がる寺院，地形等との関係を分析する際には，UTM座標系を使用する。

　以下に UTM 座標系と独自の座標系の設定を表記する。

II.2.1 Measurement Equipment
We are using the following measurement equipment:

・TPS…	TCR1205
	TCR1103

・GPS…Base Station	antenna　ATX1230 GG	
	controller　RX1250X	
Rover	antenna　AX1202GG	
	controller　RX1210T	

II.2.2 Coordinate System Setting

　We prepare two types of coordinate system settings for making the plan: UTM coordinate system used widely in the world, and the independent coordinate system of Preah Vihear Temple.

　The reason for using these two coordinate systems is that the distance and orientation are corrected in the UTM coordinate system. In the UTM coordinate system the earth are divided between 80°S and 84°N latitude into sixty zones and projected to a flat surface across the board. In this coordinate system, there is the correction factor of about max 99.96% of the distance at the central meridian, and the north in the UTM coordinate system named "grid north" and treated distinctively from "true north".

　One purpose of this survey is to assist in restoring the original design. When we analyze the original design of Preah Vihear Temple, we use the independent coordinate system to eliminate the element correction as stated above. On the other hand, for analyzing the relationship to other temples or topography or something widely arranged, we use the UTM coordinate system.

　We will show the setting of the UTM coordinate system and independent coordinate system of Preah Vihear Temple below.

Figure II.2-1 Coordinate system (UTM-48)

Figure II.2-2 Coordinate system (Preah Vihear Temple)

II.2.3 基準点の設置

　基準点を作成する際にはGPS及びトータルステーション（以下，TPSとする）を使用した。

　手順としては，まずプレア・ヴィヘア寺院の位置を定める基準となる点1点を作成し，GPSを使用し観測を行うスタティック測量を約2時間行った。Leicaを使用した場合のスタティック測量は水平方向3mm+1ppm，垂直方向6mm+1ppmの精度で測量を行うことができる。この後，Geoscience Australiaが運用しているAUSPOS（URL：http://www.ga.gov.au/earth-monitoring/geodesy/auspos-online-gps-processing-service.html）を利用してデータ解析を行い，その点を基準点として使用した。本サービスではデータを送付すると全世界に400点以上分布しているIGS（国際GNSSサービス）基準点及びIGSによる衛星軌道情報[1]を利用して送付したデータを解析する。民生用のGPSでは500km以上までしか解析できないため，その範囲内に基準点が存在しない場合，これまでは測量をそもそも行うことができなかった。しかし今後本サービスを利用すれば，基準点が近傍に存在しない遺構についても，測量を行っていくことができるだろう。

　その後，この点から環状に閉合するようGPSにて測量を行い，基準点を設置していった。その際には，20～30分の短縮スタティックにより測量を行っ

II.2.3 Installation of Base Points

　We have used GPS and Total Station (TPS) for making base points.

　First, we made a base point for the basis of the position of Preah Vihear Temple, and measured by GPS using static positioning with observation times of about two hour. Using static positioning by GPS 1200 series (Leica) assures us measurement accuracy about 3mm+1ppm for the horizontal and 6mm+1ppm for the vertical. After measurement, we requested an analysis of this result of measurement to AUSPOS (URL: http://www.ga.gov.au/earth-monitoring/geodesy/auspos-online-gps-processing-service.html) managed by Geoscience Australia. We use this result of analysis as the base point of Preah Vihear Temple. This service analyzes by both the IGS Stations Network (International GNSS Service) setting in about 400point in the world and the IGS product range1). In the past, we had not been able to do measurement work if we did not have a base point in 500km, because consumer GPS baseline analyze software is capable of analyzing GPS Data until about 500km. But for the future, if this service is available, we will be able to measure monuments without a known base point near the place to survey.

　In the next step, we made base points from the point made by AUSPOS become the measuring line between the points to closure circularly measured by GPS uses short static positioning

た。Leica GPS1200シリーズを使用した場合の短縮スタティック測量は水平方向5mm+1ppm，垂直方向10mm+1ppmである。本手法により計6点の基準点を設置した。

第1～第2伽藍周辺においてはGPSによって設置した基準点を使用し，TPSにてトラバースを組み，基準点を設置していった。本手法により設置した基準点は計17点である。

これらの基準点から，TPSにて各部の測量を行った。

II.2.4 各部の測量方法

TPSを使用した測量では，器械点から対象物まで直接目視できる場合については対象物を直接測量した。一方，器械点から対象物を直接測量することができない場合については，GPR121もしくはGMP111-0といったプリズムを使用し，間接的に対象物の位置を測量した。

この際に測量する点は比較的残存状態がいい箇所のみである。しかも原則的には建物各面に対し基座，壁面等の中から一辺を選択し数点取るのみとした。また，合わせて中心軸上に位置する測点についても測定した。それ以外の箇所に関しては残存状態のいい個所を選択し，コンベックス，曲尺を使用し，測量を行った。

with observation times of about 20-30minutes. Using short static positioning by GPS 1200 series (Leica) assures us measurement accuracy about 5mm+1ppm for the horizontal and 10mm+1ppm for the vertical. We set a total of 6 points by this process.

Around the Complex I, II, we made the base points from the points set by GPS and used TPS to make the traverse. We set a total of 17 points by this process.

We measured each point of monument from these base points or moving the instrument point several times by TPS.

II.2.4 Method of Measuring Monuments

In the case of measuring by TPS, if it is possible to see the point directly from the TPS on the instrument points, we measured the point directly by TPS. If it is impossible to see the point directly, we measured the point indirectly by TPS with prism GPR121 or GMP111-0.

For measuring by TPS, only good condition monument parts are selected because the purpose of this measurement is for making the plan for restoring the original design. Basically, we select one good condition element (wall, basement etc.) from the elements of each side of the monument. In addition, we also measure the points of the central parts of each monument. For other parts, we measured good condition parts of each monument using tape and metal measure.

3.2 Geodetic, GRS80 Ellipsoid, ITRF2008

Geoid-ellipsoidal separations, in this section, are computed using a spherical harmonic synthesis of the global EGM2008 geoid. More information on the EGM2008 geoid can be found at http://earth-info.nga.mil/GandG/wgs84/gravitymod/egm2008/

Station	Latitude (DMS)	Longitude (DMS)	Ellipsoidal Height (m)	Derived Above Geoid Height (m)
PVG4	14 23 35.9275	104 40 49.1594	599.78	619.46
BAKO	-6 29 27.79817	106 50 56.08424	158.112	139.724
COAL	22 07 14.46888	113 33 40.98735	169.450	173.871
HKFN	22 29 40.86534	114 08 17.42158	41.200	44.007
HKNP	22 14 56.63245	113 53 37.96546	350.657	354.003
HKOH	22 14 51.66872	114 13 42.80334	166.361	168.238
HKSC	22 19 19.81437	114 08 28.29218	20.215	22.671
HKSL	22 22 19.21226	113 55 40.74862	95.251	98.794
HKWS	22 26 03.41147	114 20 07.37412	63.766	65.651
LHAZ	29 39 26.39879	91 06 14.50453	3624.598	3659.289
PBRI	11 38 16.00715	92 42 43.69105	-22.553	38.381
PIMO	14 38 08.59265	121 04 39.82675	95.543	51.427
TCMS	24 47 52.74723	120 59 14.61272	77.238	58.370
TWTF	24 57 12.83282	121 09 52.21162	201.542	182.559

Figure II.2-3 Rapid Orbit Data

3.2 Geodetic, GRS80 Ellipsoid, ITRF2008

Geoid-ellipsoidal separations, in this section, are computed using a spherical harmonic synthesis of the global EGM2008 geoid. More information on the EGM2008 geoid can be found at http://earth-info.nga.mil/GandG/wgs84/gravitymod/egm2008/

Station	Latitude (DMS)	Longitude (DMS)	Ellipsoidal Height (m)	Derived Above Geoid Height (m)
PVG4	14 23 35.9275	104 40 49.1594	599.78	619.45
BAKO	-6 29 27.79817	106 50 56.08425	158.111	139.723
COAL	22 07 14.46887	113 33 40.98735	169.450	173.871
HKFN	22 29 40.86534	114 08 17.42158	41.200	44.007
HKNP	22 14 56.63245	113 53 37.96546	350.657	354.003
HKOH	22 14 51.66872	114 13 42.80334	166.361	168.238
HKSC	22 19 19.81437	114 08 28.29218	20.215	22.671
HKSL	22 22 19.21226	113 55 40.74862	95.251	98.794
HKWS	22 26 03.41146	114 20 07.37412	63.766	65.651
LHAZ	29 39 26.39880	91 06 14.50454	3624.598	3659.289
PBRI	11 38 16.00716	92 42 43.69105	-22.554	38.380
PIMO	14 38 08.59266	121 04 39.82674	95.543	51.427
TCMS	24 47 52.74723	120 59 14.61272	77.238	58.370
TWTF	24 57 12.83282	121 09 52.21162	201.541	182.558

Figure II.2-4 Final Orbit Data

Wooden Traces in the Other Temples

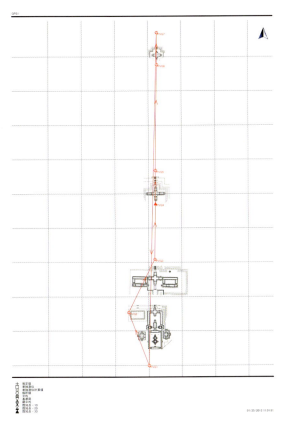

Figure II.2-5 Base point by GPS

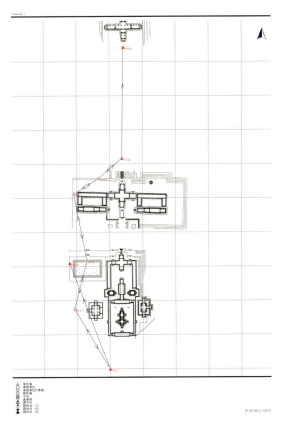

Figure II.2-6 Traverse 1 by TPS

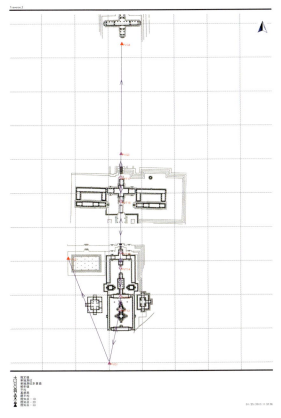

Figure II.2-7 Traverse 2 by TPS

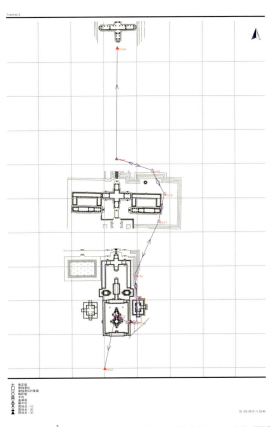

Figure II.2-8 Traverse 3 by TPS

Appx.
103

Appendix II : Measuring and Drawing Policies and Methods in Preah Vihear Temple

注

1) 基準点測量等の高精度な測量を行う場合，GPS が通常受信している衛星から常時放送されている軌道データ（放送暦）では精度的に十分ではないため，衛星軌道追跡網により分析された精密な軌道データを使用する（精密暦）。

   IGS では精密暦の中でも，超速報暦，速報暦，最終暦が定義されており，この順に精度が上がっていく。しかし，これらのデータを取得し，AUSPOS を通して分析を行う際に必要な時間がそれぞれ異なっている（超速報暦が直後，速報暦が2日，最終暦が2週間程度）。本調査においては調査の日程の都合上，速報暦を使用した。

   後日，速報暦と最終暦を比較した結果，緯度，経度においては秒の単位において小数第五位に，高さ方向は小数第三位に違いがみられる程度であったので，このまま使用しても問題ない数値であると判断した。

Notes

1) In the case of highly accurate measurement, satellite orbit data analyzed by chasing network of satellite orbit (Precise Ephemeris) is used, because the satellite orbit data usually broadcasted from satellite to GPS receiver (Broadcast Ephemeris) is not enough accuracy for calculating base point.

   IGS prepare 3 types of Precise Ephemeris: Ultra Rapid Orbit, Rapid Orbit, and Final Orbit. The highest accuracy is Final Obit, followed by Rapid Orbit, and Ultra Rapid Orbit in this order. The time taken to get this data and analyze by AUSPOS is different (Ultra Rapid Orbit: right after measurement, Rapid Orbit: 2 days, Rapid Orbit: 2 weeks). In this survey, we used the Rapid Orbit product for convenience with our schedule.

   Using Rapid Orbit product yields comparative results with the Final Orbit product, because the difference between Rapid Orbit product and Final Orbit product appears as little as a millionth of a second in latitude and longitude, and 1mm of height.

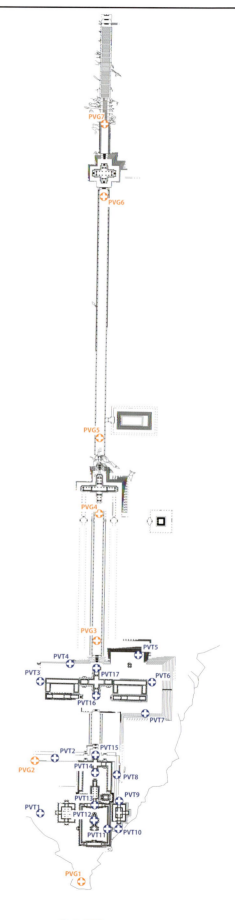

Figure II.2-9 Base Point

II.3 3次元実測調査解説
Report on Three-dimensional Measurement

大石　岳史　　影沢　政隆　　鄭　波　　佐藤　啓宏　　池内　克史

OISHI Takeshi　　KAGESAWA Masataka　　ZHENG Bo　　SATO Yoshihiro　　IKEUCHI Katsushi

II.3.1 はじめに

　本章では2012年から2015年にかけて行われたプレア・ヴィヘア寺院における3次元実測調査について解説する。カンボジア国内において我々はこれまでアンコール遺跡群においてバイヨン寺院，アンコール・ワット寺院などの3次元デジタル化を行ってきた[I][II]。これらの経験をもとに，JASA，プレア・ヴィヘア機構と協力し，レーザレンジセンサによるプレア・ヴィヘア寺院の3次元デジタル化を行った。

　本稿ではレーザレンジセンサを用いた3次元デジタル化手法について解説し，その後，得られたプレア・ヴィヘア寺院の3次元モデルの例を画像として示す。またプレア・ヴィヘア寺院の地形計測のために，新たに開発したセンサについても紹介する。

II.3.2 3次元デジタル化手法概要

　大規模な構造物を対象にした場合，高解像度・高精度の3次元計測にはレーザレンジセンサが広く用いられている。本実測においてもZ+F製Imager5010Cおよび Leica Geosystems製のC10 ScanStationを用いた。これらのセンサの最大計測距離はそれぞれ187m，300m，精度は数mm程度であり，大規模な建造物の計測に適している。これらのセンサは，ミラーの回転による縦スキャンとセンサヘッドの回転による横スキャンによって，1回のスキャンでセンサの全周を計測可能である。Figure II.3-1はこれらのセンサによって計測されたデータ例を示している。この図に示されるようにセンサ直下以外は周囲の形状を1スキャンで計測可能である。

　一方，画像中に示されるようにレーザレンジセンサはセンサから見える部分しか計測できない。つまりセンサから見て影となる部分は計測できないため，対象物体の完全な3次元モデルを取得するためには，様々

II.3.1 Introduction

　We report on the 3D measurement project in the Preah Vihear Temple that had been carried out through the missions in 2012-2015. We succeeded to digitize Angkor ruins in Cambodia such as the Bayon temple and Angkor-wat temple etc. by using 3D laser scanners[I][II]. We have conducted the 3D measurement project based on the experiences in the Angkor-ruins for the fundamental research of the Preah Vihear temple in collaboration with Japan APSARA Team for Safeguarding Angkor (JASA) and Preah Vihear Authority.

　First, we explain the 3D modeling procedures using the laser range sensors. Next, we present the results of the 3D measurement of the Peah Vihear Temple. We also introduce our new sensors, designed for scanning terrains around the temple.

II.3.2 3D Digitization Pipeline

　Laser range sensors are widely used for 3D measurement of large structures such as the Preah Vihear Temple. In this mission, we used Imager5010c (manufactured by Z+F) and C10 (manufactured by Leica Geosystems). The maximum measurement distances of Imager5010c and C10 are 187m and 300m respectively. These sensors can measure in the almost all directions at one scan by emitting laser light along a vertical line and rotating the sensor-head horizontally. Figure II.3-1 shows examples of the range images obtained by these sensors in Preah Vihear Temple. In the middle of the figures, there are circles which are the places where the sensors had been put while scanning. Only that circle areas cannot be measured because any laser beam is not emitted under the sensor.

　Moreover, as shown in the images, the sensor can measure only visible areas from the sensor. That is, there are a lot of "shadows" in the range images. The shadows are the areas where the sensor cannot see from the position of the sensor-head. Therefore, we

Appendix II : Measuring and Drawing Policies and Methods in Preah Vihear Temple

な方向から計測しなければならない。Figure II.3-2はC10による計測シーンである。この画像に示されるように建物全体を計測するために，地面だけでなく建物の屋根の上にセンサを置いて高所からも計測を行った。このような広範囲の遺跡を計測するためには後述のような移動型計測システムを用いるのが効率的である。

　様々な方向から計測された距離データはそれぞれ異なる座標系で記述されているため，座標系を統一する位置合わせ処理が必要となる。撮影時にGPSやIMUによって位置姿勢情報を取得できるが，十分な精度を得るのは難しい。そのため，部分形状データの重なり領域間の誤差を最小化する位置姿勢をソフトウェアによって求める。我々の位置合わせアルゴリズムはICP（Iterative Closest Point）のように反復計算によって相対位置姿勢を推定する。しかし，通常のICP法は2枚の距離画像を扱う逐次位置合わせ手法であるため，多数の距離データを位置合わせすると誤差の蓄積が問題となる。そのため我々の手法では，全ての距離画像間を同時に最小化する全体最適化を行っている。また距

must obtain multiple images at different positions to make the complete 3D model of the target object. The photographs in Figure II.3-2 are the scanning scenes by C10. We put the sensors not only on the ground but the top of the buildings.

Since the obtained range data are described in different coordinate systems, it is necessary to align them into a global coordinate system. Our alignment algorithm works in an iterative manner as same as ICP (Iterative Closest Point). Conventional ICP algorithm aligns the range images one by one; this is called pair-wise alignment. On the other hand, our algorithm aligns multiple range images at the same time by reducing the errors between all the rage images simultaneously. Our algorithm also accelerates the process of searching corresponding points that are required to compute the errors between two range images. The process of searching corresponding points is the most time-consuming in the alignment step. Our program uses the GPU (Graphics Processing Unit) and LUT (Look-up Table) to accelerate the searching process[III].

Figure II.3-1 Example of 3D measurements

Figure II.3-2 3D measurement scenes in Preah Vihear Temple

離データ間の距離を計算するための最近傍点探索は非常に計算コストが高いため，我々の手法では参照テーブルとグラフィックスプロセッシングユニット（GPU）を利用して高速な計算を可能としている[III]。

II.3.3 移動体による3次元計測システム

前述のように広範囲を効率的に計測するために移動体による3次元計測システムのプロトタイプを開発した。プレア・ヴィヘア寺院は山頂に広がる寺院であり，建物のみでなく地形全体をモデル化することも重要である。しかし通常のレーザレンジセンサは三脚に載せて地面に置く必要があり，さらに1スキャンに数分程度の計測時間が必要であるため，地形のような広範囲な計測には適していない。

そこで移動しながらレーザ計測可能なシステムを開発した。Figure II.3-3左に示すのは，移動台車の上にレーザプロファイラと全方位カメラを搭載した計測システムである。このシステムでは，Imager5010C をプロファイラモードで使用している。プロファイラモードでは，ヘッドが固定されているため1スキャンライン方向の計測しか行わない。そのためセンサを移動させることによって面計測を行う。図に示すように，このプラットフォームは進行方向に垂直な面をスキャンしながら移動していく。つまり移動した周囲の形状を連続的に計測することができる。一方，それぞれのスキャンラインがどの位置姿勢で計測されたか分からないため，何らかの方法でセンサの動きを推定する必要がある。

センサのモーション推定は，搭載された全方位カメラ（Point Grey Research 社製Ladybug3）からの映像を用いて行う[IV]。この全方位カメラから得られた全方位映像中の特徴点を追跡し，対応点間の整合性が取れるように移動を求めることによって連続したセンサの動きを推定する。この際，レンジセンサによって得られた奥行き値を用いることで，スケールも含めた位置姿勢が得られる。得られた動きに応じてスキャンラインを配置することによって，形状モデルを生成することが可能になる。Figure II.3-4はFigure II.3-3の移動型プラットフォームによって計測された形状データの例である。

Figure II.3-3 3D measurement system with moving platform

II.3.3 3D measurement System with Moving Platform

We have developed a new 3D measurement system that can measure wide areas with a moving platform. Preah Vihear temple is built on the top of the mountain; it is also important to archive the terrains around the buildings to obtain the complete 3D model that represents Preah Vihear. Unfortunately, conventional laser range sensors are not suitable for measuring wide areas because they are needed to be put on the ground with a tripod, and it takes a few minutes for scanning.

Therefore, we have developed a laser scanning system with a moving platform. The lower image in Fig. II.3-3 shows the measurement system with a laser profiler and an omnidirectional camera which are mounted on a handcart. We used Imager5010C for shape measurement in the profiler mode. The profiler does not rotate the head and can only measure one line, and need to be moved for wide scanning areas. The platform is moved while scanning as shown in the Figure, and obtain the shapes around the platform along the path. The sequential scan lines do not have any position information. That is, we need to estimate the motion of the sensor while scanning.

The motion is estimated by using the images taken by the omni-directional camera, Labybug3 (Point Grey Research)[IV]. Feature points in the images are tracked through the sequential images. The motion and depths of the feature points are estimated from the tracked feature points. The depths obtained by the laser scanner can be also used for estimating the absolute scale of the motion. Each scan line is ordered according to the motion to obtain the shape of the surroundings. Figure II-1.3 shows an example of obtained range data.

Appendix II : Measuring and Drawing Policies and Methods in Preah Vihear Temple

II.3.4 プレア・ヴィヘア寺院寺院の3次元モデル

2012年から2015年のミッションによって，プレア・ヴィヘア寺院の建物ほぼすべての3次元モデルを取得した。Figure II.3-5は第1ゴープラを3次元モデル化した結果である。第1ゴープラの建物は回廊によって囲まれた構造をしており，建物内や中央祠堂の上など様々な位置から計測を行った。また将来，デジタルデータによって中央祠堂を復原するため，散乱石材も詳細に計測している。Figure II.3-6は第5ゴープラの3次元モデルを示している。第5ゴープラは建物と基壇が綺麗に残されているが，それ以外の建物は倒壊しており，これらの散乱石材も含めて詳細な計測を行った。Figure II.3-7は第3ゴープラ，第1および第2ゴープラの計測結果をそれぞれ示している。Figure II.3-8は第4ゴープラをそれぞれ東西南北及び天空方向から見た画像を示している。

通常，生成された3次元モデルは任意の座標系で記述されているが，GPSデータと点群データを関連付けることによって世界座標系で記述することができる。プレア・ヴィヘア寺院においても，測量班チームがGPS点の計測を行っており，これらのデータを用いて世界座標系に修正することができる。これにより，正確な東西南北方向から直交投影した画像を生成することができる。正確な直交投影画像を生成できるのは3次元モデルだけであり，基礎資料として非常に有用である。

Figure II.3-4 An example of 3D measurement data with the moving platform

II.3.4 3D measurement in Preah Vihear Temple

We have obtained a complete 3D model of Preah Vihear temple. Figure II.3-5 shows the measurement results of Gopura I. Gopura I has a main building surrounded by the corridors. We put the sensors inside of the building and on the roofs of the Central Sanctuary and the corridors. Moreover, we measured fallen stones to virtually reconstruct the Central Sanctuary by using 3D models in the future. As shown in the images, we can easily generate orthogonal images of the buildings from the 3D models. These images should be helpful to make elevations because the complete orthogonal image cannot be obtained without 3D models.

Figure II.3-6 shows the 3D model of Gopura V. Gopura V has a beautiful gate, and the platform of the building remains. But, unfortunately, most of the building have been collapsed. We measured the gate, fallen stones, and remained pillars from the ground, and the top of the pillars.

Since the 3D models are described in arbitrary coordinate systems, they are aligned into the world coordinate system by using GPS data. We used reference points with GPS data which are taken by another measurement team. We can make orthographic images with accurate azimuth angles as shown in the figures. The images are useful for the fundamental studies of Preah Vihear temple.

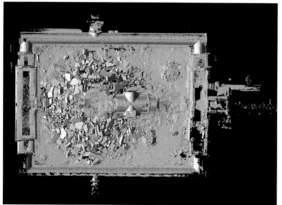

Figure II.3-5 Measurement results of Gopura I

Wooden Traces in the Other Temples

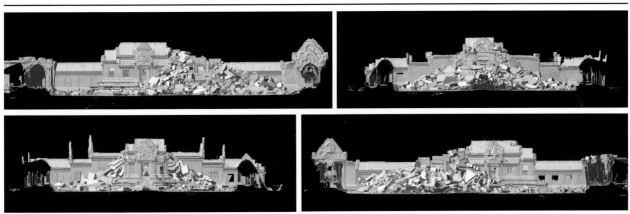

Figure II.3-5 Measurement results of Gopura I

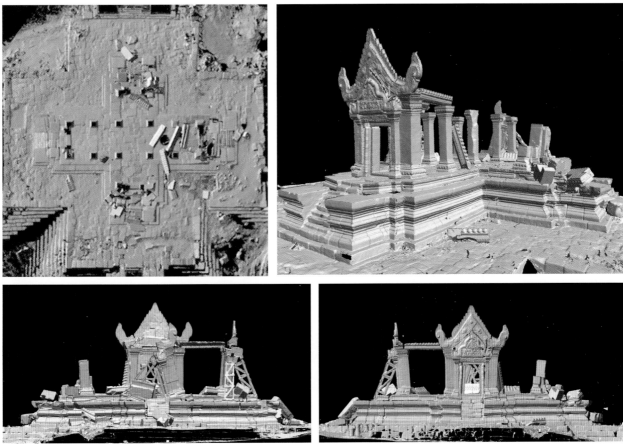

Figure II.3-6 Measurement results of Gopura V

Figure II.3-7 Measurement results of Gopura I (Left) and Gopura III (Right)

Appx.
109

II.3.5 まとめ

本稿ではプレア・ヴィヘア寺院における3次元計測プロジェクトについて概説した。高精度レーザレンジセンサによって，多数の距離データを取得し，それらを位置合わせすることによって寺院全体の3次元モデルを生成した。また寺院周辺の地形を計測するために開発した移動型レーザレンジシステムについて紹介した。地形を含めたプレア・ヴィヘア寺院全域のモデル化は今後の課題であると考えられる。

II.3.5 Conclusion

In this report, we described our 3D measurement project in the Preah Vihear Temple. The highly accurate laser range sensors were used for obtaining the 3D model of the temple. We have obtained a lot of range images from the different positions around and on the buildings. We applied simultaneous alignment method to estimate the relative measurement positions of the sensors to integrate the range images. We also introduced our new sensor system that can measure the wide areas such as the terrain around the temple. The scanning of the Preah Vihear Temple including terrains will be completed with the new sensors in the near future.

References

I) K.Ikeuchi, K.Hasegawa, A.Nakazawa, J.Takamatsu, T.Oishi and T.Masuda, "Bayon Digital Archival Project", Proc. the Tenth Int'l Conf. Virtual System and Multimedia, pp.334-343, 2004.11.

II) A.Banno, T.Masuda, T.Oishi and K.Ikeuchi, "Flying Laser Range Sensor for Large-Scale Site-Modeling and Its Applications in Bayon Digital Archival Project", International Journal of Computer Vision (IJCV), Vol. 78, No. 2-3, pp.207-222, 2008.07.

III) T.Oishi, A.Nakazawa, R.Kurazume and K.Ikeuchi, "Fast Simultaneous Alignment of Multiple Range Images using Index Images", Proc. The 5th International Conference on 3-D Digital Imaging and Modeling (3DIM 2005), pp.476-483, 2005.

IV) B.Zheng, T.Oishi, K.Ikeuchi, "Rail Sensor: A Mobile Lidar System for 3D Archiving the Bas-reliefs in Angkor Wat", IPSJ Transactions on Computer Vision and Applications (CVA), Vol. 7, pp.59-63, 2015.07.

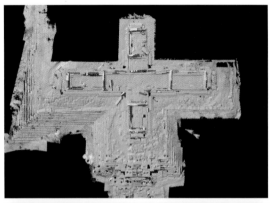
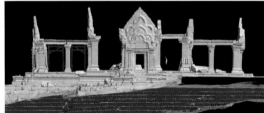

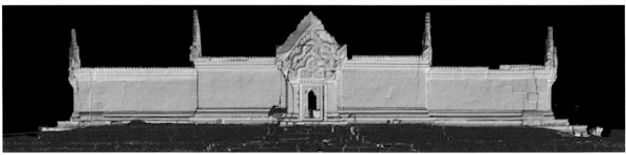

Figure II.3-8 Measurement results of Gopura IV

II.4　各種図面の作成方針
Process of Making the Drawings

石塚　充雅
ISHIZUKA Mitsumasa

II.4.1 はじめに

　プレア・ヴィヘア寺院は他の寺院と比較すると，比較的残存状態の良い遺構である。ただし，崩壊している部分はもちろん，状態が良いと思われる箇所でも，よく観察すると目地の開きや傾斜といった経年変化が見て取れる部分も多いため，現状を計測しても往時の計画を測量し，図化したことにはならない。

　こういった条件下で，今回の作図作業では，以下の2種類の図面を作成している。

II.4.2 復原平面図の作成

　今回の調査において大きな目的の一つに当時の設計計画の解明があることから，当初の寸法計画の復原的考察に耐えうる図面を作成することが必要であった。そのため，今回の調査では以下のような形で平面図を作成した。

　作成のプロセスとしては，まずトータルステーションにて測量した比較的残存状態のいい箇所の測点データを使用してエクセルのソルバー機能を用いた平均計算を行い，寺院平面配構の方位を求め，各部の基準となる辺の位置を決定した。計算の結果，寺院全体としては真北から時計回りに0.524°程度の傾きを有していた。この際に，この傾きと若干異なる傾向をみせた付属建物H-I，H'-I'（宮殿），付属建物E，第4（J）～第5ゴープラ（K）間参道，第5ゴープラ（K）北側大階段の各辺に関しては，個別に計算を行い，それぞれの傾きを求めた。その後，この辺から各部の距離についてコンベックスや曲尺を用いて計測を行い，図面を作成した。計測の際には，目地開きや傾斜といった経年変化による変位の影響がなるべく出ないよう，変位が明らかな部分は計測しない，あるいは変位量が見て取れる場合にはその分を差し引くなどして測量を行った。

　プレア・ヴィヘア寺院の建物部分は比較的残存状態が良いため，基本的にはこのようなプロセスをたどっ

II.4.1 Introduction

　Preah Vihear Temple is in better condition compared to other Khmer temples. However we can't draw the original planning by using the measurements of the present condition because if we observe these parts carefully, there are many altered parts over the years such as joint openings, wall inclinations at not only the collapsed parts, but also the parts in good condition.

　In these situations, we have drawn two types of drawing work in this study project.

II.4.2 Making the Original Plan Drawing

　The purpose of making the plan for restoring the original design in this survey is to resolve discrepancies in the conjectured plan. Therefore in this measurement survey, we need to make the plan as close to the original dimentional plan as possible. Process is as follows.

　For making the plan, we decided the position and angle of the baseline of each element by the result of an average calculation by Excel's solver function using the measuring point data by total station of points remaining in relatively good condition. As a result of the calculation, the whole temple had an inclination of about 0.524° clockwise from the true north. At this time, for the elements, Annex Building H-I, H'-I' (Palaces), Annex Building E, causeway between Gopura IV (J)- V (K), and north great staircase of Gopura V (K), having tendencies other than the main angle under the calculation, we calculate again individually. Subsequently we add other parts by using the numbers measured by tape measure and metal measure from the edge measured by Total Station. For deleting the influence of changing parts over the years such as joint openings, wall inclinations and other such signs of aging, we have implemented this measuring work such that we have not measured at the obvious changing parts, and eliminated the length of the change when we can measure the length.

て作図作業を行うことにより，完成当初の形状に近い状態を復原できると考えた。

　平面図においては各建物の平面のみならず，その周辺の階段，参道ならびに表出している遺構の痕跡，地形の概要，さらには各遺構と接している露岩の記録も行った。第5ゴープラ北階段等の変位が激しい箇所や，参道脇の石灯籠等一部欠損している箇所に関しては，残存している痕跡から，当初の計画を想定し作図を行った。地形や露岩の記録に際しては一部3Dデータも参考にした。

　また併せて寺院全体の南北方向の断面図も作成した。断面図における各建物の立面図は形状が未確定な部分も多いことから，3Dデータを使用し図面を作成した。

II.4.2 現状図面

　プレア・ヴィヘア寺院については，これまでに1930年代にH.パルマンティエによって創建時の復原図面集が作成されているが，正確な現状図面が作成されたことはない。

　本事業では将来的な修復工事計画，屋根構造解明のための木造痕跡の調査等々の理由から現状記録が必要とされるであろう現状図面の作成も進めている。図面は平面図・立面図・断面図をセットとしている。今回の図面作成に当たっては，崩壊の度合が激しい遺構及び屋根構造解明のための木造痕跡の調査対象となっている遺構の図化作業を優先的に進めるものとしている。

　図面の作成にあたっては，3次元測量によるデータを利用するが，加えてTPSのデータ，現場の採寸データ等も援用する。また，今回作成する図面は，建物を構成する部材の輪郭や主要な装飾線，石穴や木造加工跡等も含めるものとするため，3次元測量によるデータでは確認しきれない細部については写真記録を利用して図面を作成する。

　本調査においては，中央祠堂周辺，第5ゴープラ，そして第1ゴープラ及びそれに付属するホールN，擬似ゴープラの図化作業を行った。

　なお，平面図，立面図，断面図の作成に関しては，測量データにもとづき，細部装飾を含めてチャン・ヴィタロン氏が描画を担当した。

Since the building parts of Preah Vihear Temple remain ia a relatively good state, by implementing the drawing by this process, we thought we would to be able to make the plan infinitely closer to the original appearance of building at the time of initial construction.

In the drawing of the plan, we have recorded not only the plan of each building, but also each step, causeway, traces of the exhibited remains, outline of the landform around the building, and natural rock attached to the monument. Regarding parts where there are violent displacements such as the north staircase of Gopura V, or there are partially missing elements such as the stone lantern besides the causeway, we estimated the original plan from the trace remaining. For recording the outline of the landform and natural rock, we have partially used 3D data.

In addition, we also made the drawing of the entire monument in a north-south section. In this situation we have used 3D data for the elevation of each building in the drawing of sections because these elevations have many unclear parts.

II.4.2　Drawing of the Present Condition of the Each Building

Drawing of the present condition of each building has never been produced for the Preah Vihear Temple complex, although a set of the conjectural original images were prepared by H.Parmentier in the 1930s.

Our project is producing a set of drawings that are recording the present condition in order to prepare the future restoration planning, and study for the wooden trace for revealing the original wooden structure. Drawings of each building are prepared with plan, elevation and section. Order of the drawing target buildings is selected by the priority of the future restoration work or study for the wooden trace.

We are producing the drawing by using the data of three dimensional scanning, survey by TPS, and survey by hand measuring. Drawings include the line of block profile, decorative line, stone hole, traces of the missing wooden structure, and the other lines. If we cannot record these several lines by the above measuring method, photo records are applied.

In this survey, we have implemented the drawing work around the Central Sanctuary and Gopura V, Gopura I and attached Hall N, and False Gopura.

Mr. CHAN Vitharong drew the plan, eleveiton and division drawing by using measurement data and ditails of decorations.

Appendix III
付章Ⅲ

Survey Report on Preah Khan Temple of Kompong Svay
コンポンスヴァイのプレア・カーン寺院の調査報告

III.1 コンポンスヴァイのプレア・カーン寺院の調査概要
Survey Report on Preah Khan Temple of Kompong Svay

髙橋　泉美　　黒岩　千尋　　石塚　充雅　　溝口　明則
TAKAHASHI Izumi　　KUROIWA Chihiro　　ISHIZUKA Mitsumasa　　MIZOGUCHI Akinori

III.1.1 調査概要
III.1.1.1 調査背景・目的

　名城大学と早稲田大学の共同チームは2007年よりカンボジア地方遺構の調査を行ってきた。調査の主旨は，アンコール地域を中心とした調査研究や修復事業が進展しつつある現在，クメール王国を広域として理解することが，クメール学の発展にとってきわめて重要な問題であるという認識と，荒廃が進む地方寺院の基礎資料を確保することが急務であるという認識に基づいている。

　クメール地方大型遺跡として，コンポンスヴァイのプレア・カーン寺院において，まず建築学分野の学術資料として各種分析に耐えうる十分な基礎資料（図面，各種インベントリー）の作成を目的とした基礎調査を行っている。

　本節では建築学分野の現状調査報告を行う。

III.1.1.2 調査日程・メンバー
■2011年
［第0次ミッション］
調査期間：2011年4月26日〜5月5日
メンバー：中川武，下田一太，内田賢二，石塚充雅，チャン・ヴィタロン
調査内容：GPS/TPS測量による基準点作成，周辺遺構の踏査

■2013年
［第1次ミッション］
調査期間：2013年3月1日〜29日
メンバー：中川武，石塚充雅，出雲蓮人，荻原周，上條理紗，黒岩千尋
調査内容：GPS/TPS/手ばかりによる測量・図面作成

III.1.1 Introduction
III.1.1.1 Background and Objectives

 From 2007 a joint team from Meijo and Waseda Universities in Japan have implemented a survey of provincial temples. This survey was based on the realization that there is an urgent need to understanding the expansion of the Khmer empire through the collect basic data of provincial temples that are advancing to ruin as an important element for the growth of Khmer studies given the present situation that study and restoration work is mainly in the Angkor area.

 In this survey at Preah Khan Temple of Konpong Svay, one of the great provincial temple groups, the objective was to acquire basic data on architectural elements and features as well as drawings and various inventories for analyzed.

 This section of the report is introduced the present survey results from the architectural survey.

III.1.1.2 Mission schedule and Members
■ 2011
［Preliminary mission］
Schedule: 26th April - 5th May 2011
Members: NAKAGAWA Takeshi, SHIMODA Ichita, UCHIDA Kenji, ISHIZUKA Mitsumasa, CHAN Vitharong
Mission: Establish points by GPS/TPS measurement; exploration of the peripheral ruins

■ 2013
[First mission]
Schedule: 1st - 29th March 2013
Members: NAKAGAWA Takeshi, ISHIZUKA Mitsumasa, IZUMO Rento, OGIHARA Shu, KAMIJO Risa, KUROIWA Chihiro
Mission: Measuring survey by GPS/TPS/hand measurement

Appx.

115

Appendix III : Survey Report on Preah Khan Temple of Kompong Svay

■2014年
［第2次ミッション］
調査期間：2014年2月28日～3月11日
メンバー：中川武，溝口明則，石塚充雅，中村みふみ，
北井絵里沙，黒岩千尋，貞富陽介，松本奈穂
調査内容：GPS/TPS/手ばかりによる測量・図面作成

［第3次ミッション］
調査期間：2014年8月21日～9月15日
メンバー：溝口明則，石塚充雅，荻原周，古賀友佳子，
出雲蓮人，北井絵里沙，黒岩千尋，貞富陽介，松本奈穂，
中村嘉代子
調査内容：GPS/TPS/手ばかりによる測量・図面作成

［第4次ミッション］
調査期間：2014年12月9日～19日
メンバー：中川武，石塚充雅，荻原周，古賀友佳子，
出雲蓮人，貞富陽介
調査内容：GPS/TPS/手ばかりによる測量・図面作成，
建築学調査

■2015年
［第5次ミッション］
調査期間：2015年2月27日～3月2日
メンバー：溝口明則，石塚充雅，黒岩千尋，尾上千尋，
髙橋泉美，中村嘉代子
調査内容：GPS/TPS/手ばかりによる測量・図面作成，
建築学調査

［第6次ミッション］
調査期間：2015年5月5日～14日
メンバー：石塚充雅，黒岩千尋，金子達哉，髙橋泉美
調査内容：GPS/TPS/手ばかりによる測量・図面作成，
建築学調査

［第7次ミッション］
調査期間：2015年12月16日～21日
メンバー：石塚充雅，北井絵里沙，黒岩千尋，貞富陽介，
松本奈穂
調査内容：GPS/TPS/手ばかりによる図面作成，建築学
調査

■2016年
［第8次ミッション］
調査期間：2016年3月2日～19日
メンバー：小岩正樹，石塚充雅，尾上千尋，金子達哉，

■ 2014
[Second mission]
Schedule: 28th February - 11th March 2014
Members: NAKAGAWA Takeshi, MIZOGUCHI Akinori, ISHIZUKA Mitsumasa, NAKAMURA Mifumi, KITAI Erisa, KUROIWA Chihiro, SADATOMI Yosuke, MATSUMOTO Naho
Mission: Continuation of measuring survey by GPS/TPS/hand measurement

[Third mission]
Schedule: 21st August - 15th September 2014
Members: MIZOGUCHI Akinori, ISHIZUKA Mitsumasa, OGIHARA Shu, KOGA Yukako, IZUMO Rento, KITAI Erisa, KUROIWA Chihiro, SADATOMI Yosuke, MATSUMOTO Naho, NAKAMURA Kayoko
Mission: Continuation of measuring survey by GPS/TPS/hand measurement

[Fourth mission]
Schedule: 9th - 19th December 2014
Members: NAKAGAWA Takeshi, ISHIZUKA Mitsumasa, OGIHARA Shu, KOGA Yukako, IZUMO Rento, SADATOMI Yosuke
Mission: Continuation of measuring survey by GPS/TPS/hand measurement; architectural survey

■ 2015
[Fifth mission]
Schedule: 27th Feburuary - 2nd March 2015
Members: MIZOGUCHI Akinori, ISHIZUKA Mitsumasa, KUROIWA Chihiro, ONOE Chihiro, TAKAHASHI Izumi, NAKAMURA Kayoko
Mission: Continuation of measuring survey by GPS/TPS/hand measurement; continuation of architectural survey

[Sixth mission]
Schedule: 5th - 14th May 2015
Members: ISHIZUKA Mitsumasa, KUROIWA Chihiro, KANEKO Tatsuya, TAKAHASHI Izumi
Mission: Continuation of measuring survey by GPS/TPS/hand measurement; continuation of architectural survey

[Seventh mission]
Schedule: 16th-21th December 2015
Members: ISHIZUKA Mitsumasa, KITAI Erisa, KUROIWA Chihiro, SADATOMI Yosuke, MATSUMOTO Naho

髙橋泉美，成井至
調査内容：GPS/TPS/手ばかりによる測量・図面作成，建築学調査，アンコール地域の比較寺院調査

[第9次ミッション]
調査期間：2016年8月28日～9月9日
メンバー：石塚充雅，尾上千尋，金子達哉，髙橋泉美，石井由佳，宮崎瑶希
調査内容：アンコール地域の比較寺院調査

III.1.2 実測調査方針
III.1.2.1 寺院の現状

　現状のコンポンスヴァイのプレア・カーン寺院は損傷が激しく，主に調査を行った第1回廊・第2回廊においては，多くの箇所で基座を確認することができなかった。

　第1回廊内では，数基の塔状ゴープラを確認することが出来たが（Photo III.1-1を参照），中央祠堂は一部の壁体を残して崩壊（Photo III.1-2を参照）している。第1回廊は残存箇所が少ないが，一部の足元に窓枠の散乱材が確認され，壁体と窓によって構成されていたと予想される。

　第2回廊ではゴープラが崩壊しており，建物を構成していた石材が散乱している。散乱材に埋もれて，一部に壁体部や基壇を確認した（Photo III.1-3を参照）。また，回廊部は外側に2列の柱列，内側に壁を有する柱廊の形式であるが，柱列はほぼすべて倒壊しており，正確な位置や本数を把握することは困難であった。回

Mission: Continuation of measuring survey by GPS/TPS/hand measurement; continuation of architectural survey

■ 2016
[Eighth mission]
Schedule: 2nd - 19th March 2016
Members: KOIWA Masaki, ISHIZUKA Mitsumasa, ONOE Chihiro, KANEKO Tatsuya, TAKAHASHI Izumi, NARUI Itaru
Mission: Continuation of measuring survey by GPS/TPS/hand measurement; continuation of architectural survey; comparative survey in Angkor area

[Ninth mission]
Schedule: 28th August - 9th September 2016
Members: ISHIZUKA Mitsumasa, ONOE Chihiro, KANEKO Tatsuya, TAKAHASHI Izumi, ISHII Yuka, MIYAZAKI Tamaki
Mission: Continuation of comparative survey in Angkor area

III.1.2 Policies and Methods of Measuring
III.1.2.1 The Present Condition of Temple

　At present the temple buildings are almost collapsed. In Gallery I and II, where we mainly conducted the survey, the base of the buildings are almost buried in rubble.

　In Gallery I, some Gopura towers remain (see Photo III.1-1), and the Central Sanctuary is collapsed except for partial wall elements (see Photo III.1-2). The surrounding Gallery is composed of walls and windows of which little remains, however there are the window frames that are partially buried in

Photo III.1-1 (left top) The present condition of North Gopura of Gallery I
Photo III.1-2 (left bottom) Central Sanctuary in Gallery I
Photo III.1-3 (right) East Gopura of Gallery II and confronting terrace

Appendix III : Survey Report on Preah Khan Temple of Kompong Svay

廊の四隅には隅建物があるが，同様に激しい遺構の損傷が確認された。

III.1.2.2 建築学調査
III.1.2.2.1 2011 〜 2015 年

主に第1〜第2回廊周辺を対象として図面描画を行うため，GPSやTPSを用いて寺院全体の遺構測量を行った。また，各遺構の状態を記録するため，これらのエリアにおいて写真インベントリーを作成した。

III.1.2.2.2 2015 年

前述したように当該寺院は損傷が激しく，現存部を記録するのみでは往時の様相を把握するのは困難である。したがって，図面作成の上で問題となった寺院の崩壊箇所に関して，復原するための痕跡確認を行った。特に第1回廊内テラス，第2回廊の北・西ゴープラのテラスの形状確認のためのTPS測量，第2回廊列柱の配列方法，配列数を推測するための目視確認や手ばかりを行った。

III.1.2.2.3 2016 年

遺構の復原計画の妥当性を得るために，アンコール地域の寺院との比較調査を行った。特に，柱廊形式の第2回廊について，柱の配列方法や間隔の調整方法を，他寺院と比較した。対象寺院はアンコール・ワット寺院，バイヨン寺院，プレア・カーン寺院，タ・プローム寺院，バンテアイ・クデイ寺院である。

III.1.2.3 測量方針
III.1.2.3.1 TPS 測量

2011年度より，寺院の全体像を掴むために，寺院の残存状況から各建物において比較的原位置を留めている箇所を判断・選定し，TPSを用いて概形を捉えることを試みた。また，各建物のポイントをとるために，基準点を作成する際には，GPSを併用した。

III.1.2.3.2 手ばかり

上述のTPSによる測量点をプロットした測量図に細部を書き加えるため，手ばかりによる実測調査を行った。TPSによって記録したポイントを把握しつつ，図面作成上の補足調査を行った。

III.1.3 図面作成方針
III.1.3.1 図面に使用する線の分類

以上の測量調査を基に，平面図を作成した（III.2 図版を参照）。痕跡が見られる箇所についてはTPS/GPS

the ground.

In Gallery II, the Gopuras are in ruin. We confirmed a part of walls and platforms from gaps between the scuttered stone (see Photo III.1-3). The Gallery element is composed of 2 rows of pillars on the outer side and walls on the innner side. The Pillars are almost collapsed and it was difficult to confirm the exact plot and the number of pillars. There are Corner Buildings in the 4 corners of the Gallery which are near collapse.

III.1.2.2 Architectural Survey
III.1.2.2.1 2011-2015

First, we tried to understand the complete temple building alignment by GPS/TPS measurement. Subsequently, we measured existing associated elements of buildings, such as wall, platform, and base by hand. From this data, we drew the plan drawing mainly around Gallery I, II. In addition, we implemented a photo inventory to record the present condition of the temple.

III.1.2.2.2 2015

The main mission was to consider the original form of the collapsed parts by traces that we could not draw in the plan drawing in process. We conducted TPS measuring surveys of the terrace in side of Gallery I and front terraces of North and West Gopura in Gallery II. In Gallery II, we considered the number of pillars and plotted by hand measuring and inspection.

III.1.2.2.3 2016

We conducted a comparative study of Angkor temples. The method of plot and adjustment of the interval of pillars which are seen in Gallery II, were especially compared with the other temples of the Bayon period. We selected Angkor Vat Temple, Bayon Temple, Preah Khan, Ta Prohm, and Banteay Kdei Temples.

III.1.2.3 Methods of Measuring Survey
III.1.2.3.1 TPS Measuring

Since 2011we have surveyed the temple using TPS. We checked the remaining parts and took some points in each building, and tried to restore the general form. We used a GPS instrument to identify the base points.

III.1.2.3.2 Measuring by Hand

To add the details on the plan drawing, we have done measuring surveys by hand. To draw some sketches we used points that were already made by TPS.

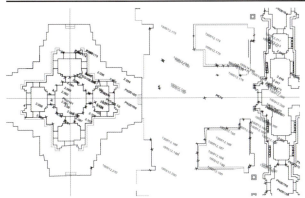

Figure III.1-1 Measured point by TPS/GPS and drawned lines

Figure III.1-2 Field note (Terrace in Gallery I)

測量と手ばかりを併用した調査結果から作図を行ったが，遺構の損傷が激しい箇所については，散乱石材や写真記録，寺院の他の箇所や既往研究等から往時の計画を復原的に判断し，描いている。そのため，以下の種類の線を区別してそれぞれの箇所を示す。

- 黒の実線：建物の要素や位置を示す痕跡が，いずれかの方法（TPS/手ばかり）で測量した箇所。
- 黒の破線：寺院内の同建物，他建物からの数値，プロポーションの反転により作図した箇所。
- 赤の破線：既往図面との比較，あるいは他寺院との比較検討から推測した箇所。

その他の不明箇所については，現状では復原研究が完了していないため，描画していない。

III.1.3.2 崩壊箇所における作図方針

図面作成にあたって，現状で不明であった箇所及び推測の結果，既往研究と異なる箇所について以下に記すとともに，作図方針を検討する。なお，既往研究として用いる図面は，EFEOが作成したものである。

① 第1回廊内のテラスと基壇について

第1回廊内にはテラスの痕跡が確認されるが，形状は完全に復原できないため，測量された数値を用い既

Photo III.1-4 Trace of Terrace in Gallery I

III.1.3 Methods and Policies of Drawing
III.1.3.1 Classification of Drawing Lines

The plan drawing was made based on the survey results (see III.2 Plate). The remaining elements were drawn from TPS/GPS and hand survey. Collapsed parts were drawn by the references obtained from scattered stones, photo inventories, other parts in same temple and previous studies. We classified 3 kinds of drawing lines based on each policy as follows:

-- Black Solid Line: The building elements or its traces can be measured by TPS or hand method.
-- Black Dotted Line: Inverse from the same building or other building in this temple.
-- Red Dotted Line: Referenced from the previous drawing or other comparative temple.

Other unidentified parts that do not suggest the original form are not drawn.

III.1.3.2 Drawing Policies of Collapsed Part

The following describes parts that were unknown in the present situation and the different suggestions from the previous drawing. We considered drawing policies for these elements. The previous drawing used for comparison were made by EFEO.

① Terrace and Platform in Gallery I

Although there are some traces of terrace in Gallery I, we draw the plan by measurement results and previous drawing (EFEO). There are some different parts from the previous drawing.

The terrace in front of the South Library was drawn as connecting to the north part in the EFEO drawing. However, the trace that turned west was confirmed on site, so the original form is unknown. Also its form is different from the terrace that is in front of the North Library. Therefore, we could not make the drawing.

Although the width of the platform of the Central Sanctuary was partially measured, the connection with the terrace is unknown.

Appendix III : Survey Report on Preah Khan Temple of Kompong Svay

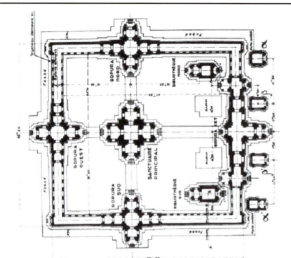

Figure III.1-3 Previous drawing of the Gallery I (©EFEO)

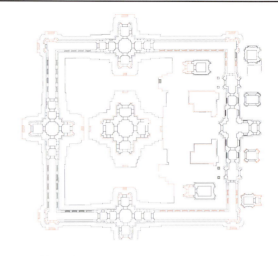

Figure III.1-4 New drawing of the Gallery I (© Meijo+Waseda)

往図面（EFEO）の形状記録から作図している。しかし，既往研究の形状と異なる箇所が数点確認された。

南経蔵の前にあるテラスは，既往研究では北に向かって繋がるように描かれているものもあるが，西方向に折れる痕跡が見つかったため形状が不明である。北経蔵前のテラスと形状が一致しないため，今回は明記しないこととする。

また，中央祠堂の基壇の出幅は一部測量した数値を利用しているがテラスとのとりつき方が不明である。第1回廊と回廊部の基壇の出幅は確認されたため，全体の形状を復原的に考える必要がある。

既往研究では，ゴープラの主室前の基壇は階段を有しているが，崩壊しているため，痕跡は確認できなかった。現状の図面では，ゴープラの形状と階段部分の基壇の幅から形状を推測して作図を行っている（Figure III.1-3，4を参照）。また，既往研究ではゴープラと隅建物の外側の基壇には階段が記されてなかったが，ゴープラの内側の基壇と同様に階段を有していたと推測し，今回は作図を行った。基壇の角の数はゴープラや隅建物の角の個数に合わせて増やしているため，既往研究よりも多く記している。

The width of the platform of Gallery I was measured.

In the past research, the platform of the inner side of the Gopura in Gallery I has a staircase, however no trace could be confirmed in this survey. Our drawing is drawn in accordance with the shape of the Gopura and measuring result of the width of the platform of the staircase element (Figure III. 1-3, 4).

Also in past research, no stairs were mentioned in the platform outside of the Gopura and the corner building, however it is presumed that it had stairs like the platform of the inside of the Gopura. The number of corners of the platform is in order to the number of corners of Gopura wall and corner building wall, therefore it is increased from the previous research.

② Windows of Gallery I

In the past study, some drawings have different dimensions and positions shown as windows restored.

The drawing we showed referenced the most detailed drawing in the concerning as to whether windows are existed or not.

Gallery I is collapsing, so the dimensions of the window length and position are measured from scattered stone. The windows that could not be positioned from TPS are aligned by using the

Photo III.1-5 Remaining part of Gallery I

Photo III.1-6 Terrace in front of Central Sanctuary of the Gallery I

② 第 1 回廊の窓について

既往研究による図面資料では，第 1 回廊の窓配列の復原に関して，個数や寸法値が統一されていない。今回の作図では，窓の有無に関しては既往図面のうち最も細緻に描かれている図面を参考にした。

第 1 回廊は崩壊が激しいため，窓幅や間隔の寸法は散乱石材等の実測データから作図を行った。崩壊によりTPSでの位置決定が不可能であった箇所に関しては，散乱石材による寸法値と隅部の関係から描画している。

東回廊も窓の痕跡がほぼ確認出来なかった。窓と壁体部の寸法の一部を測量できているが，既往研究で示される窓の数を適用させると納まりが悪く，ゴープラを挟んだ南北回廊の総長の差異も説明がつかない。

③ 第 1 回廊外側東部における付属建物と基壇について

第 1 回廊東部分における付属建物と基壇のとりつき部分の形状が不明瞭である。編年研究や他の寺院との比較研究から復原を行う必要がある。

他のアンコール遺跡の例では，回廊の東部に付属建物を有する寺院は，プレア・カーン寺院とタ・プローム寺院である。しかし，いずれも基壇部は残存しておらず，その形状について，アンコール遺跡から考察することは不可能であった。

上記の要因からコンポンスヴァイのプレア・カーン寺院の図面では描画可能な線を残し，付属建物とのとりつき方は記さないことにする（Figure III.1-5）。

④ 第 1 回廊外側のテラスについて

第 1 回廊を囲むようにテラスの痕跡が見られ，第 1 西ゴープラの外側には，それに取り付くと考えられる階段の痕跡が確認されるが，細部の形状が不明である。また，南部の付属建物周辺において，既往研究では建物に沿ってテラスが配されているが，TPS測量で建物の北部のポイントを測量しているため，このテラスは直線形として連続するものとして作図している（Figure III.1-6）。

measurement values of the windows and interval walls that we could measure to fit the corner.

East Gallery has a little evidence of windows. We partly measured the dimensions of the windows and the wall, however if we adjusts to the number of windows shown in past research, it does not properly fit and the difference between the north and south part across the Gopura is unclear.

③ Annex Building and Platform in the Eastern Part of Gallery I

The shape of the connecting part of the platform and the Annex Buildings in the eastern part of the Gallery I is unknown. It is necessary to compare with the previous research on the period temple construction, and other remaining temples.

As a result of comparative study on Angkor temples, there are 2 temples that have Annex Buildings in the eastern part of the Gallery. They are Preah Khan Temple and Ta Prohm Temple. However, neither of them have remains of the platform, so that it is impossible to consider the shape of the platform of the connecting part based on the Angkor temples.

In the previous drawing of the Preah Khan Temple of Kompong Svay, it does not mention how the connection of the platform with the Annex Building is made except for the measured part (Figure III.1-5).

④ The Terrace Line Outside of Gallery I

Traces of step are seen to surround Gallery I, and traces of the stairs that would be attached to that terrace are confirmed on the outside of the West Gopura I, but the detail of shape is unknown. Also, around the Southern Annex Buildings, the terrace line is arranged to be folded along with Annex Buildings in the past research, but since points are taken at the northern part of the building by TPS survey, this terrace line is considered to continue in a straight line (Figure III.1-6).

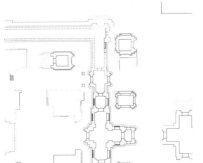

Figure III.1-5 Annexed building and platform

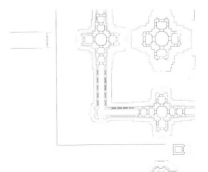

Figure III.1-6 The Step line of outside of Gallery I

Appendix III : Survey Report on Preah Khan Temple of Kompong Svay

⑤第2回廊における列柱廊

(1) 現状

　第2回廊は内側に壁体，外側に2列の列柱を有する列柱廊である。全形を通して崩壊が著しく，列柱が完形となって残存しているものは確認できていない。したがって，往時の列柱廊の計画を想定するため，測量調査を行い，復原的に列柱廊の基本計画を想定した。

　倒壊した列柱廊の中で位置のずれが少ないと推測されるものを選定し，柱間真々距離を計測したところ，隣接する柱はいずれの箇所においても約2,200〜2,600mmで近似した。一方で各隅建物における壁体付柱から列柱廊の一本目までの距離には一定の近似値は得られず，ばらつきが大きいことがわかった。柱幅に関してはいずれも420mm×460mm程度で近似することが観察された。以上の結果から，第2回廊の列柱割り付け計画が，ゴープラから一定の寸法値で配置され，各部隅建物付近で発生した誤差を許容する基本計画があったと考えられる。

(2) アンコール地域寺院遺跡の第2回廊における列柱廊

　アンコール地域に位置する大型寺院の中で，比較的状態が良く12世紀前後に築造されたと考えられる遺構をTable III.1のように選定し，列柱回廊の比較調査を行った。

　その結果，多くの遺構に関して柱間真々距離は2,200〜2,450mm程度に近似し，コンポンスヴァイのプレア・カーン寺院と大きな差は見受けられなかった。一方で，抽出箇所によっては柱間真々寸法のばらつきが大きいものが含まれ，一連の遺構調査から隅建物，あるいはゴープラ付近にてばらつきが大きくなる傾向が見られたが，遺構によってはばらつきの大きい箇所は異なり，調査遺構を通じて一貫した法則性は見られない。また柱間数に関して，調査した5遺構中3遺構で正対する箇所の間数が一致しており，他2遺構に関しても多くの箇所において同様の傾向が見られた。したがって基本計画として正対する箇所の間数を同一にする設計意図があった可能性が考えられる。

(3) 作図方針

　アンコール地域の遺構の調査を踏まえて，コンポン

⑤ Collonade in Gallery II

(1) The Present Condition of Gallery II

　Gallery II has the wall in the inner part, and collonade of two rows on the outer part. The pillars are collapsed and did not retain a semblance of their original form. Therefore, it is necessary to implement a dimensional survey at the collonade in order to imitate the initial plan.

　We selected the pillars that we estimated did not move much from the initial plan and mesured between the pillars. Many of dimensions between pillars are approximately between 2,200 to 2,600 mm. On the other hand, dimrnsions between the pillar attached with buildings of each corner to the next pillar, do not show consistent approximate values. The width of the each pillar is approximately 420 ×460 mm. Accordingly, the design plan of the collonade is predicted that the pillars are aligned with specific dimensions from each Gopuras, and the dimensional error is compensated at each corner.

(2) Colonnade in Gallery II Temple Sites in Angkor

　We select the temples that are in large scale complexes that were estimated to be designed and built around the 12th century. We researched the sites refered to in Table III.1.

　As a result, the dimensions between the pillars measured approximately 2,200~2,450 mm in many of the sites, and the dimensions do not differ to that of Preah Khan Temple in Kompong Svay. The dispersion of dimensions between the pillars are large depending on the sites. The tendency that the dimensions differ largely at or near the Gopuras or corners of buildings is observed. However the consistent tendency that the parts are near from Gopura or the buildings of the corners is not observed in research. The numbers of the space that is between the pillars are corresponding at all of each confront parts in 3 sites, and many of each confront parts in 2 sites out of 5 sites. Therefore, there is some possibility that the spaces are made corresponding at each confront parts as the basical plan.

(3) Object of Drawing the Plan of Preah Khan Temple in Kompong Svay

　Based on research in Angkor, we draw the plan of the collonade in Preah Khan Temple in Kompong Svay. The dimensions

Table III.1 Collonade in Gallery II Temple Sites in Angkor

The Cites of Resaech Object	Period	Research Parts
Angkor Vat Temple	1113~1150	Gallery II
Preah Khan Temple in Angkor	1186	Gallery II
Bayon Temple	1191	Gallery II
Banteay Kdei Temple	13c before and after	Gallery II
Ta Prohm Temple	13c before and after	middle and outer Gallery

スヴァイのプレア・カーン寺院第2回廊の作図を行った。コンポンスヴァイのプレア・カーン寺院で計測された柱間寸法はややばらつきが大きいが，アンコール地域周辺遺構で計測された寸法と大きな相違はなく，一定の柱間寸法を志向していたと想定される。したがって計測された箇所の柱間寸法を優先して調整を行い，同箇所内で柱を均等に配置した。間数に関してはコンポンスヴァイのプレア・カーン寺院では東西回廊のゴープラ形状が異なるため，南北回廊の正対する箇所で間数を一致させ，作図を行った。

この結果は復原計画ではなく，一連の傾向を踏まえて作図したものである。明確に初期計画を把握するためには，アンコール地域の遺構を含め伽藍計画順序を検討し，詳細な分析を行う必要があり，復原研究としては今後のさらなる研究に期待される。

⑥ 第2回廊東ゴープラの両脇のポーチについて

第2回廊にはゴープラの側室のさらに外側にポーチと思われる痕跡が確認されたが，形状は不明である。

既往研究ではポーチとゴープラをつなぐように壁体が配されるように描かれているが，現地において壁体の石材が発見されず，また側室周辺の柱につながる列柱があったと考えられることから，壁体ではなく柱が配置されたものと想定された。このポーチ自体の寸法は測定不可能なため，対称の位置にある，第2回廊西ゴープラのポーチの幅を転用し，作図を行なった。

⑦ 第2回廊南北ゴープラ側面の列柱について

既往研究によると，第2回廊の南北ゴープラの側室は，壁と窓によって構成されている。しかし，現地調査で確認した範囲では，窓を構成する部材が確認されず一部に列柱が確認されることから最も外側の柱列はゴープラの形状に沿ってポーチ付近まで配列されていると推測し，列柱を伴う側廊として作図した（Figure III.1-7）。

⑧ 第2回廊隅建物の形状について

第2回廊の隅建物は，南東部が崩壊しているため，直接形状を推測するのは困難だが，北東，南西と北西の隅建物で異なる形状の痕跡が見られたため，東側の2つと，西側の2つとで形状が異なると推測される。また，ポーチの外側に付属する柱は既往研究を参考に配置した。この箇所の基壇は北西隅建物にて測量しており，柱を配置するのに十分な出幅が確認された。

between the pillars in Preah Khan Temple in Kompong Svay vary widely, but the dimensions do not differ greatly. Therefore the dimensions are estimated that intension definite dimensional number. In the drawing plan, we arranged the pillars equally in some parts on rectifying the dimensions. The number of the spaces were made corresponding to the space available in the south and north collonade, because the shape of the Gopuras of east and west are difference.

This result is not restore to original state. The drawing course is based on tendency of series of research. In order to comprehend the initial plan, it is neccesary to examine the sites where the construction procedures of each building have similaraties and thoroughly analyze all construction elements. Therefore, research in the future is very important and necessary.

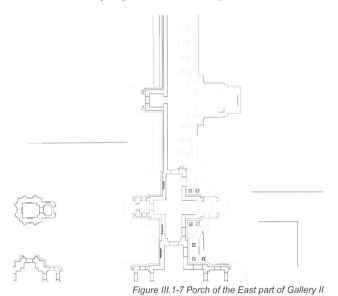

Figure III.1-7 Porch of the East part of Gallery II

⑥ Porch beside East Gopura of Gallery II

In the second Gallery, traces that appear to be a Porch were confirmed further outside of the side room of the Gopura, but the shape cannot be seen clearly.

In previous studies, a wall connects the Porch to Gopura, but the stone material of wall could not be found. Additionally, there are several pillars around the side room of the Gopura which are supposed to be connected to the colonnade beside the Gopura. For these reasons, we put pillars instead of wall.

Dimensions of this Porch follow the width of the Porch beside the West Gopura which is on other side of this Gopura in the Second Gallery (Figure III.1-7).

⑦ Colonnade beside North and South Gopura of Gallery II

In previous studies, side rooms of South and North Gopura of Gallery II consisted of walls and windows. However, we verified there was a colonnade, and no materials which made up

⑨ 第 2 回廊外の十字テラスについて

北，南，西の 3 つのゴープラの外側に十字テラスが確認されるが，いずれも崩壊している。形状を復原するために散乱石材からの考察や，他のアンコール遺跡との比較調査を行った。

アンコール遺跡における比較調査の結果，タ・プローム寺院の形状と類似しているが，テラスの各張り出し部分で幅が狭くなり，同箇所で段数も一段下げているのに対し，コンポンスヴァイのプレア・カーン寺院では，束柱の形状の変化により欄干のみの高さを下げた独特な形状が見られる。そのため，既往図面に欄干の本数や欄干の土台の形状に加え，基壇の角の位置を修正し，作図を行った（Figure III.1-8）。

また，ゴープラとの接続部分は既往図面では離れており，間に階段が 2 段設けられている。しかし，外側各所に一体の装飾のある材を確認できたことから，タ・プローム寺院同様に独立しておらず，テラスに向けて一段下がる形状とした。

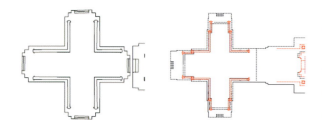

Figure III.1-8 Previous drawing（Left）and new drawing（Right）

Photo III.1-7 Scattered stone around the terrace

⑩ 第 1，第 2 回廊における軸の傾きについて

平面における回廊は，辺によって傾きが大きかったため，それぞれの軸の傾きは以下に示すように異なる値を用いている。

［第 1 回廊］全ての回廊とその付近の建物は，統一的に 28.48250 度の傾きで作図している。

［第 2 回廊］東回廊と西回廊は 28.13745 度，北回廊と南回廊東辺は 28.54971 度，南回廊西辺は 28.57079 度の傾きを用いている。

windows. Therefore, we estimated that the outermost colonnade was arranged along the shape of Gopura, and that part should be drawn as a colonnade Gallery from outside of the side room.

⑧ The shape of the Corner Building of Gallery II

Because the Southeast Corner Building of Gallery II is collapsed, it is difficult to estimate the form directly. On the other hand, traces are different between Northeast, Southwest and Northwest Buildings. Therefore it is estimated that two Corner Buildings in the East and two in West have different forms, and the line of pillars attached to the outside of the Porch follows previous studies. The platform of the Corner Building was measured at the northwest and there was enough space for pillars to be placed.

⑨ The Cruciform Terrace at the Gallery II

Although the Cruciform Terraces are confirmed on the outside of the three Gopuras in the north, south and west, they are collapsing. In other to restore the shape, consideration from scattered stones and comparative investigation in other Angkor temples must be undertaken.

These forms resemble the ones in Ta Prohm Temple whose terrace narrows at overhanging parts and is lowered at that point. However, in Preah Khan Temple of Kompong Svay the changing of that part only to change the form of a sort support and lower the height of balustrade. It seems to be a unique shape. Therefore some of the balustrades and its bases are added to the previous drawing and the positions of the corners of the platform are also modified (Figure III.1-8).

In the previous drawing the connecting part between Terrace and Gopura was separate, and there were two steps. However, that part was modified in the current drawing to be the form that the terrace was not independent like one of in Ta Prohm Temple and goes down one step from the Gopura. This was done because a series of decorated materials was found on the element.

⑩ Axis Inclination of Gallery I, II

The inclination of the axis of the Gallery differs by side in the plan.

[Gallery I]: All Galleries and buildings surrounding them are drawn with an inclination of 28.48250 degrees.

[Gallery II]:The east Gallery and the west Gallery are at the same with 28.13745 degree, the north Gallery and the east part of the south Gallery are inclined at 28.54971 degrees and the west part of the south Gallery is inclined at 28.57079 degrees.

プレア・ヴィヘア
アンコール広域拠点遺跡群の建築学的研究 2
ⓒ

発 行
2018年10月20日

監 修
中川　武
溝口明則

発行者
日野啓一

印刷
藤原印刷株式会社

製本
松岳社

中央公論美術出版
東京都千代田区神田神保町1-10-1 IVYビル6階
TEL. 03-5577-4797

ISBN978-4-8055-0858-9